T0299416

The Political Economy of Economic Growth in Africa, 1960–2000

The period from 1960 to 2000 was one of remarkable growth and transformation in the world economy. Why did most of Sub-Saharan Africa fail to develop over this period? Why did a few small African economies succeed spectacularly? *The Political Economy of Economic Growth in Africa, 1960–2000* is by far the most ambitious and comprehensive assessment of Africa's post-independence economic performance to date. Volume 2 supports and extends the analysis of African economic growth presented in the first volume by providing twenty-six case studies of individual African economies. The book is divided into three parts, based on the three main types of economy found in Sub-Saharan Africa: landlocked, coastal, and resource-rich. Eighteen of the case studies are contained in the book and a further eight are available at www.cambridge.org/9781107496262. These volumes are an invaluable resource for researchers and policy-makers concerned with the economic development of Africa.

BENNO J. NDULU is an Advisor to the Vice President in the African region of the World Bank.

STEPHEN A. O'CONNELL is a Professor of Economics at Swarthmore College.

JEAN-PAUL AZAM is a Professor of Economics at the University of Toulouse and at the Institut Universitaire de France.

ROBERT H. BATES is Eaton Professor of the Science of Government at Harvard University.

AUGUSTIN K. FOSU is Deputy Director of the World Institute for Development Economics Research at the United Nations University.

JAN WILLEM GUNNING is Professor of Development Economics at the Free University, Amsterdam, and Director of the Amsterdam Institute for International Development.

DOMINIQUE NJINKEU is Executive Director of International Lawyers and Economists Against Poverty (ILEAP), Toronto.

The Political Economy of Economic Growth in Africa, 1960–2000

VOLUME 2

Country Case Studies

EDITED BY

Benno J. Ndulu
Stephen A. O'Connell
Jean-Paul Azam
Robert H. Bates
Augustin K. Fosu
Jan Willem Gunning
Dominique Njinkeu

CAMBRIDGE
UNIVERSITY PRESS

CAMBRIDGE
UNIVERSITY PRESS

University Printing House, Cambridge CB2 8BS, United Kingdom

Cambridge University Press is part of the University of Cambridge.

It furthers the University's mission by disseminating knowledge in the pursuit of education, learning and research at the highest international levels of excellence.

www.cambridge.org
Information on this title: www.cambridge.org/9781107496262

© African Economic Research Consortium 2008

This publication is in copyright. Subject to statutory exception and to the provisions of relevant collective licensing agreements, no reproduction of any part may take place without the written permission of Cambridge University Press.

First published 2008
Third printing 2009
First paperback edition 2015

A catalogue record for this publication is available from the British Library

ISBN 978-0-521-87849-4 Hardback
ISBN 978-1-107-49626-2 Paperback

Cambridge University Press has no responsibility for the persistence or accuracy of URLs for external or third-party internet websites referred to in this publication, and does not guarantee that any content on such websites is, or will remain, accurate or appropriate. Information regarding prices, travel timetables, and other factual information given in this work is correct at the time of first printing but Cambridge University Press does not guarantee the accuracy of such information thereafter.

Contents

Files available to download from www.cambridge.org/9781107496262

Figures

Tables

Contributors

Alemayehu Geda is Professor of Economics at the Department of Economics, Faculty of Business and Economics, Addis Ababa University. Dr. Alemayehu Geda was previously an Associate Researcher and Lecturer at the School of Oriental and African Studies (SOAS), University of London, and a Principal Macroeconomist at the Kenya Institute for Public Policy Research and Analysis (KIPPRA). He has consulted and published widely on African economies, and is engaged in macroeconometric modeling work and training for governments and research institutions in Ethiopia, Kenya, and Uganda.

Ali Abdel Gadir Ali, a Sudanese national, is Deputy Director General of the Arab Planning Institute (API), based in Kuwait. He was previously Director of the Economic and Social Policy Analysis Division of the UNECA (Addis Ababa), and until 1992 was Professor of Economics at the University of Gezira, Sudan. Dr. Ali has consulted widely, including with the World Bank, the African Development Bank, UNDP, the Regional Bureau for Arab States, and UNICEF. His research in development economics includes extensive work on poverty and inequality, economic growth, policy evaluation, and the economics of civil conflict.

Ernest Aryeetey is Director of the Institute of Statistical, Social and Economic Research (ISSER) at the University of Ghana, Legon. He has held visiting positions at the School of Oriental and African Studies (SOAS), University of London, Yale University, and Swarthmore College, and has published and consulted widely, focusing on institutions and their role in development, regional integration, economic reforms, financial systems, and small enterprise development. Dr. Aryeetey is a Resource Person and member of the Program Committee of the African Economic Research Consortium (AERC) and serves on the Board of the United Nations University World Institute for Development Economics Research (UNU-WIDER).

Michael Atingi-Ego is the Executive Director of Research at the Bank of Uganda. He has published extensively on the economics of the monetary and financial sectors, and has consulted widely. Dr. Atingi-Ego occasionally works on short-term expert assignments for the International Monetary Fund (IMF), in Balance of Payments and Monetary Operations. He is a leading Resource Person in the Macroeconomic and Financial Management Institute (MEFMI) of Eastern, Central and Southern Africa.

Jean-Paul Azam is a Professor of Economics at the University of Toulouse and at the Institut Universitaire de France. He is the Director of the Atelier de Recherche Quantitative Appliquée au Développement Economique (ARQADE) in Toulouse and a Fellow of the European Development Network and the Institute for the Study of Labor (IZA) in Bonn. Dr. Azam has extensive field experience in Africa and Asia and has consulted for the World Bank and EU. His research spans a wide variety of topics, including migration, ethnic discrimination, wage determination, pro-poor growth, and the determinants of civil war and terrorism.

Robert H. Bates is Eaton Professor of the Science of Government at Harvard University. He is a member of the Political Instability Task Force of the United States Government and serves as a Resource Person for the AERC. Among recent honors, Professor Bates was a Carnegie Scholar in 2001–2 and a Moore Distinguished Scholar in 2003–4. Co-author or co-editor of thirteen books on the political economy of development, his most recent is *Prosperity and Violence* (W. W. Norton, 2001). Professor Bates has conducted research in many countries in Africa and in Colombia and Brazil.

Fodé Camara is currently an independent researcher and member of the Groupe de Recherche et d'Appui au Développement Economique in Guinea, Conakry. He has held several positions in Guinea's private or public sector (Central Bank, Ugar and Shell Guinea) as Economist or as Management Auditor. His fields of research are mainly poverty, growth, and the political economy of reforms in SSA, with a particular focus on the reconciliation between political and economic reforms.

Chinyamata Chipeta was Professor of Economics at Chancellor College, University of Malawi, until 1995. Currently he is the Executive Director of the Southern African Institute for Economic Research, which is based in Zomba. He has done consultancies for regional and international organizations on a variety of issues in development economics and policy. His main research interests and publications lie in the domain of indigenous aspects of economics.

Victor A. B. Davies is a PhD candidate in economics at Oxford University, and was previously a Senior Lecturer in Economics at Fourah Bay College, University of Sierra Leone. Mr. Davies has been a Visiting Scholar at the IMF and a consultant to the Government of Sierra Leone, UNDP, the World Bank, the International Development Research Centre (Canada), and the

Overseas Development Institute (UK). His research focuses on the economic consequences of armed conflict, the political economy of fragile states, and the role of natural resources in economic development.

Nadjiounoum Djimtoïngar is the Deputy Director for Prospective at the Executive Secretariat of the Economic and Monetary Community of Central Africa (CEMAC) in Bangui, CAR. He previously served as the Co-ordinator of the Databases and Poverty Reduction Strategy Component of the Economic Management in the Oil Era project in the Ministry of Planning and Economic Promotion in Chad. Until mid-2003, Dr. Djimtoïngar was also teaching in the Department of Management and Economic Techniques at N'Djamena University, Chad.

Sékou F. Doumbouya is Executive Director of the Groupe de Recherche et d'Appui au Développement Economique in Guinea, Conakry. He has been a visiting researcher at the Universities of Cornell (USA) and Laval (Québec), and a consultant to the UNDP, the World Bank, and the African regional communities (CEMAC, UEMOA). He serves as a Resource Person for the WTO regional course on trade policy in francophone Africa. Mr. Doumbouya's research on African development issues focuses on poverty, inequality, trade, and international negotiations.

Ibrahim A. Elbadawi, a Sudanese national, is a Lead Economist at the Development Economic Research Group of the World Bank and a past Research Director of the AERC. He is a Research Fellow of the Economic Research Forum for the Arab World, Iran and Turkey (ERF), and a member of its Advisory Committee. At the World Bank, Dr. Elbadawi managed the collaborative study *Can Africa Claim the 21st Century?* and co-ordinated the economic cluster team for the multi-donor Sudan Joint Assessment Mission following the end of the Sudanese civil war in 2005. He has published widely on macroeconomics, the economics of civil wars, and development policy.

Kodjo Evlo is a Senior Lecturer in Economics at the Université de Lomé, Togo, where he is also Chair of the Department of Economics and Director of the General Maintenance Department. Dr. Evlo has also served as short-term staff or consultant with several international organizations including UNCTAD, UNDP, UNECA, WHO, the World Bank, and USAID. Dr. Evlo's research focuses on macroeconomic management and economic growth.

Bruno Powo Fosso is an Advisor to the Executive Director of the International Lawyers and Economists Against Poverty (ILEAP), a Toronto-based non-profit organization devoted to securing pro-development outcomes in international trade negotiations. He has taught at McGill University (Canada) and has held research posts at the Institute of Applied Economics (HEC), Montreal, Canada, and the Central Bank of West African States (BCEAO). Dr. Powo Fosso's research focuses on international finance, macroeconomic management, and trade in developing countries.

Augustin Kwasi Fosu is Deputy Director of the World Institute for Development Economics Research (UNU-WIDER) in Helsinki. He was previously at the UN Economic Commission for Africa, Addis Ababa, where he served as Director of the Economic and Social Policy Division and as Senior Policy Advisor and Chief Economist. Dr. Fosu is a past Director of Research of the AERC and was a member of the Economics department at Oakland University (USA) for over two decades. He has published extensively in economic development and in labor economics.

Tchabouré Aimé Gogué is Professor of Economics at Université de Lomé, Togo. He has been a Fulbright Visiting Scholar at California Polytechnic (San Luis Obispo) and Boston University, an Associate Professor at Université de Poitiers, France, and a Visiting Professor in many French-speaking African universities. He has consulted for many international organizations and has served as the Director of the Programme de Troisième Cycle Interuniversitaire (PTCI en Economie). His research focuses on macroeconomic management, governance, and growth in SSA.

Jan Willem Gunning is Professor of Development Economics at the Free University of Amsterdam and Director of the Amsterdam Institute for International Development. Previously he was Professor of Economics and Director of the Centre for the Study of African Economies (CSAE) at the University of Oxford. Gunning has published widely on trade shocks, firm and household behavior, and macroeconomic management in Africa. He served for a decade as a Resource Person for the AERC and holds an honorary doctorate from the Université d'Auvergne where he is a Professor Associate of CERDI.

Milton A. Iyoha is Professor of Economics in the Department of Economics and Statistics, University of Benin, Benin City, Nigeria. A former Research Fellow at the Brookings Institution in Washington, DC, Dr. Iyoha has taught at the State University of New York at Buffalo and has been a Visiting Professor of Economics at the University of Lagos and the University of Botswana. He has served as a consultant to many international organizations. Professor Iyoha's research focuses on growth, trade and regional integration, and macroeconomic policy.

Louis A. Kasekende is Chief Economist of the African Development Bank (ADB). Dr. Kasekende was previously Deputy Governor of the Bank of Uganda, where he had served as Director of Research and Executive Director with responsibility for Research and Policy. From 2002 to 2004, he represented twenty-two African countries as Executive Director on the Executive Board of the World Bank. Dr. Kasekende has been a lecturer in Economics at Makerere University, Uganda, and has published widely on macroeconomic and financial policy, focusing particularly on financial and capital account liberalization, Structural Adjustment Programs, regional trade agreements, and exchange rate policy.

Georges Kobou is Dean of the Faculty of Economics and Management at the University of Yaoundé II-Soa in Cameroon. He is also Head of the Department of Quantitative Methods at the same Faculty. Professor Kobou is a member of the Executive Committee of the CODESIRA (Council for the Development of Social Science Research in Africa), where he occupies the Vice President's position. His research focuses on economic growth, labor markets, and econometrics.

Yeti Nisha Madhoo is a faculty member in the Department of Economics at the University of Mauritius. Dr. Madhoo has been a visiting researcher at the University of East Anglia, the National University of Singapore, and the University of Alberta. Her recent published research is in the areas of development economics, environmental economics, and public economics.

Gervase S. Maipose is Associate Professor and currently Head of the Department of Political and Administrative Studies at the University of Botswana. He was previously a Senior Lecturer at the University of Zambia, where he headed a similar department for three years. Professor Maipose's research interest is in development policy and management, mainly within the context of Botswana and Zambia and focusing on public finance, public sector reforms, governance, foreign aid, and recently on growth.

Thapelo C. Matsheka is the Chief Executive Officer of the Citizen Entrepreneurial Development Agency (CEDA), a parastatal institution of the Government of Botswana. Dr. Matsheka obtained his PhD from the University of Kent at Canterbury in the UK, and is a former Senior Lecturer in Economics at the University of Botswana. He has published in the area of financing growth and development in Botswana.

Mjedo Mkandawire is a Lecturer in Economics at the Malawi Polytechnic, University of Malawi. Previously he was Head of the Economics Department at the National Bank of Malawi (NBM) and Assistant Director of Research and Statistics, Reserve Bank of Malawi. His research interests and publications focus on monetary economics, poverty and macroeconomic management, and political economy and growth.

Nkunde Mwase is an economist at the International Monetary Fund (IMF). She completed her postgraduate studies at the University of Warwick and Oxford University. Since joining the IMF, she has worked on a number of countries, including Afghanistan, Algeria, Bosnia, Dominica, and St. Kitts and Nevis. Ms. Mwase previously worked at the Economics Department of the Central Bank of Tanzania. Her research interests are in the areas of international finance, public finance, and economic growth.

Francis M. Mwega is an Associate Professor of Economics at the University of Nairobi, where he has taught since the mid-1980s. He attended Makerere University (Uganda) and the University of Nairobi (Kenya) and has a PhD from the University of Illinois at Urbana–Champaign (USA). He has researched and written extensively on SSA, with a special focus on Kenya. Professor Mwega has also consulted for regional and international organizations, including the AERC (1991–2004), and has twice been a Visiting Scholar at the IMF. He is currently a Principal Analyst at the Kenya Institute for Public Policy Research and Analysis (KIPPRA) and a Resource Person at the AERC.

Shyam Nath is Professor of Economics at the University of Mauritius. Dr. Nath worked in the National Institute of Public Finance and Policy in New Delhi for more than a decade, and has served as a consultant to the World Bank, UNDP, UNCDF, and USAID. His research interests and publications focus on fiscal decentralization and local government finance, foreign aid, tax policy, and development problems in India and SSA.

Mansour Ndiaye is Head of Monetary Analysis at the Central Bank of West African States (BCEAO). He served previously as an Economist in the African Department of the IMF. His research focuses on monetary policy, economic growth, and regional economic integration in SSA.

Benno J. Ndulu is Co-ordinator (with Stephen A. O'Connell) of the Growth Project. He is an Advisor to the Vice President in the Africa Region of the World Bank. Dr. Ndulu was one of the founders of the AERC, serving as its first Research Director and later as its Executive Director. He holds an honorary doctorate from the Institute of Social Studies (The Hague), in recognition of his contributions to capacity-building and research on Africa and his intellectual contributions to the democratic change in South Africa.

He has published and advised widely on growth, adjustment, governance, and trade.

Njuguna S. Ndung'u is Governor of the Central Bank of Kenya. He is an Associate Professor of Economics at the University of Nairobi and before his appointment to the Central Bank was the Director of Training at the AERC. As Head of the Macroeconomic and Economic Modelling Division of the Kenya Institute for Public Policy Research and Analysis (KIPPRA), Dr. Ndung'u led the team that developed the KIPPRA–Treasury macro model of Kenya. He has published extensively on macroeconomic management issues in Kenya and other African countries.

Floribert Ngaruko, a Burundi national, currently works at the African Capacity Building Foundation (ACBF) in Harare, Zimbabwe. He holds a PhD in Economics and is affiliated with the Centre d'Etudes en Macro-économie et Finance Internationale (CEMAFI), Nice, France. Before joining the ACBF he worked with the World Bank in Washington, DC. Dr. Ngaruko's publications focus on the political economy of reform, the sources of conflict and civil war (particularly in Africa), and the economic and policy analysis of gender, economic growth, institutions, and governance.

Dominique Njinkeu is the Executive Director of the International Lawyers and Economists Against Poverty (ILEAP), a Toronto-based non-profit organization devoted to securing pro-development outcomes in international trade negotiations. He served previously as the Deputy Director of Research at the AERC. He has held a variety of research positions and has taught at the University of Yaoundé (Cameroon), Université Laval (Quebec), and Southern Illinois University (USA). Dr. Njinkeu's research on African development focuses on trade and regional integration and international negotiations.

Janvier D. Nkurunziza is an Economic Affairs Officer in the Office of the Special Co-ordinator for Africa, UNCTAD where he co-authors a yearly thematic report on Africa's development. Before moving to UNCTAD, he worked for the United Nations Economic Commission for Africa in Ethiopia and Cameroon. Dr. Nkurunziza has also worked at Harvard University (USA) and at the Universities of Yaoundé (Cameroon) and Burundi. He holds a doctorate in Economics from the University of Oxford where he is affiliated with the Centre for the Study of African Economies (CSAE). His research on Africa focuses on growth, macroeconomic reforms, political economy, and applied industrial organization.

Stephen A. O'Connell is Co-ordinator (with Benno J. Ndulu) of the Growth Project and Professor of Economics at Swarthmore College. He has been a visiting researcher at the Universities of Nairobi, Dar es Salaam, and Oxford, and a consultant to the IMF, the World Bank, and the Tanzanian government. He serves as a Resource Person for the AERC, where he is also a member of the Program Committee. Professor O'Connell's research focuses on macroeconomic management, governance, foreign aid, and growth in SSA.

Dickson E. Oriakhi is a Senior Lecturer in the Department of Economics and Statistics, University of Benin, Benin City, Nigeria. Dr. Oriakhi is an expert in public finance and taxation. The focus of his research has included fiscal policy, public debt, revenue allocation, and budgetary management.

Ousmane Samba Mamadou is the Minister of Primary Education of Niger. He was previously Head of the Research Division in the Research and Statistics Department of the Central Bank of West African States (BCEAO). During a secondment to the Government of Niger that began in 2004, Dr. Samba Mamadou worked in the Office of the Prime Minister, first as an "expert" within the Cellule d'Analyse et de Prospective en Développement (CAPED) and then as Senior Economic Advisor and Head of the Economic and Financial Department. Dr. Samba Mamadou has published papers on macroeconomic modeling in the countries of the West African Economic and Monetary Union (WAEMU), on monetary policy in WAEMU, and on parallel exchange rates, growth, and competitiveness.

Mahaman Sani Yakoubou is Head of the Development Department (Commissaire Chargé du Développement) in the Ministry of Finance of Niger. Mr. Yakoubou is also Economic Advisor to the President of the Republic of Niger. He has extensive experience as a practitioner in the areas of project analysis, foreign aid, and development policy.

Contributors to the downloadable resources

Massa Coulibaly is Professor of Econometrics and Research Methods at the University of Bamako, Mali. He is the Director of the Research Group in Applied and Theoretical Economics (GREAT), where he is also a Researcher. Among other topics, his research focuses on opinion polls, trade and regional economic integration, the economy of Mali, and economic policies for development and poverty reduction.

Siaka Coulibaly is an Economist at the World Bank Resident Mission in Ougadougou, Burkina Faso. He served previously as Deputy Secretary at the Secretariat for the Coordination of Structural Adjustment Program implementation in the Ministry of Finance in Burkina Faso, and as an Economic Advisor to the Minister of Environment and Water. He has contributed to the design and monitoring of a wide range of policy initiatives in public finance, macroeconomic policy, private sector development, and poverty alleviation.

Clara de Sousa is a Senior Economist at the World Bank, where she serves as the Country Economist for a number of Caribbean countries. Previously she was Executive Director in charge of monetary policy at the Bank of Mozambique and a Lecturer in the Departments of Economics, Law and Agriculture at the University Eduardo Mondlane in Maputo, Mozambique. Her research has focused on poverty, post-conflict reconstruction, governance issues in central banks, and monetary policy.

Amadou Diarra holds a PhD in Economic Science and Sociology from the University Friedrich Wilhelm in Bonn. Dr. Diarra is Financial Officer and Researcher at the Research Group in Applied and Theoretical Economics (GREAT). From 1986 to 2000, he was Professor of Economics at the University of Bamako, Mali, and before that a technical advisor to the Ministry of Industry, Trade, and Arts and Crafts (l'Artisanat) of the Republic of Mali. His research focuses on opinion polls, the economy of Mali, and economic policies for development and poverty reduction.

Antonin S. Dossou is a Statistician–Economist and is currently Chief of Staff of the Minister of Economic Development and Finance of the Republic of Benin. Mr. Dossou was previously at the Central Bank of West African

States (BCEAO), where he served as Deputy Training Director and subsequently as Director of Research and Statistics. Over the period of a decade Mr. Dossou delivered courses in applied macroeconomics, programming, financial policy, and econometrics at the West African Center for Training and Study in Banking (COFEB) of the BCEAO, and occasionally at the University Cheikh Anta Diop and the Institute of Development and Planning (IDEP), both in Dakar.

Tekaligne Godana is currently a Research Advisor at the Department for Research Cooperation, Swedish International Development Agency (SIDA). Before joining SIDA he taught for almost twenty years at the Universities of Stockholm, Zimbabwe and Namibia. He has held visiting research posts at Princeton University and Sussex University, consulted with the World Bank on education reforms, and served in economics training programs operated by the AERC and the Namibia Policy Research Institute. Dr. Godana's research focuses on public finance and the economics of education.

Marcel Kouadio Benie holds the French title of "Agrégé des Sciences Economiques" and is currently Professor of Economics at the University of Cocody, Abidjan (Côte d'Ivoire). He has served as the Director of Employment Promotion in the Agency for the Study and Promotion of Employment (Government of Côte d'Ivoire) and as the Director of postgraduate programs (Diplômes d'Etudes Supérieures Spécialisées) in labor economics and human resources in the Research and Training Unit in Economics and Management at the University of Cocody.

Coleen McCracken is an Administrative Planning Specialist at Washington State University. She has been involved in projects in Burkina Faso focusing on production and consumption of rural households and on food security issues.

Sylviane Mensah is a Macroeconomist at the Central Bank of West African States (BCEAO), where she is Head of Admissions, Competitive Examinations and Teaching in the Directorate of Training. Ms. Mensah served for three years, on a part-time basis, as teaching and research assistant in macroeconomics at the University of Paris Dauphine. She has continued on similar assignments at the Training Department of the BCEAO and the African Centre for Advanced Management Studies (CESAG), where she teaches courses in money, macroeconomics, and financial programming.

Inyambo Mwanawina is Assistant Director of the Institute of Economic and Social Research (INESOR) of the University of Zambia, where he is a Senior Research Fellow and Coordinator of the Economics and Business

Research Programme. Dr. Mwanawina is on secondment from the Economics Department of the University of Zambia, where he holds the rank of Senior Lecturer and has served as Head of Department. He has taught at the Joint Facility for Electives of the Collaborative Master Programme of the AERC. Dr. Mwanawina has consulted widely and pursues a variety of research interests in macroeconomics, trade, energy, and environmental economics.

James Mulungushi is a Permanent Secretary responsible for the Planning Division of the Ministry of Finance and National Planning (MoFNP) in Zambia. Mr. Mulungushi has served in a variety of government positions including Director of Planning and Economic Management in MoFNP, Chief Economist in the Public Investment Unit of the Budget Office in the Ministry of Finance and Economic Development (MoFED), Assistant Director in the Regional Planning Department of MoFED, District Planning Officer for Kalabo District, and Chief Regional Planner for Western Province in the National Commission for Development Planning. He has also worked as a consultant for several organizations.

John Ernest Odada is an Associate Professor of Economics at the University of Namibia. He joined the University of Namibia in 1999 following an extended academic career at the University of Nairobi, Moi University (Kenya) and the University of Botswana. During the 1980s he served as principal organizer for the Organization of African Unity (OAU) regional workshops on Africa's Priority Programme for Economic Recovery (APPER). From April 1989 to May 1991, he was Chief of the Planning Division of the Kenya Country Office of the United Nations Children's Fund (UNICEF), where he was intimately involved in the critique of structural adjustment lending and the promotion of adjustment with a human face.

Kimseyinga Savadogo is Professor of Economics at Université de Ouagadougou (Burkina Faso), where he is a past Dean of the School of Economics. He is currently on sabbatical leave at the Department of Applied Economics, University of Minnesota. Professor Savadogo teaches microeconomics, econometrics, policy analysis, and economic principles at the graduate and undergraduate levels. His research is in the areas of agricultural productivity and growth, technology adoption, rural institutions, food demand and consumer preferences, and poverty analysis.

Jean-Yves Sinzogan is Deputy Director of the Central Bank of West African States (BCEAO). He is currently with the BCEAO delegation within the West African Economic and Monetary Union (WAEMU) Commission, Ouagadougou. He served previously as Chief Advisor to the Minister of

Finance in Benin, and has also held posts within the Research and Statistics Department at the BCEAO Headquarters, Dakar, and at the Economic Forecasting Department in Benin.

José Sulemane is Advisor to the Executive Director of the Africa Constituency I in the IMF. Dr. Sulemane was previously National Director for Planning and Budget in the Ministry of Planning and Finance and National Director for Research and Policy Analysis in the Ministry of Planning and Development in Mozambique. He has taught International Economics at the Economics Faculty of University Eduardo Mondlane in Maputo, Mozambique and is a member of the Board of the Mozambican Economists Association.

Célestin Tsassa is a Senior Economist at UNDP for the Offices of Guinea-Bissau and Cape Verde. For fifteen years, Dr Tsassa was Lecturer at the University of Brazzaville (Congo). A macroeconomic and trade researcher, he has also served as Associate Lecturer at the Catholic University of Central Africa in Yaoundé. Dr Tsassa was an Economic Adviser to the President of Republic of Congo from 1992 to 1997.

Benjamin Yamb is a Senior Lecturer and the Head of the Department of International Trade and Management at the Ecole Supérieure des Sciences Economiques et Commerciales (ESSEC) of the University of Douala, Cameroon. Mr Yamb's research focuses on data analysis, international trade, and applied econometrics.

Foreword

Throughout many of the first decades following independence, Africa's economies failed to grow; indeed in 2000 *per capita* incomes in several countries were lower than they had been in 1960. In this two-volume study, the African Economic Research Consortium (AERC) probes the nature and the roots of Africa's economic performance in the first decades of independence. We seek to describe Africa's growth experience in the latter decades of the twentieth century, to account for it, and to extract lessons to guide future policy-making in the continent.

The timing of this two-volume assessment could not be more propitious. Debates over growth strategy have renewed as the region emerges from decades of economic decline and policy reform. Growth itself reignited in the mid-1990s, supported by policy reforms and also by rising commodity prices, a revival of aid flows, and the resolution of costly civil conflicts. What constitutes a pro-growth policy environment? What constrains the achievement of that environment? These questions were central to this examination of Africa's immediate past. The answers to them should feature in debates over how best to secure its economic future.

We all recognize that the forces out of our control – the vagaries of commodity prices and climatic conditions, the rigors of fierce competition in fast-changing global markets, and the uncertainties of donor priorities and commitments – place limits on what we can attain. Even at the domestic level, important factors constrain our choices. The political reforms of the 1990s widened the scope for popular restraints on government, for example; but they also increased the level of uncertainty regarding the direction of future policy choices. And in a number of countries, the pursuit of growth awaits the end of armed conflict. Despite such limitations, however, policymakers can identify country-specific opportunities for growth and build upon them, drawing lessons from a country's own history and from experiences elsewhere in Africa and the developing world. In these volumes, the scholars of the AERC seek to make the historical and comparative record available to those whose choices will affect our economic future.

The core of the "Explaining African Economic Growth" Project appears in volume 2, which contains eighteen detailed country studies (plus an additional eight available from www.cambridge.org/9781107496262) conducted by African research teams. These case studies use a common methodology that identifies key turning points in the governance environment and grounds each country's experience in the global evidence on growth. In volume 1, the project's steering committee draws on the country evidence to analyze the determinants of growth. With its two-fold emphasis on geography and governance – or, more broadly, on growth opportunities and choices – the synthesis provides a platform for the analysis of country-specific and region-wide growth strategies in contemporary Africa. Taken together, these two volumes constitute the most ambitious and comprehensive study of the African growth experience to date.

This study would not have been possible without the continuing support of AERC Core funders. We are very grateful to them for their unflinching support of the abiding goals of the AERC, namely, strengthening the African capacity to conduct rigorous, independent, and policy-relevant research which is grounded in local realities and, hence, provides support for evidence-based policy-making in Africa, especially in the context of a dynamic and evolving environment. This mission rests on two basic premises. First, that development is more likely to occur where there is sustained sound management of the economy. Second, that such management is more likely to happen where there is an active, well-informed cadre of locally based professionals to conduct policy-relevant research.

The AERC is building that cadre of professionals through a program that has two primary components, one devoted to policy-relevant research and the other to graduate training in economics. The research component, in turn, comprises thematic research, as the bedrock of capacity-building, and collaborative research, which is designed to engage senior African researchers with their colleagues from outside the continent in conducting research into topical and policy-relevant issues pertinent to enhancing economic development in Africa. This study is a sterling example of the AERC's collaborative research program. It received specific financial support from the Swedish International Development Co-operation Agency (Sida), the Swiss Agency for Development Cooperation (SDC), the Norwegian Agency for Development Cooperation (NORAD), the UK's Department for International Development (DFID), the United States Agency for International Development (USAID), and the World Bank (IBRD) through the Global Development Network, and for this support we are very grateful.

We are also grateful to a variety of research organizations for their contributions over the course of the study. In this regard, we thank the Weatherhead Center for International Affairs at Harvard University, for supporting the launching conference in 1999 and the culminating conference in March 2005; Stanford University's Institute for Advanced Study in the Behavioral and Social Sciences, for hosting a week-long meeting in August 2003 during which the basic structure of the synthesis was developed; the Ford Foundation, for supporting the Stanford meeting through the Institute for International Education; Dr. Pauline Boerma, for hosting an editors' conference in

Goelo, France, in August 2004; and the Rockefeller Foundation, for sponsoring an editors' meeting at the Bellagio Study Center in October 2005.

We owe a debt of gratitude to Robert Bates, Paul Collier, Benno Ndulu and Ademola Oyejide, who designed the Project; and to the Project's Steering Committee, which was intimately involved at all stages of the research. Members of the Steering Committee included Olusanya Ajakaiye (the current Director of Research) and Augustin Fosu (his predecessor), Jean-Paul Azam, Robert Bates, Paul Collier, Shantayanan Devarajan, Jan Willem Gunning, Dominique Njinkeu (former AERC Deputy Director of Research), Benno Ndulu, Stephen O'Connell, and Chukwuma Soludo. We are grateful also to Robert Bates and Macartan Humphreys for conducting a key training session on political economy analysis.

The project was co-ordinated by Benno Ndulu, Stephen O'Connell, and Chukwuma Soludo, whose intellectual guidance and high standards of excellence are evident throughout these pages. Particular thanks go to Steve, who managed the revision of draft chapters and their preparation for publication.

Dr. Joseph Karugia, Ms. Angelina Musera, Ms. Pamellah Lidaywa, and, indeed, the entire staff of AERC Secretariat deserve special thanks for providing superb technical and administrative support. We thank Swarthmore College students Elizabeth Upshur, Matthew Meltzer, Dann Naseemullah, Isaac Sorkin, Daniel Hammer, Sikandra Christian, Bree Bang-Jensen, and Jennifer Peck for excellent research and editorial assistance, and our copyeditor, Barbara Docherty, for her great patience and expertise. We thank the scholars and policymakers – too many to enumerate here – who provided comments on work-in-progress; we trust that they will find, in these volumes, an ample return on their efforts. Finally, we are very grateful to Chris Harrison, our commissioning editor at Cambridge, for his guidance and support throughout the publication phase of this study.

Olusanya Ajakaiye
Director of Research, AERC

William Lyakurwa
Executive Director, AERC

Acronyms

ACCT	Agence pour la Coopération Culturelle et Technique (Togo)
ACGSF	Agricultural Credit Guarantee Scheme Fund (Nigeria)
ACP	African, Caribbean, and Pacific Group of States
ADMARC	Agricultural Development and Marketing Corporation (Malawi)
ADP	Agriculture Development Project (Nigeria)
AERC	African Economic Research Consortium
AGOA	Africa Growth and Opportunity Act
AGRIMA	National Import Agency for Agricultural Implements (Guinea)
ALP	Average labor productivity
AMC	Agricultural Marketing Corporation (Ethiopia)
ANC	African National Congress
AOF	Afrique Occidentale Française
APC	All People's Congress (Sierra Leone)
ASAC	Agricultural Sector Adjustment Credit (Malawi)
AU	African Union
BCEAO	Banque Centrale des Etats de l'Afrique de l'Ouest
BCL	Bamangwato Concessions Limited (Botswana)
BDP	Botswana Democratic Party
BDRN	Development Bank (Niger)
BEAC	Banque des Etats de l'Afrique Centrale
BNF	Botswana National Front
BWI	Bretton Woods Institutions
CAA	Caisse Autonome d'Amortissement (Chad)
CAR	Central African Republic
CBG	Compagnie des Bauxites de Guinea
CBK	Central Bank of Kenya
CBN	Central Bank of Nigeria
CEAC	Communauté Economique des Pays d'Afrique Centrale
CEET	Compagnie Energie Electrique du Togo
CEMAC	Communauté Economique et Monétaire de l'Afrique Centrale (Economic and Monetary Community of Central Africa)
CEPGL	Communauté Economique des Pays des Grands Lacs
CESAG	Centre Africain d'Etudes Supérieures en Gestion

CET	common external tariff
CFA	Communauté Financière d'Afrique
CFAF	CFA franc
CFDT	Compagnie Française des Textiles
CMA	Capital Markets Authority (Kenya)
CMS	Conseil Militaire Supreme (Niger)
CNCA	Agricultural Bank (Niger)
CNPC	China National Petroleum Corporation
COGERCO	Compagnie de Gérance du Coton (Burundi)
COFEB	Centre Ouest Africain de Formation et d'Etudes Bancaires
COMESA	Common Market for Eastern and Southern African States
CPI	Consumer Price Index
CPI	Corruption Perception Index
CPIA	Country Policy and Institutional Assessment (World Bank)
CPP	Convention People's Party (Ghana)
CSA	Central Statistical Authority (Ethiopia)
CSO	Central Selling Organization (Botswana)
CSO	Central Statistical Office (Mauritius)
CSON	Conseil Supérieur d'Orientation Nationale (Niger)
CTMB	Compagnie Togolaise des Mines du Bénin
CUT	Comité de l'Unité Togolaise
DBM	Development Bank of Mauritius
DDF	Domestic Development Fund (Botswana)
Derg	Amharic: "the committee of soldiers" (Ethiopia)
DFI	Development Financial Institutions (Kenya)
DFRRI	Directorate for Foods, Roads, and Rural Infrastructure (Nigeria)
DGM	deputy general manager
DIFZ	Dakar Industrial Free Zone
DRC	Democratic Republic of Congo
DSD	Direction de la Statistique et de la Démographie Niger
EAC	East African Community
EACB	East African Currency Board
EAGER	Equity and Growth through Economic Research
EC	European Community
ECOWAS	Economic Community of West African States
ECU	European Currency Unit
EEA	Ethiopian Economic Association
EEC	European Economic Community
EFF	extended financing facility (IMF)
ELF	ethno-linguistic fractionalization measure
EP	Enquête Prioritaire
EPA	Economic Partnership Agreement (EU)

EPRDF	Ethiopian People's Revolutionary Democratic Front
EPZ	Export-Processing Zone
ERP	Economic Recovery Program (Ghana)
ERP	effective rate of protection
ESAF	Enhanced Structural Adjustment Facility
FAO	Food and Agriculture Organization
FASR	reinforced facilities for structural adjustment (IMF)
FDI	foreign direct investment
FEAP	Family Economic Advancement Programs (Nigeria)
FEPA	Federal Environmental Protection Agency (Nigeria)
FF	French franc
FG	Guinean franc
FIAS	Foreign Investment Advisory Services (World Bank)
fob	free on board
Forex C	Foreign Exchange Bearer Certificate
FRDP	Fiscal Restructuring and Deregulation Program (Malawi)
Frolinat	Front de Libération Nationale du Tchad
FSP	Financial Stabilization Program (IMF)
FSRCC	Financial Services Regulatory Co-ordinating Committee (Nigeria)
FSU	former Soviet Union
FTZ	free-trade zone
GATT	General Agreement on Tariffs and Trade
GDN	Global Development Network
GDP	gross domestic product
GEC	Groupement d'Etudes Communistes
GFCF	gross fixed capital formation
GM	general manager
GNI	gross national income
GNPOC	Great Nile Petroleum and Oil Corporation
GTU	Gezira Tenants' Union (Sudan)
HDI	Human Development Index
HIPC	Heavily Indebted Poor Countries
HPAEs	High-Performing Asian Economies
HRD	human-resource development
ICG	International Crisis Group
ICOR	Incremental capital/output ratio
ICPC	Independent Corrupt Practices Commission (Nigeria)
ICRG	International Country Risk Guide
IDA	International Development Association
IDEP	Institut de Développement et de Planification
IEO	Independent Evaluation Office (Senegal)
IFC	International Finance Corporation

IFPRI	International Food Policy Research Institute
IFS	*International Financial Statistics*
IIF	Indispensable Institutional Framework
ILO	International Labor Organization
IMC	index of market connectivity
IMF	International Monetary Fund
IMG	Independent Monitoring Group (Tanzania)
INEC	Independent Electoral Commission (Nigeria)
ISI	import-substituting industrialization
ISSER	Institute of Statistical, Social, and Economic Research
IT	information technology
ITPAC	Industry and Trade Policy Adjustment Credit (Malawi)
IUP	Imam faction (UP)
JUVENTO	Mouvement de Jeunesse Togolaise (Togo)
JV	joint venture
KFA	Kenya Farmers' Association
KNFU	Kenya National Farmers' Union
KY	*Kabaka Yekka* (Uganda)
LDC	less-developed country
LPDA	Lettre de politique de développement agricole (Guinea)
MAP	Mass Agricultural Projects (Nigeria)
MCCI	Malawi Chamber of Commerce and Industry
MEDac	Ministry of Economic Development and Co-operation (Ethiopia)
MESC	Middle East Supply Corporation (Sudan)
MFA	Multi-Fiber Agreement
MFDC	Mouvement des Forces Démocratiques de la Casamance (Senegal)
MFDP	Ministry of Finance and Development Planning (Botswana)
MIPA	Malawi Investment Promotion Agency
MLP	Mauritian Labor Party
MMM	Mauritius Militant Movement
MNC	multinational corporation
MNSD/Nassara	Mouvement National pour la Société de Développement-Nassara (Niger)
MOFED	Ministry of Finance and Economic Development (Ethiopia)
MP	Member of Parliament
MPC	Ministère du Plan et de la Cooperation (Guinea)
MPDR	Ministère de la Planification du Développement et de la Reconstruction
MSM	Mauritius Socialist Movement

mt	metric tonne
NACB	Nigeria Agricultural and Co-operative Bank
NAFCOM	National Fertilizer Company (Nigeria)
NAFPP	National Accelerated Food Production Program (Nigeria)
NARC	National Rainbow Coalition (Kenya)
NBC	National Bank of Commerce (Tanzania)
NBE	National Bank of Ethiopia
NBFI	non-banking financial institution
NCMB	Nigerian Cocoa Marketing Board
NCPB	National Cereal and Produce Board (Kenya)
NDDC	Niger Delta Development Commission
NDE	National Directorate of Employment (Nigeria)
NDIC	Nigerian Deposit Insurance Corporation
NDMC	National Diamond Mining Company (Sierra Leone)
NDP	National Development Plan
NEAC	National Economic Advisory Council (Botswana)
NEMIC	National Employment, Manpower, and Incomes Council (Botswana)
NEPA	National Electric Power Authority (Nigeria)
NGO	non-government organization
NIF	National Islamist Front (Sudan)
NPI	new industrial policy (Senegal)
NPMB	National Produce Marketing Board (Cameroon)
NPRC	National Provisional Ruling Council (Sierra Leone)
NRM	National Resistance Movement (Uganda)
NRPS	National Poverty Eradication Strategy (Tanzania)
NSE	Nairobi Stock Exchange
NSS	National Seeds Service (Nigeria)
NTB	non-tariff barrier
NUP	National Unionist Party (Sudan)
NYSC	National Youth Service Corps (Nigeria)
OAU	Organization of African Unity
OCIBU	Office des cultures industrielles du Burundi
ODA	Official Development Assistance
ODC	Overseas Development Council (US)
OECD	Organization for Economic Co-operation and Development
OFN	Operation Feed the Nation (Nigeria)
OFY	Operation Feed Yourself (Ghana)
OFYI	Operation Feed Your Industries (Ghana)
OGL	Open General License
OLF	Oromo Liberation Front (Ethiopia)
OMO	open market operations

OMPADEC	Oil Mineral Producing Area Development Commission (Nigeria)
ONC	Office National de Commerce (Burundi)
ONCAD	Office National Pour la Commerce Agricole au Développement (Senegal)
ONDR	Office National de Développement Rural
OPAT	Office des Produits Agricoles du Togo
OPEC	Organization of Petroleum-exporting Countries
OPTT	Office des Postes et Télécommunications du Togo
OTB	Office du Thé du Burundi
OTP	Office Togolais des Phosphates
PAE	Programme d'Aide à l'Emploi (Guinea)
PAMSCAD	Programme of Action to Mitigate the Social Costs of Adjustment (Ghana)
PBN	People's Bank of Nigeria
PCII	*Per capita* income index
PCME	Programme de Création de Micro-Entreprises (Guinea)
PDG	Parti Démocratique de Guinée
PDSF	Public Debt Service Fund (Botswana)
PE	public enterprise (Senegal)
PMSD	Mauritian Social Democratic Party
PNDC	Provisional National Defence Council (Ghana)
PPI	political polarization index
PPN/RDA	Parti Progressiste Nigérien–Rassemblement Démocratique Africain
PPP	purchasing power parity
PRI	Political Risk Index
PRSs	Poverty Reduction Strategies (Uganda)
PRSP	Poverty Reduction Strategy Paper (Tanzania)
PS	Parti Socialiste (Senegal)
PSIF	Programme Special d'Insertion des Femmes (Guinea)
PSM	Parti Socialiste Mauricien (Mauritius)
PTP	Parti Togolais du Progrès
PWT	Penn World Tables
QR	quantitative restriction
RBDAs	River Basin Development Authorities (Nigeria)
RDA	African Democratic Rally (Niger)
RER	real exchange rate
RMA	Rand Monetary Area
RPED	Regional Program on Enterprise Development (World Bank)
RPT	Rassemblement du Peuple Togolais
RSF	Revenue Stabilization Fund (Botswana)

RSP	Republican Socialist Party (Sudan)
RUF	Revolutionary United Front (Sierra Leone)
SACU	Southern African Customs Union
SAL	Structural Adjustment Loan (Malawi)
SAM	Social Accounting Matrix
SAP	Structural Adjustment Program
SBA	stand-by arrangement (IMF)
SCOA	Société Commerciale de l'Ouest Africain (Togo)
SDF	Social Democratic Front (Cameroon)
SDR	Special Drawing Right (IMF)
SEC	Securities and Exchange Commission (Nigeria)
SGGG	Société Générale du Golf de Guinée
SLPMB	Sierra Leone Produce Marketing Board
SLPP	Sierra Leone People's Party
SLST	Sierra Leone Selection Trust
SME	small- and medium-sized enterprise
SMI	small and medium industry
SNWA	Sudanese Nationals Working Abroad
SOBECOV	Société Burundaise d'Entreposage et de Commercialisation des Produits Vivriers
SODECOTON	Société de Développement du Coton du Cameroun (Cameroon)
SOE	state-owned enterprise
SONACOM	Société Nationale de Commerce (Togo)
SONACOS	Société Nationale de Commercialisation des Oléagineux du Sénégal (Senegal)
SONAGRAINES	Société National d'Approvisionnement en Graines (Senegal)
SONARA	Société Nigerienne de Commercialisation de l'Arachide (Niger)
SOTOCO	Société Togolaise de Coton
SPLA/M	Sudan People's Liberation Army/Movement
SPS	Sudan Plantation Syndicate
SSA	Sub-Saharan Africa
STT	Société Textile du Tchad
SUP	Sadig faction (UP)
SWTUF	Sudan Workers Trade Union Federation
TAS	Tanzania Assistance Strategy
TFP	total factor productivity
TFPG	total factor productivity growth
TPLF	Tigray People's Liberation Front
TUC	Trades Union Congress (Ghana)
UBE	Universal Basic Education Program (Nigeria)

UCB	Uganda Commercial Bank
UCSS	Uganda Credit and Savings Society
UDI	Unilateral Declaration of Independence (Rhodesia)
UEMOA	Union Economique et Monétaire Ouest Africaine
UMOA	West African Monetary Union
UNAMSIL	United Nations Mission in Sierra Leone
UNDP	United Nations Development Program
UP	Umma Party (Sudan)
UPC	Uganda People's Congress
UPC	Union des Populations du Cameroun
UPE	Universal Primary Education (Uganda)
UPRONA	Union pour le Progrès National (Burundi)
UPS	Union Progressiste Sénégalaise
VAT	value added tax
WAMU	West African Monetary Union
WAEMU	West African Economic and Monetary Union
WDI	World Development Indicators
WHO	World Health Organization
WTO	World Trade Organization

1 | Overview

Stephen A. O'Connell

1. Introduction

In 1999, the African Economic Research Consortium (AERC) launched a project (henceforth the "Growth Project") designed to produce the first major assessment by African research economists of the post-independence growth performance of the countries of Sub-Saharan Africa (SSA). The country studies assembled here constitute the core of that effort. Together they account for over three-quarters of the region's population and span the full variety of its growth experience.

The companion synthesis volume (vol. 1) distills the evidence presented here into a unified analytical account of the political economy of economic growth in SSA from 1960 to 2000.[1] I outline that synthesis below, as a guide to the cross-cutting relevance of each of the country studies. But synthesis

Swarthmore College, USA. This chapter was written with financial support from the NSF (Grant SES-0213754) and from a Swarthmore College Lang Faculty Fellowship. I draw liberally here from chapters 1, 2, and 12 of volume 1 (see n. 1). I am grateful to Benno Ndulu for many helpful comments and to Robert Bates, Jan W. Gunning, and Growth Project researchers for contributions to section 5. Any errors or omissions are my own.

[1] Ndulu *et al.* (2007). The steering committee of the Growth Project was composed of Benno Ndulu and Stephen O'Connell (co-ordinators); Jean-Paul Azam,

Table 1.1 *Countries in the Growth Project*

| Country | Average growth in real GDP *per capita* (1961–2000) | Percentage share in total SSA | | Ratio of GDP *per capita* to SSA average (1960) | Authors of country study (chapter in vol. 2 in parentheses) |
		Population (1960)	GDP (1960)		
Coastal opportunity (CO) group					
Benin	0.63	1.03	0.82	0.74	Antonin S. Dossou and Jean-Yves Sinzogan, with Sylviane Mensah (22)
Côte d'Ivoire	0.57	1.73	2.06	1.10	Marcel Kouadio Benie (23)
Ghana	−0.21	3.11	1.91	0.57	Ernest Aryeetey and Augustin K. Fosu (9)
Kenya	1.23	3.82	2.20	0.53	Francis F. Mwega and Njuguna S. Ndung'u (10)
Mauritius	3.70	0.30	0.69	2.11	Shyam Nath and Yeti Nisha Madhoo (11)
Mozambique	−0.38	3.42	3.96	1.07	Clara Ana de Sousa and José Sulemane (24)
Senegal	−0.24	1.46	1.98	1.25	Mansour Ndiaye (12)
Tanzania	1.83	4.68	1.32	0.26	Nkunde Mwase and Benno Ndulu (13)
Togo	0.86	0.70	0.46	0.61	Tchabouré Aimé Gogué and Kodjo Evlo (14)
CO group	**0.89**[a]	**20.24**[b]	**15.39**[b]	**0.92**[a]	
Landlocked (LL) opportunity group					
Burkina Faso	1.25	2.12	1.20	0.52	Kimseyinga Savadogo, Siaka Coulibaly, and Coleen A. McCracken (20)
Burundi	0.20	1.35	0.51	0.35	Janvier D. Nkurunziza and Floribert Ngaruko (2)
Chad	−0.72	1.40	1.22	0.80	Jean-Paul Azam and Nadjiounoum Djimtoïngar (3)
Ethiopia[c]	0.41	10.44	4.05	0.36	Alemayehu Geda (4)
Malawi	1.36	1.62	0.50	0.29	Chinyamata Chipeta and Mjedo Mkandawire (5)
Mali	−0.27	1.99	1.46	0.68	Massa Coulibaly and Amadou Diarra (21)

(cont.)

Table 1.1 (*cont.*)

Country	Average growth in real GDP *per capita* (1961–2000)	Percentage share in total SSA		Ratio of GDP *per capita* to SSA average (1960)	Authors of country study (chapter in vol. 2 in parentheses)
		Population (1960)	GDP (1960)		
Niger	−1.65	1.46	1.74	1.11	Ousmane Samba Mamadou and Mahaman Sani Yakoubou (6)
Sudan[c,d]	0.75	5.22	3.89	0.69	Ali Abdel Gadir Ali and Ibrahim A. Elbadawi (7)
Uganda	1.40	3.01	1.24	0.38	Louis A. Kasekende and Michael Atingi-Ego (8)
LL group	**0.31**[a]	**28.61**[b]	**15.83**[b]	**0.58**[a]	
Resource-rich (RR) opportunity group					
Botswana	6.33	0.22	0.16	0.67	Gervase S. Maipose and Thapelo C. Matsheka (15)
Cameroon	0.66	2.43	3.03	1.16	Georges Kobou, Dominique Njinkeu, and Bruno Powo Fosso (16)
Congo, Rep.	1.33	0.45	0.15	0.31	Célestin Tsassa and Benjamin Yamb (25)
Guinea	0.02	1.44	2.92	1.88	Sékou F. Doumbouya and Fodé Camara (17)
Namibia	0.62	0.28	0.69	2.24	Tekaligne Godana and John E. Odada (26)
Nigeria	0.32	18.71	14.30	0.71	Milton A. Iyoha and Dickson E. Oriakhi (18)
Sierra Leone	−1.36	1.03	0.82	0.74	Victor A. B. Davies (19)
Zambia	−1.25	1.44	1.24	0.80	Inyambo Mwanawina and James Mulungushi (27)
RR group	**0.83**[a]	**26.00**[b]	**23.31**[b]	**1.06**[a]	
Total	**0.67**[a]	**74.85**[b]	**54.53**[b]	**0.84**[a]	

Notes: [a]Average for category; [b]Total for category; [c]LL since 1994; [d]Included in LL for analytical purposes. The comparisons are *vis-à-vis* all forty-two countries in SSA for which we have data on population and real GDP at international prices. The *RR* group contains all countries classified in chapter 2 of volume 1 as resource-rich for more than half of the 1960–2000 period.

inevitably means compression, and there is much in these case studies that remains to be exploited. As detailed narratives of growth opportunities seized or missed, policy choices rewarded or gone awry, and struggles played out by firms and households at the microeconomic level, these chapters constitute an ongoing resource for growth scholars. In previously under-studied cases – including Burundi, Chad, and Togo, among others – they provide the foundation for a country-based empirical literature that has not previously existed.

Table 1.1 lists the research teams that participated in the Growth Project. To ensure comparability and support a synthesis of the country evidence, these teams adopted a common methodology grounded in the growth econometrics literature and the rational-choice tradition in political science.[2] I outline that methodology in section 2, as a guide to the structure of the country chapters. At the synthesis stage, the episodes identified and ana-lyzed in these chapters became the raw materials for analysis. In section 3, I describe the taxonomic approach adopted by the steering committee, in which "opportunities" and "choices" proxy for the forces of geography and governance that powerfully shaped Africa's growth experience after 1960. Section 4 summarizes the main lessons of the synthesis. I close this chapter in section 5 with a brief substantive introduction to the individual country studies, and make some final observations in section 6.

2. Grounding country research

The case study methodology has its foundation in the global growth econo-metrics evidence, which provides comparability across studies and addresses the "degrees-of-freedom" problem characteristic of single-country analysis, and in the rational-choice tradition in political economy analysis, which provides a conceptual basis for analyzing policy choice and reform.

Collier and Gunning (1999b) organized their survey of African growth experience around the growing complementarity between cross-country regression evidence and the microeconomic evidence on African economies.

Olusanya Ajakaiye, Robert Bates, Paul Collier, Shantayanan Devarajan, Augustin Fosu, Jan Willem Gunning, Dominique Njinkeu, and Chukwuma Soludo. T. Ademola Oyejide collaborated in developing the project's methodology, and Chukwuma Soludo served as co-ordinator during the initial phase of the project.

[2] The methodology was developed in four framework papers presented at the Growth Project's inaugural meeting at Harvard University in 1999 and published in the AERC's Working Papers series: Collier and Gunning (2001), O'Connell and Ndulu (2001), Oyejide and Soyibo (2001), and Bates and Devarajan (2001). The Global Development Network subsequently adopted the methodology and used it to structure a set of parallel Growth Projects in six regions (see www.gdnet.org).

Within the Growth Project, this complementarity became a central feature of the case study methodology. By the late 1990s, as Collier and Gunning (1999b) observed, the growth literature had virtually eliminated the "African dummy variable," which had typically soaked up between 1 and 2 percentage points of annual growth in global regressions. The systematic contours of African experience, it appeared, were increasingly well captured by differences in observable growth determinants. Meanwhile, microeconomic and sectoral evidence often existed to document the detailed operation, within Africa, of linkages that featured prominently in the cross-country evidence.[3] This complementarity suggested that cross-country evidence could be used to discipline the search for leading themes at the country level, while country evidence, in turn, would "feed back" into the broad account of African growth that was emerging from the growth literature. As described below, country teams used the cross-country literature to locate their own country in the global distribution of growth and its determinants. Detailed country-level analysis, in turn, provided sharper measures of key variables – particularly measures of policy and governance – and traced out their influence at the microeconomic and sectoral level. It also gave potential scope to expectations, policy reversals, leadership transitions, and other dynamic phenomena poorly proxied in cross-country econometric models.

Cross-country evidence is particularly useful in addressing the "degrees-of-freedom" problem confronted by single-country analysis. In analyzing the persistent growth slowdown that got underway in Kenya around the 1980s, for example, a short list of plausibly important determinants would have to include the global recession, changes in coffee and oil prices, structural adjustment policies, and political succession. Slower-moving candidates would also have to be considered, including institutional quality and distributional politics. With forty or fewer data points, however, the scope for untangling the contributions of a large set of potentially relevant determinants is very limited. Cross-country econometrics takes the natural approach of treating each country's experience as a partial counterfactual for Kenya's. The assumption is heroic, but where pooling is roughly valid it greatly expands the sample of relevant evidence. The magnitude of Kenya's policy adjustment, for example, can be compared to that of other countries, and its growth contribution scaled by a coefficient that is consistent with cross-country experience; the confounding effects of terms of trade shocks and global recession can be controlled for; and some sense can be gained of the net underlying influence of Kenya's institutions. Country analysis can then come into its own, marshaling the detailed country- and period-specific

---

[3] Thus, for example, openness to trade had emerged as a globally relevant determinant of growth; this was consistent with an existing country-level literature documenting the response of African cocoa farmers to export taxes.

evidence on the Kenyan growth environment and its evolution over time (see Mwega and Ndung'u, chapter 10).

Drawing on the framework paper by O'Connell and Ndulu (2001), therefore, country teams used a combination of growth accounting and cross-country regression models to formulate the key themes of their research. For most countries, growth accounting decompositions were available from Collins and Bosworth (1996), as updated by the same authors through 2000.[4] These decompositions track the potential contributions of factor accumulation to growth, using an aggregate production function. Any growth (or decline) in output per worker that cannot be accounted for by human or physical capital deepening is interpreted as a change in total factor productivity (TFP), a broad measure of country-level technological progress. Regression-based decompositions (using five-year non-overlapping periods) came from two sources, one based on the parsimonious neoclassical growth or "augmented Solow" model estimated by Hoeffler (2002) and the other on a looser, Barro-style specification developed for the project by O'Connell and Ndulu (2001) and referred to in the country chapters as the "pooled full specification." Country teams used these data, in combination with the existing country literature, to characterize the evolution of the growth environment in their country and identify the key stylized facts and puzzles to be addressed.

The second methodological foundation of the country studies lies in the neoclassical or "rational-choice" approach to the political economy of policy and institutions (Bates and Devarajan 2001). A central objective of the project was to understand the linkages between governance and growth, where governance embodies the full set of economic roles undertaken by the state as producer, consumer, provider of public goods, and regulator of economic activity. Our working hypothesis was that firms and households allocate resources within an incentive environment that is shaped in fundamental ways by the state (Collier and Gunning 1999b), and that the political processes that produce and support this incentive environment typically retain substantial autonomy relative to economic outcomes, at least over extended periods. Our interest was in how these processes work. Why do they sometimes produce growth-promoting incentives, and other times not?

The neoclassical political-economy tradition approaches this question by interpreting political competition as competition for economic resources. In this view, any interest the political elite may have in promoting long-run growth is conditioned by its own interest in accumulation and its obligation to adjudicate competing demands for economic resources (Rodrik 1999).

---

[4] See Ndulu and O'Connell (2000, 2003).

Salient groups include the incumbent elite itself, competing elites, and broader selectorates whose influence is determined by their success at negotiating internal free-rider problems and by the institutional rules that limit their access to power (Bates and Devarajan 2001). We challenged country teams not just to observe what had happened with respect to growth and its determinants, but to analyze why government actors took the decisions they did.

Within each case study, these two elements of the project methodology – the location of country-level themes within the cross-country econometric evidence, and the search for major transitions in the governance environment for growth – come together in a *periodization* of the governance environment between 1960 and 2000. Country teams divided each country's experience into a small set of episodes corresponding to major changes in the incentive structure facing private economic activity, particularly with respect to government intervention in markets. Within each episode, researchers focused on two questions:

- First, how did policies and shocks combine to produce the observed growth outcomes? Researchers were to develop microeconomic evidence linking policies and shocks to the resource allocation decisions of firms and households, and in particular to the scale and efficiency of investment in human and physical capital. Where growth appeared to be dominated by factors poorly proxied in cross-country growth regressions, these factors were to be identified and evidence brought to bear on their importance.
- Second, why were these policies chosen? Researchers were asked to develop evidence on the beliefs of the political elite, the interests to which they responded, and the institutions through which political competition was mediated.

3. Synthesizing the evidence

At the synthesis stage, the evidence to be distilled took the form of growth episodes, each analyzed in detail by the country authors for patterns of government intervention, microeconomic responses by firms and households, and the political economy of policy choices and transitions. With a view to extracting lessons for growth strategy, we developed a two-way taxonomy of these episodes, according to the growth opportunities and policy choices they embodied.[5] On the opportunity dimension, the global

---

[5] In chapter 1, vol. 1, Ndulu and O'Connell (2007) survey the growth literature under the broad headings of demography and human resources, geography, and governance. Collier and O'Connell (2007) develop the synthesis taxonomy.

evidence since 1960 gives prominence to locational and endowment-based variables that influence how countries engage in global markets. Our classification stresses physical remoteness and natural resource wealth; in the synthesis volume (vol. 1), we show that the growth opportunities open to coastal, landlocked, and resource-rich countries differ systematically during the period of study, and that controlling for these differences is a crucial step in interpreting growth performance. On the choice dimension, policy variables feature prominently in the growth literature and have been a focal point of the conditionality dialog between African governments and the international financial institutions (IFIs) since the late 1970s. We construe "policy" broadly here, to include all the major ways in which African governments have shaped the incentive environment for resource allocation. This approach encompasses conventional concepts of macroeconomic and sectoral policy, but also includes the performance of public sector institutions and the emergence of systemic violence and state breakdown.

We use the three opportunity groups to structure the presentation of country studies in the current volume; our analysis of recurring policy patterns provides the organizing framework for volume 1.

3.1   Growth opportunities

In grouping countries by an analytical geography we are intentionally departing from the conventional division of SSA into East, West, Central, and Southern regions. The conventional approach evokes continuities of physical geography and colonial history, but its over-riding appeal is that it is non-controversial. Our aim in adopting an approach based on economic structure is to provide a more powerful basis for interpreting Africa's growth experience and thinking about growth strategy.

Our first distinction is between landlocked, low-opportunity economies and coastal, high-opportunity economies. The most dramatic feature of landlocked developing countries on a global basis is their relative poverty (Faye *et al.* 2004). Outside of the industrial world, the average *per capita* income of landlocked countries in the late 1990s was nearly 40 percent below that of coastal countries, and the income differential remains almost 30 percent if we restrict the comparison group to contiguous coastal neighbors.[6] In

---

[6] The 40 percent figure comes from a regression of the log of average real *per capita* GDP (PPP-adjusted) between 1997 and 1999 on a landlocked dummy variable and a non-SSA dummy variable. The non-SSA dummy is highly significant with a coefficient of 1.22 ($p = 0.00$), reflecting the generally higher incomes of non-SSA developing countries. The landlocked dummy is -0.46 ($p = 0.01$), implying that predicted landlocked income is 63 percent of predicted coastal income. The regression has 129 non-industrial-country observations and an R^2 of 0.42. To derive the "coastal neighbors" comparison we calculated the average log income of contiguous coastal neighbors and subtracted the log

neoclassical growth models, lower initial income is associated, other things equal, with faster growth. But this "conditional convergence" effect is easily overcome if the factors that reduce current income also reduce growth opportunities. This is powerfully true for landlockedness. The most obvious factor is high transport costs, which separate landlocked states from the trade exposure that has a causal impact on growth in global samples (Frankel and Romer 1999; Gallup and Sachs with Mellinger 1999) and which appear to have an even larger impact on growth in SSA than elsewhere (Block 2001; O'Connell and Ndulu 2001). But levels of human development also condition growth opportunities, as do measures of demographic burden, including the relative size of the working age population and its evolution over time. In our survey of the growth evidence Benno Ndulu and I (chapter 1, vol. 1) show that landlockedness exerts a strong and negative indirect impact on predicted growth via these channels.[7]

The growth challenges of landlocked countries are mirrored, of course, by the advantages of a coastal location. The spectacular growth of Asian coastal exporters of manufactured goods is the development success story of the post-Second World War period and the driving force behind the convergence of the population-weighted distribution of global income during this phase of globalization (Firebaugh 2003; Sala-i-Martin 2006).

A second distinction cuts across the landlocked/coastal divide to separate "resource-rich" countries, whether landlocked or coastal, from all others. Resource-rich economies are economies whose growth is driven more powerfully by primary commodity endowments, typically in minerals or energy resources, than by location. Global experience suggests that commodity wealth holds out growth opportunities that are unavailable even to the coastal, high-opportunity economies: in Africa, Botswana provides a potent example of these opportunities. But natural resource abundance also undermines the competitiveness of other sectors producing traded goods (the "Dutch disease"), increases the risk of civil war (Collier and Hoeffler 2004), and may divert resources into zero-sum distributional struggles on an ongoing basis (Ross 2003). On a global basis, the adverse influences dominate: the econometrics literature finds strong evidence of a "natural

---

of own income from this for the thirty landlocked countries in the sample (the advantage of the late 1990s is to include a large number of countries in Central Asia). Regressing this on a constant, the constant term is –0.33 and highly significant ($p = 0.01$); the predicted ratio of landlocked to contiguous coastal income in this regression is 72 percent. There is no evidence in these regressions that the income premium on coastal location is different in SSA than in the rest of the developing world: an interaction term landlocked*non-SSA is small and insignificant in the first regression (coefficient 0.10, $p = 0.78$), and a non-SSA dummy variable is small and insignificant in the second (coefficient –0.03, $p = 0.88$).

[7] In a similar vein O'Connell (2004) finds that predicted annual long-run growth based on "deep" econometric instruments for trade exposure and institutional quality is fully half a point higher for the coastal group than the landlocked or resource-rich groups.

resource curse" in the period since 1960, with primary commodity exporters tending systematically to grow more slowly than exporters of manufactures and/or services (Sachs and Warner 2001).

The analytical geography reviewed here suggests that landlocked, resource-scarce, coastal, resource-scarce, and resource-rich countries face systematically different growth opportunities. In the synthesis volume we use a time-varying classification to operationalize these distinctions: coastal or landlocked countries become resource-rich in the first year they exceed a pair of thresholds for the shares of primary commodities in exports and primary commodity rents in GDP.[8] A country like Nigeria is therefore classified as coastal, resource-scarce until 1971, and as resource-rich thereafter. For the present volume, the natural approach is to group countries according to their dominant opportunity classification over the entire post-independence period (see table 1.1). We place Ethiopia, not politically landlocked until 1994, and the Sudan, with its Red Sea coastline, among the landlocked countries; this judgmental adjustment reflects the vast internal territories of these countries and their limited access to the sea.[9]

Figure 1.1 looks at differences in export structure and development level by opportunity group (using the time-invariant classification), for SSA and an aggregate representing "all other developing areas." Figure 1.1 uses all countries with continuously available observations. Two observations on export structure stand out. First, although resource wealth varies along a more/less continuum rather than by the either/or classification we are using, our definition captures sharp structural differences in economic endowments. Many of our resource-scarce countries have appreciable commodity exports – gold in Ghana, phosphates in Togo – but the resource-rich countries are, by comparison, a highly non-diversified group on average. Second, African resource-rich countries have hardened their primary commodity specialization over time – they are in fact the only group in figure 1.1 to have a higher share of primary commodities in exports at the end of the period than at the beginning. This reflects a broader phenomenon within Africa: in each of the opportunity groups, African countries reduced their primary export share over time by less than other developing regions. Dramatic cases in point include the emergence of new African oil exporters in the 1990s from

---

[8] Collier and O'Connell (2007; chapter 2, volume 1) define a country as resource-rich in the first year if satisfies the following three conditions, and in all subsequent years (i.e. the classification is irreversible): (1) current rents from energy, minerals and forests exceed 5 percent of gross national income (GNI); (2) a forward moving average of these rents exceeds 10 percent of GNI; (3) the share of primary commodities in exports exceeds 20 percent for at least a five-year period following this initial year.

[9] Ethiopia became politically landlocked with Eritrea's independence in 1994, but this was preceded by three decades of armed conflict with Eritrean forces.

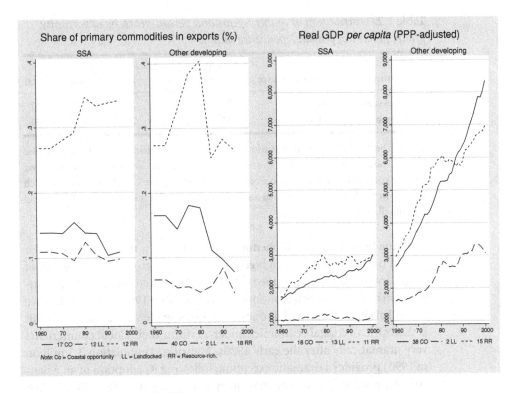

Figure 1.1 Export structure and real GDP, by opportunity group, 1960–2000
Sources: Share of primary commodities in exports from Collier and Hoeffler (2004).
Real GDP *per capita* from PWT6.1, supplemented with growth rates of constant local
currency real GDP *per capita* from the World Bank.

among the resource-scarce groups, including Chad, Equatorial Guinea, and
the Sudan.

The real GDP charts illustrate three observations analyzed in detail by
Collier and O'Connell in volume 1 (Collier and O'Connell 2007). First,
the African landlocked, resource-scarce countries are not only the poorest
group on a global basis but also the slowest-growing group: on average, their
incomes fall over time.[10] Malawi does best in the African landlocked group
over the 1960–2000 period, but at 1.4 percent even Malawi's growth was
well below the median long-run growth rate for all developing countries
(2.3 percent). Second, starting in the early 1980s the relative fortunes of
coastal and resource-rich economies differ systematically between SSA and
the rest of the developing world. Outside Africa, the coastal economies

---

[10] Collier and O'Connell (2007) do their analysis on a population-weighted basis. The
generalizations we are making here are not affected by population weighting, except
where noted.

Table 1.2 *Distribution of country-years and person-years, by opportunity group, percent of post-independence sample*

Distribution by	Coastal, resource-scarce	Landlocked, resource-scarce	Resource-rich	Total
Country-years	46.0	29.8	24.2	**100**
Person-years	44.4	31.1	24.5	**100**

Notes: The table uses all observations for forty-seven African countries, from the year of independence to 2000. The opportunity-group classification is time-varying because coastal or landlocked resource-scarce countries are re-classified as resource-rich starting in the first year they exceed a set of resource-wealth thresholds (see Collier and O'Connell 2007).

continue to surge ahead, a phenomenon that is even more dramatic when viewed on a population-weighted basis given the growth accelerations of China and India starting in the mid-1980s. Africa's coastal economies out-perform its resource-rich economies on average after 1980, but the difference is small and the benchmark is one of nearly complete stagnation. The result is that Africa's coastal economies under-perform their global counterparts very dramatically after the early 1980s. Mauritius (population 3.5 million in 1990) provides a dramatic exception, following its adoption of an Asian-style outward-oriented growth strategy starting in the early 1970s. Collier and O'Connell (2007) argue that the under-performance of Africa's large coastal economies deprived Africa's landlocked countries of a key engine of growth during much of the 1960–2000 period.[11]

Finally, these charts convey a stylized fact that influences all broad growth comparisons between SSA and other regions: by comparison with the rest of the developing world, SSA is unusually landlocked and resource rich. Table 1.2 shows the distribution of countries and population, by opportunity group, for the sample of countries used by Collier and O'Connell (2007).[12] To the degree that landlockedness and resource wealth proxy for structurally adverse growth opportunities, the observed growth performance of African countries is partly a consequence of their objectively limited opportunities. Collier and O'Connell (2007) find that a full percentage point of the population-weighted growth differential between SSA and

[11] They find that on a global basis, a 1 percent increase in the growth rate of *per capita* GDP among contiguous neighbors raises the home country's growth by nearly 0.4 percentage points. Outside of SSA, this spillover effect is particularly strong for landlocked, resource-scarce economies, because for these economies coastal neighbors represent not just a transport barrier but also an enticing export market.

[12] Figure 1.1 draws directly from the Penn World Tables (PWT) 6.1 dataset, which includes a full run of data for only two landlocked developing countries outside of SSA, Bolivia and Nepal. Collier and O'Connell (2007) expand the dataset slightly using World Bank data on growth rates of constant local currency GDP.

other developing regions – 0.96 points out of a total differential of 3.50 – can be traced to the unusually high prevalence of resource wealth and land-lockedness in the region.

Before turning to patterns of governance I note a second dimension of geography that is too fluid and contingent to serve as a basis for classifying growth opportunities but that came forcefully to our attention as the country evidence was being developed. As Ndulu and I note in volume 1 (Ndulu and O'Connell 2007), the political geography that emerges from the country studies is more often defined on broadly ethno-regional lines than by economic sector or urban/rural location. The salience of ethno-regional interests may have deep roots in the region's physical geography and colonial history. Collier (2002) argues that the predominance of subsistence risks and low population density in SSA favored the historical emergence of strong and localized identities based on kinship. The colonial powers then re-posed issues of economic and political management on a larger spatial scale, encouraging the reorganization of collective action around the more fluid and socially determined categories of tribe and ethnicity. By late in the colonial period, Collier argues, these "imagined identities" had acquired a powerful salience, often underpinned by a common language and/or religion. When issues of political self-determination came to the fore, ethno-regional political parties were the dominant basis for political competition in many countries.

By global standards, the character of ethnic diversity in African countries is unusual in two respects. First, African countries tend to display an unusually high level of ethno-linguistic fractionalization, as measured by the probability that two randomly chosen individuals speak a different first language. Easterly and Levine (1997) showed that higher degrees of ethno-linguistic fractionalization were associated with slower growth in global samples, largely through a deterioration of the quality of national policy and measures of institutional performance. Subsequent work has produced a more nuanced picture; Rodrik (1999) and Collier (2000) find that fractionalization has deleterious effects only in the absence of democratic institutions, a combination characteristic of much of SSA between the mid-1970s and the early 1990s. Second, however, many African countries display a polarized pattern of sub-national identity consistent with what Collier (2002) calls "ethnic dominance." This is a situation in which individual groups are large enough either to constitute a permanent majority or to contest for the control of national sovereignty on an ongoing basis. In countries characterized by *ex ante* polarization, sub-national cleavages have often had a strongly geographical dimension, raising fundamental issues of nation-building and culminating in cases such as Burundi, Chad, Nigeria, and the Sudan in secessionist movements and/or civil war. In these arenas fractionalization *per se* has a protective effect: Collier and Hoeffler (2004) find, for example, that high levels of fractionalization reduce the risk of civil war.

3.2   Patterns of governance

Choices constitute the second axis of our synthesis taxonomy. Fiscal deficits, black market premia, and other economic policy outcomes tend to be correlated with growth in global samples, and during the 1990s policy variables played a substantial role in the growth econometrics literature as sources of predicted growth differentials across countries and regions. As Ndulu and O'Connell argue in volume 1, however, the deeper message of that literature is to identify a core set of functions the public sector must perform adequately if sustained growth is to occur. Moreover, the degree to which these functions are performed – in effect, the nature of the governance environment – is often poorly proxied by individual measures of policy or institutional performance. This is in part because institutions vary across countries, so that policy variables that do well at capturing the thrust of policy in one setting may do poorly in another. The rate of inflation, for example, does not provide a useful measure of macroeconomic stability in the African countries of the CFA zone, where exchange rates were irrevocably fixed to the French franc until 1994. But policy variables also tend to be endogenous to actual growth performance, so that an adverse macroeconomic shock can produce an apparent deterioration in policy even when policy settings remain broadly unchanged (the black market premium is an example). For analytical purposes, we needed a way to characterize choices that was robust to institutional variations and plausibly predetermined with respect to growth outcomes.

As described above, the country studies were designed with a view to tracking the major features of the governance environment over time on a country-by-country basis. After an intensive review of the country evidence, the steering committee identified four recurring patterns, each recognizable in terms of the overall thrust of policy as distinct from the setting of individual policy instruments. As outlined by Ndulu and O'Connell:

[t]hese include control or *regulatory* regimes that severely distort productive activity and reward rent-seeking, regimes of *ethno-regional redistribution* that compromise efficiency in order to generate resource-transfers to sub-national political interests, and regimes of *intertemporal redistribution* that aggressively transfer resources from the future to the present. The fourth [regime], *state breakdown*, refers to situations of civil war or intense political instability in which a government fails to provide security or to project a coherent influence in a substantial portion of the country. (Ndulu and O'Connell 2007: 12)

In a two-stage process, the steering committee compiled an initial judgmental classification of all country-years based on the case study evidence, and then finalized this classification in consultation with the country teams. Based on the case study analysis, the steering committee then extended the classification to twenty-one additional African countries. The resulting

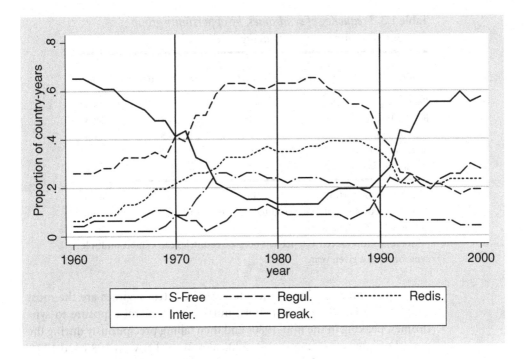

Figure 1.2 The policy environment over time, 46 countries of SSA, 1960–2000
Source: Collier and O'Connell (2007).
Notes: Figure 1.2 shows the judgmental classification developed by the Growth Project's
editorial committee, based on the country studies and the broader literature. Episodes
are characterized as S-Free = Syndrome-free; Regul. = Excessive regulatory controls;
Redis. = Inefficient redistribution; Inter. = Unsustainable intertemporal
redistribution; Break. = State breakdown. The full classification appears in Collier and
O'Connell (2007), table 2.A2.

classification is explained in detail in Collier and O'Connell (2007) and
covers forty-seven countries for the period 1960–2005.[13]

The four anti-growth "syndromes" capture a substantial fraction of the
observed variation in policy choice in Africa, both across countries and
over time. One or more of the syndromes is present in nearly two-thirds
of the country-years in our twenty-six-country sample. As indicated in
figure 1.2, the syndromes show a decided evolution over time, with
syndrome-free status eroding rapidly starting in the late 1960s and returning

[13] The classification was undertaken by Jean-Paul Azam, Robert Bates, Paul Collier,
Augustin Fosu, Jan Willem Gunning, Benno Ndulu, Dominique Njinkeu, and Stephen
O'Connell. The case study countries were completed between August and November
2003, in an iterative process involving the country teams. The remainder of SSA was
completed by the editorial committee in August 2004. A final set of revisions was
undertaken by the committee in October 2005.

Table 1.3 *Frequency of syndromes, by opportunity group (percent of country-years displaying syndrome[a])*

Syndrome	Coastal, resource-scarce	Landlocked, resource-scarce	Resource-rich	Total
Regulatory	48.5	45.6	33.8	**44.0**
Redistributive	23.9	34.9	30.3	**28.8**
Intertemporal	10.0	7.9	18.5	**11.5**
State breakdown	10.7	18.8	13.1	**13.7**
Syndrome-free	32.2	27.6	46.0	**34.2**

Notes: [a]The opportunity group classification is time-varying (see note to table 1.2). For a population-weighted version of this table, see Collier and O'Connell (2007), table 2.7.

Column sums exceed 100 percent because countries can exhibit multiple syndromes in a given year.

with equal force starting in the late 1980s. Control regimes are the most common by far; their time pattern mirrors the general exposure to syndromes, peaking in the mid-1980s and then falling precipitously during the period of intense economic and political reforms between 1988 and 1994. State breakdown is the only marked exception to the generally "hump-shaped" distribution of syndromes over time. It worsens during the 1990s in the face of a sharp change in the external aid and security environment (with the collapse of the Soviet Union in 1989) and a wave of economic and political reforms.

3.3   Interactions between opportunities and choices

In chapter 3 of volume 1, Fosu (2007) draws on the case material to provide extended examples of the syndromes and study the dynamics of their adoption and abandonment. I provide some canonical examples in section 4. Here I focus instead on what can be learned from the interaction of syndromes with our opportunity categories.

Table 1.3 shows the frequencies of each syndrome, by opportunity group, and table 1.4 uses probit regressions to control for year effects and check for statistical significance. The most powerful general observation in tables 1.3 and 1.4 is the correlation of landlockedness with poor governance. Coastal and especially resource-rich countries are significantly more likely to be syndrome-free than are landlocked and resource-poor countries. The differences are largest with respect to ethno-regional redistribution and state breakdown. The greater tendency of landlocked countries to choose redistribution over growth is consistent with a simple political-economy model

Table 1.4 *Incidence of syndromes, by opportunity group, controlling for year effects*

Opportunity group	Probit regressions controlling for year effects, for dependent variable:				
	Syndrome-free	Regulatory	Redistributive	Intertemporal	State breakdown
Coastal	0.170**	0.057	−0.350***	0.127	−0.384***
Resource-rich	0.602***	−0.356***	−0.185**	0.503***	−0.292***
N	1,677	1,677	1,677	1,677	1,677
Pseudo R^2	0.122	0.101	0.039	0.138	0.071
chi^2	230.66	219.71	72.94	107.81	92.12
Prob>chi^2	0.000	0.000	0.002	0.000	0.000
Marginal impact of category on probability of syndrome:					
Coastal	0.060**	0.022	−0.117***	0.018	−0.074***
Resource-rich	0.224***	−0.137***	−0.061**	0.085***	−0.053***
Significance test for equality of coastal and resource-rich coefficients:					
Prob>chi^2	0.000	0.000	0.046	0.000	0.366
Reject $CO = RR$?	Yes	Yes	Yes	Yes	No

$p < 0.1$; **$p < 0.05$; ***$p < 0.01$.

Note: ^{a}Coastal means coastal, resource-scarce. The omitted category is landlocked, resource-scarce.

The dependent variable is a dummy variable for the occurrence of the syndrome. Coefficients are from probit regressions with year effects included, for forty-seven SSA countries for all years from independence to 2000. Collier and O'Connell (2007), table 2.8, reports a similar table using all years 1960–2000 and weighting by population.

in which the political elite sets the level of distortionary taxes so as to achieve its preferred balance between current and future revenues. Redistribution pays off in the short run but undermines growth; given this trade-off, it is more likely to be chosen if growth opportunities are already limited (Gallup and Sachs, with Mellinger 1999). Within the redistributive syndrome, moreover, the landlocked countries are unusually exposed to its most predatory forms. Our system distinguishes adverse ethno-regional redistribution, as practiced during some episodes by northern-dominated governments in Nigeria and Sudan, from acute cases of self-aggrandizement by a narrow political elite, as in Uganda under Idi Amin or Burundi under the Bururi faction. The landlocked countries are disproportionately exposed to the latter phenomenon. Their disproportionate exposure to state breakdown is consistent with an empirical literature on the incidence of civil war, which finds large effects not just of low income but also of slow growth (Collier and Hoeffler 2004; Miguel, Satyanatah, and Sergenti 2004).

Second, the coastal, resource-scarce economies, whose growth opportunities are best illustrated by Mauritius and the outward-oriented Asian exporters of manufactured goods, are in fact the most strongly exposed to regulatory regimes. From a normative viewpoint this result is extraordinary. Returning to the Gallup and Sachs, with Mellinger (1999) framework, the economic costs of tight controls on production and trade are greatest in this group, precisely because growth opportunities are both favorable and sensitive to policy. The global evidence suggests that an alternative combining core infrastructural services with market-based incentives is likely to spur diversification into the higher-opportunity areas of labor-intensive manufacturing and services. Bates (2007; vol. 1, chapter 4) identifies three driving forces behind control regimes in Africa, each of which appears to apply with particular force to the coastal, resource-scarce economies. The first is ideology. Bates (2007) and Ndulu (2007; vol. 1, chapter 9) stress the widespread influence of Fabian socialism and, in a few cases of revolutionary Marxism, in encouraging a dominant state presence in the economy. While this operated world-wide and independently of opportunity structure, it was used to justify particularly sharp market distortions in Africa's coastal economies, where trade offered not only the dominant source of revenue but also an opportunity to make the transfer of colonial assets and the repudiation of colonial patterns a matter of national development strategy (Ake 1996). The second explanation lies in the rent-generating nature of controls and the tendency of narrow but well-organized interests to capture national policy in the absence of broad electoral competition (Bates 1981). Independently of opportunity structure, the rents created by control regimes produce a set of vested interests that comes to oppose the removal of controls. But among the coastal economies, nascent import-competing and urban rent-seeking interests – small-scale industrialists, an educated civil service, labor unions – were in place already at independence; their presence may have added an interest-based impetus to the original adoption of controls. Finally, regional wealth inequalities may have encouraged the adoption and maintenance of control regimes. While the coastal, resource-scarce group is not disproportionately exposed to such inequalities, those that exist tend to separate a trade-based and relatively high-income coastal region from a relatively poorer interior (a theme developed by Azam 2007; vol. 1, chapter 6).[14] Bates (2007) finds that in countries characterized by large regional wealth disparities, controls were more likely to be imposed when the President or national executive originated from the poorer regions. In the coastal, resource-scarce

[14] Azam (2007) focuses mainly on West Africa. Bates (1989) argues that in East Africa, where mountain regions support high-value cash crops, it is altitude more than proximity to the coast that separates rich and poor regions.

economies, intervention in markets would have provided a mechanism for diverting resources from the coastal regions to the interior.

Ideology began to lose its impetus within Africa during the economic crisis of the late 1970s and early 1980s, and with the collapse of the Soviet Union in 1989 the idea of an African socialism virtually evaporated as context for policy. But controls had by then acquired their own impetus as a political equilibrium. Collier *et al.* (2007; vol. 1, chapter 12) argue that the market-based reform programs that got underway starting in the mid-1980s ultimately required a parallel process of political reforms. By enfranchising a wide electorate, political reforms could potentially break a political equilibrium in favor of continued controls.

I turn last to the intertemporal redistribution syndrome. The "resource curse" literature emphasizes the exposure of natural-resource exporters to public spending booms that undermine the efficiency of investment and leave a legacy of external debt and fiscal imbalances. On a population-weighted basis, resource-rich countries experience the highest exposure to this pattern, including most notably Nigeria which displays it from 1970 to 1987. But unsustainable spending can also be supported by what Nkurunziza and Ngaruko (chapter 2) call the "rents to sovereignty" – aid, foreign borrowing, or revenues from the taxation of export crops like coffee in Burundi. On a population-unweighted basis – taking country-years as observations – landlocked countries were as likely to succumb to intertemporal redistribution as were resource-rich countries.

4. Lessons from the synthesis

Figure 1.3 juxtaposes the diversity of Africa's growth experience with the central puzzle that any assessment of the region's experience must confront. Dots show long-run growth rates, with countries arranged in declining order from left to right. The range of long-run outcomes is wide – from Botswana's 6.3 percent per annum to the Democratic Republic of Congo's (DRC) –3.3 percent (Liberia, not shown, grew at –3.5 percent). There is also substantial diversity within countries, as indicated by the upper and lower labels, which show the fastest and slowest ten-year growth period for each country: well over half of the countries of SSA have achieved an average growth rate exceeding the global median of 2.3 percent for at least a decade, and many have grown twice as fast. But the dominant long-run pattern, by far, is one of stagnation and divergence relative to the rest of the developing world. Rapid growth, when it did occur, was very seldom sustained. Over the full 1960–2000 period, SSA lost its initial income advantage *vis-à-vis* South Asia and fell further behind the regions that were already richer in 1960. A

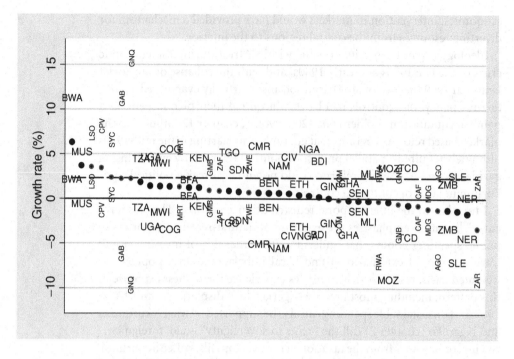

Figure 1.3 Country-level growth performance, SSA, 1960–2000

Source: Ndulu and O'Connell (2007).

Notes: Figure 1.3 ranks the countries of SSA from left to right, in descending order of the long-run average growth rate of real GDP *per capita*. Heavy dots indicate the country-specific long-run averages, and the dashed horizontal line shows the global median (2.3 percent). For each country, three-letter labels indicate the upper and lower extremes of medium-term growth experience, measuring these as the fastest and slowest ten-year moving averages of growth over the course of the sample. Thus for example: Botswana (the left-most country) has the highest long-run growth, at above 6 percent per annum; its fastest ten-year moving average was above 11 percent and its slowest was just below the global mean. Horizontal (vertical) labels and dark (lighter) dots indicate case study (non-case study) countries. We exclude Somalia for lack of data and Liberia for scaling purposes (a moving average of its logarithmic growth rate from 1985 to 1995 is –25.7): Liberia's long-run growth is –3.5, slightly below that of the Democratic Republic of Congo (DRC) at –3.3. Annual growth rates are log differences of real GDP *per capita* in local currency units from the World Bank, supplemented in a few cases of unavailable World Bank data, by log differences of real GDP *per capita* in constant international dollars from the PWT6.1. For Tanzania, we use the PWT6.1 series, but treat 1988 as a missing observation because the series shows a massive downward adjustment in that year due to a revision in the national accounts. The resulting long-run average, with this observation excluded, is close to the average calculated using the PWT5.6.

few small countries did well, but the collective population of the five African countries that exceeded the global median long-run growth rate (the dashed line in figure 1.3) was fewer than 5 million people in 2000.

Cross-country growth accounting comparisons reveal that slow capital accumulation and slow growth in TFP have been roughly equal contributors to the region's growth performance, each accounting for about half of the long-run growth differential relative to other developing regions (table 1.5). While these calculations do not resolve causality, the quantitative importance of lagging productivity is striking. A growing productivity shortfall points to aspects of the incentive environment that affect the deployment of existing assets, the allocation of available investment resources, and the incentives for acquiring technological capability. Evidence on capital flight suggests further that a substantial portion of saving effort is diverted abroad in many African countries (Collier, Hoeffler, and Pattillo 2001), whether in search of higher *ex ante* returns or to avoid detection of illegal activity.

The central message of the Growth Project is that securing the core functions of market-friendly governance – Ndulu and O'Connell (2007) contrast the anti-growth syndromes with Adam Smith's famous trilogy of "peace, easy taxes, and a tolerable administration of justice" – is critically important for long-run growth. Collier and O'Connell (2007) show that syndrome-free status was worth roughly 2 percentage points of predicted annual growth between 1960 and 2000, an amount equivalent to more than half of the population-weighted growth differential between SSA and other developing regions after accounting for differences in opportunity structure. Viewed differently, maintaining syndrome-free status was virtually a *sufficient* condition for avoiding episodes of economic collapse and virtually a *necessary* condition for achieving rapid growth on a sustained basis (see also Fosu and O'Connell 2007).

With their focus on core functions, the syndromes highlight what Collier and Gunning (1999b) call "errors of commission" – choices that actively undermined the quality of governance and the prospects for long-run growth, in favor of the stated or unstated objectives of the political elite. We find evidence of such errors in two-thirds of the country-years in the post-independence period and demonstrate that the prevalence of these patterns provides a powerful account of Africa's overall growth shortfall (Collier and O'Connell 2007). The bulk of the synthesis volume (vol. 1) is devoted to understanding the political and institutional origins of these patterns: why they emerged, why they persisted, and how some countries managed to avoid them. The single deepest task of growth strategy, the evidence implies, is to provide the core functions of market-friendly governance in the short run while strengthening the institutional capacity for securing them on a continuing basis.

Table 1.5 *Regional growth-accounting decompositions, annual growth rates except where noted*

Region	N	Real GDP	Population	Real GDP per capita	Workers per capita	Real GDP per worker	Contributions of		
							Growth in physical capital per worker	Growth in education per worker	Residual
SSA	18.0	3.25	2.70	0.54	−0.07	0.61	0.36	0.25	0.00
Other developing:									
LAC	21	3.49	2.17	1.32	0.39	0.92	0.41	0.34	0.18
SASIA	4	4.45	2.23	2.22	−0.32	2.54	1.11	0.32	1.11
EAP	7	6.21	2.04	4.17	0.22	3.95	2.11	0.49	1.35
MENAT	9	4.84	2.19	2.65	0.13	2.52	1.19	0.44	0.90
Total	**59**	**4.01**	**2.32**	**1.68**	**0.14**	**1.54**	**0.76**	**0.34**	**0.43**
SSA minus Other Developing		−1.10	0.55	−1.64	−0.31	−1.33	−0.57	−0.13	−0.63

Source: Ndulu and O'Connell (2007).

Note: Data on real GDP per worker, population, and investment are from the Penn World Tables (PWT6.1) and are in constant PPP-adjusted dollars. The initial capital stock and the contribution of growth in education per worker are from Susan Collins; see Collins and Bosworth (1996). LAC is Latin America and the Caribbean; SASIA is South Asia; EAP is East Asia and the Pacific; MENAT is Middle East, North Africa, and Turkey.

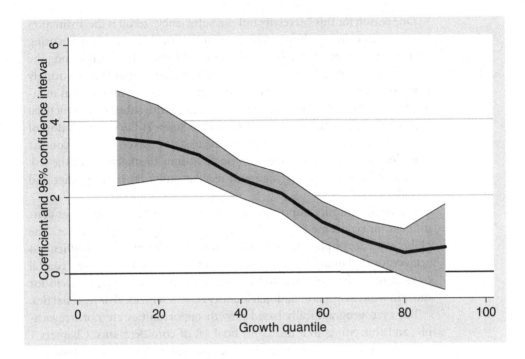

Figure 1.4 Estimated growth impact of avoiding syndromes
Source: The estimated specification appears in column (1) of table 2.12 of Collier and O'Connell (2007).

In fully a third of the country-years after independence, however, governments steered clear of recognizable anti-growth patterns. This is in sharp contrast to the pejorative thrust of much of the African political economy literature. Yet while growth collapse was rare in such cases, truly rapid growth (e.g. at a sustained rate of 5 percent or more) was also rare. Figure 1.4, from Collier and O'Connell (2007), conveys this point by showing the estimated impact of syndrome-free status at various quantiles of the conditional distribution of annual growth rates. At each quantile we model the growth rate as a linear function of opportunity group and economic shocks; the upper quantiles contain observations of rapid growth conditional on these variables, and the lower quantiles, slow growth. At the conditional median, the impact of syndrome-free status is consistent with standard regression estimates (which model the conditional mean rather than the median): an extra 2 percent of growth. At the lower quantiles, the impact is even larger. But in the highest quantiles, where growth is rapid for unobserved reasons, the presence or absence of syndromes makes considerably less difference. Over the 1960–2000 period, syndrome-free status allowed but did not guarantee sustained rapid growth.

One reason for this "necessity but not sufficiency" result is the distinction between achieving syndrome-free status and securing it over time. Focusing on regulatory controls, Collier and O'Connell (2007) show that among the coastal economies, the degree of export diversification after 1980 is strongly correlated with the duration of reforms. Reforming governments that managed to stay the course were rewarded over time with substantial structural change, a phenomenon that itself tended to support the consolidation of reforms. A similar result holds with respect to state breakdown: post-conflict episodes are by definition free from outright state breakdown, but the risk of renewed conflict is very high and recedes only over time (Collier and Hoeffler 2004).

A second critically important reason for the spread of outcomes conditional on syndrome-free status is that growth opportunities differ. The global evidence implies that sustained rapid growth will be more difficult to achieve for the landlocked, low-opportunity countries than for their coastal or resource-rich neighbors, and for politically polarized societies than for those in which aspects of national identity coexist with local or regional ties.

But even geographically based growth opportunities are not irrevocable, and this points to a third and final set of considerations. Chapters 1 and 12, vol. 1, widen the analysis to accommodate "errors of omission" – failures to intervene in a purposive manner to overcome locational disadvantages and other critical constraints to rapid growth. In volume 1, Ndulu and O'Connell (2007) focus on public infrastructure investment and human-resource development; Collier et al. (2007) focus on opportunity-specific interventions and the political institutions required to support them.

Ndulu (2004) draws on the growth literature to motivate public investments geared to reducing the unusually high cost of development in SSA. Consistent with our analytical geography, the costs associated with low population density, sparse networks of navigable waterways, long overland distances, and a multiplicity of national borders point to national and regional transport infrastructure as a key element in long-term growth strategy.

Ndulu and O'Connell (2007) argue that the contribution of human resources to Africa's growth is poised to be considerably larger in the region's second forty years of independence than it was in the first. The cross-country growth literature provides modest support for this argument: educational attainments and (until the early 1990s) life expectancies grew more rapidly than incomes did over the period, gradually strengthening the initial conditions for subsequent growth. The broad move to syndrome-free status meanwhile began to improve the *ex ante* social efficiency of private investments in secondary education and job experience, as the lure of remunerative public sector employment was replaced, by the late 1980s in most countries, by more uncertain prospects based in the private sector. Evidence from outside of Africa suggests that bursts of rapid investment and growth have in a number of cases been preceded by a cumulative increase in the ratio of human to physical capital (Hayami 2001; Berthélemy 2006) – a finding that, if generally valid, may help explain the weak performance of educational variables in panel-growth econometrics. Citing such threshold effects, Ndulu and O'Connell argue that:

the steady advance of educational attainment in Africa may have brought the region closer to supporting the rapid expansion of new and more education-intensive activities in the manufacturing and services sector. (Ndulu and O'Connell 2007: 68)

Demographic developments present a more complicated picture, with opposing tendencies presented by the HIV/AIDS epidemic and the beginnings of a fertility transition. These developments have qualitatively similar implications for population growth but sharply divergent implications for overall economic growth, via their impacts on age dependency ratios and the incentives for human-capital investment. African fertility rates were comparable to those in the rest of the developing world in 1960 but then stagnated before beginning a slow decline starting in the early 1980s. Outside of SSA, fertility was cut in half between 1960 and 2000, falling by over three births as compared to roughly one in SSA. Dependency ratios began to fall sharply outside of SSA by the early 1970s, while in SSA they continued to rise until the early 1990s. Dependency ratios did begin to fall in SSA during the 1990s, however. Progress in containing HIV/AIDS can help secure a major demographic dividend from Africa's entry into the final stage of the demographic transition.

Collier et al. (2007) use the "opportunities and choices" framework to develop an integrated analysis of opportunity-specific growth strategies and the political or institutional choices required to implement them. We focus here on a few highlights.

Resource-rich countries face the simplest challenge, if not the easiest. Their task is to spend public money effectively. Political democracy can contribute to this end, but the evidence suggests a sharp distinction between two of the leading attributes of democracy – public scrutiny and electoral accountability. Under conditions of low income and ethnic diversity, electoral accountability provides little bulwark against the misuse of commodity rents. Public scrutiny, in contrast, is essential to the successful management of resource rents. This can be supplied via a free press, quasi-independent mechanisms of project evaluation, and other mechanisms for enhancing the transparency of public management.

Coastal, resource-scarce countries have the Asian model to emulate; their task is to create an effective platform for export diversification. Maintaining syndrome-free status will provide a critical enabling environment for private investment in new activities. But success in bringing costs down to world levels may also require a "big-push" approach to improvements in infrastructure and public services, with individual infrastructure projects evaluated in light of an overall strategy of export promotion. Meanwhile the costs of late arrival imply that establishing a foothold in industrial-country markets is almost certainly more difficult now than it would have been in the early 1980s, due to the agglomeration benefits that have accrued to successful Asian exporters into these markets. Collier *et al.* (2007) argue that temporary trade preferences can help address this situation, but only if existing frameworks (Europe's Everything but Arms initiative and the Africa Growth and Opportunity Act (AGOA) in the USA) are extended to middle-income African countries and modified to adopt looser rules of origin (both), wider participation criteria (Everything but Arms), and longer horizons (AGOA).

The landlocked, resource-scarce countries pose the deepest structural challenges. One reason is that they depend on their coastal neighbors for local export markets and for transport access to world markets. This gives these countries an intense interest in both the overall prosperity of their coastal neighbors and the quality of their transport infrastructure. As Collier *et al.* (2007) point out, the relationship is largely a non-reciprocal one: holding security aside, Kenya's governance environment (and its transport network) matters more for Uganda than Uganda's does for Kenya. This makes the landlocked group a natural lobby for regional integration initiatives in both the transport and trade arenas. Regional customs unions should be outward-oriented and, crucially, not bound by their own internal rules of origin, if they are to serve the interests of the landlocked countries. They should seek low external tariffs so as to avoid the costly diversion of import trade from low-cost global suppliers to highly protected coastal industries.

The landlocked, resource-scarce group differs from the others, however, in lacking a single dominant strategy for moving to middle-income status. Particularly where coastal labor markets do not offer reliable and remunerative options for temporary labor exports, foreign aid will be critical in raising agricultural productivity and building the infrastructure and human-resource base for diversification into non-traditional export areas. Collier *et al.* (2007) emphasize that landlocked countries do not need to be air-locked and E-locked: high-quality airport and telecommunications services may allow these countries to exploit seasonal, time-of-day, and language advantages in delivering agricultural and E-service exports to industrial-country markets. Large aid flows have a critical ongoing role to play in these countries given their narrow resource base and high cost of development; this places a significant premium on institutional innovations that increase absorptive capacity by integrating donor financing into the domestic budgetary process.

5. The country studies

I turn briefly now to some highlights of the country studies, focusing on the political economy of policy and the interactions between geography and governance.[15] Further references to the country evidence appear throughout the synthesis volume. In chapter 3 of volume 1, Fosu draws on the country studies to provide extended illustrations of the policy syndromes (Fosu 2007).

5.1 Landlocked, resource-scarce economies

Of the three opportunity groups, the landlocked, resource-scarce group is the least thoroughly studied in the economics literature. The work of Jeffrey Sachs and his co-authors has brought to prominence the unusually high cost of development in this group, a phenomenon illustrated most dramatically in our case studies by the Sahelian economies Burkina Faso, Chad, Mali, and Niger (Gallup and Sachs, with Mellinger 1999; Faye *et al.* 2004). The most striking feature of the landlocked group, however, is its exposure to fundamental weaknesses in governance. The incidence of state breakdown is double that of other opportunity groups, and in many cases the patterns of ethno-regional polarization emphasized by Azam (1995, 2007) play a central role. Growth takes place "in the shadow of conflict," with incumbent regimes choosing a mixture of repression and redistributive transfers to suppress or buy off opposition. Enlightened leaders seek ways of investing in national public goods, but a temporarily stable equilibrium may be destroyed by economic shocks, outside intervention, or irregular political succession. The investment environment reflects not just the current settings of policy and the relative weakness of growth opportunities, but also the high *ex ante* risk of conflict and policy reversals.

The forces of geographical opportunity and governance may be mutually reinforcing within the landlocked, resource-scarce group. Remoteness and resource scarcity reduce income, which in turn lowers the opportunity cost of violence and distributional conflict relative to that of production (Hirshleifer 1994). The security environment disarms institutions of restraint and favors the emergence of autocratic leaders. The ability of these leaders to reconcile growth with the retention of political power then drives the growth process – favorably in a few cases, such as Uganda under Museveni and (arguably) Malawi under Hastings Banda, but more often unfavorably. In the latter cases a narrow political elite chooses private accumulation over the provision of public goods, including costly initiatives capable of addressing geographical constraints; and the circle is complete.

---

[15] Table 1.1 contains a list of countries and authors.

The geography/governance trap is most acute under conditions of *ex ante* ethno-regional polarization. Burundi, Chad, the Sudan, Uganda, and Ethiopia provide potent illustrations. In **Burundi**, Belgian colonial policy created a social hierarchy based on perceived ethnicity, with political authority and human-capital investment concentrated in the minority Tutsi tribe. The promise of national reconciliation disappeared with the assassination of Burundi's founding leader in 1962 and the accession to power of the Bururi Tutsi faction in 1966. As documented in detail by Nkurunziza and Ngaruko in chapter 2, a succession of military dictators deployed the instruments of policy and state patronage to repress opposition by the majority and concentrate the "rents to sovereignty" in the Bururi region. Adam and O'Connell (1999) relate the severity of policy distortions to the narrowness of the ruling elite and the discount rate they apply to future benefits; in the case of Burundi, the patent unsustainability of minority domination generated spectacular distortions of public employment and investment.

Chad illustrates a pattern of regional conflict recognized by Arab historian Ibn Khaldun in the fourteenth century and reproduced throughout West and Central Africa. As outlined by Azam and Djimtoïngar in chapter 3, colonial policies reinforced existing tensions between a low-income, pastoral Northern society and a sedentary "useful Chad" (*Chad utile*) in the South characterized by higher levels of productivity and human capital. In the absence of a credible power-sharing arrangement, regional animosities erupted into open civil war twice during the post-independence period. The accession of Idriss Déby to power in the 1990s finally initiated a period of stable rule by the South, in a bargain analyzed in general terms by Azam (2007); the North's interests were guaranteed through the incumbency of a Northern rebel leader as Vice President. The arrangement provided the basis for foreign investment to exploit oil reserves in the South, whose existence had been known since the 1950s. Exploitation of these reserves enhanced growth opportunities but also raised new issues of political coexistence and economic management, as indicated by the experience of resource-rich countries.

In **the Sudan**, the reluctance of the Black and largely Christian/Animist South to submit to political control by the Arab and Muslim North created a state of civil war from the earliest days of independence. By contrast with Chad and some other regionally polarized countries, Ali and Elbadawi in chapter 7 emphasize the highly factionalized nature of Northern rule through much of the post-independence period, a feature that lent a short-term and opportunistic bias to economic policy against a background of consistent Northern domination. Discovery of oil reserves in the South of the country led the North to abrogate a 1972 power-sharing accord that had initiated a period of relative peace and stability. Growth in the late 1990s was based almost solely on oil. Armed conflicts continued in the South and West of the country, reflecting a Northern policy of repressing Southern demands for political and economic autonomy.

Consistent with its analytically landlocked status, temporary labor exports (mainly to Gulf states) have constituted an important source of foreign exchange earnings for the Sudan since the 1970s. The destination of labor remittances provides a sensitive barometer of the policy environment. Ali and Elbadawi document the diversion of remittances into the black market during periods of exchange rate misalignment and their retention abroad, as capital flight, during periods of political instability.

In **Ethiopia**, a revolutionary Marxist regime (the Derg) displaced the slowly modernizing Imperial regime in 1974 and implemented a broad program of state controls. While the attendant market distortions undermined the efficiency of resource allocation, Ethiopia's deep institutional history – with the church, military, and civil service all operating at national scale since at least the eighteenth century, and without significant interruption by European colonial powers – provides the background for some striking continuities of policy. Alemayehu in chapter 4 cites the maintenance of macroeconomic discipline across widely divergent regimes, as well as the willingness of subsequent regimes to restore the autonomy of successful state enterprises (like Ethiopian airlines) after initially subjecting them to tight political control.

Ethiopia was, of course, not politically landlocked for most of the post-1960 period, the result of a 1951 UN arrangement that federated Ethiopia with coastal Eritrea, in part to guarantee the former's access to the sea.[16] But although successive Ethiopian governments pushed for full union, this was actively contested by Eritrean forces during a three-decade war that ended with the union's peaceful dissolution in 1993.

Uganda, finally, illustrates the growth potential of landlocked countries in the wake of state breakdown. By prioritizing core functions and learning from early policy mistakes, the Museveni government initiated a cumulative process that encouraged the re-deployment of labor and capital to productive activities while creating a cumulatively decisive improvement in the investment environment. Kasekende and Atingi-Ego in chapter 8 document the key features of the Ugandan package, including the establishment of security, the stabilization of high inflation, and the removal of punitive export taxes. An essential feature of the Ugandan experience was the restoration of critical agencies of restraint within the public sector, including the Ministry of Finance, Planning, and Economic Development and the Central Bank.

---

[16] The Sudan is not politically landlocked either; as discussed earlier, we include it here to reflect the realities of a largely interior population.

Burkina Faso, **Chad**, **Mali**, and **Niger** illustrate the high cost of development in the landlocked economics of the Sahel. Growth is volatile, highly sensitive to fluctuations in rainfall (reflecting the sparsity of irrigation networks) and to the world prices of export commodities, particularly cotton and, in Niger, groundnuts. Transport costs to global markets are extremely high, with a large proportion representing the overland costs of transit through coastal neighbors. Burkina Faso's tenuous political status before independence – the country was shared out (as Upper Volta) between neighboring countries before being reconstituted as a separate state – illustrates the financial and political appeal of integrating these weak economies with stronger neighbors. The opposite, of course, happened at independence: the economic zones of French West Africa broke apart and the costs of isolation rose sharply as each state imposed its own structure of taxes and duties. The disintegration of regional markets was reproduced throughout landlocked Africa, with the exception of a few small states that remained tightly integrated with South Africa.[17] Labor exports to more favorable coastal economies continued to generate remittance incomes for the landlocked economies – Savadogo, Coulibaly, and McCracken report in chapter 20 that some 400,000 Burkinabe worked in the Ghanaian and Ivorian plantations at independence, out of a total population of 3.6 million – but outside of Southern Africa these arrangements proved unreliable, subject to economic contraction and populist repudiation in the host economies.

Malawi emerges as a high-growth performer after benchmarking for the adverse opportunities of the landlocked, resource-scarce group and the added isolation enforced by the destruction of transport lines through Mozambique during the early 1980s. We stress two reasons for this. One is that governance was relatively good – among the landlocked, resource-scarce countries only Malawi, Lesotho, and Swaziland maintained syndrome-free status throughout the entire post-independence period. As noted by Chipeta and Mkandawire in chapter 5, President Banda built a political base in export agriculture, drawing members of parliament and other high government officials into the profitable estate tobacco sector. Second, Malawi's relative success illustrates the influence of coastal neighbors on the character of growth opportunities among landlocked, resource-scarce countries. Here the contrast with Burkina Faso is instructive. Both have benefited from remittance incomes generated by temporary labor migration to coastal neighbors. But Ghana's economy contracted sharply during the 1970s and

---

[17] Botswana, Lesotho, Swaziland, and later Namibia, retained their membership in SACU. The policy-driven fragmentation of regional trade markets is well documented and survived many attempts at regional integration; see Oyejide, Elbadawi, and Collier (1999). Examples include the breakup of the East African Community (EAC) in 1977, which further isolated Uganda, and the 1963 dissolution of the Federation of Rhodesia and Nyasaland as Zambia and Malawi came to independence.

early 1980s, as did Côte d'Ivoire's for the entire period from 1979 to 1994. By comparison, although the South African economy stagnated starting in the mid-1970s, that economy nonetheless continued to represent a major regional market for the landlocked states of Southern Africa as well as a high-quality transport option for trade with industrial-country markets. Banda's willingness to continue political and economic relations with the apartheid regime generated major benefits, including investments in infrastructure, access to the talents of skilled technicians, and continued access to the richest market in SSA.

Burkina Faso and **Niger** illustrate the endogeneity of vested interests and the influence of these interests on the political and economic reforms that swept the continent between the late 1980s and mid-1990s. Burkina Faso's democratic transition in 1991 came virtually simultaneously with the government's acceptance of structural adjustment reforms. Both followed nearly two decades of acute policy and political instability, including a brief period of hard economic controls under the agrarian populist military regime of Thomas Sankara. Urban groups had played a supporting role in the removal of corrupt governments by military coup, but neither they nor the rural constituency Sankara sought to create exerted serious pressures on the course of policy after the mid-1980s. Structural adjustment reforms therefore confronted few vested interests. The second half of the decade witnessed an unprecedented combination of modest economic growth and political stability. Niger's period of political stability, by contrast, came earlier. As described by Samba Mamadou and Yakoubou in chapter 6, governments used groundnut and then uranium revenues to create alliances with traditional chiefs and buy the support of key interest groups, via free education and guaranteed public sector employment to secondary school graduates. Political liberalization occurred as the end of the uranium boom erased the revenue base on which the government had maintained its core functions and satisfied key interests. The 1990s were a decade of state breakdown punctuated by permanent strikes, violent political demonstrations, military coup, and regional rebellions.

5.2 Coastal, resource-scarce economies

By global standards, Africa's coastal, resource-scarce economies suffered the largest gap between opportunities and performance (Collier and O'Connell 2007). **Mauritius** is the only consistent high performer in the group, and the trajectory of this country is instructive. In 1961, future Nobel laureate James Meade submitted a major report to the British colonial government of Mauritius, advocating a turn to import-substituting industrialization. The existing sugar monoculture, Meade warned, was incapable of forestalling growing unemployment and social unrest in the face of rapid population growth.

Nor did the country's resource endowment favor diversification within agriculture. Meade also rejected a labor-intensive manufactured export drive, citing human capital requirements and the difficulty of securing the inter-ethnic co-operation that would be necessary to integrate sectors typically occupied by different races (Meade *et al.* 1961). Meade's advice carried the day, and the government implemented a classic import-substitution program that combined sugar taxes with high import tariffs. The outlines of this program were meanwhile being implemented throughout independent Africa, reflecting the post-war sympathy for state intervention, the influence of Fabian socialist ideology on Africa's founding political leaders, prevailing concepts of the agricultural "surplus" that could be leveraged in favor of industrialization, and, in some cases, the political salience of urban as opposed to rural political interests (Bates 2007; Ndulu 2007).

Import substitution failed to create significant employment or growth in Mauritius, and in the midst of a renewed employment crisis following independence in 1968 the ruling Labor Party adopted a two-track policy of export promotion. At center stage was the construction of an Asian-style platform for labor-intensive textile exports, an effort supported by massive investment in education throughout the 1970s and 1980s, generous subsidies and duty-free imports for firms operating in the Export-Processing Zone (EPZ), low minimum wages for women, the maintenance of a competitive exchange rate, and preferential access to industrial-country textile markets. Meanwhile the government joined the Yaoundé Convention in 1972, which provided large rents on sugar exports to Europe; and it continued selectively to protect firms producing for the domestic market. Nath and Madhoo in chapter 11 describe the strategy as one of "shared growth."

The half-life of import-substituting industrialization was much longer in the rest of coastal Africa, where it became tied up with the nationalization of industry and with macroeconomic imbalances and exchange rate over-valuation. Ghana, Tanzania, and Senegal implemented socialist regimes in the 1960s and retained tight economic controls through the mid-1980s. In Kenya and Côte d'Ivoire, policy was initially favorable to export agriculture, but sought also to expand the manufacturing sector through import protection; the period of export promotion did not survive the 1970s, falling prey in Côte d'Ivoire to debt problems and exchange rate over-valuation and in Kenya to a political succession that disenfranchised dynamic interests in the export sector. Only in Côte d'Ivoire did the import-substituting path show even temporary promise as a component of growth strategy, but as in Tanzania and Kenya its viability had eroded by the mid-1970s, to be prolonged only temporarily by the tropical beverages boom of 1976–7.

Outside of Mauritius, an inward-looking development strategy was displaced by attrition rather than by a decisive adoption of outward orientation. The case evidence suggests that, in contrast to Mauritius, the instruments of protection and control in the bulk of coastal Africa facilitated powerful and ultimately relatively narrow combinations of interest between governments and protected entities in the private and state enterprise sectors. The interests most damaged by these regimes – in the agricultural sector and in potential areas of export development – had little recourse within a domestic political sphere that had narrowed sharply during the 1970s: Ndulu and O'Connell (2007) document the replacement of multi-party systems with one-party states throughout coastal Africa. Commitments to export promotion remained superficial, and trade liberalization was frequently reversed (Oyejide, Elbadawi, and Collier 1999). Exchange controls were dismantled outside of the CFA zone during the 1980s, removing a substantial barrier to export diversification, but within the CFA countries devaluation was postponed until 1994. Only in the mid-1990s – in the wake of democratization and two decades after Mauritius made its decisive move to export promotion – could it be said that liberalizing reforms had begun to acquire an irreversible momentum in parts of coastal Africa. Collier and O'Connell (2007) show that the duration of syndrome-free status after 1980 is a powerful predictor of export diversification into manufactures and services.

Kenya's favorable coastal opportunities were dogged from the outset by a tribally based politics that concentrated power in the executive and converted the state sector into an instrument of patronage and exclusion. The promotion of non-traditional exports was never supported politically; under President Kenyatta, policy favored incumbent Kikuyu interests in export agriculture and, in a pattern reminiscent of Malawi under Hastings Banda, sought to enfranchise these interests in both the state enterprise sector and the civil service. His successor, Daniel Arap Moi, represented lower-income interests in the food crop sector and, as documented by Mwega and Ndung'u in chapter 10, turned increasingly against export agriculture in the early 1980s. Both leaders maintained an accommodation with politically excluded Kenyans of Indian descent who dominated international trade but had neither the leverage nor the interest to champion the creation of an effective platform for manufactured exports – a process that could upset a tenuous and reasonably lucrative political equilibrium.

Despite its initial advantages in human-capital formation – **Senegal** was the administrative center of French West Africa – and its broad maintenance of democratic institutions, Senegal remained a poorly diversified groundnut economy through much of the period, suffering the Sahel drought starting in the late 1970s, the oil shocks of the 1970s, and the cumulative effects of CFA franc over-valuation between 1985 and 1994. Ndiaye in chapter 12 describes a social structure that gave substantial influence to local Islamic religious leaders as intermediaries between the Dakar government and its rural constituencies; this structure helped to underpin political stability but may also have slowed the economy's diversification into non-traditional exports. The economy was characterized by "soft controls" through the early 1990s and turned to market-based reforms and outward orientation only with the CFA devaluation of 1994.

Ghana's trajectory was established early on by President Nkrumah's pointed rejection of the advice of W. Arthur Lewis, who wrote in 1953 that

The main obstacle to development [in the Gold Coast] is the fact that agricultural productivity per man is stagnant. Very many years will have elapsed before it becomes economical for the government to transfer any large part of its resources towards industrialization and away from the more urgent priorities of agricultural productivity and public services. (Lewis 1953: para. 255, reprinted in Kay 1972: 88)

Nkrumah's strategy, by contrast, embraced rapid industrialization and the promotion of a state-run agriculture. His removal by coup in 1966 initiated a period of political instability, continued economic controls, and policy disarray that lasted nearly two decades. As in Tanzania, Mozambique, and other countries that sought to repudiate market prices as a means for resource allocation, price controls and public marketing agencies ultimately lost their traction as instruments of resource allocation and revenue: by the early 1980s two-thirds of Ghana's cocoa crop was being smuggled to neighboring Côte d'Ivoire. Controls were abandoned by the Rawlings government in the early 1980s; this occurred in the depths of a macroeconomic crisis as the leverage of experience and donor financing finally overwhelmed urban interests that had been weakened by attrition.

Ex post, Ghana's policy reversal was decisive and the transformation of its growth experience was remarkable. After 1984 the average annual growth rate of real GDP *per capita* rose by 2.9 percent and, perhaps more revealingly, its standard deviation fell by nearly 90 percent. As Aryeetey and Fosu point out in chapter 9, however, the private investment response to reforms remained very weak, at least through the mid-1990s. This is consistent with the tenuous credibility of reforms, against a background of policy instability and perhaps Rawlings' own continued ambiguity regarding their status (Aryeetey 1994). Ghana's experience poses a central issue of growth strategy in coastal Africa: having achieved two decades of political and policy stability, what further steps are required to build an export platform that will attract high levels of investment, including the re-entry of flight capital and of professional Ghanaians abroad?

Côte d'Ivoire presents a remarkable picture of sustained rapid growth until 1979, followed by equally sustained and rapid decline. The death of founding President Houphouët-Boigny in 1995 set off a succession crisis, ending a long period of political stability and initiating a period of armed rebellion in the North and state breakdown. As documented by Kouadio

Benie in chapter 23, however Houphouët-Boigny's death was preceded by a long period of exchange rate over-valuation, fiscal crisis, and economic decline. The seeds of decline had been sown in Houphouët-Boigny's turn towards import-substituting industrialization in the early 1970s and his use of commercial borrowing to finance patronage projects and ride out the oil shocks.

Interpretation of the Houphouët-Boigny era remains contentious. Azam (2007) regards Houphouët-Boigny as a master of high economic states-manship, for his inclusion of the low-income North in a national system of state patronage. Against a counterfactual of civil war, "mere" long-run stagnation may constitute a victory of sorts, and the preservation of political stability during fifteen years of outright decline (1980–94) speaks of first-order political skills. But the succession crisis and renewed decline in the late 1990s suggests a much less favorable bargain over the four decades of Houphouët-Boigny's rule, one in which regional identities were appeased but not disarmed and Houphouët-Boigny's personalized guarantee of stability was never institutionalized.

Tanzania illustrates a mismatch between ideology and opportunity that was particularly corrosive among Africa's coastal countries, where it under-mined the core elements of a pro-growth strategy even where leaders dis-played high personal character and commanded broad popular support. President Nyerere sought early on to free Tanzania from Kenyan domina-tion in the East African community, and from a dependence on foreign capital and markets. He established a separate currency soon after indepen-dence and nationalized the "commanding heights" of the economy in the Arusha Declaration of 1967. The public sector grew rapidly, subsisting on foreign aid and the coffee boom of 1976–7, while in agriculture Nyerere sought to control both exports and domestic distribution via price controls and mandatory sales to government marketing boards. As documented by Mwase and Ndulu in chapter 13, a combination of shocks in the late 1970s – including the second Organization of Petroleum-exporting Countries (OPEC) oil price increase and a costly war with the Idi Amin regime in Uganda – revealed the unsustainability of the system. The government responded to a balance of payments crisis by tightening its exchange control regime, rationing consumer goods, and running a public-relations cam-paign against "economic saboteurs" operating in the black market. Output collapsed, with producers starved of imported intermediates in the manu-facturing sector and driven into subsistence activity and smuggling in agri-culture. To his credit, Nyerere sponsored a protracted domestic debate on exchange rate policy in the early 1980s – a debate won by technocrats whose victory was sealed by Nyerere's resignation in 1985 and the country's accep-tance of structural adjustment reforms including a maxi-devaluation. Trade and financial reforms and the privatization of state enterprises dominated the subsequent decade, proceeding at a halting but resolute pace and becoming irreversible with the introduction of multi-party elections in 1995.

Nyerere's more lasting legacy may be Tanzania's long-standing political stability. Comparing Tanzania with Kenya, Miguel (2004) argues that Nyerere's deeper commitment to nation-building – expressed in a wide variety of ways, including the adoption of Swahili as the language of primary education and government – succeeded over time in subordinating sub-national identities to national ones, creating a durable social capital that supported higher levels of public goods provision at both the local level and nationally.

Mozambique's trajectory was dominated by state controls and conflict following an abrupt transition to independence in the wake of the Portuguese Revolution of 1974. The Marxist–Leninist regime rapidly nationalized industry and adopted widespread economic controls, in a pattern consistent with the coercive practices of Portuguese colonialism but ideologically grounded (as in Tanzania) in a repudiation of markets and private accumulation. President Machel's hard line against the apartheid regime in South Africa ran in sharp contrast to the pragmatically accommodating stances of both Malawi and Botswana, and as Sulemane and de Sousa observe in chapter 24, it cost the country dearly: transport services and labor exports had been major sources of export revenues, and South Africa cut off its imports of both in retaliation for the country's support of the African National Congress (ANC). As the civil war spread in the early 1980s, South African supported rebels destroyed the major transport lines through Mozambique, further disabling the service economy. By the early 1980s, officially marketed agricultural output had nearly disappeared and consumer goods were rationed in urban areas, amid widespread black market activity. Economic crisis drove the country to join the Bretton Woods institutions in 1984 and to adopt structural adjustment reforms starting in 1987. Growth awaited the resolution of conflict, which came in 1992, followed in quick succession by democratic elections and major aid inflows.

Among the coastal, resource-poor economies, **Togo**'s phosphate resources have given rise to features mainly associated with resource-rich countries. Policy in the 1960s initially followed the conservative and market-oriented principles of the French colonial regime, reflecting the business background of founding President Sylvanus Olympio. Olympio nonetheless sought to assert the country's independence from French influence; he was replaced in 1963 in SSA's first military coup, widely thought to have been supported by the French government. Popular dissatisfaction produced a second coup in 1967, installing the Northerner Gnassingbe Edayema and setting the country on a course of increasingly predatory and repressive autocracy through the end of the century. The phosphate boom of 1973 played a crucial transitional role by financing a rapid expansion of the state enterprise sector and the introduction of widespread economic controls. Gogué and Evlo in chapter 14 document the concentration of state benefits in favor of the Kabye, an ethnic minority, and the systems of repression employed by Edayema to retain power in the face of popular democractic movements in the 1990s.

Benin's growth opportunities have been influenced by its position as a transit point for landlocked countries such as Burkina Faso and Niger, but even more so by its long and porous border with Nigeria. Much of Nigeria's trade with coastal West Africa passes through Benin, and for a substantial portion of the 1960–2000 period the port of Conotou provided a major transit point for Nigeria's global trade, both on the export side – Dossou and Sinzogan, with Mensah (chapter 22) note that smuggled cocoa amounted to nearly 30 percent of Benin's exports in the early 1970s – and as oil-based spending drove up effective protection rates in Nigeria's import-substituting regime, on the import side. Re-exports of foodstuffs and restricted consumer goods to Nigeria played such a central role during the 1970s and 1980s that Benin's Marxist–Leninist regime (1972–89) not only invested heavily in overland transport between Conotou and the Nigerian border, but also implemented a relatively open tariff regime that would satisfy revenue needs while preserving a strong price differential in favor of the re-export trade. Nigeria's progressive economic liberalization, starting in 1994 and affecting trade incentives both directly (via reduced effective protection rates) and indirectly (via exchange rate unification and a substantial real depreciation of the naira) constituted a major adverse shock to Benin's service sector and its public revenue base early in the country's democratic transition.

5.3 Resource-rich economies

While there is nothing inevitable about the "natural-resource curse" – witness Botswana, for decades the fastest-growing economy in the world – the global evidence suggests that resource wealth often induces economic mismanagement. The political economy literature points to two important channels.[18] First, the property rights over resource wealth are worth fighting for. Where resource wealth is geographically concentrated, the contest over its control may raise fundamental issues of sovereignty, pitting regions against one another in a struggle for control of the national government. Secondly, as emphasized by Collier and Gunning (2007), resource rents are an attractive source of revenue for non-representative regimes, absolving them from the need to provide effective public services in return for tax revenues. In effect, resource rents release the government from domestic scrutiny of how it spends its money.

---

[18] The "Dutch disease," mentioned earlier, is a third.

The existence or emergence of large resource rents therefore tends to exacerbate the very institutional weaknesses that must be overcome if rents are to be deployed in the service of economic growth. There is a partial analogy with foreign aid, the resource component of which has similar effects on domestic scrutiny. But aid comes with outside scrutiny by donors and it may be denied outright to a government that acquires sovereignty illegitimately; these differences are critical to its broadly more favorable growth impact. For the resource-rich economies, of course, commodity rents undermine the scope for external as well domestic scrutiny, by reducing the need for aid. The latter point is apparent in figure 1.5, where we use our time-invariant classification to track the main components of import capacity for resource-rich countries and a composite of all others (landlocked, resource-scarce and coastal countries), over the 1960–2000 period.[19] *Per capita* aid levels are very similar for the resource-rich and non-resource-rich groups in Africa, but by comparison with real exports and the income effect of the terms of trade they are much smaller among the resource-rich countries than the non-resource-rich countries.

Africa's resource-rich economies have grown more slowly than their global counterparts on both an unweighted and a population-weighted basis (Collier and O'Connell 2007). Figure 1.5 suggests that commodity price shocks were less favorable for this group, on average, than for its non-African counterparts: terms of trade increases were less dramatic during the 1960s and 1970s, while the cumulative collapse following the late 1970s was comparable in magnitude. But the larger story is in real exports *per capita*, which rose sharply during the 1960s and 1970s as these economies acquired resource-rich status. Exports than stagnated in real terms through the remainder of the century, suggesting a set of economies subsisting on natural-resource rents and undergoing very little structural transformation.

Collier and O'Connell (2007) argue in volume 1 that the relative under-performance of Africa's resource-rich economies is associated with the combination of ethnic diversity and political autocracy that characterized these economies during much of the 1960–2000 period. Global evidence implies that this combination is particularly damaging to long-run growth (Collier 2000; Alesina and La Ferrara 2004). Theory relates this observation to the choice between providing public goods and making transfers to special interests: autocracy removes constraints on the use of policy instruments, while ethnic diversity increases the likelihood that the government in power will serve narrow interests. The geography of opportunity is at work here at a deep level; Collier and Hoeffler (2005) find that autocracy

---

[19] Commercial borrowing is an important omitted further source of import financing for the non-African sample. In the SSA case, it has been relevant for only a few countries including Côte d'Ivoire, Nigeria, and South Africa.

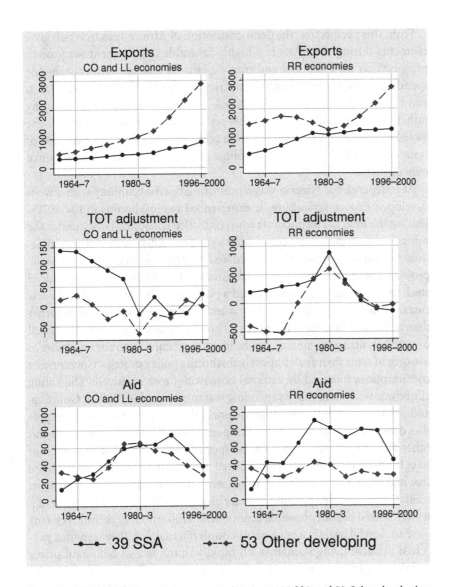

Figure 1.5 Capacity to import, by opportunity group, 39 SSA and 53 Other developing
countries, constant international dollars *per capita*, 1960–2000.
Notes: Exports and the terms of trade adjustment are in constant 1996 international
dollars *per capita*, and are from the PWT6.1. Aid in current dollars is from the World
Bank, deflated by the USA GDP deflator.

is significantly more likely to emerge when resource rents are large than
when they are not. These observations suggest a geography–governance
trap similar to the one we analyzed among the landlocked, resource-scarce
countries.

From this perspective, the democratization of African resource-rich governments during the 1990s is a highly favorable development for growth prospects on the continent and may explain the absence of unsustainable spending episodes among these countries after 1990. Ndulu, Collier, Bates, and O'Connell (chapters 1 and 12, vol. 1) argue that it is public scrutiny rather than electoral accountability *per se* that promotes this effect; the global evidence suggests that electoral accountability alone, in a context of resource wealth, can give rise to populist pressures that undermine resource management.

At independence **Nigeria** was a promising coastal economy with a well-developed export agriculture. It experienced two oil booms in the 1970s. During the first, the technocrats who controlled economic policy under the military government were committed to import-substituting industrialization. Accordingly, oil wealth was used for investment in large-scale industrial projects, including a massively expensive steel mill which never produced steel. In effect, the oil boom financed a policy experiment, in one of the few cases of public spending driven by a technocratic economic vision rather than by the self-interest of the regime. During the second oil boom, presided over by a civilian government, public investment continued but now more as a source of rents than as an import-substituting policy strategy. Government consumption, financed by external borrowing, rose massively. The ruling clique was well aware that its spending was unsustainable; Collier, Gunning, and Associates (1999) argue that the prevailing competitive patronage politics drove those with power into rampant embezzlement. Devaluation and other adjustment measures were postponed for so long that the shock of structural adjustment became associated not with the unsustainable policies that had produced the need for adjustment, but with structural adjustment itself. Unsustainable spending therefore left a costly legacy, in the form of a widely shared hostility towards economic liberalization. Economic reforms were successful against a reasonable counterfactual, but they were not perceived as such: living standards fell rapidly in the face of falling oil prices and debt repayment. In this sense, Nigeria's case is similar to that of Zambia: there, too, liberalization was greatly hampered by the legacy of the past. Nigeria serves as a spectacular example of the damage resource wealth can do in the absence of institutions for screening government spending proposals, including parliamentary scrutiny.[20]

At a deeper level Nigeria illustrates the challenges of natural-resource management under conditions of *ex ante* ethno-regional polarization. As

---

[20] We argued above that electoral accountability provides little guarantee against natural-resource mismanagement in the absence of scrutiny. Consistent with this argument, the democratically elected Shagari regime (1979–83) presided over what Collier and Gunning (2007) characterize as Africa's single biggest missed growth opportunity of the post-independence period.

emphasized by Iyoha and Oriakhi in chapter 18, Nigeria rushed to independence as an uneasy federation of a militarily powerful but economically weak interior (the North) and two smaller coastal regions, each home to a dominant ethnic group. Oil hardened regional political identities, replacing the North's development agenda with one of continued political domination and placing issues of revenue allocation at the center of political competition.

The case of the **Republic of Congo** is somewhat similar. As in Nigeria, the oil boom had the effect of relaxing a borrowing constraint. As documented by Tsassa and Yamb (chapter 25), the government responded with substantial and unsustainable borrowing. The proceeds were invested in a heavily regulated non-oil sector, dominated by state enterprises. The results cannot, of course, be attributed entirely to oil wealth (which could have been used quite differently). Rather, oil wealth enabled a government intent on adopting misguided policies to do so on a truly grand scale.

Cameroon started oil exports in the late 1970s, and initially this boom was managed remarkably well. This may well have reflected the government's interpretation of what had gone wrong in other countries during the oil boom of 1973–4. Spending pressures were resisted, in part by keeping the size of the windfall a secret, even from the Ministry of Finance. The Ahidjo government saved a very large fraction of its windfall income and held its savings largely in the form of foreign assets; Cameroon was one of the few oil producers to use foreign assets in this way (Collier, Gunning, and Associates 1999). However, upon repatriation these assets were poorly allocated. Kobou, Njinkeu, and Powo Fosso in chapter 16 note that government spending was increasingly used to subsidize state enterprises and, after 1985, to maintain cash crop prices in real terms when world prices had declined substantially. In the end oil wealth, and the borrowing that it enabled, served mainly to prolong an unsustainable policy stance. At a deeper level, what outlasted Ahidjo (the transition occurred in 1982) was not his personal prudence in managing resource rents but his evisceration of institutions of public scrutiny. During the 1980s public corruption emerged as a major and continuing feature of economic management in Cameroon.

In the economic history of **Guinea**, the key period is that of economic decline in 1978–84, following the discovery of bauxite in 1973. This reflected a combination of policy choices – Guinea had a highly interventionist socialist regime – and bad luck, in the form of a negative oil shock and a debt-servicing crisis. The government then embarked upon unsustainable redistribution, protecting the urban wage earning elite with rice subsidies and public employment guarantees and financing this through heavy taxes on peasant producers. As in Tanzania, however, peasants could shift resources from production of export crops to food crops, and Guinea was not in a position to offset the resulting fall in exports through borrowing. Doumbouya and Camara in chapter 17 document the resulting economic implosion, in which private agents retreated from the formal economy into subsistence and informal-sector activities. This process ended with a military coup in 1984. The ability of peasants to survive while shifting out of export production is a limit on government power which many African regimes have failed to recognize.

In **Zambia**, copper wealth came to be seen after independence as a means of financing Kaunda-type socialism. This included pan-territorial pricing, inefficient parastatals, exchange controls, and public ownership of firms. These policy choices (combined with a decline in copper prices) produced stagnation. In the 1990s Zambia adopted economic reforms. The process proved extraordinarily difficult, as documented by Mwanawina and Mulungushi (chapter 27): reform started with very low copper prices, a huge public debt, and an unsustainably large public sector. In addition, the legacy of pan-territorial pricing and other *dirigiste* interventions in the Kaunda period left the rural economy in a poor state to respond to changing price incentives. Major investments in rural roads and marketing institutions were required to reap the fruits of reform, but at the time the country could not afford such investments. In these circumstances it would have been extremely difficult to grow even if macroeconomic reforms had not been mishandled, as in fact they were (leading to hyperinflation and a collapse of investment). A possible interpretation is that the government simply could not deliver what voters had come to expect, given the poor hand it had been dealt by history. As a landlocked economy with copper- and aid-induced "Dutch disease," Zambia's opportunities for breaking into manufactured exports were extremely limited.

Sierra Leone had excellent opportunities – a coastal location plus mineral wealth – and was indeed better placed than landlocked Botswana. But Sierra Leone became a case of state collapse in the 1990s, with rapid economic decline. What explains the difference? First, diamond wealth had strong "dutch disease" effects in Sierra Leone, penalizing food production to the extent that the staple had to be imported. To some extent this reflected restrictive trade policies which made much of domestic production effectively non-tradable. By contrast, no such mechanisms operated in Botswana where borders are so open (and transport costs so low) that in fact all production is tradable. In chapter 19, Davies emphasizes a second difference rooted in technology: unlike in Botswana, diamonds in Sierra Leone are alluvial, making it extremely difficult for the government to control resource rents while at the same time making fighting for these rents relatively cheap. Finally, Sierra Leone fell under the influence of Khadafi, who attempted to export the Libyan revolution. While the last two differences may be classified as bad luck for Sierra Leone, the first difference has a clear policy implication.

In **Namibia** a legacy of very high inequality plays a continuing role in limiting investment outside of a diversified non-fuel mining sector that accounts for some 20 percent of GDP. Prior to independence in 1990, this inequality induced expectations of redistribution as apartheid was seen to be coming to an end. However, anticipated redistribution continues to characterize the post-independence period, since white settlers remain in control of much of the economy. The result is that in spite of formal protections of property rights, investors (both domestic and foreign) adopt a wait-and-see attitude, reckoning that inequality cannot be sustained at the present level and that property rights might well be violated when the inevitable change occurs.

Botswana started with poor opportunities but succeeded spectacularly. Superficially, this is not surprising. In our taxonomy Botswana remained syndrome-free throughout the period. The government was extraordinarily careful in its responses to diamond shocks, effectively treating positive shocks as temporary and negative shocks as permanent, and it imposed rigorous cost-benefit criteria in the allocation of public investment. In both respects, the difference with Nigeria is striking: Nigeria borrowed during windfalls while Botswana saved, and Nigeria invested in domestic projects with extremely low returns while Botswana limited the pace of investment to its absorptive capacity. But why did Botswana manage to avoid the mistakes of so many other resource-rich countries? There is no single answer. Botswana's leadership was involved in export agriculture, which limited the appeal of import-substituting industrialization and, unlike Malawi, Kenya, and Côte d'Ivoire, where founding leaders had similar political roots, Botswana forswore even the instruments of import protection by retaining its membership of the Southern African Customs Union (SACU). Botswana's political elite had acquired a prudent attitude towards the management of economic shocks, first from its experience with livestock and second, before diamonds emerged in the 1970s, with copper; oil producers, in contrast, had little experience with the large and transitory price movements that began in the 1970s. Third, Maipose and Matsheka stress in chapter 15 the lack of ethno-regional polarization and the participatory and consensual nature of traditional "Tswana" leadership, features that President Khama and his successor sought to accommodate alongside the institutions of a modern democracy. Finally, Botswana's leaders demonstrated a willingness to learn from what they perceived as the policy errors of other countries, including Zambia's copper policy.

6. Final observations

The decade after 1995 saw a broad revival of growth in Africa, with the median country growing at 1.3 percent in *per capita* terms and nearly two in five countries exceeding the developing-country median for 1960–2000 (2.3 percent). In light of experience – recall figure 1.3 – the critical question is whether patterns now underway will be sustained and deepened over the long run. Here and in volume 1 we have argued that growth outcomes will be shaped by the interaction of opportunities with choices. With respect to choices, the country evidence places Africa at the cusp of a potentially epochal change. By the mid-1990s, economic reforms had improved the growth environment across the continent, with nearly two-thirds of countries achieving syndrome-free status. Maintaining this status will open the possibility of truly rapid growth, while protecting countries from the episodal collapses that have undermined sustained progress in the past.

Economic transformation will require strong political leadership and here, too, forty years' experience provides a clarity unavailable in previous decades. African leaders began to dismantle domestic agencies of restraint in the late 1960s, citing considerations of development and national unity. But in sharp contrast to experience in much of Asia, political autocracy failed to produce development in Africa. As argued in detail in volume 1, the impact of democratization goes beyond the short-run uncertainties it created, starting in the late 1980s, and the vigorous resistance it provoked in countries such as Niger and Nigeria. By broadening the accountability of political leaders and widening the scope for public scrutiny of policy, these reforms hold the promise of supporting political programs based on national public goods rather than private or regional accumulation.

We have emphasized the importance of regional integration for Africa's landlocked economies. Within our framework of opportunities and choices, however, the scope for regional co-operation is considerably wider. Regional security co-operation is critical to containing armed conflict and limiting its spillover effects. Regional approaches are also appropriate for addressing the under-provision of agricultural research, transport infrastructure, and other cross-national public goods. The investment environment itself is subject to neighborhood effects, providing a rationale for peer review mechanisms such as those being developed by African regional organizations. While these benefits have long been relevant, the dominant pattern since independence has been one of disintegration rather than integration. Developments in the 1990s were fundamentally favorable to deeper co-operation, including the convergence of policy regimes in favor of outward orientation and private sector development and the emergence of Africa's largest economy, South Africa, from its long exile within the continent.

Growth opportunities are multi-faceted and country-specific, and most countries display a combination of the features we have associated with landlockedness, coastal location, and resource abundance. The salience of these features, moreover, evolves over time, in response to changes in global technology and trade. In the final decade of our 1960–2000 period, developments in information technology (IT) began to erode some of the costs of remoteness; meanwhile, the development of export platforms in India and especially China heightened the comparative resource intensity of Africa's endowment, enhancing the attractiveness of resource-based exports – with their attendant challenges – while creating tough new competition in markets for labor-intensive manufactures and services. Against this evolving background, successful national growth strategies will be those that bring the global evidence and the evidence from Africa's own experience to bear in the particular and changing circumstances of individual countries. In volume 1, we sought to inform that effort by extracting lessons of cross-cutting relevance from the country evidence. Here, the country experiences speak for themselves. We commend these studies to scholars and practitioners alike, and particularly to those whose strategic choices will shape the environment for growth in the coming decades.

References

Adam, Christopher S. and Stephen A. O'Connell (1999), "Aid, Taxation, and Development in Sub-Saharan Africa," *Economics and Politics* 11(3), November: 225–54

Ake, Claude (1996), *Democracy and Development in Africa.* Washington, DC: The Brookings Institution

Alesina, A. and E. La Ferrara (2004), "Ethnic Diversity and Economic Performance," NBER Working Papers 10313. Cambridge, MA: National Bureau of Economic Research, Inc.

Aryeety, Ernest (1994), "Private Investment under Uncertainty in Ghana," *World Development* 22(8), August: 1211–21

Azam, Jean-Paul (1995), "How to Pay for the Peace? A Theoretical Framework with References to African Countries," *Public Choice* 83(1/2): 173–84

(2007), "The Political Geography of Redistribution," chapter 6 in Benno J. Ndulu, Stephen A. O'Connell, Robert H. Bates, Paul Collier, and Chukwuma C. Soludo, eds., *The Political Economy of Economic Growth in Africa, 1960–2000,* vol. 1. Cambridge: Cambridge University Press

Bates, Robert H. (1981), *Markets and States in Tropical Africa: The Political Basis of Agricultural Policies.* Berkeley, CA: University of California Press

(1989) *Beyond the Miracle of the Market: The Political Economy of Agrarian Development in Kenya.* Cambridge: Cambridge University Press

(2007), "Domestic Interests and Control Regimes," chapter 4 in Benno J. Ndulu, Stephen A. O'Connell, Robert H. Bates, Paul Collier, and Chukwuma C. Soludo, eds., *The Political Economy of Economic Growth in Africa, 1960–2000,* vol. 1. Cambridge: Cambridge University Press

Bates, Robert H. and Shantayanan Devarajan (2001), "Framework Paper on the Political Economy of African Growth," *AERC Working Papers Series.* Nairobi: African Economic Research Consortium

Berthélemy, Jean-Claude (2006), "Convergence and Development Traps: How Did Emerging Economies Escape the Underdevelopment Trap?," in François Bourguignon and Boris Pleskovic, eds., *Growth and Integration: Annual World*

Bank Conference on Development Economics 2006. Washington, DC: The World Bank: 127–56

Block, Steven A. (2001), "Does Africa Grow Differently?," *Journal of Development Economics* 65: 443–67

Collier, Paul (2000), "Ethnicity, Politics and Economic Performance," *Economics and Politics* 12(3), November: 225–45

(2002) "Implications of Ethnic Diversity," *Economic Policy* 32, April: 129–66

Collier, Paul and Jan Willem Gunning (1999), "Explaining African Economic Performance," *Journal of Economic Literature* 37, March: 64–111

(2001), "The Microeconomics of African Growth," Framework paper for the Explaining African Economic Growth Project. Nairobi: African Economic Research Consortium

(2007), "Sacrificing the Future: Intertemporal Strategies and their Implications for Growth," chapter 5 in Benno J. Ndulu, Stephen A. O'Connell, Robert H. Bates, Paul Collier, and Chukwuma C. Soludo, eds., *The Political Economy of Economic Growth in Africa, 1960–2000*, vol. 1. Cambridge: Cambridge University Press

Collier, Paul, Jan Willem Gunning, and Associates (1999), *Trade Shocks in Developing Countries*. Oxford: Oxford University Press, 2 vols.

Collier, Paul, Jan Willem Gunning, Stephen A. O'Connell and Benno J. Ndulu (2007), "Harnessing Growth Opportunities: How Africa Can Advance," chapter 12 in Benno J. Ndulu, Stephen A. O'Connell, Robert H. Bates, Paul Collier, and Chukwuma C. Soludo, eds., *The Political Economy of Economic Growth in Africa, 1960–2000*, vol. 1. Cambridge: Cambridge University Press

Collier, Paul and Anke Hoeffler (2004), "Greed and Grievance in Civil War," *Oxford Economic Papers* 56(4), October: 563–95

(2005), "Democracy and Natural Resources," CSAE, Department of Economics, Oxford University

Collier, Paul, Anke Hoeffler, and Catherine Pattillo (2001), "Capital Flight as a Portfolio Choice," *World Bank Economic Review* 15(1): 55–80

Collier, Paul and Stephen A. O'Connell (2007), "Opportunities and Choices," chapter 2 in Benno J. Ndulu, Stephen A. O'Connell, Robert H. Bates, Paul Collier, and Chukwuma C. Soludo, eds., *The Political Economy of Economic Growth in Africa, 1960–2000*, vol. 1. Cambridge: Cambridge University Press

Collins, Susan and Barry P. Bosworth (1996), "Economic Growth in East Asia: Accumulation versus Assimilation," *Brookings Papers on Economic Activity* 2: 135–203

Easterly, William and Ross Levine (1997), "Africa's Growth Tragedy: Policies and Ethnic Divisions," *Quarterly Journal of Economics* 92: 1203–50

Faye, Michael, John McArthur, Jeffrey Sachs, and Thomas Snow (2004), "The Challenges Facing Landlocked Developing Countries," *Journal of Human Development* 5(1), March: 31–68

Firebaugh, Glenn (2003), *The New Geography of Global Income Inequality*. Cambridge, MA: Harvard University Press

Fosu, Augustin Kwasi (2007), "Anti-growth Syndromes in Africa: A Synthesis of the Case Studies," chapter 3 in Benno J. Ndulu, Stephen A. O'Connell, Robert

H. Bates, Paul Collier, and Chukwuma C. Soludo, eds., *The Political Economy of Economic Growth in Africa, 1960–2000*, vol. 1. Cambridge: Cambridge University Press

Fosu, Augustin Kwasi and Stephen A. O'Connell (2006), "Explaining African Economic Growth: The Role of Anti-growth Syndromes," in François Bourguignon and Boris Pleskovic, eds., *Growth and Integration: Annual World Bank Conference on Development Economics 2006*. Washington, DC: The World Bank: 31–66

Frankel, Jeffrey A. and David Romer (1999), "Does Trade Cause Growth?," *American Economic Review* 89(3), June: 379–99

Gallup, John Luke and Jeffrey D. Sachs, with Andrew Mellinger (1999), "Geography and Economic Development," in Boris Pleskovic and Joseph E. Stiglitz, eds., *Annual World Bank Conference on Development Economics 1998*. Washington, DC: The World Bank

Hayami, Yuhiro (2001), *Development Economics: From the Poverty to the Wealth of Nations*, 2nd edn. Oxford: Oxford University Press

Hirshleifer, Jack (1994), "The Dark Side of the Force," *Economic Inquiry* 32

Hoeffler, Anke (2002), "The Augmented Solow Model and the African Growth Debate," *Oxford Bulletin of Economics and Statistics* 64(2), May: 135–58

Kay, G. B., ed. (1972), *The Political Economy of Colonialism in Ghana: A Collection of Documents and Statistics 1900–1960*. Cambridge: Cambridge University Press

Lewis, W. Arthur (1953), *Report on Industrialization and the Gold Coast*. Accra: Government Printing Department

Meade, James E. *et al.* (1961), *The Economic and Social Structure of Mauritius – Report to the Government of Mauritius*. London: Methuen

Miguel, Edward (2004), "Tribe or Nation? Nation-Building and Public Goods in Kenya versus Tanzania," *World Politics* 56, April: 327–62

Miguel, Edward, Shanker Satyanatah, and Ernest Sergenti (2004), "Economic Shocks and Civil Conflict: An Instrumental Variables Approach," *Journal of Political Economy* 112(4): 725–53

Ndulu, Benno J. (2004), "Infrastructure, Regional Integration and Growth in Sub-Saharan Africa: Dealing with the Disadvantages of Geographical and Sovereign Fragmentation," Paper presented at the AERC Plenary Session, Nairobi, December

 (2007), "The Evolution of Global Development Paradigms and their Influence on African Economic Growth," chapter 9 in Benno J. Ndulu, Stephen A. O'Connell, Robert H. Bates, Paul Collier, and Chukwuma C. Soludo, eds., *The Political Economy of Economic Growth in Africa, 1960–2000*, vol. 1. Cambridge: Cambridge University Press

Ndulu, Benno J. and Stephen A. O'Connell (2000), "Background Information on Economic Growth," AERC Growth Project, Nairobi, April (downloadable: www.aercafrica.org)

 (2003) "Revised Collins–Bosworth Growth Accounting Decompositions," AERC Growth Project, Nairobi, March (downloadable: www.aercafrica.org)

 (2007), "Policy Plus: African Growth Performance, 1960–2000," chapter 1 in Benno J. Ndulu, Stephen A. O'Connell, Robert H. Bates, Paul Collier, and

Chukwuma C. Soludo, eds., *The Political Economy of Economic Growth in Africa, 1960–2000*, vol. 1. Cambridge: Cambridge University Press

O'Connell, Stephen A. (2004), "Explaining African Economic Growth: Emerging Lessons from the Growth Project," Paper presented at the AERC Plenary Session, Nairobi, May 26

O'Connell, Stephen A. and Benno J. Ndulu (2001), "Explaining African Economic Growth: A Focus on Sources of Growth," *AERC Growth Working Paper Series*, African Economic Research Consortium, Nairobi (downloadable: www.aercafrica.org)

Oyejide, T. Ademola, Ibrahim Elbadawi, and Paul Collier, eds. (1999), *Regional Integration and Trade Liberalization in Africa*. New York: St. Martin's Press

Oyejide, T. Ademola and A. Soyibo (2001), "Markets and Economic Growth in Africa," Framework paper for the Explaining African Economic Growth Project, Nairobi: African Economic Research Consortium.

Rodrik, Dani (1999), "Where Did All the Growth Go? External Shocks and Growth Collapses," *Journal of Economic Growth* 4(4), December: 384–412

Ross, Michael (2003), "The Natural Resource Curse: How Wealth can Make you Poor," in I. Bannon and P. Collier, eds., *Natural Resources and Violent Conflict*. Washington, DC: The World Bank

Sachs, Jeffrey D. and Andrew Warner (2001), "The Curse of Natural Resources," *European Economic Review* 45(4–6): 827–38

Sala-i-Martin, Xavier A. (2006), "The World Distribution of Income: Falling Poverty and . . . Convergence, Period," *Quarterly Journal of Economics* 121(2), May: 351–97

PART I

Landlocked economies

2 | Why has Burundi grown so slowly? The political economy of redistribution

Janvier D. Nkurunziza and Floribert Ngaruko

1. Introduction

Burundi is a "low-opportunity" economy. The country is small and over-populated, with more than 6 million people divided into three ethnic groups: the Hutu (about 84 percent), the Tutsi (about 15 percent) and the Twa

UNCTAD, Geneva; Université de Nice Sophia Antipolis and ACBF, Harare.
  This chapter is based on a study carried out in the framework of the AERC Global Project on "Explaining Africa's Growth Performance." AERC's financial assistance is gratefully acknowledged. The study has greatly benefited from comments by Jan W. Gunning on several drafts; his contribution is highly appreciated. We also thank Léonce Ndikumana, William Easterly, Randall Filer, Vittorio Corbo, Paul Collier, Robert Bates, Stephen O'Connell, Chukwuma Soludo, Dominique Njinkeu and all those who provided comments

(1 percent).[1] With an urbanisation rate of only 7 percent, Burundi is essentially rural. Furthermore, Burundi's location in the tropics, where malaria and other debilitating tropical diseases are prevalent, imposes a heavy constraint on the country's development potential.[2] In addition, Burundi is landlocked and dependent on its neighbors' wrecked road and rail infrastructure in the conduct of its international trade. The country's isolation within a geographically isolated continent (Fafchamps 2003) compounds the challenges to Burundi's economic growth.

Instead of responding to the country's adverse natural environment by adopting pro-growth policies, Burundi's political leaders have isolated the country even further through catastrophic governance. The main argument developed in this chapter is that from the early 1960s, poor governance has been at the heart of Burundi's dismal economic performance. Putting the state at the center of economic activity, the ruling elite have ensured that their hold on political power guarantees them total control over the economy and its rents. Although the country is poor, there are "rents to sovereignty" that have motivated policy choices. The sovereign has appropriated part of foreign aid and international borrowing. The leaders have allocated public investment and public employment to benefit members of their group. Even taxation of the domestic economy and the organization of markets have been shaped not to encourage production and growth but to generate rents enjoyed by those in power.

As a result, the traditional economic determinants of growth such as investment and human capital have been endogenous to political imperatives. In response to the predatory policies pursued by successive governments, households have retreated into a subsistence economy while the modern private sector has remained rudimentary. Consequently, Burundi's economic performance over the last four decades has been catastrophic, even by African standards. In absolute terms, GDP per capita fell from about US$620 to US$370 between 1960 and 1998.

Most of post-colonial Burundi's history has been dominated by military dictatorships. Three military Tutsi presidents from Rutovu, a commune

---

at the conferences where the original paper has been presented: GDN conference in Brazil; HILR at Harvard University; CGD in Washington, DC; AERC in Nairobi; University of Ngozi in Burundi; and American University in Washington, DC. However, the authors alone remain responsible for the study's contents.

[1] These figures as well as the notion of ethnicity should be taken with caution. All Burundians speak the same language (Kirundi), share the same culture, live side by side in the different regions of the country, and do not present systematic differentiating physiological features. The differences between groups may have to do with "imagined" or "created" identities rather than the usual factors used to empirically define ethnic groups (see Horowitz 1985). This caveat should be kept in mind when interpreting ethnicity in Burundi.

[2] Easterly and Levine (2003) provide an interesting contrast between Burundi and Canada in terms of the two countries' geographic location and physical environment.

of the Southern province of Bururi, were at the helm of the country for thirty-four years out of forty-one since the country's independence in 1962.[3] These are Michel Micombero (1966–76), Jean-Baptiste Bagaza (1976–87) and Pierre Buyoya (1987–93, 1996–2003), all of whom took power through *coups d'états*. Increasingly, the leadership's greed and poor governance have generated grievances which, in turn, have led to a cycle of civil wars. From independence, the country has recorded five episodes of civil war that have claimed more than 500,000 lives and have produced about a million refugees. The latest civil war has been raging for ten years so it is hardly surprising that the country's economy is currently in tatters.

This chapter is organized in four sections. First, it reviews Burundi's growth based on traditional macroeconomic analysis to highlight the limitation of this approach and to show the position of Burundi relative to other developing regions. Secondly, the chapter discusses how the organization of market institutions by the state has been responsible for the poor performance of the economy. Thirdly, the behavior of agents, both firms and households, faced with a discouraging environment, is analyzed. Lastly, the chapter develops a political-economy argument to explain why Burundi's economy has performed so poorly and why the leadership hardly cared.

The chapter contributes to the literature on Africa's growth in many respects. First, it is the first comprehensive study of Burundi's growth experience of which we are aware. Secondly, the chapter shows the central role played by politics in explaining the lack of growth and its underlying characteristics such as equity, poverty, and income distribution. Thirdly, the chapter clarifies the nature of one of the most misunderstood conflicts in Africa by showing that the simplistic interpretation of the Burundi conflicts as ethnic contests is flawed. Different groups fight to control important economic rents and they use ethnicity as an instrument for their propaganda.

2. Burundi's growth in comparative perspective

This section provides a brief historical background of Burundi's pre-independence growth performance. It proposes three episodes of the growth experience and, finally, discusses the results of growth accounting in comparison with other developing regions.

2.1 Historical background

Before independence, Burundi's economy was integrated under Belgian rule with those of Rwanda and Congo. Bujumbura – later the capital of

---

[3] Lack of information on the period before 1960 did not allow us to start the analysis from 1950. Even for the period 1960 to 1970, statistical information is sketchy.

independent Burundi – served as the industrial base for Burundi, Rwanda, and Eastern Congo. Until Congo's independence in 1960, this area used a common currency. Congo adopted its own currency after independence in 1960, but currency union between Burundi and Rwanda was terminated only in 1964, two years after the two countries' independence in 1962.[4] As economic independence was thought to give teeth to political independence, Rwanda and Eastern Congo decided to create their own industries. Disintegration of the common market was damaging to Burundi's economy; following the loss of the Rwandese and Eastern Congolese markets in addition to the loss of qualified manpower after the Belgians left Burundi, firm capacity utilization dropped to about 25–50 percent in 1962–3 (Ngaruko 1993).

At the political level, Belgium's colonial policy was based on *divide et impera*. Playing the Hutu against the Tutsi reinforced group distinctions that had traditionally been relatively innocuous. The Hutu versus Tutsi rivalry existed before colonization, and to a large extent, the Tutsi ethnic group enjoyed relatively more economic privileges and political power. However, this state of play was institutionally regulated through sophisticated rules that prevented ethnic confrontations. The colonial power institutionalized the domination of Hutu by Tutsi through extremely rigid rules and policies clearly biased against the Hutu.

For instance, in the 1920s, there were twenty-seven Hutu chiefs ruling Hutu and Tutsi alike in their chiefdoms. By 1945, after a colonial administrative reform implemented from the late 1920s, all Hutu chiefs had been replaced (Reyntjens 1994). In the same vein, Belgian "scholars" went out of their way to show that Tutsi were a superior race born to rule while Hutu were inferior (De Lespinay 2000). It is ironic that instead of dismissing the colonial propaganda many Hutu and Tutsi, especially the elites, perpetuated it, often using it to advance their own interests. This perception of the superiority/inferiority of the two groups has shaped their relations ever since. The Belgian colonial government, for its own part, turned against the Tutsi in the 1950s because they adopted a more openly rebellious attitude towards the colonial power.

Belgium's education policy in Burundi reflected the perceptions of the colonial masters. For every Hutu student admitted into the Butare colonial institute, there were five Tutsi students in 1932, fifteen in 1945, three in 1954, and two in 1959 (Lemarchand 1994). Not surprisingly, at independence in 1962, some Tutsi leaders believed they had a special prerogative to rule the country. Moreover, the removal of Tutsi from leadership in Rwanda in the 1959 Belgian-orchestrated bloody social revolution profoundly affected Burundi. With the same ethnic configuration as in Rwanda, Burundi could

---

[4] See Nkurunziza (2001) for a summary of Burundi's monetary history.

not remain unscathed by the events. Not only did the country play host to vast numbers of Tutsi refugees who attempted to destabilize Rwanda a few years later, but also Tutsi and Hutu in Burundi started seeing each other through the Rwandese prism.

Radical Hutu leaders in Burundi saw it as the model to replicate, arguing that their numeric majority should guarantee them *de facto* control of political (and hence economic) power. On the other hand, most Tutsi leaders viewed the events in Rwanda as the scenario to avoid by all means, arguing that power in the hands of the Hutu would inexorably lead to their extermination.[5] This fundamental difference of perception explains, to date, the cycle of wars in Burundi and the actions of many of the elite of both groups.

Despite Belgian efforts to divide Burundians, the struggle for independence assembled politicians from the two major ethnic groups in the Union for National Progress (Union pour le Progrès National, UPRONA), a nationalist partly founded and led by Prince Louis Rwagasore. The party won legislative elections in September 1961, leading to independence on July 1, 1962. UPRONA was largely built on democratic values and included Hutu as well as Tutsi in its highest leadership structures. The assassination of Rwagasore in October 1961 and the political crisis that ensued changed the political atmosphere. King Mwambutsa IV lost control and the unity Rwagasore had instilled in his followers gave place to merciless political fights among the political elite. The loss of Rwagasore, a unifying figure at such a sensitive time in the country's history, is arguably the most important determinant of the country's political trajectory to date.[6]

For most of the 1960s and early 1970s, politicians were so busy fighting against each other that they devoted little time to economic growth. Rarely did governments between 1962 and the early 1970s last for more than a year. Amid this chaos, it was easier for political elites to seek an immediate gain than to speculate on some uncertain long-term or even medium-term economic benefit they would get by fostering economic growth. In retrospect, it is clear that this period set the standard for political competition and economic management for the following decades. Short-term gain and predatory politics have remained the most distinctive characteristics of Burundi's political culture.

2.2   Periodization of Burundi's growth experience

Burundi's economic policies evolved in three different periods. The period from 1960 to 1972 was characterized by policy instability, resulting in economic decline. The second period, from 1972 to 1988, saw the expansion

---

[5] The 1994 Rwandan genocide has to some degree vindicated those holding this view.
[6] This argument is well developed in Ngaruko and Nkurunziza (2000).

of the basis for economic rents to provide for the needs of young members of the elite. Per capita GDP increased, but the cost was massive borrowing and alarming inefficiencies. The third period, from 1988 to date, has been characterized by war and an unprecedented economic crisis. A brief discussion of each period follows.

2.2.1   1960–1972: institutional instability and economic decline

Most of the factors explaining economic decline during this period are a consequence of the chaotic departure of Belgians from their three colonies. First, the legacy of high ethnic tensions inherited from the Belgians paralyed institutions, culminating, in 1965, in the first large-scale political violence. Secondly, as already noted, Congo and Rwanda's independence spelled the end of the economic union, resulting in the loss of most of Burundi's export markets. Large trade deficits ensued. Thirdly, the scarcity of qualified manpower and capital stock following decolonization resulted in a sluggish economy, especially within the modern sector. During this period, Burundi's economic growth was lower than the African average and much lower than the average for highly performing Asian countries.

2.2.2   1972–1988: political repression and expansion of the basis for rents

On the political front, this period was characterized by the relative calm warranted by a highly repressive regime. The 1972 massacre, in which thousands of Tutsi were killed by Hutu rebels, triggered a horrendous repression directed against the Hutu by the Tutsi-dominated army. Most Hutu able to exercise any political, administrative, or economic power were physically eliminated. The massacre was followed by a long period of political repression, until the fall of Colonel Jean-Baptiste Bagaza and his replacement by Major Pierre Buyoya in September 1987.

From 1975, the country embarked on a massive program of investment, financed mostly by foreign resources in addition to increased export revenue following the coffee boom of the 1970s. A large number of public corporations were created and used to collect and distribute rents to the members of the political elite. The management of these loss-making corporations involved massive transfers of subsidies, crowding out resources for productive investment. Although this period experienced positive rates of economic growth, the widening budget deficits and the cost of servicing the resulting debts made this growth unsustainable in the 1980s. As a result, Burundi adopted a Structural Adjustment Program (SAP) in 1986. To economic difficulties was added the 1988 civil war, a result of political tensions that had been brewing during the preceding period of repression.

2.2.3   1988 to date: war and economic decline

Despite the fact that the war in 1988 was shorter and less costly in terms of human loss relative to 1972, it opened the way for increasing grievances from a new generation of Hutu, who had been excluded from political and economic participation since 1972. Facing an international community that conditioned more and more of its external aid on political inclusion of the Hutu, Burundi experienced a volatile political and economic environment (Reyntjens 1994). In 1993, another civil war erupted after the assassination by the army of the first democratically elected President.

In August 1996, the crisis deepened when Burundi's neighboring countries imposed a total economic embargo in reaction to a new military coup by Major Pierre Buyoya, the officer who had lost the 1993 elections. The international community followed suit by suspending its co-operation with Burundi. As a result, economic agents, including the government, attempted to import and export some strategic products illegally, criminalizing economic activity. Transactions costs multiplied as speculation and corruption reached new heights. The Burundi franc plummeted and inflation reached levels never seen before. Not surprisingly, Burundi recorded its highest levels of poverty during this period. Today, although the embargo has been suspended and the war has subsided in most parts of the country, the economy is in a shambles.[7] The destruction of physical, human, and social capital has been so deep that it will take many years to reconstruct them. However, there is renewed hope now that the country is slowly engaging in a process of democratization. In August 2005 a new class of democratically elected politicians took over the mantle to lead the country through its reconstruction era and beyond. Unfortunately, the first impressions are that these new leaders are not immune to the corrupt practices associated with the previous dictatorial regimes. Indeed, so much time has been wasted quarreling on how to share government positions that the new leadership has not been able to present to the nation a clear reconstruction and development strategy.

2.3   *Growth accounting and cross-country comparison*

Using the secondary school enrollment ratio as a proxy for human capital despite the inherent limits of this indicator (Gemmell 1996), and adopting the usual assumptions on the measurement of the number of workers, capital

---

[7] In order to have an idea of what Burundi would have become if it had not experienced its civil wars, we have assumed that the country would have had the mean growth rate of African countries, including those that have experienced war. It turns out that by 2000, GDP *per capita* would have been more than 70 percent higher than the actual figure. Taking the mean growth rate of countries that have experienced no war would increase the gap. This simple figure gives an idea of the cost of Burundi policies in the post-1960 period.

Table 2.1 *Decomposition of the contribution to growth, 1960–1997, period annual average, percent*

Period	$\dfrac{q}{l}$	$\dfrac{k}{l}$	H	A
1960–72	−2.50	105.80	15.40	−49.50
1973–88	1.56	13.40	3.30	−5.27
1989–97	−2.80	2.10	2.70	−5.25
1960–97	−0.74	40.56	7.01	−19.47

depreciation, and the elasticity of capital to output (see Collins and Bosworth 1996; Ndulu and O'Connell 2000), we find the following. GDP *per capita* decreased by more than 40 percent between 1960 and 1997; physical capital *per capita* was multiplied by 58 and human capital by 5; TFP was divided by 25. Overall, these figures conform to Burundi's reality. While investments made before independence to cater for Belgian colonial needs were made with efficiency in mind, the pattern changed after independence. Investment was generally allocated based on non-economic objectives to respond to such needs as rent-seeking, regionalism, clientelism, nepotism, and patronage.

This picture limits the relevance of the textbook growth model, which assumes that resources are efficiently allocated. When cronies rather than qualified managers are running the economy, when priority is given to investment projects in function of their location rather than the objective needs of the economy, it is not surprising that TFP decreases (Easterly 2001). Consequently, despite an apparently large increase in public investment since the 1970s, the effective increase in productive physical capital has been modest.

In table 2.1, the enormous rates of increase of physical and human capital *per capita* between 1960 and 1972 were due to particularly low initial conditions rather than high investment rates. Furthermore, the specification of capital depreciation does not seem to be appropriate for war economies. Taking into account the massive destruction of human and physical capital due to repetitive wars, the figures in table 2.1 should be lower.

HIV/AIDS has become another important source of human capital destruction. Recent figures show that HIV prevalence accelerated during the current civil war as a result of population displacements, army and rebel movements, and promiscuity in displacement camps. The prevalence rate in cities increased from 1 percent in 1983 to 15.1 percent in 1993 and to 21 percent in 1997, against 0.73 percent in 1989 to 5.9 percent in 1997 in rural areas (World Bank 1999). Educated urban elites are among the most affected.

Conflicts have also caused huge losses of physical capital. The killing and looting of livestock caused its decline from 2.6 million head to 1.8 million head from 1993 to 1999, a fall of 31 percent in just six years. Given the importance of livestock for land productivity through its supply of organic fertilizer, looting and killing of livestock not only deprived rural households of an important source of food but also an important source of agriculture input. The rates of growth of physical and human capital in Burundi are thus likely to be over-estimated, as their computation does not take these factors into account.

In a comparative perspective, it is notable that the evolution of Burundi's economic performance is atypical (see table 2.2). Whereas most African economies were growing in the period following independence, Burundi's was declining. The main reason was the political instability that followed the assassination of Prince Louis Rwagasore, who had spearheaded the country's struggle for independence. Rwagasore was charismatic and visionary; arguably, it was thanks to his leadership that the events in Rwanda in 1959 did not spread to Burundi (see Ngaruko and Nkurunziza 2000). His assassination robbed the country of a leader who would have put Burundi on a different course. Had other countries absorbed similar losses, their trajectories would probably have been similar to Burundi's.[8]

In the 1970s and 1980s, Burundi's economy grew at a faster rate than the African average, another departure from the norm. The government embarked on a large-scale program of modernization of the country's infrastructure – roads, dams, schools, etc. – partly in view of the rents these projects generated for the elites. The country experienced no civil war after the 1972 tragedy, but despite the prevailing relative calm it is during this period that exclusion based on ethnicity and regionalism was institutionalized. At the same time, and probably in reaction to these exclusionary policies, the period saw an intensification of clandestine Hutu opposition to the Tutsi political regimes, both from within and outside the country. This political unrest resulted in the 1988 and 1993 wars, which reversed the gains from the previous periods. Most of the variables considered in table 2.2 show that Burundi was worse off than the group of developing countries during this period.

Other growth determinants, such as the age dependency ratio, black market premium and inflation from 1990 to 1997, are consistent with a war economy – as noted, for example in Cukierman, Edwards, and Tabellini (1992). These variables are also consistent with the typology of African economies proposed by Hugon (1993). As table 2.3 shows, the deviation in Burundi's actual economic growth from the sample mean is correlated with war occurrence, suggesting that Burundi's economic dynamics are largely

---

[8] The current chaos in Côte d'Ivoire, more than forty years after independence but only a few years after the loss of their charismatic leader, is revealing.

Table 2.2 *Factors of growth, Burundi compared to Africa and Asia, 1975–1997*

Explanatory factors of growth	Expl. power[a]	Position of Burundi relative to SSA and HPAEs							
		1975–9		1980–4		1985–9		1990–7	
		SSA	HPAE	SSA	HPAE	SSA	HPAE	SSA	HPAE
Real GDP *per capita* growth rate	–	c	a	c	a	c	b	a	a
Initial income (expressed in log)	High	a	a	a	a	b	a	b	a
Landlocked	High	d	d	d	d	c	d	d	d
Cumulative terms of trade shocks	None	c	d	c	c	b	c	c	b
Black market premium	High	b	d	b	d	b	d	d	d
Initial life expectancy	High	b	a	b	a	b	a	a	a
Age dependency ratio	High	c	d	c	d	c	d	c	d
Growth in potential labor force	High	d	a	c	a	a	a	b	a
Trade-weighted growth rate of GDP *per capita*, trading partners	High	b	a	b	a	b	a	b	a
Political instability	High	b	a	b	b	b	d	c	d
Inflation	Low	c	d	b	b	c	c	d	d
Extended Barro–Lee gov. spending (% GDP)	High	b	d	b	d	n.a.	n.a.	n.a.	n.a.
Ln ratio investment to GDP (%)		b	a	c	a	c	a	n.a.	n.a.

Notes: [a]High, low, and none explanatory power refer to statistical significance levels of 1 percent, 25 percent, and more than 50 percent, respectively. The estimated parameters are from an OLS regression of real GDP *per capita* on several explanatory variables. Blanks mean that the variables are not included in the regression: they are included in table 2.2 for comparative purposes of Burundi's position relative to SSA and HPAE groups of countries; a: Burundi falls below the mean of the group of countries and below the 1 standard deviation margin; b: Falls below the mean of the group of countries but within the 1 standard deviation margin; c: Falls over the mean of the group of countries but within the 1 standard deviation margin; d: Falls over the mean of the group of countries and over the 1 standard deviation margin; n.a.: Not available; SSA: Sub-Saharan Africa; HPAEs: High-Performing Asian Economies.

explained by war. Moreover, while table 2.3 confirms the importance of traditional economic variables in explaining growth, it also highlights the role of policies, with a particular effect attributed to government spending. Section 3 analyzes how government intervention affected the structure of markets underlying this poor macroeconomic performance.

Table 2.3 *Burundi, fits and residuals from pooled conditional model, 1970–1997*

Period	Fits and residuals			Actual and predicted growth deviation				Breakdown of policy contribution, by variable		
	Actual growth	Fitted growth	Residual	Actual growth deviation from sample mean	Contribution to predicted growth deviation			Inflation >500%	Black market prem. >500%	Barro–Lee gov. spending as ratio to GDP
					Base Variables	Political Instability	Policy			
1970–4	3.80	–	–	1.60	0.11	0.00	–	0.04	–	−0.70
1975–9	2.07	2.06	0.01	−0.13	−0.05	0.13	−0.43	−0.01	0.01	−0.44
1980–4	0.46	0.29	0.17	−1.74	−0.95	0.20	−0.45	0.03	−0.01	−0.47
1985–9	2.50	–	–	0.30	−0.69	0.13	–	0.04	0.01	–
1990–7	−4.18	–	–	−6.37	−1.16	−0.13	–	0.00	−0.09	–
Total	**0.93**	**1.18**	**0.09**	**−1.27**	**−0.55**	**0.07**	**0.14**	**0.03**	**0.00**	**−0.06**

Source: Based on Ndulu and O'Connell (2000).

3. Government intervention and market structure

Markets are normally institutions that facilitate exchange and hence foster production and growth. In Burundi, markets respond to political objectives. This section looks at three different markets, namely those for goods and services, financial services, and labor, and the way they have been used as political tools.

3.1 Markets for goods and services

Traditionally, the government has been involved in the goods markets through its parastatals. Prominent among them are OCIBU, OTB, and COGERCO[9] which, together, control almost 100 percent of the country's total exports.[10] Through these three parastatals the government controls the determination of producer prices, thus providing a way to appropriate an important proportion of export earnings. For instance, during the fifteen years preceding the adoption of an SAP in 1986, coffee farmers were paid, on average, 40 percent of the world price, the lowest share in the region. The difference was appropriated by different agents and institutions, many of them controlled by the government or politically connected individuals.

The government has several other indirect ways of controlling the goods market, including taxation and exchange rate controls. Burundi's tax system lacks all three characteristics of an efficient tax system: certainty, simplicity, and transparency. The frequent changes in tax rates and the ad hoc use of quantitative import restrictions and import licenses illustrate the lack of certainty. Anecdotal evidence purports to show that non-connected businesses are sometimes denied licenses even when they do not require foreign currency from the central bank to pay for their imports. Moreover, the multiplicity of tax rates within each category of taxes makes the tax system overly complex. In terms of transparency, extremely widespread tax exemptions provide a leeway for abuses, increasing the potential for corruption.

For instance, in 1993, import duty exemptions made up 50 percent of total potential import duty revenue. The undefined category of "other exemptions" represented 3.3 billion Burundi francs in 1996, accounting for as much as 42 percent of total exemptions. The problem is that most officials

---

[9] OCIBU is Office des cultures industrielles du Burundi; OTB is Office du thé du Burundi, and COGERCO is Compagnie de gérance du coton.

[10] In the late 1970s the government also established parastatals to regulate the commercialization of consumer goods. SOBECOV (Société Burundaise d'entreposage et de commercialisation des produits vivriers) was tasked with the marketing of local produce while ONC (Office national de commerce) marketed imported consumer goods, from needles to motor vehicles. These state firms were eventually ruined in the 1980s by bad management, corruption, and nepotism.

making these decisions do not hesitate to trade on them for monetary gain. This complicated tax system leaves the determination of tax levels to the discretion of senior tax officers, a power they may use to extract and distribute rents.

3.2 Financial markets

For most of the post-independence period, the financial sector was dominated by two commercial banks, owned partly by the state and partly by Belgian banks. There was also a government savings bank, a government development bank, and a few non-banking financial institutions (NBFIs). With financial liberalization in the late 1980s and early 1990s, Burundi's financial sector has become more diversified. However, the country has no stock market and no dynamic informal financial markets, implying that most financial transactions are carried out through banks. Financial institutions are concentrated in Bujumbura, the capital city, but the main banks have branches in a number of provinces.

Despite some progress in terms of diversification, the financial sector remains under-developed. The average ratio of M2 to GDP was only 15 percent in the period between 1965 and 1998, 7 percentage points lower than the African average and less than half that of other less-developed countries (LDCs). The level of M2/M1, which stands at 1.35, is almost half of the means for both Africa and other LDCs. Furthermore, credit allocation is socially inefficient, as it does not reflect sectoral contributions to the economy.[11] In 1995, credit to agriculture represented only 1.7 percent of total credit, in comparison with 35 percent for trade, 14 percent for civil engineering and other services, and 10.5 percent for industrial activities. During the same year, the agriculture-dominated primary sector contributed about 50 percent to GDP against 6 percent, 3 percent, and 9 percent for trade, other services, and manufacturing, respectively. The high proportion of credit to the trading sector is in line with the rent-sharing model: since trade itself is partially controlled by the government through the issuance of import licenses, the financing of trade activities implies that banks are either part of the game, more interested in speculative activities, or both. Either way, the financial sector has a limited contribution to the process of economic growth.

With respect to the distortions in exchange rate markets, Burundi is the only country in the region that still controls the allocation of foreign currency; all other countries in the region were able to unify their foreign exchange markets in the early 1990s. In Burundi, the average premium more

---

[11] Credit allocation may, however, be efficient for banks, because their returns are high and they limit their lending to sectors with very low risk.

than doubled in the 1990s, reaching 45 percent per annum between 1990 and 2000. Controlling who may have access to cheap foreign currency from the central bank creates a two-tier system where importers incur different costs for the same imported products. Since the same imported product is sold at the same price on the local market, importers using cheaper foreign currency have larger profit margins. This is another way of allocating rents.

The large spreads between lending and borrowing rates are usually a symptom of both an inefficient and an oligopolistic financial sector. In Burundi, lending and borrowing rates were fixed by the government for most of the sample period. From 1975 to 1998, the average interest rate spread was 8.7 percent for average lending and deposit rates of 12.5 and 3.8, respectively. The average ratio of the spread to the lending rate was 0.70, a value that is higher than most African countries including Kenya (0.4), Ghana (0.5), Malawi (0.6), and Nigeria (0.65).[12] The lending rate is 2.5 points lower than the mean for Africa, or 83 percent of the latter, while the deposit rate is 4.5 percentage points lower, or only 46 percent of the African average, with an average real rate of −6.19 percent between 1970 and 1998. These large spreads and the negative real deposit rate reflect the objective of a government interested in extracting rents from depositors, most of whom are not able to borrow from the same market. Indeed, high spreads raise banks' profits while benefiting the government through the inflation tax.

3.3 Labor markets

The labor market does not function as a competitive market. In rural areas only 24 percent of households employ any form of paid labor, often without a clear wage contract. Employment opportunities are essentially limited to public employment, accounting for 80 percent of total formal employment. Public sector jobs are a major source of accumulation through indirect benefits such as subsidized credit and housing, free or subsidized transportation, frequent international travel, and other rents extracted through corruption and patronage. As a result, the conditions in the labor market reflect largely political rather than economic fundamentals. Large parts of the population are excluded from participation in public employment by direct ethnic and regional selection, or indirectly by discriminatory access to education, as we discuss later.

It is not clear that there is a proper labor market in Burundi even in the modern sector. The matching of demand and supply is done more informally than through the allocative function of an open and competitive market.

---

[12] These comparative data are from Nkurunziza (2004).

Firm-level workers' data from a survey of 120 firms carried out in 1993 in the context of the World Bank's Regional Program on Enterprise Development (RPED) show that firms recruited only about 20 percent of employees through formal channels, namely job advertisement and recruitment agencies. About 75 percent of workers were recruited through informal channels such as friends and relatives of the manager, word of mouth, friends of other workers, etc.

Although recruitment does not appear to be based on economic considerations, wages generally seem to be determined by economic factors. This does not imply that economic factors alone explain workers' compensation. In addition to wages, private sector employment entitles workers to a number of additional benefits, including interest-free borrowing from the firm, and allowances for housing, transportation, food, health care, etc. Table 2.4 presents the results of earnings equations based on worker-level information as well as the characteristics of the firms they work for.[13]

The main message of the findings is that workers' wages are driven by the same economic factors that drive wages elsewhere. The main determinants are workers' education, age, or tenure, and the size and age of the firm. Firms in Bujumbura appear to offer better wages than those in the interior, and formal firms offer higher wages than informal ones, even after controlling for firm size. Workers hired through informal and formal channels do not seem to earn different wages. The reason may be that once a worker is hired, the wage is determined on the basis of an implicit pay scale used by the industry. However, differences may be noticeable once allowances are taken into account, especially those at the discretion of the employer.

These findings have implications for economic growth. First, the results confirm the argument of a dual economy: rural versus urban and formal versus informal. Secondly, given that schooling is the most important variable explaining the level of wages, unequal access to education has a strong effect on social inequality. Thirdly, even if it were true that workers recruited through informal channels do not earn more than those recruited through formal channels, those recruited informally occupy positions that could have been taken by others, who might remain unemployed or opt for lower-paid jobs. In addition, the fact that employees recruited informally tend to pledge their loyalty to the individuals who recruited them rather than the firms employing them creates an incentive problem that is harmful to firm performance. In the end, individuals may benefit from informality but, on the whole, the economy at large loses.

---

[13] Given that worker-level information on non-wage benefits is not available, the following results may be biased. Such allowances could be important in determining the relationship between an employee and his firm or his employer.

Table 2.4 *Burundi, earnings function, workers in the manufacturing sector, dependent variable is log of monthly wage in Burundi francs*

Variables	Model 1		Model 2		Model 3	
	Coefficient	t-test	Coefficient	t-test	Coefficient	t-test
Constant	4.833	12.71***	7.241	45.63***	5.061	11.66***
Age	0.761	6.99***	–	–	0.694	5.36***
School	0.841	16.59***	0.821	15.01***	0.823	15.58***
Tenure	–	–	0.164	4.06***	0.055	1.23
Size	0.114	3.96***	0.142	4.73***	0.109	3.72***
Firm age	−0.082	−2.59***	−0.151	−3.91***	−0.111	−2.92***
Formal/Informal	0.147	1.49	0.241	2.27**	0.178	1.72*
Bujumbura	0.151	1.91*	0.168	1.99**	0.167	2.06**
Metal	0.236	2.49**	0.198	1.92*	0.218	2.18**
Textiles	0.125	1.31	0.098	0.96	0.101	1.02
Food	0.153	1.74*	0.132	1.41	0.143	1.57
Foreigner	0.000	0.70	0.000	0.67	0.001	1.08
Public	0.003	2.91***	0.003	2.73***	0.003	2.98***
Recruit	0.014	0.18	−0.034	−0.43	0.025	0.33
Adjusted R^2	0.561		0.547		0.577	
Obs.	426.000		400.000		399.000	
Heteroskedasticity test	$Chi^2 (1) = 8.87$		$Chi^2 (1) = 3.86$		$Chi^2 (1) = 8.87$	
OV test	$F (3,410) = 16.76$		$F (3,384) = 8.59$		$F (3,382) = 13.90$	

Source: Data from World Bank (1992).

***, **, * are significant at 1, 5, and 10 percent probability level, respectively.

Notes: The variables are the log of wage (dependent variable) and, following the order in the table: log age of the worker (Age), log of the number of years of schooling (School), log of the number of years the worker has worked for the current firm (Tenure), log of firm size, proxied by the number of permanent employees (Size), log of the age of the firm (Firm age), and a number of dummies: a Formal/Informal sector dummy with value 1 when the sector is formal and 0 otherwise; a location dummy with value 1 for firms located in Bujumbura and 0 otherwise; three sectoral dummies: Metal, Textiles, and Food if the firm is in these sectors (wood work is the omitted category of firms), and two ownership dummies (Foreigner and Public) which represent the majority ownership of the firm (Burundi private ownership is the omitted category). We have also added a dummy variable (Recruit) to test whether the way a worker is recruited has a significant impact on his wage. It takes value 1 if he was recruited through job advertisement or through a recruitment agency and zero otherwise.

The OV test is a RESET test (Regression Specification Error Test) of the null hypothesis of no omitted variables.

4.   The response of firms and households

The market structure discussed above defines the opportunities available to firms and households, as well as the constraints they must confront.

4.1   Firm response

We briefly discuss three constraints facing firm development in Burundi and the associated responses of firms. These are the small size of the domestic market and the difficulty of accessing external markets, the legal framework supporting firm activity, and the risks associated with Burundi's geographic and political environment.

4.1.1   Size of domestic and external markets

With 6 million people who are among the poorest in the world, Burundi is one of the smallest economies in Africa. In this light, it is difficult to envisage a development strategy based on domestic markets. Burundi's external markets were largely Rwanda and the Eastern provinces of Congo under colonial rule. In this regard, firms established during colonial times were tailored to meet the demand of this relatively large market. Firms created before 1960 have an average production capacity of 240 kW in comparison to 98.5 kW for firms created after 1960. Although the pre-1960 firms did not grow, they are still among the biggest in Burundi, suggesting that the collapse of the economic union in the early 1960s had a limited long-term impact on the firms.

By 1993, these larger firms were, on average, more active than the group of firms created after 1960. Their average capacity utilization was 87 percent, in comparison to 66 percent for the post-1960 firms. In addition, 33 percent of firms in the first group were exporting, relative to 13 percent in the second group. This difference in performance may be the result of two different managerial cultures. Pre-1960s firms were created and run by Belgians. After independence, these firms were run either by their Belgian owners who decided to stay in the country or they were taken over by Burundian managers who had worked under the original owners. On the other hand, post-1960 firms were mostly created by the government with little regard for efficiency, or by former politicians who converted to business in order to use their valuable political networks, but without managerial experience or expertise.

The fact that the country is landlocked increases transportation costs and hence total production costs. This constraint limits firm competitiveness in international markets. One opportunity for the country to increase its exports could be to devise a strategy targeting regional markets. Since

Burundi is signatory to a number of regional trading blocs, firms should strive to take advantage of the preferential provisions offered by such bodies to increase their businesses across the region.[14] However, mistrust among the countries' leaders, and their nationalist shortsightedness and egoistic interests have, so far, undermined attempts to establish vibrant regional markets.

4.1.2 Regulatory framework

Firm efficiency is hampered by an inappropriate regulatory framework, particularly the weak legal system that fails to enforce commercial contracts and property rights. For instance, when a bank takes a defaulting borrower to court, the case may take up to ten years to be settled. Judges tend to sympathize with the plight of defaulting borrowers at the expense of "those silly bankers."[15] This increases the cost of lending, which may partly explain the large interest rate spreads observed in Burundi. Hence, 86 percent of firms interviewed in 1993 preferred to settle their conflicts with clients through direct negotiations while only 15 percent of the conflicts were taken to court.[16]

In addition to legal institutions, firms also need government business support services. However, as in the case of import licenses, government discretionary measures have often not been transparent. For example, large firms are more likely to benefit from the tax and duty exemptions provided for in the Investment Code than small firms. By 1993, 31 percent of firms in the RPED sample had applied for the benefits. Successful firms represented 60 percent of the applicants but what is striking is that, as for credit, smaller firms not only applied fewer times but were also less successful than bigger ones when they applied. The importance of returns to size when dealing with government institutions is also highlighted by Gauthier and Gersovitz (1997). They show that, in Cameroon, large firms are more able to save through tax evasion than smaller firms, because they are powerful enough to lobby tax administrators.

4.1.3 Risk and uncertainty

Burundi is characterized by high economic and political risk. Economic risk is partly due to bad policies – for instance, exchange rate uncertainty resulting from the controlled regime increases uncertainty about future

---

[14] Attempts to create regional institutions include the Communauté Economique des Pays des Grands Lacs (CEPGL), Communauté Economique des Pays d'Afrique Centrale (CEAC), and the Common Market for Eastern and Southern African States (COMESA). Of the three institutions, only the last functions at some level of normalcy.

[15] Personal discussions with Burundi bank managers.

[16] This is not particular to Burundi. Bigsten *et al.* (2000) find comparable findings in a study covering Burundi, Cameroon, Côte d'Ivoire, Kenya, Zambia, and Zimbabwe.

prices and costs, limiting firms' involvement in medium- and long-term activities. Devaluations increase the cost of imports. Since devaluations are essentially unpredictable, firms face unexpected additional costs that may affect their capacity to honor commitments towards banks and suppliers. Between 1990 and 1993, RPED data show that 53 percent of firms failed to pay their loans in time, while 40 percent failed to pay at all.

The effects of geographical isolation add to policy-induced uncertainty. Burundi is fully dependent on its neighbours' wrecked roads, ports, and railways for the conduct of its international trade. As a result, firms have to invest in large stocks of raw materials to minimize the cost of supply interruptions. On average, RPED data show that firms held inventories of raw material worth 39 percent of the value of their yearly production, or the equivalent of 87 percent of their raw material needs for a year. This strategy has a high opportunity cost as large financial resources are tied up in unproductive use.

With respect to political risk, the cycle of civil wars has created an extremely volatile political environment with a heavy toll on manufacturing activity. For instance, as a result of the current war, manufacturing production has declined by an average of 13 percent per annum between 1993 and 1997 (World Bank 1999). In 1994, only one year into the current political crisis, a sample of eighty-four firms showed that only 45 percent had kept their pre-crisis size or had reduced it by less than 10 percent; 15 percent shrank by 10–25 percent, and 21 percent declined by more than 25 percent (MPDR 2001).

In addition to the immediate effects of war, its recurrence increases instability, eroding the credibility of government announcements about its capacity to sustain long-term peace. This lack of credibility is one of the most important deterrents of investment in countries at war or those recovering from it (Collier and Pattillo 2000). By nature, war economies are short-term-oriented. Post-war economies inherit a destroyed infrastructure, social disorder, a pattern of resource allocation penalizing productive sectors by diverting resources to war financing, dis-saving, portfolio substitution in favor of foreign assets, degradation of moral standards, activity choices skewed towards the short-term, and other kinds of disruption. Most of these problems have a strong persistence effect (Collier 1999). In this light, it is not surprising that Burundi witnessed disinvestment rather than investment in the 1990s. The rate of gross investment declined from 17.5 percent in 1990 to a mere 5.6 percent in 1998 (MPDR 2001).

4.2 Household response

The lack of appropriate incentives and a limited support environment – in particular, an inadequate infrastructure – as well as government policies skewed against the rural sector, have hampered the development of a rural economy. The lack of a basic market infrastructure in rural Burundi has been a major cause of market failure and probably the single most important factor affecting production. As De Janvry, Fafchamps, and Sadoulet (1991: 1401) remark: "a market fails when the cost of a transaction through market exchange creates disutility greater than the utility gain that it produces, with the result that the market is not used for the transaction."

According to the Enquête Prioritaire carried out in 1998 (hereafter, EP 1998), farmers in rural areas walk an average of 1 hour to get to the nearest market place while it takes them 30 minutes to reach the nearest grocery. Including the facts that there is only one market day per week in many rural areas, and that there are no storage facilities for perishable agriculture produce, farmers have no incentive to produce marketable surpluses. Communication infrastructure that could help integrate markets is either inexistent or poor, especially during periods of insecurity. For instance, with three mainlines per 1,000 persons, Burundi has the lowest telephone density in Africa. The few lines that exist are concentrated in urban areas, so they do not help the rural economy. The same may be said for electricity and other types of infrastructure.[17] To cap it all, government predatory policies and the lack of financial and insurance markets heavily constrain household activities.

Farmers have responded to this adverse environment by retreating into subsistence production in line with De Janvry, Fafchamps, and Sadoulet (1991). EP1998 data show that producers consume on average 64 percent of their own food produce. In regions where climatic conditions permit diversified production, this average is as high as 80 percent. In addition, as suggested by Ghosh (1986), the fear of market exposure and ensuing taxation has induced many households to transform their surpluses into in-kind savings in the form of cattle. This policy has prevented accumulation in agriculture and its transformation into a more productive sector, thus leading to stagnation (Benhabib and Rustichini 1996).

Coercion has not been capable of reversing this trend. Extension workers have sometimes behaved as policemen, using their power as area representatives of the single party and informers of the state security apparatus to impose their choices on farmers. This method has failed to induce increase in production. In general, households are better off producing staple crops rather than coffee, tea, or cotton (see table 2.5), three crops favored by government.[18] For instance, the preference of many farmers we surveyed in the cotton-growing Imbo region was to grow tomatoes, which generated three

---

[17] These problems are not limited to Burundi (see Collier and Gunning 1999).

[18] Even taking into account the different levels of taxation of the different crops in table 2.5, food crops are generally much more productive than industrial crops for the same quality of land.

Table 2.5 *Burundi, land and labor returns, main crops, 1985*

Crops	Average yield (kg/ha)	Price 1985 (Fbu/kg)	Income (000Fbu/ha)	Work days	Daily income
	(1)	(2)	(3) = (1)*(2)	(4)	(5) = (3)/(4)
Food crops					
Corn	800	41.9	33.5	232	144.5
Sorghum	780	33.4	26.1	177	147.2
Rice	1,410	30.0	42.3	590	71.7
Wheat	410	40.0	16.8	274	61.2
Beans	800	46.5	37.2	210	177.1
Peas	550	82.6	45.4	210	216.3
Sweet potatoes	5,240	10.1	52.9	372	142.3
Cassava	6,370	21.1	134.4	342	393.0
Potatoes	5,750	18.9	108.7	435	249.8
Palm oil	2,520	7.9	19.9	244	81.6
Groundnuts	790	74.5	58.9	240	245.2
Bananas	11,240	11.0	128.6	253	488.7
Industrial crops					
Coffee	240	160.0	38.4	500	76.8
Dry tea	731	17.0	12.4	526	23.6
Cotton	1,185	35.0	41.5	255	162.6

Note: Fbu = Burundi francs.
Source: World Bank (1988).

times more income than cotton. But as they did not have the opportunity to choose what to grow and as monitoring by government agents was regular, the farmers were forced to adopt "cheating" strategies by growing tomatoes under the cover of the wide cotton leaves.

Forced specialization by government has thus failed because it is ill advised, ignores the basic cost-benefit economic principle, is not incentive-compatible and, above all, is biased against the food sector that is of more direct interest to farmers. In the euphoria that followed the 1993 democratic elections, farmers in some regions manifested their displeasure with previous regimes by destroying their coffee stands, an offense that had been traditionally punishable by a long prison sentence.

5. Political economy of growth

The question that arises from these discussions is why Burundi's leadership perpetrated policies that were so economically disastrous. To understand the logic underlying the government's choices, we discuss the problem of politicization of the economy, and how it undermined market efficiency. First, we discuss the formation of interest groups and the patterns of distributive politics. Secondly, we analyze the policies underlying the predatory system that defines the modalities of governing rent-sharing among the members of the ruling elite. Thirdly, we propose our perspective on the question why the system has been stable for such a long time.

5.1   Interest groups and patterns of distributive politics

The early 1960s saw the emergence of two political groups divided along ethnic lines. In November 1966, in the midst of this politically charged period, Captain Michel Micombero, a young Tutsi officer from the Southern province of Bururi, deposed the centuries-old monarchy in a military coup, instituting a republican regime. The Micombero government dissolved parliament and established a repressive single-party system. Slowly, political institutions were purged of Hutu, leaving Tutsi – especially those from the President's province – at the helm of the country's institutions.

Although to some extent non-Bururi Tutsi may have benefited from power more than Bururi Hutu (Nkurunziza and Ngaruko 2003), from Micombero's coup in 1966 until very recently, the presidents, key ministers and their advisors, managers of public firms, as well as the army commanders, have mostly been from Bururi. What is called "regionalism" in Burundi was born with the 1966 coup. Interestingly, as the group of Bururi Tutsi claiming a share of rents widened, political fights started among the ruling elite, this time within a narrow intra-ethnic and intra-regional space. These opposed those from Matana to those from Rutovu communes of Bururi. In the mid-1980s, in-fights occurred between the Bayanzi and the Bashingo clans of Bururi Tutsi. Although some prominent politicians or army officers were thrown in jail, the fighting groups never resorted to violence against each other.

5.1.1   Using education to filter entry into the elite group

Offering Bururi Tutsi a privileged access to primary, secondary, and university education, including access to overseas scholarships, guaranteed that power remained in the hands of the Southern ruling elite. Jackson (2001), for example, notes that the Mugamba commune of Bururi, out of a total of 114 communes nationwide, accounts for a disproportionate 15 percent of the 6,000 students of the government-run national university. The fact that the latter was the country's single institution of higher education until some five years ago shows that denying non-Bururi students access to the national university was tantamount to economic and political

Table 2.6 *Burundi, distribution of social infrastructure and returns to regionalism*

Variables	Bururi province	Average 15 provinces	Std dev.	Bururi rank
Overall school enrollment ratio	0.39	0.245	0.105	1.00
Teachers per classroom	2.00	1.00	0.3	1.00
Illiteracy rate	57.00	64.00	5.0	14.00
Population/hospital ratio (000)	107.00	266.00	134.0	2.00

Source: Data are from Ministère de la Planification du Développement et de la Reconstruction (MPDR) and UNDP (1999). Data on *per capita* tax are from Ministère de l'Administration du Territoire et du Développement Communal (2001).

marginalization.[19] Safeguarding the privileges of the elite became the bedrock of government policy, resulting in the marginalization of the majority of the population.

For instance, to ensure that Bururi produced the most educated people who would be the future leaders, Jackson (2001: 31–5) finds that Bururi accounted for 15 percent of all primary school teachers, 19 percent of the country's secondary school students and 36 percent of secondary schools. In short, Bururi boasts the best educational infrastructure in the country (see table 2.6): the provinces of Bururi and Bujumbura, the capital city, host 11 percent of the country's population, but account for 32 percent of all secondary school students. In contrast, the five least endowed provinces account for only 10 percent of secondary school students, almost half of the number for Bururi. Jackson (2001: 35) notes that in the late 1980s the government allocated about 60 percent of donor aid to education to Bururi alone.[20] Since the modern labor market is dominated by public employment, and given that access to public employment depends on the level of education,[21] those denied education at an early age are denied access to most opportunities offered by the economic system.

[19] Pritchett and Filmer (1999) have shown, in a detailed multi-country study, that access to education increases wealth and that wealth increases the level of education. The implication is that lack of access to education perpetuates poverty, especially in countries such as Burundi where access to education opens the doors to the civil service, the best and almost only opportunity to escape poverty.

[20] These statistics are so embarrassing that, according to Jackson (2001), the Belgian minister for development co-operation, reacting to a government request for aid to education, asked to be given the number of colleges and students in Bururi in 2000 in order to send the required aid; he never got a response from the government.

[21] For instance, every job in the public sector, up to district level, requires knowledge of French. Since the language is taught only in schools, those who do not attend school, or those who do not go far enough, are automatically excluded from job opportunities.

The transfers to Bururi have also taken other forms. Guichaoua (1991) reports that out of the country's fifteen provinces, the Fifth Five-Year Plan allocated 66 percent of gross fixed capital formation to a geographical area comprising Bujumbura, the capital city, and its surrounding areas and the province of Bururi. The regions that are the breadbasket of the country are the ones that benefit the least from state resources. At a tender age, due to the lack of schools, many young Burundians from the North, the East, and the West engage in agriculture, trading, and other productive activities when in the South children of their age attend school to be prepared for future leadership. Those from the South who are not successful in school enrole in the army or join their relatives in Bujumbura and in other regions where they work in government-controlled institutions.[22] Rather than preparing future entrepreneurs, the education system has been shaped to prepare rent-seekers. Politicization of the education system has had a devastating impact on growth.

Most of the schools were built and run with the use of foreign aid; an interesting question is why the donors acquiesced in these discriminatory policies. The answer is that, since the 1960s, the doctrine underlying inter-national development assistance was that the new sovereign nations would be entrusted with domestic allocation of aid, regardless of their internal institutions and governance standards. Insofar as the agenda of the donors was not compromised (containment of communism, buying off diplomatic support in international institutions, etc.) the groups in power could use foreign aid as they wished, regardless of the impact on growth (Herbst 2000: 97–132). Conditioning external assistance on "good" domestic policies is a recent development still timidly applied.

5.1.2   The army at the heart of the rentier state

The army plays a prominent role as both an actor and guarantor of the mechanism of rent collection and distribution within the elite group. It also ensures that the rentier system is not threatened by outsiders. Public expenditures allocated to the army rose by more than 100 percent between the mid-1970s and the mid-1980s, reflecting a strengthening of the institu-tion protecting the predatory system. The army also acts as a distributive machine. From the early 1970s, it has been overwhelmingly dominated by Bururi Tutsi at all levels. According to the International Crisis Group (ICG) (2001), all the thirty-seven highest command positions are held by Tutsi,

---

[22] There is a story in Burundi about a manager who had just replaced a Southerner in a managerial position of a government institution in the North of the country. He realized that all the drivers, cleaners, and night watchmen were from the South. He once asked the watchmen: "Why did you come all the way from the South to be watchmen here? Do you mean there are no thieves in the South?"

twenty-seven of whom (or 73 percent) are from Bururi. Policies privileging the army, parastatals, or public servants target a specific group within the population and anyone threatening the status quo is mercilessly suppressed. When Melchior Ndadaye, the first civilian, first Hutu, and first non-Bururi democratically elected President attempted to change the system in 1993, he was murdered by members of the army only three months after taking power.

Reyntjens (1994) notes that the factors which induced members of the army to assassinate the President included the following: first, the new government had a plan to reduce bid bonds by 80 percent to allow small businessmen, including many Hutu, to benefit from privatization of state-owned enterprises (SOEs).[23] Secondly, the Belgian firm Affiment had been authorized to refine and export gold under an Export-Processing Zone (EPZ) license a few weeks before the June 1993 elections. The attempt to redesign the conditions of this arrangement was against the interests of influential people from both the firm and the previous government. Thirdly, the attempt by returning Hutu refugees to recover their property – some of it in powerful hands – was obviously too sensitive. Fourthly, the intention of the President to reform the army did not please those who felt threatened – above all, the Bururi civilian and military oligarchy, in view of the benefits they stood to lose. In this light, it is clear that regionalism is not just a political phenomenon but also has an important economic dimension.

5.2 The policies underlying rent-sharing

Behind the merciless fights for political control are important economic rents. The ultimate aim of political factions fighting for the control of the state is to control public institutions which have become the center of a system of rent-sharing. We illustrate how this system works using two examples: public employment and trade policy.

5.2.1 Public employment and parastatals as sources of economic rents

Unlike most African bureaucracies, Burundi's public sector is relatively small. While many populist governments used public employment to provide revenue to a maximum number of followers, Burundi's public sector has remained elitist. The successive governments reserved the relatively high-paying jobs for their political clients. In Burundi, the mean income of a civil servant puts him among the richest 6 percent of the population,[24] against an average of 13 percent in SSA, 30 percent for the Middle East and

---

[23] In the privatization context, a bid bond is a deposit required of any entity that seeks to participate as a bidder for a particular public enterprise. The bond is returned to losing bidders and is forfeited by the winning bidder if that bidder does not go through with the acquisition.

[24] The percentile would be even smaller if other "rents to power" are taken into account.

Table 2.7 *Burundi, ethnic disparities, public sector civil service posts, 1987*

	Hutu[a]	Tutsi[a]	Twa[a]
Office of the President	1	98	0
Central Committee of Single Party (UPRONA)	2	50	0
Administration of Single Party	3	52	0
Ministers	5	13	0
Ministerial Cabinet Directors	1	17	0
Ministry Permanent Secretaries	0	40	0
Province Governors	2	13	0
Ambassadors	1	21	0
Embassy Diplomats	0	88	0
Army Barrack Commanders	0	20	0
Army High Ranking Officers	2	398	0
Army Sergeant and Privates	30	11,970	0
State-Owned Company Directors	5	252	0
Hospital Directors	1	19	0
University Lecturers	10	80	0
Secondary School Directors and Inspectors	6	89	0
Prosecutors	0	66	0
Magistrates	5	92	0
High Court Presidents	1	7	0
Judiciary Police Officers and Inspectors	0	400	0

Source: Ntibazonkiza (1993).

Notes: Hutu, Tutsi, and Twa reportedly represent 85 percent, 14 percent and 1 percent of the population, respectively.

[a]Although it is difficult to ascertain the accuracy of these statistics, they should be interpreted on showing that the Tutsi have dominated all government institutions, which is a non-controversial fact.

North Africa region, 33 percent for Asia, 40 percent for Latin America and the Caribbean, 76 percent for Eastern Europe and the former USSR, and 63 percent for Organization for Economic Co-operation and Development (OECD) countries. Hence, individuals in the highest civil service jobs are among the richest Burundians.

Table 2.7 gives information on the ethnic identity of the highest civil servants and army officers. Although it is difficult to ascertain the accuracy of the data, it is clear that the Tutsi group dominates in all government institutions. However, the reality is that this generalization of ethnic dominance masks a more subtle discrimination pattern based on regionalism. Disaggregated data on some of the positions in table 2.7 unveil Bururi's dominance.

Table 2.8 shows the ethnic and regional background of the managers of state-owned corporations. The dominance of Tutsi from Bururi supports

Table 2.8 *Burundi, ethnic and regional distribution, public firm managers, percent*

| Region of origin | Ethnic Group | | | Total |
	Tutsi	Hutu	Twa	
Bururi Province	60	3	0	63
Remaining Provinces	29	8	0	37
Total	**89**	**11**	**0**	**100**

Source: Based on data from "La Lumière," a Burundian weekly, and reported in International Crisis Group (ICG) (2001).

Table 2.9 *Burundi, external borrowing, domestic savings, and investment, 1975–1998, percent of GDP*

| | Burundi | | | SSA | | |
	1975–84	1985–9	1990–8	1975–84	1985–9	1990–8
Investment	15.6	16.3	11.9	17.8	16.3	17.0
Public	14.1	13.6	9.6	7.9	7.0	6.1
Private	1.5	2.7	2.3	9.9	9.3	10.9
Domestic savings	4.1	3.3	−2.9	23.9	20.2	16.1
Net long-term borrowing	4.8	7.5	4.7	3.0	2.4	1.0

Source: The World Bank (2000).

our hypothesis that the firms were created to enlarge the rent basis in order to fulfill the needs of the new members of the elite.

The government embarked on an active economic policy program, raising the share of public investment from 5.6 percent to 42.8 percent of total investment between 1971 and 1980. The program was funded by both internal and external debt (see table 2.9). As Nyamoya (1998) notes, from 1977 to 1982, about 100 state-owned companies were created and put in the hands of cronies. Most of the corporations were mismanaged and had cash flow problems from their inception, resulting in large infusions of subsidies that imposed a high cost on the economy. World Bank (1998) shows that although they produced only 9 percent of the country's GDP in 1990, state firms accounted for 31 percent of formal sector employment, 25 percent of outstanding domestic credit, and benefited from 3.4 percent of GDP in subsidies from the government.

Furthermore, IMF (1997) shows that by 1995, the equity capital of thirty-six such firms with majority state participation represented 20 percent of the country's GDP but, overall, these corporations posted a net loss equivalent to 6 percent of GDP or 14 percent of government revenue, excluding grants. These losses and subsequent government transfers are illustrations of the ways that resources have been transferred from taxpayers, including farmers, to bail out firms that served group rather than national interests.

It could be argued that those discriminated against in the public sector have better opportunities in the private sector, suggesting some type of specialization. However, government policies have not allowed the development of a private sector in Burundi. Using the data on private investment as a measure of private sector involvement in economic activity, table 2.9 shows that between 1975 and 1984 (when massive investments in the public sector were undertaken), private investment, at a mere 1.5 percent of GDP compared to 9.9 percent for SSA, was almost ten times lower than public investment. The contrast is staggering given that private investment is higher than public investment in other African countries. As a result, given that most of the public investment is funded by foreign resources, investment is highly dependent on foreign aid.

5.2.2   External trade policy as a source of economic rents

The real motive for external trade controls is far from the official objective of guaranteeing low prices for strategic imports. These controls confer a huge amount of economic rents. Using a sample of thirty-three imported commodities, Greenaway and Milner (1990) have found that in 1984 the amount of rents associated with the distribution of quota import licenses was about 2 billion Burundi francs, the equivalent of 17 percent of government revenue. These controls benefit a small circle of individuals, including a pool of former high-ranking civil servants turned businessmen who capitalize on their links with the government to make money. Any effort towards relaxation of the controls erodes these privileges, so reforms are fiercely resisted.

For instance, following the adoption of an SAP in 1986, the country adopted trade liberalization measures culminating in an Open General License (OGL) for both imports and exports in 1992. As a result, the number of licensed importers grew from 145 in 1985 to 400 in 1991. This increase, by almost 200 percent in six years, suggests that very substantial rents were being captured by protected importers.[25] The country's export sector has also been a victim of this lopsided policy, as demonstrated by the main export product, coffee, accounting for more than 80 percent of total exports. Although producer price stability has been the main justification of the government's intervention in the coffee sector, the government did not isolate peasants

---

[25] Some of these liberalization measures have been reversed during the current political crisis.

Table 2.10 *Burundi, economic benefits underlying regionalism*

Variables	Bururi province	Average 15 provinces	Std. dev.	Rank of Bururi province
Per capita income (1998) in US PPP$	444.00	328	99.00	2
Food prod. *per capita* (tons)	0.41	1	0.15	14
Per capita tax (1999)	268.00	366	90.00	14

Source: Data on the first two variables are from: Ministère de la Planification du Développement et de la Reconstruction (MPDR) and UNDP (1999). Data on *per capita* tax are from Ministère de l'Administration du Territoire et du Développement Communal (2001).

from fluctuating international prices. The correlation coefficient between producer and world prices is 0.90, suggesting that, as Bates (1981) notes, "what was stabilized is the off-take of the marketing boards rather than incomes of farmers."

The previous examples suggest that ultimately the justification for the predatory behavior of the elite is economic. As table 2.10 illustrates, being a Bururi Tutsi confers material economic gain. Though the Bururi province ranks fourteen in a total of fifteen provinces in terms of both its contribution to central government's tax revenue and of food production *per capita*, its income *per capita* puts it in the second highest place.

The absence of any specific natural resource Bururi may claim to explain its high *per capita* income leaves one explanation. The province benefits from large transfers, both directly from the central government and from remittances of Bururi natives running the country from Bujumbura and outlying areas.

5.3   Why has the predatory system been so stable for so long?

In Burundi, narrowly based governing elites tend to promote policies that distort the economy because they benefit from the distortions without incurring their cost. Adam and O'Connell (1999) show that when the elite group is small, economic distortions are largely borne by the non-favoured group, and a small distortion may have large payoffs for each member of the elite. Therefore, in the absence of political punishment of poor performers, narrowly based political elites have an incentive to distort the economy, especially when such distortions are illegitimate and privilege immediate gain.

As to why such illegitimate regimes can last for so long, Humphreys and Bates (2002) provide useful insights. In countries where a selectorate – a small group of citizens such as the army in Burundi – enjoys monopoly power to change governments, a bad leader may remain in power unchallenged for a long time. The condition to conserve power is to ensure that the selectorate's reservation utility is satisfied; this is the single criterion against which the performance of an incumbent leader is measured. In Burundi, the selectorate – the Bururi elite – has no incentive to remove a leader from power when he satisfies their needs. Instead, the army is used to quell any opposition to the selectorate's policies.

These two models have two results that perfectly fit Burundi. First, the probability of distorting the economy and engaging in predation is highest for governments at war. Secondly, regionally based governments engage more in predation and in disequilibrating macroeconomic policies. We have seen that households respond by retreating into subsistence agriculture. How do agents in other productive sectors respond? Faced with predatory leaders, citizens move their wealth outside the economy. But, fearing this move, predatory governments impose restrictions on factor mobility, particularly capital. Ironically, narrow-based elites themselves are more engaged in capital flight as they live with a constant fear of losing their illegitimate power. The case of General Sani Abacha, his family, and their associates in Nigeria is an illustration of this fact.

In Burundi, despite strict controls on capital mobility even before the current war, capital flight was relatively high, representing 30 percent of government total revenue between 1985 and 1992.[26] It is probable that those involved in capital flight were chiefly members of the Bagaza regime before it was deposed in 1987, and subsequently, the elites around Buyoya, for two reasons. First, strict capital controls meant that one needed the complicity of those enforcing the controls to violate them; such complicity could be easily obtained by those in power and their associates. The data on the parallel exchange rate show no important increases until the last two years (1991 and 1992), suggesting that the market was not widely used to make these transfers.

Secondly, it was the members of the elite who had substantial capital to send abroad, considering that most other Burundians lived in poverty. These hypotheses illustrate Adam and O'Connell's (1999) proposition that economic distortions benefit the elites.[27] Since 1993, there has been a pattern among the elites in Burundi to send their children to Europe or North

---

[26] We are grateful to Paul Collier for suggesting that capital flight could explain why Burundi's political elite do not seem to care about political stability and economic efficiency.

[27] These distortions should not be confused with the taxes discussed by Azam (1995) in the case of Côte d'Ivoire. In his analysis, taxes are collected from rich members of the ruling ethnic group in the South to be invested in the poor North in projects that may be economically non-viable, in order to maintain social cohesion.

America. The parents stay in Burundi, well protected by armed bodyguards. These people continue preaching that those in the country should keep fighting the "enemy" as it is others who bear the brunt of the war.

It is too easy, *ex post*, to wonder why Burundian leaders have been so "irrational" for almost four decades. We should not forget that this "irrational" system was put in place in the 1960s and survived four civil wars. It was a stable system that could have withstood the recent shocks (and we would probably not be questioning it) if the external events that destabilized the system had not taken place. These include the wave of democracy that swept the continent in the early 1990s, the genocide in Rwanda in 1994, and the war in the Democratic Republic of Congo (DRC) (see Ngaruko and Nkurunziza 2000; Nkurunziza and Ngaruko 2003). We would be mistaken to think that the system has imploded; its internal dynamics are still relatively intact. The slow but remarkable changes that are taking place are due to pressure from the international community. However, it is not clear how far the elite is prepared to abandon its benefits, nor whether the pressure will weaken, leading to a reversal of what has been achieved.

6. Conclusion

This study has analyzed the process of economic growth in Burundi over the period 1960–2000. The growth pattern followed closely the country's political trajectory represented in three sub-periods: 1960–72, 1972–88, and 1988 to date. Economic decline during the first sub-period was largely due to political instability and the loss of Burundi's export markets in neighboring Rwanda and Congo following decolonization. During the period 1972–88, economic growth was fueled by an increase in coffee export revenues in the second half of the 1970s, and by massive foreign borrowing. Most of the funds were exploited to create inefficient state firms exploited by the ruling elite as a source of economic rents. During the third sub-period, economic decline was a result of three civil wars, a total economic blockade, the freezing of aid by international donors, and the collapse of investment and infrastructure.

On the whole, growth has been a failure because it has not been the priority of Burundi's leadership. Blending traditional macroeconomic growth analysis with microeconomic, institutional, and political-economy approaches, the study has shown that economic outcomes have been endogenous to political imperatives. Controlled access to education and to the civil service and the army, the creation of a large number of state corporations, monetary policy, trade policy, and a myriad of other policies were used to ensure that resources were allocated to the members of the ruling elite. The overarching objective of the leadership was the government's desire to maintain its grip over the different sources of economic rents. In this light, political economy is a more appealing approach in explaining Burundi's dismal economic performance.

The main contribution of the study to the cross-country growth literature has been not only to provide the first detailed study of growth in Burundi but also to highlight the centrality of the oft-neglected political factors in explaining growth outcomes. A traditional analysis of growth focusing on macroeconomic variables such as investment and schooling is not only limited, but may also be misleading. This study has shown that economic growth is the outcome of a complex process in which the political objectives of the individuals in power play a central role. The challenge is, therefore, to develop new growth analytical frameworks integrating political and traditional economic and policy variables.

If Burundi's track record remains unchanged, Ali (2001) has calculated that it would take 225 years to cut the country's poverty level by half. This suggests that the status quo is a hopeless option; the question is rather how to change this situation and put Burundi on a better growth path. When the current war broke out in 1993, the country was seven years into an SAP that had been hailed by the World Bank as a success in Africa. However, economic reforms were built on a shallow political foundation, and economic policy and political infrastructure collapsed in 1993. Therefore, without pretending to have a miracle solution to the deeply rooted problems facing the country, we think it is not appropriate to advocate economic reforms in Burundi without accompanying structural political reforms.

It will not be easy to achieve this objective, but there is no better alternative. In Burundi as elsewhere, economic agents respond to incentives. Burundians' contribution to economic growth will in large part depend on the extent to which the structure of incentives, both political and economic, can be aligned with people's preferences (Easterly 2001). In the process, the protection of human life and the socio-economic integration of all Burundians without distinction based on regional or ethnic background should be the basic principle guiding political and economic reforms. It remains to be seen whether the ongoing political reforms will bring about such changes. The co-operation of the members of the traditional ruling class will be needed to make such change possible, but their track record suggests that they cannot credibly commit to change. In this context, external pressure will be needed to force change (Addison and Murshed 2002). To a certain extent, this is already happening. The positive political developments geared towards the establishment of an accountable and democratic system were almost imposed by external actors. The most visible have been the leaders of Burundi's neighboring states, the United Nations, the African Union (AU) and, most particularly, South Africa, which sent a contingent of its army to Burundi to make these changes possible.

Currently, all but one of the rebel groups have joined the country's political institutions. However, it is not clear that these new leaders have all the required skills to run the country, especially in this sensitive post-conflict period. There are also some early indications that some of these leaders may want to "get even" and indulge in corruption to accumulate wealth as quickly as possible. Changing the standards of leadership that have prevailed for more than four decades will take time. Until this happens, the leaders may change, but the tradition of state capture and exclusion may persist.

References

Adam, C. S. and S. A. O'Connell (1999), "Aid, Taxation and Development in Sub-Saharan Africa," *Economics and Politics* 11(3): 225–54

Addison, T. and S. M. Murshed (2002), "Credibility and Reputation in Peace Making," *Journal of Peace Research* 39(4): 487–501

Ali, A. G. (2001), "Can Africa Cut its Poverty Level by Half by 2015?," United Nations Economic Commission for Africa, *Economic Report on Africa 2000*, Addis Ababa

Azam, J.-P. (1995), "How to Pay for Peace? A Theoretical Framework with Reference to African Countries," *Public Choice* 83(1/2): 173–84

Bates, R. H. (1981), *Markets and States in Tropical Africa: The Political Basis of Agricultural Policies*. Berkeley, CA: University of California Press

Benhabib, J. and A. Rustichini (1996), "Social Conflict and Growth," *Journal of Economic Growth* 1(1): 125–42

Bigsten, A., P. Collier, S. Dercon, M. Fafchamps, B. Gauthier, J. W. Gunning, M. Soderbom, A. Oduro, R. Oostendorp, C. Pattillo, F. Teal, and A. Zeufack (2000), "Contract Flexibility and Dispute Resolution in African Manufacturing," *Journal of Development Studies* 36: 1–37

Collier, P. (1999), "On the Economic Consequences of Civil War," *Oxford Economic Papers* 51: 168–83

Collier, P. and J. W. Gunning (1999), "Explaining African Economic Performance," *Journal of Economic Literature* 37(1): 64–111

Collier, P. and C. Pattillo (2000), *Investment and Risk in Africa*. Basingstoke: Macmillan

Collins, S. M. and B. P. Bosworth (1996), "Economic Growth in East Asia: Accumulation versus Assimilation," *Brookings Papers on Economic Activity* 2: 135–91

Cukierman, A., S. Edwards, and G. Tabellini (1992), "Seignorage and Political Instability," *American Economic Review* 82(3): 537–55

De Janvry, A., M. Fafchamps, and M. Sadoulet (1991), "Peasant Household Behaviour with Missing Markets: Some Paradoxes Explained," *Economic Journal* 101(409): 1400–17

De Lespinay, C. (2000), "Les Eglises et le génocide dans la région des Grands Lacs est-africains," http://www.u-paris10.fr/gdr1178/lesp-egl.htm

Easterly, W. (2001), *The Elusive Quest for Growth*. Cambridge, MA: MIT Press

Easterly, W. and R. Levine (2003), "Tropics, Germs, and Crops: The Role of Endowments in Economic Development," *Journal of Monetary Economics* 50(1): 3–39

Fafchamps, M. (2003), "Engines of Growth and Africa's Economic Performance," in Emmanuel Nnadozie, ed., *African Economic Development*. London: Academic Press: 65–98

Gauthier, B. and M. Gersovitz (1997), "Revenue Erosion through Exemption and Evasion in Cameroon, 1993," *Journal of Public Economics* 64: 407–24

Gemmell, N. (1996), "Evaluating the Impacts of Human Capital Stocks and Accumulation on Economic Growth: Some New Evidence," *Oxford Bulletin of Economics and Statistics* 58: 9–28

Ghosh, D. (1986), "Savings Behaviour in the Non-monetized Sector and Its Implications," *Savings and Development* (10)2

Greenaway, D. and C. R. Milner (1990), "Policy Appraisal and the Structure of Protection in a Low-income Developing Country: Problems of Measurement and Evaluation in Burundi," *Journal of Development Studies* 27(1): 22–42

Guichaoua, A. (1991), "Les travaux communautaires en Afrique Centrale," *Revue Tiers Monde* 32(127): 551–73

Herbst, J. (2000), *States and Power in Africa: Comparative Lessons in Authority and Control*. Princeton, NJ: Princeton University Press

Horowitz, D. L. (1985), *Ethnic Groups in Conflict*. Berkeley, CA: University of California Press

Hugon, P. (1993), *L'Economie de l'Afrique*, Paris: Repères–La Découverte

Humphreys, M. and R. Bates, (2002), "Political Institutions and Economic Policies: Lessons From Africa," Working Paper, Center for International Development, Harvard University, Cambridge, MA

IMF (1997), "Burundi: Recent Economic Developments," *IMF Staff Country Report* 97/114, November 17

International Crisis Group (ICG) (2001), *Burundi: Breaking the Deadlock: The Urgent Need for a New Negotiating Framework*, Africa Report 29, May 14, Brussels and Nairobi

Jackson, T. (2001), "L'Egalite d'accès à l'éducation: un impératif pour la paix au Burundi," *International Alert*, manuscript

Lemarchand, R. (1994), *Burundi: Ethnic Conflict and Genocide*. Cambridge: Cambridge University Press

Ministère de l'Administration du Territoire et du Développement Communal (2001), Recettes fiscales communales, Bujumbura, Burundi

Ministère de la Planification du Développement et de la Reconstruction (MPDR) and UNDP (2001), *Programme National d'Action pour le Développement du Burundi 2001–2010*, Troisième Conférence des Nations Unies sur les Pays les Moins Avancés, Brussels, 13–20 May

Ndulu, B. J. and S. A. O'Connell (2000), "Background Information on Economic Growth," Explaining African Economic Growth Project. Nairobi: African Economic Research Consortium (downloadable: aercafrica.org)

Ngaruko, F. (1993), "L'Industrie et l'accumulation au Burundi," *Mondes en Développement* 21(92): 85–91

Ngaruko, F. and J. D. Nkurunziza (2000), "An Economic Interpretation of Conflict in Burundi," *Journal of African Economies* 9(3): 370–409

(2004), *The Effect of Credit on Firm Growth and Survival in Kenyan Manufacturing*, D.Phil thesis, University of Oxford

Nkurunziza, J. D. (2001), "Exchange Rate Policy and the Parallel Market for Foreign Currency in Burundi," *African Journal of Economic Policy* 8(1): 69–121

Nkurunziza, J. D. and F. Ngaruko (2003), "War and Its Duration in Burundi," World Bank/Yale Project on The Economics of Political and Common Violence, Yale University, New Haven, CT

Ntibazonkiza, R. (1993), *Au Royaume des Seigneurs de la Lance: une approche historique de la Question Ethnique au Burundi*, vol. 2. Brussels: Bruxelles-Droits de L'Homme

Nyamoya, P. (1998), *Pour un modèle original de privatisation des entreprises publiques au Burundi*, RIDEC 2(2), September, Bujumbura

Pritchett, L. and D. Filmer (1999), "What Educational Production Functions Really Show: A Positive Theory of Education Spending," *Economics of Education Review* 18(2): 223–39

Reyntjens, P. (1994), *L'Afrique des Grands Lacs en Crise: Rwanda et Burundi, 1988–1994*. Paris: Karthala

World Bank (1988), "Burundi: Structural Adjustment and Development Issues," Background Paper Report 67-54-Bu, Washington, DC: The World Bank

(1992), "Regional Program on Enterprise Development (RPED), Burundi," Original Dataset

World Bank (1998), *African Development Indicators 1998/1999*. Washington, DC: The World Bank

(1999), *Burundi: Poverty Note. Prospects for Social Protection in a Crisis Economy*, Report 17909-Bu, Washington, DC: The World Bank, February 23

(2000), *African Development Indicators 2000*. Washington, DC: The World Bank

3 | Cotton, war, and growth in Chad, 1960–2000

Jean-Paul Azam and Nadjiounoum Djimtoïngar

1. Introduction

Chad is a small Sahelian economy of 7.7 million inhabitants (in 1999), which is landlocked, partly a desert, and whose political life is dominated by the perennial rivalry between the northern semi-nomadic Muslims and the southern Animist/Christian farmers. Like many other African countries, Chad has a highly polarized society, where identity and differences are defined along ethnic, cultural, religious, and economic lines. The northerners speak an Arabic dialect and, in their majority, rejected western education during colonial days and afterwards. The southerners, in contrast, seized what they saw as a unique opportunity to develop, and speak Sara and French. The northerners live on cattle-raising and other livestock, as

University of Toulouse (ARQADE and IDEI), Institut Universitaire de France, and CSAE, Oxford; CEMAC, Bangui (CAR).

This chapter was partly written while Jean-Paul Azam was visiting N'Djamena, during January 20–30, 2001, and Nadjiounoum Djimtoïngar was with the Ministry of Economic Promotion and University of N'Djamena (Chad). We wish to thank Etienne Moïta, deputy general secretary of the presidency, for an illuminating discussion spanning the whole post-independence period, as well as Georges Diguimbaye, for his long and rich memory. Written comments by Steve O'Connell were very helpful, and are also gratefully acknowledged, without implication.

well as on trade and smuggling with neighboring Algeria, Libya, Sudan, and Egypt (via Sudan) in the north, as well as with Cameroon, the Central African Republic (CAR), Niger, and Nigeria in the south. The southerners produce the main export crop, cotton, and own most of the productive human capital; and their land contains huge oil reserves, which have been known since the mid-1970s and began to be exploited after 2003. At that point, Chad switched from being a landlocked, resource-scarce country to a resource-rich country. However, this change in economic opportunities was partly endogenous, as shown below. It is only after peace was secured, and institutions were put in place to make it credible, that foreign oil companies ventured into exploiting the oil.

Until then, the growth experience of this country was dominated by the cotton sector, often disturbed by civil war, and complicated by the Libyan intervention. This is brought out strikingly by section 2, which shows econometrically that, after controlling for shocks due to political violence, growth in Chad simply reflects the evolution of growth in other cotton-driven Sahelian economies. These economies are quite similar to one another, all belonging to the CFA zone and heavily dependent on the cotton sector. The cotton sector was dominated for most of the period by a French company, the Compagnie Française des Textiles (CFDT). Hence, a large component of Chad's growth experience can be regarded as determined exogenously, reflecting only the ups and downs of the Sahelian cotton economy. In the case of Chad, this can also be checked econometrically by a direct analysis of the impact of the output of the cotton sector on the whole economy, which is also performed in section 2. Cotton also provides the transmission channel through which the 1994 devaluation of the CFA franc, an event that owes nothing to Chadian history itself, impacted the country's growth path. The devaluation triggered a cotton-led export boom that pulled the economy upwards, for a while.

Political shocks provide the idiosyncratic features of Chadian growth history. The most important one occurred in 1979–84, comprising three years of outright civil war followed by two years of near-genocidal massacres perpetrated in the cotton-growing area. This is by all accounts a watershed in Chadian history. Section 3 shows that the pattern of growth is different before and after this period. Hence, a natural periodization of Chad's economic history emerges, as war draws a clear separation between two contrasted growth episodes. There was a gradual build-up leading to the outbreak of the civil war, when GDP *per capita* was on average decreasing. This superimposed a downward trend on the cotton-led growth path between independence in 1960 and the outbreak of the civil war, reflecting the pessimistic expectations of potential investors. This may be called the "expected disaster" episode, when the shadow of conflict loomed large over the Chadian economy. Potential investors anticipated the probable breakdown of the post-independence political equilibrium, with a potentially dramatic redistribution of property rights and political power. The post-conflict period shows a different profile, with mere stagnation or a slight recovery, at a significantly lower income level than before. The new political equilibrium only emerged with a lag, after the civil war ended. While the 1980s were still highly unstable and violent, including an attempted invasion by Libya, Idriss Déby imposed a lasting settlement in 1990. It was based on a degree of power-sharing and a relatively credible framework for sharing the benefits of economic growth between the two ethno-regional groups.

As cotton and war will have been shown in sections 2 and 3 to be the crucial determinants of Chad's growth history, sections 4 and 5 will describe in greater detail the history of the cotton sector (section 4) and the political history that led, through the civil war, to a change in power from the (relatively) rich and educated southerners, who ran the country just after independence, to the poorer northerners, after the turmoil period of the war (section 5).

2. Cotton-led Sahelian growth in Chad

A large part of the growth experience of Chad is shared with other Sahelian economies. This comes out clearly in figure 3.1. As mentioned above, we take a regression-based approach to identifying the relevant growth episodes in Chad, using only variables that can reasonably be regarded either as exogenous to Chad's growth process, such as the growth experience of other Sahelian countries, or at least as unquestionably predetermined, like the outbreak of political violence. The latter might arguably be regarded as influenced to some extent by Chad's cumulated growth experience over a distant past.

Figure 3.1 shows that a remarkable tracking of the growth rate of this economy over the 1970–96 period can be achieved by using a very simple econometric equation, presented in column (1) of table 3.1. Figure 3.1, and column (1) of table 3.1 from which it is derived, show clearly that the growth rate of GDP in Chad, measured at constant 1987 local prices, can be tracked rather closely by taking into account only the growth experience of Burkina Faso and the various episodes of political violence. The series comes from World Bank (1998). Although episodes of fighting or massacre have occurred in Chad from 1965 up until almost the present, we have identified 1979–84 as the most acute period of civil war in constructing the dummy variable "War" used in table 3.1. In fact, the years 1983–4 witnessed more a series of massacres perpetrated in the south of the country than a civil war proper. Similarly, Libya occupied a portion of Chad, the Aouzou Strip

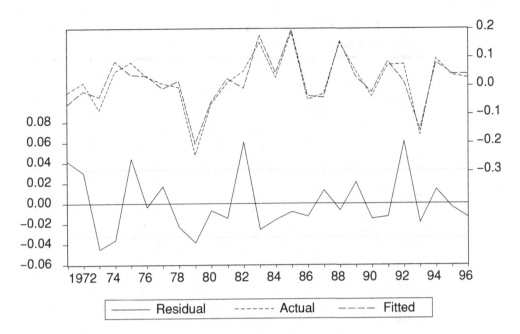

Figure 3.1 Chad, residual, actual, and fitted GDP growth rate, constant local 1987 currency, 1972–1996.

just across the border, beginning in 1973; but it was only in 1986 that the Libyan army launched a massive attack in the center of the country. This triggered the victorious counterattack of 1987, which removed all Libyan presence from Chad. Hence, the "WarLib" dummy in table 3.1 indicates the years 1986–7. Some killings of southerners had taken place ever since the outbreak of the civil war in 1979. But they took another, much larger, dimension in 1982–4, after the victory of the northerners in the civil war, under Hissein Habré, and again in 1993, under Idriss Déby. During that year of political trouble, the "National Conference" took place for venting popular resentment (see Buijtenhuijs 1998). The two episodes of massacre are captured by the "RepSouth" dummy variable in table 3.1.

The estimated equation has a simple implicit error-correction specification à la Banerjee et al. (1993), with the GDP of Burkina Faso being included both as the current growth rate and as the lagged level, in logarithm, while the lagged value of Chad's GDP is also included. Hence, these equations are based on the so-called "one-step Hendry" method for estimating error-correction models and testing co-integration. As Banerjee et al. (1993) show using Monte-Carlo simulation, this method is clearly preferable to the more common "two-step" Engle–Granger approach (Engle and Granger 1987) when using a sample size below 200 observations. In this case, the two-step method is liable to produce highly biased estimates.

Table 3.1 *Chad, GDP growth rate at local 1987 constant prices, dependent variable GyChad*

	(1)	(2)	(3)	(4)	(5)	(6)
Intercept	1.44	1.04	1.70	1.03	1.38	1.44
	(6.47)	(2.88)	(6.27)	(1.65)	(6.12)	(5.74)
War	−0.26	−0.29	−0.22	−0.26	−0.25	−0.26
	(11.15)	(6.62)	(7.38)	(9.72)	(11.68)	(10.84)
WarLib	−0.13	−0.09	−0.14	−0.12	−0.13	−0.13
	(4.98)	(2.21)	(5.38)	(4.74)	(5.61)	(4.70)
RepSouth	−0.09	−0.07	−0.11	−0.10	−0.10	−0.09
	(4.40)	(2.2)	(4.70)	(4.29)	(4.98)	(4.17)
LyChad(−1)	−0.73	−0.83	−0.68	−0.72	−0.74	−0.73
	(10.85)	(6.26)	(8.41)	(10.29)	(12.10)	(10.56)
GyBur	1.01		0.84	0.90	0.79	0.85
	(3.81)		(4.41)	(4.17)	(4.39)	(4.22)
LyBur(−1)	0.85		0.60	0.40	0.45	0.42
	(4.34)		(4.62)	(8.22)	(7.40)	(9.26)
GyMali		0.49	0.00			
		(1.90)	(0.00)			
LyMali(−1)		0.56	−0.27			
		(5.51)	(1.43)			
GyNiger				−0.01		
				(0.09)		
LyNiger(−1)				0.07		
				(0.69)		
GySudan					0.22	
					(2.40)	
LySudan(−1)					−0.04	
					(0.53)	
Devaluation						0.00
						(0.07)
No. obs.	26.0	26.0	26.0	26.0	24.0	26.0
R^2	0.90	0.73	0.92	0.91	0.94	0.90
DW	2.28	1.92	2.30	2.30	2.29	2.29
LM2	1.85	2.73	1.12	1.50	1.49	1.86
Rho	−0.22	−0.04	−0.21	−0.17	−0.28	−0.23
	(0.86)	(0.12)	(0.80)	(0.58)	(0.99)	(0.90)

Note: *t*-ratios in parentheses. Gy-Country Name is the growth rate of GDP at constant 1987 local prices, and Ly-Country Name is GDP at constant 1987 local price. War is a dummy equal to 1 in 1979–84, to capture the civil war, while WarLib takes the value 1 in 1986–7, to capture the Libyan attempted invasion and eventual defeat, the Libyan army being thrown out of Chad in 1987. RepSouth is a dummy variable that indicates the dates when bloody repression by the army was inflicted on the south (1982–4, 1993). *N* is the number of observations, R^2 is the standard goodness-of-fit measure, DW the Durbin–Watson test, which is biased here, LM2 the Lagrange-Multiplier auto-correlation test up to the order 2, and Rho the coefficient of residual auto-regression estimated by the Cochrane–Orcutt method.

This equation suggests that GDP in Chad and Burkina Faso are co-integrated. This is confirmed by a direct application of the Johansen cointegration test, including War, WarLib, and RepSouth as exogenous forcing variables. The likelihood ratio found for this test is 1.54, to be compared with a 5 percent critical value of 3.76. The co-integration equation reads: LyChad = 1.74 + 0.59 LyBur. Notice the small slope of this equation, which implies that for each 1 percent of additional growth in Burkina Faso, Chad gets 0.59 percent additional growth, on average, over the period of analysis. However, this estimate is probably biased, as it is much smaller than the corresponding slope that can be retrieved from column (1), namely 0.86, which, unlike the direct estimate, does not suffer from omitted variable bias. In particular, the error-correction representation that is implicit in the columns of table 3.1, à la Banerjee et al. (1993), entails a complicated auto-regressive/distributed-lag process. The latter allows for long-drawn-out effects of the shocks affecting the right-hand side variables on the growth of Chadian GDP, which are neglected in the direct method.

Column (2) of table 3.1 shows that a nearly similar econometric performance can be achieved by using Mali instead of Burkina Faso, but with a less impressive fit. Moreover, in the encompassing equation of column (3), the Malian variables become insignificant. Columns (4) and (5) show that neither Niger nor Sudan, the closest Sahelian neighbors of Chad, provide significant additional variables, although the growth rate of Sudanese GDP is significant, but not its level, suggesting that the two series are not co-integrated. This suggests that what is at stake here is a "similarity effect," rather than a "contagion effect" à la Easterly and Levine (1998). Both Burkina Faso and Mali are strongly reliant on cotton as their almost exclusive export crop. The closer fit obtained with Burkina Faso is due to the political troubles that affected Mali mainly around 1980 and again in the early 1990s, and that are omitted from this equation. This also suggests that what is at stake here is not simply a CFA zone effect, as neither Mali nor Niger can be used to substitute for the Burkina Faso effect. Similarly, the uranium boom in Niger does not seem to have had a significant spillover on the Chadian economy, nor does the Sudanese oil boom or civil war.

This interpretation of the results can be tested directly by looking at the impact of the output of cotton on GDP. More precisely, table 3.2 presents two regressions that explain the growth rate of Chad's GDP over the period 1963–95 as a function of the level of cotton production. The dependent variable is the growth rate of GDP at constant local prices, from Azam et al. (1999). Column (7) includes first as regressors the three variables representing political violence: War, WarLib, and RepSouth, defined above. It turns out that War is the only one to remain significant, while the other two drop out. Column (8), in part of table 3.2, shows the result obtained by the parsimonious equation resulting from the deletion of these two variables.

Table 3.2 *Chad, the impact of cotton on GDP growth*

	(7)	(8)
War	−0.22	−0.21
	(5.81)	(5.66)
WarLib	−0.02	−
	(0.66)	
RepSouth	0.04	−
	(1.34)	
Gprod	0.11	0.11
	(3.00)	(2.90)
Lprod(−1)	0.20	0.20
	(3.85)	(3.66)
Lgdp(−1)	−0.88	−0.88
	(5.83)	(6.02)
Lpop(−1)	0.38	0.39
	(3.70)	(3.87)
Ltot(−1)	−0.15	−0.14
	(2.19)	(2.06)
AR(1)	0.72	0.73
	(4.81)	(5.00)
R^2	0.76	0.74
F-LM2	0.64 ($p = 0.53$)	1.53 ($p = 0.24$)

Note: See note to table 3.1.

This implies that the impact of these two shocks is entirely captured by the level of cotton production, with no additional impact. This is not true of the War variable, suggesting that some additional effects, beyond the fall in cotton production, are significant.

The other regressors are the growth rate and the log of cotton production, the latter lagged once, and then the logs of GDP, population, and the terms of trade, also lagged once. Therefore, this equation must be interpreted as implicitly comprising an error-correction mechanism *à la* Banerjee *et al.* (1993). This implies that there exists a co-integration equation linking the latter four variables. The sign of the long-run impact of the terms of trade on GDP, given the level of cotton output, is a bit unexpected: columns (7) and (8) imply that cotton output and population affect GDP positively in the long run, while the terms of trade affect it negatively. However, care must be taken to avoid interpreting this effect as the total effect of the latter on GDP, as what is captured here is the marginal effect, given the level of cotton output. As this sector is heavily taxed (as explained in section 3), the most probable mechanism for explaining this effect works as follows. A terms of trade improvement is to a large extent taxed away

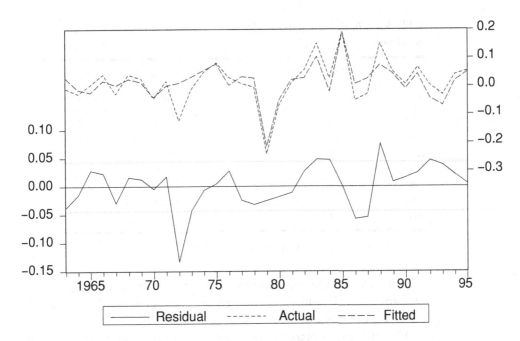

Figure 3.2 Chad, residual, tracking of GDP growth, 1963–1995
Note: See table 3.2, column (8)

from the producers, and the proceeds are used to expand employment in the civil service and the public sector. This draws away some labor from the other productive sectors, with a negative impact on output. Lastly, an auto-regressive residual term is included, estimated by the Cochrane–Orcutt method.

Figure 3.2 represents the tracking of GDP growth that is achieved by column (8). The fit is quite good for most of the period, with the exception of 1972. In Chad, the drought of the early 1970s was at least as damaging as in the rest of the Sahelian region. However, it is generally admitted that 1970 and 1971 were the worst years, and not 1972, which shows an unexplained fall in figure 3.2. The most probable explanation is that our three political violence variables fail to capture the effects of the lower-intensity fighting that was going on in some other years. For example, in 1971 and 1972, some severe fighting took place between the two main factions of the northern rebellion, while the 1969–71 "pacification" campaign performed by the Chadian army with some French support reached a climax in 1971 (see Azam *et al.* 1999). An additional potentially important factor is that the cotton sector was subjected in the course of 1971 to a major institutional change. The parastatal in charge of the sector changed status, becoming Cotontchad, with 75 percent of the capital owned by the Chadian government, the French involvement falling to 19 percent, a change described in more detail in section 3. Such an

Table 3.3 *Chad, growth and inflation in the wake of the 1994 devaluation, 1994–2000*

Year	Real GDP growth rate (%)		Inflation rate (%)	
	Chad	CEMAC	Chad	CEMAC
1994	4.0		49.2	41.7
1995	0.9	4.2	8.3	5.5
1996	2.9	5.0	10.5	2.8
1997	4.4	5.2	0.6	5.4
1998	6.5	4.9	3.0	3.3
1999	0.5	0.1	−4.7	−0.2
2000	−0.3	3.5	13.0	2.1

Source: Banque de France: *Rapport Zone Franc,* various issues.

institutional change might have entailed some degree of temporary disorganization, which reduced the positive externalities normally provided by this sector to the rest of the economy.

While the shadow of conflict gradually faded away, strengthening property rights and incentives to some extent, Chad saw its currency devalued in January 1994, together with all the other CFA zone member countries. This occurred at the end of 1993, a year which saw both a lot of killing in the south by the governmental army, and the national conference, which started a sort of democratic dialog. In addition, an (ESAF) agreement was signed with the International Monetary Fund (IMF) on September 1, 1995, as well as an SAP with the World Bank, signed in June 1997. The devaluation did not attract as much attention from the ordinary citizen as it did in many other CFA countries. Nevertheless, figures 3.6 and 3.7 (pp. 100 and 102) show that the supply response was spectacular in the cotton sector and triggered an export boom. This response was distributed over several years, peaking in 1997–8. The same pattern can be found in the GDP series, as could be expected from the econometric exercises presented above. Table 3.3 shows how the growth of GDP and the rate of inflation evolved in Chad in the wake of the 1994 devaluation, together with the corresponding averages for the Economic and Monetary Community of Central Africa (CEMAC) to which it belongs. This table clearly shows that Chad is a slow grower, by CEMAC standards, with a more volatile rate of inflation. However, the export boom finished in 1999, due to excessive rains in the south, as well as to an expansion of food crops as the price of cereals increased. Not surprisingly, GDP followed suit, starting a recession.

In summary, the econometric exercises performed so far single out clearly the two main points around which a historical account of the Chadian

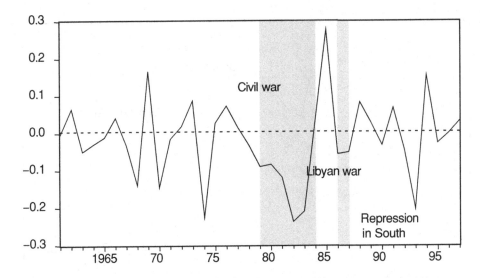

Figure 3.3 Chad, residual, growth rate of *per capita* GDP, constant international prices, 1961–1997

growth experience must be built: the development of the cotton sector, and the political economy of war and political violence. Section 3 gives a first account of this impact, by showing that the civil war separates clearly the periods that run before and after its occurrence. Section 4 presents a history of the cotton sector, while section 5 looks at the political history of this country, showing how the south failed to keep the control of the country, which it inherited from the French at independence, before the civil war gave it to the northerners.

3. The three main phases of Chadian growth history

A slightly different picture of the growth experience of Chad comes out of an examination of the time profile of GDP *per capita* measured at international or local prices, mainly after 1979. Over the whole period, episodes with positive growth are pretty rare and far apart, as seen from figure 3.3. Strongly negative growth rates occur in some years, like 1968, 1970, 1974 (the year of the oil shock), then 1979–83, during the civil war, and again in 1993, when massacres were perpetrated in the south. Figure 3.4 shows the resulting time profile of *per capita* GDP at international prices.

Over this period of time, one can clearly identify three sub-periods with different characteristics: from independence in 1960 until the outbreak of

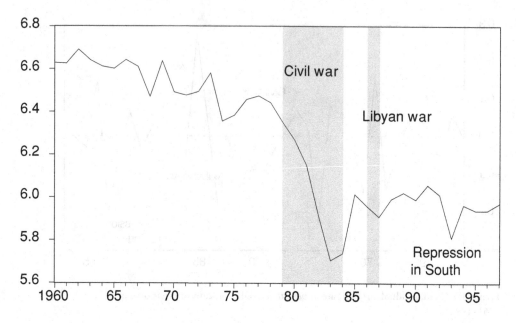

Figure 3.4 Chad, residual, *per capita* GDP, international prices, 1960–1997, log scale

the civil war in 1979, we observe a slow reduction in *per capita* GDP, with wide swings in the short run. The first oil shock, in 1974, seems to have a significant negative impact. This was also a period of drought, which decimated the herds in the north. When the war broke out, *per capita* GDP was 27.5 percent lower than in 1960. This fall cannot be blamed only on external shocks, and was probably mainly the result of pessimistic expectations and the anticipated collapse of the political equilibrium.

We then have the civil war years, which witnessed a collapse of the economy. By 1983 *per capita* GDP had fallen to 50 percent of its 1962 value. This was followed from 1985 onwards by a period of stagnation of *per capita* GDP, at slightly above 55 percent of its 1962 value, with some years of positive growth, disturbed by the Libyan war and by the 1993 bloodbath in the south, the cotton-production area. The 1994 devaluation of the CFA franc gave an additional impetus to growth, especially because of its fiscal effects and the renewed aid effort that it triggered, which together allowed the government to pay the salaries of civil servants, to invest, and to clear some arrears. It might therefore be useful to split the post-civil war period 1985–97 into pre- and post-devaluation periods. However, the sketch presented above is sufficient to illustrate the positive growth response that occurred.

Figure 3.5 compares the *per capita* GDP series at international and local prices, from Azam *et al.* (1999), expressed in log terms. The two series have been normalized to have the same base year, in 1960. This type of comparison is a bit awkward, as the two series obey a different logic: while the local price

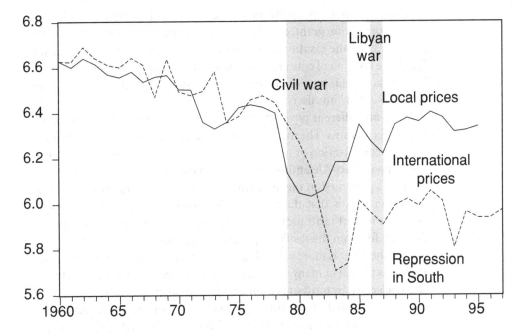

Figure 3.5 Chad, comparison of *per capita* GDP, local and international prices, 1960–1996, log scale

data are based on value added, the international price series is based on the expenditure side (consumption, investment, etc.). However, the latter is nevertheless supposed to be an accurate indirect measure of GDP, the two being related by an accounting identity. Two main differences emerge immediately from this chart: the impact of the civil war seems both delayed and deeper in the international prices series, while the latter also indicates a much deeper fall in *per capita* GDP after the end of the civil war. This type of divergence between the local price GDP series and the international price ones can be explained by the differences in the structure of relative prices between the two series. In particular, in economies where there exists a significant non-traded goods sector, the real exchange rate might play an important part. However, as shown by Azam (1991) and Azam and Wane (2001), this is not the case in the small open economies of the CFA zone. In particular, the latter show that the 1994 devaluation of the CFA franc had a negligible impact on the structure of relative consumer prices in several CFA zone member countries. This suggests that most of these countries are price takers on the world market for most of their consumption goods, and thus that non-traded goods can be neglected as a first-order approximation. Similarly, this devaluation has no impact on the series presented in figure 3.5, suggesting that the real exchange rate cannot be the cause of their divergence.

A more important factor in Africa over most of this period is the implicit protection granted to the capital-intensive import substitution sector, mainly by the taxation of export crops, as well as by other means. In Chad, the taxation of cotton and livestock, described below, played this part. The impact of this type of distortion on economic growth was at the center of the so-called "immiserizing growth theory."

There are different types of immiserizing growth models, based on different mechanisms. The most relevant ones for the problem at hand analyze the impact of taxation or tariffs, and were produced by Johnson (1967) and Brecher and Diaz-Alejandro (1977), which extends it. A sketch of these two models is presented in the appendix (p. 113). The central intuition of this line of analysis is that the relative price distortion entailed by an export tax or an import tariff provides an incentive to produce more of the good that benefits from the resulting protection, and less of the other good, even though the latter is more valuable at world market prices. Severe export taxation was typical in many African countries, while the industrial sector was often protected by tariffs, tax exemptions, and other means. The Rybczynski theorem states that, under these conditions, an increase in the capital stock will result in an increase in the size of the protected sector, which already produces too much at international prices, and a contraction of the more labor-intensive sector, which already produces too little.

Investment was positive during most of this period (except, of course, during the war years), assisted in part by external funding from France, and growth at domestic prices was regarded as positive, slightly above population growth in the early phase (World Bank 1971). It is remembered as such by the people who lived through that period. Nevertheless, at both local and international prices, the overall trend seems to be negative, but much less so at local prices, where some recovery seems to occur after the war. Such a divergence can be explained within the Johnson (1967) and Brecher–Diaz-Alejandro (1977) framework by the fact that the export sectors (cotton and cattle) were massively taxed, while the other sectors (import substitution industry and services), were much less taxed, or even sometimes subsidized. The divergence of the two series shown in figure 3.5 after 1984 suggests that the post-war recovery may have entailed some immiserizing growth, of the type described above, as investment may have been concentrated in the protected sector. Similarly, the puzzling desynchronized dips in the series during the civil war suggest that a wide swing in the relative importance of the different production sectors, which are weighted by very different relative prices in the two series, occurred then. However, this effect does not seem to matter before the civil war, as the two series remain quite close to each other.

The dynamics of GDP before the war, during the anticipated disaster episode, are probably best explained by the pessimistic expectations of potential investors. Collier (1999) offers an analysis of changes in the sectoral composition of output due to civil war. He emphasizes the role of the stock-adjustment of the capital stock to the political risk as perceived by entrepreneurs. However, the gradual fall in output before the outbreak of the civil war proper in 1979 suggests that the more sporadic violence that occurred before that had already damaged the investment climate. Moreover, the end of this gradual fall after the war, and its outright recovery at local prices even earlier, suggest that the stock-adjustment of the capital stock to the risk of war emphasized by Collier (1999) had been completed by then. Hence, the shadow of conflict probably grew larger and larger before the war, over nearly two decades, while the war itself did not provide investors with a lot of relevant information.

Nevertheless, the same periods can be clearly identified in the two series, with a roughly similar interpretation, although the post-civil war fall in *per capita* GDP is much stronger when evaluated at international prices. Similarly, the post-civil war recovery is more evident at local prices than at international prices.

4. The history of the cotton sector

The cultivation of cotton was introduced during the colonial period in 1928, under the forced labor regime. A similar policy was pursued by the French in most Sahelian areas; Bassett (2001) gives a rich account of the experience of northern Côte d'Ivoire. Many similarities can be found with the case of Chad. In both cases, the evolution of the sector was tightly controlled by a parastatal, which provided the seeds and other inputs as well as doing research for selecting the most appropriate seeds and providing extension services. As in most Sahelian countries, the French CFDT was heavily involved in the sector. An important change occurred in 1971 with the creation of Cotontchad, which replaced Cotonfran as the firm in charge of the cotton sector. The capital of Cotontchad is owned mainly by the Chadian government, which holds 75 percent, the rest being shared between the CFDT, which holds 19 percent, and several local banks, together accounting for 6 percent. In 1985, this parastatal encountered serious problems because of a fall in the world price of cotton. Output was limited to 100,000 tons, the producer price was reduced to a low CFAF 100, and seven ginning plants had to be closed out of the twelve in operation up to that date. Further serious problems emerged in the early 1990s and persisted until a combination of the 1994 devaluation and a rise in world prices helped to restore the financial position. The producer price was then increased from CFAF 90 to CFAF 120, for the 1994–5 campaign.

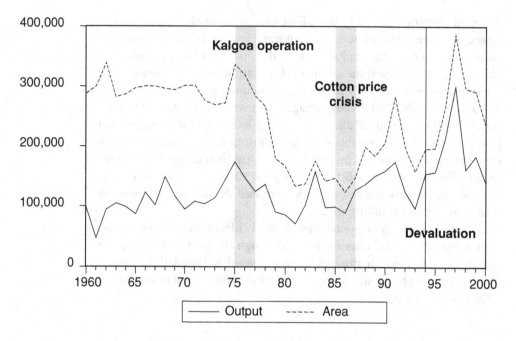

Figure 3.6 Chad, cultivated area and cotton-seed output, 1960–2000

During the colonial period, output grew from 18 tons of cotton-seed during the 1928–9 campaign to 80,500 tons in 1957–8. After independence, output went from almost 98,000 tons in 1960–1 to 145,750 tons in 2000–1. This growth is related to that of the average yield per hectare, which has increased steadily as a result of research into the choice of seed varieties and agricultural techniques, which drew largely on the experience of the CFDT throughout the Sahelian area. From 120 kg per hectare on average over 1928–39, yields reached 200 kg during 1940–50, then 280 kg in 1956–61. The average yield per hectare in 2000 was 592 kg.

Figure 3.6 shows the area devoted to cotton and its output level. The impact of the civil war is evident on the area cultivated, as well as on the output level, where it must be appreciated against the positive trend characterizing this series. It falls over 1979–81, while a positive spike occurs in 1983. Just before the war, in 1974–5, a special operation, called the Kalgoa operation, was launched by the government, aiming at pushing output to a record 150,000 tons for that campaign. This was meant to increase revenues for the purposes of intensifying the fighting in the north and funding oil prospecting in the south. It had some positive effects in the following two years, with output reaching 174,062 tons and 147,384 tons, respectively. Figure 3.6 also shows the impact of the droughts that affected this sector especially in 1970–1 and 1984.

Table 3.4 *Chad, exports and cotton exports, 1980–2000 CFAF billion*

		Cotton				Cotton
Year	Total exports	Exports		Year	Total exports	Exports
1980				1991	54.6	24.0
1981				1992	48.2	25.0
1982				1993	45.9	14.5
1983	29.8	23.1		1994	78.7	26.3
1984	47.7	40.7		1995	12.3	63.7
1985	44.7	22.4		1996	12.9	47.0
1986	34.1	14.6		1997	138.1	63.0
1987	32.8	12.3		1998	157.0	78.0
1988	42.9	23.1		1999	150.0	60.0
1989	49.5	23.4		2000	129.4	50.7
1990	52.6	26.0				

Source: BEAC, IMF.

Cotton was the main source of income in Chad during the colonial period, and it remained so from independence until oil revenues began to flow in 2003. The primary sector, and in particular cotton and livestock, is the mainstay of the Chadian economy. Despite its recent decline, the share of the primary sector in GDP is about 40 percent, that of industry about 15 percent, and that of the service sector between 45 percent and 50 percent. It follows that GDP is severely exposed to climatic shocks, mainly through cotton and livestock. Cotton directly employs 300,000 households in the southern part of the country. This sector has been the subject of special attention by successive governments since independence, because it is the main source of fiscal revenues. Cotton is also the main export crop and provides at least 80 percent of the foreign exchange earning for most of the period, until the recent relative decline. Table 3.4 and Figure 3.7 show the series for total exports and cotton exports since 1983. Some of the cotton was transformed locally by the Société Textile du Tchad (STT), which was one of the main industrial firms in the country between 1965 and its closure in 1991.

The determination of the Chadian government to develop the cotton sector is well illustrated by the 1966–70 Five-Year Plan. Investment in the production sectors, including rural development and industry, amounted to 42 percent of the total expenditures of the plan; 28.3 percent of the resources were allocated to the modernization of agriculture, and were almost entirely devoted to the cotton sector, the growth of which was meant to provide the fiscal resources for supporting the state.

Government involvement in the cotton sector did not stop with the end of the 1966–70 Plan, or with the switch of power into the hands of northerners

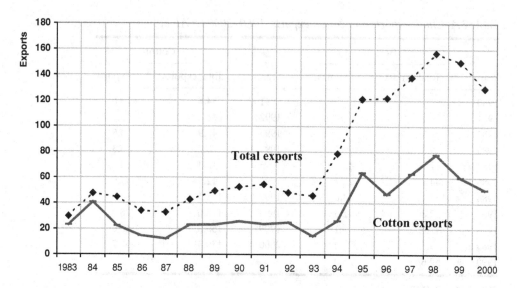

Figure 3.7 Chad, total exports and cotton exports, 1983–2000, CFAF billion

after the civil war. The 1985 Convention, the 1988 Plan-contract, and Decrees 022 and 023/PR/MCI/90 passed on February 9, 1990, all aimed at restoring the competitiveness of the cotton sector. The 1994 devaluation gave a new boost to exports, as illustrated by figure 3.7, and in particular to cotton exports. Currently, the government is examining the possibility of privatizing the Cotontchad company, and of separating the marketing and ginning functions from the production of oil and soap from cotton seeds.

The government levies three kinds of revenues from the cotton sector:

- An export tax on cotton-fiber exports
- A company tax and profits tax on Cotontchad
- Dividends.

In the days of Cotonfran, the export tax amounted to CFAF 17,000 per ton of cotton fiber exported. In 1971, this was raised to CFAF 21,500 per ton, and this amount has fluctuated ever since, following changes in the world price. According to the computations made by Madengar and Farris (1991) for the 1985–6 period, the state levied CFAF 53,739 as export tax, CFAF 6,060 as levy for the "Caisse Autonome d'Amortissement" (CAA), a direct contribution to the reimbursement of the national debt, and CFAF 7,000 for the "Office National de Développement Rural" (ONDR), a parastatal in charge of rural development. This amounts to a total of CFAF 66,799 per ton, i.e. FF 1,336 at that time. Table 3.5 shows the time

Table 3.5 *Chad, revenues from export tax on cotton fiber, 1985–1986*

| Month | Quantity exported (tons) | Shares in CFAF 000 | | | |
		Treasury	CAA	ONDR	Total
12:85	4,173	224,253	25,288	29,211	278,753
01:86	5,959	320,232	36,112	41,713	398,057
02:86	7,203	387,077	43,650	50,420	481,146
03:86	2,499	134,282	15,143	17,491	166,916
04:86	3,305	177,604	20,028	23,135	220,767
05:86	2,618	140,693	15,866	18,327	174,886
06:86	2,048	110,043	12,409	14,334	136,786
07:86	9,081	488,017	55,032	65,568	608,618
Total	**36,886**	**1,982,202**	**223,527**	**260,200**	**2,465,929**

Source: Madengar and Farris 1991.

profile of these revenues over the relevant part of the 1985–6 period. It suggests that the harvest is highly seasonal, with peaks in February and July.

After the 1985 Convention, the government levied a direct tax, and left 80 percent of the profit to the "Caisse de Stabilization des Prix au Producteur" – i.e. the stabilization fund for the producer price – and 20 percent to Cotontchad. The latter 20 percent was in turn taxed at 50 percent by the profit tax, the rest being distributed to the shareholders (of which 75 percent went to the Chadian state). Moreover, as in most other Francophone African countries, the resources of the stabilization fund were in fact used to finance various government expenditures. One can therefore estimate that, behind this administrative veil, the state in fact levied more than 90 percent of the profits of the cotton sector. This nevertheless left southern farmers at an income level well above that of the northern herdsmen.

The cotton sector impacts the economy in many other ways. Although it was initially introduced by force, it has become a major factor influencing the life of most people in the south of Chad. It gives them access to three of the crucial characteristics of a modern economy: credit, technical progress, and insurance. Cotontchad provides the various inputs – be they annual ones such as seeds, fertilizers, and pesticides, or longer-lasting ones such as plows and weeders, at credit. Reimbursement is then recovered directly out of the crop sale. Extension services are provided by the ONDR, which also provides credit for buying the pair of oxen required for cultivation. Animal traction has in fact been promoted since 1966 as a means of boosting production; moreover, the use of fertilizers and other modern inputs, as well as animal traction and various cultivation techniques introduced for cotton, spill over to other crops. The output of rice trebled over 1966–95, and a new crop emerged in the 1980s, namely sugar cane, which expanded rapidly (Azam *et al.* 1999). Lastly, Cotontchad ensures the marketing of the crop, thanks to its own fleet of trucks, at a known price.

The cotton sector also provides incentives for the expansion and maintenance of the road network in the south, with positive spillovers on the local economy. Earth roads are regularly maintained there, unlike in the rest of the country, giving farmers and other producers some access to markets. Schools and dispensaries are created in the neighborhoods of ginning plants, which primarily benefit the children of the employees of these plants, but are also available to the children of the farmers. There were eight such ginning plants in 1945, rising to twenty-three in 1966. Since the 1985–6 cotton crisis *à la* figure 3.6, only eight of these plants have remained in operation. But some of the related socio-economic infrastructure has outlasted the closure of the others. Of course, this bundling of services provided by the local monopsony firm has some well-known drawbacks, which have been well identified in the case of transition economies and are subject to the attacks of the IFIs, as in many other Sahelian countries.

The cotton sector also provides activity to the local banking sector and to local transport companies. Cotontchad borrows a short-term campaign credit each year worth between CFAF 40–60 billion, at a rate of interest of at least 12 percent, and all the cotton fiber is transported by private truckers to the port of Douala in Cameroon.

No positive externality of this kind has been sustained by the livestock sector in the north of the country, where the involvement of the state has always been more distant. The feeling that there existed a *Tchad utile* or "useful Chad," in the south, distinct from the "useless Chad" of the north, helped fuel the resentments that eventually led to the civil war and the transfer of political power from southerners to northerners. We now analyze how this happened.

5. The political history

The southern part of the country, south of the Chari river, was cut off in 1936 from the Oubangui-Chari territory (now the CAR), part of the French Equatorial Africa territory, and added to the Chad territory. This measure aimed to provide fiscal resources to the French administration in Fort-Lamy, now N'Djamena, which had been unable to raise any from what is now northern and central Chad. From independence and until the civil war, the country was ruled by southerners, first by François Ngarta Tombalbaye and after a 1975 *coup d'état*, by General Félix Malloum. The latter was regarded with some sympathy by the French government, as Tombalbaye had adopted a fairly independent and despotic attitude. Most of the administrative staff were from the south, because of their educational advantage, fueling north-ern perceptions of favoritism towards the south.

Endless debates have taken place to determine what caused the eruption of political violence between the north and the south. Many emphasize grievances – and, in particular, that the northerners had developed a sense of superiority over the southerners because nomads had for centuries used the south as a reserve for slaves, which they captured by occasionally raiding the villages south of the Chari river. This would then explain the resentment of the uneducated northerners faced with a post-colonial government dom-inated by southerners (e.g. Lanne 1996). Roné (2000), however, points out that the capture of slaves is a reciprocal exercise, one that all groups perform to the detriment of all other groups and that even occurs between neigh-boring villages within each group. Lanne (1996), a former French adminis-trator from the colonial period, recalls that various skirmishes between the northerners and the southerners erupted well before independence. Riots took place between southerners and northerners in 1946 and 1947 in Fort-Lamy (now N'Djamena) and Fort-Archambault (now Sarh) in the south. In particular in 1947 in Sarh, the fight was led on the southern side by a school master called François Tombalbaye. The southern contingent sought revenge for some insults addressed to southerners by northerners during a political meeting.

At that point, the flooding of the civil service by southerners was far from evident. In fact, during the colonial period the French administration could be more accurately described as favoring northerners reflecting the traditional fascination with desert people that partially explains the pattern of French penetration in Africa, from Senegal eastward. The first Chadian civil servants in the 1920s were Muslims from the north: Hanoun Othman and Béchir Sow. The first schools were created in the north, in the 1920s (Lanne 1996). At that time, the south was still part of the Oubangui-Chari territory, where the French were not pursuing such a development policy. As late as 1966, when the rebellion started to gain momentum, more than 55 percent of the medical infrastructure was in the north, as shown by table 3.6. However, this attraction was in fact one-sided, as the northerners voluntarily kept their distance from the French schooling system, where neither Arabic nor the Koran were taught and where boys and girls were educated on a par, side by side. After a French-imposed civil service reform in 1956–7 made recruitment dependent on competitive exams "à la française," open only to educated people, 70–80 percent of the civil servants turned out to be from the south.

A fairly natural selection process thus led southerners to hold the gov-ernment at independence. At that point, the challenge was to build a nation under the threat of ethnic conflict. As shown by Azam (2001) and Azam and

Table 3.6 *Chad, distribution of health infrastructure between North and South, 1966*

	Hospitals	Medical centers	Infirmaries	Dispensaries	Epidemiological units	Polyclinics	Social centers	Total
North	2	6	19	51	5	1	6	90
South	2	5	8	42	3	0	3	63
Total	**4**	**11**	**27**	**93**	**8**	**1**	**9**	**153**

Source: Diguimbaye and Langue (1968).

Mesnard (2003), the crucial factor in such a process, when the government does not exert an obvious military domination over the excluded group, is to put in place a credible redistribution system in favor of the excluded group. The aim of such a system has nothing to do with philanthropy, and is instead meant to avoid the social costs of war by giving potential rebels at least as much as what they could expect to capture by waging a war. This is the fundamental participation constraint that bears on the social contract required for maintaining peace in a divided society (Azam and Mesnard 2003). In Côte d'Ivoire, for example, the high wages of the civil service, combined with a broad-based education policy and a commitment to selecting the elite from the groups, played a large part in such a framework (Azam 2001; Azam and Koidou 2002). The reluctance of northerners to join the French schooling system in Chad closed that avenue for credible redistribution in their favor. As discussed above with regard to the cotton sector, most of the investment in infrastructure was consistently done in favor of the "useful Chad," with very little benefit to the north, where the social rate of return was admittedly much lower, from a narrow economic point of view. This closed a second major potential avenue for redistribution across regions. The only avenue left was patronage, a common system in most African countries, with power-sharing in government aimed at making it as credible as possible. Tangri (1999) provides a richly documented analysis of patronage in several Anglophone countries that sheds light on the various possibilities that were probably still open to the Chadian government, had it wished to use them.

However, other aspects of the government's behavior suggest that Tombalbaye was not convinced of the value of such a redistribution policy, and was instead paying only lip service to the regional balance between ethnic groups. This was noticed very early on by some observers. In its 1971 *Country Economic Memorandum*, the World Bank wrote: "the question of livestock taxation occupies an important place in the conflict between northern and southern population groups" (World Bank 1971: 7). Combining the cattle head tax with other levies bearing on the livestock sector, this report estimates the contribution of this sector to public finance at CFAF 631 million in 1966, while the cotton sector, the main foreign exchange earner, was contributing only CFAF 90 million in the same period. However, many observers deny that economic motivations triggered the uprising of the northerners, pointing out in particular that the head tax on livestock had been created by the French colonial authority in 1910 (Roné 2000). Nevertheless, although taxes were collected in the north by local chiefs on behalf of the government, partly deflecting the potential resentment, the imbalance in tax revenues described above certainly aggravated the tension between the two groups. Moreover, the government issued bonds in 1964, borrowing money locally for the first time and making it compulsory for all Chadians to subscribe. This action was perceived by poor farmers and herdsmen as a doubling of their tax liability (Lanne 1996). Some southern cotton growers committed suicide in desperation, seeing their yearly income obliterated by this levy. In the north, the response was more positive, as many were soon to take to the bush and join the rebellion.

The most spectacular political events happened just after the creation of the single party, the "Parti Progressiste Tchadien" (PPT). Before independence, the PPT was merely the local branch of the "Rassemblement Démocratique Africain" (RDA), the party that had nurtured the whole political elite of most Francophone African countries before and after independence. As he became President in 1962, Tombalbaye aimed at turning it into the sole political party, as was done in so many other countries in Africa at that time. The northerners were very wary of this move, and many of them were in favor of keeping a separate political party. However, Tombalbaye won initially, and the principle of a single party was adopted at a plenary congress in Fort-Archambault in January 1963. The national political board of this new party was manned equally by northerners and southerners. However, a small number of northerners turned down the offer to join, and the prestigious Minister of Foreign Affairs had to be replaced one month later. Tombalbaye chose a southerner to replace this important political leader from the north, and this was regarded as a flagrant violation of the principle of regional balance. Many separate meetings were convened by the northerners, which Tombalbaye tried to prevent. A series of arrests and condemnations followed, and this sealed the fate of the consensual single party. On September 16, 1963, a march organized by the northerners was fiercely repressed, killing a few demonstrators and leading to the arrest of three more political leaders from the north. At that point Tombalbaye lost all his credibility, and his attempt at cementing national unity by imposing the single-party regime ended up with the opposite effect. Dissent emerged in the north less than two years later, leading eventually to the civil war and the replacement of southerners by northerners at the head of the country.

Tombalbaye became gradually more and more despotic, and lost most of his support. In a strange attempt to reduce the weight of religious antagonism, he tried to impose a return to the roots and to impose traditional initiation on all southerners. Several resisting Christians, mainly protestants, were summarily executed. This is the time when he took the title of "Ngarta," normally reserved to traditional chiefs. He was overthrown by a *coup d'état* on April 13, 1975, led by General Félix Malloum, a prominent southerner. The latter tried to launch a policy aiming at restoring a degree of regional balance between the north and the south. He thus chose Hissein Habré, one of the leaders of the rebellion movement in the north, to become his Prime Minister. This was an attempt at finding a more acceptable political system for involving northerners in the sharing of the benefits from power. Habré accepted, and this raised hopes. A new constitution organizing the sharing of power between the President and the Prime Minister was passed on August 29, 1978. The French Prime Minister Raymond Barre sent a telegram of congratulation. However, the two men failed to get on, as Habré turned rapidly into a radical aiming at cleaning up the "stables," and fighting corruption by drastic measures. The old guard of southern civil servants naturally felt under threat. The civil war broke out on February 12, 1979, with a lot of fighting in N'Djamena. Inter-ethnic massacres occurred, and the state collapsed. The new constitution, probably enacted too late, thus turned out to be a Trojan horse, rather than the seal of a new alliance.

Ever since 1965, a low-intensity insurrection had been happening in the north, run by the Front de Libération Nationale du Tchad (Frolinat), which was led by the two Toubou rivals Goukouni Oueddeï and Hissein Habré. Goukouni is the son of the highest traditional authority of his group, the Gedré, while Habré is from a lower caste of the same group, the Goranne. A finer ethnic division is sometimes used to distinguish the Teda and the Daza among the Toubou. Goukouni Oueddeï is a Teda, from the very north, south of the Libyan border, while Hissein Habré is a Daza, from the east, by the border with Egypt and Sudan (Azam *et al.* 1999). The former developed a very close relationship with the Libyan ruler, Khadafi, while the latter is an inflexible nationalist, who has always fought hard to keep Khadafi out of Chad. At times this won Habré serious US support, which exerted a competitive pressure on France to adopt a firm stance on these matters and to provide Habré with the required military support, including arms and the discreet assistance of "technical advisors," when it came time to push the Libyan army out of the country. Habré lost French support by selling captured high-tech Soviet military hardware to the USA in 1987 without letting the French look at it. He was thus dumped by Paris when Idriss Déby launched an attack from the Sudanese territory, and seized N'Djamena very quickly in 1990.

Idriss Déby comes from the Zarghawa group, whose territory lies on either side of the Sudanese border, with only about 30–40 percent of its population living inside Chad. The presidential guard is now staffed with a large proportion of Sudanese Arab-speaking elite soldiers. The Zarghawa are Muslim Arab speakers, with natural relations with the Goranne. A blow-by-blow account of the extremely complicated game of alliances and antagonism between the different players during the first thirty years of independence, which has at times a chaotic flavor, is provided by Lemoine (1997), and falls outside the scope of the present study. For example, Habré was the last Prime Minister of the Malloum days, while the latter was trying to avoid the war, and the second President of the post-war period, until 1990. This occurred when the northerners began to rule the country, after a short interim leadership of Goukouni. Until the civil war proper, most of the fighting took place in the northern half of the country.

After the civil war, the country was not perfectly peaceful either. Besides the failed Libyan invasion described above, this period saw much military activity in the south. The "codos" (short for "commandos") rebellion movements emerged in the south, from 1983 to 1986, and then from 1992 to 1999 (Roné 2000). These triggered two massive waves of very harsh repression, first by the Habré government and then by the Idriss Déby government, in which innocent civilians were massacred and many villages were burnt to ashes and deleted from the map. Buijtenhuijs (1998) does not hesitate to characterize these massacres as "genocidal." He estimates that more than 1,000 southerners were killed every year during those two episodes. As seen above in the econometric exercises, these massacres made a significant dent in the growth history of the country.

Moreover, over-armed herdsmen from the north, where most of the fighting took place for more than a decade, started to cross the Chari river in order to feed their cattle in the cotton fields, shooting resisting farmers dead with impunity. Neither the administration nor the judicial authority, now dominated by the northerners, would take any action against this type of roving banditry, because quite a lot of this cattle is in fact owned by high-ranking officials. Thus, crime can now be viewed in the south as "the continuation of war by other means." Ironically, these incursions became possible only after the donors funded a massive project for eradicating the tse-tse fly, which had for centuries provided a natural protection for the south against vagrant northern herds and the entailed extension of the desert. There are no precise estimates of the number of southern peasants who have emigrated to neighboring Cameroon, CAR, and Nigeria. However, to the surprise of most observers, the northerners got the majority in the electoral census prior to the 1996 elections (see Buijtenhuijs 1998). Some claim that many farmers have deserted their fields because of this threat, and that this is the root cause of the ending of the post-devaluation cotton-led boom. No data are available to examine statistically the exact significance of these claims, as most of these assaults are left unreported.

Nevertheless, the Déby regime has persisted since 1990 and is rightly regarded as a more satisfactory regime than its predecessors. The key to its relative success is that it has established a degree of regional balance at the head of the state. Tombalbaye had consciously destroyed the prospect of regional balance, probably over-estimating his political or military strength. Malloum had attempted the strategy, but too late; Habré was already too strong to consider it. Déby chose Wadel Abdelkader Kamougué, the General who organized resistance in the south, during the civil war and the subsequent massacres, as the President of the national assembly. This is formally the second position in the state hierarchy, and Kamougué represents a genuine personal power, as he could mobilize several military units in case of need. In addition, some decentralization was adopted with the new constitution approved by referendum on March 31, 1996. Three levels of local governments were created on the French pattern, with communes (both rural and urban) at the bottom, departments at the intermediate level, and regions. Hence, Déby based his peace-keeping strategy partly on credible power-sharing with the southerners, and succeeded in halting the downward spiral that had characterized the economy before the civil war. We saw above that the economy recovered partially in the 1990s, with some positive growth of *per capita* GDP, when measured at local constant prices. In the oil sector, at least, investors have now recovered enough confidence to launch the exploitation of the oil fields, more than twenty-five years after their discovery. The strategy of regional balance was reinforced in April 2001 by the selection as Prime Minister of Nagoum Yamassoum, a southerner, while Déby was re-elected in May 2001, with 67.35 percent of the votes.

However, it remains to be seen whether the arrival of the oil money into the public coffers as of 2003 will leave this equilibrium untouched, or whether it will trigger a new round of political violence, aimed at determining the shares of the spoils going to each group. The Chadian national assembly passed a law, on December 30, 1998, aimed at providing various guarantees about the use of the oil money. It allocated the various direct or indirect revenues from oil to different accounts in the government budget, in an attempt to avoid diversion of this money. Moreover, it created a watchdog, called the "Collège de Contrôle et de Surveillance des Ressources Pétrolières," in charge of monitoring the use of the oil money. A law passed on June 21, 2000 reinforced the presence of civil society in this supervision committee, beside the representatives of the parliament, the central bank and the treasury, the Supreme Court, etc. Nevertheless, in view of the sporadic violence that still occurs in some parts of the country, epitomized by the killing of the chief of staff of the Chadian army in an ambush in the north of the country in early 2001, it seems that peace and the enforceability of this legal device are jointly determined.

6. Conclusion

The growth experience of Chad provides several lessons for understanding the political economy of African development. For most of Chad's post-colonial history, growth depended on a heavily controlled and taxed export crop sector, whose evolution was in turn driven by a parastatal company. Growth was concentrated in a small part of the country, the "useful Chad" in the south, while the rest was left with a minimal presence of the state and with no spillovers from the relative prosperity of the south. Independence gave political power to the southerners, who had benefited from the French presence by producing an educated elite which controlled the state apparatus. The southerners failed to understand the need to share some of their prosperity with the powerful northerners, made more efficient at fighting by their nomadic life and their involvement in livestock-raising. Alternatively, they may have understood this participation constraint as a matter of principle, but under-estimated the northerners' relative efficiency at fighting, and thus their chances of overthrowing the southerners' rule. Nomadic herdsmen have been known as better at fighting than sedentary farmers since time immemorial, and the great fourteenth-century Arab social thinker Ibn Khaldun emphasized it in *Al Muqqadima* (1958[1392]). Herders are better at fighting for two reasons. First, they are poorer than farmers, so that their opportunity cost of labor is lower. Moreover, their livelihoods are more uncertain, and climatic shocks such as drought have always pushed them occasionally into relying on "*razzia*" (raiding) for their survival. Second, Keegan (1994) emphasizes that spilling blood is part of the everyday life of herders, while sedentary farmers tend to develop a specialized caste or profession of butchers, which relieves them of this unpleasant task. He argues that this makes the former more determined fighters, who kill humans more easily.

The exclusion of northerners from sharing the spoils of the peaceful economy resulted in a long-standing state of political violence, which could be restricted to the north only until the 1979–84 civil war. Massacres were then perpetrated in the south, in 1982–4 by the Habré government, and in 1993 by the Déby government, resulting in the destruction of many villages and a collapse in cotton production, the mainstay of the economy. However, the social cost of this political violence is under-estimated by looking only at these contemporaneous events (the killing of farmers and the ensuing fall in cotton production). The most important lesson from a careful analysis of Chad's economic history is that the outbreak of the civil war was probably anticipated by potential investors. This superimposed a downward trend on GDP, which was otherwise determined as elsewhere in the Sahel by the cotton economy. As a result of that gradual decline, Chadian *per capita* GDP was

27.5 percent lower, at the onset of the civil war in 1979, than it had been at independence in 1960. The shadow of conflict was thus a fundamental brake on growth for nearly two decades. The civil war proper, and the massacre that followed in the cotton-growing area, deepened the damage, leaving *per capita* GDP at the end of 1984 at about 50 percent of its level reached at the time of independence. This figure provides a rough estimate of the social cost of the failure by the Tombalbaye government to understand the need to pursue a credible redistribution strategy in a polarized country like Chad.

Some form of democratization took place under Idriss Déby, and some protection of the political rights of the defeated southerners was made credible by the election as President of the National Assembly of General Kamougué, who has consistently been the main leader of the southern resistance, ever since the beginning of the civil war. He is known to be able to raise military units rapidly, and therefore to give the south some chance of resisting a massive attack by the northerners. As a result, some economic recovery took place after the civil war, halting the downward slide of the pre-war era. However, this recovery is more noticeable when GDP is measured at constant local prices than at international prices, at which a mere stagnation is observed. The peace so purchased seems to be credible enough to the oil companies, which have at long last invested in the development of Chad's oil fields, the existence of which had been known for more than twenty-five years. Oil exports began in 2003, providing the country with the much-needed financial means to invest in infrastructure and other productive capital and finally giving development a chance in this very poor country. One hopes that the lessons of two decades of decline, violence, and destruction have taught the political elite how to share resources to ensure some lasting prosperity.

Nevertheless, the protection of the southerners' rights is still far from perfect. Vagrant herdsmen from the north have been reported crossing the Chari river to graze their herds in the cotton fields of the south, on many occasions killing any farmers who resisted. This is made possible by two factors. First, the herds can now survive in the south because donors have funded a program for eradicating the tse-tse fly, which for centuries had provided a natural protection against this type of invasion; and, second, these herdsmen now benefit from almost perfect impunity, as the political power, including the judiciary system, is now dominated by northerners. Moreover, as oil revenues are expected to carry on flowing in the foreseeable future, the protection of the cotton growers is losing some of its previous prominence in the eyes of the political elite, and is gradually becoming a concern of secondary importance. The sustainability of the political equilibrium established by Idriss Déby will therefore rest on his reputation, on the one hand, and on the credibility of the institutions put in place for controlling the sharing of oil revenue, on the other. The backing of these institutions by the donor community seems to be a necessary prop for their sustainability, the price that must be paid for keeping the forces of greed and violence at bay.

Appendix 1: The Johnson–Brecher–Diaz-Alejandro immiserizing growth model

The impact of trade policy on the returns to capital accumulation has been brought out forcefully by Johnson (1967), who shows that a tariff protecting the capital intensive sector in a standard Hecksher–Ohlin two-sector trade model can result in capital accumulation having a negative impact on the international purchasing power of the country. Brecher and Diaz-Alejandro (1977) extended this model by showing that this impact is necessarily negative if the additional capital is imported. These results gave a fatal blow to the doctrine of import substitution policy and the related "tariff-jumping" industrialization strategy. They can be presented very simply as follows. Let

$$q = x + pz \quad \text{and} \quad q^* = x + p^*z \tag{A1}$$

represent GDP *per capita* at domestic and international prices, respectively, where x is the *per capita* output of the labor-intensive sector and z the *per capita* output of the capital-intensive sector both assumed to be strictly positive, p and p^* being the domestic and international relative producer price of z, taking x as the numeraire. We assume that $p > p^*$, either because of the trade policy protecting the capital-intensive sector, or because the x-sector is heavily taxed, as is typical of poor countries exporting agricultural products. Using duality theory, perfect competition ensures (see Dixit 1976):

$$q = q(k, p), \text{ with } \frac{\partial q}{\partial k} = r(k, p) \text{ and } \frac{\partial q}{\partial p} = z(k, p), \tag{A2}$$

where k is the *per capita* capital stock and r is the domestic rental rate of capital. From (A2), it is easily shown that $q^* = q(k, p) + (p^* - p) z (k, p)$, so that:

$$\frac{\partial q^*}{\partial k} = r + (p^* - p)\frac{\partial z}{\partial k}. \tag{A3}$$

By the Rybczynski theorem,

$$\frac{\partial z}{\partial k} > 0,$$

so that the impact of capital accumulation on q^* is ambiguous, as $p^* - p < 0$. This ambiguous impact is the core of the contribution made by Johnson (1967).

Now, assume that the capital stock is partly owned by foreign residents, so that:

$$k = k_D + k_F, \tag{A4}$$

where k_D and k_F are, respectively, the domestic and foreign capital stocks. Then *per capita* national income at domestic and world prices respectively may be written as:

$$y = q - rk_F \quad \text{and} \quad y^* = q^* - rk_F, \tag{A5}$$

so that:

$$\frac{\partial y^*}{\partial k_D} = r + (p^* - p)\frac{\partial z}{\partial k_D} \text{ is ambiguous and}$$

$$\frac{\partial y^*}{\partial k_F} = (p^* - p)\frac{\partial z}{\partial k_F} < 0. \tag{A6}$$

Hence, the impact of domestic investment on national income at international prices is ambiguous, while the impact of foreign investment is necessarily negative in this case. The intuition for these results is that the price distortion provides an incentive to invest the additional capital in the sector whose production is inefficient at international prices, which is already producing too much relative to the optimum, and this entails a contraction of the efficient sector, as labor is reallocated.

References

Azam, J.-P. (1991), "Niger and the Naira: Some Monetary Consequences of Cross-Border Trade with Nigeria," in Ajay Chhibber and Stanley Fischer, eds., *Economic Reform in Sub-Saharan Africa*. Washington, DC: The World Bank: 66–75

(2001), "The Redistributive State and Conflicts in Africa," *Journal of Peace Research* 38(4): 429–44

Azam, J.-P. and C. Koidou (2002), "Rising Threats: Containing Political Violence in Côte d'Ivoire," paper presented at the World Bank/Yale University Conference on 'The Economics and Politics of Civil War', Yale University, April 13–14

Azam, J.-P. and A. Mesnard (2003), "Civil War and the Social Contract," *Public Choice* 115(3): 455–75

Azam, J.-P., C. Morrisson, S. Chauvin, and S. Rospabé (1999), *Conflict and Growth in Africa, Volume 1: The Sahel*. Paris: Development Centre Studies, OECD

Azam, J.-P. and W. Wane (2001), "The 1994 Devaluation and Poverty in the WAEMU." Washington, DC: The World Bank, April

Banerjee, A., J. Dolado, J. W. Galbraith, and D. F. Hendry (1993), *Co-Integration, Error-Correction, and the Analysis of Non-Stationary Data*. Oxford: Oxford University Press

Banque de France. *Rapport Zone Franc*. Paris

Bassett, T. J. (2001), *The Peasant Cotton Revolution in West Africa: Côte d'Ivoire 1880–1995*. Cambridge: Cambridge University Press

Brecher, R. A. and C. F. Diaz-Alejandro (1977), "Tariffs, Foreign Capital and Immiserizing Growth," *Journal of International Economics* 7: 317–22

Buijtenhuijs, R. (1998), *Transitions et élections au Tchad 1993–1997: restauration autoritaire et recomposition politique.* Paris: ASC–Karthala

Collier, P. (1999), "On the Economic Consequences of Civil War," *Oxford Economic Papers* 51: 168–83

Diguimbaye, G. and R. Langue (1968), *L'Essor du Tchad.* Paris: Presses Universitaire de France

Dixit, A. K. (1976), *The Theory of Equilibrium Growth.* Oxford: Oxford University Press

Easterly, W. and R. Levine (1998), "Troubles with the Neighbours: Africa's Problem, Africa's Opportunity," *Journal of African Economies* 7(1): 120–42

Engle, R. F. and C. W. J. Granger (1987), "Co-integration and Error Correction: Representation, Estimation and Testing," *Econometrica* 55: 251–76

Johnson, H. G. (1967), "The Possibility of Income Losses from Increased Efficiency or Factor Accumulation in the Presence of Tariffs," *Economic Journal* 77: 151–4

Keegan, J. (1994), *A History of Warfare.* London: Pimlico

Khaldun, I. (1958)[1392], *Al Muqqadima: An Introduction to History*, trans. F. Rosenthal, New York: Pantheon Books

Lanne, B. (1996), "Conflits et violences au Tchad," *Afrique contemporaine* 180: 52–61

Lemoine, T. (1997), *Tchad 1960–1990: trente années d'indépendance.* Paris: Lettres du Monde

Madengar, B. and M. Farrris (1991), "Etude juridique et financière sur l'endettement de la caisse de stabilization des prix du coton," Ministère du Commerce et de l'Industrie, N'Djamena

Roné, B. (2000), *Tchad: l'ambivalence culturelle et l'intégration nationale.* Paris: L'Harmattan

Tangri, R. (1999), *The Politics of Patronage in Africa.* Oxford: James Currey

World Bank (1971), *Current Economic Situation and Prospects of Chad.* Report AW-24a. Washington, DC: The World Bank, April 9

(1998), *World Development Indicators 1998 CD-ROM.* Washington, DC: The World Bank

4 | The political economy of growth in Ethiopia

Alemayehu Geda

1. Introduction

With a population of over 70 million in 2005, Ethiopia is the second most populous country in Africa. Its history as a political entity stretches back to antiquity, and almost uniquely within SSA, it has never been colonized. Yet Ethiopia is one of the poorest countries in the world. Rainfall and commodity prices have a major influence on year-to-year growth, but I argue in this chapter that the detrimental impact of these exogenous factors has been accentuated by a policy environment that has reflected the narrow and shifting influences of politically dominant interest groups. At the microeconomic level, investment behavior has reflected the pervasive influence of both exogenous and policy-generated risks to income and property. In the

Associate Professor, Department of Economics, Addis Ababa University. I would like to thank Abebe Shimeles, Daniel Zerfu, and Steve O'Connell for their assistance and comments.

aggregate, poverty and slow growth have reproduced themselves over time. Each reflects the joint influence of structural vulnerabilities and weaknesses in governance. Against this background, key public sector institutions have provided a critical minimum level of policy continuity in Ethiopia. In their absence, the impact of a volatile political economy on growth would have been even greater.

The literature on Ethiopia's long-run economic growth is limited. Useful but largely descriptive macroeconomic reviews appear in Eshetu and Mekonnen (1992) for 1974–90, the papers edited by Alemayehu and Berhanu (1999) for 1991–9, and MEDaC (1999), EEA (2000), and Berhanu and Seid (1999). Comprehensive empirical studies of the growth process are limited to those of Netsante (1997) and Seyoum (1997), who estimate augmented Solow growth models; and Seid (2000).[1] Physical capital fails to have a strong impact on growth in all three of these studies. Results for human capital are less conclusive, suggesting problems of data and method: thus Netsante (1997) finds a substantial contribution of education to growth, but Seyoum (1997) and Seid (2000) do not.

The present study differs from these in several ways. It constructs a detailed empirical and analytical narrative of the growth record, and emphasizes political economy factors, the role of institutions, and the behavior of microeconomic agents. It also benchmarks Ethiopia's growth performance against that of all other developing countries.

I begin in section 2 by placing growth in Ethiopia in its politico-economic and historical contexts. I distinguish three successive policy regimes in the post-1960 period and use growth accounting and cross-country econometrics to characterize the growth record across these regimes. Section 3 turns to explanation; I examine the nature of product and factor markets, the roles of institutions and political economy, and the behavior of microeconomic agents. I argue that growth in Ethiopia is largely determined by political-economy factors, climatic risks, the strength and efficiency of institutions, the quality of public policies, and risks related to war and property rights. Product and input markets are found to be not only thin but inflexible. Combined with the unstable political environment, this has greatly limited both the potential for long-run growth and the sustainability of individual growth episodes. At the same time, the analysis suggests a potentially powerful role for Ethiopia's long and unique history, operating through the continuity provided by a few key public sector institutions. In the absence of such continuity – and notwithstanding the manifest inefficiencies of these institutions in other respects – the growth record may well have been worse than observed. Section 4 concludes the chapter.

---

[1] These three papers are graduate research papers from the Department of Economics, Addis Ababa University.

2. Growth experience in cross-country perspective

2.1 Historical background and policy episodes, 1960–2000

Ethiopia's modern history reflects the institutional legacy of centuries of internal conflict and external threat. Internally, religion, regional location, ethnicity, and nationality have each, at various times and in varying combinations, served as focal points in the contest for power and control over economic resources. Land remains an economically critical and politically contested resource, reflecting the age-old antagonism between a landed aristocracy (including the church, a major presence since the fourth century) and the peasantry (Addis 1975; Gebru 1995). Externally, although the country was never colonized, hostile and powerful colonial forces encircled it from the last quarter of the nineteenth century and rendered its independence a besieged one. The country fought three times with the Egyptians, four times with the Dervishes, five times with the Italians, and once with the British in the period from 1868 to 1896 (Pankhurst 1963b; Bahru 2001). As a result, Ethiopia developed as a militaristic state[2] with an economy dependent on the export of primary commodities and the import of manufactures, especially weapons. The acquisition of firearms from nearby European powers by Ethiopia's regional lords also shaped the pattern of internal conflict and the regional balance of power. The institutional legacies of conflict and militarization are generally identified as the major internal constraints on growth and development in Ethiopia (Gebre-Hiwot 1912; Pankhurst 1963a, 1963b; Alemayehu 2002a, 2004).

Economic performance in Ethiopia is therefore highly correlated with conflict and the political processes that accompany it. The period 1960–2000 breaks down readily, *ex post*, into the Imperial, Derg, and Ethiopian People's Revolutionary Democratic Front (EPRDF) sub-periods, reflecting the divergent policy regimes implemented by a succession of ruling cliques. The political process that brought first the Derg and then the EPRDF to power (in 1974 and 1991, respectively) was both unpredictable and violent. Economic insecurity pervades Ethiopia's modern history, with the rule of law, the enforcement of contracts, and the security of property each configured on a shaky political base. It is within this broader framework that the three regimes outlined below need to be understood.

---

[2] According to Pankhurst (1963a, 1963b), by the late nineteenth and early twentieth century the Emperor of Ethiopia commanded an army of between 100,000 and 225,000 soldiers. The overall population at the beginning of the twentieth century was below 9 million (Pankhurst 1968). If each of five regional kings commanded an army of (say) 100,000, and we assume an entourage of five persons per soldier (including the soldier's family), the military as a whole, which is dependent on the peasant sector's output, amounted to over a quarter of the total population and a third to one-half of the economically active population.

2.1.1   The imperial regime, 1930–1974

The "imperial regime" refers to the reign of emperor Hayla-Sellase I (1930–74) in particular, and to its predecessors in general. The landed aristocracy and the majority of peasants (tenants) constituted the major socio-economic agents during this period. Land was the critical resource, the control of which was invaluable for any economic agent that aspired to power. In this period an attempt was made to modernize the country through the expansion of modern schools and health facilities, the promulgation of a constitution, the development of infrastructure, and the beginning of medium-term planning. The imperial regime pursued a market-based economic policy, which in Collier and O'Connell's terminology (chapter 2, vol. 1) can be characterized as "syndrome-free" (Collier and O'Connell 2007). GDP growth averaged 4 percent over the final phase (1960–74), which is the first period for which we have data; the average *per capita* growth was roughly 1.5 percent.

2.1.2   The Derg regime, 1974–1991

The Derg (meaning "the committee [of soldiers]" in Amharic) came to power after toppling the imperial regime in the 1974 popular revolution. In terms of ideology and general policy, the Derg opted for a socialist economic system where market forces were deliberately repressed and socialization of the production and distribution process vigorously pursued. By all measures, they adopted a "hard-control" regime. Between 1974/5 and 1989/90, growth decelerated to 2.3 percent (−0.4 percent in *per capita* terms). Growth was also extremely irregular given its dependence on the agricultural sector, which is vulnerable to the vagaries of nature (see Alemayehu 2003a). The Derg regime was also characterized by intense conflict, which accentuated the dismal growth performance.

2.1.3   The EPRDF regime, 1991–

This period began following the accession to power of the EPRDF in May 1991, following the demise of the Derg. The Tigray People's Liberation Front (TPLF) formed the core of the regime. The EPRDF adopted the typical structural adjustment policies of market liberalization, with the support of the Bretton Woods institutions. Although these reforms countered the regulatory syndrome characteristic of the Derg, the EPRDF regime can be viewed as displaying the "redistributive" syndrome, with power, policy-making, and resources controlled by, and in the direct interests of, the TPLF, which originated from the North of the country.

Economic growth during this period (1990/1–1999/2000) was quite impressive. Real total and *per capita* GDP grew at average rates of 3.7 and 0.7 percent per annum, respectively, figures that rise to 5.6 and 2.6 percent,

Table 4.1 *Ethiopia, Collins–Bosworth growth-accounting-based decomposition of sources of growth, 1960–2000*

| Period | Growth in real GDP per worker | Contribution of | | |
		Physical capital per worker	Education per worker	Residual
1960–4	2.72	3.23	0.05	−0.55
1965–9	1.68	2.32	0.05	−0.68
1970–4	1.71	0.88	0.11	0.73
1975–9	−0.20	−0.29	0.13	−0.04
1980–4	−0.55	1.42	0.27	−2.25
1985–9	−2.35	0.93	0.31	−3.58
1990–4	−0.14	0.25	0.28	−0.67
1995–2000	2.96	1.13	0.28	1.55
Total: 1960–2000	**0.73**	**1.18**	**0.19**	**−0.63**

Source: Author's computation based on O'Connell and Ndulu (2003).

respectively, if one excludes the abnormal years 1990–2. The revival of growth appears to be the combined result of the reforms and favorable weather. Growth performance has nonetheless been fragile and uneven; on a year-to-year basis, growth was heavily dependent on both the vagaries of nature and on external shocks, including the war with Eritrea (see Alemayehu 2003, 2005).

In sum, the last four decades have witnessed a cyclical evolution of policy regimes in Ethiopia. The environment for growth evolved from a fairly market-oriented one to a highly controlled one before being liberalized in the third period. This cyclical policy stance is associated with a growth cycle which was favorable in the first and third periods, and very poor in the second.

2.2   Determinants and sources of growth

In table 4.1 I have employed the Collins–Bosworth (1996) benchmark estimation to carry out a growth-accounting exercise. I seek to estimate the contribution of physical capital, education, and the residuals to growth under the three political regimes.[3]

---

[3] In Collins and Bosworth (1996), the stock of physical capital was derived by applying the perpetual inventory method using initial (1950) capital stock from Nehru and Dhareshwar (1993). Similarly, the labor quality index imputed a rate of return of 7 percent to an additional year of average schooling attainment in the adult population (see O'Connell and Ndulu 2000).

The results in table 4.1 appear to substantiate our periodization. Although the average share of investment in total GDP was fairly stagnant in the first two regimes at 12.6 (1962/3–1973/4) and 12 percent (1974/5–1989/90), respectively, it attained a high level in early 1960s (1962/3–1965/6): 13.2 percent of GDP. The highest contribution of capital to growth occurred in the 1960s, partly reflecting the large investment in infrastructure under the three development plans of the imperial regime. In addition, this was also a period in which the age-old feudal aristocracy began to change into a nascent entrepreneur class by investing in capital-intensive farms and food-processing firms. The process of capital formation was interrupted, however, by the 1974 revolution and the coming into power of the Derg, which imposed hard controls. The contribution of physical capital to growth abruptly declined under the Derg; this decline may reflect the disruption caused by the revolution, compounded by the radical institutional changes[4] that disrupted the operation of productive economic agents.

With the rise to power of the EPRDF, the early 1990s also witnessed another political change. The change was violent, briefly bringing back the instability that accompanied the coming of the Derg. This led to the lower contribution of physical capital to growth in the first half-decade of the EPRDF regime. Thanks to the return of external finance, which had dried up during the Derg regime, and the liberalization policy pursued by the EPRDF, the share of investment in GDP rose to about 17 percent between 1990/1 and 1999/2000. The result was the strong contribution of physical capital and TFP to growth in the late 1980s (see table 4.1).

The contribution of education per worker was very weak over the whole period. In the imperial regime, the quality of education was extremely poor; nearly 90 percent of the population remained illiterate. By contrast, the Derg invested heavily in education, in particular through the expansion of schools in rural areas and by launching an adult education program called the "Literacy Campaign." These efforts reduced the illiteracy rate to 38 percent by 1990 (see Gebru 1992). Although the drive for expanding primary education continued in the post-Derg period, the "Literacy Campaign" was stopped, helping to explain the recent rise in the level of illiteracy. Given these trends, it is not surprising to see the positive contribution of education per worker in the period 1989–90, where relatively speaking the literacy rate is highest (see table 4.1).

Note that the contribution of TFP to growth remained negative throughout the period 1974–94. One reason might be political instability and the regulatory policies adopted by the Derg. Another is that TFP growth in rain-dependent African countries is closely related to the weather and to external

---

[4] For example, the changes in the land tenure system, the role of public institutions, the formation of peasant associations, and the policy of repressing the private sector.

shocks. Note in particular the year 1984, where we witness the lowest TFP growth: 1984 was one of the worst drought years in Ethiopia.

The growth-accounting exercise reinforces our three-way partition of Ethiopia's post-1960 experience. It points to the detrimental effect of systemic instability, as well as to Ethiopia's vulnerability to weather shocks. The latter vulnerability is partly explained by lack of structural change in the economy, which remained overwhelmingly dependent on rainfed agriculture

Following the growth-accounting exercise, I have used coefficients derived from two cross-country regression-based growth models. On the basis of Hoeffler's (2002) augmented Solow and O'Connell and Ndulu's (2000) conditional growth models I have attempted to frame Ethiopia's position within the context of a cross-country growth regression based on a sample of eighty-five developing countries (see Ndulu and O'Connell 2000). The results are given in tables 4.2 and 4.3.

The comparison of actual with predicted growth rates in table 4.2 demonstrates that the rate of growth in Ethiopia lay below expected levels in all periods. During the imperial regime, this deviation is to a large extent explained by initial level of income. Under the Derg, both investment in and the replacement of capital equipment contributed to Ethiopia's deviation from the mean rate of growth of all developing countries. The high residual observed in the previous period persisted in this era and reached its historic minimum (−1.45) in 1980–4. The post-Derg period is characterized by some degree of improvement in all variables. The positive value of the time dummy may reflect the effect of reforms initiated in 1992 and favorable weather during this period. Investment and education also made a positive contribution.

Table 4.3, which is based on Ndulu and O'Connell (2000), provides additional information. It suggests the dramatic extent to which Ethiopia's growth lagged behind that of other countries. This deviation was the highest during the imperial regime. The base variables (demographic, trade shocks, and initial endowments) made the greatest contribution to this deviation. Political stability contributed to growth in the imperial period, while subsequent instability detracted from it, with 1975–9 representing the nadir.

The contribution of policies to growth deviation is negative throughout the three periods, but was at its worst under the Derg. In that period, over-valuation of the exchange rate and government spending weakened Ethiopia's growth performance. Public spending, much of it unproductive, remained a problem in the other two periods as well. Defense spending consumed half the budget during the Derg regime. Additional policy failures resulted in inefficient public enterprises, a bias against the private sector, the slow diffusion of farm technology, import compression, and low capacity utilization (below 50 percent in most industries).

Table 4.2 *Ethiopia, Hoeffler's augmented Solow model (SYS–GMM estimates), decomposition, 1960–2000*

| | | | | Actual deviation | Estimated contribution of | | | | |
| | | | | | | | | Replacement | |
Period	Actual growth (per capita)[a]	Predicted growth	Residual	of growth from sample mean	Initial income	Investment rate	Initial education attainment	investment term	Residual
1960–4	1.13	2.49	−1.36	0.03	0.34	−0.01	−0.01	−0.01	−1.33
1965–9	1.02	2.36	−1.34	−0.08	0.32	−0.03	−0.01	−0.04	−1.36
1970–4	1.03	2.22	−1.18	−0.07	0.32	−0.09	0.00	−0.03	−1.27
1975–9	1.05	2.27	−1.21	−0.05	0.31	−0.07	0.00	−0.04	−1.28
1980–4	0.93	2.38	−1.45	−0.17	0.31	−0.01	0.00	−0.05	−1.47
1985–9	1.08	2.29	−1.21	−0.02	0.32	−0.03	0.00	−0.07	−1.27
1990–4	1.10	2.49	−1.39	0.00	0.30	0.01	0.00	−0.01	−1.36
1995–2000	1.10	2.57	−1.47	0.00	0.30	0.04	0.00	−0.01	1.00
1960–2000	1.06	2.38	−1.33	−0.05	0.32	−0.02	0.00	−0.03	0.13

Note: [a] At 1985 international prices. Note the variation from table 4.5 which is consistent with MEDaC data. This is attributed to variation in the method of growth computation and the coverage of years, and the use of different prices in the two models.

Source: Author's computations based on models estimated in O'Connell and Ndulu (2000).

Table 4.3 *Ethiopia, Ndulu–O'Connell pooled conditional model-based results, 1960–2000*

| | Fits and residuals | | | Actual and predicted growth deviations | | | | | | |
| | | | | | Contribution to predicted growth deviation | | | Breakdown of policy contribution by variable | | |
Period	Actual growth (per capita)	Fitted growth	Residual	Actual growth deviation from sample mean	Base variables	Political instability	Policy	Inflation (>500%)	Parallel market premium (>500%)	B/L govt spending/ GDP
1960–4	2.7	5.1	−2.4	0.5	2.4	0.1	−0.2	0.0	0.1	−0.3
1965–9	1.7	4.4	−2.7	−0.5	2.2	0.2	−0.2	0.1	0.0	−0.3
1970–4	1.7	3.6	−1.9	−0.5	1.4	−0.3	−0.3	0.0	0.0	−0.4
1975–9	−0.2	1.9	−2.1	−2.4	1.6	−1.0	−1.0	0.0	−0.4	−0.6
1980–4	−0.6	1.2	−1.7	−2.7	0.6	−0.1	−0.7	0.0	−0.4	−0.4
1985–9	−2.4	−12.9	10.6	−4.5	1.6	−0.2	−1.7	0.0	−1.0	−0.7
1990–4	−0.1	−13.3	13.2	−2.3	0.4	0.0	−1.2	0.0	−0.9	−0.3
1995–2000	3.0	−13.2	16.1	0.8	0.4	0.0	−1.2	0.0	−0.9	−0.3
1960–2000	0.4	−4.0	4.5	−1.8	1.2	−0.2	−0.9	0.0	−0.5	−0.4

Source: Author's computations based on models estimated in O'Connell and Ndulu (2000).

Many of the policies of the Derg were altered in 1992. Although the EPRDF still engages in excessive and inefficient public spending, the detrimental impact of these policies appears to have declined. This may be a reflection of the declining share of defense expenditure during this period.[5] Recent data show that the parallel market premium rate declined from its highest level of 358 percent in 1992 to just 15.5 percent in 1997, thus suggesting a favorable alteration in exchange rate policies (see Alemayehu, Berket, and Shumeles 2003).

Although growth and policy performance seem to have improved in the 1990s, the sustainability of this growth remains in question. This is because of the economy's continued dependence on rainfed agriculture, its vulnerability to external shocks, and the high level of political instability.

3. Markets, institutions, agents, and the political economy of growth

3.1 The political economy of growth

By the late 1960s, the educated elite that had emerged in the imperial period began to challenge the political system. The result was the downfall of the imperial regime and of Hayla-Sellase I (its last emperor). Those who overthrew the imperial government formed a military junta called the Derg, which soon endorsed socialism, the ideology of the Ethiopian educated elite of the period (see Clapham 1988). Its first important policy decision was to nationalize land and other private property (rental property), financial institutions, and manufacturing firms. The Derg began to build a socialist state and a strong army. It also began to consolidate its grip on power by introducing new institutions of economic and political control, including peasant associations and co-operatives, marketing boards, and a workers' party.

A growing number of opposition groups among the intelligentsia began to oppose the Derg, however: *Meison*, EPRP, TPLF, Eritrea People's Liberation Front (EPLF)[6] (see Clapham 1988). The Derg managed to destroy most of these organizations, except the TPLF and EPLF, who eventually toppled it

---

[5] Notwithstanding the post-1998 rise following the Ethiopian–Eritrea war.

[6] *Meison* refers to the Amharic abbreviation for "All Ethiopia Socialist Movement"; EPRP is the Ethiopian People's Revolutionary Party. Both were multi-ethnic parties. The EPLF (Eritrea People's Liberation Front – a nationalist group dominated by Tigregna-speaking Christian highlanders of Eritrea) is a secessionist organization, established following the abolition of a UN-sponsored federation of the Italian colony of Eritrea with Ethiopia by Emperor Hayla-Selasse I in 1961. After a protracted guerrilla war with the Derg, and with the help of the TPLF – an ethno-linguistic front), it *de facto* managed to secede from Eritrea by 1991. The TPLF was a Marxist guerrilla opposition established with the help of

in 1991. As all were Marxist organizations, ideology appears to have played little part in this conflict. Although grievances over the cultural/linguistic domination by Amharic speakers over others did play a role, the fundamental feature was competition for power and control of resources.[7] In the case of ethno-linguistic groups, ethnicity is conveniently deployed in this competition for power (see Alemayehu 2004).

The abrupt political change in 1974, the nationalization of the productive assets and the inability of the new owners to run them, the disruption in both industrial and agricultural activity following the revolution, and the 1984–5 drought, resulted in the deceleration of growth. The Derg imposed a control regime that implemented policies aimed at benefiting the socialized (and penalizing the private) sector. As a result, the period witnessed deteriorating economic conditions and mounting discontent. Following the military failure of the Derg, especially in the North of the country, the regime was finally toppled in 1991. Following its ascent to power, the EPRDF pursued a liberalization policy aimed at revitalizing the devastated economy, a process that had been initiated by the Derg virtually at the end of its reign.

Three fundamental political trajectories informed this reform (see Alemayehu 2005). First was the collapse of the USSR. Secondly, the government inherited a shattered "socialist" economy with no foreign exchange reserves. While the reform did not directly address the problem, it did elicit inflows of international aid.[8]

The third was an attempt by the political elites of the EPRDF to weaken the national bureaucracy through expenditure reduction and retrenchment programs. The ruling EPRDF was dominated by the TPLF (Tigregna speakers

the EPLF to fight the Derg. The TPLF initially flirted with the idea of secession but later (in the 1980s) changed its objective to creating a democratic Ethiopia. It began to organize other ethno-linguistic-based organizations (including the Amhara Nation Democratic Movement, the Oromo People's Democratic Organization, and the South Nations, Nationalists and People's Organization) to form the Ethiopian People Revolutionary Democratic Front, EPRDF, which is the current government. It initially accommodated the other important ethno-linguistic organization, the Oromo Liberation Front (OLF), but chased it out later. The EPRDF reorganized the country as a federal state structured along ethno-linguistic lines (see Alemayehu and Befekadu 2005).

[7] This hypothesis is confirmed by a book authored by an opposition leader who was arrested following the 2005 election and wrote his book from prison (Berhanu 2006). Berhanu describes the infighting by organizations within his opposition coalition, who sought to register as many of their own candidates as possible in order to maximize financing from their diasporas. He also notes that one of the opposition leaders told him that members of his party desperately needed the salary they would get by being parliamentarians. More generally, few individuals appear to have embraced the ideology pursued by the rebels and committed themselves to the betterment of the majority; this was particularly true among the rank and file of the insurgent movements.

[8] The need to address the distributional dimension of this policy stance is empirically substantiated in Alemayehu, Shimeles, and Weeks (2002).

from the North). It adopted the position of "self-determination including secession"[9] for regions organized along ethno-linguistic lines[10] while
many political groups, including the majority of the inherited bureaucracy,
opposed radical decentralization. Its political core came from a relatively
resource-poor and drought-prone northern part of the country and the
EPRDF regime used state power to effect the redistribution of resources
away from the central and southern part of the country (whose main actors
are Amharic and Oromingna speakers). The shift of power in 1991 thus
marked the change from a regulatory syndrome to "a redistributive syndrome." One implication was increased uncertainty for investors. Another
was that the domination of the TPLF might mark the substitution of sub-
national, ethnic interests for national ones.

   In identifying the political process that shapes policy choice in Ethiopia,
it is worth emphasizing the cycles of revolt and conflict. These conflicts,
though apparently ethnic, were essentially regional and class-based. The
evidence for this is that they were structured by:

- The "king of kings" system, where the strongest regionally-based king[11]
  became the king of all regional kings and occupied the central position
  of power. The king of kings did not necessarily come from an ethnically
  homogenous region, and maintained his power by drawing officials from
  different regions (usually tying regional lords through marriage to his
  offspring).
- The subjugation of *all* peasants from *all* ethnic groups by the ruling elite.[12]
- Civil conflict among the intelligentsia, who were drawn from different
  ethnic groups.

   Evidence of the impact on growth can be seen in figure 4.3 (p. 131), where
we plot the index of *per capita* income against an indicator of political risk.[13]

---

[9] This political factor implicitly addresses the so-called "Eritrean question" – that is, the
   fact that EPRDF opted for the country's independence, a position opposed by many other
   political groups.

[10] In Ethiopian politics (especially of the EPRDF) these groups are referred as nations,
   nationalities, and people without any conceptual basis for distinction. The Gebre–Hiwot
   model refers these groups by the term "*Neged*," and its use would have been broad and
   relevant (see Alemayehu 2002b).

[11] An important evidence here is the fierce regional competition and war between the
   Shewan and *Gojam* kings, who ethnically speaking belong to *Amhara*, in the late
   nineteenth century to control regions that lie in today's South Western Ethiopia (this is
   called the battle of *Embabo* in Ethiopian history).

[12] This argument in no way denies the historic domination of the highlanders' language and
   culture over the others but takes it, compared to the power-grabbing motive, as secondary.

[13] The political risk rating is based on "International Country Risk Guide" (ICRG), which
   uses twelve political risk indicators (government stability, socio-economic condition,
   investment profile, internal conflict, external conflict, corruption, military in politics,

Clearly the premium on reducing political risk (which can also be taken as an indicator of the quality of governance and institutions) is huge – an improvement in this index by 1 unit brings about an 0.4 point increment in the index of the *per capita* income (see figure 4.3).

Each regime created institutions to help it to sustain its grip on power. At the core of the imperial regime lay the church and the military; at the core of the Derg, mass organizations such as peasant associations, as well as market-ing boards and the military; and at the core of the EPRDF, ethno-linguistic parties, party-affiliated companies and the military. Some institutions have been nourished by every regime: the Ethiopian airline, the National Bank and Ministry of Finance (which maintained a prudential macro-policy stance in all regimes), the air force, the civil service, the church, and other indigenous institutions including the *Iqub* (informal money market) and the like.[14] However inefficient they might appear, these institutions have contributed to the continuity of the Ethiopian state.

3.2   Institutions in the growth process

Given this dismal growth performance, what has kept Ethiopia from col-lapsing as a nation? Perhaps one of the positive outcomes of the long history of Ethiopia is the creation and retention of institutions which averted such collapse. This has resulted in a fairly professional, but unfortunately largely inefficient, civil servant class that has managed to prevail across different regimes. This may perhaps explain why the country survived as a nation and was able to have a prudent macro-policy across the different regimes despite pervasive poverty, internal conflict, and external aggression.

The imperial regime sought to create institutions to support financial and product markets: central, commercial, and development banks; private banks; and import-substituting industries. As noted above, by promoting capital formation this effort appears to have contributed to the growth performance of the economy. The nascent development of such institutions was interrupted by the 1974 revolution and the Derg's rise to power. The Derg

religion in politics, law and order, ethnic tensions, democratic accountability, and bureaucratic quality). Points given for each item range from 0 to 12. The first five indicators have a maximum score of 12 each; the next six items have a maximum score of 6 each; the last has a maximum score of 4. The higher the number, the better the performance (i.e. the less the political risk).

[14] What happened to the Ethiopian national airline in the last two regimes (the Derg and EPRDF) is quite informative. Immediately following each regime shift, the incumbents fired professionals and installed "their men." This resulted in an immediate decline in profits of the airline, prompting the two regimes to re-hire the professionals and restore management autonomy, actions that succeeded in reversing the airline's collapse. The reason for these turnabouts may relate to (a) the foreign exchange-generating capacity of the airline, which the incumbent has an interest in preserving, and (b) its symbolic nature and the political costs associated with its collapse, given its long institutional history.

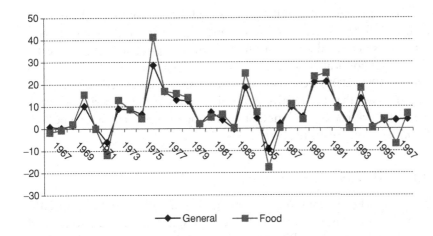

Figure 4.1 Ethiopia, inflation, 1967–1998, percentage change over previous year
Source: Based on data obtained from the CSA.

nationalized all financial institutions, and biased the allocation of foreign exchange and credit against the private sector. It also maintained a fixed exchange rate (see Alemayehu 1999 for more detail).

The EPRDF liberalized the previous control regime. It also sought to revitalize the private sector. It devalued the currency and subsequently introduced an auction-based exchange rate system. It liberalized the interest rate, with the government now setting only the floor. It introduced an inter-bank market for foreign exchange. The period of the EPRDF is characterized by efforts to promote the market and the institutions that are compatible with a liberalized economy.

There has thus been a policy cycle: from liberalization to control regime back to liberalization. The last four decades have also witnessed the formation of a dual economy with associated institutions. While the modern institutions, such as commercial and central banks, cater to the needs of the modern sector,[15] informal (traditional) money markets called "*Iqub*" serve the majority of the private sector: the rural farming community, the urban informal sector, and micro-enterprises (see Dejene 1995; Mengestu 1998; Alemayehu 2005).

The professionalism of modern institutions is revealed by the manner in which civil servants have maintained macroeconomic stability in spite of the changes in political regimes and the attendant political strife. This can be illustrated by the pattern of inflation shown in figure 4.1.

---

[15] For instance, not more than 5 percent of the credits extended by the formal financial institutions targeted the rural sector. These were often channeled through public enterprises that supplied small farmers with inputs such as fertilizers and improved seeds on credit basis (see Alemayehu and Befekadu 2005).

Figure 4.1 shows that inflation exceeded 20 percent when there was a regime shift. However, the persistent and continuous functioning of institutions, as described above, ensured a return to price stability. Figure 4.2 shows that political episodes such as the war with Somalia (1977–8), and Eritrea (1998–2000) were associated with a sharp rise in defense spending. It also shows that the relative political stability of the imperial regime is associated with stable and modest level of public spending, as can be seen from the trend during the period 1960–73.

3.3   Markets and the growth process

The imperial regime was based upon the landed gentry. Driven by socialist ideology, the Derg was bent on the destruction of the private sector and markets. Officially, the EPRDF has reinstated the market and endorsed the private sector, but by examining production and factor markets we see that the departure from the control regime has not been as comprehensive as has often been claimed (Alemayehu and Befekadu 2005).

3.3.1   The product and land markets

In the imperial period, land was privately owned. The church was also in possession of a good share. Political power is largely linked to the size and quality of land owned. The emperor rewarded local and regional authorities for their support by handing out land. The Northern part of the country was characterized by a communal ownership (the *rist* system), yet the peasants were the subjects of the regional lords to whom they had to provide nearly all of their produce. In the south, the peasants were made serfs, under the *gabar* system of land rights.[16] The end of the imperial regime witnessed the rise of an active land market in both rural (usually for emerging commercial farms) and urban areas. The product market was also a liberalized one. These changes remained in effect until the 1974 revolution.

The Derg nationalized both urban and rural lands and distributed them freely, but granted only usufruct rights. This policy effectively put an end to the imperial structure of power and to the emerging land market. Through its control over land and the Agricultural Marketing Corporation (AMC), the Derg was able to procure the agricultural surplus by force. The result was a decline in marketed surplus throughout that period (see Alemayehu 1987, 1992).

The EPRDF regime liberalized most of the product markets, but state ownership of the land is explicitly incorporated in the EPRDF's constitution. Notwithstanding official policy, however, the last two periods witnessed an emergence of a parallel market for land. Berket and Croppenstedt (1995),

---

[16] See Teshale (1995) for an insightful analytical approach to these issues.

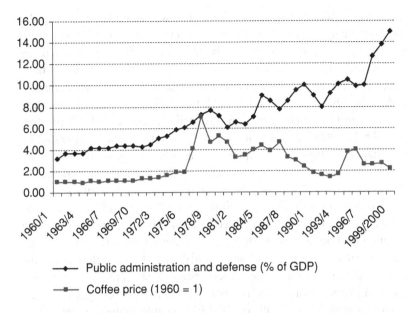

Figure 4.2 Ethiopia, defense expenditure and external shocks, 1960/1–1999/2000
Source: MOFED for public administration, and defense data and IMF, *International Financial Statistics*, for coffee price.

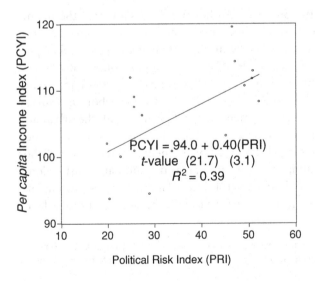

Figure 4.3 Ethiopia, political risk and *per capita* income growth, 1984–2000

for instance, found that in areas where land was acquired following the nationalization, the incidence of sharecropping increased and in most cases, sharecropped land was of average or better quality. They inferred that the parallel market was thus generating an efficient allocation of land. Abebe (2000), however, reports a lack of efficiency in land use. Alemayehu, Berket, and Shimeles (2003) also found a small, but statistically significant, negative coefficient for the effect of land re-distribution on cereals output (see below). Abebe (2000) noted that the informal land market is operated by differentiated (as opposed to impersonal) agents with different bargaining power. Moreover, its operation is closely linked to other input markets.

Using a simple model, Haile (2000) ran a simulation of what the level of output would have been with and without the 1974 land reform. He found that the land reform was accompanied by a rise in output in the first seven years and a decline thereafter. He rightly attributed the former to possible positive incentives to farmers following land distribution and the latter to the forced co-operativization and regulated price policies of the government.[17]

Whether privatization of land offers a solution to Ethiopia's growth problem in the current political context is highly debatable. In the short run, there seems to be a need for experimenting with a range of tenure systems.[18] In the long run, however, an active land market is needed if a meaningful and dynamic social and economic transformation is to be effected.

3.3.2   The labor market

Data from the Central Statistical Authority (CSA) show that the unemployment rate in the rural areas increased from 0.4 to 0.7 percent between 1984 and 1994. The comparable figures for urban areas were 8 and 22 percent, respectively (MEDaC, 1999). Using a survey of some 1,500 households, Krishnan, Gebre, and Dercon (1998) estimated the urban unemployment rate in 1997 to be about 29.9 percent. The national labor force survey (1999) puts the total unemployment rate at 8 percent, with the urban and rural unemployment rate being 26.4 and 5.14 percent, respectively. Open unemployment is thus largely an urban phenomenon. Since the rural labor market is also very thin, people in rural areas use alternative institutional arrangements: household labor and traditional labor-sharing arrangements. As it functions largely in non-market fashion, the operation of the labor

---

[17] As noted before, good weather out turn is also crucial. Since Haile's regressions do not control for this it is difficult to attribute the negative dummy he used to the land reform alone.

[18] Desalegne Rahmato, one of the best rural development researchers in the country, has worked on rural issues for the last four decades. He has suggested what he called "associated ownership," where community ownership could skillfully be configured with a market for land. It is an ingenious idea in the current political context of Ethiopia (see www.FSSEthiopia.com).

market is limited and highly seasonal (see Alemayehu, Berket, and Shimeles 2003; Alemayehu and Alem 2005).

In the formal sector, wages have shown small gains since the 1990s (Krishnan, Tesfay, and Dercon 1998). Taye (2001) has found that skill formation yields greater job mobility and increased earnings. But Krishnan, Tesfay, and Dercon (1998) find that the labor market is rigid and unresponsive to the growing queue of educated job seekers.

3.4 Behavior of economic agents and the growth process

The imperial regime was characterized by relative political and economic stability. Economic agents had relatively less risk, in terms of both policy shock and natural shock such as drought. This resulted in a fairly buoyant economy with respectable growth.

In contrast, the Derg regime was actively engaged in eliminating private economic activity. Private ownership was legally prohibited and entrepreneurship openly discouraged. Its policies constituted a major shock and reduced economic activity in the private sector. Peasants, moreover, were forced to supply their produce at fixed prices to the government marketing board, the AMC. The agents responded by withholding investment, curtailing entrepreneurial activity, and reducing production to a level just sufficient to feed themselves and to satisfy the compulsory delivery targets imposed by the government.

While the EPRDF regime reintroduced the market paradigm, it nevertheless generated new risk factors. The most important was the remapping of the administrative framework on ethno-linguistic lines and the affording of these ethno-linguistic entities constitutional guarantees for secession any time the majority felt like doing so. This reconfiguration is likely to limit labor and capital mobility across the ethnic enclaves, to heighten the risk of investing outside the "ethnic home region," and to increase the fear of political succession.

Such factors bear upon the productivity of rural agents and the rate of growth in their output. To explore this issue, we estimate a model that empirically captures these issues, using data from a rural household survey conducted in 1999 (see the appendix, p. 137, for the model and the data). Since the rural households represent more than 90 percent of the population, the result can fairly be generalized not only for the country as a whole, but also for the Derg period, when the land policy resembled that of the EPRDF (see table 4.4). The model explores cereal production, which accounts for more than 80 percent of the total agricultural production (CSA 1999). It employs a Cobb–Douglas production function.

Column (3) introduces a measure of the expectation of land redistribution. The coefficient on land declines when this variable is entered into the

Table 4.4 *Ethiopia, Tobit estimates, dependent variable: output*

Variable	(1)			(2)			(3)		
	Coeff.	*t*-value	Slope[a]	Coeff.	*t*-value	Slope[a]	Coeff.	*t*-value	Slope[a]
Constant	4.29	49.5		4.19	50.3		4.05	44.6	
ln (labor)	0.21	9.0	0.21	0.15	6.54	0.15	0.15	6.61	0.15
ln (Land)	1.51	17.0	1.49	1.38	16.16	1.37	1.11	11.54	1.10
ln (Oxen)	0.36	5.44	0.35	0.33	5.25	0.33	0.28	.52	0.28
Credit				0.14	2.0	0.14	0.11	1.5^	0.11
Fertilizer use				0.63	10.9	0.63	0.58	10.1	0.57
Land quality				0.04	50.0	0.04	0.014	0.70^	0.01
Redistribution							−0.08	1.65	−0.08
Climate							0.01	5.8	0.01
Diagnostic tests	LR $\chi^2(3) = 770.54$			LR chi^2 (6) = 917.39			LR χ^2 (8) = 928.27		
	Prob > $\chi^2 = 0.0000$			Prob > $\chi^2 = 0.000$			Prob > $\chi^2 = 0.0000$		
	Log likelihood = −1757.29			Log likelihood = −1683.86			Log likelihood = −1678.43		
	Pseudo $R^2 = 0.1798$			Pseudo $R^2 = 0.2141$			Pseudo $R^2 = 0.2166$		
							^Not significant		

No. obs. = 1,291 (11 left-censored observations at ln(output) ≤ 0; 1,280 uncensored observations).
Note: [a]Marginal coefficients.

model. In addition, the expectation about future land redistribution has a negative impact on production, though the size of the coefficient is not large. The data also reveal that farmers who associate the future with risk tend to be reluctant to conserve and upgrade their land. Cross-tabulation of soil conservation practices with expectation about the size of land holding shows that about 60 percent of those who rate the future as risky do not practice soil conservation. Using a small sample (about 500 rural households), Tekie (2000) reports similar results.

In the urban areas, small- and medium-scale firms are largely engaged in food-processing activities. They make a limited contribution to GDP, as the manufacturing sector as whole contributes less than 5 percent. These firms expanded during the imperial regime but were nationalized by the Derg, after which they performed poorly. Following liberalization under the EPRDF, the sector revived. The government yielded management autonomy to some publicly owned firms, privatized others, and created incentive schemes to motivate the private sector.

Modeling the production function of manufacturing firms as a Cobb–Douglas function with two basic inputs – labor and capital – we can explore the impact of the real exchange rate (RER) and tariffs (see Alemayehu *et al.* 2004). The Central Statistical Authority (CSA) manufacturing sector survey reports data on food products and beverages, tobacco products,

Table 4.5 *Ethiopia, results, general model of manufacturing sector*

Variable	(1)		(2)		(3)	
	Coefficient	Prob.	Coefficient	Prob.	Coefficient	Prob.
Constant	7.014341	0.0000	6.224008	0.0000	5.531277	0.0000
Labor	0.284343	0.0005	0.197014	0.0277	0.238453	0.0072
Capital	0.303248	0.0000	0.359461	0.0000	0.315886	0.0000
Dummy/Regime change	−0.217327	0.0454	−0.241697	0.0254	−0.461365	0.0004
Tariff			0.267489	0.0287	0.231010	0.0537
RER					0.719319	0.0025
Diagnostic tests	Adjusted R^2 = 0.4913		Adjusted R^2 = 0.5028		Adjusted R^2 = 0.5268	
	DW = 0.1458		DW = 0.1816		DW = 0.1748	
	Log likelihood = 14.0667		Log likelihood = 2.8908		Log likelihood = 11.2736	
	Prob. (*F*-stat) = 0.0000		Prob. (*F*-stat) = 0.0000		Prob. (*F*-stat) = 0.0000	

textile, leather, wood, paper and paper products, chemical products, non-metallic products and metal products for the period 1980/1 to 1998/9. The customs authority provides data on tariff rates. The National Bank of Ethiopia provides data for foreign prices, domestic prices, and the nominal exchange rate, allowing us to calculate the real exchange rate as

$$RER = NER^* \frac{p^f}{p^d},$$

where *NER* is the nominal exchange rate and p^f and p^d are foreign and domestic prices, respectively. All nominal variables are deflated by the price level to have them in real terms. We estimate the coefficients of this model using pooled time-series data for the nine sectors and nineteen years with 171 balanced observations. To capture the liberalization of 1991, we enter a dummy variable that takes a value of 0 before 1991 and 1 otherwise.

The estimation results are reported in table 4.5. As column (1) shows, both labor and capital play a significant role in the dynamics of the manufacturing sector. The coefficient on the dummy variable shows that a regime shift negatively affects the sector's performance. However, the impact of the regime shift is not the same across the different sectors. Its negative effect was not observed on the food, leather, and tobacco industries. On the other hand, textile, wood, paper, and non-metal-producing industries were among the worst affected by the policy of liberalization.[19] Column (2) of table 4.5 shows that tariff rate is positively related to manufacturing output. This result is particularly strong for the metal, chemical, and tobacco industries, while being insignificant for the food, paper, leather, and

---

[19] This result is not surprising as most of the producers in these sectors were or are going out of the market because of the stiff foreign competition following the regime shift of 1991.

Table 4.6 *Ethiopia, growth accounting, manufacturing sector, 1980/1 to 1998/9*

Period	Growth rates			Contribution to growth (%)		
	Output	Capital	Labor	Capital	Labor	TFP
1980/1–1989/90	−6.18	2.93	1.30	0.98	0.87	−8.03
				(15.85%)	(14.07%)	(−129.93%)
1990/1–1998/9	9.67	12.63	1.36	3.16	1.02	5.49
				(32.7%)	(10.6%)	(56.7%)

non-metallic-producing industries. In column (3), the real exchange rate has a strong and significant positive impact on output, demonstrating the importance of the macroeconomic environment for industrial development.

We can also employ this model in a growth-accounting exercise. As seen in table 4.6, TFP accounted for more than 56 percent of the growth during the period 1990/1–1998/9. For comparison, TFP turned negative during the period 1980/1–1989/90.[20] This indicates the notoriously distorted policy of the Derg's "hard-control" regime. However, this trend is reversed during 1990/1–1998/9. In this period, privatized large- and medium-scale industries saw improvements in efficiency due to changes in ownership: publicly owned industries enjoyed a newly accorded management autonomy. These changes, coupled with access to imported inputs and the need for being competitive in the liberalized environment, led to a remarkable increase in the contribution of TFP.

Notwithstanding the positive effect of the reform, the foreign direct investment (FDI) flows to Ethiopia remain negligible and are dominated by one firm (MIDROC Ethiopia), which is owned by a Saudi-Arabian tycoon who was born in Ethiopia and whose mother is Ethiopian. The company has invested in a range of industries, services, and agro-processing.

4. Conclusion

This chapter has shown that growth performance in Ethiopia has been disappointing, especially compared to that of other developing countries. The rate of growth has varied across the three regimes, the Derg regime's performance being the worst. GDP growth was the highest during the imperial era (averaging 4 percent and 1.5 percent *per capita*), declined during the military regime of 1974–91 (2.3 percent and −0.4 percent *per capita*) and

[20] The average α value during this period is estimated to be 0.33; and capital was found not to be statistically significant in two of the nine manufacturing sectors. Moreover, capital also bears a negative sign in the other two sectors.

revived during the post-Derg period 1992–9 (3.7 percent and 0.7 percent *per capita*). TFP growth was negative under all the three regimes, with the military era scoring the lowest and the post-Derg era the highest.

There has been a marked absence of structural transformation during the past four decades, due to structural problems and initial conditions, especially in the last two regimes. Applying the augmented Solow model and its "conditional" variant to the Ethiopian data shows that the sources of GDP growth were intensive use of resources, especially labor. Productivity growth played little part and, when it did, its impact was negative. This finding should not come as a surprise given an economy that is operating with backward technology embedded in an often hostile policy environment, and vulnerable to external shocks, some meteorological and some originating in foreign markets.

The lessons from the last four decades are that the market-oriented policies provide the best opportunities for growth. The more the market has been tuned to local conditions and capacities, the better has been the outcome. Markets require institutional defenses, however. The long history of Ethiopia has bequeathed such institutions: the state, the military, the church, the Ministry of Finance, and the central bank, as well as indigenous self-help associations. Most are archaic, however, and have been riven with conflict, as one group or the other seeks to control them to advance its own interests. This, in turn, has led to cycles of violence and created levels of risk sufficient to thwart the growth of the economy.

Appendix: A model of constraints on rural microeconomic agents

In order to investigate factors that constrain the productivity of the rural households, a simple Cobb–Douglas production function is specified. The output of household i is given by:

$$Y_i = \prod_j \left(x_{ij}^{\beta_j} \right) \prod_k \left(z_{ik}^{\alpha_k} \right) e^{\gamma + \mu_i}, \tag{A1}$$

where Y_i is the output of the ith household, x_{ij} is the ith household's use of the jth input, z_{ik} is the effect of other variables k on the ith household, β_j and α_k are elasticities of Y with respect to x_j and z_k, and γ and μ_i are the constant term and the stochastic disturbance term, respectively.

For estimation purpose (A2) can be linearized as

$$\ln Y_i = \Sigma \beta_j \ln x_{ij} + \Sigma \alpha_k \ln z_{ik} + \gamma + \mu_i. \tag{A2}$$

Equation (A2) can, thus, be augmented, in a semi-log form, to capture the effects of other variables apart from the physical inputs:

$$\ln Y_i = \gamma + \beta_1 \ln(labor)_i + \beta_2 \ln(Land)_i + \beta_3 \ln(OX)_i + \beta_4(fert)_i$$
$$+ \beta_5(landquality)\beta_6(climate)_i + \beta_7(redistribution)$$
$$+ \beta_8(credit)_i + \mu_i, \tag{A3}$$

where:

Output	Measured as total cereal production by household i.
Land	Area of land used for cereal production by household i.
Labor	Total adult equivalent man-days including family and non-family members' labor.
OX	Number of animals used in cereal production by household i.
Fertilizer	Chemical fertilizers used. For the purpose of estimation this variable is used as a dummy variable in which those households who used chemical fertilizer are assigned 1 and 0 otherwise.
Land quality	Three types of land quality are identified in the survey (see below). These are fertile, infertile, and intermediate. The land quality is indexed from 1 to 3, in which 3 indicates fertile land, 2 intermediate land, and 1 indicates the infertile or least fertile land.
Credit	Loan acquired by household i for agricultural activities.
Redistribution	In the questionnaire the households are asked about their future expectation about their land holding size. The response is categorized into four groups: "increase," "decrease," "no change," and "do not know." Those households with the response of "decrease" and "do not know" are considered to be uncertain about the future and hence categorized as one group and considered to associate some risk premium about their land holding while the rest – those with the response of "increase" and "no change" – do not expect future risk in relation to their land size and are hence classified as one group. Thus, this variable is treated as a dummy variable in which 1 indicates negative expectation and 0 otherwise.
Climate	This variable is a combination of environmental variables including total rainfall, distribution of rainfall, availability of rain near harvest season, prevalence of storm, hail, frost, and flood. To get a reasonable measure of the impact of such natural factors, the above indicators are indexed as indicated in table 4.A1.

Table 4.A1 *Ethiopia, climate variables*

Total rainfall	Distribution of rainfall	Rainfall near harvest	Natural calamities					
			Response	Storm	Hail	Frost	Flood	Total
Good 3	Excellent 3	Yes 2	No	2	2	2	2	16
Shortage 2	Good 2	No 1	Yes	1	1	1	1	9
Excess 1	Poor 1							2
Can't recall 0	Can't recall 0							0

Data and estimation

The relevant variables are extracted from the 5th round (1999) Ethiopian Rural Household Survey conducted by the Department of Economics of Addis Ababa University. The survey covered 1,681 households in eighteen villages spanning fifteen districts. The sample was selected using a systematic sampling method in which the households in the villages were selected randomly after the villages were identified so as to capture the major farming regions (see Negus 2001[21] and Croppenstedt and Mulat 1997 for a good summary of the survey structure).

For the initial sample 1,681 households, we selected 1,291 major cereal-producing households for estimation purposes (*a priori* truncation). In addition, the outliers in the data set are filtered following Mukherjee, White, and Wuyts (1998) defining an observation Y_0 as an outlier if $Y_0 < Q_L -$ 1.5^*IQR or $Y_0 > Q_U + 1.5^*IQR$, where IQR is the inter quartile range and Q_L and Q_U are the lower and upper quartiles, respectively. This process entails censoring the sample. The resulting dataset is both truncate and censored, implying that OLS give biased and inconsistent estimates of the parameters (Maddala 1983); to take care of this, we used Tobit regression.

References

Abebe Haile-Gabriel (2000), "Thriving Informal Land Markets and Patterns of Entitlement Redistribution among Peasant Households: The Case of Cereal Producing Central Ethiopian Highlands," in Mekonnen Alemu and Aredo Dejene, *Institutions, Resources and Development in Ethiopia*. Addis Ababa: EEA and Department of Economics, Addis Ababa University

Addis Hiwot (1975), *Ethiopia: From Autocracy to Revolution*. London: Review of African Political Economy

Alemayehu Geda (1999), "The Structure and Performance of Ethiopia's Financial Sector," in Alemayehu Geda and Berhanu Nega, *The Ethiopian Economy:*

[21] Unpublished MSc thesis, Addis Ababa University.

Performance and Evolution. Addis Ababa: Department of Economics, Addis Ababa University

(2002a), *Finance and Trade in Africa: Macroeconomic Response in the World Economy Context*. London: Palgrave Macmillan.

(2002b), "The Gebre–Hiwot Model: A Pioneer African (Ethiopian) Development Economist," *Ethiopian Journal of Development Research* 24(1):1–28

(2003), "The Macroeconomic Environment and Ethiopian Agriculture," Addis Ababa: Department of Economics, Addis Ababa University.

(2004), "Does Conflict Explain Ethiopia's Backwardness? Yes! and Significantly." Paper presented at Making Peace Work Conference, WIDER, Helsinki

(2005), "Macroeconomic Performance in Post-Reform Ethiopia," *Journal of Northeast African Studies* 8(1): 159–85.

Alemayehu Geda and Alem Abreha (2005), "Macro Policy, Labor Market and Poverty in Ethiopia: A Microsimulation Approach," Department of Economics, Addis Ababa University, mimeo.

Alemayehu Geda and Befekadu Degefe (2005), "Explaining African Economic Growth: The Case of Ethiopia," African Economic Research Consortium, mimeo; also at www.alemayehu.com

Alemayehu Geda and Berhanu Nega (1999), *The Ethiopian Economy: Performance and Evolution*. Addis Ababa: Department of Economics, Addis Ababa University

Alemayehu Geda, Berket Kebede, and Abebe Shimeles (2003), "Rural Poverty in Ethiopia: The Role of Institutions in a Globalized Economy," Foundation for Advanced Studies on International Development, Tokyo

Alemayehu Geda, John Weeks, Daniel Zerfu, and Dawit Weldeyesus (2004), "Source of Growth in Ethiopia," Policy Research Paper for Ministry of Finance and Economic Development, Addis Ababa

Alemayehu Lirenso (1987), "Grain Marketing and Pricing in Ethiopia: A Study of the Impact of Grain Quotas and Fixed Grain Prices on Grain Producers," *IDR Research Report* 28, Addis Ababa University.

(1992), "Economic Reform and Agricultural Deco-operativization in Ethiopia: Implications for Agricultural Production in the 1990s," in Mekonen Taddesse, *The Ethiopian Economy: Structure, Problems and Policy Issues*, Proceedings of the First Annual Conference on the Ethiopian Economy, Addis Ababa: EEA and Department of Economics, Addis Ababa University

Bahru Zewde (2001), *A History of Modern Ethiopia: 1855–1991*, 2nd edn. Oxford: James Currey

Berhanu Nega (2006), *Yenesanet Gohe Siked: Likelebes Yetemokerwu Ye Ethiopia Democracy (When the Dawn of Freedom Comes: The Attempt to Abort the Ethiopian Democracy)*. Kampala: MM Publishers, in Amharic

Berhanu Nega and Seid Nuru (1999), "Performance of the Ethiopian Economy: 1991–1998," in Alemayehu Geda and Berhanu Nega, eds., *The Ethiopian Economy: Performance and Evaluation*. Addis Ababa: EEA and Department of Economics, Addis Ababa University

Berket Kebede and A. Croppenstedt (1995), "The Nature of Share-cropping in Ethiopia: Some Preliminary Observation," in Dejene Aredo and Mulat Demeke,

Ethiopian Agriculture: Problems of Transformation. Addis Ababa: EEA and Department of Economics, Addis Ababa University.

Central Statistical Authority (CSA) (1999), *Agricultural Sample Survey*. Addis Ababa.

Clapham, C. (1988), *Transformation and Continuity in Revolutionary Ethiopia*. Cambridge: Cambridge University Press

Collier, P. and S. A. O'Connell (2007), "Opportunities and Choices," chapter 2 in B. J. Ndulu, S. A. O'Connell, R. H. Bates, P. Collier, and C. C. Soludo, eds., *The Political Economy of Economic Growth in Africa, 1960–2000*, vol. 1. Cambridge: Cambridge University Press

Collins, S. and B. Bosworth (1996), "Economic Growth in East Asia: Accumulation versus Assimilation," *Brookings Papers on Economic Activity* 2: 135–203

Croppenstedt, A. and Mulat Demeke (1997), "An Empirical Study of Cereal Crop Production and Efficiency of Private Farmers in Ethiopia: A Mixed Fixed-random Approach," *Applied Economics*, 29: 1217–26

Dejene Aredo (1995), "The Informal and Semi-formal Sectors in Ethiopia: A Study of Iqub, Ider and Savings and Credit Cooperatives," AERC Research Paper 21. Nairobi: African Economic Research Consortium

Eshetu Chole and Mekonnen Manyazewal (1992), "The Macroeconomic Performance of the Ethiopian Economy," in Mekonen Taddesse, *The Ethiopian Economy: Structure, Problems and Policy Issues*. Addis Ababa: EEA and Department of Economics, Addis Ababa University

Ethiopian Economic Association (EEA) (2000), *Annual Report on Ethiopian Economy, I, 1998/1999*. Addis Ababa: Ethiopian Economic Association

Gebre-Hiwot Baykedagne (1912), *Emperor Minilik and Ethiopia*. Asmara: in Amharic

Gebru Getahun (1995), "Issues of Human Resource Development in Ethiopia: With Particular Reference to Education," in Mekonen Taddesse, *The Ethiopian Economy: Structure, Problems and Policy Issues*. Addis Ababa: EEA and Department of Economics, Addis Ababa University

Haile, Kibret (2000), "Land Reform: Revisiting the Public versus Private Ownership Controversy," in Alemu Mekonnen and Dejene Aredo, *Institutions, Resources and Development in Ethiopia*, Proceedings of the Ninth Annual Conference on the Ethiopian Economy. Addis Ababa: EEA and Department of Economics, Addis Ababa University

Hoeffler, A. (2002), "The Augmented Solow Model and the African Growth Debate," Oxford, *Bulletin of Economics and Statistics* 64(2), May: 135–58

Krishnan, Pramikla, Tesfay Gebre, and Stefan Dercon (1998), "The Urban Labor Market during Structural Adjustment: Ethiopia 1990–1997," CSAE Working Paper Series WPS/98–9, University of Oxford

Maddala, G. S. (1983), *Limited-dependent and Qualitative Variables in Econometrics*. Cambridge: Cambridge University Press

MEDaC (Ministry of Economic Development and Co-operation) (1999), *Survey of the Ethiopian Economy: Review of Post-reform Development, 1992/93–1997/98*. Addis Ababa: MEDaC

Mengestu Bediye (1998), "Overview of the Ethiopian Financial Sector: Review of and Comments on Informal Finance, Semi-formal Finance and Formal Finance,"

Background Paper for the First Annual Report on the Ethiopian Economy, Addis Ababa

Mukherjee, C., White, H., and Wuyts, M. (1998), *Econometrics and Data Analysis for Developing Countries*. London and New York: Routledge

National Bank of Ethiopia (1999/2000), *Annual Report*. Addis Ababa: NBE

Ndulu, Benno J. and S. A. O'Connell (2000), "Background Information on Economic Growth," Paper for the Explaining African Economic Growth Project. Nairobi: African Economic Research Consortium

Negus, N. (2001), "The Role of Education in Enhancing Agricultural Productivity: The Case of Teff Production in Selected Villages of Ethiopia," Unpublished MSc thesis, Department of Economics, Addis Ababa University

Nehru, V. and A. Dhareshwar (1993), "New Database on Physical Capital Stock: Sources, Methodology, and Results," *Revista de Analisis Economico* 8: 37–59

Netsaute Walelign (1997), "Human Resource Development and Economic Growth in Ethiopia," unpublished MSc thesis, Department of Economics, Addis Ababa University

O'Connell, S. A. and Benno J. Ndulu (2000), "Africa's Growth Experience: A Focus on Source of Growth," AERC Growth Working Paper No. 10, Nairobi: African Economic Research Consortium, April (downloadable: www.aercafrica.org)

—— (2003), "Revised Collins/Bosworth Growth Decompositions," Paper for the AERC Growth Project (downloadable: www.aercafrica.org)

Pankhurst, Richard (1963a), "The Ethiopian Army of Former Times," *Ethiopian Observer* 2(2): 118–42

—— (1963b), "The Effect of War in Ethiopian History," *Ethiopian Observer* 2(2): 143–62

—— (1968), *Economic History of Ethiopia, II*. Addis Ababa: Hayla-Selassie University Press

Seid Nuru (2000), "Determinants of Economic Growth in Ethiopia," unpublished MSc thesis, Department of Economics, Addis Ababa University

Seyoum Chane (1997), "Economic Performance of Ethiopia (1972–1995): Growth Determinants and Implications," unpublished MSc thesis, Department of Economics, Addis Ababa University

Syrquin, M. and H. Chenery (1989), "Three Decades of Industrialization," *World Bank Economic Review* 3(2): 145–81

Taye Mengistae (2001), "Skill Formation and Job Matching Effects in Wage Growth in Ethiopia," *Journal of African Economies* 10(1): 1–36

Tekie Alemu (2000), "Farmers' Willingness to Pay for Tenure Security," in Alemu Mekonnen and Dejene Aredo, *Institutions, Resources and Development in Ethiopia*, Proceedings of the Ninth Annual Conference on the Ethiopian Economy. Addis Ababa: EEA and Department of Economics, Addis Ababa University

Teshale Tibebu (1995), *The Making of Modern Ethiopia: 1896–1974*. Trenton, NJ: The Red Sea Press

5 | Man-made opportunities and growth in Malawi

Chinyamata Chipeta and Mjedo Mkandawire

1. Introduction

According to the country classification used in the Growth Project, Malawi is a low-opportunity, landlocked, resource-scarce nation. Despite lack of rents from oil, minerals, and other natural resources, the absence of a coastline to facilitate export of manufactures, and high transport costs, Malawi's rate of growth exceeded the African average between 1960 and 2000 (table 5.1). The rate of growth of real GDP per worker was particularly high during the period 1960–79, averaging 3 percent per annum (table 5.2). Malawi's relatively high rate of growth between 1960 and 1979 was accompanied by structural change, with agriculture decreasing its share in GDP from 36.37 percent during 1965–9 to 31.89 percent during 1975–9, and that of manufacturing rising from 4.5 percent to 12.06 percent.

The rate of growth achieved between 1960 and 1979 was not sustained, however. From 1980 to 2000, the rate of growth of real GDP per worker averaged 0.16 percent per year. This was on account of a lower average

Southern African Institute for Economic Research.

Table 5.1 *Malawi, growth-accounting decomposition, by half-decade, 1960–2000*

Period	Growth in real GDP per worker	Contribution of		
		Physical capital per worker	Education per worker	Residual
1960–64	0.33	4.46	0.06	−4.19
1965–69	5.11	4.45	−0.02	0.67
1970–74	3.59	4.25	0.24	−0.90
1975–79	2.96	2.52	0.13	0.30
1980–84	−1.65	0.07	0.24	−1.96
1985–89	−0.97	−0.90	0.18	−0.25
1990–94	−0.65	−0.11	0.20	−0.74
1995–2000	3.90	−1.29	0.39	4.80
Total	**1.67**	**1.54**	**0.19**	**−0.06**
1960–2000				
SSA	0.51	0.36	0.25	−0.09
LAC	0.76	0.44	0.33	0.00
SA	2.18	1.04	0.31	0.82
EAP	3.89	2.20	0.48	1.21
MENA	2.37	1.10	0.44	0.84
INDU	2.23	0.96	0.32	0.96
All countries	**1.63**	**0.83**	**0.34**	**0.47**

Notes: SSA = Sub-Saharan Africa; LAC = Latin America and Caribbean; SA = South Asia; EAP = East Asia and Pacific; MENA = Middle East and North Africa; INDU = Industrialized countries.
Source: Ndulu and O'Connell (2003).

contribution of physical capital per worker, caused by a reduction in the rate of investment (tables 5.1, 5.2, and 5.4).

This study explains Malawi's growth performance mainly in terms of physical capital accumulation, in relation to the growth of the labor force, the accumulation of human capital, and productivity growth. It also emphasizes the role of policy, and accounts for policy choices in terms of the interaction of interest groups and the incentives created by the structure of political competition.

2. Historical background

Malawi became a British Colony in 1891. A governor, appointed by the Colonial Office, ran the affairs of the country with the assistance of expatriate civil servants, but effective control of the country remained with the Colonial

Table 5.2 *Malawi, growth-accounting decomposition, pre-SAP (1960–1979) and SAP (1980–2000) periods, percent*

| Period | Growth in real GDP per worker | Contribution of | | |
		Physical capital per worker	Education per worker	TFPG residual
1960–79	3.00	3.12	0.10	−1.03
1980–2000	0.16	0.56	0.25	0.46

Source: Ndulu and O'Connell (2003).

Office. The country became independent in 1964. Initially, independent Malawi was a multi-party state with a Prime Minister as the head of government. In 1966, Malawi became a republic with a President as the head of state and government. Later, the country was declared a one-party state and in 1971, Dr. Hastings Kamazu Banda became Life President, a position he held until 1994, when he was defeated by Bakili Muluzi in the country's first democratic elections.

During the colonial period, the country was a member of the Federation of Rhodesia and Nyasaland. Federation with Rhodesia had been imposed against the wishes of the majority African people and resistance to it provided the focus for nationalist politics from 1953 to 1963.

2.1   Periodization

Malawi's growth story can be divided into two periods. The first covers the colonial (including Federal) era and the independence period up to about 1979. The second period is from 1980 to the year 2000. Until independence, the first period was characterized by mild restrictions based on race on entry into certain industries and markets. Throughout the period, the government imposed quantitative restrictions (QRs) on imports and exports of goods and services; minimum price controls on smallholder agricultural products, and maximum price controls on most locally produced and imported manufactured goods; restrictions on changes in wage rates; controls on interest rates; exchange controls that restricted demand for foreign exchange while ensuring that foreign exchange receipts found their way into the hands of banks; and pegging of the exchange rate of the local currency to other currencies or to a basket of other currencies.

As shown in table 5.3, these policies resulted in a fairly stable economic environment. On average, budget deficits as percent of GDP were relatively low, the rates of inflation and interest were comparatively low, the price of foreign exchange was low, and gross domestic savings and investment rates were high. Rates of growth of GDP and formal sector employment were also

Table 5.3 *Malawi, selected pre-SAP (1971–1979) and SAP (1980–2000) period macroeconomic indicators*

Indicators	Pre-SAP (1971–9) period	SAP (1980–2000) period
Rate of growth of real GDP (% per annum)	6.1	3.0
Rate of growth of formal sector employment (% per annum)	7.1	3.6
Gross domestic savings/GDP (%)	13.0	7.7
Gross domestic investment/GDP (%)	26.2	16.6
Commercial bank prime lending rate (%)	9.8	25.4
Rate of inflation	9.5	24.4
Current account deficit of the balance of payments/GDP (%)	13.1	9.4
Broad money/GDP (%)	16.8	17.2
Exchange rate (Malawi Kwacha per US Dollar)	0.8	13.1
Budget deficit excluding grants/GDP (%)	−7.3	−10.2
Budget deficit including grants/GDP (%)	−5.3	−5.7

Sources: Malawi Government, *Economic Report* (various issues); Reserve Bank of Malawi, *Financial and Economic Review* (various issues); World Bank, *World Development Report* (various issues).

high. However, the economy ran a fairly high current account deficit on its balance of payments.

As stated above, this period was associated with a high average rate of growth of real GDP per worker (tables 5.1 and 5.2) and a high average rate of investment (table 5.4). Except for the period 1960–4, the average rate of investment remained high.

During the 1960s and 1970s, Malawi's development plans included large-scale projects that required huge expenditures. Among these were the New Capital City in Lilongwe, the Lakeshore Road, and the University of Malawi. The political leadership conceived these projects when in political detention at Gwelo Prison in Southern Rhodesia (now Zimbabwe) and they came to be known as the Gwelo Plan. Later, the Nacala Railway Project was added. Other projects included in the country's development plans were the Blantyre–Lilongwe Road, the Nkula Hydroelectric Project, and the National Rural Development Programme. Planned development expenditure over the 1971–80 period amounted to K374 million (Malawi Government 1971). In sectoral terms, most of the actual development expenditure over the period 1974–9 went into transport (50 percent), agriculture and natural resources (19.4 percent), government buildings (9.4 percent), and utilities (7.9 percent). Bilateral and multilateral donors financed between 70 and 85 percent of public investment from 1964 to 1977 (Malawi Government 1983).

Table 5.4 *Malawi, investment rates,[a] 1960–1964 to 1995–2000, %*

Period	Private investment rate	Public investment rate	Total investment rate
1960–64	–	–	9.78
1965–69	–	–	15.88
1970–74	15.31	8.49	23.80
1975–79	14.39	16.28	30.67
1980–84	9.05	10.84	19.89
1985–89	8.90	8.39	17.29
1990–94	11.4	5.3	16.7
1995–2000	5.2	8.9	14.1

Note: [a]Gross domestic investment as a percent of GDP.
Source: Malawi Government, *Economic Report* (various issues).

Changes in savings also passed through distinct phases since 1960. During the 1960s, national savings were negligible in Malawi; foreign savings financed virtually all capital expenditure. The 1970s ushered in a new period. Gross national savings grew fairly rapidly, averaging 11.2 percent of GDP during 1970–4 and 13 percent during 1975–9. This change was partly a result of a policy decision to save part of government revenues and public enterprise profits. Corporate and household savings also increased. During the 1980s, however, the trend was reversed, and gross national savings declined to 10 percent of GDP during 1980–4 and to 7.4 percent during 1985–9. The rate remained about the same during the 1990s, averaging 7.5 percent between 1994 and 1999.

A series of exogenous shocks brought an end to the first period. These shocks included disruptions and, eventually, closure of short routes to the sea through Mozambique, which are believed to have reduced growth by 1.5 percent per year (Sahn 1996); a worsening in the external terms of trade; a drought that adversely affected the 1979–80 crop growing season; and a remittance shock due to the marked reduction in the number of Malawians going to the South African mines.[1] These shocks came on top of the oil price shock of 1979–80 and the accumulation of foreign debt.

During the second period, the government implemented a series of structural adjustment reforms, gradually dismantling the mild controls of the first period. The current account deficit of the balance of payments as percentage of GDP fell (table 5.3), but budget deficits as percent of GDP increased, inflation and interest rates rose, the price of foreign exchange accelerated,

---

[1] From a peak of 123,845 workers in 1972, the number fell to less than 22,000 between 1975 and 1992. The cession of recruitment after 1992 led to a decline in total remittances from K33 million in 1988 to less than K6 million per year from 1990 in real terms.

savings and investment rates declined, and GDP and formal sector employ-ment growth rates plummeted.

The implementation of SAPs has coincided with the spread of HIV/AIDS in Malawi. As in other Southern African countries, the HIV/AIDS epidemic has reached crisis proportions; at the end of 1999, the adult prevalence rate made Malawi one of the sixteen countries with the highest HIV/AIDS infection rates in the world.

Over the whole period (1960–2000) under study, however, Malawi remained syndrome-free. State actors avoided choosing a control or reg-ulatory regime that would have distorted productive activity and rewarded rent-seeking. They avoided the ethno-regional redistribution that would have compromised efficiency in order to effect resource transfers. They avoided creating a regime of intertemporal redistribution that would have aggressively transferred resources from the future to the present. And, lastly, they avoided state breakdown.

3. Cross-country perspectives on growth

In this section, we seek to explain the trends in economic growth in Malawi using two cross-country approaches; one using differences in the accumu-lation of productive factors and the other using differences in the policy stances (see the appendix, p. 163).

Table 5.1 presents a growth-accounting decomposition for Malawi for the period 1960–2000, using half-decade intervals to control for short-term influences (see Ndulu and O'Connell 2003). The data show that over the 1960–79 period, the average rate of growth of real GDP per worker was high, averaging about 3 percent per annum. The main determinant of this growth record was the contribution of physical capital per worker. During the three half-decades after 1979, growth in real GDP per worker turned negative on account of the low or negative contribution of physical capital per worker and the residual. During 1995–2000, growth of real GDP per worker was once again high and positive, largely due to the large contribution of the residual.

Over the entire 1960–2000 period, growth in real GDP per worker aver-aged 1.67 percent, about the average for all the countries included in the Collins–Bosworth study (Ndulu and O'Connell 2003). The contribution of physical capital per worker, at 1.54 percent, to the average annual growth rate of 1.67 percent in real GDP per worker, was larger than the contribu-tion of education per worker, at 0.19 percent, while that of the total factor productivity growth (TFPG) residual was negative at –0.06 percent. The overall contribution of education per worker, though small, remained pos-itive throughout most of the review period. The contribution of the TFPG

Table 5.5 *Malawi and other countries, initial average years of schooling,*
1960–1997

Malawi	Initial average years of schooling	Other countries (1994)	Initial average years of schooling
1960–4	1.9	China	5.3
1965–9	2.0	East Asia	7.2
1970–4	1.9	South Asia	3.4
1975–9	2.5	Africa	3.5
1980–4	2.7	Middle East	4.9
1985–9	2.8	Latin America	5.5
1990–7	2.7	Industrialized countries	9.8

Source: Collins and Bosworth (1996); and Barro and Lee (1993).

residual alternated between positive and negative, but was negative during a greater part of the review period – i.e. during 1960–4, 1970–4 and 1980–94.

The decline in Malawi's economic growth from the early 1980s appears to be due to a reduction in physical capital accumulation (table 5.4), a delayed demographic transition, slow accumulation of human capital (table 5.5) and slow productivity growth (table 5.1). The reduction in physical capital accumulation depressed capital and income per worker, indicating that an increase in the rate of physical capital accumulation will be required to reverse the country's fortunes. In the absence of a demographic transition, the rapid growth of the working population – mainly through natural increases in the population that have averaged 2.8 percent per annum since 1960 – has also depressed the rate of growth.

Relevant to the accumulation of human capital was the low priority that the government placed on education – allocating, for example, 0.5 percent of planned development expenditure to education between 1971 and 1980. The gross primary school enrollment ratio remained below 80 percent, while secondary school gross enrollment stagnated at 4 percent, with the tertiary education enrollment ratio remaining below 1 percent. As a result of the introduction of free primary education and an expansion in secondary school enrollment, the average number of years of schooling has increased since the mid-1990s, but it is still below the world average.

The low or negative average TFPG residual for the entire 1960–2000 period reflects the impact of a series of more or less permanent factors: among others, a low rate of adoption of productive technologies, the impact of malaria and HIV/AIDS, and the impact of tax and tax-like policies in producing an inefficient composition of aggregate investment. Large negative residuals have also been due to temporary or periodic factors, such as disruptions in the supply of electricity and water, transport route disruptions, droughts, floods, and trade shocks. Large positive residuals have been caused by an improvement in these temporary or periodic factors.

When we turn to the policy equations, we find that the net effect of the baseline variables has been negative (table 5.6): low initial life expectancy, a high age dependency ratio, landlockedness, and the terms of trade have more than offset the boost implied by low initial income, growth in the potential labor force, trading partner growth, and political stability.

The effect of the policy variables, including the black market premium and the Barro–Lee non-productive government expenditure (Barro and Lee 1993), has also been negative. The black market premium rose from an average of 8.6 percent during 1960–4 to 81.6 percent during 1975–9, before declining to an average of 28.8 percent during 1985–9.

Another factor contributing to the decline in the rate of growth was the decrease in the real value of migrants' remittances originating abroad, falling from a peak level of K54.1 million in 1974. Between 1976 and 1979, the level of these remittances remained fairly flat. Although it recovered subsequently, in real terms it never reached the earlier high levels. Another was a decline in real consumer demand, caused by stagnation in the growth of real incomes of wage earners and smallholder farmers, compounded by rising levels of poverty. The proportion of the population falling below the national poverty line increased from 54 percent in 1991 to 65 percent in 1998 and 68 percent in 2003, thus increasing inequality in the distribution of income. The national Gini coefficient rose from 0.48 in 1968 to 0.62 in 1995 (data on regional Gini coefficients is not available). At independence in 1964, it was thought that the Southern Region was more developed because most of the modern economic activities were located there, but there were no data on *per capita* income or levels of poverty to substantiate this. The government attempted to correct the perceived regional imbalance in economic development by shifting the capital from Zomba in the Southern Region to Lilongwe in the Central Region, with the Central Region gaining at the expense of the South. On the basis of the Human Development Index (HDI) and poverty headcounts, the most developed region is the Northern, which suffered relative neglect under both colonial and independent governments, followed by the Central.

4.   Evidence on markets, agents, and political economy

4.1   *Markets*

4.1.1   Agricultural markets

From the time of colonial rule, Malawi's agricultural markets have been dualistic. For a greater part of the colonial period, the large farming sub-sector dominated commercial farming. Painful lessons, including the 1949 famine,

Table 5.6 *Malawi, fits and residuals from Ndulu–O'Connell pooled full specification model, 1960–1997*

| | Fits and residuals | | | Actual and predicted growth deviation | | | | | | |
| | | | | | Contribution to predicted growth deviation of | | | Breakdown of policy contribution variables | | |
Period	Actual growth per capita	Fitted growth per capita	Residual	Actual growth deviation from sample mean	Base variables	Political instability	Policy	Inflation (<500%)	Black market premium (<500%)	Non-productive government spending/GDP
1960–4	0.03	–	–	–2.17	–	–	–0.70	0.06	0.10	–0.86
1965–9	5.03	1.31	3.72	2.83	–0.53	0.20	–0.60	0.06	0.07	–0.72
1970–4	3.44	2.44	1.00	1.25	–0.15	0.20	–0.41	0.03	–0.04	–0.40
1975–9	2.67	0.16	2.51	0.47	–1.56	0.20	–0.89	0.04	–0.43	–0.49
1980–4	–1.62	–1.16	–0.45	–3.82	–1.53	0.13	–1.25	0.01	–0.36	–0.89
1985–9	–1.18	–	–	–3.38	–0.91	0.20	–	–0.01	–0.04	–
1990–7	1.78	–	–	–0.42	–1.25	0.20	–	–0.06	–0.10	–
Total	**1.45**	**0.69**	**1.69**	**–0.75**	**–0.99**	**0.19**	**–0.77**	**0.02**	**–0.11**	**–0.67**

Source: Ndulu and O'Connell (2000).

led to the colonial administration's increased commitment to the expansion of smallholder agriculture (Kydd and Christiansen 1981). According to Chanock (referred to by Pryor 1990), this policy stance was supported by educated Africans. Thus, at independence in the early 1960s, the prevailing view was already in favor of agricultural development, which was strengthened by the orientation towards agriculture of Dr. Hastings Kamuzu Banda, the first President of Malawi, who was to dominate the country's political and economic scene for three decades to May 1994.

Estate crops

The estate sub-sector produces mainly tea, tobacco (flue-cured and burley varieties), and sugar. In 1989, there were 14,700 estates in the country, with each estate having about 58 hectares of land (Malawi Government 1987), some of which had been developed out of unused common customary land. By 2004, there were 30,000 estates with land holdings of between 10 and 500 hectares (World Bank 2004). The colonial government promoted estate agriculture because it was the main source of exports and employment. The independent government of Dr. Banda had similar motives; in addition, it was driven by the need to create and retain political support among the Malawian elite who went into estate tobacco growing. Under both colonial and independent regimes, estates producing these major cash/export crops benefited from access to large tracts of arable land which they could lease at low rents; access to cheap labor backed by low wage policies; and, for tobacco estates in particular, access to large amounts of domestic bank credit at subsidized interest rates.

Estate crops have always been sold under competitive market forces. An important exception has been tobacco, which estate growers sell at the local auction floors. There is a small number of buyers, representing tobacco merchants with close connections to powerful tobacco multinationals, who are believed to collude to the detriment of growers. Particularly in recent years, estate owners have lobbied the government to intervene when tobacco auction prices have been unprofitably low.

Another important exception is burley tobacco, which is partly grown by smallholders on tenant schemes. The estate owners purchase tobacco from the tenants at prices that are much lower than those fetched on the auction floors; in so doing, they are helped by the government, which sets a ceiling on the prices paid by the estate owners.

Despite the unfavourable characteristics of the estate tobacco market, tobacco, tea, and sugar have contributed substantially to the growth of formal employment in the country and the growth of total exports. Tobacco, tea, and sugar comprise over 70 percent of total exports.

Smallholder crops

In 1984–5, the 1.6 million smallholder farm households cultivated an average of 1.1 hectares of land. About 56 percent of these households cultivated less than 1 hectare, with 30.9 percent between 1 and 2 hectares and 14 percent more than 2 hectares (Malawi Government 1987). In 2002, there were between 1.8 and 2.0 smallholder farm households cultivating an average of 1 hectare of land, with 48 percent cultivating less than 1 hectare, 25.4 percent between 1 and 2 hectares, and 16 percent more than 2 hectares (World Bank 2004). It would appear, therefore, that smallholders have been able to acquire more land.

Smallholders produce food crops and keep livestock. They have always exchanged a portion of their crops for cash or other goods or services. Successive governments have promoted smallholder agriculture in order to ensure that the people avoid famine and generate a cash income. The independent governments had the additional motive of winning and retaining the support of rural dwellers, who now constitute 85 percent of the total population.

With the introduction of estate farming from the late 1800s, smallholder farmers concentrated on the production of fire-cured and oriental tobacco and grew the bulk of the cotton and coffee. In terms of volume and value, smallholders have always produced most of the crops, but estates dominate in terms of export value.

Before market liberalization, smallholders had two market outlets for selling their commodities: private outlets and the dominant official outlet. The first consisted of informal sales to consumers at small produce markets in rural areas, usually along roadsides, or in large urban produce markets. They also sold to private traders. Through licensing, the government has heavily regulated the export of agricultural commodities, especially food crops and at times of drought.

The dominant official outlet is the Agricultural Development and Marketing Corporation (ADMARC), a parastatal. The government and ADMARC jointly fix producer prices at guaranteed minima and at uniform levels for the whole country. They announce these prices to smallholders before the planting season. Smallholders transport their commodities to ADMARC and other markets on foot, on bicycles or, more rarely, on ox-drawn carts.

ADMARC has also been involved in the transporting, storing, cleaning, grading, milling, and shelling of smallholder crops and in arranging for their domestic sale and export. Domestic sales have been made to agro-based industries (such as grain-millers and textile manufacturers) as well as directly to consumers in the case of major food crops, including smallholders who may have run out of food in the period before harvest.

Like estate tobacco growers, ADMARC also sells on the local auction floors. For a long time, the prices at which ADMARC has sold smallholder crops domestically and abroad have been much higher than the prices the corporation has paid smallholders. ADMARC's network of hundreds of seasonal and permanent markets has also facilitated the extension of agricultural credit to smallholders and the recovery of loans.

The smallholders' domestic markets have thus not been competitive. Prices for goods sold to ADMARC have been officially set. In the case of the sales through private outlets, traders are more mobile and better informed than farmers. Private markets for smallholder crops are fragmented, and whereas traders travel and gather information, smallholders remain in their own areas and remain poorly informed. Within any segment of this market, there are few traders and many farmers. Traders are thus in a stronger bargaining position than smallholders and this is reflected in the low level of producer prices.

4.1.2 Financial markets

Formal financial credit markets

During the post-colonial period, the formal financial market has been marked by financial repression, with the government exerting direct controls on the interest rate, rationing credit, and regulating entry.

Competition Before financial sector reform, competition in the formal financial market was constrained. Commercial banks were over-exposed to the estate tobacco growing sub-sector, which took a large share of their lending. Banks and NBFIs perceived a lack of good lending opportunities in the economy, resulting in high liquidity ratios. The use of direct monetary policy instruments also constrained competition between banks.

With financial sector reform, the number of players in the market has risen; banks' over-exposure to estate tobacco growers has decreased; some of the NBFIs which were not accepting deposits have been allowed to do so; and direct monetary policy instruments have become indirect, thereby ending financial repression.

Fragmentation Particularly before reform, fragmentation of the formal financial sector was reflected in the inadequate flow of resources within and between the commercial bank and NBFI segments of the market. A number of factors were behind this fragmentation. First, commercial banks specialized in short-term lending, and did little medium-term lending, while NBFIs specialized in medium- and long-term lending and did little short-term lending. While specialization promotes efficiency, the institutions in each of the segments often failed to explore lending opportunities beyond their traditional spheres. Development finance institutions mainly relied on foreign sources of capital funds, even when some domestic institutions had excess loanable funds: evidence of this was the excess liquidity of commercial banks and insurance companies. Moreover, the money and capital markets were too underdeveloped to facilitate efficient flow of funds amongst financial institutions. Following reform, there are indications of some decrease in fragmentation of the financial market, particularly after the establishment of the first discount houses in the late 1990s.

Informal financial credit market

The majority of small-scale operators are unable to access credit at formal financial institutions, and even when it is available, the procedures for its access are generally time-consuming and cumbersome (Chipeta and Mkandawire 1991). There has been even more fragmentation within the informal financial market than in the formal; rarely do funds flow between market institutions, and information about each other and about their clients is rarely shared. For these same reasons, the informal financial market is not meaningfully competitive.

4.2   Agents

4.2.1   Agricultural households

In 1960, agriculture accounted for about 45 percent of GDP. By 1979, agriculture's share had declined to about 32 percent, where it has remained. Whereas estates received most of their loans from banks, smallholder farmers accessed most of their credit from the informal financial sector, mainly in the form of interest-free loans from friends, relatives, and neighbors. In many cases, smallholder farmers also made use of income transfers or remittances from relatives. Most of the estates used leasehold land for which they paid rent, while most of the smallholder farmers used customary land to which they had free usufruct rights. Value added in estate agriculture grew at an average rate of 13 percent per annum between 1965 and 1979; in contrast, value added in the smallholder sub-sector grew at a lower average annual rate of 8 percent between 1965 and 1979. These different rates largely reflected the marked expansion in estate tobacco growing following the Unilateral Declaration of Independence (UDI) by Rhodesia; the expansion in tea production, partly as a result of the opening of a new tea estate in the Northern region; and the coming onstream of sugar production.

Employment on estates grew rapidly, induced by the growth of value added, from 43,000 workers in 1968 to 178,804 in 1979. However, these workers benefited little from the growth of value added, as their average monthly earnings remained low. Average monthly earnings of agricultural workers, for example, were K14.41 in 1979, as against K9.76 in 1972. Tenants on burley tobacco estates fared little better. They were advanced loans for production and consumption by the estate owners, on which they paid interest. Estate owners paid them low prices for the tobacco that they produced, resulting in low net earnings. As a result, tenants could hardly feed and clothe their families.

After 1980, capital formation in agriculture declined. On the basis of data reported in the *Annual Economic Survey*, in real terms gross capital formation on the estates fell from an annual average of K40.3 million during 1975–9 to K12.2 million during 1980–4, K10.1 million during 1985–9, and to K8.8 million during 1990–4. Like manufacturing firms, agricultural enterprises now face high costs of imported and domestic inputs, interest, and transport. But unlike manufacturing firms, agricultural enterprises also suffer from an erratic rainfall pattern. As a result, many tobacco estates have either ceased production or scaled down their operations.

From the early 1980s, the government carried out a number of reforms affecting smallholders. The principal objectives of the reforms were to ensure an appropriate price policy (Structural Adjustment Loan I or SAL I) and adequate incentives (SAL II), expand the role of the private sector in the marketing of smallholder crops (SAL III), increase efficiency and improve incomes of smallholders, increase efficiency of land use, and protect the environment (Agricultural Sector Adjustment Credit or ASAC), and to complete the removal of remaining pricing and marketing constraints on smallholder agriculture (Fiscal Restructuring and Deregulation Program or FRDP). To achieve these objectives, the government rationalized and increased smallholder producer prices; removed fertilizer subsidies; reduced the role of ADMARC in favor of private competition in marketing inputs and outputs; and allowed smallholder farmers to grow burley tobacco. Supporting macroeconomic policies stressed the control of inflation and the liberalization of the exchange rate, thus removing the implicit tax on agricultural exports.

Under SAPs, there has been no increase in yields of most cash and food crops, necessitating food imports and increasing the risk of food insecurity.

The liberalization of the growing and selling of burley tobacco has adversely affected the quality of the crop and led to lower prices. There is less quality control on smallholder farms compared to estates; anybody can obtain a license to purchase burley tobacco as an intermediate buyer, and as most do not know how to handle the crop, they mix different grades of tobacco. A by-product of the decline in quality is a reduction in bank lending. In the past, the banks used to recover their loans at the auction floors. Now the crop can be sold through intermediate buyers, so banks have no way of recovering their loans.

SAPs have not adequately addressed the problems of inadequate producer incentives, unfavorable internal terms of trade, and inadequate credit and ineffective extension services. Certainly, they have not addressed non-price constraints, such as infrastructure, feeder roads, or extension services.

A sign of increasing stress in agriculture is the high rate of crime that emerged after the 1994 multi-party elections (Pelser, Burton, and Gondwe 2004). Most of the crimes in rural areas concern theft of food and cash crops, livestock, and personal property, and can be called "crimes of need." The date of the rise reflects the sudden weakening of political institutions that had maintained discipline among the people, and the dismantling of civilian structures that had supported the police force.

4.2.2   Manufacturing firms

During the pre-SAP period, the economic environment was generally favorable to manufacturing. Improvements in infrastructure included expansion in electricity generating capacity and in urban water supplies; the construction of the Nacala Railway to the Mozambican coast and extension of the domestic railway; and improvement to the country's main road network, among other developments. The economy itself experienced relative stability: the rate of inflation averaged less than 10 percent; financial policies resulted in interest rates that were low and not volatile; and the pegging of the currency consecutively to the pound sterling, the US dollar, and the pound sterling, and then to the Special Drawing Right (SDR), gave the exchange rate a measure of relative stability.

The 1966 Industrial Development Act set out the conditions under which industrial firms could be licensed and the incentives for stimulating them. The emphasis on a minimum efficient scale in the Act meant that large firms were favored at the expense of small-scale firms. Also favoring large-scale firms were generous investment and depreciation allowances, which were given to them to reduce their tax liability. The provisions relating to tariff and exclusive protection bred monopolies and infant industries that could not survive if protection were lifted.

Between 1960 and the mid-1980s, the government set maximum prices for several manufactured products, whose prices could not be raised in line with increases in costs without government approval. Sometimes approval was denied or, when it was granted, the price adjustment was inadequate. As in the case of sugar and cooking oil, some industries reacted by reducing supply, which resulted in rationing; the result for the firms was lower profits and little investment. Because the political elite had no direct business interests, the Malawi Chamber of Commerce and Industry (MCCI) failed to convince the government to abolish maximum price controls.

For most firms, the economic environment remained generally favorable during the pre-SAP period. There was a marked increase in gross capital formation in manufacturing. Real gross capital formation among large-scale firms increased from an average annual amount of K102.45 million during 1965–9 to K182.40 million during 1970–4 and K282.34 million during 1975–9, according to data provided by the National Statistical Office. During 1970–4, inventory investment was 68.56 percent of gross capital formation, implying that there was less investment in equipment and machinery. But during 1975–9, the situation changed, with inventory investment accounting for only 23.02 percent of total manufacturing investment. Available evidence also indicates that, initially, investment in manufacturing was largely financed from foreign saving because domestic savings were negligible (World Bank 1985). The early 1970s witnessed large gains in private sector savings, and so the share of domestic financing in manufacturing investment increased (Malawi Government 1983).

The growth of manufactured output during the 1970s averaged 5.6 percent per annum. As percent of GDP, the manufacturing sector increased its share from 7 percent at independence to 13 percent in 1980. Employment in the manufacturing sector, in turn, increased by a high, average rate of 6.8 percent per year. These developments were very closely related to the performance of the economy as a whole, with GDP growing at an average annual rate of 6.1 percent.

In response to the changed economic environment after 1980, the average half-decadal rate of investment in manufacturing declined in real terms from K282.34 million during 1975–9 to K227.60 million during 1980–4 and K183.08 million during 1985–9. Although the half-decadal rate of investment subsequently increased and reached K230.54 million during 1990–4, it never reached the peak level attained during 1975–9. During the 1995–7 period, it fell again. A notable development was a steep decline in the share of inventory investment in the total, to 2.82 percent during 1980–4. However, this was short-lived, as inventory investment climbed to 35.44 percent during the 1985–9 period and subsequently remained high. The relatively large inventory investment reflects the uncertainties faced by manufacturing firms because of transport and foreign exchange constraints. Manufacturing firms are also spending more money on security and electric generators than before, but the quantitative magnitude of this is not known.

The unfavorable economic environment raised transaction costs. Manufacturing firms face high imported input costs due to exchange rate depreciation, high domestic input costs due to the high rate of inflation, and inefficiency in the provision of electricity, water, and telecommunications; high finance costs due to high rates of interest; and high transport costs due to the high cost of external (table 5.7) and internal transport.

Transport costs account for 47 percent of the price of fertilizer (based on delivery at Kasungu), 24 percent of the pump price of diesel (inland costs from Beira only), and 12.5 percent of the auction price of tobacco (excluding

Table 5.7 *The cost of insurance and freight in relation to the fob value of Malawi's imports, 1971–1999*

Period	Cost of insurance and freight in real terms MKmillion.	Cost of insurance and freight as percent of imports fob
1971–5	33.7	15.4
1976–80	68.2	24.8
1981–5	108.8	51.8
1986–90	121.1	64.3
1991–5	179.8	81.1
1996–9	106.1	44.4
Average	**103.0**	**47.0**

Source: Calculated from data available in Reserve Bank of Malawi, *Financial and Economic Review* (various issues).

transport from farms to the auction floors). Domestic transport rates in Malawi are equivalent to about US$0.065–US$0.075 per km. Comparable rates in South Africa and Zimbabwe are much lower, at about US$0.02 on trunk roads and US$0.035 on rural roads (World Bank 2004).

The high external transport costs can partly be explained by Malawi's long and uncertain links to the sea. The shortest routes to the sea are Nacala (815 km by rail from Blantyre) and Beira (640 km by rail, which is not currently operating, and 884 km by road). But over 70 percent of Malawi's trade goes through Durban (2,600–3,806 km away, depending on the route, and 50 percent more expensive than the routes through Mozambique) and Dar-es-Salaam (3,030 km by road). The shortest rail route through Nacala is not being fully used because of security problems, including theft of cargo during transit; the unpredictability and inefficiency of the port authority; bureaucratic delay in processing customs documents; lack of flexibility in scheduling shipments; and occasional derailments during bad weather. In addition, Nacala is off the standard international routes, implying that unless the shipment is large enough to warrant making a call, goods must disembark at Durban or Maputo and be trans-shipped by coastal steamer.

Malawi's internal transport costs are high due to the poor network of secondary roads, trucking cartels that keep prices high, restrictions on the operations of foreign vehicles, and high taxation on the transport sector.

Corruption is another factor contributing to the cost of doing business in Malawi. On a scale where 10 is the least corrupt, Malawi scored 4.1 on the Corruption Perception Index (CPI) in 2000, ranking forty-third out of ninety countries. The activities most vulnerable to corruption are public procurement, management of land, and provision of public services such as police and immigration.

Reforms in the manufacturing sector were aimed at encouraging efficient import substitution (SAL I and SAL II) and improving the policy environment for the sector (Industry and Trade Policy Adjustment Credit or ITPAC). Under SAL II, prices of 41 percent of manufactured products to which controls applied were decontrolled. Under SAL III, the prices of the remaining items were decontrolled, except those of petrol, low-grade beef, fertilizers, sugar, and motor vehicle spare parts. Later, beef, sugar, and fertilizer prices were decontrolled. As of 2005, only petroleum products are subject to price controls. Other policy measures for reforming the manufacturing sector included reduction of the scope of industrial licensing requirements, elimination of authority to grant exclusive product rights, revision of the duty drawback system, establishment of the Malawi Investment Promotion Agency (MIPA), simplification of the process for registration and incorporation of companies, elimination of the industrial licensing process for investments except for a short list, and establishment of export-processing zones (EPZs).

These policy measures have not led to a marked expansion in manufacturing output in the country. Between 1981 and 1996, manufacturing value added increased at an average annual rate of 3.9 percent, while in the 1971–80 pre-SAP period, it grew at a much higher average annual rate of 13.6 percent. As a result, the manufacturing sector has not increased its share in GDP since 1980; in fact, it has fallen to about 11 percent, nor has it increased its share in total formal sector employment since that date. Measured by the index of production, total manufactured output is lower now than it was in 1991, as is that of the sub-sectors of export goods, intermediate goods, and consumer goods (except food and beverages). Greater efficiency in import substitution has not been achieved either. Among other things, this has been due to lack of domestic competition, with most industries dominated by monopolies and oligopolies; and price controls, which were retained on some products after the authorities had started to dismantle the controls system.

The liberal policy environment has exposed domestic manufacturing firms to stiff foreign competition. In reaction to high transaction costs and foreign competition, many manufacturing firms have stopped normal operations, scaled down their operations, or turned to trading in the goods that they formerly made themselves.

4.3 Political economy

For the three decades before May 1994, the country's political and economic story revolved around one man, Dr. Hastings Kamuzu Banda. Banda chose to follow a capitalist orientation, spearheaded by the promotion of commercial agriculture, which was also a continuation of the colonial approach.

4.3.1   Interest groups

During Banda's one-party rule, interest groups did not appear to have any significant political impact (Pryor 1990: 384). Policy-making remained centralized and precluded the participation of broader interest groups (Kaunda 2002: 2). A small ruling clique emerged which handed down policies and decrees (Mhone 1992).

The influence of local interest groups on policy-making in the multi-party era, though not yet significant, is likely to be more than in the one-party era. In both periods, the donor interest group, particularly the IMF and the World Bank, has exerted considerable influence on policy-making.

Below we discuss some of the major interest groups, paying particular attention to some examples of their preferences and whether or not their lobbying has had any influence on the making of policy choices. Smallholder farmers and estate farmers were discussed under agricultural markets above.

Political parties and politicians

Members of Parliament (MPs) had an interest in seeing that their constituencies received a fair share of development activity, because their re-election to some extent depended on it; their capacity to influence matters was constrained by bureaucratic decision-making (Kaunda 2002: 69). Each also sought private benefits: appointments to jobs in the public sector, including the few ministerial positions; diplomatic posts; directorships in the expanding parastatal sub-sector; and access to opportunities for doing business, particularly in the estate tobacco growing sub-sector. All this was part of the extensive patronage system set up by Banda. Banda consolidated his political support among senior politicians by promoting estate tobacco growing in all the three regions of the country.

Regional sentiments existed during Banda's rule. The Central region, Banda's home, was the most favored in the distribution of public resources. Several of the largest infrastructural projects and the upgrading of major roads took place there.

During the post-Banda multi-party era, regionalism has strongly impacted political competition. Voting for presidential candidates followed regional lines in the elections of 1994, 1999, and 2004. On the basis of anecdotal evidence, appointments to positions in the civil service and parastatals have gone mainly to politicians from the Southern region, the home of the head of state in the first ten years of multi-partyism.

The post-Banda era has witnessed an increasingly unproductive use of public resources; there have been some well-publicized major cases of corruption involving high-ranking public servants. In several recent fiscal years, publicly targeted spending has resulted in large budget deficits.

Bureaucrats

With the approach of independence, civil servants had high hopes for better remuneration. These were, however, dashed by Banda's adoption of the harsh recommendations of a report prepared by a Briton, Thomas Skinner. The report proposed a set of fiscal measures which effectively reduced net take-home pay of many African civil servants, whose salaries were to remain lower than those of expatriates doing the same job. Civil servants also resented Banda's policy of slow Africanization, and his banning of public sector unions.

In spite of these measures, civil servants had considerable influence on policies. Even in the multi-party era, many of the government budget documents they prepared were passed on to parliament after only brief debate by politicians.

Expatriates

What influence, if any, European expatriates had on Banda's policy choices is not clearly known. What is clearly known is that Banda trusted them more than he trusted his fellow Africans.

Donors

Because of his pro-capitalist and anti-communist stance, Banda was welcomed in the international financial community. From the early 1980s and the era of adjustment, the donor community, especially the IMF and the World Bank, worked closely with the government of Malawi. They have had considerable influence on government policy choices, both macro- and sectoral.

Among the areas of particular interest to donors have been human rights, good governance, and transparency. They have even provided grants to non-government organizations (NGOs) and other civil society organizations dealing with these issues. Donor groups thus serve as agencies of restraint on political leadership, as well as agents of political change.

Private enterprises

Established in the early days of colonial rule, the MCCI has continued to represent the economic/business interests of the private enterprise sector. During a good part of Banda's rule, the MCCI continued to be dominated by whites, but it posed no political threat, as whites were a minority and the country had adopted a one-party system of government, and the MCCI's influence on policy choices was marginal during Banda's rule.

The end of single-party rule reinvigorated the MCCI, now called the Malawi Confederation of Chambers of Commerce and Industry (MCCCI). It has become openly more critical of unsound macro- and sectoral economic policies, and in recent years, its proposals appear to have more noticeably influenced government policy.

5. Conclusion

Malawi's growth record has seen two episodes: one characterized by a high average rate of growth of real GDP per worker from 1960 to 1979, followed by another with a low average rate of growth of real GDP per worker between 1980 and 2000. Despite being low-opportunity, landlocked, and resource-scarce, Malawi achieved a high rate of economic growth from 1960 to 1979 because the government took advantage of opportunities created by changes in neighboring countries and made choices that induced high levels of invest-ment. The benefits of growth were unequally distributed, however, and no conscious attempt was made to reduce dualism in agriculture and other sec-tors of the economy, or to increase investment in education and other social services. As revealed by the reversals in the early 1980s, it proved difficult to maintain a high growth rate, as a low rate of domestic savings rendered the economy dependent on external financial resources.

During the whole 1960–2000 period, the average rate of growth of real GDP per worker in Malawi equaled the average rate of growth of real GDP per worker for all countries included in the Collins–Bosworth (1996) study. In fact, it was far higher than that of either SSA or Latin America and the Caribbean. The average physical capital per worker contributed more to the average rate of growth of real GDP per worker than either education per worker or the TFP residual. The contribution of physical capital exceeded that of all countries and all regions in the Collins–Bosworth sample, except East Asia and the Pacific. The average rate of growth of real GDP per worker should have been higher, but for the low average contribution of educa-tion per worker and the negative TFP residual. The average contribution of education per worker was lower than that of all countries and regions included in the Collins–Bosworth study (1996), including SSA, as was the contribution of the TFP residual.

Appendix

Growth accounting

Tables 5.1 and 5.2 show growth-accounting decompositions for Malawi using data supplied by Susan Collins and Barry Bosworth (Collins and Bosworth 1996; see Ndulu and O'Connell 2003 for details). The underlying framework is a Cobb–Douglas aggregate production function of the form

$Y = AK^{0.35}(h \cdot L)^{0.65}$, where K and $h \cdot L$ are physical capital and effective labor input and h is an index of human capital per worker (measured by imputing a 7 percent return to years of schooling), respectively. In per-worker terms, $y = Ak^{0.35}h^{0.65}$, where $y \equiv Y/L$ and $k \equiv K/L$. The level of TFP, A, is unobservable; its contribution to growth is calculated as a residual. Taking logs, the growth in real GDP per worker (*growth*) can be expressed in terms of the contributions of physical capital per worker (*kcontrib*), human capital per worker (*hcontrib*), and the residual (*tfpg*):

$$\ln y(t) - \ln y(t - 1) = [\ln A(t) - \ln A(t - 1)]$$
$$+ 0.35^*[\ln k(t) - \ln k(t - 1)]$$
$$+ 0.65^*[\ln h(t) - \ln h(t - 1)]$$
$$growth(t) = tpfg + kcontrib + hcontrib.$$

Regression-based decomposition

Ndulu and O'Connell (2000) estimate panel growth regressions of the form

$$growth_{it} = \ln y_{it} - \ln y_{i,t-1} = -\alpha \cdot \ln y_{i,t-1} + x_{it}\beta + z_{it}\gamma + \varepsilon_{it},$$

where i and t index countries and years and x and z are vectors of time-varying and time-invariant growth determinants. In table 5.6 we decompose the period-by-period deviation between Malawi's five-year average growth and the sample average growth for all eighty-five countries into the contributions of (groups of) right-hand-side variables and the residual. The contribution of each variable to the predicted deviation of $growth_{it}$ from its sample mean is given by the deviation of Malawi's value from the sample mean, multiplied by the relevant regression coefficient. As indicated in table 5.6, the global regression tended to under-state Malawi's actual growth performance; predicted growth was below actual growth except during the 1980–4 half-decade.

References

Barro, R. and J. W. Lee (1993), "International Comparisons of Educational Attainment," *Journal of Monetary Economics* 32(3): 363–94

Chipeta, C. and M. L. C. Mkandawire (1991), "The Informal Financial Sector and Macroeconomic Adjustment in Malawi." Nairobi: African Economic Research Consortium

Collins, S. M. and B. P. Bosworth (1996), "Economic Growth in East Asia: Accumulation versus Assimilation," *Brookings Papers on Economic Activity* 2: 135–203

Kaunda, Jonathan Mayuyuka (2002), *The Developmental Role of the Bureaucracy in a Centralised State: Policy and Administration during the One-party Era in Malawi*. Gaborone: Bay Publishing

Kydd, J. G. and R. E. Christiansen (1981), "Trends in the Distribution of Income in Malawi since Independence," Working Paper 2, African Economic Research Consortium, Nairobi

Malawi Government (1971), *Statement of Development Policies 1971–80*. Zomba: Government Printer

(1983), *International Conference of Partners in Economic Development: Past Performance and Prospects for 1983–1987, Volume I*. Lilongwe: Ministry of Finance

(1987), *Statement of Development Policies 1987–1996*. Lilongwe: Office of the President and Cabinet, Department of Economic Planning and Development

Mhone, Guy C. Z. (1992), "The Political Economy of Malawi: An Overview," in Guy C. Z. Mhone, ed., *Malawi at the Crossroads: The Post-colonial Political Economy*. Harare: SAPES Books: 1–33

Ndulu, B. J. and S. A. O'Connell (2000), "Background Information on Economic Growth," Background paper for the Explaining African Growth Project. Nairobi: African Economic Research Consortium (downloadable: www.aercafrica.org)

(2003), "Revised Collins–Bosworth Growth Accounting Decompositions," Background paper prepared for the Explaining African Growth Project. Nairobi: African Economic Research Consortium (downloadable: www.aercafrica.org)

Pelser, E., P. Burton, and L. Gondwe (2004), *Crimes of Need – Results of the Malawi National Crime Victimisation Survey*. Zomba: National Statistical Office

Pryor, F. L. (1990), *The Political Economy of Poverty, Equity and Growth: Malawi and Madagascar*. New York: Oxford University Press

Sahn, D., ed. (1996), *Economic Reform and the Poor in Africa*. Oxford: Oxford University Press

World Bank (1985), *Malawi Economic Recovery: Resources and Policy Needs: An Economic Memorandum*. Washington, DC: The World Bank

(1989), *World Development Report*. New York: Oxford University Press

(2004), *Malawi Country Economic Memorandum Policies for Accelerating Economic Growth*. Washington, DC: The World Bank

6 | Climate vulnerability, political instability, investment, and growth in a landlocked, Sahelian economy: Niger, 1960–2000

Ousmane Samba Mamadou and Mahaman Sani Yakoubou

1. Introduction

Niger is a landlocked, Sahelian,[1] and resource-scarce economy, where growth dynamics have been constrained by two kinds of instability over the last four decades: climate instability and political instability.

Seventy-five percent of Niger's population, estimated at around 11 million with an annual growth rate of 3.3 percent, live in rural areas. Niger

---

[1] A semi-arid, north central African country located south of the Saharan desert.

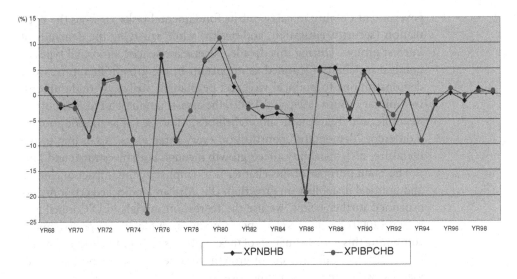

Figure 6.1 Niger, growth rates of GDP (XPNBHB) and GNP *per capita* (XPIBPCHB), 1968–1999

is among the poorest countries in the world based on the percent of the population living on less than 1 dollar *per capita* per day. Over 15 percent of the population is younger than fifteen years old, and women represent 50.3 percent of the population. Density averages 7.26 habitants/km^2 and varies from 80 habitants/km^2 (in the South) to 0.4 habitant/km^2 (in the Northern part of the country).

The performance of Niger's economy has been volatile since the 1960s, with only ten years of positive growth and four years of near zero growth (see figure 6.1). Due to the dominance of the agricultural sector, the years of negative growth rates generally coincided with the occurrence of droughts. The economic performance of the country is thus very dependent upon rainfall availability.

During the period 1960–89, climate instability represented the main constraint upon growth performance, while the political environment was relatively stable. Governments avoided political instability through "soft controls" of prices and redistribution policies designed to appease various vocal groups. For example, the government provided free education to students, guaranteed employment to all educated people, and created alliances with traditional chiefs by appointing their educated relatives to the highest posts in the civil service. These redistribution policies were supported first by groundnut revenues (1960–73) and then by the uranium boom (1974–89). However, both the groundnut and the uranium booms ultimately proved unsustainable.

In the 1990s, political instability became the main constraint on economic growth in Niger. The end of the uranium boom considerably reduced the government's ability to carry out its fundamental tasks *vis-à-vis* the population (security, education, and health) while satisfying the demands of interest groups. During this decade, Niger experienced almost all types of political instability identified as important in the growth literature, from demonstrations to political violence: permanent strikes by trade unions, two military coups (1996 and 1999), the assassination of a President of the Republic, and Tuareg and Tubu rebellions. All these led to the adoption of a different "democratic" constitution every three years. According to the literature, such instability affects growth through both investment and TFP.

The main purpose of this chapter is to emphasize the impact of climate and political instability on growth in this African landlocked economy. As explained further below, we use the regression models in O'Connell and Ndulu (2000) to place Niger's performance in a global perspective and – combining this with an analysis of the country's social and political history – to identify the main drivers of growth on a period-by-period basis.[2] We identify two main policy regimes over the 1960–2000 period:

- **1960–89**: a period characterized by "soft controls" and government intervention in all areas of the formal economy (through development planning systems, increasing public expenditures, and price controls). The country experienced two non-democratic but relatively stable political regimes; a one-party system, the *Parti Progressiste Nigérien – Rassemblement Démocratique Africain* (Nigerian Progressive Party/African Democratic Rally, PPN/RDA) from 1960 to 1974, under the presidency of Hamani Diori, and a military regime as of April 1974, led by Colonel Seyni Kountché. Each political regime benefited from the presence of a major export product – respectively, groundnuts and uranium – to finance its economic and social interventions and avoid political instability. Climatic rather than political instability was thus the most important constraint on growth during this period;
- **1990s**: a politically unstable period characterized by the weakness of the state and the failure of both the democratization process and economic reforms. Unlike the first period, the absence of any major export product undermined the ability of the government to conduct its redistribution policies. Confronted by financial constraints, the government had

[2] A parsimonious model (the augmented Solow model) emphasizes physical and human capital as the main drivers of economic growth. This model, taken from Hoeffler (2002), treats technological progress as exogenous and does not take the effects of policy variables on growth into account. Ndulu and O'Connell develop an extended model that takes a wider range of factors including political and other exogenous factors into account. This model extends the Hoeffler model by taking the role of the institutional and political environment, external shocks (in terms of trade and for trading partners), geographic position, demography (of which age dependency and ethnic diversity), and economic policy variables into account.

to reduce its expenditures on security, education, and health, and to liberalize certain sectors. However, all the reform initiatives were opposed by interest groups such as trade unions and civil society. As a result, the period witnessed turmoil, a National Conference, rebellions in the North, two *coups d'état*, the assassination of a President, and adoption of three Constitutions (in 1993, 1996, and 1999).

These changes in policy regime had consequences for Niger's economic performance. In sections 2 and 3 we analyze the determinants of the country's economic growth over the two periods, combining model-related data with extra-model information. In these sections we stress the supply-side determinants of growth. Section 4, devoted to the structural composition of growth in Niger, analyzes the drivers of growth from the demand side by focusing on the tradable sectors (agriculture and industry). This section is based on an approach developed by Chenery and Syrquin (1985). The final section 5 presents some basic conclusions.

2. Climate instability, commodity booms, and growth, 1960–1989

Three main features characterized Niger's economy at its independence:

- The rural sector dominated the economy, with groundnuts as a main engine of growth
- Modern activities were dominated by the public sector, with the government substituting for what it perceived as a lack of private entrepreneurship in all major categories of economic activity
- The economy was highly dependent on external trade, in terms of both imported manufactured products and of export revenues from groundnuts.

During the 1960–89 period, the main characteristics of Niger's economy were extreme vulnerability due to the predominance of the rural sector in an arid, Sahelian context, and strong dependence upon uranium exports for foreign exchange, in the context of declining demand and prices for uranium in world markets.

On the political level, the episode from 1960 to 1989 was a non-democratic period ruled by a single-party regime from 1960 to 1974 and then by a military regime from 1974 to 1989. It was, nonetheless, a relatively stable period, with very few socio-political troubles. A marked feature of the entire period was the dominance of the public sector in economic activity and the strongly redistributionist role of economic policy. The uranium boom resulted in unsustainable economic growth due, in part, to the "Dutch disease" phenomenon, which undermined the competitiveness of the tradable sector.

Table 6.1 *Niger, regression-based growth decomposition, augmented Solow model, 1960–1989*

Variables	1960–4	1965–9	1970–4	1975–9	1980–4	1985–9
Log (Initial real GDP *per capita*)	6.28	6.46	6.69	6.39	6.58	6.33
Investment/GDP	9.20	7.65	9.27	11.38	8.13	6.04
Replacement investment	−2.54	−2.65	−2.59	− 2.50	−2.47	−2.51
Average years of schooling	0.28	0.27	0.30	0.46	0.55	0.67
Dummy (1965–9)	0.00	1.00	0.00	0.00	0.00	0.00
Dummy (1970–4)	0.00	0.00	1.00	0.00	0.00	0.00
Dummy (1975–9)	0.00	0.00	0.00	1.00	0.00	0.00
Dummy (1980–4)	0.00	0.00	0.00	0.00	1.00	0.00
Dummy (1985–9)	0.00	0.00	0.00	0.00	0.00	1.00
Intercept	1.00	1.00	1.00	1.00	1.00	1.00
Actual growth	**2.12**	**−2.45**	**−3.44**	**2.11**	**−7.43**	**1.19**
Predicted growth	**2.06**	**2.38**	**2.84**	**2.07**	**1.56**	**1.47**
Residual, of which:	0.06	−4.83	−6.28	0.04	−9.00	−0.28
– *country average*	−3.36	−3.36	−3.36	− 3.36	−3.36	−3.36
– *period deviation*	−3.45	1.46	2.84	− 3.40	5.63	−3.08

Source: O'Connell and Ndulu (2000).
Note: The table shows the values of explanatory variables on a period-by-period basis. Predicted growth is calculated using coefficients estimated by Hoeffler (2002) and reported in O'Connell and Ndulu (2000), table 4.1, column (3). Investment/GDP is measured using 1985 international prices. The replacement investment term is measured as $\ln(0.05 + n)$, where n is the growth rate of the population. Years of schooling pertain to the population greater than fifteen years of age.

2.1 Accounting for Niger's real GDP per capita growth, 1960–1989

Tables 6.1 and 6.2 show Niger's evolution over time using the growth determinants employed by Hoeffler (2002) and O'Connell and Ndulu (2000). In the bottom panel of each table we compare the fitted and actual growth rates, using the regression coefficients reported in O'Connell and Ndulu (2000). We divide the 1960–89 period into six sub-periods in order to isolate the drought years (1965–9; 1970–4; 1980–4), the boom periods (1960–4; 1975–9), and the structural adjustment period (1985–9).

The results in tables 6.1 and 6.2 provoke the following remarks:

- For the sub-periods corresponding to groundnut (1960–4) and uranium (1975–9) booms, both models predict the positive average growth rates of real GDP *per capita* reasonably well. However, the augmented Solow model (Hoeffler's 2002 model) seems to replicate the actual growth rates of Niger's economy better, with residuals closer to zero. The extended model consistently under-predicts growth in Niger.
- A similar result holds for the structural adjustment sub-period (1985–9), during which both models correctly predict the positive average growth;

Table 6.2 *Niger, regression-based growth accounting, extended model, 1960–1989*

Variable	1960–4	1965–9	1970–4	1975–9	1980–4	1985–9
Log (Initial real GDP *per capita*)	6.277	6.463	6.691	6.390	6.575	6.326
Initial life expectancy in years	35.960	36.735	38.410	39.760	41.680	43.460
Age dependency ratio	91.042	93.340	94.175	95.371	96.898	98.826
Growth of potential labor force participation	−0.248	−0.088	−0.126	−0.161	−0.201	−0.188
Cumulative income effect of terms of trade, % GDP	0.246	−0.882	1.355	3.677	−0.931	2.031
Trading partners' growth rate	3.453	3.348	4.212	2.036	−0.320	2.724
Landlocked status	1.000	1.000	1.000	1.000	1.000	1.000
Political instability	0.067	0.000	0.000	0.067	0.067	0.000
CPI inflation	1.078	4.620	6.050	14.652	10.146	−3.008
Black market premium	4.995	9.089	0.194	3.264	2.542	1.922
Barro–Lee measure of govt. consumption, % of GDP	19.866	15.872	14.738	16.948	13.758	15.142
Dummy (1965–9)	0.000	1.000	0.000	0.000	0.000	0.000
Dummy (1970–4)	0.000	0.000	1.000	0.000	0.000	0.000
Dummy (1975–9)	0.000	0.000	0.000	1.000	0.000	0.000
Dummy (1980–4)	0.000	0.000	0.000	0.000	1.000	0.000
Dummy (1985–9)	0.000	0.000	0.000	0.000	0.000	1.000
Intercept	1.000	1.000	1.000	1.000	1.000	1.000
Actual growth	**2.121**	**−2.447**	**−3.435**	**2.110**	**−7.432**	**1.192**
Predicted growth	**1.183**	**0.859**	**1.770**	**0.394**	**−1.703**	**0.691**
Residual, of which:	0,939	−3,307	−5,205	1,716	−5,729	0,500
– country average	−1,900	−1,900	−1,900	−1,900	−1,900	−1,900
– period deviation	−2,839	1,407	3,305	−3,616	3,829	−2,401

Source: O'Connell and Ndulu (2000) and authors' calculations.

Note: The table shows the values of explanatory variables on a period-by-period basis. Predicted growth is calculated using using the coefficients of the pooled full specification estimated by O'Connell and Ndulu (2000), table 5.1.1, column (1). Growth of potential labor force is the difference between the growth of the population of working age and the growth of total population. Political instability is measured by the sum of strikes, revolutions, and assassinations, divided by 3. CPI inflation and the black market premium are truncated at 500 percent, so that observations above this threshold are excluded. For other variables, see O'Connell and Ndulu (2000).

again the augmented Solow model shows a somewhat lower residual in absolute terms.
- For the boom and structural adjustment sub-periods (1960–4; 1975–9; 1985–9), the fact that the augmented Solow model appears to fit better implies that investment (excluded from the extended model) is an important driver of growth. In fact, the young government decided to base its

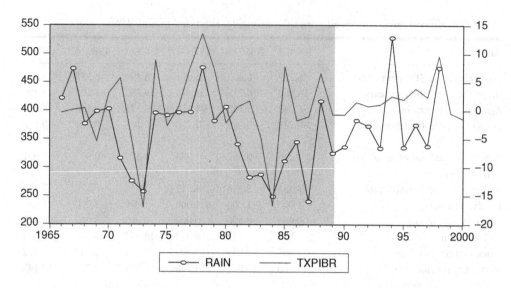

Figure 6.2 Niger, real growth rate of GDP and rainfall level, 1966–2000

development strategy on a system of planning, and to enhance its role in the process of development of the modern sector.

• During the drought sub-periods (1965–9; 1970–4; 1980–4), actual growth rates were negative, but both models predict positive growth rates. The substantial negative residuals may reflect the impact of the extreme vulnerability of Niger's economy to rainfall instability, since neither model includes this variable. Figure 6.2 displays a strong correlation between real growth rates and the average level of rainfall in Niger.[3]

2.2   A Sahelian rural economy subject to climate instability

By 1960, around 95 percent of Niger's population lived in rural areas and earned income from rural activities (DSD 1991). Despite the rapid urbanization of the country, with urban population growing from 5.2 percent in 1960 to 10 percent in 1970 and 12.4 percent in 1975, the rural basis of Niger's economy remains significant.

2.2.1   Characteristics of Niger's rural sector

Rural activities are composed mainly of agriculture and livestock. Sedentary people specialize in agricultural production in the southern regions of the country, while livestock are mainly raised by nomadic people.

---

[3] It is worth noting that the 1980–4 sub-period also corresponds to the financial crisis period that followed the uranium boom.

As with all Sahelian countries, Niger is subject to great climate instabilities, with a rainy season that lasts only three–four months (June–September) in good years. A large part of the country receives less than 300 mm of rainfall per year. Niger's agriculture is rainfed and production conditions differ greatly from the South to the North. Production is concentrated on a thin part of national territory: the extent of potentially arable land is estimated at less than 12 percent of the total area of Niger. In addition to this lack of arable land, an inadequate overall rainfall and rainfall irregularity seriously affect both crop performance and overall economic performance.

Rural households use rudimentary techniques of production, with the majority of peasants relying on fallow and manuring. Archaic techniques of production, poor use of fertilizer, and inadequate seeds exacerbate the negative effects of droughts on the agricultural sector. The agriculture sector's share in GDP fell from 49 percent in 1975 to 41 percent by 1981, and stabilized at around 36 percent in 1984. Agriculture, nonetheless, continues to provide employment to some 85 percent of the active population.

Recurring droughts, continuing drops in cash crop prices (in particular for groundnuts), and food insecurity led farmers to rely increasingly on the production of staple foods. Areas devoted to cereals – in particular, millet and sorghum – increased significantly after the 1984 drought, and the share of these cereals in Niger's agricultural production increased to more than 80 percent.

Livestock represents the second source of export earnings (after uranium), and accounts for about 15 percent of Niger's GDP. The 1973 and 1984 droughts seriously affected Niger's livestock; indeed, cattle, sheep, and goats had hardly recovered to their 1972 levels when the 1984 drought further devastated the herd size. The slow recovery of Niger's livestock sector after 1984 may reflect the impact of recurrent severe droughts on long-established patterns of agricultural subsistence.

2.2.2   The impact of instability on growth

First, because of the recurrent droughts, some of the traditionally nomadic herdsmen adopted sedentary patterns, while those that continued to breed and move livestock were obliged to substitute big ruminants (such as cattle) for small ruminants (such as goats). Second, because of continuous lack in rainfall, nomadic herders who chose to continue breeding big ruminants were obliged to migrate southwards into Nigeria, Cameroon, Côte d'Ivoire, and other countries where pasture was available. Some would return to Niger during the rainy seasons and descend again to the south when pasture availability was reduced.

The impact of instability on growth has long been studied in the literature (Guillaumont 1987; Gymah-Brempong 1991; Fosu 1992; Combes 1993). Climatic shocks are among what Guillaumont, Guillaumont, and

Brun (1999) call "primary" sources of instability because of their structural, rather than political, nature. Using cross-section econometric models on a sample of African and non-African countries and two pooled decades, they found that this kind of instability affects growth more through the TFP channel than through investment. Climatic instability may therefore be considered one of the most important determinants of the weak performance of Niger's economy between 1960 and 1989. During this period, the country experienced its most important drought episodes, while its economy was dominated by the rural sector. In figure 6.2, the positive correlation between real growth rates and rainfall in Niger, is particularly notable during the 1960–89 period.

2.3   Commodity booms, controls, and unsustainable growth, 1960–1989

2.3.1   The groundnut boom and "soft controls," 1960–1974

We indicated earlier that investment was an important driver of growth in Niger during the boom periods. However, during the colonial period no local private entrepreneur actually emerged with the financial capacity and intellectual ability to take advantage of opportunities in the newly independent country and expand the modern sector. So the government had to intervene heavily in the economy within the framework of a five-year development planning strategy. The objective was to make up for the lack of private entrepreneurship and contribute to the creation of a diversified, modern sector through public enterprises.

Public enterprises were created in various sectors, from traditional public service activities (electricity, communication, etc.) to more competitive sectors that could be left to private investors. Most public enterprises held a monopoly in their respective activities. Until 1970, revenues from the groundnut sector (around 70 percent of exports) facilitated the development of the public sector in commerce and other related modern activities. The importance of groundnuts in Niger's development strategy had been emphasized since 1962, when the government created a company called SONARA. This public enterprise was given a monopoly in the export of groundnuts, with the official justification that revenues raised should be used to support infrastructure programs and make up for the lack of private enterprise.

As of 1975, uranium supplanted groundnuts as the major export product. The military regime continued its previous policy strategy of using uranium revenues to undertake massive public investment expenditures in the modern sector and in infrastructure. As part of development strategy, both the civilian (PPN–RDA) and the military regimes adopted a system of administrative prices for all goods. An administrative structure was created to fix the price of each good and to monitor private sector's activities with the "Direction des contrôles des prix."

2.3.2 The uranium boom, investment, and unsustained growth, 1975–1989

In analyzing the impact of the uranium boom, Azam (1999) distinguishes one windfall component associated with unexpectedly high prices and another associated with the corresponding supply response. Both components were large in Niger's uranium boom. Following the sharp increase in global uranium demand in the late 1970s, the world market price quadrupled while the bilateral rate agreed between France and Niger tripled, from CFA franc 8,000 per kg in 1975 to CFA franc 24,000 in 1980. Thus, both the price and the quantity of Niger's uranium exports sharply increased during the boom.

In 1975–80, following a substantial increase in revenues from the uranium sector and good rainy seasons, Niger's economy experienced an unprecedented prosperity. Real GDP grew at nearly 6 percent for the period. With the share of the mining sector more than doubling between 1975 and 1979 (from 5.9 percent to 14 percent), a construction and public works boom took place (Azam 1992): the share of construction and public works in GDP doubled from 3 to 6 percent between 1975 and 1988.

Perceiving uranium as a sustainable source of export revenue, the government launched ambitious investment and expenditure programs, with heavy recourse to external borrowing. Despite its positive nature, however, the uranium boom did not pave the way for long-term growth. As discussed below, most of the investments undertaken appeared to be inefficient. Moreover, as predicted by the "Dutch Disease" arguments, the boom resulted in the contraction of non-uranium tradable sectors – agriculture and manufactures – and in the expansion of non-tradable activities. This boom in aggregate spending boosted Niger's inflation above the inflation rates of its major trading partners, so that from 1975 to 1978 the effective real exchange rate appreciated by an average of 7.1 percent per year.[4] By late 1980, Niger's domestic performance and external competitiveness were so weak that adjustment measures became unavoidable. When the uranium boom suddenly ended in the early 1980s, the economy experienced a deep and long-lasting financial crisis. As a result of this crisis, private investment fell sharply, with clear consequences for growth (see figure 6.3).[5]

The fact that the uranium boom did not result in a sustained increase in private investment is evidence of the unsustainable spending growth

---

[4] In real terms, total exports decreased on average by about 8.6 percent per annum during the period 1980–4 and by 4.4 percent from 1985 to 1989 (see DSD 1991). The rates of growth of handicraft exports were −2.4 percent and −7.1 percent, respectively.

[5] The private sector demand for labor also reduced during the period, as shown in figure 6.7.

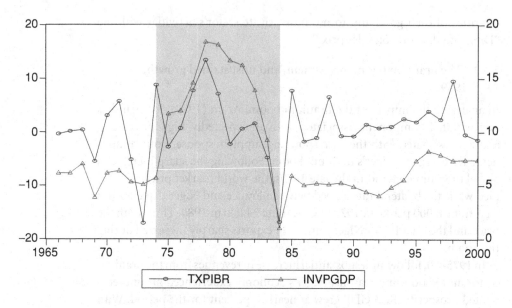

Figure 6.3 Niger, real GDP growth and ratio of private investment:GDP, 1966–2000

syndrome. The inefficiency of the investment – in particular, public investment – during the period also points to this syndrome. In figure 6.4, we use
a simple definition of the marginal efficiency of investment to show that the
productivity of investment was very weak (near zero) during the uranium
boom.[6]

2.4   Socio-political stability and growth in Niger: the role of redistribution

2.4.1   The PPN–RDA's system, 1960–1974

After its independence, Niger was ruled by a one-party regime. To consolidate the power of the PPN–RDA as the sole political party, the government subsidized the population through free schooling, free health care,
and price controls to preserve people's purchasing power. These subsidies
mainly benefited the urban population. Moreover, the political leaders developed alliances with the traditional chiefs in rural areas by nominating their
sons and relatives for high posts within the civil service or in parliament.
These "elites" would redistribute part of their income to their kin groups
or direct public investment to their regions. This policy illustrates the "triangular predation game" described by Azam (2002), which emphasizes the
role of resource distribution among ethno-regional groups in maintaining

---

[6] We define the marginal efficiency as $(Y_t - Y_{t-1})/I_{t-1}$ where Y is GDP and I is investment.

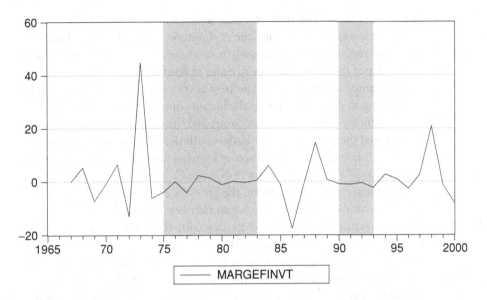

Figure 6.4 Niger, marginal efficiency of capital, $[100*(Y_t - Y_{t-1})/I_{t-1}]$, 1966–2000

peace, increasing popular support, and buying the loyalties of the dominant classes in the regions. The system linked the chiefs, their relatives, and the government in a way that ensured social stability. Only one trade union was authorized, and its leaders were linked to the party and the government. To complement these policies, employment was guaranteed for all educated people.

These devices, among others, allowed Hamani Diori's government to remain in power for fifteen years (1960–74). However, in the mid-1970s, a persistent decline in real GDP due to recurrent droughts and problems in the groundnut sector created distress among rural and urban people, while limiting the ability of the government to pursue its redistribution policy. Corruption developed as the political elites had to redistribute money in their regions in order to buy the support of their ethnic group and reinforce their regional power. Corruption also developed within the government and among political leaders, because neither a political opposition nor an effective civil society existed to criticize such behavior. The only structure that criticized the government was the students' trade union. In April 1974, following the drought and its social impacts, the PPN–RDA regime became unpopular and a military council took power.

2.4.2   Military government, 1974–1989

Good luck greeted the military regime, in the form of a uranium boom. Taking advantage of the substantial increase in international prices, the new government renegotiated its contract with French partners and extended its productive capacity through the exploitation of new deposits. Though a repressive regime, the military used its revenues to continue the redistribution policy of the former regime in order to reinforce the image of the army and guarantee social stability. The new government went even further, by suspending all direct taxation of the income of rural households.

The military government also controlled the civil servants' trade union and favored the election of new leaders with ties to the military. These new leaders galvanized workers into voting for what was then called "responsible participation" ("*la participation responsable*") in the development efforts of the military regime. In return, the government increased civil servants' salaries by at least 10 percent each year between 1975 and 1980.

The government maintained its ties with traditional chiefs and their relatives. However, in contrast with Diori's regime, the new government announced a set of anti-corruption objectives and followed this by reinforcing legal sanctions against corruption. In 1985, for example, the government announced that any embezzlement of more than CFAF 200 million would result in capital punishment.

Rent-seeking behavior by military officers was nonetheless widespread during the uranium boom. The income of military officers increased substantially through both official and unofficial means; as an example of the latter, officers regularly received unofficial bonuses directly from the President's office. It became gradually clear that the army would never leave power. Official speeches made it clear that military officers would participate in the management of public affairs: it was publicly declared that they had the right to participate in the political life of the country and to serve in political organs in collaboration with civilians, most of whom represented their regions through connections with traditional chiefs. The former "Conseil Militaire Supreme" (CMS), constituted exclusively of army officers, was replaced by a "Conseil Supérieur d'Orientation Nationale" (CSON), to include civilians, but its continued domination by the military was clear.

In June 1987, the "Charte Nationale" was adopted as the first step in creating a single-party system linked to the army. In October 1987, President Kountché died of cancer. His successor, General Ali Saibou, confirmed the role of the army in political management and continued the process of putting a single-party regime into place. In September 1989, a referendum was organized to adopt the Constitution of the Second Republic, and three months later Ali Saibou was officially elected as the first President of the Second Republic. General Saibou presided over a single-party regime, the *Mouvement National pour la Société de Développement-Nassara* (MNSD-Nassara).

From 1960 to 1989, Niger experienced two non-democratic regimes, each of which lasted roughly fifteen years (1960–74 and 1974–89, respectively).

Until the death of President Kountché in 1987, both could be characterized as "strong" regimes following Rodrik's classification (Rodrik 1992; see discussion below). Both governments increased public expenditures on social sectors in order to avoid social crisis in the country. In each case, the credibility of the public spending program and of the regime itself was reinforced by revenue from a major export product – groundnuts during the first regime and uranium during the second.

Although growth rates were positive during the commodity booms, the uranium boom did not pave the way for sustained and diversified growth. Real appreciation undermined the competitiveness of the traded goods sectors – the "Dutch disease" – and led to a decline in private investment from 1978 to 1989. The country remained vulnerable to climate instability and so suffered severely from recurrent droughts during the 1960–89 period.

3. Political instability, devaluation, and growth, 1990–2000

Democracy is often cited as a contributor to social stability. Based on a global sample, however, Collier and Hoeffler (1999) find a non-linear relationship between democracy and the risk of civil war: the risk of civil war is highest when the democratic process is at an intermediate level. In Niger, the 1990s were dominated by the fluid and highly uncertain democratic process that got underway in the aftermath of a national conference in 1991. During the 1990s, Niger's real GDP *per capita* showed very low and often negative growth rates. The devaluation of the CFA franc in 1994 appears to have had little impact on growth, which displayed considerably lower volatility than during the 1960–89 period, but nonetheless hovered around zero from 1995 to 1999 (figure 6.2, p. 172). Yet, unlike the earlier period, rainfall levels remained near or above their long-run averages after 1990 (figure 6.2). In this section we argue that Niger's economic under-performance during the 1990s must be linked to the political instability that characterized this decade.

3.1   Accounting for Niger's real GDP per capita growth, 1990s

We divide the 1990s into two sub-periods. The first (1990–3) is a period of political transition following the National Conference. The second, as of 1994, witnessed the CFA franc devaluation (decided in January 1994) and the beginning of the democratic process. Both periods are characterized by frequent turmoil, social unrest, and political trouble.

Proceeding as we did earlier, the regression-based decompositions in tables 6.3 and 6.4 suggest the following observations:

Table **6.3** *Niger, growth accounting, augmented Solow model, 1990–1997*

Variable	1990–3	1994–7	1990–7
Log (Initial real GDP *per capita*)	6.18	6.06	6.18
Investment/GDP	4.62	6.51	5.56
Replacement Investment	−2.48	−2.48	−2.48
Average years of schooling	0.82	0.82	0.82
Dummy (1965–9)	0.00	0.00	0.00
Dummy (1970–4)	0.00	0.00	0.00
Dummy (1975–9)	0.00	0.00	0.00
Dummy (1980–4)	0.00	0.00	0.00
Dummy (1985–9)	0.00	0.00	0.00
Intercept	1.00	1.00	1.00
Actual growth	**−4.75**	**−1.08**	**−2.10**
Predicted growth	**1.26**	**1.75**	**1.50**
Residual, of which:	**−6.01**	**−2.83**	**−3.59**
– country average	−3.52	−3.52	−3.52
– period deviation	2.48	−0.69	0.07

Notes: See notes to Table 6.1.

- Unlike 1960–89, the augmented Solow model does poorly during the 1990s, consistently predicting positive growth rates while actual rates are negative. This over-prediction may reflect the impact of political instability during the first half of the 1990s. It may also reflect deteriorating standards of governance associated with the arrears on civil servants' salaries. These seriously affected the civil servants' financial capacities, as well as those of domestic formal and informal enterprises. Within the public sector, corruption and absenteeism expanded during the period, and turmoil became endemic.
- The extended model also over-predicts growth in the 1990s, but by a smaller margin; and for the 1990–3 sub-period it correctly predicts outright contraction. During the political transition period (1990–3), the growth rate predicted by this model (−0.43) has the same sign as the actual one (−4.75). This advantage over the augmented Solow model may reflect the inclusion of a political instability variable in the extended model (table 6.4).

3.2   Interest groups and socio-political instability, 1990s

Azam (2001) considers conflicts to be motivated by the failure of a government to carry out its fundamental tasks of security and basic social services (e.g. education and health). In this view, the inability of a government to implement certain categories of public expenditure with a clear

Table 6.4 *Niger, growth accounting, extended model, 1990–1997*

Variable	1990–3	1994–7	1990–7
Log (Initial real GDP *per capita*)	6.180	6.059	6.180
Initial life expectancy in years	45.470	45.470	45.470
Age dependency ratio	101.437	103.541	102.489
Growth of potential labor force participation	−0.269	−0.261	−0.264
Cumulative income effect of the terms of trade, % GDP	1.103	1.103	1.103
Trading partners' growth rate	0.535	2.460	1.498
Landlocked status	1.000	1.000	1.000
Political instability	0.250	0.250	0.250
CPI inflation	−3.578	13.705	5.064
Black market premium	1.922	1.922	1.922
Barro–Lee measure of govt. consumption, % of GDP	16.380	14.329	15.354
Dummy (1965–9)	0.00	0.00	0.00
Dummy (1970–4)	0.00	0.00	0.00
Dummy (1975–9)	0.00	0.00	0.00
Dummy (1980–4)	0.00	0.00	0.00
Dummy (1985–9)	0.00	0.00	0.00
Dummy (1990–7)	1.00	1.00	1.00
Intercept	1.00	1.00	1.00
Actual growth	**−4.746**	**−1.080**	**−2.099**
Predicted growth	**−0.433**	**0.876**	**0.115**
Residual, of which:	−4.313	−1.956	−2.214
– country average	−1.900	−1.900	−1.900
– period deviation	2.412	0.056	0.314

Note: See note to table 6.2.

redistributive content may weaken state authority and increase the risk of social and political conflict. Azam, Berthélemy, and Calipel (1996), using a probit model on a panel data from twenty-one African countries, find that increases in public expenditure on health reduce the risk of political violence. Redistribution and public expenditures are, therefore, among the most important factors in determining social stability in a country. This suggests that, in Niger, the decline in government resources during the 1990s, which limited the government's capacity to undertake expenditures with redistributive content, may have contributed substantially to the increased political instability.

3.2.1 Financial constraints and the decline in state authority, 1990s

During the 1990s, the devices employed by former regimes to achieve political stability were no longer feasible due to government financial constraints.

Table 6.5 *Niger, external trade structure, 1980–1997*

| | Exports of goods | | | |
	Agriculture	Industry	Handicraft	Mine
1980–4	12.6	87.4	6.55	80.83
1985–9	7.9	92.1	7.37	84.77
1990–3	23.3	76.7	10.88	65.82
1994–7	23.4	76.6	24.83	51.78
	Imports of goods			
	Agriculture	Industry	Handicraft	Mine
1980–4	22.7	77.3	62.00	15.32
1985–9	23.8	76.2	67.13	9.06
1990–3	11.8	88.2	81.97	6.24
1994–7	6.9	93.1	83.27	9.81

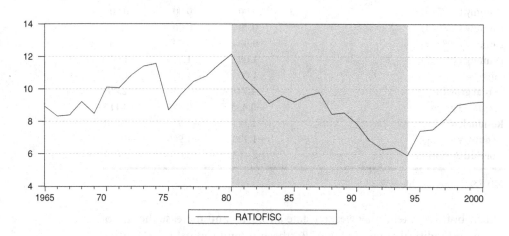

RATIOFISC

Figure 6.5 Niger, ratio of fiscal revenue: GDP, 1965–2000

The share of uranium in total export revenue fell from 85 percent in 1985–9 to 66 percent in 1990–3, and to only 51 percent in 1994–7 (see table 6.5) and, in contrast to 1960–89, the government found no other source of income with which it could buy loyalties and avoid socio-political troubles.

The 1990s was a decade of severe budgetary constraints not only because no other sector emerged as an alternative source of income for the government, but also due to a decrease in conventional fiscal revenues. The ratio of fiscal revenue to GDP fell to 6 percent in 1994, before gradually recovering to 9 percent of GDP by the end of the decade (see figure 6.5).

Tax evasion was a leading cause of the decline in fiscal revenues during the 1990s. Private economic agents – many of whom operated as contractors to the government, constructing roads and schools, supplying imported cars, and the like – evaded tax obligations both by shifting to the informal sector and by bribing public officials. Wealthy entrepreneurs also moved aggressively to acquire political influence, both by financing political parties and by becoming political leaders in their own regions. The participation of private entrepreneurs in parliament illustrates the latter phenomenon. During the period of the First Republic (1960–5), parliament was the domain of the civil service and there was only one private entrepreneur in the national assembly. After the 1993 elections, the number of private entrepreneurs in parliament reached eleven (of eighty-three, or 13 percent), rising further to twenty-six (31 percent) in 1996, and thirty-six (43 percent) in 1999.

As parliamentarians or heads of regional political parties, these new "political entrepreneurs" developed opportunistic alliances within the civil service and the government, using their electoral influence and the fact that high-level civil servants and ministers owed their positions to these entrepreneurs' interventions. The source of redistribution therefore changed during the 1990s, from the government itself to a set of wealthy economic agents who used their incomes – a portion of which continued to be generated by lucrative government contracts – both to evade tax obligations and to buy political support. The resulting lack of fiscal resources, together with the growing corruption of civil servants and the political ambitions of army leaders, considerably limited the authority of the government and its ability to maintain social and political peace in the country.

3.2.2 Failed redistribution, conflict, and rebellion in the North

Due to the government's inability to raise enough resources, Niger experienced almost every type of political instability during the 1990s, ranging from simple demonstrations to political violence. Many demonstrations were instigated by trade unions and political interest groups. Two *coups d'état* took place, in 1996 and 1999, the latter resulting in the assassination of President Ibrahim Bare. In contrast to the previous thirty years, during which only two political regimes had existed, the decade of the 1990s saw three new constitutions promulgated in only six years (1993, 1996, 1999).

Azam (2001, 2002) and Rodrik (1992) make a distinction between strong governments with the credibility and capacity to supply public services, and weak governments that respond to social grievances with repression due to their inability to address these issues. Such behavior increases the risk of political violence. In the early 1990s, military forces repressed some Tuareg families suspected to be connected to what the government then called "armed bandits." The Tuareg, a nomadic ethnic group residing in the northern part of the country where uranium is exploited, rebelled for about five years (1990–5).

Economic grievance[7] seems to have been the principal motivation for the Tuareg rebellion in Niger. Many young, jobless Tuareg had returned to Niger from Libya after being fired by Khadafi's government (Azam 2002). They soon associated the lack of job opportunities in Niger with a failure by former governments to invest the uranium revenues in the northern regions where the mineral was located. Lacking the technical knowledge to compete for jobs in the cities, these young rebels decided to "voice" their discontent using arms and the military experience they had acquired in Libya. The rebellion was led, in turn, by a set of Tuareg intellectuals looking for "better places in the sun." In January 1992, the rebels announced the creation of the "Front de Libération de l'Ar et de l'Azawak." The Tuareg rebellion ended in 1996 as a result of an agreement between the rebels and the government: the government promised to find employment for the rebels in the civil service, army, police, and customs offices, and to appoint rebel leaders to high-level positions in the government.

3.2.3   Social troubles and failed reforms

In addition to the Tuareg rebellion, a large number of strikes took place in the country starting in 1989, particularly in the education sector. Strikes were organized by interest groups (teachers and students) who had lost economic privileges due to the fiscal austerity measures adopted by the government in 1986 as part of its adjustment programs. There were also strikes in the banking sector, where the World Bank called for a complete financial liberalization and the closure of the Development Bank (BDRN) and the Agricultural Bank (CNCA). Both banks belonged to the government, and had been poorly managed due to political interventions. It was clear that the adjustment policies would result in a substantial increase in unemployment. Consequentially, both student and worker trade unions engaged in campaigns against the adjustment programs and the government. In 1989, the government was forced to suspend the SAP it had adopted with the Bretton Woods institutions. Niger entered a period of forced and disorganized adjustment. Figure 6.6 shows that suspension of the program succeeded in preserving employment, at least in the public sector.

---

[7] Unlike other rebellions in African countries with mineral resources, and due to the fact that uranium is not as easily tradable and transportable as gold or diamonds, there was little scope for looting of mineral resources by rebel groups in Niger. However, rebels attacked peasants and other nomads groups (in particular, Arabic ethnic groups) living in or near the northern regions to steal their livestock and other goods.

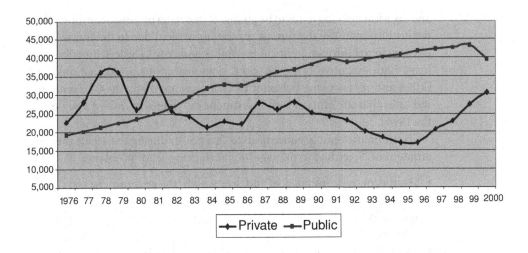

Figure 6.6 Niger, private and public employment, 1976–2000

3.3   Socio-political instability and growth in Niger, 1990s

A large part of the under-performance of Niger's economy during the 1990s can be explained by social conflicts and political instability. A variety of indicators have been used to analyze the impact of political factors on growth, including the number of assassinations, the number of coup and demonstrations, the number of months of war, and the number of years that political leaders spent in office (Nkurunziza and Bates 2003). Nkurunziza and Bates (2003) estimate the impact of political instability on growth in African countries. They extend Hoeffler's (2002) augmented Solow model to include political instability variables; they find that political stability is good for growth, and that the inclusion of these variables reduces the estimated residuals. Social conflicts impose costs to growth by diverting resources from economically productive activities, hampering social co-operation (co-ordination failure), preventing the adoption of mutually beneficial projects, and leading government to delay required adjustments (Rodrik 1999). Rodrik (1999) finds that shocks to terms of trade are more damaging to growth in countries with deep latent social conflicts and poor institutions for conflict management. These countries are more vulnerable to shocks. Niger's experience is strongly consistent with this line of argument: between 1990 and 1993, postponement of the reforms agreed upon with the Bretton Woods institutions led to steep declines in growth rates (see figure 6.1, p. 167).

Weak institutions may also have a direct effect on growth by reducing the efficiency of investment. In an environment where the enforcement of property rights is not reliable, firms tend to be small and labor-intensive, and decision-making tends to be guided by short-term considerations. Weak institutions may also discourage private investment due to the transactions costs incurred through political instability and coup, weak democratic systems, high executive turnover, riots, demonstrations, assassinations, and bribes and rent-seeking behavior of civil servants (Aron 2000). Figure 6.4 indicates that the efficiency of investment in Niger was indeed low during the 1990s.

To summarize our argument up to this point, during the 1990s the government of Niger had to manage an interlocking set of problems:

- Macroeconomic imbalances and tax evasion: the government was unable to collect sufficient tax revenues from politically powerful economic agents, particularly in the face of increasing corruption among tax collectors.
- Social problems: the government had little authority to fight against corruption and absenteeism. Many civil servants justified their behavior by appealing to the outstanding arrears on their own salaries.
- Political instability: the average duration of a government was less than nine months due to frequent shifts in alliances between political parties. One government lasted only four months.

The end of the uranium boom therefore resulted in the abandonment of the redistribution system. This led to social instability and to prolonged conflicts between the government and some key interest groups, particularly trade unions. Even the 1994 devaluation did not put the economy onto a sustainable growth path due to its weak diversification.

3.4 Competitiveness and growth in the 1990s: the CFA franc devaluation

Samba Mamadou, Garba, and Mahaman (2005) and Samba Mamadou et al. (2005), using traditional price and quantity indicators, assess Niger's competitiveness in the 1990s in the agricultural and industrial sectors. Niger's price-competitiveness, as measured by the real exchange rate, declined during the period 1990–3 because domestic inflation exceeded inflation among foreign trading partners. This result holds for the overall real effective exchange rate and separately for the agricultural and the industrial sectors (see figure 6.7). A similar pattern of declining competitiveness holds with respect to Nigeria, Niger's main informal trading partner.

In 1994, the 50 percent CFA franc devaluation restored competitiveness. However, this improvement lasted only four years (from 1994 to 1998) principally due to the following phenomena:

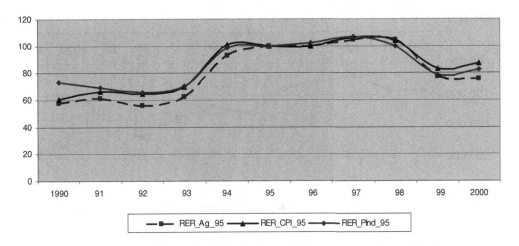

Figure 6.7 Niger, real effective exchange rates, agriculture and industry, global CPI, 1990–2000

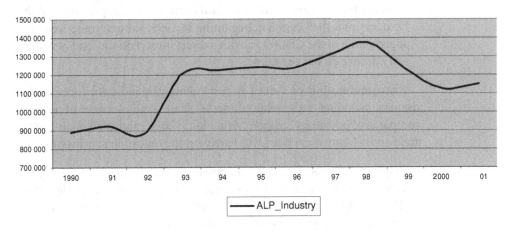

Figure 6.8 Niger, average labor productivity, 1990–2001, constant CFAF

- Productivity decreased significantly during the 1990s. Labor productivity in the industrial sector, for example, declined significantly during the decade (see figure 6.8);
- As part of their commitment to deepen the process of integration within the Economic Community of West African States (ECOWAS), some member states decided in 1999 to create a second monetary zone in West Africa. This obliged member states, in particular Nigeria, to undertake vigorous actions to contain inflation. The inflation differential with Nigeria therefore declined, reducing Niger's competitiveness *vis-à-vis* one of its dominant trading partners;

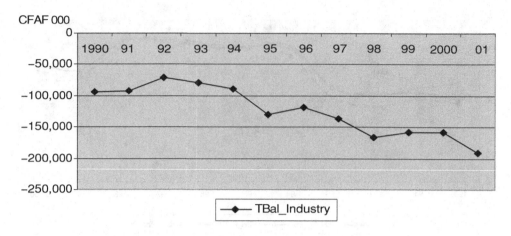

Figure 6.9 Niger, trade balance, manufactured goods, 1990–2001

- 1999 marked a shift in the exchange rate peg for the CFA franc zone, from the French franc to the new Euro currency. The appreciation of the Euro *vis-à-vis* the US dollar, beginning in 1999, led to a trade-weighted appreciation of the CFA franc, with a direct impact on the level of Niger's real effective exchange rate.

After careful study of a set of *ex post* quantitative indicators of competitiveness, including trade balances, market shares, and measures of revealed comparative advantage, Samba Mamadou, Garba, and Mahaman (2005) and Samba Mamadou *et al.* (2005) arrive at the following conclusions:

- Despite the restored price competitiveness due to the 1994 CFA franc devaluation, Niger's trade balance was in deficit during the whole period (1990–2000). Both the agricultural and the industrial sectors had a serious problem of competitiveness (see figures 6.9, 6.10).
- Niger's revealed comparative advantage is in the agricultural sector, and particularly in certain goods including onions, livestock, and hides and skins. This advantage has been unexploited, in part due to Niger's extreme vulnerability to climate instability. No revealed comparative advantage has been identified in the manufacturing sector, which is not surprising considering the structure of Niger's economy.

4. Growth and structural change: an accounting analysis from the demand side

In Niger, real GDP *per capita* growth rates were negative, on average, throughout the 1990s. This is partly due to the lack of diversification in

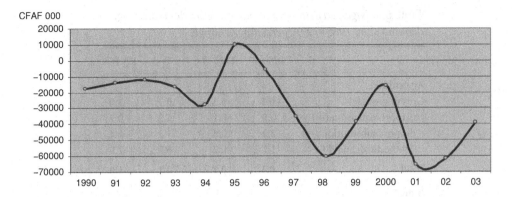

Figure 6.10 Niger, trade balance, agricultural products, 1990–2003

the economy: to be substantial and sustained, growth should go hand-in-hand with a change in the economic structure of the country.

The economic performance of a country depends upon its ability to improve its competitiveness, particularly through export-led growth. To assess the role of this strategy in addition to that of import substitution or domestic demand expansion in explaining Niger's growth performance, we adopt a variant of growth accounting introduced by Chenery and Syrquin (1985). This approach focuses on tradable sectors, and starts from the identity:

$$Y_i = D_i + X_i - M_i,$$

where Y_i is the output of tradable sector i (agriculture, industry), D_i is domestic demand in that sector (comprising both consumption and investment demand), and X_i and M_i are, respectively, the exports and imports of sector i goods. The growth performance of each sector can therefore be disaggregated into three main components: the growth in domestic demand ($\hat{D}_i$), the rate of export expansion ($\hat{X}_i$), and the rate of import substitution ($-\hat{M}_i$), each weighted by its share in sectoral value added. This leads to the following growth accounting equation for tradable sector i:

$$\hat{Y}_i = sd_i \cdot \hat{D}_i + sx_i \cdot \hat{X}_i - sm_i \cdot \hat{M}_i,$$

where sd, sx, and sm are the respective shares of each component in sectoral value added.

Table 6.6 uses this approach to assess the main drivers of growth in Niger's tradable sectors. Table 6.6 indicates that both agriculture and industry experienced poor growth performance between 1980 and 1993. Growth resumed only after the 1994 devaluation, after which the manufacturing industry grew at around 5 percent per annum in real terms and agriculture grew at only 1 percent. Weak growth outcomes between 1980 and 1993, particularly in the industrial sectors, are generally attributable to weak export

Table 6.6 *Niger, structural changes and growth accounting, demand side, 1980–1997, percentage changes*

	1980–4	1985–9	1990–3	1994–7
Agriculture				
Output growth	−0.1	0.1	0.1	1.0
Export expansion (+)	0.5	−0.1	5.3	−0.7
Import substitution (−)	−2.3	0.4	1.3	−0.4
Domestic demand (+)	1.7	−0.2	−6.6	2.0
Total	**−0.1**	**0.1**	**0.1**	**1.0**
Industry				
Output growth	−0.5	−3.4	−2.0	4.8
Export expansion (+)	−5.5	−2.8	−5.2	4.9
Import substitution (−)	9.3	2.9	9.0	−0.3
Domestic demand (+)	−4.3	−3.4	−5.8	0.2
Total	**−0.5**	**−3.4**	**−2.0**	**4.8**
Manufacturing				
Output growth	19.0	−2.7	−1.7	4.4
Export expansion (+)	−0.7	−1.1	4.2	32.2
Import substitution (−)	23.2	−0.2	25.6	0.6
Domestic demand (+)	−3.5	−1.4	−31.5	−28.4
Total	**19.0**	**−2.7**	**−1.7**	**4.4**

expansion – suggesting the absence of any effective export-led growth strategy – and to weak domestic demand. During the post-devaluation period (1994–7), the positive growth rate observed in the agricultural sector stems principally from the increase in domestic demand, while the industrial sector performance improved due to an expansion of exports of manufactured goods. In short, despite the tradability of agriculture and particularly industry, domestic demand expansion accounts for a dominant share of sector growth in these sectors. This reveals the necessity of improving household income and designing a good poverty-reduction strategy to promote economic growth in Niger.

5. Conclusion

Niger offers an interesting case study of a country with a very volatile and low real income *per capita*. The growth rate of real GDP *per capita* in Niger is a stationary variable with a zero mean. Yet growth constitutes a precondition for any poverty-reduction strategy. The volatility of Niger's GDP is attributable, in substantial part, to the agricultural sector, which is subject to rainfall instability and characterized by rudimentary techniques of production.

This chapter identifies the main factors behind Niger's weak performance. It emphasizes Niger's extreme vulnerability to climatic and political instabilities. Climatic instability explains the episodes of negative growth recorded during the period 1960–89: years of negative growth rates coincided with the occurrence of droughts. During the 1990s, however, socio-political instability explains Niger's growth under-performance. The vulnerability of the economy is further aggravated by its weak diversification, which makes adjustments difficult to achieve during shocks.

Each modestly sustained episode of positive growth in Niger was associated with a commodity boom, whether from groundnuts or uranium. However, growth driven by the uranium boom ultimately proved unsustainable, due to the economy's inability to cope with exogenous shocks such as droughts.

Since 2000, Niger has recovered some socio-political stability. The rebellion has ended and the wage bill is regularly paid, giving civil servants less opportunity to call for strikes. In December 2004 the President was re-elected for a second five-year term. For the first time in Niger's recent political history, a democratic mandate has been completed with no disruption by a coup. Thanks to this political stability, the real growth rate averaged 5 percent per annum from 2000 to 2003. However, the economy of Niger remains fragile and vulnerable to climate instability. The food crisis experienced in 2005, resulting from insufficient rainfall in 2004 and serious locust attacks, provides a recent example.

The augmented Solow model estimated by Hoeffler (2002) provides a useful benchmark for explaining the determinants of growth in Niger, and its performance improves when political instability is taken into account; incorporating rainfall fluctuations would probably improve it further. From this model, we conclude that investment is an important driver of growth in Niger, but that its impact and efficiency are often impeded by the extreme vulnerability of the country, particularly to droughts.

Given the frequency of droughts in the Sahelian zone, a public investment program designed to reduce Niger's vulnerability to droughts, through agricultural research, investment in irrigation infrastructure, and other means, may have a high growth return both directly, by enhancing agricultural productivity, and indirectly, by increasing the return to private investment.

References

Aron, J. (2000), "Growth and Institutions: A Review of Evidence," *World Bank Research Observer* 15(1), February: 99–135

Azam, J.-P. (1999), "The Uranium Boom in Niger (1975–1982)," in P. Collier and J. Gunning, eds., *Temporary Trade Shocks in Developing Countries*, 1. Oxford: Oxford University Press: 351–98

    (2002), "Statecraft in the Shadow of Civil Conflict," *International Forum of Economic Perspectives*, ADB-OECD, Paris, February 4–5

    (2001), "The Redistributive State and Conflicts in Africa," *Journal of Peace Research* 38, July: 429–44

Azam J.-P., J. C. Berthélemy, and S. Calipel (1996), "Risque politique et croissance en Afrique," *Revue Economique* 47(3): 819–29

Chenery and Syrquin (1985), *Industrialization and Growth*. Oxford: Oxford University Press

Collier, P. and A. Hoeffler (1999), "Justice-seeking and Loot-seeking in Civil War," World Bank, Washington, DC, mimeo

Combes, J. L. (1993), "Instabilité des révenus et épargnes dans les pays en voie de développement: le rôle de la politique de stabilisation du prix des produits agricoles d'exportation," PhD thesis, University of Clermont Ferrand, I

Direction de la Statistique et de la Démographie Niger (DSD) (1991), *Annuaire statistique: séries longue*. Ministère du Plan, Niamey

Fosu, A. (1992), "Political Instability and Economic Growth: Evidence from Sub-Saharan Africa," *Economic Development and Cultural Change* 40(4), July: 829–41

Guillaumont, P. (1987), "From Export Instability Effect to International Stabilization Policies," *World Development* 15(5): 633–43

Guillaumont, P., S. Guillaumont, and F. Brun (1999), "How Instability Lowers African Growth," *Journal of African Economies* 8(1), March: 87–107

Gymah-Brempong, K. (1991), "Export Instability and Economic Growth in Sub-Saharan Africa," *Economic Development and Cultural Change* 39(4): 815–28

Hoeffler, A. (2002), "The Augmented Solow Model and the African Growth Debate," *Bulletin of Economics and Statistics*: 64(2), May: 135–58

Nkurunziza, J. and R. Bates (2003), "Political Institutions and Economic Growth in Africa," WPS 2003–03, CSAE, University of Oxford

O'Connell, S. and B. Ndulu (2000), "Africa's Growth Experience: A Focus on the Sources of Growth," AERC Growth Working Paper No. 10. Nairobi, April (downloadable: www.aercafrica.org)

Rodrik, D. (1992), "Political Economy of Development Policy," *European Economic Review, Papers and Proceedings* 36, April: 329–36

    (1999), "Where Did All the Growth Go? External Shocks, Social Conflict and Growth Collapses," *Journal of Economic Growth* 4(4): 385–412

Samba Mamadou, O., M. A. Garba, and H. M. Mahaman (2005), "La compétitivité du secteur manufacturier nigérien," Etude CAPED/02/05, December

Samba Mamadou, O., M. A. Garba, H. M. Mahaman, and M. Sani (2005), "La compétitivité du secteur agro-pastoral du Niger," Etude CAPED/01/05, June

7 | Explaining Sudan's economic growth performance

Ali Abdel Gadir Ali and Ibrahim A. Elbadawi

The rule of growth in developing countries is that anything can happen and often does.   (Pritchett 2000: 247)

Sudan, an international pariah with no democracy and no international assistance, is doing as well as anyone these days, with a current growth rate of more than 7 percent. Much of Africa is ruled more by rainfall than politics.

     (*The Economist,* May 13–19, 2000: 24)

Arab Planning Institute; The World Bank, Washington, DC.
    We are grateful to Khalid Affan for comments on an earlier draft of this version of the chapter. We would also like to express our gratitude to Professor R. H. Bates for encouragement and insightful comments, and to Professors S. O'Connell and C. Soludo for guidance in development of the chapter. All of them, however, are not to be held accountable for any remaining errors and inaccuracies.

1. Economic background

Prior to independence in January 1956, Sudan had been subjected to over sixty years of Turko-Egyptian rule and then governed by the Condominium formed by Britain and Egypt. During Ottoman rule, a centralized administration emerged in the northern part of the country, with Khartoum serving as the capital. In the southern (Equatoria in British colonial parlance) and western (Darfur) parts of the present country, less formal, and traditional, administrations prevailed. The second half of the nineteenth century witnessed improvements in transport and communications that resulted in the opening of the country to foreigners. As a result trade in goods (e.g. gum-Arabic) and slaves (at the hands of Egyptians, British, and Austrian traders) increased rapidly, although this was severely disrupted during the Mahdist rule of 1885–98.

The period of British colonial administration witnessed the laying of the foundations of the modern economy of Sudan. The foundations rested on long-staple cotton. Brown (1992: 80) summarized the story succinctly by noting that in

1913 the Condominium administration, backed by the British government, raised a loan to finance the construction of a dam at Sennar on the Blue Nile. Work began in 1914, was interrupted by the First World War, and in 1925 was completed. The Gezira irrigated cotton scheme, located in the triangle of land south of the confluence of the two Niles thus came into being. Ultimately covering an area of over two million feddans, it was to become the world's largest single farming enterprise under one management, and the most important source of foreign revenue for Sudan.[1]

Drawing on the traditions of crop-sharing in northern and central Sudan, the Gezira scheme was organized as a partnership between the Sudan Plantation Syndicate (SPS, a British management company representing British shareholders), the colonial government, and the tenants. The net profits of the scheme (after deducting the costs of non-labor inputs, overhead production costs, transportation, and marketing from the gross proceeds of cotton sales) were distributed between the three partners such that tenants received 40 percent, the government received 35 percent, and SPS received 25 percent. In 1925, the total irrigated area of the scheme was 240,000 feddans, increasing to about 1 million feddans by independence in 1956.

Replication of the Gezira model in the eastern part of the country led to cotton becoming the economic foundation of the colonial administration. Unlike the gravity-irrigated Gezira, the Gash delta cotton scheme was developed on the basis of flush irrigation. While the annual area fluctuated depending on rain levels, the total area increased from about 9,100 feddans

[1] One feddan = 1.038 acres = 4,201 m^2. For the detailed history of the Gezira scheme, see Gaitskell (1959).

Table 7.1 *Sudan, GDP composition, 1955–1956 current prices*

Sector	GDP (million Ls.)	GDP share (%)
Agriculture	172.6	60.7
Industry	3.0	1.1
Construction	16.2	5.7
Transport	37.6	13.2
Public utilities	1.0	0.4
Government	17.2	6.0
Real estate	8.2	2.9
Other	28.4	10.0
Total	284.2	100.0

Source: Brown (1992: 86, table 3.1).

in 1920 to about 68,800 in 1956. A smaller scheme was also initiated in the delta of the Baraka river in eastern Sudan, with a total area of 30,000–40,000 feddans. Private pump schemes were established on the White and Blue Niles, their number increasing from 372 (with an area of 170,000 feddans) in 1944 to 2,229 (with an area of 770,000 feddans) in 1957.

The rise of the cotton economy led to the rise of the transport and communications industries. It is estimated that between 1919 and 1939 about 56 percent of total government capital expenditure was devoted to the Gezira scheme and 24.1 percent to the development of the railway system. The limited investment that was undertaken in industry was devoted to cotton ginneries (large ones in Port Sudan, Sennar, and Atbara and six smaller ones in other parts of the country).

Mechanized agriculture provided the second leg of the Sudanese economy. Large-scale mechanized production of sorghum (dura), the main food staple of the northern part of the country, was started in 1945 near Gedaref in eastern Sudan; it covered about 12,000 feddans and was managed by the Middle East Supply Corporation (MESC). Labor difficulties encountered by the MESC resulted in the government taking over the scheme in 1947, introducing a sharecropping arrangement similar to the Gezira formula. Under the government, the scheme covered 25,000 feddans and involved about 1,000 cultivators, up to 1953. During the period 1947–53 a number of entrepreneurs expressed interest in investing in mechanized farming under a different land tenure system. Eventually, the crop-sharing arrangement was abandoned and leaseholds were sold to private investors. At independence in 1956 there were more than 300 private mechanized schemes covering about 388,000 feddans. Along with cotton production, the mechanized schemes constitute the second pillar of Sudan's agrarian economy.

Table 7.1 summarizes the production structure of the Sudan economy at the time of independence (1956). Not surprisingly, the economy was dominated by agriculture, which contributed about 61 percent of GDP. There was virtually no industrial sector to speak of (a contribution of about 1.1 percent of GDP). The services sector accounted for the remaining 37.9 percent of GDP.

It is estimated that total investment amounted to about Ls. 21.1 million in current prices. The bulk of this investment was in the real estate sector (38.7 percent), followed by the government sector (21.7 percent), transport (19.7 percent), and agriculture (8.5 percent). Investment in manufacturing amounted to only 2.5 percent of the total. Of the total investment in 1955–6, it is estimated that 54 percent was contributed by the public sector, leaving a balance of 46 percent for the private sector. Of the private sector's total investment, 84 percent was devoted to the real estate sector, 5 percent to manufacturing, 4 percent to agriculture, and 3 percent to transport.

Given the structure of the economy, the composition of Sudan's exports at independence was dominated exclusively by primary products. Total exports amounted to about Ls. 65.4 million in current prices (about 23 percent of GDP). Cotton dominated Sudan's exports, with a share of 80 percent of total exports. Gum-Arabic and groundnuts ranked second to cotton, with a share of 7 percent each, while melon-seed, hides, and skins ranked third, with a share of 2 percent each.

The economy was dual in structure, with a vast traditional sector and a small modern sector, and this production structure influenced the fiscal system. Public revenues derived from a land tax (introduced in 1925 on all irrigated land, except that which was irrigated seasonally by rain or flood, as a fixed charge on land value or the value of the products); a date tax (1925 on date trees bearing fruits); an animal tax (1925 on livestock at a specified rate per head of each type); "ushur," an Islamic tax on rainfed agriculture (1924, at 10 percent of the value of the product of rain lands); a poll tax (1925, on almost all adult males in the subsistence part of the economy, at 1 Sudanese pound per head); and a house tax (1918 at a rate of 1/12 of the annual rental value of the house, irrespective of it being rented or occupied). Other direct taxes were levied upon the modern part of the economy. The most important among these was the business profits tax which was introduced in 1913. Not surprisingly, however, indirect taxes were the most important source of government revenue under the colonial state. Among these, taxes on international trade were central. Import duties, export taxes, and royalties were imposed in 1939. Excise duties, imposed upon certain locally produced commodities, and consumption taxes on selected imported goods, were imposed in 1924.

At independence, on January 1, 1956, Sudan was composed of nine administrative units called provinces: six in the north of the country (Northern, Khartoum, Blue Nile, Kassala, Kordofan, and Darfur) and three in the south (Bahr El Ghazal, Upper Nile, and Equatoria). Table 7.2 gives the distribution of population according to the 1956 census.

Table 7.2 *Sudan, population by province, 1956*

Province	Population	% population
Blue Nile	2,069,646	20.17
Kassala	941,039	9.17
Khartoum	504,923	4.92
Darfur	1,328,765	12.95
Kordofan	1,761,968	17.17
Northern	873,059	8.51
Bahr El Ghazal	991,022	9.66
Equatoria	903,503	8.80
Upper Nile	888,611	8.65
Total	**10,262,536**	**100.00**

Source: Balamoan (1981: 58, table 4).

Table 7.3 *Sudan, GDP, by region, 1956*

Region	Provinces	GDP (Ls. 000)	GDP share (%)	Population	Population share (%)	GDP *per capita* (Ls.)
North-East	Northern, Kassala, Khartoum	75,786	26.67	2,319,021	22.60	32.68
Blue Nile	Blue Nile	86,032	30.27	2,069,646	20.17	41.59
North-West	Kordofan, Darfur	83,777	29.48	3,090,733	30.11	27.11
South	Bahr El Ghazal, Equatoria, Upper Nile	38,610	13.59	2,783,136	27.12	13.87
Total		**284,205**	**100.00**	**10,262,536**	**100.00**	**27.69**

Source: based on Balamoan (1981: 244, table 39).

At independence, Sudan's GDP was estimated as amounting to Ls. 284 million (US$795 million). Per capita GDP amounted to Ls. 28, or about US$78, leaving Sudan among the poorest countries in the world. The distribution of GDP over regions is given in table 7.3.

Table 7.3 shows that the Blue Nile region, the heart of agricultural development during the colonial period, was relatively better off than other regions, with a *per capita* GDP that amounted to about Ls. 42 (US$118), followed by the North-East region, which includes the capital city of Khartoum, with a *per capita* GDP of about Ls. 33 (US$92), and the North-West region with a *per capita* GDP of Ls. 27 (US$76). The South fared much worse, with a *per capita* GDP of about Ls. 14 (US$39), reflecting years of neglect and marginalization during the colonial period. The poorest northern sub-region has almost twice the income *per capita* of the South.

Table 7.4 *Sudan, sectoral composition and regional distribution of GDP, 1956, Ls. 000*

Sector	North-East	Blue Nile	North-West	South	Total	GDP share (%)
Agriculture	23,434	63,117	58,454	27,603	172,608	60.73
	(13.58)	(36.66)	(33.86)	(16.00)		
Industry	5,302	3,134	2,819	2,533	13,788	4.85
	(38.45)	(22.73)	(20.45)	(18.37)		
Services	47,050	19,781	22,504	8,474	97,809	34.42
	(48.10)	(20.22)	(23.01)	(8.66)		
Total	**85,786**	**86,032**	**83,777**	**38,610**	**284,205**	**100.00**

Source: compiled from Balamoan (1981: 246, table 40).

The development gap between the northern and southern parts of the country is echoed in the sectoral distribution of GDP. Table 7.4 provides the distribution among the regions, where figures in parentheses are the shares of the regions in sectoral GDP.

Thus, at independence, the northern part of the country contributed 84 percent of agricultural output, about 82 percent of industrial output, and about 91 percent of the services sector output. In the southern part of the country, agriculture contributed 72 percent of the GDP of the region, services 22 percent, and industry the rest.

2. Economic growth in Sudan

Our data on real GDP *per capita* in 1985 PPP come from the database of the Global Development Network (Easterly and Sewadeh 2002). Visual inspection suggests four sub-periods of growth, each of different length. Table 7.5 reports the trend growth rates for each of the sub-periods and the mean, the standard deviation, and the coefficient of variation. The figures in parentheses are the standard deviations of the sub-period growth rates.

Arrayed in this manner, we find alternating sub-periods of negative and positive growth. The negative growth periods are the longest, but with relatively low negative growth rates. By contrast, the positive growth sub-periods are shorter, but with relatively high *per capita* growth rates. For the whole period, there was a positive, but insignificant, growth trend with a very low R^2 coefficient.

During the sub-periods in which the rate of growth was negative, it nonetheless fluctuated. During the negative growth episode of 1960–73, for example, real *per capita* GDP increased in 1965, 1966, 1970, and 1971. Similarly, during the 1984–94 episode, real *per capita* GDP increased for

Table 7.5 *Sudan's growth episodes, per capita GDP growth rates, 1960–1998*

Growth episode (1)	Trend growth rate (%) (2)	Average growth rate (%) and (std dev.) (3)	Coefficient of variation (4)	# of years with growth<0 (total years)(5)
1960–73	0.89*	−1.43 (5.13)	3.59	9 (13)
1974–83	1.27	2.57 (7.54)	2.93	2 (10)
1984–94	−0.11	−0.60 (4.97)	8.28	6 (11)
1995–98	2.96*	2.60 (1.12)	0.43	0 (4)
1960–98	0.02	0.29 (5.69)	19.62	17 (38)

Source: Own calculations. Trend growth rates are based on regressions of the form $\ln y = a + bt$, where y is *per capita* GDP in PPP 1985 dollars and t is time.
*indicates significance at 1 percent level or better. Note that in column (5) year-on-year growth rates are calculated and as such 1960 is lost in recording the number of years.

the years 1986, 1989, 1991, 1992, and 1994. During these two episodes the magnitude of the rates of growth also varied. During the 1960–73 episode, for example, the highest negative growth rate is recorded for 1973 (−12 percent) while the lowest negative growth is recorded for 1967 (−0.8 percent); the highest positive growth rate is recorded for 1971 (5.1 percent) while the lowest positive growth rate is recorded for 1970 (3.4 percent). On the other hand, for the positive growth episodes, only 1974–83 recorded negative growth rates for the years 1978 (−3 percent) and 1979 (−11.6 percent).

Sudan's growth record is thus highly volatile. Looking at the coefficient of variation, we see that the positive growth periods had relatively low variability while the negative growth periods were volatile. For the whole period the coefficient of variation is fairly high, confirming the overall volatility of the country's growth experience.

To decompose the sources of growth, we replicate the Collins and Bosworth (1996) global cross-country regressions. To estimate the capital stock, we build on previous estimates by Ali (1974: 126–33) for the initial 1960 capital stock. In line with the literature, we assume a depreciation rate of 0.06.[2] Using the ratio of the estimated capital stock in real terms to GDP for 1960 we convert the initial capital stock to 1985 PPP dollars. We calculate

---

[2] Where K is capital stock, δ is the depreciation rate, and I is investment, the formula used to estimate the capital stock for Sudan is $K_{t+1} = (1 - \delta)K_t + I_t$. The initial capital stock is US$7.2 billion, equivalent to 0.75 of 1960 GDP.

Table 7.6 *Sudan, growth-accounting decompositions, 1960–1999, percentages*

Period	GDP per worker growth rate: G(y)	Growth rate of capital stock per worker: G(k)	Growth rate of human capital per worker: G(h)	Contribution of physical capital: 0.35 G(k)	Contribution of human capital: 0.65G(h)	TFP resid.
1960–4	−1.38	9.60	4.05	3.36	2.63	−7.37
1965–9	−0.67	2.60	4.40	0.91	2.86	−4.44
1970–4	−1.69	−0.05	6.00	−0.02	3.90	−5.57
1975–9	4.48	4.63	6.55	1.62	4.26	−1.40
1980–4	−0.51	1.28	3.29	0.45	2.14	−3.10
1985–9	−0.45	2.45	4.12	0.86	2.68	−3.99
1990–4	−0.54	−0.42	3.31	−0.15	2.15	−2.54
1995–9	1.97	−0.46	2.09	−0.16	1.36	0.77
1960–99	0.19	2.27	4.23	0.79	2.75	−3.35

Source: Own calculations.

the growth rate of human capital variable from Barro and Lee (2000), who provide the number of years of schooling in the population age fifteen years and above for five-year intervals starting 1960 up to 2000.[3] Consistent with prevailing usage, we use real GDP per worker (1985 PPP US$) as our indicator of development performance.[4] Table 7.6 presents the results of the calculations for Sudan.

The column reporting GDP per worker confirms the pattern of alternating negative and positive growth sub-periods established for GDP *per capita*, with the 1990–4 half-decade recording a negative growth rate for output per worker. The overall average growth rate of labor productivity is positive, but rather low at 0.19 percent per annum, implying a doubling time for labor productivity of about 368 years! The growth of labor productivity is volatile, with a coefficient of variation of 30.3 for the whole period.

It is instructive to look at the data on capital per worker and human capital per worker. The column in table 7.6 reporting capital per worker shows relatively high rates of growth during the first two half-decades, followed by a negative growth rate of 0.05 percent per annum for the 1970–4 half-decade. The 1975–89 period was one of positive growth for capital per worker, with the 1975–9 half-decade recording the second highest growth

[3] Barro and Lee (2000: appendix table A2) estimate the average years of schooling per person of fifteen years and above as 0.41 for 1960; 0.50 for 1965; 0.62 for 1970; 0.83 for 1975; 1.14 for 1980; 1.34 for 1985; 1.64 for 1990; 1.93 for 1995; and 2.14 for 2000.

[4] As would be expected, the per-worker GDP growth series is also found to be stationary. The result, where Gw is the per-worker GDP growth rate, is as follows:

$$\Delta Gw = 0.11 - 1.143Gw(-1) + 0.305\Delta Gw(-1),$$

with an augmented Dickey–Fuller test-statistic of −5.276, which is significant at the 1 percent level (for a critical value of −3.621).

rate for the whole period. For the 1990s the growth rate of capital stock per worker was negative. For the whole period, however, capital per worker increased by an annual rate of 2.27 percent, implying a doubling time of 30.8 years. Moreover, the pattern of increase is fairly stable, with a coefficient of variation of about 1.5. As for human capital per worker, table 7.6 shows positive growth for all decades. This is as should be expected in a developing country. The highest rates of growth of human capital stock are recorded for the 1970–9 decade. For the whole period, the average rate of increase of human capital per worker is 4.23 percent per annum, implying a doubling time of 16.5 years.

Turning to TFP, we note that in 1960–94 growth in GDP per worker was caused by a relatively large decline in total factor productivity. Negative TFP growth caused growth to slip, on average, by about 5.8 percentage points per annum for the period 1960–74, and by about 2.41 percentage points per annum for the period 1975–94. Save for a brief period in the mid-1990s, negative TFP growth characterizes the entire history of modern Sudan.

3. Growth and development transformation

Over the entire period 1960–98, the share of agriculture declined from 55.35 percent of GDP in 1960 to 39.29 percent in 1998. Thus, even at the end of the period, agriculture continued to play a major role in the production structure of Sudan. The pattern of decline, however, was not uniform. For the whole period 1960–87, we estimated a trend annual rate of decline of 1.67 percent (with a t-value of 8.1 and an R^2 of 72 percent). During the period 1960–73, an annual rate of decline of 2.1 percent (with a t-value of 2.83 and an R^2 of 40 percent) is estimated. However, the period saw the share of agriculture declining from 55.4 percent in 1960 to a low of 36.8 percent in 1968 before increasing to 44.9 percent in 1973. Over the period 1973–7 the share of agriculture declined in a sustained fashion at a trend rate of decline of 3.7 percent per annum (with a t-value of 3.4 and an R^2 of 80 percent). The share declined from 44.9 percent in 1973 to 39.9 percent in 1977. During the period 1977–87, a rate of decline of 1.5 percent was estimated (with a t-value of 2.43 and an R^2 of 40 percent), and the share declined from 39.9 percent in 1977 to 32.8 percent in 1987.

For the entire period 1960–87, we estimate the average rate of increase of industry's share of GDP at 0.35 percent (with a t-value of 1.67 and an R^2 of 9.7 percent), not significantly different from zero at the 10 percent level. During this period, the share of industry increased from about 13.5 percent of GDP in 1960 to about 16.3 in 1987. The increase in the share of industry was not significantly different from zero for the sub-period 1960–73 (a trend rate of increase of 0.51 percent with a t-value of 0.83 and an R^2 coefficient of

Table 7.7 *Sudan, structural transformation, actual and predicted sectoral shares, 1960–1997, percent*

Period	Agriculture		Industry		Services	
	Actual	Predicted	Actual	Predicted	Actual	Predicted
1960–4	52.42	32.42	13.56	25.52	34.02	42.06
1965–9	39.83	31.63	15.59	25.17	44.58	43.20
1970–4	44.33	31.42	13.79	24.34	41.88	44.24
1975–9	38.77	30.94	13.11	23.88	48.13	45.18
1980–4	34.12	28.58	14.87	25.18	51.01	46.24
1985–9	33.06	29.11	16.08	23.76	50.92	47.12
1990–7	38.34	28.93	15.79	22.91	45.36	48.17

Source: Ndulu and O'Connell (2000: 16) for the predicted shares.

5.5 percent). For the period 1973–7, the share of industry recorded a decline at an average rate of 2.12 percent, also not significantly different from zero (with a t-value of 1.69 and an R^2 coefficient of 49 percent). The period 1977–87 recorded a significant average rate of increase of 3.12 percent (with a t-value of 12 and an R^2 coefficient of 94 percent). By 1998, the share of industry amounted to 18.2 percent of GDP.

For the whole period 1960–87, the share of the services sector in GDP increased at an annual average rate of 1.55 percent (with a t-value of 8 and an R^2 coefficient of 71 percent), and the share increased from 31.1 percent of GDP in 1960 to 50.9 percent in 1987. Significant average rates of increase are estimated for the two sub-periods 1960–73 (2.54 percent with a t-value of 3.95 and an R^2 coefficient of 56 percent) and 1973–7 (4.1 percent with a t-value of 5.4 and an R^2 coefficient of 91 percent). The share of services fluctuated along an increasing trend during the period 1977–87. Thus, during this period, the share of services registered a non-significant rate of increase of 1.7 percent (with a t-value of 0.44 and an R^2 coefficient of only 2.2 percent). By 1998, the share of services amounted to 42.6 percent of GDP.

The estimates of Ndulu and O'Connell (2000: 10–17, table 3.3.A) provide actual and predicted sectoral shares for the economy. In table 7.7, we replicate their efforts for Sudan. We use the data in table 7.8 to compute the means for the half-decades and compare them with the predicted shares. At this stage, our results should be taken as indicative.

On the basis of tables 7.7 and 7.8, we can note that:

(1) Sudan's growth experience does not conform to the observation that "agricultural output shares are just slightly higher in Sub-Saharan Africa than predicted on the basis of income and population" (Ndulu and

Table 7.8 *Sudan, GDP per capita, structural composition, and macro/institutional factors, averages for various time periods, 1960–2000*

Year	Real GDP per capita (US$; PPP 1985)	GDP per capita growth rate (%)	Share of agriculture in GDP (%)	Share of industry in GDP (%)	Share of services in GDP (%)	Investment/ GDP (%)	Inflation rate (%)	Real over-valuation index	Trading partner per capita GDP growth rate (%)	Terms of trade index	Political rights score	Civil liberties score	Freedom status	Average annual rain
1960–4	50.404	−0.012	2.417	3.561	4.022	5.440	0.766	18.352	0.852					59.491
1960–8	34.587	−0.009	6.844	4.465	8.691	4.411	0.414	18.830	0.750	46.540				46.109
1960–73	20.259	−0.014	5.605	4.355	0.040	3.435	0.084	19.668	0.881	43.193				23.801
1960–98	33.424	0.003	0.206	4.778	4.919	5.945	5.149	46.827	0.397	26.437				91.524
1960–2000	39.584	0.005	0.591	4.964	4.353	5.964	5.149	46.827	0.397	26.437				91.524
1965–8	14.815	−0.005	9.877	5.595	4.528	3.125	0.062	19.428	0.647	46.540				29.381
1965–9	09.920	−0.006	9.830	5.593	4.577	3.100	0.571	19.185	0.070	47.775				21.566
1969–73	94.469	−0.022	3.374	4.159	2.467	1.678	0.357	21.175	0.092	42.524				83.648
1970–4	78.800	−0.018	4.330	3.793	1.877	2.758	2.067	28.129	0.121	45.602	0.00	0.00	0.00	90.759
1974–7	41.000	0.090	0.930	3.403	5.668	9.038	7.218	69.389	0.032	53.825	0.00	0.00	0.00	08.145
1974–8	65.200	0.066	0.534	3.204	6.262	8.100	7.620	73.053	0.419	49.720	0.00	0.75	0.88	16.488
1975–9	92.800	0.041	8.766	3.107	8.128	7.436	8.616	81.372	0.950	42.540	0.75	0.50	0.63	11.434
1978–83	84.000	−0.017	5.730	4.010	0.261	5.537	6.100	67.097	0.617	24.917	0.00	0.20	0.10	91.498
1979–90	31.700	−0.017	3.465	5.277	0.941	7.823	8.209	73.161	0.132	18.750	0.09	0.45	0.27	70.886
1980–4	65.200	−0.003	4.120	4.871	1.009	6.118	8.075	54.928	−0.397	22.000	0.00	0.25	0.13	54.800
1985–9	06.200	−0.005	3.061	6.081	0.918	0.000	4.368	51.584	0.865	12.620	0.50	0.25	0.88	94.211
1986–9	10.000	0.007	2.941	5.974	1.160	9.600	4.108	58.912	0.264	10.575	0.00	0.00	0.50	94.023
1990–4	04.880	0.003	4.140	6.740	8.280	6.580	4.630	20.046	0.745	11.960	0.00	0.00	0.00	76.263
1991–4	12.750	0.015	5.150	7.100	7.725	6.175	14.498	87.358	0.510	09.100	0.00	0.00	0.00	94.084
1991–2000	63.290	0.024	2.150	6.320	1.530	6.233	0.368	38.463	0.866	05.650	0.00	0.00	0.00	50.392
1995–8	65.625	0.026	6.175	4.400	9.450	6.175	6.238	9.568	0.222	08.750	0.00	0.00	0.00	06.700
1995–2000	96.983	0.029	6.817	5.800	7.400	6.280	6.238	9.568	0.222	08.750	0.00	0.00	0.00	06.700

O'Connell 2006: 6). As table 7.7 shows, for all half-decades, the actual share of agriculture in GDP is markedly higher than the predicted share. The difference narrowed for some periods but has also widened for others.

(2) Sudan's growth experience does not conform to the observation that given income and population the size of industry is "markedly larger than would be predicted based on cross-country norms" (Ndulu and O'Connell 2000: 6). As table 7.7 shows, for all half-decades, the actual share of industry in GDP is markedly lower than what is predicted by the cross-country norms.

(3) Sudan's growth experience partly conforms to the observation that "given income and population, the size of the services sector is markedly lower than would be predicted based on cross-country norms" (Ndulu and O'Connell 2000: 6). As table 7.7 shows, the observation applies to the half-decades of 1960–4, 1970–4 and 1990–7; for the remaining periods the actual share of services is higher than the predicted share.

Thus, our analysis of Sudan's growth experience shows that little or no development transformation has occurred over the period 1960–98.

4. Politics, institutions, and growth

Political scientists and historians generally agree that at independence and during the subsequent post-independence period three major social groups came to dominate the political, social, and economic life of northern Sudan and thus of the country as a whole: religious leaders, tribal leaders, and merchants. Their origins lay in the domination of religious life in northern society by Muslim Sufi religious orders and in the colonial policy of indirect rule.

4.1 Political parties

At independence, the most prominent and politically involved religious orders included the Ansar, followers of Sayed (Mr.) Abdel Rahman al-Mahdi; the Khatmiyyah, followers of Sayed (Mr.) Ali al-Mirghani; and the followers of Sharif (Honorable) Yusuf al-Hindi. Given their social status and influence, the colonial state followed a deliberate policy of enhancing the business interests of these families by preferential allocation of productive assets (mostly land), business contracts, and bank loans (converted into grants), with the objective of minimizing the risk of resistance to the colonial regime.

Tribal leaders were the cornerstone of the indirect rule policy, and as such their economic influence increased under the colonial state. As noted by Niblock (1987):

Under the condominium, then, the tribal leaders (some more than others) encountered new opportunities for accumulating funds and investing in profitable enterprises. The formal support from a strong centralized government improved their
ability to collect dues which had been their traditional rights; the expansion of
their authority to cover some semi-urban areas gave them some control over trade
licenses and some other aspects of commercial life (and the process of land registration) made it possible for tribal leaders to establish ownership rights over land
which had in fact been communal property, belonging to the tribe as a whole, not to
the tribal leader. Where the land which tribal leaders acquired was fertile and could
be irrigated, the way was open for them to invest in pump schemes, dividing the
land into share-cropping tenancies. (1987: 53)

The merchant class grew over the years under the colonial state. While
export and import trade were dominated by British companies with Egyptians, Syrians, Lebanese, and Greeks sharing in the spoils, Sudanese merchants were allowed to trade in gum-Arabic, livestock, and oilseeds. Some
of these merchants had the foresight to invest their profits in related manufacturing ventures such as oilseed pressing and cotton ginning.

The political life of the country prior to independence started to
revolve around the most prominent two religious leaders: al-Mahdi and
al-Mirghani, with the other two social groups appropriately aligning themselves with one or the other group. The most influential civil society organization of that time, the Graduates' Congress, which purported to articulate
the social and political demands of the society on a non-sectarian basis,
eventually found itself split along the same sectarian divide. Two major
parties emerged eventually: the Umma Party (UP), with largely Mahdist
followers, and the National Unionist Party (NUP), with largely Khatmiyyah
followers. The political platforms of the two major parties that were identified at the time of the struggle for independence revolved around the future
of independent Sudan, with the UP arguing for independence from the two
condominium powers (Britain and Egypt) and the NUP arguing for a union
with Egypt.

As Brown (1992) notes, the two main religious leaders

combined their existing popular support and growing economic power, with substantial political influence among the leadership of the country's educated elite. In
turn, this meant that the main constituencies of the political parties lay within the
social groups at the core of the economic elite, and not among the popular masses.
In this way the values and objectives of the economic elite came to predominate and
thus determine the political orientation of the main tendencies within the nationalist movement as the country approached its independence. It also implied that
Sudan's political leadership, during most of the post-independence era, remained
the captive of its major clients among the economic elite. (1992: 96)

One important consequence of these historical developments was that
the policies pursued by the post-colonial state in Sudan were not designed

Table 7.9 *Sudan, regional basis of political parties, 1953, parliamentary seats from geographic constituencies*

Province	NUP	UP	Republican Socialist Party	Southern Party	Others	Total
Blue Nile	6	10	2	0	0	18
Kassala	6	1	0	0	1	8
Khartoum	9	0	0	0	0	9
Darfur	2	6	1	0	2	11
Kordofan	11	6	0	0	0	17
Northern	7	0	0	0	0	7
Bahr El Ghazal	1	0	0	2	4	7
Equatoria	0	0	0	5	2	7
Upper Nile	4	0	0	2	2	8
Total	**46**	**23**	**3**	**9**	**11**	**92**

Source: Compiled from Niblock (1987).

to bring about radical changes to the existing socio-economic structure, nor were they designed to attract popular support:

Political parties maintained themselves in power by their ability to forge alliances with those elements among the economic elite whose religious, tribal or other bases of social prominence enabled them to command the support of the mass of the population. (1992: 97)

In 1953, the first parliamentary elections for a self-rule government were contested by the two major parties, the NUP and the UP, in addition to a number of small parties including the Republican Socialist Party (RSP). The RSP was composed of tribal leaders and its creation is credited to the British administration; however, 75 percent of the seats from geographic constituencies went for the two parties aligned with the two major religious sects. Twenty-two of the 92 geographic constituencies were allocated to the South and the remainder to the North. In addition to these geographic constituencies, five additional constituencies were reserved for "graduates of secondary schools" in Sudan. These five graduate constituencies were open for competition at the national level. The details are reported in table 7.9.

From tables 7.3 and 7.9, it becomes clear that NUP's regional base lay in the Northeast of the country (together with Kordofan) while that of the UP lay in the Blue Nile and the Northwest.[5]

---

[5] For more detailed analysis of the economic interests of the parties see, for example, Ali (1989).

Table 7.10 *Sudan, social groups, members of the first elected parliament*

Social group	Northern constituencies	Southern constituencies	Graduate constituencies	Total
Tribal and religious leaders	31	3	0	34
Ex-employees and ex-soldiers	19	10	1	30
Merchants and farmers	14	1	0	15
Teachers and others	6	8	4	18
Total	**70**	**22**	**5**	**97**

Source: Compiled from Niblock (1987).

Niblock's (1987) description of the social origins of MPs is consistent with our interpretation of the economic base of the dominant parties. Classifying their backgrounds into four major categories – tribal and religious leaders; ex-government employees and ex-army officers, merchants, and farmers; and teachers and others – he reports the data summarized in table 7.10.

The results of the 1953 self-rule elections necessitated rule by coalition governments, a pattern of weak and divided civilian governments that was to become characteristic of post-independence Sudan. A major reason is the high degree of economic, cultural, and ethnic polarization in the country.

The degree of economic polarization, with the poorest northern sub-region enjoying almost twice the *per capita* income of the South, has already been noted. To that can be added ethnic polarization. The first population census of Sudan, conducted in 1956, enumerated seven major ethnic groups comprising Arabs, Beja, Nubiyin, Southern Nilotic, Southern Nilo-Hamitic, Southern Sudanic, and Westerners. Excluding foreigners, Sudanese people with known Arab origins constituted about 39.88 percent of the total population in 1956; those of African origin comprised 30.12. Excluding foreigners, the ethnic polarization index thus stands at 0.625.[6] Given that a polarization index in excess of 0.5 is considered high, Sudan is an ethnically polarized country.

At the time of independence, approximately 2.24 percent of the population followed the Christian faith while 72.88 percent were Muslim. The balance of the population, 24.88 percent, followed indigenous beliefs. More recent estimates put the shares as 70 percent Muslim, 25 percent followers of

---

[6] The index of ethnic polarization (IEP) is defined as:

$$\text{ethnic polarization index} = \text{IEP} = 1 - 4\Sigma(0.5 - \pi_i)^2 \pi_i,$$

where π_i is the share of the population group in the total population and the summation is over population groups. Maximum polarization attains at a value of $I = 1$, when a country is composed of two groups with equal weights.

indigenous beliefs, and 5 percent Christian. At independence, the religious polarization index therefore stood at 0.772.

According to the most recent research, 134 languages are spoken in Sudan. African languages belong to five families: Afro-Asiatic; Nilo-Saharan; Niger–Congo; Khoisan; Austronesian.[7] Sudan's 134 languages belong to the first three families, with the share of the population speaking Afro-Asiatic languages being 73.24 percent, that speaking Nilo-Saharan languages 22.45 percent, and that speaking Niger–Congo languages 4.3 percent. The linguistic polarization index for Sudan therefore stands at 0.738.[8]

The high degree of economic, cultural, and religious polarization led to a high level of political polarization. As noted above, politics in the northern part of the country started off as factional and conflict-ridden and hence fairly highly polarized. It remains so today. Using a political polarization index that has a maximum value of unity where there are only two parties with equal weights,[9] we find the value of this index ranging from a high of 0.8842 for the 1958 elections to a low of 0.6616 for the 1968 elections. Table 7.11 portrays the geographic distribution of the support in Sudan, while Table 7.12 provides the index of political polarization for each national election.

The level of partisan conflict thus remains high and democratically elected governments find it difficult to legislate in a coherent manner. A major result has been frequent military intervention, in response either to appeals from civilian dissidents or to frustration at the ineptitude of the incumbent regime. From 1956 to the late 1990s, Sudan experienced six alternations between democratic and military regimes (see table 7.13).

[7] For a fascinating summary of the development of African languages see, for example, Diamond (1997: 381–6).

[8] It is perhaps interesting in this regard to note that the above polarization measure is not different from the standard ethno-linguistic fractionalization measure (ELF) frequently used by economists

The measure is reported for 1960 in Mauro (1995: 710) for a large sample of countries including Sudan. ELF measures the probability that two randomly selected persons from a given country will not belong to the same ethno-linguistic group. For Sudan, the measure is reported as 0.73, confirming the polarization of the country.

[9] A political polarization index (PPI) is defined as follows:

$$\text{political polarization index} = PPI = 1 - 4\Sigma(0.5 - \pi_i)^2 \pi_i,$$

where π_i is the percentage of seats secured by a given party in an election and the summation is over the number of political parties. The maximum political polarization, an index value equal to 1, obtains when there are only two parties with equal weights in the elections. The index is calculated for the number of seats secured by given parties as reported in the literature. Where there are numerous small parties a category called "others" is used in the calculation of the index.

Table 7.11 *Northern Sudan, number of geographical constituencies, 1953 and 1958*

Province	1953	1958	% change	Party political influence
Northern	7	16	128.0	Khatmiyyah sect
Kassala	8	16	100.0	Khatmiyyah + Ansar
Darfur	11	22	100.0	Ansar
Blue Nile	18	35	94.4	Ansar + Quasi-secular
Kordofan	17	29	70.6	Quasi-secular + Ansar
Khartoum	9	9	0.0	Quasi-secular

Source: Niblock (1987).

Table 7.12 *Sudan, political polarization index (PPI), 1953–1986*

Year	Number of parties	Number of constituencies	PPI	Governments formed during the period
1953	5	97	0.7798	NUP formed the first government. A coalition NUP–UP government was formed in February 1956. In June 1956 Khatmiyyah loyalists broke away from the NUP and formed the Peoples' Democratic Party (PDP). An UP–PDP government was formed in July 1956.
1958	3	127	0.8842	UP–PDP coalition government. UP handed over the government to the army generals on November 17, due to a threat of being deposed by a NUP–PDP coalition.
1965	6	173	0.7867	UP–NUP coalition for May 1965–June 1966. UP split into two parties: Sadig faction (SUP) and the Imam faction (IUP). SUP–NUP coalition government for June 1966–May 1967. IUP–NUP coalition for May 1967–June 1968.
1968	9	218	0.6616	IUP–NUP coalition for June 1968–May 1969.
1986	7	260	0.7323	UP–NUP two coalition governments (June 1986–May 1987 and June 1987–May 1988); UP–NUP–NIF coalition government (May 1988–December 1988); UP–NIF coalition government (December 1988–March 1989); and National Unity Government (March 1989–June 1989).

Note: NUP = National Unionist Party; UP = Umma Party; NIF = National Islamist Front.
Source: Own calculation and compilation from various sources. In all coalition governments there were ministers from the South though not necessarily representing it.

Table 7.13 *Sudan, political regimes and policy orientation, 1956–2002*

Period	Regime type	Duration in (months)	Ideology	Policy stance
January 1, 1956–November 16, 1958	Parliamentary–democratic	35	No identified ideological stance Dominant traditional parties with Islamic–sectarian popular support Dominant agricultural–economic interests	• Private sector and export orientation • Agricultural development • Fine tuning fiscal and monetary policy
November 16, 1958–October 25, 1964	Military (generals)	71	No identified ideological stance	As above
October 26, 1964–May 24, 1969	Parliamentary–democratic	55	As per period (1)	As above
May 25, 1969–April 5, 1984	Military (young officers)	178	Arab Nationalism and Arab Socialism with support from the Left. Subsequent adherence to Islamic Orientation.	• Up to 1972, socialist policies • From 1972, liberalization and private sector orientation; inflow of foreign capital • Debt crisis • IMF/World Bank adjustment policies
April 6, 1984–June 30, 1989	Parliamentary–democratic	63	As per the first period with coalition with Islamic Oriented Political Forces.	Ad-hoc policies
June 30, 1989–end 2000	Military–civilian	138	So-called Islamic Civilizing Project	• Up to 1995 confused policy stance • From 1995 to the present, home-grown adjustment policies of the IMF/World Bank variety with no financial support • Oil exports from September 1999
Total	–	**540**	–	–

Source: Own compilation.

4.2   The trade union movement

A modern, democratic, economically conscious, and politically active trade union movement developed in Sudan as early as 1946 and was involved in the struggle for independence. According to the most authoritative account of the rise of this movement, it started at Atbara, the headquarters of Sudan railways, when an informal association of workers agitated to be recognized as the sole representative of the railways workers (Fawzi 1957). The railways union was eventually registered in 1949 as the largest trade union in the country with a dominating membership of more than 17,000 workers, accounting for 45.7 percent of the total members of the trade union movement in 1951. On the basis of this legislative instrument the number of workers' trade unions increased from 5 in 1949 to 62 in 1950 to 86 in 1951 to 99 in 1952 to 123 in 1953. The railways trade union was instrumental in the eventual establishment of an umbrella organization for workers' trade unions, first in the form of the Workers Trade Union Congress and later in the form of the Sudan Workers Trade Union Federation (SWTUF) in 1950.

The farmers also organized. The Nuba Mountains Tenants' Union was the first farmers' union to achieve government recognition in 1952. The Gezira Tenants' Union (GTU), the largest and by far the most influential, came into existence in 1954. While workers' unions were mainly concerned with issues of wage, pay, and conditions of service, tenants' unions were concerned with the distribution of net proceeds of cotton and other crops between various partners in agricultural schemes. They were also concerned with issues of marketing of crops and pricing policies for inputs and outputs.

In addition to workers and farmers, professionals also organized in trade unions and professional syndicates as early as the 1950s. These included doctors, engineers, administrators, civil servants, and bank employees.

In the period since independence, the role of the trade union movement in politics became extremely controversial, especially from the point of view of the dominant parties. In contrast to the political parties, the union movement has very clear views on a number of economic issues; moreover, relative to the total population, the trade unions were much more politically sophisticated, being able to follow major political debates through the media and their own organized meetings. They therefore gained power that was disproportionate to their numbers. Over the period 1960–98, the trade union movement was involved in all the major challenges to military rule and in the overthrow of military governments. In that sense, one of the causes of political instability in the country is the hyperactive role of the trade union movement.

The political environment in post-independence Sudan can be looked at in terms of a political freedom indicator produced by Freedom House: an

Table 7.14 *Sudan's growth episodes and political freedoms, 1960–1998*

Episode	Average growth rate (%)	Political rights	Civil liberties	Freedom score
1960–73[a]	−1.43	6.00	6.00	6.00
1974–83	2.56	6.00	5.75	5.88
1984–94	−0.60	5.50	5.83	5.67
1995–8	2.60	7.00	7.00	7.00
1960–98[b]	0.29	5.89	6.00	5.95

Source: Own calculations.
Notes:
[a]Refers to 1972–3 only.
[b]Refers to the period 1972–98.

indicator of political rights and civil liberties. These measures are scored on a scale ranging from unity (for "free" status) to 7 (for "not-free" status). The composite indicator is the average of the two scores. The political rights' component measures the extent to which a government is chosen by means of free and fair elections of representatives of the people. The civil liberties' component measures the extent of freedom from government oppression and covers four broad categories of freedoms: "freedom of expression and belief," "association and organization rights," "rule of law and human rights," and "personal autonomy and economic rights." Averaging over the two components, countries are classified into freedom status such that a country is judged "free" if the average freedom score is in the range 1–2.5, "partly free" if the score is in the range 2.5–5.5, and "not free" if the average score is greater than 5.5. Freedom indicators have been compiled since the early 1970s. Table 7.14 relates Sudan's achievements on these scores to its growth performance.

Table 7.14 shows that the average rating of Sudan in the post-independence period was 5.95, or "not free." During the first positive growth episode, the freedom score of 5.88 reflects the dominance of the military regimes. During the negative growth episode that followed, the freedom score improved slightly to 5.67; reflecting the democratic interlude of 1985–9, the score still marks Sudan as "not free." Sudan's score of 7 for the two categories of freedom remained unchanged over the period 1989–98, which included the second period of positive growth. This rating reflects the military nature of the regime and its Islamic fundamentalist posture.

Recent research suggests a method for constructing aggregate institutional and governance indicators that more directly incorporate relevant measures of institutional quality.[10] The method is based on a compilation of a large

---

[10] See Kaufmann, Kraay, and Zoido-Lobaton (1999a, 1999b).

Table 7.15 *Sudan and SSA, governance indicators of institutional structure, 1997*

Region	Government effectiveness	Regulatory burden	Rule of law	Graft	Average
Sudan	−1.697	−0.823	−1.348	−1.061	−1.232
Central	−0.763	−0.716	−1.019	−0.826	−0.831
Eastern	−0.905	−0.680	−0.813	−0.821	−0.805
Southern	−0.435	−0.014	−0.062	−0.141	−0.163
Western	−0.342	−0.504	−0.593	−0.508	−0.487
SSA	−0.611	−0.479	−0.622	−0.574	−0.572
Best	0.221	0.570	1.279	0.535	0.501
Worst	−1.769	−2.340	−2.153	−1.567	−1.955

Source: Based on Kaufmann, Kraay, and Zoido-Lobaton (1999a, 1999b) data files. The indicated numbers measure the distance from the average quality in terms of standard deviations.

data set from thirteen specialized agencies that monitor various aspects of institutions of governance covering 155 to 173 countries all over the world.[11] Factor analysis suggests that the thirty-one ratings can be grouped into six clusters. Two refer to the governance process and can be called "voice and accountability" and "political instability and violence"; two refer to capacity and can be called "government effectiveness" and "regulatory burden"; and two refer to the rule of law and can be called "rule of law" and "graft."

For each indicator, higher values correspond to better outcomes. Each is re-scaled by subtracting the minimum possible score and dividing by the difference between the maximum and minimum, so that each indicator is on a scale from 0 to 1. Standardization yields a distribution such that each indicator has a mean of 0 and a standard deviation of 1 and range from about −2.5 to about 2.5.

Sudan's governance indicators in 1997 lie below the global average. On voice and accountability Sudan was 1.498 below the average, quality; on political instability it was 1.732 below the average; on government effectiveness it was 1.697 below the average; on government regulatory burden it was 0.823 below the average; on the rule of law it was 1.348 below the average; and on graft it was 1.061 below the average. As seen in table 7.15, these values lie below the Sub-Saharan average as well.

---

[11] The sources used are: Business Environment Risk Intelligence; European Bank for Reconstruction and Development; Economist Intelligence Unit; Freedom House; Gallup International; Heritage Foundation; Institute of Management Development; Political Economic Risk Consultancy; Political Risk Services; Standard and Poor's; World Bank; World Economic Forum; *Wall Street Journal.*

Table 7.16 *Sudan, policy and growth, results from a pooled sample of countries*

Detail	Specification (1)	Specification (2)	Specification (3)	Specification (4)
Financial depth (M2/GDP)		0.021		
		(2.842)		
Inflation rate	−0.004		−0.003	−0.002
	(1.830)		(1.170)	(0.766)
Black market premium	−0.007	−0.008	−0.008	−0.009
	(2.403)	(2.687)	(2.399)	(2.293)
Government non-productive consumption/GDP	−0.113	−0.105	−0.113	−0.100
	(4.555)	(3.931)	(4.210)	(3.681)
Fiscal deficit after grants/GDP				−0.103
				(2.928)
No. of obs	422	364	363	258
R^2	0.407	0.402	0.417	0.467

Source: Ndulu and O'Connell (2000: table 5.3.1)

4.3   Policy, politics, and growth

4.3.1   Overall picture

Controlling for a number of initial, geographic, and institutional variables, Ndulu and O'Connell (2000) relate the choice of public policies to the rate of economic growth.[12] Table 7.16 summarizes the relevant results for the macroeconomic policy variables, where figures in parentheses are absolute *t*-values and the dependent variable is the growth rate of real GDP *per capita*.

Specifications (1) and (2) suggest that the three indicators of macroeconomic policy – inflation, currency valuation, and government consumption – are significantly related to *per capita* growth. As specifications (3) and (4) make clear, however, the impact of the inflation rate is not precisely estimated. Further, specification (4) indicates that the ratio of the fiscal deficit after grants to GDP is also significantly related to growth.

Using relevant macroeconomic policy indicators, table 7.17 summarizes the evidence for Sudan, focusing on the inflation rate, the budget deficit, and exchange rate misalignment, as proxied by the index of over-valuation.

---

[12] For all specifications the non-policy variables included in the regression are: the logarithm of initial income (initial with respect to the half-decade); life expectancy; age dependency ratio; growth of the potential labor force; terms of trade shock; trading partner growth; landlocked status; political instability.

Table 7.17 *Sudan, policy and growth, 1960–1998*

Episode	Real over-valuation	Inflation rate	Budget deficit/GDP (%)	GDP *per capita* growth rate (%)
1960–73	119.67	5.08	4.31[a]	−1.43
1974–83	168.01	16.94	6.64	2.56
1984–94	182.94	70.83	5.62	−0.60
1995–8	89.57	66.24	2.00	2.60
1960–98	146.83	35.15	5.29[b]	0.29

Source: Own calculations based on Global Development Network (GDN) data base for the over-valuation index and the inflation rate (see Easterly and Sewadeh 2002); IMF (2000) for the budget deficit for the period 1995–9; official figures as reported to the Arab Monetary Fund *et al.* (2000) for the fiscal deficit 1990–4; and table 7.5 for the growth rates.

Notes:

[a]Average for the period 1970–3.

[b]Weighted average for the period 1970–98.

The growth experience of Sudan thus provides further evidence of the impact of macroeconomic policy.[13]

4.3.2   Political cycles and policy

As noted earlier, Sudan has had five unscheduled regime changes during its short post-independence history, including three successful coup (1958, 1969, 1989), which led to the installation of military regimes, and popular uprisings in 1964 and 1985, which replaced military regimes with civilian governments.

It has been argued that such a military–civilian regime cycle could represent a form of political business cycle (Abdel-Rahman 1997). The military dictator, lacking the legal basis for power, would attempt to manipulate the macroeconomy in order to strike at targets of high unemployment and low inflation. Being unable to simultaneously attain both objectives, the military regime would tend to choose high growth. Provided that it could direct subsidies to constituencies whose support was necessary for its survival, the military would not be averse to inflation. As inflation reached crisis proportions, however, growth collapsed. Moreover, as agents exercised the option of diversifying away from domestic money, the seigniorage revenue

---

[13] Over the past few years the Sudan has been collaborating with the IMF under an arrangement called the "medium-term staff monitored program." In 2002, a staff appraisal of the program noted that macroeconomic "policy now appears roughly on track with the basic objectives of moderate growth and lower inflation achieved" (IMF 2000: 34), thus confirming the association observed in the text.

declined over time, making it difficult to sustain transfer programs. The regime therefore collapsed.

Democratic regimes inherit the macroeconomic crisis of their military predecessors; they have no option but to focus on restoring macroeconomic stability and shoring up shattered business confidence. In the case of Sudan, democracy brought political parties back into power; but as the trade and professional unions had played a decisive role in engineering the uprising that swept these parties to power, they exercised substantial influence on civilian policy-making by civilian governments. In the absence of a workable "social contract" among highly polarized stakeholders, democratic regimes thus found it difficult to concur on growth-oriented policies and came to favor distributional policies instead.

To what degree does the Sudan record exhibit the characteristics of Abdel-Rahman's (1997) political business cycle? Regression results (for want of space, not reported here, see Ali and Elbadawi 2002) suggest that the first and third military regimes as well as the second civilian regime generated positive (albeit marginal) contributions to growth; the others failed to do so. Second, seigniorage was used as a form of finance by both military and civilian regimes, but significantly by the third military regime and the first civilian democracy. The second and third military regime, the second transitional regime (essentially a military government) and the third civilian regime appear to have resorted to an inflation tax; the first and second civilian administrations reduced that tax. The evidence on inflation acceleration mirrors that of the inflation tax. The evidence suggests that monetary surprises were strictly confined to the last two military regimes. Finally, the evidence on the quasi-fiscal deficit suggests that, except for the last civilian administration, all other regimes had significant impact on expansionary budgets. The failure to detect difference between military and civilian regimes in this case could be explained by the difficulty of controlling budgets in weak coalition governments.

The above analysis suggests that while the military–civilian regime cycle in the Sudan explains a large part of the story of the political economy of macroeconomic policy, it does not fully account for it. We identify four issues that require further analysis. First, there are differences between the second (1964–8) and third (1985–9) civilian democracies, and between the first (partially covered by the period 1961–4) and the other two military regimes (1969–84 and 1989–present, respectively). Second, there are similarities between the first military regime and the second civilian regime. Third, there are differences between phases within the last two military regimes. Fourth, relative to all regimes, the first phase of the Salvation regime (1989–94) stands out in terms of its excessive use of inflationary finance.

4.3.3   A second look

The first three regimes that ruled Sudan—the first civilian democracy (1956–8), the first military regime (1958–4), and the second civilian administration (1964–9) – lacked a transformative political agenda and adopted similar economic policies. The first coup was a palace coup, mounted at the behest of the political establishment to restore political stability to the country. The coup-makers quickly acquiesced to popular pressure and handed over power to a transitional government, which prepared the country for an elected civilian administration. The second democracy pursued economic policies similar to the first.

The political philosophy of the first military regime is reflected in its macroeconomic policy. It relied only modestly on inflationary finance, which yielded an average seigniorage revenue of 1.4 percentage points of GDP and below 5 percent inflation rate. The second democracy (1965–8) showed even further commitment to macroeconomic stability, with no inflation tax and a decline in seigniorage revenue to less than 1 percent. This was made possible by reducing the rate of monetary expansion by more than 50 percent (from about 15 percent during the military regime to 7 percent). In these two periods, all recurrent and development budgets were financed domestically. The civil war continued at a very low level of violence with limited economy-wide consequences.

The military regime evolved through four distinct phases, each of which has distinct features in terms of political economy and the associated economic policies.

The first phase (1969–73) was dominated by a socialist ideology, which came with a radical program for restructuring Sudanese society and the economy. However, due to strong opposition from the main political establishment as well as divisions within the rank of the leftist junta, the regime could not implement its radical agenda. Inflation remained in single digits and foreign aid (at $1.50 *per capita*) was negligible. Growth declined much further to a low of −2.2 percent per annum, compared to −0.5 percent for 1965–8.

Following a failed coup in 1971 by the Sudanese Communist Party, General Gaafar al-Nimeiri, the head of the military regime, moved his regime closer to the West. The regime also started to intensify its efforts to reach a peaceful resolution to the civil war. In 1972, it negotiated the Addis Ababa peace agreement, which brought an end to the first civil war.

In terms of economic performance, the period 1974–7 – which we identify as the second phase of this regime – recorded the most impressive growth (9 percent annual *per capita* growth rate) in post-independence history. While inflation rose to more than 17 percent and the rate of monetary expansion almost doubled (from 17 percent to 30 percent), the value of foreign aid increased massively from $1.50 *per capita* in the previous period to more than $14 *per capita* in 1974–7. This was the most dramatic development in the Sudanese economy.

The resolution of the conflict and the ability of the country to realize a handsome "peace dividend," reflected in the dramatic rise in aid, facilitated a period of "catch-up" growth following the end of the civil war. In addition, the regime embarked on an ambitious development strategy, a substantial part of it devoted to post-conflict reconstruction in the South. During this period, the share of gross investment in GDP reached more than 19 percent, up by more than 6 percentage points of GDP from the average for 1970–4. Most of this investment was accounted for by FDI.

Important, too, was Sudan's position in the geopolitics of the region. Following the 1973 Arab–Israeli war, the oil-surplus countries of the Arab world endorsed a development strategy that promised to transform the country into a "bread basket" for the Arab world. This strategy augured well with pan-Arab political thinking at the time.

To maintain the pace of its ambitious development plan, while at the same time continue to provide for substantial outlays to the Regional Government in the South, the regime also relied on monetary expansion, especially as external financing tapered off toward the end of the period. In addition to rising macroeconomic instability (Elbadawi 1997, 1992), gross implementation and planning deficiencies not only brought growth to a halt but had also led the country by 1978 to the brink of a major economic crisis.

In 1979, Sudan became one of the first countries to adopt International Monetary Fund (IMF) and World Bank macroeconomic stabilization and structural adjustment programs (SAPs). However, the economy continued to slide further throughout 1978–84, which precipitated very active adjustment operations. Growth collapsed during this period to an average annual rate of –1.7 percent *per capita*, while macroeconomic policy continued to worsen. Inflation shot to more than 27 percent, and for the first time the inflation tax (at 6.2 percent of GDP) exceeded seigniorage revenue by more than 1 percentage point, indicating the increasing inefficiency of monetary finance (see table 7.18). The reforms emphasized two central policies: successive devaluations, and trade liberalization measures that shifted imports (and to some extent exports) from the official market to the free market. These reforms were also motivated by the emerging role of Sudan as a major labor-exporting country to the oil-surplus economies of the Middle East. Remittances from Sudanese nationals working abroad averaged more than three times the dollar value of official exports during 1983–4. These huge foreign exchange resources prompted the government to adopt reforms to unify the exchange rate. Having failed to attract further investment from the oil-surplus economies in the Arab region, these reforms aimed at mobilizing

Table 7.18 *Sudan, seigniorage, inflation tax, and foreign aid, 1961–1999*

Macroeconomic policy	1961–4	1965–8	1969–73	1974–7	1978–84	1985–9	1990–4	1995–9
Seigniorage revenue (% of GDP)	1.4	0.9	2.3	4.0	5.0	6.5	5.4	2.31
Inflation tax revenue (% of GDP)	0.6	0.0	1.5	3.0	6.2	8.9	14.1	4.25
Inflation rate	4.8	0.1	9.4	17.2	27.2	44.4	104.6	56.2
% change in M1	14.6	6.8	16.9	30.0	28.1	47.4	67.7	48.5
M1 to GDP (%)	12.2	14.0	16.0	17.4	23.0	20.8	13.7	7.1
Foreign aid								
Aid ratio (as % of GNI)	1.0	1.3	0.9	4.5	7.8	6.4	7.2	2.7
Aid *per capita* (current US$)	1.1	1.6	1.5	14.2	32.9	40.1	24.2	7.20

the remittances from these countries. However, these efforts were largely unsuccessful, and Sudanese nationals continued to send the bulk of their remittances through the parallel foreign exchange market, attracted by its more depreciated exchange rate (Elbadawi 1992).

Given the obvious failure of reforms, an important question to ask at this juncture is: why had adjustment lending continued all the way until the collapse of the regime in April 1985, causing the country to inherit one of the highest external debt burdens in Africa?

The fundamental factor was that under the regime, Sudan was a key ally of the West in the Cold War politics of the Horn of Africa and the Middle East (Brown, 1992). Political rather than economic considerations appeared to have been the key motivation behind the commitment to support the failed reform program of the Nimeiri regime.

The professional unions and political parties launched a popular uprising in April 1984, and when the armed forces switched loyalty to the rebellious masses, the regime collapsed. Following a one-year transitional government, the third elected civilian democracy assumed power. In addition to inheriting a violent civil war, the third democracy also inherited an economy in deep crisis. Unfortunately, the government was compromised by a weak and fractious partisan coalition, uncooperative professional unions, and a still aggressive military. A lack of political consensus prevented the government from undoing the economic legacy inherited from the previous sixteen years of the Nimeiri regime. The economy, therefore, continued to slide. Inflation reached more than 40 percent due to continued recourse to inflationary finance, despite a significant rise in foreign aid by about $7 *per capita*.

In June 1989, a military take-over put an end to the short-lived third democracy. This time, the army acted on behalf of the Islamic Front, which managed to install the so-called "Salvation" regime which remains in power at the time of writing. This era brought to Sudan major and sweeping changes. The objectives of the regime included purging the civil service, police, and especially the military of non-Islamist elements; creating a new entrepreneurial class through massive redistribution to party loyalists; using fiscal and monetary policy, including the inflation tax, to mobilize domestic resources to implement the political agendas of the party; and creating a strong economy, army, and state that could end the civil war in the South by imposing a military defeat on the rebels.

In pursuing these objectives, the regime had to contend with the reaction of the international community, which immediately scaled down foreign aid by almost 50 percent to about $24 *per capita* (table 7.18). When the IFIs suspended all lending, the regime then took recourse in inflationary finance. Because inflation averaged more than 100 percent, seigniorage revenue amounted to little, despite the massive growth in money supply. In this period financial deepening was reversed, as agents diversified away from holding banking deposits. The narrow money stock (as a share of GDP) declined from 21 percent in 1985–9 to 14 percent in 1990–4. Contributing to the loss of confidence and the decapitalization of banks was the announced surprise decision to change the currency in 1991.

A major part of the appropriated resources were used to finance war. Anecdotal evidence suggest that massive transfers may also have served the economic interests of the ruling party and the "new" private sector. Following the first five chaotic and unstable years, the regime was able to sharply cut inflation to about 56 percent during 1995–9. While the rate was about half that of 1990–4, seigniorage revenues declined even further to about 2.3 percent, almost a third the revenue share generated by the last civilian administration. The main factor behind the collapse of inflationary finance was massive financial disintermediation, leading to a reduction of the monetary ratio from 14 percent in the previous period to an all-time-low of only 7 percent. Clearly the regime had to face up to the limits of predatory monetary financing. Moreover, and as a result of imposition of formal sanctions by western countries, aid declined to just $7 *per capita*, almost one-sixth of the level in during the third democracy.

During this period, however, the regime was able to reap the benefits of a major strategic initiative in the form of the commercial exploitation of oil following strategic economic agreements with China, Malaysia, and other smaller countries, including the building of massive infrastructure in support of the oil industry. This development, which brought substantial FDI to Sudan, spurred a turnaround in the growth rate. Moreover the regime had also started to change its war strategy, and had been actively engaged in peace initiatives and sought to mend fences with the international development community.

5. Markets and growth

5.1   The food market

During the year 1984–5, Sudan experienced a famine. A study by the International Food Policy Research Institute (IFPRI) (Teklu, von Braun, and Zaki
1991) subjected the famine of 1984–5 to careful scrutiny, using survey data
from western Sudan as well as aggregate data at the country level. Some of
the findings of this study relate to the food market in Sudan.

The study notes that rainfall levels declined during the period 1960–86,
and that year-to-year fluctuations increased. These fluctuations resulted in
low growth in cereal production, largely because of the short-run effects on
yields. The researchers find that a 10 percent drop in annual rainfall from
the mean was associated with a 5 percent drop in cereal production and a
3.7 percent drop in yield. Sorghum was more affected by rainfall compared
to millet, the staple of some parts of western Sudan, with the elasticity of
yield to rainfall estimated as 0.73 for sorghum and 0.3 for millet.

The study shows that the markets for cereals in Sudan were highly respon-
sive to changes in production. A 10 percent drop in production resulted in a
26 percent increase in the real price of cereal while a 10 percent reduction in
stocks increased prices by 8 percent. Real cereal prices increased more than
three times in 1984–5 compared to 1982–3.

To further explore the characteristics of the food market, the researchers
estimated a price movement model of the following form, where the relevant
variables are in logarithms:

$$P_{it} = \alpha_i\, P_{i,t-1} + \beta_i(R_t - R_{t-1}) + \theta_i\, R_{t-1}$$
$$+\phi_i\, D_{85} + \gamma \cdot X + \varepsilon_{it}, \tag{1}$$

where P is the monthly wholesale price in a given market at a point in
time; R is the wholesale monthly price in a reference market; D is a dummy
variable for 1984–5, taking the value of 1 if the month belongs to 1984–5
and 0 otherwise; and X is a vector of local specific market factors. β therefore
measures the change in the local prices caused by a change in price in the
reference market. A positive value indicates that the local market prices track
movements in the reference market prices, implying that local traders monitor changes in the reference market and adjust accordingly. The parameter
θ is supposed to capture the influence of the reference market price level on
local prices. A summary of the results is reported in table 7.19, where figures
in parantheses are t-values.

The statistical significance of the β and θ coefficients suggests that commodity markets are not segmented. The relatively high β for sorghum and
cattle indicates that the regional markets in the western part of the country integrate strongly with the principal markets in the central and eastern

Table 7.19 *Sudan, information flows in the food market, index of market connectivity (IMC)*

Commodity	Regional market	Central market	α	β	θ	IMC (α/θ)
Sorghum	Elobeid	Gedaref	0.55	1.08	0.45	1.22
			(5.0)	(18.5)	(3.6)	
Cattle	Elobeid	Omdurman	0.72	0.78	0.24	2.98
			(8.2)	(12.1)	(2.3)	
Cattle	Nyala	Omdurman	0.75	0.73	0.20	3.68
			(8.6)	(8.1)	(1.7)	
Cattle	Nyala	Elobeid	0.43	0.95	0.60	0.71
			(3.8)	(12.8)	(4.5)	

Source: Teklu, von Braun, and Zaki (1991: 75–6, tables 44, 45).

regions. The implication is that traders have a well-functioning information network for monitoring price developments in various parts of the country.

The ratio of the local market coefficient, α, to the reference market coefficient, θ, is defined as the index of market connectivity (IMC) (i.e. IMC = α/θ). An IMC greater than unity indicates poor connections across markets, or that the relative contribution of local price history is the primary factor in the current level of local prices. Market segmentation obtains when θ approaches zero. An IMC less than unity implies a high degree of market connection. For sorghum, the regional market of Elobeid, in the west, is compared to the central market of Gedaref, in the east. The index of market connection is found to be 1.22. For cattle, two regional markets in the west, Elobeid and Nyala, are compared to two central markets in Omdurman and Elobeid. Except for the Elobeid–Nyala cattle link, which exhibits a relatively high connection with an IMC of 0.7, cattle market links have IMCs in excess of unity, indicating poor connectivity. The major explanation for poor market connectivity is the distance between markets. Nyala, for example, is about 1,400 km away from Omdurman, and the journey takes about two months during the rainy season.

The study comments that markets

appear to operate and to transmit price signals across regions. Even though such long-term regional price relations exist and remain unaffected in periods of acute production shortfalls, poor market connections preclude markets from clearing because of high market transaction costs. (Teklu, von Braun, and Zaki 1991: 76)

5.2 The labor market

Sudan possesses a fairly large market in the rural, traditional, sector and a small, but growing, urban modern market. The rural labor market is perceived to be largely competitive, or flexible, with self-employment as the dominant form of employment. The urban labor market started out as protected, but has experienced increasing flexibility since the late 1970s.

The migration and labor force survey of 1996 provides the latest detailed information on the labor market (Ministry of Manpower 1996). The survey shows that the rural labor market accounted for 69 percent of the total labor force of age ten years and above and for 71 percent of employment, and that 69 percent of the total labor force was male – 75 percent for the urban sector and 65.7 percent for the rural. Women's involvement in economic activity is thus higher in rural areas, as would be expected given the agricultural nature of the economy.

The labor force has a low level of educational achievement: 43 percent of the total labor force had no education (13.4 percent for the urban sector and 56 percent for the rural); only 19.5 percent could read and write (13.7 percent for the urban sector and 22 percent for the rural); 11.8 percent had primary education (14 percent for the urban sector and 10.8 percent for the rural); 12.8 percent had secondary education (29.8 percent for the urban sector and 5.3 percent for the rural); and only 5.3 percent had higher education (15.6 percent for the urban sector and 0.7 percent for the rural). The educational levels of the employed labor force were almost identical to those of the total labor force. As would be expected in a developing country like Sudan, there are substantial gender differences. Suffice it to note that of the employed labor force, 34.9 percent of the males and 65.9 percent of the females had no education.

The primary sector accounted for 55.3 percent of employment, with services accounting for 38.7 percent and the secondary sector for only 6 percent. In the urban areas 82.9 percent of the employment is accounted for by the tertiary sector, with 12.3 percent for the secondary sector and 4.8 percent for the primary sector. By contrast, in the rural areas, 76.6 percent of employment is accounted for by the primary sector, 20 percent by the tertiary sector, and only 3.4 percent by the secondary sector.

The private sector accounted for 75 percent of employment, the government sector accounted for 17.4 percent, and the public enterprise sector accounted for 3.1 percent, with the remainder employed in co-operative and other unidentified sectors. In the urban areas, the private sector accounted for 52.3 percent of urban employment with the government sector accounting for 39.2 percent and the public enterprise sector accounted for 4.5 percent. In the rural areas, by contrast, the private sector accounted for 84.6 percent of total employment, while the government sector accounted for 8.2 percent and the public enterprise sector accounted for 2.6 percent of total employment.

According to the survey, 42.5 percent of the employed labor had permanent employment, with seasonal employment accounting for 48.3 percent and occasional and temporary employment accounting for 10 percent and 1.2 percent, respectively. In the urban labor market permanent employment accounted for 80.2 percent of the employed labor with occasional employment accounting for about 13 percent, while seasonal and temporary employment accounted for 5.5 percent and 1.2 percent of urban employment, respectively. By contrast, in the rural labor market, permanent employment accounted for 26.7 percent while seasonal employment accounted for 63.5 percent of rural employment, with occasional and temporary employment accounting for 8.7 percent and 1.1 percent, respectively. These differences highlight the greater flexibility of the rural labor market relative to the urban labor market.

Of the employed labor, 84.1 percent worked in very small establishments (defined as employing between one and nine workers). Employment in small enterprises (employing between ten and twenty-nine workers) accounted for 7.8 percent; that in medium enterprises (thirty–forty-nine workers) accounted for 1.2 percent; and that in large enterprises (employing fifty workers and more) accounted for 7 percent of the total. In urban areas, very small enterprises accounted for the employment of 65.8 percent of the employed urban labor force, while small, medium, and large enterprises accounted for 15.2 percent, 3.2 percent, and 15.8 percent, respectively. In the rural areas, very small enterprises accounted for the employment of 91.8 percent of the employed rural labor force, with small, medium, and large enterprises accounting for 4.5 percent, 0.4 percent, and 3.3 percent, respectively.

Only 35.8 percent of the total employed labor were working for a wage: 71.9 percent in the urban sector and 19.5 percent in the rural. The average monthly wage in 1996 amounted to Ls. 26,320 in the rural sector (equivalent to US$19.60) and Ls. 50,024 in the urban sector (equivalent to US$37.30) thus implying an urban–rural wage differential of 1.9 per month. Note that the average wage rate in the rural sector was below the international poverty line of US$30 per person per month while that in the urban areas is slightly above this benchmark. According to the Ministry of Manpower (1996: xiii) the rate of unemployment increased from about 5.5 percent in 1973 to 16.6 percent in 1996, recording an annual rate of increase of 5.2 percent. Table 7.20 provides information concerning the unemployment rate, by level of education, as given in 1996.

The rural unemployment rate is lower than that for the urban sector, but still quite high. Unemployment increases with the level of education, though the pattern of increase is not uniform. In the urban sector, the highest unemployment rate is recorded for an intermediate level of education, with the university level ranking second. In the rural sector, there is a clear tendency for the rate of unemployment to increase up to the primary level and then to decline.

In response to the rising rate of unemployment, the rate of emigration increased, especially to the oil-producing countries. As a result of the first oil price increase, these countries started ambitious development programs and created a regional labor market to which labor flocked from all over the

Table 7.20 *Sudan, unemployment rates, by level of education and labor market, 1996, percent*

Educational level	Urban	Rural	Total
No education	18.9	14.1	14.6
Read and write	19.1	16.0	16.6
Primary	19.7	19.3	19.4
Intermediate	23.0	18.1	20.6
Secondary	17.6	15.1	16.9
University and higher	21.8	7.5	22.6
Total	**19.6**	**15.3**	**16.6**

Source: Calculated from Ministry of Manpower (1996: 48–52, table 8).

world. No exact numbers of Sudanese Nationals Working Abroad (SNWA) has been reported in the relevant literature or the official sources. However, field surveys yield time-series data (Brown 1992: 227). According to these estimates, the number of emigrants increased from about 185,000 in 1978 to about 350,000 in 1984 and stabilized thereafter. As would be expected, such an emigration process was highly selective in terms of educational levels, skill levels, and age groups.

In 1983, 0.4 percent of SNWA were highly trained administrators compared to 0.2 percent for the labor force; 9 percent were professionals compared to 3 percent; 7 percent were clerks compared to 2.4 percent and 4.3 were unskilled workers compared to 11.9 percent. In terms of educational level, only 16.6 percent of SNWA were illiterate compared to 68 percent of the labor force; 32.4 percent had primary education compared to 6 percent; 17 percent had intermediate-level education compared to only 2.1 percent; and 26 percent had secondary or higher qualifications compared to 4.8 percent. Indeed, in 1983 it was officially reported that out of 5,815 doctors 2,254 left the country (39 percent); out of 2,640 engineers 950 migrated (36 percent); and out of 1,665 trained teachers, 965 opted to migrate (58 percent).[14]

5.3 The foreign exchange market

Emigration is closely linked to developments in the foreign exchange market. From independence up to 1979, this market was tightly controlled; the central bank was the sole body authorized to deal in foreign exchange.

In response to increased emigration to the Gulf states, the government introduced an incentive exchange rate for the remittances of SNWA and a nil-value import system. Under the latter, the government issued import licenses to people who had access to foreign exchange outside of official

[14] For similar survey-based results see, among others, Choucri (1985) and Galaledin (1987).

sources. Importers could borrow their foreign exchange requirements from workers abroad against the promise of paying the equivalent in Sudanese pounds. On June 8, 1978, the official exchange rate was devalued from Ls. 0.36/US$ to Ls. 0.4/US$ and the effective rate, applied on all transactions except cotton, was devalued from Ls.0.4/US$ to Ls.0.5/US$. The incentive rate for remittances was kept at Ls.0.57/US$.

In September 1979, foreign exchange controls and the nil-value system were abolished. A dual exchange rate system was established with an official rate (now depreciated from Ls.0.4/US$ to Ls.0.5/US$) and a parallel rate (of Ls. 0.8/US$) to be applied to a selected list of imported goods. By 1980 about 60 percent of total imports were channeled through the parallel market. On July 15, 1981 a free foreign exchange market was created and black market foreign exchange dealers were licensed.[15] The working of the black market, on the one hand, and the structural weakness of the economy, on the other, led to a depreciation of the official exchange rate from about Ls.0.35/US$ for the period 1960–77 to Ls.25.5/US$ in 1999. According to the Global Development Network (GDN) database, the black market premium, starting from 20 percent in 1960, fluctuated in an increasing trend to reach a maximum of 915.4 percent in 1990, and then declined to almost zero in 1999.[16]

Depending on conservative estimates of the number of SNWA as being about a quarter of a million workers, it has been estimated that over the period 1978–87 their average total earnings ranged between US$2.5 billion– 3 billion per year, with an average saving ratio of 60 percent of total income. This implies that potential remittances ranged from US$1.5 billion–1.8 billion per year. For the year 1983–4 it is estimated that actual cash remittances flowing into the country were US$1.64 billion: 76 percent of the remittances came through unofficial channels, 15 percent through Sudanese banks, and 9 percent through foreign banks. According to estimates reported in Hussain (1986: 25–6), black market resources contributed to the financing of about 55 percent of total imports during the mid-1980s.

The behavior of the black market exchange rate provided incentives for capital flight. Using an adjusted National Accounts framework to account for unofficial remittances, Brown (1992: 228–9) estimates that about US$11 billion left the economy as capital export over the period. "This is equivalent to 17 percent of Sudan's adjusted GNY [gross national income] over the same period, and approximately equal to the economy's accumulated foreign

[15] The official and parallel exchange rates were unified at Ls.0.9/US$ on November 19, 1979. A detailed description of the various stages of the development of the black market, as well as an analysis of the major determinants of the black market premium, is to be found in Elbadawi (1992).

[16] Elbadawi (1992: 57, table 9) reports average black market premiums of 71.9 percent for the period 1970–3; 77.8 percent for the period 1974–7; 77.7 percent for the period 1978–87; and 449.3 percent for the period 1988–90.

debt, which stood at US$11.1 billion at the end of 1987." Using a similar methodology, Elbadawi (1992: 52, table 4) estimates capital flight over the period 1973–88 as US$11.9 billion. According to these results annual capital flight as a ratio of GDP ranged between a low of 4.5 percent for 1984 to a high of 21 percent for 1975.

More recent estimates for capital flight are provided in Boyce and Ndiku-mana (2001) for the period 1970–96, where adjustments are made for exchange rate changes, the misinvoicing of trade transactions, and inter-est earnings. The estimates are made in terms of real 1996 prices using IMF trade statistics. Sudan ranked fourth in terms of average annual unadjusted capital flight of US$513 million (with Nigeria leading with an annual aver-age of US$2.3 billion, followed by Angola, US$1.5 billion, and Côte d'Ivoire, US$616). Allowing for trade misinvoicing, Sudan's accumulated real capital flight amounted to US$6.98 billion and allowing for imputed interest earn-ings it amounted to US$11.61 billion. Average annual capital flight as a ratio of GDP is calculated as 1.6 percent while the accumulated capital flight with interest earnings amounted to 161 percent of 1996 real GDP, equivalent to US$428 *per capita* for the same year (compared to a real GDP *per capita* of US$265). Relatively large amounts of capital flight are recorded for the years 1974 (US$674 million), 1979 (US$545 million), 1984 (US$1.4 billion), 1987 (US$599 million), 1989 (US$1.2 billion), and 1990 (US$846 million).

6. Special factors

6.1 Education and growth

The stock of human capital is usually measured as the average number of years of schooling in a population. The most recent estimates of human capital are provided in Barro and Lee (2000). The results for Sudan are reported in table 7.21.

Table 7.21 shows that the average years of schooling for the relevant population category in Sudan was only 0.41 years in 1960, but increased to reach an estimated 2.14 years by 2000. For 2000, the educational achievement of Sudan was much lower than that of the world (an average of 6.7 years), that for the developing world (an average of 5.1 years), that for South Asia (an average of 4.6 years), and that for SSA (an average of 3.5 years).

Despite this very limited achievement, the stock of human capital per worker in Sudan has recorded rather impressive growth. The annual growth rates of human capital stock ranged between 6.55 percent for the period 1975–80, to a low of 2.09 percent for the period 1995–2000 (see table 7.6, p. 200). For the whole period 1960–2000 the annual rate of growth is 4.23 percent. Recalling the fluctuating *per capita* growth record during the period since 1960, the experience of Sudan seems to conform to an emerging puzzle in the empirical growth literature: despite the rather impressive expansion

Table 7.21 *Sudan, educational achievements of population over fifteen years, 1960–2000*

Year	Population over age 15 (million)	% of Population with no schooling	% of Population with first level of schooling	% of Population with second level of schooling	% of Population with post-secondary level of schooling	Average years of schooling
1960	6.2	87.5	10.9	1.5	0.1	0.41
1965	6.9	85.3	12.7	1.8	0.2	0.50
1970	7.7	82.7	14.4	2.6	0.3	0.62
1975	8.9	79.0	16.2	4.3	0.5	0.83
1980	10.3	74.3	19.0	6.0	0.7	1.14
1985	11.8	69.5	23.7	6.2	0.6	1.34
1990	13.6	65.9	24.7	8.4	0.9	1.64
1995	15.8	62.8	26.1	9.7	1.4	1.93
2000	18.3	60.0	27.4	10.7	1.9	2.14

Source: Based on Barro and Lee (2000: appendix table A2).

Table 7.22 *Sudan, human capital and growth, 1960–2000*

Period	Growth rate of human capital per worker (%)	Growth rate of *per capita* GDP (%)	Output elasticity with respect to human capital
1960–5	4.56	−1.25	−0.27
1965–70	4.39	−0.61	−0.14
1970–5	6.01	−1.85	−0.31
1975–80	6.55	4.09	0.63
1980–5	3.29	−0.34	−0.10
1985–90	3.87	−0.45	−0.12
1990–5	3.31	0.33	0.10
1995–2000	2.09	2.94	1.41

Source: Based on table 7.21 and estimates of growth rates for the half-decades.

in the stock of human capital as measured by the average years of schooling in the population, GDP *per capita* did not show a similar trend.

Using the results on *per capita* GDP growth rates in Sudan, together with the results on human capital, confirms the ambiguity of the relationship between the increase in capital stock per worker and GDP *per capita* growth (table 7.22).

6.2 Civil war and growth

Sudan has endured one of the longest (1956–73 and 1983–present), and more recently one of the bloodiest, wars in Africa.[17] Elbadawi (1999a)

---

[17] A study of the economics of civil war in Sudan is that of Ali, Elbadawi, and El-Battahani (2002), which provides historical as well as analytical insights on this war.

Table 7.23 *Sudan, cost of civil war, forgone per capita growth, 1963–1997*

Period	Designation	5-year moving average *per capita* growth rate (%)	Change in *per capita* growth rate (percentage points)	Implied GDP growth rate (%)
1963–72	First civil war	1.52	–	4.32
1973–83	Addis Ababa peace interlude	4.24	2.72	7.04
1984–94	Second civil war without oil	2.11	−2.13	4.91
1984–97	Second civil war with oil	2.63	−1.86	5.43
1995–7	Oil and second civil war	4.27	0.03	7.07

Source: Own estimation.

simulates the possible costs incurred by the Sudan due to: (1) the intensity of the war, which is assumed to lead to political instability, erosion of the state and civil society instruments, and the consequent decline in property rights and the enforcement of contracts; and (2) the diversion of the limited human, financial, and physical resources to military ends. The first effect is proxied by the number of war casualties per 1,000, while the ratio of military expenditure to GDP proxies for the second. Using global panel data estimates of the determinants of growth and investment, which account for the two channels, Elbadawi[18] finds that the high military expenditure ratios in Sudan for 1989/90–1993/4, averaging roughly 7.9 percent of GDP by comparison with an average of 2.5 percent for SSA as a whole in 1986–90, result in a decline of 16 percent in investment/GDP and a loss of 2 percent in *per capita* GDP growth. When the war intensified from a relatively low level of casualties (an average of 956 non-civilian casualties in 1984) to more than 4,000 in 1989,[19] the investment ratio declined by 49 percent and GDP *per capita* growth slowed down by 6 percentage points. The civil war thus appears to have caused the country's investment ratio to be less than one-third of its potential level under normal conditions and has reduced *per capita* GDP by a cumulative rate of 8 percentage points. On average, therefore, the cost of war can be looked at as having been 2 percent in real *per capita* GDP growth. This is consistent with the estimates in Collier (1999).

The effect of the civil war on the growth performance of the economy can be looked at in a different fashion. In table 7.23, the average growth rate for the 1973–83 period is used as the peace counterfactual. The difference between the observed average growth rate and the counterfactual suggests the opportunity cost of the civil war. For the second civil war, a distinction

[18] Holding constant other determinants of both investment and growth.
[19] By all accounts, these are extremely conservative estimates. Furthermore, the war casualties have risen significantly over the five years since the advent of the current military government in June 1989.

is drawn between two sub-periods: 1984–94 is designated as "without oil" while 1984–97 is designated "with oil."

The five-year moving average real *per capita* growth rate during the peace period 1973–83 was 4.27 percent per annum, compared to a moving-average growth rate of 1.52 percent per annum for the war period 1963–72. This difference implies that the cost of the first civil war was about an 2.73 percentage points reduction in real *per capita* growth. During the second civil war, prior to the inflow of oil investments, the average real *per capita* growth rate was 2.11 percent per annum, implying that the cost of war was 2.13 percentage points. With the inflow of oil-related investments, *per capita* growth over the period 1984–97 averaged 2.63 percent per annum, implying a cost of war of a 1.86 percentage points reduction in the growth rate. The weighted average cost of war comes to a 2.22 percentage points reduction in the *per capita* rate of growth. Despite the difference in methodology, the result supports Collier's (1999) conclusions.

The pure effect of oil production is given by comparing the average for the period 1995–7 with the peace counterfactual. A remarkable feature of the above results is that the five-year moving average for the peace-duration period is almost identical to the five-year moving average for the period where there was civil war with oil.

6.3 Growth, distribution, and poverty

While there are both conceptual and practical problems regarding the measurement of poverty, there is general agreement that measures should be based on the cost of basic needs. This method involves identifying a typical diet for the poor that is necessary for leading a healthy life, as defined in terms of nutritional requirements recommended by the World Health Organization (WHO) and the Food and Agriculture Organization (FAO) (2,500 calories per adult per day). When the required quantities of the goods supplying the required calories are appropriately priced, a monetary value for the poverty line can be defined.[20]

Once a poverty line has been established, one measure of poverty is the ratio of the number of those who are poor to the total population, or the head-count ratio. It is the most widely used, and easily understood, measure

---

[20] Anand and Nur (1984) used this method to estimate an absolute poverty line for Sudan for 1984. According to their estimates the absolute poverty line was Ls.1.2 per person per day, equivalent to US$ 0.92. Subsequent studies in Sudan used the typical food basket for the poor identified by Anand and Nur (1984) to estimate poverty lines by appropriate re-pricing of the quantities involved that provide the recommended per person daily calorie intake.

Table 7.24 *Sudan, real per capita consumption expenditure, 1968–1999*

Year	GDP *per capita* ($ 1985 PPP)	Private consumption as % of GDP	*Per capita* consumption expenditure ($ 1985 PPP)	Annual growth rate of *per capita* consumption expenditure (%)
1968	798	0.679	542	–
1978	962	0.815	784	3.76
1987	817	0.778	636	−2.30
1988	763	0.713	544	−14.47
1989	808	0.890	719	32.17
1990	773	0.833	644	−10.43
1991	798	0.937	748	16.15
1992	817	0.721	589	−21.26
1993	815	0.932	760	29.03
1994	820	0.933	765	0.66
1995	833	0.782	651	−14.90
1996	846	0.810	685	5.22
1997	876	0.874	766	11.82
1998	908	0.913	829	8.22
1999	944	0.857	809	−2.41

Source: GDN data base (see Easterly and Sewadeh 2002). Figures for *per capita* GDP are appropriately adjusted using real GDP growth rates. Figures for private consumption as a ratio of GDP from 1988 onwards are from the Arab Monetary Fund *et al.* (2000).

of poverty. Another measure is the poverty gap. The two measures are special cases of a general class of additively separable poverty measures.

Changes in poverty over time can be looked at in terms of the elasticity of the poverty measure with respect to consumption expenditure. A poverty equation is estimated where the logarithms of relevant poverty measure are the independent variables and *per capita* consumption expenditure and the Gini coefficient are the explanatory variables. Table 7.24 presents estimates of real *per capita* consumption expenditure for a number of years, including the 1990s decade, using the estimates of private consumption to GDP from National Income Accounts. The ratio of the head-count to real *per capita* consumption expenditure is estimated on the basis of 1985 PPP USD.

From the above information it is clear that *per capita* private consumption expenditure fluctuated widely over the period. As table 7.24 shows, during the period 1968–78, *per capita* consumption expenditure increased by an annual rate of 3.8 percent, followed by a decline at an annual rate of 2.3 percent over the period 1978–87. Despite the fluctuations during the period since the mid-1980s, *per capita* consumption expenditure recorded positive

Table 7.25 *Sudan, growth and poverty, 1990s, change in head-count ratio*

Period	Initial per capita expenditure: μ ($ PPP)	Elasticity of H wrt $\mu = \gamma$	Initial Gini coefficient: G (%)	Elasticity of H wrt $G = \nu$	Per capita expenditure growth rate (%)	Growth in the Gini coefficient (%)	Change in poverty (%)
1990–9	773	−1.26	65.61	0.81	2.21	4.51	0.87
1990–8	773	−1.26	65.61	0.81	2.72	4.51	0.23
1990–4	773	−1.26	65.61	0.81	2.88	4.51	0.24
1995–8	833	−1.36	81.81	1.01	1.59	4.51	2.39

Note: wrt = With respect to.
Source: Own calculations.

growth for the various sub-periods of the 1990s. The average annual growth rates of *per capita* consumption are as follows: 2.21 percent for 1990–9 (with a standard deviation of 15.2 percentage points); 2.72 percent for 1990–8 (with a standard deviation of 16 percentage points); 2.88 percent for 1990–4 (with a standard deviation of 20.24 percentage points); and 1.59 percent for 1995–8 (with a standard deviation of 10.6 percentage points).

While high-quality information on the distribution of expenditure exists only for 1968, there is comparable information for 1978 and 1987. On the basis of this information, Gini coefficients for the distribution of expenditure are reported as 38.72 percent for 1968; 40.4 percent for 1978; and 57.48 percent for 1986.[21] The expenditure Gini coefficient thus recorded an annual increase at the rate of 0.42 percent over the period 1968–78, and at the rate of 4.51 percent over the period 1978–86. In what follows use will be made of the rate of increase in the Gini coefficient of 4.51 percent for the 1990s period. Table 7.25 reports the results for the rate of increase in the head-count ratio during the 1990s.

The results suggest that an increase of 1 percent in *per capita* consumption expenditure leads the head-count ratio to decline by 1.26 percent for the periods that have 1990 as the base year and by 1.36 for the periods that have 1994 as the base year. Improvements in the distribution of consumption expenditure, as reflected in a decline in the Gini coefficient, display a similar pattern.

Table 7.25 shows that the spread of poverty increased during the 1990s despite the overall growth in *per capita* GDP. For the period 1990–9, poverty increased by an annual rate of 0.87 percent. For the first half of this period, poverty increased only marginally, at an annual rate of 0.24 percent. For the second half of the 1990s, however, the rate of increase in the head-count ratio rose to 2.4 percent.

[21] See Ali (1994) for data sources.

6.4   Oil and growth: was there an investment transition in the 1990s?

In August 1999, Sudan exported its first shipment of oil.[22] According to an IMF report, proven reserves are estimated to range from about 1 billion to 5 billion barrels.[23]

According to recent estimates total yearly production amounted to about 52.8 million barrels, of which total cost of production amounted to 22.18 million barrels (i.e. 42 percent of total production). Oil profits thus amounted to about 30.62 million barrels, of which the government received 22.05 million barrels (i.e. 72 percent of total profits). Of this total, 15 million barrels were allocated for local consumption (3 million for the El Obeid refinery and 12 million for the Khartoum refinery), 4.7 million represented the transportation fees (i.e. 31.4 percent of the total local consumption or 21.3 percent of the total share of the government), and 2.34 million represented exports (i.e. 10.6 percent of the total share of the government).

The export price realized by the government averaged about US$20.75 per barrel. On the basis of this export price, it is estimated that the total gross revenue generated by the government from oil in 2000 amounted to about US$360 million (US$49 million from exports, US$62 million from the El Obeid refinery and US$249 from the Khartoum refinery). After deducting oil-related loan repayments, net government revenue from oil amounted to US$292 million. Oil has already started to dominate the Sudan's exports; it reached 35.4 percent in 1999, having been US$275.9 million out of US$780 million.

Given the above, the sustained growth that was registered during the second half of the 1990s could have been related to private investment flows to the oil sector. The distinct growth record of this sub-period thus raises the question as to whether the Sudan was able to engineer an investment transition during this period.

An "investment transition" is defined as a sustained increase in the investment rate of 5 percentage points or more. Investment transitions are shown to be associated with significant increases in rates of economic growth. In particular, it is shown that countries that experience an investment transition see their real *per capita* GDP growth rate increase from an average of

---

[22] According to an Amnesty report, the major companies currently active in the oil sector are the Great Nile Petroleum and Oil Corporation (GNPOC), which holds the concession for the two main oil-producing areas, the China National Petroleum Corporation (CNPC) which holds a 40 percent share in the project, Petronas Bhd of Malaysia with a 30 percent share, Talisman Energy of Canada with a 25 percent share, and Sudapet of Sudan with a 5 percent share.

[23] A reference to estimated reserves came in the context of the report by the US special envoy J. Danforth to President Bush on the civil war in Sudan. The figures are reported in the *St. Louis Post-Dispatch* (http://home.post-dispatch.com) on April 29, 2002.

Table 7.26 *Sudan, five-year moving-average investment rates and growth, 1960–1996*

Period	Investment rate (%)	GDP *per capita* growth	Capital output ratio	Rate of return to capital (%)
1960–4	15.31	1.61	9.5	10.5
1965–9	13.43	1.62	8.3	12.1
1970–4	13.17	2.05	6.4	15.6
1975–9	16.96	6.86	2.5	40.0
1980–4	16.79	1.70	9.9	10.1
1985–9	19.51	1.15	17.0	5.9
1990–6	16.28	3.26	5.0	20.0
1960–96	16.00	2.73	5.9	17.0

Source: Own calculations.

Table 7.27 *FDI flows into Sudan, 1996–2000*

Year	GDP (US$ million)	UNCTAD FDI flows (US$ million)	UNCTAD FDI/GDP ratio (%)	IMF FDI flows (US$ million)	IMF FDI/GDP ratio (%)
1996	7,586	0	0.00	70	0.92
1997	8,237	98	1.19	180	2.19
1998	8,830	371	4.20	670	7.59
1999	9,903	371	3.75	224[a]	2.26
2000	11,414	392	3.43	150[a]	1.31

Sources: UNCTAD (2001); IMF (2000).
Note: [a]Projections.

0.8 percentage points less than the world average growth rate to one that is 1.4 percentage points more than the world average growth rate, implying an increase of 2.2 percentage points.

Available information permits the investigation of an investment transition in Sudan. Table 7.26 summarizes the results for the half-decade five-year moving-average investment rates and the corresponding average growth rates of real *per capita* GDP, where figures in parentheses are standard deviations.

Compared to the half decade 1990–4, an investment transition would have required the investment rate for the 1995–8 sub-period to be in excess of 22.7 percent of GDP. There is evidence to suggest that FDI flows related to the oil sector were indeed substantial during the second half of the 1990s. However, the World Bank and IMF offer different estimates of FDI flows than UNCTAD does. Table 7.27 provides the relevant information.

The time pattern of the flow of FDI is almost identical for the two sources, but FDI flows peaked in 1998, amounting to 4.2 percent of GDP according to UNCTAD and about 7.6 percent of GDP according to the IMF. Despite the difference in estimates, the flow of FDI seems to be associated with the reported jump in the growth rate of the economy in 1997. On an annual average basis, however, the resulting FDI rate for the period 1996–2000 of 2.5 to 2.9 percentage points of GDP falls short of the minimum 5 percentage points required for an investment transition.

7. Conclusions

A case-based analysis of growth performance can be expected to provide answers to questions such as: What patterns of investment, learning, and innovation were observed? Why were these chosen by economic agents (households, firms, and governments)? How did these choices feed into the growth outcomes? Our responses to these questions can be related to the growth episodes identified above.

(1) **The devil they knew (1960–9):** The pattern of investment chosen by the various regimes since independence and up to May 1969 was dictated by the inherited institutional structure of the colonial state. The democratic governments, as well as the first military regime, continued with major investments in the agricultural sector and some investment in the transport sector. Economic policy sought to encourage the private sector to invest in the import-substituting industrial sector, with the government investing in factories with the intention of privatizing them in the future. The emerging private sector invested in real estate, cotton pump schemes, and mechanized rainfed agriculture. There was little technological progress, little innovation, and little learning. The result was volatile growth.

(2) **External influence and the bread-basket mirage (1969–73 and 1974–84):** During the remainder of the first growth episode (1969–73), the government attempted to copy the Arab socialist model of Egypt. The pattern of investment was heavily biased towards the public sector, with large-scale nationalization and confiscation of manufacturing firms. Investment in agriculture continued to focus on irrigated agriculture and mechanized rainfed farming. Incentives for the private sector were negative, however, and it adopted a "wait and see" attitude. Foreign businessmen, especially those associated with the import and export trade, began winding down their business in Sudan and relocating outside, while retaining links with business agents inside the country. The military regime made a dramatic change in political alliances, veering

from "socialist" policies towards liberalization and opening up to foreign investment. This change largely reflected the political interests of external parties including Saudi Arabia and the Arab countries and the USA. Conservative Arab regimes wanted to extricate Sudan from the throes of a so-called radical Arab camp while the USA wanted an ally for Egypt.

The "wait and see" attitude taken by private investors paid off in less than four years. The growth episode 1974–84 was largely based on joint ventures, with the government targeting transport, telecommunications, and agriculture in the name of the so-called "bread-basket strategy." A relatively high inflow of net resources was recorded during this period, including both private capital and official foreign assistance. If there was an investment pattern, it was largely dictated by the IMF and World Bank in the context of policy-based lending of the SAPs.

The result was a growth episode dependent on foreign official capital and a subsequent accumulation of debt. When the credibility of the government eroded, capital flight ensued, facilitated by high levels of emigration to the Gulf states.

(3) **Party politics and ideology (1985–94):** There were no clear investment patterns during this period for reasons due to the highly polarized political practices of the democratic regime (1986–9) and the highly ideological stance of the military regime (1989–94). Incentives to the private sector did not change during the democratic regime, and were dealt a shattering blow during the first phase of the third military regime with its Islamic ideological rhetoric and its biased economic practices, and the period saw high levels of capital flight. The US identification of the regime as one harboring "terrorism" increased the risks associated with the economy. In addition, the intensification of the civil war in the southern part of the country continued its pressure on the public treasury and further distorted the allocation of investment funds.

(4) **The lure of oil (1995–8):** This period saw the inflow of relatively large amounts of FDI related to the oil sector, despite the negative incentives to the private sector resulting from the intensification of the civil war and the continued non-credibility of the governing regime. A major move to stabilize the economy was started in 1996 by the adoption of a home-grown stabilization program based on the IMF stabilization model, with devaluation, privatization, and the adoption of stringent monetary and fiscal policies. Investment in the oil sector has already had an impact on the growth performance of the economy. As a result the period since 1995 has been the only sustained growth episode in the history of the country.

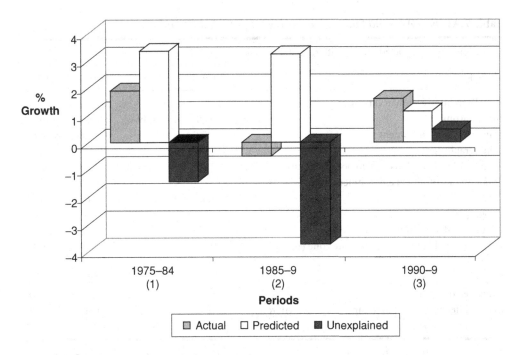

Figure 7.A1 Sudan, growth relative to East Asia, 1975–1999, *per capita* growth in East Asia minus *per capita* growth in Sudan

Appendix: Why has Sudan grown so little?

In addition to a sound macroeconomic and institutional environment and the rapid accumulation of human and physical capital, growth has been linked to factors associated with "geography and ecology," "demographic transition," and political and criminal violence. As we shall show, all three are likely to be strong determinants of growth in the Sudan. We take the East Asian economic performance as defining the development frontier and estimate an endogenous growth model (due to Elbadawi 2005) to probe further the reasons for Sudan's lack of growth.

Figure 7.A1 depicts the growth differentials in *per capita* GDP growth between East Asia and Sudan for three periods: 1975–84, 1985–9, and 1990–9.[24] The first period approximates period (2) (1974–83) of table 7.5, which was the longest period of peace in post-independence Sudan. During this period, average annual *per capita* growth in East Asia exceeded that of the Sudan by more than 4.6 percentage points. The model predicts a growth

[24] The periodization is dictated by the fact that the regression data, which cover seventy countries, are averaged over the following periods: 1965–9, 1970–4, 1975–9, 1980–4, 1985–9, 1990–4, 1995–2000 (cf Elbadawi 2005: table 7).

Table 7.A1 *East Asia and Sudan, accounting for growth differential*

Contributions to predicted growth differential, East Asia Sudan, 1975–99

Variable	1975–84	1985–9	1990–4	1995–9
Initial conditions/Human capital				
Initial income	−9.80	12.49	−14.35	−16.70
Primary school enrollment	2.09	2.01	2.06	1.83
Demographic gift				
Proportion of labor force size to population size (in log)	2.58	3.56	3.69	3.57
Policy and institutional environment				
CPIA	1.45	2.05	2.65	3.03
Geography				
Population density at the coastal/sea-navigable river	6.72	6.72	6.72	6.72
Proportion of land in non-temperate zone (in log)	0.17	0.17	0.17	0.17
Conflict				
Civil war	0.15	1.21	1.51	1.21
Explained difference	3.35	3.24	2.44	−0.18
Actual difference = Difference in average growth rate	1.90	−0.50	0.30	2.90
Unexplained difference	−1.45	3.74	−2.14	3.08

Notes: The simulation is based on the difference in magnitude of the variable in question between the two regions, multiplied by the coefficient taken from model 2a of Elbadawi (2005). The coefficients are reproduced above.

differential of only 3.4 percent, suggesting an unexplained growth rate of about 13 percent. During 1985–9 the growth differential (at 6.48 percent) widened further in favor of East Asia. The model, however, predicts a growth differential of only 3.24 percent, leaving more than 3.2 percentage points unexplained. This period approximates period (3) in table 7.5 (1984–94), which follows the collapse of peace and the start of the second and much more violent episode of the civil war. During period (3) in figure 7.A1 (1990–9), average growth has improved considerably, virtually matching that of East Asia.

Sudanese growth in this latter period was not uniform, however, with the first half of the period (1990–4) experiencing negative growth and the period 1995–9 a positive growth rate of almost 8 percent per annum. More importantly, however, in this period the production and export of oil and the huge inflow of foreign investment associated with the oil sector are likely to have been the key contributors to growth. At the same time, most East Asian countries experienced a substantial decline in growth during this period.

In table 7.A1, we apportion the determinants of growth between "traditional growth fundamentals" – initial income, human capital, and institutions – and factors associated with demography, geography, and civil war.

The exercise suggests that because Sudan's initial income was much lower than that of East Asia, it benefited from a huge catch-up effect. This effect is partially reduced, however, by the impact of East Asia's more favorable institutional and policy environment and its greater accumulation of human capital. These two factors translate into a growth advantage for the latter ranging from 3.5 to 4.6 percent. Though substantial, the "net" catch-up effect is still substantial and favors the Sudan.

We now turn to two non-conventional growth determinants, geography and physical ecology, and the "demographic gift."

(1) **Geography and physical ecology:** Jeffrey Sachs and his research associates[25] argue that favorable geography and ecology – in terms of access to long coastal lines or sea-navigable rivers and temperate climate – are robustly associated with superior growth record. This literature suggests several channels through which favorable geography and ecology could promote overall economic growth. A high share of a country's area around coastal lines or sea-navigable rivers and high economic density along the coast are important determinants of competitiveness, especially for transaction-intensive exports, such as manufactures. A high share of non-tropical (especially temperate) regions is associated with a reduced prevalence of vector-borne diseases and high agricultural productivity. The literature also suggests that natural openness is associated with "good" institutions.

Easterly and Levine (2002), using cross-country regression models of growth, test the effect of endowment (tropics, germs, and crops), institutions, and policy, and find that endowment affects growth through institutions; they fail to find a direct effect for the former, however. Using a panel of manufacturing firm-level data from a sample of African and non-African countries, Elbadawi and Sambanis (2001, 2002) find strong evidence linking geography-based measures of "suppliers' access" and "market access" to productivity and export performance, while controlling for institutions. Elbadawi (2005) finds that geography and climate are robustly and directly associated with growth, though institutions associate with growth as well.

Geography appears to be a very significant source of growth differentials between East Asia and Sudan. According to the estimates of Figure 7.A1, the effect of the population density along coastal lines and sea-navigable rivers (100 km radius) accounts for more than 6.7 percent of the growth differential in favor of East Asia.[26] Despite the small

---

[25] Sachs and Warner (1997), Bloom and Sachs (1998), Gallup and Sachs (1998). See also Elbadawi (1999b).

[26] The variable accounts for the combined influence of the land area along the coast and its population density. The population density was based on the average for the 1980s.

share of its coastal area (only 2 percent compared to 60 percent for East Asia), the density of population along the Sudanese coast is negligible even by African standards. At 15 people per km^2, it stands at less than one-sixteenth of the East Asian average. Since most of East Asia and the Sudan are non-temperate, however, the factor accounts for only 0.17 percentage points of the growth differential in favor of East Asia.

(2) **The demographic gift:** The demographic transition experienced by East Asia manifests itself in a steadily rising share of the working-age population relative to the rest of the population. This type of demographic transition offers "a demographic window of opportunity," where the high shares of the working-age population foster accelerated and sustained economic growth by increasing labor force participation and savings (Yousif 1997). The resulting rise in income, in turn, further consolidates the demographic transition, hence completing the virtuous circle. For most SSA countries, including the Sudan, this "demographic gift" is not yet in sight. Over the last thirty years, the share of the working-age population in this region has remained virtually stable. Even where such a transition has taken place, such as Egypt, the opportunity may not be realized because either growth has been sluggish or has not created enough jobs to absorb the huge increase in its working-age population.

It is therefore not surprising that the "demographic gift" has generated handsome growth dividends for East Asia relative to the Sudan. It explains about 2.6 percentage points of the growth differential in 1975–84, and about 3.6 percentage points for the remaining periods of 1985–9, 1990–4, and 1995–9.[27]

---

[27] The predicted growth differential is based on the following growth regression estimated by Elbadawi (2002):

$$grwth = \begin{array}{cccc} -6.90\ln y_{t-1} + & 0.04prim + & 15.08\ln\left(\dfrac{labor}{pop}\right) + & 0.90CPIA \\ (-7.88) & (2.46) & (4.72) & (3.65) \end{array}$$

$$+ \begin{array}{ccc} 2.14pdensty - & 0.15temp - & 1.51Cwar + 67.9 \\ (7.35) & (-8.38) & (-2.82) \end{array}$$

No. of Observations 669, no. of Countries 113, R^2 0.60; $grwth = per capita$ growth, $prim$ = primary school enrollment, $CPIA$ = Country Policy and Institutional Assessment (from the World Bank), $pdensity$ = population density, $temp$ = proportion of land in non-temperate zones, and $Cwar$ = Civil War Dummy. The CPIA is composed of twenty components covering four categories: macroeconomic management and sustainability of reforms; policies for sustainable and equitable growth; policies for reducing inequality; and public sector management and service delivery.

References

Abdel-Rahman, A-M. M. (1997), "The Partisan Theory and Macroeconomic Policy under Unscheduled Regime Transfers: A Case Study of an LDC," *Journal of Economic Study* 24: 223–42

Ali, A. A. G., I. Elbadawi, and A. El-Battahani (2002), "On the Causes, Consequences and Resolution of the Civil War in Sudan." Unpublished case study for the World Bank/Yale University project on the Economics of Political and Criminal Violence

Ali, M. A. R. (1974), *Government Expenditure and Economic Development: A Case Study of the Sudan.* Khartoum: Khartoum University Press

(1989), *The Cultivation of Hunger: State and Agriculture in Sudan.* Khartoum: Khartoum State University

(1994), *Adjustment Programmes and Poverty in Sudan.* Cairo: Arab Research Center (in Arabic)

Anand, V. I. and E. M. Nur (1984), "The Absolute Poverty Line in the Sudan: Estimates and Analysis," Faculty of Economic and Rural Development, University of Gezira

Arab Monetary Fund, League of Arab States, Arab Fund for Economic and Social Development, and the Organization of Arab Petroleum Exporting Countries (2000), *Unified Arab Economic Report 2000.* Abu Dhabi: Arab Monetary Fund

Barro, R. and J. W. Lee (2000), "International Data on Educational Attainment: Updates and Implications," CID Working Paper 42. Harvard University, Cambridge, MA

Bloom, D. and J. Sachs (1998), "Geography, Demography and Economic Growth in Africa," *Brookings Papers on Economic Activity* 2: 207–95

Boyce, J. and L. Ndikumana (2001), "Is Africa a Net Creditor? New Estimates of Capital Flight from Severely Indebted Sub-Saharan African Countries, 1970–96," *Journal of Development Studies* 38: 27–56

Brown, R. (1992), *Public Debt and Private Wealth: Debt, Capital Flight and the International Monetary Fund in Sudan.* London: Macmillan

Choucri, N. (1985), *Study of Sudanese Nationals Working Abroad.* Khartoum: Ministry of Finance and Economic Planning

Collier, P. (1999), "On the Economic Consequences of Civil War," *Oxford Economic Papers* 51: 168–83

Collins, S. and B. Bosworth (1996), "Economic Growth in East Asia: Accumulation versus Assimilation," *Brookings Papers on Economic Activity* 2: 135–91

Diamond, J. (1997), *Guns, Germs and Steel: The Fate of Human Societies.* New York: W. W. Norton

Easterly, W. and R. Levine (2000), "It's not Factor Accumulation: Stylized Facts and Growth Models," *World Bank Economic Review* 11: 33–58

(2002), "Tropics, Germs, and Crops: How Endowments Influence Economic Development." Unpublished paper, Washington, DC: Center for Global Development and Institute for International Economics

Easterly, W. and M. Sewadeh (2002), Global Development Network Growth database, www.worldbank.org.

Economist (2000), "The Heart of the Matter," May 13–19: 22–4

Elbadawi, I. (1992), "Macroeconomic Management and the Black Market in Foreign Exchange in Sudan," Working Paper 859, Washington, DC: The World Bank

(1994), "Macroeconomic Management and the Black Market for Foreign Exchange in Sudan," in M. Kiguel, S. Lizondo, and S. A. O'Connell, eds., *Parallel Exchange Rates in Developing Countries*. Houndmills: Macmillan and New York: St. Martin's Press

(1999a), "The Tragedy of the Civil War in the Sudan and its Economic Consequences," in K. Wohlmuth *et al.*, eds., *Empowerment and Economic Development in Africa: African Development Perspectives Year Book*. New Brunswick, NJ and London: Transactions Publishers

(1999b), "Can Africa Export Manufactures? The Role of Endowment, Exchange Rates and Transaction Costs," Working Paper 2120, Washington DC: The World Bank

(2005), "Reviving Growth in the Arab World," *Economic Development and Cultural Change* 53(2): 293–326

Elbadawi, I. and N. Sombanis (2000), "Why are there so many Civil Wars in Africa? Understanding and Preventing Violent Conflict," *Journal of African Economies* 9: 244–69

(2002), "How Much War Will We See? Explaining the Prevalence of Civil War," *Journal of Conflict Resolution* 46: 307–34

Fawzi, S. E. (1957), *The Labor Movement in the Sudan*. Oxford: Oxford University Press

Gaitskell, A. (1959), *Gezira: A Story of Development in the Sudan*. London: Faber & Faber

Galaledin, M. E. (1987), "Remittances of Sudanese Working in the Oil Countries," in Arab Planning Institute, *Remittances of Arabs Working Abroad*. Kuwait: Arab Planning Institute (in Arabic)

Gallup, J. L. and J. Sachs (1998), "Geography and Economic Growth," in B. Pleskovic and J. E. Stiglitz, eds., *Proceedings of the World Bank Annual Conference on Development Economics*. Washington, DC: World Bank

Hussain, M. N. (1986), "Remittances: A Synthesis of Information and Analyzes." Unpublished Paper, Development Studies and Research Center, University of Khartoum

International Monetary Fund (IMF) (2000), Sudan: Staff Report for the 2000 Article IV Consultation and Fourth Review of the First Annual Program under the Medium-term Staff-monitored Program. International Monetary Fund, Washington, DC

Kaufmann, D., A. Kraay, and P. Zoido-Lobaton (1999a), "Governance Matters," Working Paper 2195, The World Bank, Washington, DC

(1999b), "Aggregating Governance Indicators." Unpublished paper, The World Bank, Washington, DC

Mauro, P. (1995), "Corruption and Growth," *Quarterly Journal of Economics* 110: 681–712

Ministry of Manpower (1996), *Migration and Labor Force Survey 1996: Statistical Tables*. Khartoum: Ministry of Manpower

Ndulu, B. J. and S. A. O'Connell (2000). "Background Information on Economic Growth." Background paper prepared for the Explaining African Growth Project. Nairobi: African Economic Research Consortium (downloadable: www.aercafrica.org)

Niblock, T. (1987), *Class and Power in Sudan: The Dynamics of Sudanese Politics, 1898–1985.* Albany, NY: State University of New York Press

O'Connell, S. A. and B. J. Ndulu (2000), "Africa's Growth Experience: A Focus on Sources of Growth." AERC Growth Working Paper No. 10. Nairobi: African Economic Research Consortium, April (downloadable: www.aercafrica.org)

Pritchett, L. (2000), "Understanding Patterns of Economic Growth: Searching for Hills among Plateaus, Mountains, and Plains." *World Bank Economic Review* 14: 221–50

Sachs, J. and A. Warner (1997), "Sources of Slow Growth in African Economies," *Journal of African Economies* 6: 335–76

Teklu, T., J. von Braun, and E. Zaki (1991), "Drought and Famine Relationships in Sudan: Policy Implications." Research Report 88, IFPRI, Washington DC

UNCTAD (2001), *World Investment Report 2001.* Geneva: Promoting Linkages

Yousif, T. (1997), "Demography, Capital Dependency and Globalization in MENA." Unpublished paper, Economic Research Fund, Cairo

8 | Restarting and sustaining growth in a post-conflict economy: the case of Uganda

Louis A. Kasekende and Michael Atingi-Ego

1. Introduction

At the beginning of the 1960s, Uganda's *per capita* income was close to that of most of the economies of Southeast Asia. During the 1960s, the country experienced impressive economic performance based largely on inward-looking policies, with an emphasis on import-substitution industries and greater regulation on the part of government. The external shocks of the 1970s, arising from deterioration in Uganda's terms of trade, reversed this impressive economic performance. As with most SSA countries, the inability to adjust economic policies in the face of worsening terms of trade, highly restrictive economic policies in the OECD countries, dwindling access to external finance, and the consequent external debt crisis, did little to spur growth in the 1980s. Until the early 1990s, growth was further undermined by a legacy of poor governance that began to emerge soon after independence, undermining social capital and increasing the perceived risks of private investment. These factors changed in the 1990s, however, mainly driven by increasing democratization and an improved economic policy environment. Indeed, the Ugandan economy has been one of the frontrunners in recovery in the continent, reversing the earlier trends of economic growth.

Growth analysts agree that the sustainability of growth in an economy is a function of the levels of investment and TFP. Key determinants of these factors include initial income, savings rates, geography (or the degree of natural protection), demography, and governance – the latter including both policy and institutions (Sachs and Warner 1997; Collier and Gunning 1997; Ndulu and O'Connell 2007). While TFP growth has shown striking variations over time in Uganda, the level of aggregate investment has tended uniformly to be rather low. We will argue that both outcomes reflect a high-risk environment characterized by insufficient social capital and prone to wide swings in the quality of governance. Low investment levels may also, however, reflect the impact of landlockedness and resource scarcity on investment returns. In weighing alternative explanations, we borrow substantially from the findings of EAGER (2000) and from Reinikka and Collier (2000).

Uganda's growth experience is strikingly correlated with the evolution of its political economy, and we organize our analysis accordingly. In section 2 we begin by presenting a brief sketch of the political economy of Uganda as a prelude to identifying a set of distinct episodes in the governance environment. We interpret these episodes in terms of the four policy syndromes identified by Collier and O'Connell (2007): excessive state controls (or "regulatory" regimes), inefficient redistribution, intertemporal failures, and state breakdown. In sections 3–5 we take up the leading syndromes in turn, exploring their origins, the details of their operation, and their impacts on resource allocation. In section 6 we return to the basic periodization to assess the impact of the evolving policy environment on investment and growth. Section 7 has some concluding remarks and lessons.

2. Uganda's political economy

Conflicts between political, institutional and market interests, and control economics characterized the Ugandan political economy during the period 1962–2000. These conflicts resulted in various governance styles, conflicts, policy environments, and degrees of market functioning, which ultimately affected the process of structural transformation of the economy.

Table 8.1 *Uganda, GDP performance, 1961–1970*

Industry	1961	1962	1963	1964	1965	1966	1967	1968	1969	1970	Average
Sectoral growth rates (%)											
Monetary sector	**0.5**	**−0.8**	**15.0**	**4.8**	**1.8**	**10.6**	**3.2**	**1.6**	**12.0**	**2.9**	**5.2**
– Primary[b]	−2.2	−5.1	20.7	6.7	−4.0	10.4	0.0	−1.1	19.6	1.5	4.7
– Secondary[c]	5.2	−1.1	22.0	−2.0	10.0	7.1	6.8	6.1	9.4	4.5	6.8
– Tertiary[d]	1.5	3.2	7.9	5.4	4.5	12.1	4.7	2.2	7.0	3.5	5.2
Non-monetary sector	**−4.9**	**9.1**	**0.7**	**4.4**	**5.8**	**1.2**	**3.8**	**3.2**	**7.6**	**−0.4**	**3.1**
– Agriculture	−5.9	11.4	0.7	4.2	6.3	1.1	3.6	4.3	8.0	−1.1	3.3
– Other	−1.2	0.6	0.9	5.6	3.5	1.7	4.4	−1.3	5.9	2.8	2.3
Total GDP	**−1.3**	**2.5**	**10.0**	**4.7**	**3.1**	**7.6**	**3.4**	**2.1**	**10.7**	**1.9**	**4.4**
Of which agriculture	−3.9	2.5	10.4	5.1	1.1	6.2	1.8	1.2	14.1	0.0	3.8
Inflation[a]	...	3.0	5.8	4.6	12.3	−5.5	5.8	4.7	7.5	−10.4	0.42
Sectoral contribution (%)											
Monetary sector	**67.2**	**65.1**	**68.0**	**68.1**	**67.3**	**69.2**	**69.1**	**68.7**	**69.6**	**70.3**	**68.0**
– Primary	27.2	25.2	27.7	28.2	26.3	26.9	26.1	68.7	27.3	27.2	26.8
– Secondary	6.2	6.1	7.5	7.3	8.2	8.7	9.2	25.3	12.7	13.7	8.7
– Tertiary	30.0	30.2	29.7	29.9	30.3	31.6	32.0	10.2	30.9	31.4	30.6
Non-monetary sector	**32.8**	**34.9**	**32.0**	**31.9**	**32.7**	**30.8**	**30.9**	**32.0**	**30.4**	**29.7**	**32.0**
– Agriculture	25.9	28.2	25.8	25.7	26.5	24.9	25.0	25.5	24.9	24.2	25.8
– Other	6.9	6.7	6.2	6.2	6.3	5.9	6.0	5.8	5.5	5.6	6.2
Total GDP	**100.0**	**100.0**	**100.0**	**100.0**	**100.0**	**100.0**	**100.0**	**100.0**	**100.0**	**100.0**	**100.0**
Of which agriculture	50.5	50.5	50.7	50.9	49.9	49.3	48.3	48.1	49.6	48.6	49.9

Notes: [a]Based on the Kampala Cost of Living Index for the Middle-Income Group (January 1961=100).
[b]Primary category includes agriculture, forestry, hunting, mining, and quarrying.
[c]Secondary category includes cotton ginning, coffee curing and sugar manufacturing, food products manufacturing, miscellaneous manufacturing, and electricity generation and construction.
[d]Tertiary category includes commerce, transport and communications, government services, miscellaneous services, and rent.
Source: Background to the Budgets (various issues).
... Data are unavailable.

The entrenchment of the state/public sector in factors of production and factor allocation in the late 1960s and the 1970s resulted in a deteriorating policy environment and economic contraction (see tables 8.1 and 8.2). These were accompanied by increasing political instability that began with the 1966 abrogation of the 1962 Constitution and the resultant weakening of institutions, and culminated in conflict, with the associated risk to the economy. Problems were exacerbated by the ascent of Amin to power in 1971, and the declaration of Economic War in 1972, which raised the levels of these parameters in the economy. All this lowered Uganda's investment levels further, reduced economic activity through destruction/dis-saving and capital flight, and hence diminished the outstanding stock of human and physical capital.

Table 8.2 *Uganda, GDP performance, 1971–1980*

Industry	1971	1972	1973	1974	1975	1976	1977	1978	1979	1980	Average
Sectoral growth rate (%)											
Monetary sector	3.4	−1.3	−2.9	−1.3	−4.3	−0.6	0.4	−8.5	−11.0	−1.4	−2.8
– Primary[a]	−7.2	2.1	4.8	−6.8	−3.9	−3.7	0.0	−5.5	−10.7	−6.3	−3.7
– Secondary[b]	4.1	−3.8	−6.6	0.4	−14.3	−4.3	−1.8	−18.5	−32.4	7.1	−7.0
– Tertiary[c]	12.2	−2.8	−7.5	2.9	−1.5	2.7	1.2	−8.1	−6.3	0.6	−0.7
Non-monetary sector	2.7	4.3	3.7	4.0	2.5	3.2	3.6	2.5	−13.6	−6.5	0.6
– Agriculture	2.3	4.6	3.7	4.2	2.4	3.2	3.7	2.7	−18.3	−7.4	0.1
– Other	4.3	3.2	3.7	3.2	3.3	3.6	3.5	1.3	6.2	−3.8	2.8
Total GDP	3.2	0.4	−0.9	0.4	−2.0	0.7	1.6	−4.5	−12.0	−3.4	−1.6
Of which agriculture	−3.1	3.8	5.2	−1.2	−0.4	0.1	2.3	−0.6	−15.0	−7.0	−1.6
Inflation rate (p.a.)	24.8	1.2	12.9	49.5	18.9	38.8	74.9	47.6	216.6	11.9	55.5
Sectoral contribution (%)											
Monetary sector	70.1	69.0	67.5	66.4	64.8	63.9	63.2	60.5	61.2	62.5	64.9
– Primary	24.5	24.9	26.3	24.4	23.9	22.9	22.5	22.3	22.6	21.9	23.6
– Secondary	11.3	10.8	10.2	10.2	8.9	8.5	8.2	7.0	5.4	6.0	8.6
– Tertiary	34.4	33.2	31.0	31.8	32.0	32.6	32.5	31.3	33.3	34.6	32.7
Non-monetary sector	29.9	31.0	32.5	33.6	35.2	36.1	36.8	39.5	38.8	37.5	35.1
– Agriculture	24.0	25.0	26.2	27.1	28.3	29.0	29.6	31.9	29.6	28.4	27.9
– Other	5.9	6.3	6.3	6.5	6.9	7.0	7.2	7.6	9.2	9.1	7.2
Total GDP	100.0	100.0	100	100.0	100.0	100.0	100.0	100.0	100.0	100.0	100.0
Of which agriculture	45.7	47.3	50.2	49.4	50.2	49.8	50.2	52.2	50.4	48.5	49.4

Notes: [a] Primary category includes agriculture, forestry, hunting, mining, and quarrying.
[b] Secondary category includes cotton ginning, coffee curing and sugar manufacturing, food products manufacturing, miscellaneous manufacturing, and electricity generation and construction.
[c] Tertiary category includes commerce, transport and communications, government services, miscellaneous services, and rent.
Source: Background to the Budgets (various issues).

The immediate post-Amin political economy was largely guided by the need to stabilize and restart economic growth. In that period, the main focus was on stabilizing the economy; other objectives played a subordinate role. Consequently, in 1981, a package of far-reaching economic policy reforms supported by the IMF/World Bank was introduced that were biased towards market-oriented policies and private sector-led economic growth. The peace dividend and these policy reforms improved economic performance, at least until 1984. The suspension of the monetary program by the IMF and the escalation of the civil conflict resulted in the renewed slowdown of the economy between 1984 and 1986. Conflict and its associated risks again reduced the quality and efficiency of domestic investment, while also diverting government expenditures from productive to security sectors.

The post-1986 period, the Museveni era, started with the end of civil war and was initially marked by adoption of a control economic regime (1986), followed by a partial implementation of the reform program between 1987 and 1992. The post-1992 period saw full ownership of the reform program together with political will; these ensured consistency in implementation and resistance to any form of policy reversal. Uganda's reform program between 1986 and 2000 has been one of the most successful in SSA. This also ensured that the policy environment was conducive to supporting private sector-led growth. Institutions were strengthened and more attempts to resolve conflict peacefully were adopted. Government emphasis on reducing poverty led to further improvements in social capital, which deepened, integrated, and sustained the growth process, and raised the opportunity cost of conflict. As a result, Uganda recorded strong economic performance during the 1990s.

Because Uganda is a landlocked country and possesses limited extractive resources where substantial rents can be earned, it is disadvantaged in terms of growth opportunities. Its landlocked nature constrains easy entry into the global market for manufactures and without high-value resources it is left to depend on rainfed agriculture, whose rents are much lower. In addition, its economy is exposed to the vagaries of weather and international commodity price decline. Uganda is also vulnerable to political instability. Prolonged armed conflicts and a resort to arms to change governments has characterized its political history. Only during the period 1986–2000 have efforts to build and strengthen democracy resulted in a sustained period of implementation of economic reforms. Even then, Uganda has had to cope with an insurgency in Northern Uganda for most of this period. Notwithstanding this, Uganda needs to stay and strengthen the course in setting up viable and coherent institutions that can be used to resolve internal conflicts and promote good relations with neighbors.

Based on these facts, a number of syndromes that led to poor growth performance can be identified: entrenchment of public ownership of factors of production (regulatory), conflicts (state breakdown), and inefficient redistribution.

3. Regulatory syndrome

A debate about market versus control economics, public versus private ownership of the means of production, and Africanization/Ugandanization versus multinational/foreign ownership characterized the discussion of Ugandan political economy during the post-independence era. Economic and political direction was dictated by the relative strength and influence of different interest groups. This had at times resulted in rapid changes in policy and direction after only a short implementation experience. It is noteworthy, however, that the period 1992–2000 has been characterized by a predictable and consistent policy environment.

The first development plan for the period 1961/2–1966/7 was modeled on the recommendations made by the World Bank Mission invited by the government of Uganda in 1961. After extensive consultative discussions with a number of stakeholders, the Mission drew up the first Five-Year Development Plan with several major recommendations. First, it noted that Uganda had a comparative advantage in the production of coffee and cotton, so the post-independence government should seek all possible ways to sustain the production of these commodities. Second, given that domestic savings could not match the required levels of investment, the importance of external financing was highlighted. Third, to stimulate and promote domestic savings, there was a need to promote the local entrepreneurial class as a means of domestic resource mobilization. The plan also recommended increased government expenditure on education and health, although the levels of social expenditure were to be maintained. It also took into account the need for an orderly evolution from a traditional to a modern economy, and increased production and wealth-creating activities. This was in addition to requesting government to prop up private investment through encouraging active investors and creating incentives to attract new ones, including African entrepreneurs.

In its assessment, the second Five-Year Development Plan (1965–9) noted that considerable economic progress had been recorded as a result of implementing the first Five-Year Development Plan as average growth in real GDP *per capita* accelerated from 0.37 to 1.54 percent per annum (see table 8.3). Targets on aggregate output growth and capital investment were achieved. Major setbacks during the period, however, included both the unsatisfactory expansion of employment opportunities during the five years, and the unsuccessful efforts aimed at reducing income dependence on coffee and cotton.

Seeking ways to overcome these shortcomings, the second Five-Year Development Plan (1965–9) instituted some radical changes to promote the dominance of the public sector in economic development. This was a major shift from the leading role accorded to the private sector in the first Five-Year Development Plan. In addition, the plan was more ambitious, and called for higher targets in real sector growth and import substitution. Other reforms including changes in foreign policy, monetary reform, and nationalization were emphasized. The monetary reform disbanded the East African Currency Board (EACB) by setting up a central bank, the Bank of Uganda, to which it assigned more control over monetary policy. The *Move to the Left* that was outlined by the 1969 "Common Man's Charter" led to the Nakivubo Pronouncements which called for the nationalization of key

Table 8.3 *Uganda, Ndulu–O'Connell pooled conditional growth decomposition, 1960–1997*

| Period | Growth in real GDP per capita | | Contribution of | | | | |
	Actual growth	Predicted growth	Base variables	Political instability	Policy variables inflation	Black market premium	Barro–Lee govt. spending/GDP
1960–4	0.37	3.80	−11.50	−0.022	−0.021	−	−
1965–9	1.54	3.60	−11.15	−0.108	−0.024	−	−
1970–4	1.54	3.66	−11.37	−0.390	−0.034	−	−
1975–9	−1.81	2.87	−11.80	−0.260	−0.124	−	−
1980–4	6.92	1.10	−12.52	−0.260	−0.252	−	−
1985–9	−0.88	1.93	−11.48	−0.324	−0.649	−	−
1990–7	3.10	1.83	−12.60	−0.081	−0.080	−	−

Note: Base variables include life expectancy, age dependency, growth of potential labor force, terms of trade shock, trading partner growth, and a dummy for landlockedness.

industries, indigenization of labor, and emphasis on centralized planning.[1] Significant forms of soft control[2] were thus introduced.

Atingi-Ego and Kasekende (1998) refer to the late 1960s and the 1970s as a period when inward-looking policies that promoted state ownership, financial repression, and trade protection hampered the efficient allocation of resources and capital formation. While, for instance, authoritarian political regimes transferred resources to areas that were politically prioritized, trade protection through high import taxes created sector resource misallocation that favored import-substituting industries. In general, the period 1967–79 saw increased controls that promoted the role of the public sector in development. In the absence of institutions to promote accountability and transparency, corruption set in and eroded the asset value and return to public investments. This provides a partial explanation for the growth trend below that realized in the immediate post-independence

[1] The abrogation of the 1962 Constitution was seen as a mechanism to contitutionalize the change to African socialism that was sweeping the region at that time. The President used the powers entrusted to him by the 1967 Constitution to establish a new political order, which aimed at radically increasing the participation of the state in economic production. In the same manner, President Nkrumah had earlier created state farms in Ghana; the 1967 Arusha Declaration basically socialized all means of production in Tanzania using the Ujamaa Villagization program, and the Mulugushi Declaration in 1968 pursued similar objectives using Block Farms in Zambia. The 1962 Constitution would not have given the President these sweeping powers (see EAGER 2000).

[2] A situation where some parts of economic activity are regulated by the state, nationalization of productive enterprises, and the ambition or efficiency of policies is moderate. This is compared with the *hard controls*, which are close to Communism.

Table 8.4 *Uganda and SSA, Collins–Bosworth (1996) growth decomposition, 1960–1997*

| | UGANDA | | | | SSA | | | |
| | Growth in | Contribution of | | | Growth in | Contribution of | | |
Period	real GDP *per capita*	Physical capital	Education	TFP residual	real GDP *per capita*	Physical capital	Education	TFP residual
1960–4	1.97	0.67	0.13	**1.17**	1.26	0.86	0.14	**0.26**
1965–9	0.35	1.24	−0.22	**−0.67**	1.60	1.03	0.18	**0.39**
1970–4	−0.55	0.78	0.14	**−1.47**	2.29	1.22	0.20	**0.87**
1975–9	−6.21	−0.24	0.35	**−6.32**	−0.10	0.81	0.27	**−1.18**
1980–4	0.22	−0.19	0.29	**0.13**	−1.28	0.41	0.30	**−1.99**
1985–9	0.13	−0.10	0.26	**−0.03**	0.64	0.06	0.30	**0.28**
1990–7	2.50	0.06	0.16	**2.29**	−1.55	−0.14	0.18	**−1.59**
Total	**−0.23**	**0.31**	**0.16**	**−0.70**	**0.41**	**0.61**	**0.23**	**−0.42**

Table 8.5 *Uganda and SSA, Hoeffler (1999) augmented Solow decomposition, 1960–1997*

| | Growth in real GDP *per capita* | | Contribution of | | | | |
Period	Actual growth	Predicted growth	Initial income	Investment rate	Initial education attainment	Replacement investment	Residuals
1960–4	0.53	−3.66	4.24	−7.97	−0.24	−2.20	4.17
1965–9	1.05	−6.64	4.16	−7.03	−0.23	−2.09	3.67
1970–4	−0.92	3.83	4.00	−8.68	−0.19	−0.81	2.90
1975–9	−2.92	−4.10	4.14	−9.48	−0.19	−0.74	1.16
1980–4	0.22	−5.05	4.58	−9.93	−0.19	0.10	5.25
1985–9	0.51	−5.45	4.55	−10.82	−0.17	−1.02	5.94
1990–7	3.28	−4.44	4.47	−10.02	−0.14	−1.26	7.70
Total	**0.25**	**−4.17**	**4.31**	**−9.13**	**−0.19**	**−1.16**	**4.40**

period (tables 8.3, 8.5 show a general contraction in the economy during the period).

The 1970s witnessed an entrenchment of the political-economy views that had begun in the late 1960s. Ugandanization and Nationalization were expanded through the declaration of Economic War by Amin in 1972. This act was intended to oust foreign interests and shift the means of production to indigenous Ugandans. Indeed, after the expulsion of the Asian community from Uganda in 1972, a new social class locally referred to as the *Mafutamingi*[3] was created. Given that most of the new managers were either

---

[3] Beneficiaries of Asian properties.

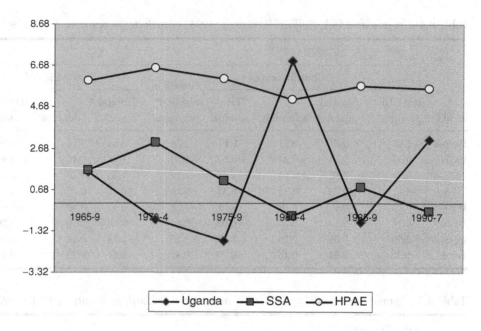

Figure 8.1 Uganda, growth in real GDP *per capita*, 1965–1997
Source: Ndulu and O'Connell database.
Note: SSA = Sub-Saharan Africa; HPAE = High-performing Asian Economies.

illiterate or lacked business acumen, there was a rapid decline in the business sector. Productivity fell due to the loss of management expertise and entrepreneurial capacity. Gross mismanagement of productive enterprises ensued, resulting in a rapid decay of existing capital assets. The sub-optimal policies pursued at the time had major costs for the monetary economy, especially the industrial sector. The decline in the share of monetary GDP in total GDP shown in table 8.2 demonstrates this.

Economic policies pursued in the second half of the 1970s evolved around the third Five-Year Development Plan and the *Action Plan* of 1975. This still emphasized the importance of the public sector in development. In particular, the plan included the goals of Ugandanization of the economy, realization of equitable distribution of income, and generation of employment. Following the expulsion of Asians, the enhanced state ownership of productive enterprises and increased public sector involvement in such enterprises resulted in higher inefficiency in production and the collapse of public service delivery. These, together with the pursuit of imprudent macroeconomic policies, the breakdown of law and order, the resultant deterioration in financial discipline, and the misallocation of resources through price distortions, were the main reasons for continued contraction in activity (see figure 8.1).

The major outcomes of the economic mismanagement included extensive misallocation of resources, emergence of parallel markets, rent-seeking, and speculation. Given the highly regulated environment, internal and external imbalances resulted in financial repression, in the emergence and intensification of negative real interest rates, and in over-valued exchange rates. Together with the prevailing political instability, these resulted in massive capital and human resource flight, leading to a contraction of the economy. At the same time, while coffee and cotton remained the main export crops, the failure of the marketing structure, poor policy, and extensive taxation led to a contraction in the production of these crops. The rise in oil prices in 1973–5 increased the import bill (see table 8.6), compounding the already existing problems reflected in the contraction of the economy, which posted an average decline in real GDP of 1.6 percent per year in the 1970s (see table 8.2).

The coffee boom of 1976–7 should have boosted the economy, but potential benefits were not realized due to the poor policy environment. The current account improved to a record surplus of USD 43.2 million and USD 68.1 million in 1976 and 1977, respectively (table 8.6). The increase in both official and private capital outflows, however, produced only a marginal increase in gross reserves. In 1978 the current account balance deteriorated to a deficit of USD 137.4 million. With the end of the coffee boom in 1978, the economy returned to its contracting trend, with growth rates recorded at −4.5 and −12 percent per annum in 1978 and 1979, respectively.

In summary, the first Five-Year Development Plan following the recommendations made by the World Bank saw the economy grow in real terms at an average of 5.2 percent per annum during the period 1962–6, higher than the growth target of 4.5–5.0 percent. The growth momentum slowed during the second Five-Year Development Plan period when the economy on average grew by 3.2 percent per annum following the significant introduction of soft controls. This was mainly on account of effects of the 1969 Nakivubo Pronouncements and the declaration of Economic War in 1972 that resulted in loss of confidence among private sector investors and security of investment in Uganda. The Nakivubo Pronouncements called for the nationalization of industries, which affected a number of foreign-owned firms, in which the government acquired a 60 percent stake. Despite the improvement in the current account linked to good export performance, the massive outflow of private capital in 1970 that followed the Nakivubo Pronouncements resulted in a reduction in fixed capital formation by the private sector. As discussed in the following sections, the ascent of Amin to power entrenched public ownership, and together with a loss of entrepreneurial skill and weakened institutions caused the economy to severely contract.

Table 8.6 *Uganda, balance of payments position, 1971–1980, US$ million*

Industry	1971	1972	1973	1974	1975	1976	1977	1978	1979	1980
Current account	**−85.8**	**16.4**	**43.0**	**−24.1**	**−56.1**	**43.2**	**68.1**	**−137.4**	**39.5**	**−83.1**
Merchandise account	−3.8	92.0	99.7	57.7	8.9	116.8	181.2	16.7	131.5	1.8
− Exports	243.9	263.8	275.1	294.0	237.2	323.6	547.8	323.0	397.2	319.4
− Imports	−247.7	−171.9	−175.5	−236.3	−228.4	−206.8	−366.6	−306.3	−265.7	−317.6
Services and income	−77.1	−69.7	−55.3	−80.6	−77.6	−75.7	−110.4	−151.1	−104.4	−120.8
Private transfers	−7.4	−9.0	−3.9	−5.1	−3.4	−5.7	−4.7	−8.8	−16.7	−2.2
Official transfers	2.6	3.1	2.6	3.8	16.0	7.7	2.0	5.9	29.1	38.1
Capital account	**41.3**	**−12.0**	**−51.7**	**5.9**	**56.0**	**−40.7**	**−67.6**	**144.7**	**−72.0**	**27.9**
Official capital	37.8	30.8	−15.9	29.9	20.6	−14.2	−41.6	62.0	112.2	92.4
Private capital	3.5	−42.8	−35.8	−24.0	35.4	−26.5	−26.0	82.7	−184.2	−64.5
Overall balance	**−44.4**	**4.4**	**−8.6**	**−18.1**	**−0.1**	**2.5**	**0.5**	**7.2**	**−32.6**	**−55.2**
Financing	**44.4**	**4.4**	**8.6**	**18.1**	**0.1**	**−2.5**	**−0.5**	**−7.2**	**32.6**	**55.2**
Of which reserves Δ	40.6	−9.0	8.0	18.6	−4.3	−3.8	−0.8	−7.3	26.3	32.4
Curr. account/GDP	**−5.9**	**1.04**	**2.33**	**−1.07**	**−1.85**	**1.35**	**1.16**	**−1.65**	**0.31**	**−0.46**
Trade/GDP	**−0.26**	**5.8**	**5.4**	**2.6**	**2.6**	**3.7**	**3.1**	**0.02**	**1.02**	**0.01**
Exchange rate ($hs/$)	7.14	7.02	7.14	7.42	8.27	8.26	7.74	7.48	7.42	

Source: Background to the Budgets (various issues).

3.1   Dismantling "soft controls"

A package of far-reaching economic policy reforms was introduced in 1981 under the support of three successive one-year stand-by arrangements with the IMF, which later culminated in the Economic Recovery Program (1982–4). As shown in table 8.4, the average rate of increase in *per capita* income of 0.22 percent[4] over the period 1981–4 starkly contrasted with the average decline of 1.28 percent in the Sub-Saharan region during this period.

During 1984–5, Atingi-Ego and Kasekende (1998) observe that neither the structural policies to address budgetary issues nor the arsenal of monetary policy instruments to deal with the resulting liquidity overhang was sufficient to promote macroeconomic stability. Furthermore, commitment by the government to the program was weak, denying the reform program the desired credibility. A number of performance benchmarks in the monetary program were violated, which culminated in the suspension of the IMF program as more resources were diverted to military expenditures. Armed conflict took a further toll on economic activity, both directly (via destruction of existing capital) and indirectly (by distorting the volume and allocation of saving). As a result of these developments, the economy contracted by 4.7 percent and grew by 0.5 percent in 1984 and 1985, respectively, while inflation soared to 101 and 91 percent, respectively (see table 8.7).

In January 1986, the National Resistance Movement (NRM) took power and implemented a ten-point program, a broad vision for political and economic change for the country. The political economy developments in the post-1986 period are discussed in Holmgren *et al.* (2002), who point out that there was a lack of consensus on certain key areas of macroeconomic management – in particular, the choice between a closed and open economy. In summary, the reform process was initially marked by rejection of market-based reforms in 1986 in favor of continued controls and regulation, followed by reluctant implementation of the reforms between 1987 and 1992.

As part of the reform process, the government convened a consultative conference in December 1989 to critically discuss Uganda's economy under the new government. All stakeholders in the economy were invited and the conference turned out to be another landmark in the reform process. The recommendations ranged from liberalization of the financial sector, to privatization and divestiture, to reduction of excessive government expenditure. It also laid the foundation for a radical liberalization of the foreign exchange market system, which internal observers viewed as a key reform. A combination of policy ownership and political will preserved the momentum of reforms even during exogenous shocks such as the deteriorating terms of trade (Henstridge and Kasekende 2001). It also meant that conditionality,

---

[4] The growth rate of total GDP averaged 3.9 percent per annum during this period.

Table 8.7 *Uganda, GDP, sector contribution, 1981–1989, percent*

Industry	1981	1982	1983	1984	1985	1986	1987	1988	1989	Average 1981–89
Sectoral growth rates (%)										
Monetary sector	0.0	7.2	6.0	−3.7	−1.5	0.4	8.2	7.9	6.9	3.49
– Primary[a]	−1.0	4.0	7.0	−5.6	0.3	−0.8	4.8	6.7	5.9	2.37
– Secondary[b]	0.8	14.4	3.1	−3.9	−5.0	0.4	24.4	10.0	8.6	6.98
– Tertiary[c]	0.4	6.4	6.4	−8.5	5.1	2.4	6.0	8.0	7.1	3.70
Non-monetary sector	10.3	5.8	5.7	−6.7	1.4	2.4	4.0	5.6	5.4	3.77
– Agriculture	13.2	6.4	6.4	−8.5	5.1	2.4	4.1	6.1	5.9	4.57
– Other	1.4	2.7	2.3	2.8	1.4	2.5	3.4	3.0	3.0	2.44
Total GDP	3.9	6.7	5.9	−4.7	0.5	1.1	6.7	7.1	6.4	2.28
Of which agriculture	7.2	5.4	6.9	−8.4	3.1	1.0	4.3	6.5	6.3	3.59
Inflation	164.2	34.8	21.2	100.9	90.9	358.4	163.0	118.9	81.1	125.9
Sectoral contribution (%)										
Monetary sector	64.9	65.2	65.2	65.9	64.6	64.2	65.1	65.6	65.9	65.0
– Primary	25.9	25.2	25.3	25.3	25.2	24.8	24.3	24.3	24.1	25.3
– Secondary	9.4	10.1	9.8	9.9	9.4	9.3	10.8	11.1	11.4	9.6
– Tertiary	29.5	29.8	29.9	30.8	30.0	30.1	29.9	30.2	30.4	30.0
Non-monetary sector	35.1	34.8	34.8	34.1	35.4	35.8	34.9	34.4	34.1	35.0
– Agriculture	29.4	29.3	29.5	28.3	29.6	29.9	29.2	28.9	28.8	29.3
– Other	5.7	5.5	5.3	5.8	5.8	5.9	5.7	5.5	5.3	5.7
Total GDP	100.0	100.0	100.0	100.0	100.0	100.0	100.0	100.0	100.0	100.0
Of which agriculture	52.1	51.4	51.9	50.0	51.2	51.2	50.0	49.8	49.7	51.3

Notes: [a]Primary category includes agriculture, forestry, hunting, mining, and quarrying.
[b]Secondary category includes cotton ginning, coffee curing and sugar manufacturing, food products manufacturing, miscellaneous manufacturing, and electricity generation and construction.
[c]Tertiary category includes commerce, transport and communications, government services, miscellaneous services, and rent.
Source: Background to the Budgets (various issues).

which had earlier been used by the reformists in 1987–92 to break the back of interest groups, was now less relevant for inducing reforms.

Decisions to change the direction in economic management were undertaken with a greater role for market-based allocation of resources as opposed to the controls used earlier. These decisions mainly arose from the consultative conference in 1989, whose outcome was biased in favor of the adoption of market-oriented policies and private sector-led growth. This set the basis for the pursuit of prudent macroeconomic and structural policies during this

Table 8.8 *Uganda, GDP performance, 1990–1999*

Sector contribution for the period 1990–9

Industry	1990	1991	1992	1993	1994	1995	1996	1997	1998	1999
Sector growth rates (%)										
Monetary sector	7.5	7.5	6.1	7.7	10.7	12.9	6.7	7.0	8.2	5.7
– Primary[a]	8.1	5.4	55.1	6.7	8.2	6.2	3.4	3.7	8.9	3.9
– Secondary[b]	5.3	9.4	6.8	11.1	21.9	18.2	13.2	13.0	9.6	7.8
– Tertiary[c]	8.0	8.5	6.6	7.2	12.6	11.2	6.1	6.3	7.1	5.9
Non-monetary sector	1.6	0.4	1.1	3.2	4.7	2.0	−1.2	0.4	5.4	2.6
– Agriculture	1.2	−0.1	0.7	3.2	4.7	1.2	−2.7	−1.0	5.3	2.0
– Other	3.7	3.0	3.3	3.2	4.4	6.2	6.1	6.1	5.6	5.1
Total GDP	5.5	5.2	4.5	6.3	10.4	8.3	4.7	5.3	7.5	5.0
Of which agriculture	3.5	2.2	2.6	4.9	7.0	3.4	−0.2	0.8	7.4	3.3
Inflation	33.3	27.8	54.5	5.1	10.0	6.6	7.1	8.2	0.6	5.8
Sectoral contribution (%)										
Monetary sector	67.2	68.6	69.7	70.6	72.1	73.7	75.2	76.4	76.8	77.4
– Primary	24.7	24.8	24.9	25.0	24.5	24.0	23.7	23.4	23.7	23.4
– Secondary	11.3	11.8	12.0	12.6	13.9	15.2	16.4	17.6	18.0	18.4
– Tertiary	31.1	32.1	32.1	33.0	33.7	34.5	35.0	35.3	35.2	35.5
Non-monetary sector	32.8	31.4	30.3	29.4	27.9	26.3	24.8	23.6	23.2	22.6
– Agriculture	27.6	26.3	25.3	24.5	23.3	21.7	20.2	19.0	18.6	18.1
– Other	5.2	5.1	5.0	4.9	4.6	4.5	4.6	4.6	4.6	4.6
Total GDP	100.0	100.0	100.0	100.0	100.0	100.0	100.0	100.0	100.0	100.0
Of which agriculture	48.8	47.4	46.5	45.9	44.5	42.5	40.5	38.8	38.7	38.1

Notes: [a]Primary category includes agriculture, forestry, hunting, mining, and quarrying.
[b]Secondary category includes cotton ginning, coffee curing and sugar manufacturing, food products manufacturing, miscellaneous manufacturing, and electricity generation and construction.
[c]Tertiary category includes commerce, transport and communications, government services, miscellaneous services, and rent.
Source: Background to the Budgets (various issues).

growth process. The IMF and World Bank were invited by the government of Uganda to assist it in designing a program based on the recommendations of the consultative forum, and Uganda's reform program since 1992 has been one of the most successful in SSA.

As shown in table 8.8, GDP grew by an average of 6.4 percent during 1992–9, and inflation was reduced from more than 100 percent in 1987 to single-digit figures. The developments outlined in this section could explain why Uganda out-performed SSA as a region, particularly through the contribution from TFP (see table 8.4). In spite of this stabilization effort, there were a host of challenges to sustainable macroeconomic stability, including fluctuating weather patterns, deterioration in terms of trade, and internal conflicts. Nonetheless, the period 1990–9 is characterized by sustained positive growth rates, as shown in table 8.8.

4. State breakdown

Although state breakdown is a syndrome that is characterized by the failure of the state to maintain internal security, we argue that Uganda has had a number of similar episodes which may not perfectly fit the definition but have had consequences for growth. We specifically point to governance and large-scale conflicts. Poor governance increases opportunism, civil strife, and political strife, which constrains the proper functioning of government policy. Contract enforcement, law and order, and the general standard of conduct can break down in an environment of poor governance. This leads to a decline in private sector investment. Armed conflict and its associated risks undermines growth via the channels emphasized earlier: a straight destruction of the human and physical stock, reductions in national savings, and diversion of available saving into capital flight. We therefore argue that the state breakdown that led to or increased the risk of conflict in the case of Uganda was characterized by poor governance, weak institutions, ethnicity, and external factors.

4.1   Governance

The 1962 Constitution promulgated just before independence provided a basis for the evolution of the country's post-independence political governance. According to EAGER (2000), this Constitution emphasized the observance and preservation of human rights and property rights, in addition to democratic leadership. It also provided for different levels and details of powers, authority, and functions of administration including central government, local government, the legislature, the executive, and the judiciary. Despite these attributes, there were shortcomings in the Constitution that affected the governance of the country. First, given the divergent political, social, and economic environments, and especially the regional resource endowments in Uganda, the compromises embodied in the Constitution could not last. Second, the consultations in the run-up to the promulgation of the Constitution were not inclusive enough to enlist broad support from the grass-roots. Third, Museveni (1997) observes that the foundation of political organization in Uganda was opportunistic and sectarian, given that it was based on divisions along religious and tribal lines. Indeed, the alliance between the *Kabaka Yekka* (KY) and the Uganda People's Congress (UPC) was short-lived, and by 1964 strains based on ideological, tribal, and ethnic interests had emerged.

The ideological differences within the UPC as a party led to the arrest and detention of four ministers including the Secretary General of the party and the Army Commander in 1966 (Museveni 1997). Earlier, allegations of gold-looting linked to Amin and Obote following Ugandan troops' involvement in Congo led to a motion in parliament accusing them of the offense. A near-unanimous vote to set up a commission of inquiry and suspend Amin was reversed by Obote (*Parliamentary Hansards* 1966). No action was taken against Amin; instead, he was later elevated to the rank of Army Commander after the detention of his predecessor (Museveni 1997).

The political crisis in Uganda thus deepened in 1966 when arrests, detentions without trial, and killings of civilians degenerated into states of emergency being placed on some parts of Buganda (Mudoola 1993). EAGER (2000) observes that these events culminated in the suspension of the 1962 Constitution in 1966 and in a military showdown; the *Kabaka's* palace was attacked forcing him into exile. Obote declared himself the Executive President.

EAGER (2000) further notes that the abrogation of the 1962 Constitution destroyed institutions that had promoted cultural values, attitudes, morals, and ethics in the community. As a result, opportunism, civil strife, and political strife began to reign in the post-1966 period, which constrained the proper functioning of government policy. Contract enforcement, law and order, and the general standard of conduct broke down. In such an environment, private sector investment could not thrive and it leveled off during the period 1965–9 as shown in figure 8.2.

4.2   Weak institutions

The role of interest groups in national politics is critical in molding institutions for the resolution of internal conflicts. Mudoola (1993) observes that institution-building has partly been distorted by the unbalanced allocation of resources along ethnic, regional, and religious lines. He points out that the use of resources by a particular group of people for their political advantage at the expense of other groups has provoked resentment from marginalized groups. In the 1960s, for example, Obote played one institution off another for political survival. The army, Mudoola argues, was not built into a national institution with national values because it was seen as necessary for political survival.[5] Thus while the military's intervention in domestic

---

[5] After the army mutiny in 1964, Obote made no effort to reform the army, as opposed to Nyerere who transformed the Tanzanian army into a national institution.

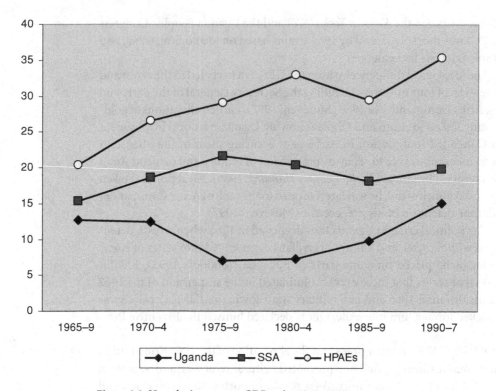

Figure 8.2 Uganda, investment:GDP ratio, 1965–1997
Source: Ndulu and O'Connell database.

affairs was largely responsible for the collapse of civil order in Uganda, this intervention had its roots in a fundamental political disorder, of which it was a symptom rather than a cause. This was the case when the government placed a state of emergency on Buganda subsequent to the storming of the *Kabaka*'s palace by the Army in 1966. The army was thus used against the parliament, the constitution, and the people of Uganda and later against the UPC government itself in 1971 (Mudoola 1993).

The coup by Idi Amin in 1971 elevated the army as an institution to a supreme organ of the state and was used to defend the ruling class and remove any obstacles that stood in the way of their search for wealth and power (see Mamdani 1983). The rule of law and order completely collapsed in 1972 as Amin assumed both legislative and executive powers with most legislation in the form of presidential decrees, while military tribunals judged major violations of the law. To remain politically safe and economically buoyant, senior civil servants sought connections with the agents of the regime. As long as Amin and his core team ran the government in a manner that would satisfy their personal and financial advantage, they did not care what happened to others. This resulted in the breakdown of law and order, while incentives for private investment, contract enforcement, and property rights completely disappeared. This is a situation described by Collier and O'Connell (2007) as a "looting" regime.

In the immediate post-Amin era, institutions necessary to promote good governance and accountability, though existing, were ineffective because they had been left to run down and stagnate during the Amin regime. Consequently, the capacity to implement good governance necessary for the effective functioning of government was constrained.

Institutions for good policy-making were not resilient to the developments that affected other institutions during the 1970s. Many of them subordinated their role to emerging informal institutions – for example, the parallel credit and foreign exchange markets. These developments were due to the controls that existed in the formal institutions, so they were merely motivated by the desire to circumvent the bureaucracies in the formal institutions. As earlier mentioned, poor governance also affected the standards of good conduct, such as filing of tax returns, and corporate governance. As a result, tax-collection efforts were constrained, informal sector activities increased, and institutional management generally weakened. The impact of these factors on economic performance was catastrophic, as evidenced by the developments in the 1970s. Table 8.2 provides evidence of increased informal activities and deceleration in GDP growth (i.e the evolution of non-monetary GDP).

4.3   Ethnicity

Ethnicity has also contributed to the conflicts in Uganda. Mudoola (1993) notes that ethnic groups were the most powerful historical, social, and political forces in determining the terms of the 1962 constitutional arrangements. Ethnic balancing characterized the immediate post-independence period because no single social force was yet strong enough to dictate terms to others. As such, a political–institutional structure arose from the situation of a balance of power that transcended particularistic interests. Following the abrogation of the Constitution in 1966, ethnic balancing ceased to play this important role and the risk of conflict thus increased.

With institutions strained, ethnic groups used whatever political resources were available to them to promote their own interests at the expense of less fortunate groups. The consequence of this dynamic relationship between the formal political groups, their leaders, and other interest groups was a highly polarized political situation in which interest groups and formal institutions were not insulated. Mudoola (1993) therefore argues that Ugandan politics became an institution-less arena in which groups with political resources seized power and dictated their terms, thus provoking violent reactions and grievances from others.

4.4 External factors

As mentioned in section 1, Uganda is a landlocked country and located in a region that has been characterized by conflict. The 1990s saw conflicts in Uganda's neighborhood, and these had implications for Uganda's economic performance. Despite its abundant agricultural resources, Uganda is geopolitically vulnerable and therefore its first line of defense should be viable and coherent institutions that are a means of resolving internal conflicts and establishing good relations with its neighbors. Unfortunately, political institutions remain largely weak. As a result, external influences have been important factors in explaining conflicts in Uganda. As we observed earlier, the presence of Ugandan troops in Congo and the resultant allegations of gold-looting by Obote and Amin was one of the trigger factors of the 1966 crisis. The bad relationship with Tanzania in the period 1972–8 contributed to the 1979 war. During the late 1980s and 1990s, Uganda has at different times had tensions with neighboring countries, particularly Kenya, Rwanda, the Democratic Republic of Congo (DRC), and Sudan. In the case of Rwanda, the tension culminated in a military confrontation within the DRC.

The effect of external factors was particularly important in the 1990s when some governments in the region believed others to be sympathetic to rebels. As a result, suspicion between governments in the region promoted conflicts internally and regionally, and thus introduced a new and complex regional dynamism to conflict. This made it possible for rebels to launch cross-border offensive moves against the governments they opposed, and receive financial and military support from host governments. The long duration of the conflicts in the region, such as the *Kony War* in Northern Uganda, that has lasted over a decade, could largely be attributed to this regional dimension. While this may not have seriously affected growth in general, its socio-political impact, diversion of resources to the military, and incidence of poverty in affected areas weighs heavily on the country.

4.5 Conflict and its resolution

As observed earlier, weak institutions and ethnicity have promoted both the risk and actual occurrence of conflict in Uganda. This appears to have been the case during the 1962–79 period. These risks on average appear to have lessened during the 1986–2000 period, although persistent insurgency continued in Northern Uganda. Indeed, Reinikka and Collier (2001) note that, since 1986, the Ugandan government has faced two policy challenges: reducing the risks of conflict in a conflict-prone society and reducing poverty in a very poor economy.

In addition, the inherited political economy that ensured a north–south divide, characterized by an unequal resource endowment between the north and south, has kept the risk of conflict reasonably high. Government efforts to mitigate this have been aimed at diversifying the economy, to ensure that the north becomes an integral part of Uganda's growth (Atingi-Ego and Sebudde 2005). A number of measures to address conflict and its reoccurrence were put in place during the 1990s, and these seem to have reduced the probability of an internal large-scale conflict:

- Addressing the problems that had, in the past, caused grievances in a number of groups that had contested for political and economic power between 1962 and 1986
- Building viable and durable institutions, and increasing the penalty for wrongdoing
- Political measures, such as the Amnesty Act, that offer blanket forgiveness to all those who renounce rebellion for civilian life
- Liberalization of economic activities, including privatization, that has generally eliminated rent-seeking behavior among the politically well-placed, and raised the opportunity cost of war
- Regional Peace Accords, such as the Lusaka Peace Accord with Congo and the peace agreement pursued by Kenya between the Sudanese government and the Sudan People's Liberation Army/Movement (SPLA/M), are a step in the right direction for ending conflicts in Uganda.

These appear to have reversed agents' expectations and could probably explain the recovery in the investment ratios as shown in figure 8.2. Indeed, Reinikka and Collier (2001) observe that, by the close of the 1980s, Ugandan society was considerably safer from internal large-scale conflict than it had been at both independence and at the start of the decade. During the 1990s, the economy staged a remarkable recovery from the collapse that had occurred during the conflict and has recently experienced respectable growth rates. The Ndulu and O'Connell model estimated, in table 8.3, that the reduction in GDP *per capita* growth rate accounted for by the political instability variable greatly declined from the 0.324 recorded from 1985 to 1989 to only 0.08 during the most recent period, 1990–7.

5. Redistribution

Collier and O'Connell (2007) allude to two types of redistribution in which growth is sacrificed to the objective of redistribution. These are vertical and regional distributions where vertical redistribution transfers resources from the rich to the poor households. In the case of Uganda, it may be difficult to identify episodes when either form of redistribution led to a deceleration of growth. Nonetheless, we argue that other forms of redistribution that resulted from macroeconomic policy management have been more relevant in explaining deceleration of growth. Redistribution through economic policy management transferred resources across sectors. For example, the current comprehensive development strategy that places emphasis on poverty reduction has resulted in the reallocation of a substantial amount of resources to poverty-reducing sectors. In addition, the management of economic policy has also seen resource transfer between both factor and product markets, and between Ugandans and non-Ugandans.

5.1   The Economic War

The process of the declaration of Economic War was akin to the Nakivubo Pronouncements, and was seen as a crusade against imperialism and its agents. Following the soft controls that were introduced in the 1969 Nakivubo Pronouncements, efforts at nationalization continued, culminating in the expulsion of the Asian community from Uganda. This was seen as a way of rewarding the Amin regime supporters and expanding its ranks. The property expropriated from Asian capitalists was mainly distributed to the agents of the regime commonly known as the *Mafutamingi*. To the extent that Economic War was designed to create an indigenous business and entrepreneurial class, a number of young Ugandans warmly embraced its declaration. Its implementation resulted in the transfer of economic wealth and power from foreigners, especially of Indian origin, in favor mainly of the state and politically connected individuals.

We mentioned earlier that the coup of 1971 transformed the army from a notionally national institution into an instrument of the ruling class. The Amin regime recruited young, unemployed, and uneducated men (the urban riff-raff) into the army and increasingly employed terror to eliminate the obstacles to wealth accumulation by a narrow elite. As depicted in table 8.2, economic deceleration began in 1972 and lasted until the end of the regime in 1979. The major outcome of this redistributive regime included:

(1) Extensive misallocation of resources – e.g. flow of resources to sectors which were profitable only because they were regulated.
(2) Emergence of parallel markets to meet the supply shortages and cater to agents who were rationed out of the regulated markets.
(3) Rent-seeking and speculative activities became more profitable and preferred to the production of goods and services. Short-term investment became more profitable as economic uncertainty increased. This resulted in distortions in the savings–investment relationship.

(4) Given the highly regulated environment, and the internal and external imbalances prevailing, financial repression in the form of negative real interest rates and over-valued exchange rates emerged and intensified.
(5) Massive capital and human resource flight.

5.2   Poverty reduction

Increased budgetary allocations and enhancement of the incomes of the poor were the strategies used to reduce the level of poverty. The organization of markets, for both products and factors of production, has been influenced by largely rural-based production and also by the prevailing policy environment. The change of rural households and firms in response to developments in the policy environment and political economy is discussed in Reinikka and Collier (2001). This development seems to explain the sustained satisfactory economic performance in the 1990s. The main aspects relevant to this chapter are that five recent Ugandan household surveys show that the number of people living below the poverty line fell from 56 percent in 1992 to 34 percent in 2001, though an increase to 38 percent was registered in 2003. The reduction in poverty can be explained mainly by economic growth, and partly by falling income inequality. The authors show that imperfections decreased in both factor and product markets, resulting in increased agricultural output and productivity by poor rural households during the period 1990–9. This is mainly attributed to the Poverty Reduction Strategies (PRSs) and the trade liberalization policies pursued by the government during this period. Policies that strengthened the property rights to resources already owned by the poor enhanced their asset position and had a significant impact on the functioning of factor markets. The involvement of the poor in the overall growth process was critical through increasing their access to productive resources and enhancing their productivity in a market friendly environment. This not only sustained economic growth, but also addressed the issues of income inequality among people, sectors, and regions.

5.3   Implications for markets

The economic management discussed above had implications for both the product and the factor markets, and the way resources were distributed among them.

5.3.1   Product markets

During the 1960s Uganda supplied raw materials to British firms and imported finished consumer goods from Britain. Growth was driven mostly by the agricultural sector, which was also in line with the first post-independence plan initiated by a World Bank Mission. The plan was based on the assumption that Uganda had a comparative advantage in the production of coffee and cotton. In line with the preference for government direct participation in the economy at the time, export marketing of crops through the formation of statutory boards such as the Coffee Marketing Board and the Lint Marketing Board was promoted.

At the local level, the processing factories (cotton ginneries and coffee factories) originally owned and run by non-Africans were handed over to the co-operative unions managed mainly by Africans. This continued into the 1970s when the major export (cotton and coffee) processing and marketing were handled entirely through state-owned marketing boards (government monopolies).

Furthermore, the welfare of the military rulers largely depended on the performance of the export–import connection, while the welfare of the workers and rural households hinged on their ability, at the individual level, to break out of the export–import confines. This was mainly attributed to the poor export polices that saw the state skim off a bigger surplus of the rural household export crop value. The poor policy environment indirectly taxed the peasant farmers; this not only reduced producer price incentives but also promoted smuggling of primary commodities out of the country for better returns. As a result, peasant farmers resorted to subsistence agriculture as shown by its increasing share in table 8.2. The peasants responded by moving out of the production of export crops and crops marketed by the state in favor of those that could be privately marketed. In other words, there was a shift from the production of tradable to non-tradable products, given the barriers that existed in the payment and exchange mechanisms. Even during the coffee price boom of 1976–7, the peasants responded by increasing smuggling of whatever they produced. The implication of this was the rise in the informal (subsistence) share of the economy, thereby reducing the multiplier effects of growth through sustainability and integration of economic activities (see table 8.2).

In the 1980s, attempts at reviving production were made, but these were short-lived. While the implementation of prudent macroeconomic policy was a step in the right direction, the absence of structural reforms to comprehensively address marketing problems ensured that marketing inefficiencies continued to reign. In the economic recovery program initiated in 1987, marketing was considered one of the priority areas of reform in order to revive economic growth. On the exchange rate and trade policy reform front, the government conformed to the obligations of Article VIII of the IMF agreement that placed no restrictions on international transactions. Consequently, in July 1990, the authorities legalized the buying and selling of foreign currencies at a market-determined rate through the establishment of foreign exchange bureaux. Finally, in 1994, the auction and the surrender requirements were abolished, and replaced with a unified foreign exchange system with the commercial banks and foreign exchange bureaux as the key institutions on the market. In addition, in July 1997, the capital account of the balance of payments was opened up in an attempt to increase private capital inflows. The major aim of the authorities was to reduce the share of informal activities.

Indeed, measures taken to revamp export earnings included the liberalization of export commodity marketing. A number of private companies and co-operative unions were licensed to compete with the once monopolistic marketing boards. The major impact has been on the spot delivery of money for value offered by the producers instead of the one-time issuance of promissory chits to pay for value delivered by the producers. On the macro-front, the central bank financing of the marketing boards, often associated with the injection of high-powered money into the system and accounting quite heavily for the inflationary episodes witnessed earlier, ceased. Competition within this marketing arrangement improved the efficiency of marketing and eliminated the need for central bank financing.

The liberalization of agricultural commodity prices and the increased competition in marketing increased revenues to farmers and lowered marketing costs. Additionally, the progressive liberalization of the exchange system and the abolition of surrender requirements on export proceeds from non-coffee exports resulted in much higher returns to producers, processors, and exporters. Liberal marketing policies increased competition and largely contributed to the increasing incomes of the poor through higher prices paid to farmers. In addition, one of the main aims of government policy of improving rural road networks was to ensure that rural households were well integrated into the market economy. Crop marketing provides a link between subsistence-oriented households and the rest of the economy.

There is also evidence that investment in infrastructure can significantly explain average crop prices among communities. Access to telecommunications and credit improved greatly during the 1990s, not only in the urban centers but also in the rural markets (see table 8.9). Larson and Deininger (2001) provide evidence that access to a fixed telephone line within 10 km raises rural prices, on average, by about 5 percent as information asymmetries between rural and urban markets are reduced.

Strengthening the infrastructure and marketing institutions for agricultural commodities integrated the poor into the overall growth process, besides enhancing their incomes; earlier policies that weakened these marketing institutions had had the converse effects on the poor and the entire growth process. Another important aspect of a liberalized market is the price transfer. Larson and Deininger (2001) show that the current market conditions encourage households to produce for export rather than produce food crops. The absence of extension services and of rural markets,

Table 8.9 *Uganda, evolution of telecommunication services, 1988–2001*

Indicator	1988	1990	1992	1994	1996	1998	2001
Fixed telephone lines connected	59,503	44,757	12,603	62,753	46,207	55,749	60,000
Fixed telephone line in rural areas	...	...	...	...	9,735	...	10,000
National telephone operators	1	1	1	1	1	2	2
Mobile cellular operators	0	0	0	0	1	2	3
Mobile lines	0	0		0	3,500	40,000	260,000
Mobile lines in rural area	0	0	0	0	0	...	40,000
Internet service providers	n/a	n/a	n/a	0	2	7	20
Public pay phone	0	0	0	0	0	1,115	3,116

Source: Uganda Communications Commission (Uganda Post and Communications Corporation for data prior to 1996).

especially in land and labor rentals, reduced agricultural output. In addition, information imperfections among rural households gave rise to high levels of credit rationing where neither the formal nor the informal money market existed. As a result, the capacity of the household to use recurrent inputs in agriculture as well to invest in non-farm activities was reduced. As pointed out earlier, the over-valued exchange rate and administered export prices caused a shift of resources to the production of non-traded goods. Unfortunately, markets for non-traded goods could not develop because of high transfer costs and risks that drove a wedge between rural and urban prices.

5.3.2 Factor markets

Land

The pattern of land ownership and its use prior to 1975 did not hamper agriculture production. The Land Decree of 1975, however, affected the rural households because all land now fell under the control of the state. Absolute ownership of land and the power of the customary tenant to stand in the way of development were abolished as all land became a state property held on a 99-year lease. The Land Commission was empowered to terminate any lease on under-developed land and give it to a potential developer. Such a leaseholder was free to evict a tenant occupying any part of the granted leasehold to permit the development of the land.

   This led well-to-do individuals, who had benefited from trade and property given away by the Amin regime (*Mafutamingis*), to grab large tracts of land, particularly in areas where land was scarce. Rural households were frequently driven away and the whole area fenced off. The practice of "absentee landlords" in the country was expanded because potential developers were not actually capitalistic farmers. Unfortunately, the wealth they amassed in form of land did not result in increased production; indeed, it eroded output by the rural households. Together with other factors, this may explain the deceleration in agricultural production during the 1975–9 period, as reflected in table 8.2.

The strengthened property rights after the fall of Amin in 1979 could partly explain the strong rebound in subsistence agriculture. It became increasingly difficult to evict the peasant tenant, and this ensured the continuity of production. The interests of tenants were further reinforced by the Land Act of 1998, which replaced the Land Decree of 1975. At the same time, however, acquisition of land for commercial purposes has become very difficult.

Labor

Human-capital formation has been influenced by a number of key factors: population growth rates, political economy, conflicts, education, and health. In addition, the organization of labor markets and how well they functioned affected productivity. Whereas the population growth rate has averaged 3.1 percent per annum over the last four decades, other demographic factors such as initial life expectancy, age structure of the population, education, and the social and political environment have had major implications for human capital and its productivity. The initial life expectancy that had peaked at 49.75 years in the period 1970–5, and trended above the SSA average in the first two decades after independence, has since declined and even fallen below the continent's average (see figure 8.3).

As a result of social and political instability, the demographic structure, and hence labor productivity, was adversely affected, especially by civil war in the 1970s and 1980s and by HIV/AIDS in the 1990s. Partly due to this, Uganda's demographic structure reveals a heavy degree of dependency in the population, even by SSA standards, throughout the study period. The trends in figure 8.4 show the dependency ratio[6] rising from the 97.5 percent recorded in the early 1960s to 103.4 percent in the late 1990s. These ratios are far higher than the SSA and High-performing Asian Economies (HPAEs) averages. Consequently, these have reduced Uganda's savings and investment rate when compared to other regions.

Additionally, the stock of human capital has been abysmal even by SSA and other developing-country standards, irrespective of whether this is proxied by years of education attainment at primary level, years of education attainment at secondary level, or secondary enrollment at relevant age. As shown in figures 8.5 and 8.6, the quality of human capital in Uganda, which was at almost the average level for SSA economies in the early 1960s, stagnated in

[6] Slower growth of the working-group population, compared to the dependent population (i.e. population outside the age brackets of sixteen–sixty-five years of age).

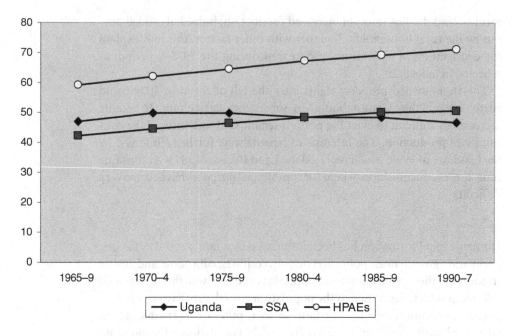

Figure 8.3 Uganda, initial life expectancy, in years, 1965–1997
Source: O'Connell and Ndulu data.

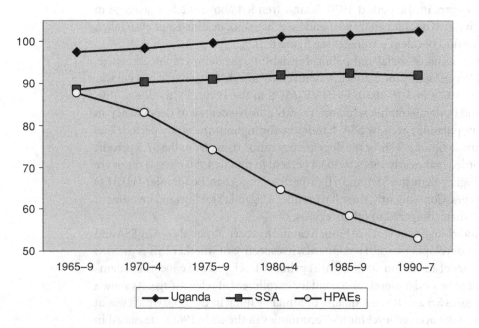

Figure 8.4 Uganda, age-dependency ratio, 1965–1997
Source: Ndulu and O'Connell data.

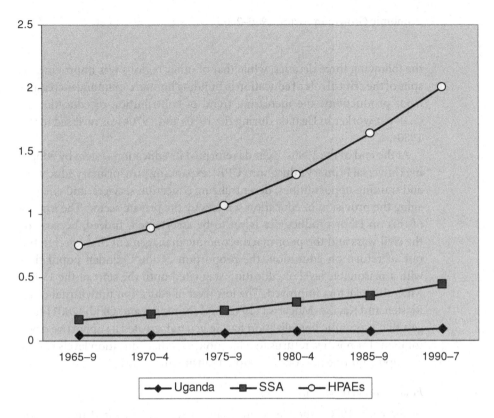

Figure 8.5 Uganda, average secondary school years attained, 1965–1997
Source: Ndulu and O'Connell data.

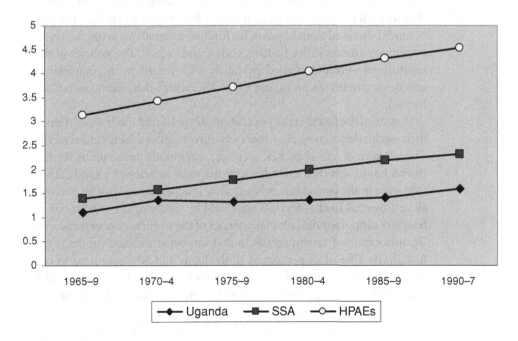

Figure 8.6 Uganda, average primary school years attained, 1965–1997
Source: Ndulu and O'Connell data.

the following three decades, while that of other regions was improving. In spite of the critical role of education in building human capital and increasing labor productivity, the increasing trend of contribution of education to GDP per worker in Uganda during the 1960s and 1970s was reversed in the 1980s.

At the end of the 1990s, Uganda reformed its education system by adopting Universal Primary Education (UPE), expanding post-primary education and training opportunities, decentralizing education services, and encouraging the provision of education services by the private sector. The impact of this on labor productivity is yet to be ascertained. Indeed, because of the civil wars and the poor macroeconomic management that lowered the rate of return on education, the proportion of the Ugandan population with a reasonable level of education stagnated until the start of the 1990s, when these factors improved. The low level of education notwithstanding, Bigsten and Kayizzi-Mugerwa (1992) and Deininger and Okidi (2001) suggest that economic liberalization has, in general, created a supportive environment for positive returns to education, and that education levels played an important role in economic growth during the 1990s.

Finance and credit markets

In the early 1960s, the Ugandan financial sector comprised three major commercial banks (Barclays, Grindlays, and Standard) and a few other deposit-taking institutions. Most financial institutions were expatriate banks (branches of international institutions), which provided credit on the basis of funds borrowed from London, for funding internal marketing and export of primary commodities (cotton, coffee, and sugar). The policies of these institutions were determined primarily with regard to the financial and economic conditions prevailing in the UK, where their headquarters were located.

In spite of the fact that the population still preferred other ways of storing their wealth (land, cows, etc.), there was a growing need for financial services. The network of sub-branches, agencies, and mobile units run by the three British banks was thus extended into the rural interior of Uganda. Therefore, even in the period immediately after independence, over 80 percent of all commercial banks' deposits were held by these British institutions that basically supported the colonial interests of the export–import trade where Uganda exported raw materials to and imported finished products from Britain. By 1966, 41.2 percent of all the loans and advances went to commerce (principally the export–import trade), 41 percent to industry, which was mainly under the control of British companies, and only 8 percent was extended to crop-financing for co-operatives.

In 1965, in an effort to promote local interests in the banking sector, the first indigenous bank, the Uganda Commercial Bank (UCB), was established when the Uganda Credit and Savings Society (UCSS)[7] was converted into a commercial bank. This raised the number of banks to nine, all expatriate except UCB. When the Bank of Uganda was being set up in 1966 as the monetary authority to issue a national currency, the need to open up upcountry branches and encourage indigenous savings mobilization was at the top of the agenda. This was coupled with the desire to allocate hard-earned foreign exchange in a manner that would see maximum returns in the development plans that necessitated the introduction of exchange controls.

In line with the nationalization objectives at the time, the Banking Act of 1969 required expatriate banks to be locally incorporated. The ensuing mergers and complete pullout of some commercial banks reduced the size of the banking system to five banks. Moreover, as the government decided to increase its control in a number of firms, government ownership in the commercial banks was forcefully increased to 60 percent in June 1970. All these developments were in support of the Nakivubo Pronouncements that sought to increase the level of government participation in production and allocation of resources (see p. 249). In spite of these developments, both deposits and credit to the economy increased considerably. With inflation recorded at an average of 0.42 percent over the period 1966–70, there is no doubt that the growth in both deposits and domestic credit of 69 percent and 80 percent, respectively, was on account of the increasing real sector activity.

In the 1970s, financial repression created disintermediation in the financial system. As a result, the capacity of formal financial markets to efficiently intermediate resources was lost and the parallel market (locally referred to as a *magendo* economy) emerged (see, for example, Kasekende and Atingi-Ego 1996). Further disruptions in the economy were witnessed through the early 1980s with the "go and stop" macroeconomic policies, the civil war, the overvalued shilling, and the high level of non-performing loans in the banking system. Financial institutions were inefficiently run, not properly supervised, and the administered interest rates offered no incentive for savings. The parallel financial market activity intensified and caused further disintermediation in the formal financial market.

By the beginning of the 1990s, the Ugandan economy had already undergone some macroeconomic stabilization and reform of some sectors. Within the financial system, interest rates had been partially liberalized and the banking system opened to competition. However, this sector was faced with weaknesses and inefficiencies that created a vicious cycle of macroeconomic

---

[7] UCSS had been in operation since 1950 to finance entities that had no access to regular commercial bank loans through either legal or institutional constraints. Due to administrative difficulties and high costs of operating programs for entities scattered in the rural areas, its lending programs had not progressed well.

instability. The business environment was still uncertain, with high inflation and no other credible initiatives needed for sustained production. In order to address these problems, the government implemented a financial sector reform program aimed at completing interest rate liberalization, restricting the role of government in the allocation of financial resources (including crop financing and divestiture of the government's ownership in the commercial banking system), and creating a conducive environment for competition in the financial system. This process was complemented by parallel measures to strengthen bank supervision and foster financial discipline through new legislation and regulations, and policies to improve the efficiency and profitability of financial institutions. The foreign exchange market was liberalized and the exchange rate became market-determined.

Following the initiation of financial sector reforms in 1994, considerable growth was realized in the levels of intermediation. In spite of a short-lived hiccup in the system in 1998–9, when the central bank intervened in some banks and others closed, this growth persisted. Apart from the enhanced regulations, supervision, and surveillance, the improved fiscal performance has been key in building confidence in the economy and achieving stabilization through lower inflation, hence affecting savings, investment, and credit behavior. The act of government increasing its savings with the banking system has created a potential for crowding in private sector credit.

As shown in table 8.10, it would seem that some relative degree of structural transformation took place when market-oriented policies were pursued – i.e. 1960–6 and the 1990s. The period 1960–6 saw the implementation of the first development plan and policies, modeled along recommendations of the World Bank, characterized by market-friendly policies and emphasis on private sector-led growth. The 1990s implemented similar policies, but with increased emphasis on building social capital so that growth was deepened and integrated and therefore sustained over a longer period. Structural transformation in the case of Uganda appears to be linked to the periods when market-oriented and private sector-led growth took place.

The political economy developments during Obote's Nakivubo Pronouncements and Amin's Economic War that saw the increased shift towards public sector participation and halted the private sector-led growth limited any possible transformation. The allocative inefficiency of resources under this "control regime" accompanied by the poor policy environment appears to have compromised structural transformation during this period.

6. Evidence

The motivation for this section is to ascertain the extent to which the identified syndromes explain the performance of the Ugandan economy. We use

Table 8.10 *Uganda, sectoral contribution to GDP and share of labor in agricultural and non-agricultural output, 1960–1997*

	Agricultural output/GDP			Industrial output/GDP			Services output/GDP		
Period	Actual	Fitted	Residual	Actual	Fitted	Residual	Actual	Fitted	Residual
1960–4	54.0	39.15	14.85	16.2	17.16	−0.96	29.8	43.69	−13.89
1965–9	52.2	37.65	14.55	16.5	17.90	−1.40	31.3	44.45	−13.15
1970–4	48.7	35.69	13.01	18.8	19.02	−0.22	32.4	45.29	−12.89
1975–9	50.6	35.58	15.02	17.1	18.21	−1.11	32.3	46.21	−13.91
1980–4	50.8	37.40	13.40	18.3	15.68	2.62	30.9	46.93	−16.03
1985–9	50.4	36.26	14.14	19.5	15.62	3.88	30.1	48.12	−18.02
1990–7	44.4	34.82	9.58	22.3	16.02	6.28	33.4	49.15	−15.75

	Manufacturing output/GDP			Share of labor force in agriculture			Ratio of ALP[a] in non-agricultural to ALP in agriculture		
	Actual	Fitted	Residual	Actual	Fitted	Residual	Actual	Fitted	Residual
1960–4	7.49	8.38	−0.90	92.21	55.51	36.70	...	5.18	...
1965–9	8.34	9.25	−0.91	90.86	52.10	38.76	...	4.58	...
1970–4	8.70	10.28	−1.58	89.43	48.35	40.78	...	4.07	...
1975–9	8.70	10.19	−1.49	88.01	46.35	41.65	...	3.31	...
1980–4	5.30	9.43	−4.13	86.60	44.48	42.12	4.58	2.14	2.44
1985–9	5.10	9.45	−4.35	85.33	42.40	42.94	4.38	1.68	2.79
1990–7	6.90	9.95	−3.05	...	39.70	...	...	1.15	...

Note: [a]ALP = Average product of labor (= real value added per person).

the real GDP *per capita* growth, and the investment–GDP and dependency ratios for Uganda and compare these with the SSA averages to determine the extent to which these syndromes can explain the deviations between the two numbers. Figures 8.1, 8.2 and 8.4 show the results of this comparison.

According to figure 8.2, Uganda's investment ratios have been trending below those of other SSA African countries and high-performing Asian countries. In part, this reflects the direct effect of armed conflict but even in the absence of ongoing conflict, past conflicts may continue to undermine the perceived security of investment. In addition, in periods when poor macroeconomic policies prevailed, as was the case in the 1970s, we see further contraction in these rates. Following the 1966 abrogation of the 1962 Constitution, opportunism and civil and political strife increased, which constrained the proper functioning of government policy. In this environment, the breakdown of contract enforcement, law and order, and the general standard of conduct impaired the promotion of private sector investment. This could probably explain its leveling off, decline, and leveling off again during the 1964–9, 1970–9, and 1980–4 periods, respectively.

In figures 8.1 and 8.2, we observe that the level of investment was consistently low and declining during the period 1965–85, and these developments also coincide with the period when the real GDP *per capita* growth in Uganda was not only declining but trailing that of the SSA average. It is worth noting that risks of either internal large-scale conflict or economic mismanagement were quite significant during this time. The nature of governance discussed in section 4.2 seems to have influenced the occurrence of conflict, economic policy, and the level of capital formation. These in turn appear to have combined to affect the rate of investment and utilization of existing capacity and the rate of economic growth. In addition, as seen in figure 8.2, the investment–GDP ratios further declined between 1970–9 on account of the expulsion of Asians in 1972 that resulted in a loss of confidence in the economy. As earlier discussed, a "looting" syndrome also severely affected growth. During this period, the proper functioning of government policy appeared not insulated from poor governance.

The events of 1982–4 highlight the fact that economic reforms in a situation of conflict can easily be derailed. The peace dividend that followed the 1979–80 war, together with the implementation of market-based policies, delivered some improved economic performance at least until 1984, as shown in figure 8.1, in addition to halting the decline in investment–GDP ratios. As a result of the escalation of the conflict, there was a diversion of resources from the production of goods and services into military expenditures, which led to the suspension of the program with the IMF. With the widening conflict and the deteriorating economic environment, economic performance declined. The developments in 1966–86 capture the regulatory, state breakdown and redistributive syndromes identified in this chapter.

This, however, contrasts with the developments in the 1990s, when economic recovery was achieved against the backdrop of insurgency in the northern part of the country. This insurgency has, to some extent, also diverted resources from the production of goods and services to military expenditures, thus denying the economy of the full benefits of the reform. It would appear that risks of large-scale internal conflicts occurring were minimized in the 1990s, and due to this, along with prudent macroeconomic management, investment made a recovery to close the gap with the SSA average. The regulatory and state breakdown syndromes that had earlier negated growth were now weakened.

The political, social, and economic strife associated with the conflicts and poor macroeconomic management probably explains why the dependency ratios in Uganda trended above the average of other SSA countries. This continued into the 1990s, the period when Uganda's economic performance outperformed the SSA averages, probably on account of the HIV/AIDS epidemic that hit Uganda during this period. These events had a direct impact on savings, thus affecting investment. External financing that could have closed the gap was not forthcoming, particularly in the period 1966–79. As seen in tables 8.6 and 8.11, private capital outflows dominated, largely because of the loss of confidence in the economy which followed the nationalization/Ugandanization drives that characterized the period. In table 8.12, and 8.13 under Other capital (net), we continue to see significant outflows of capital, a situation that reversed only in 1990 on account of reduced large-scale internal conflict and improved macroeconomic management. The regulatory syndrome that characterizes this episode could explain these developments.

In the 1990s, which is our third phase derived from the syndromes, Uganda made a post-conflict recovery underpinned by increased democratization and an improved economic policy environment. We see a weakening of all three syndromes during this period and associated economic improvement. Both the investment–GDP ratios and real GDP *per capita* growth rates began to improve, due to the changes in political management and economic reform that took place in the post-1987 period. During the 1992–7 period, private sector-led growth increased because of a conducive environment, political commitment to reforms, conflict resolution, and strengthened institutions. The government's commitment to reforms and poverty reduction saw further improvements in social capital, which deepened, integrated, and sustained the growth process. This redistribution in favor of poverty reduction sustained growth, and as a result Uganda recorded strong economic performance throughout this period, as shown in the period 1989–97 in figures 8.1 and 8.2. This contrasts with the redistribution witnessed during 1966–72 through nationalization/Ugandanization that eroded private sector confidence in the Ugandan economy.

Despite low levels of investment that trended below the SSA averages, Uganda's economic performance has, in the past, sometimes surpassed the average of other SSA countries. We examine this performance in terms of the evolution of the TFP. Table 8.4 uses the Collins and Bosworth (1996) growth decomposition for Uganda and SSA and shows the change in TFP. In the period 1960–4, the TFP for Uganda and the SSA average was 1.17 and 0.26, respectively, while during the 1990s it was 2.29 and 1.59, respectively, for our first and third growth phases. Between 1966 and 1989, our second phase, the averages were −1.67 and −0.32 for Uganda and SSA, respectively, which neatly fits the periodization generated by the syndromes. Between 1966 and 1979, the contribution of TFP was negative and continued to decline because of the political conflict and economic mismanagement at the time, compared to other SSA countries where TFP was increasing. Another important explanation for the evolution of TFP is the functioning of both product and factor markets, as discussed in section 5. The functioning of markets is largely driven by political-economy developments that fit into our periodization. In addition, the economic policies also affected the returns

Table 8.11 *Uganda, balance of payments position, 1960–1970, US$ million*

Industry	1960	1961	1962	1963	1964	1965	1966	1967	1968	1969	1970
Current account	...	...	...	...	...	...	**-15.2**	**-10.1**	**-3.1**	**-5.4**	**20.3**
Merchandise account	47.5	39.4	39.4	61.4	83.2	45.2	43.0	49.1	47.6	47.7	83.3
– Exports	138.9	134.7	134.5	175.8	213.2	206.4	205.8	209.5	208.8	220.9	261.6
– Imports	-91.5	-95.2	-95.1	-114.4	-130.0	-161.2	-162.8	-160.4	-161.2	-173.2	-178.3
Services and income	...	...	...	...	...	...	-59.2	-59.2	-50.3	-50.7	-57.6
Private transfers	...	...	...	...	...	...	-3.0	-2.9	-4.6	-4.9	-6.9
Official transfers	...	...	...	...	...	...	4.0	2.9	4.2	2.5	1.5
Capital account	...	...	...	...	...	...	**36.1**	**20.1**	**13.7**	**16.0**	**-21.6**
Official capital	...	...	...	...	...	...	25.8	14.8	12.6	18.7	19.7
– Inflows	...	...	...	...	...	...	...	...	...	...	...
– Outflows	...	...	...	...	...	...	...	...	...	...	...
Private capital	...	...	...	...	...	...	10.3	5.3	1.1	-2.7	-41.3
Overall balance	...	...	...	...	...	...	**20.9**	**10.0**	**10.7**	**12.9**	**-1.3**
Financing	...	...	...	...	...	...	**-20.9**	**-10.0**	**-10.7**	**-12.9**	**1.3**
Of which reserves Δ	...	...	...	...	...	...	-13.5	6.0	-14.1	-3.2	-4.4
Curr. account/GDP	...	...	...	...	...	...	2.32	1.45	0.30	0.46	1.53
Trade/GDP	42.1	40.0	40.1	45.7	48.7	45.9	45.1	43.5	40.2	37.6	37.0
Exchange rate (Shs/$)	7.14	7.14	7.14	7.14	7.14	7.14	7.14	7.14	7.14	7.14	7.14

Source: Background to the Budgets (various issues).

Table 8.12 *Uganda, balance of payments position, 1981–1990, US$ million*

Industry	1981	1982	1983	1984	1985	1986	1987	1988	1989	1990
Current account	**−170.6**	**−69.9**	**−72.3**	**107.1**	**77.1**	**6.9**	**−112.0**	**−195.2**	**−259.5**	**−263.3**
Merchandise account	−169.2	−74.9	−60.4	–	115.0	−68.5	−142.0	−257.2	−310.6	−313.2
– Exports	245.5	347.1	367.7	407.9	379.0	407.5	333.6	266.3	277.7	177.8
– Imports	−414.7	−422.0	−428.1	−312.2	−264.0	−476.1	−475.6	−523.5	−588.3	−491.0
Services and income	−122.0	−102.3	−115.4	−44.0	−98.9	−133.2	−236.2	−260.4	−260.5	−243.1
Official transfers	120.6	107.3	103.5	85.4	61.0	208.7	266.2	322.4	311.6	293.0
Capital account	**−51.5**	**14.6**	**27.7**	**−88.3**	**−27.4**	**75.8**	**31.2**	**3.6**	**213.0**	**211.8**
Official medium and long term (net)	−101.8	26.2	23.9	32.1	14.6	64.5	79.6	33.5	213.8	257.6
Other capital (net)	50.3	−11.6	3.8	−120.4	−42.0	11.3	−48.4	−29.5	−0.8	−45.8
Overall balance	**−118.1**	**−32.9**	**−36.4**	**−58.4**	**67.0**	**127.1**	**−54.4**	**−36.7**	**−84.5**	**−41.9**
Financing										
Of which reserves	−30.7	−34.3	−28.4	56.2	29.5	0.8	−20.3	2.4	1.8	5.2
Curr. account/GDP	...	...	...	...	...	...	2.1	...	...	...
Trade/GDP	...	...	...	...	...	...	...	...	...	...
Exchange rate (Shs/$)	−3.8	−5.5	−22.6	...	...	...	42.8	106.1	223.1	428.9

Source: Background to the Budgets (various issues).

Table 8.13 *Uganda, balance of payments position, 1991–2000, US$ million*

Industry	1991	1992	1993	1994	1995	1996	1997	1998	1999	2000
Current account	**−169.8**	**−99.6**	**−166.06**	**−168.7**	**−246.2**	**−200.1**	**−335.7**	**−399.16**	**−421.2**	**−467.5**
Merchandise account	−203.9	−270.7	−401.62	−436.9	−609.1	−610.9	−718.7	−956.8	−865.2	−1123.6
− Exports	173.2	151.2	200.0	462.9	556.4	641.8	592.6	510.2	500.1	413.7
− Imports	−377.1	−421.9	−601.6	−899.8	−1165.5	−1252.7	−1311.4	−1467.0	−1365.3	−1537.3
Services and income	−294.9	−297.4	−130.1	−235.5	−280.4	−302.2	−270.7	−295.8	−288.1	−282.6
Private transfers	–	–	79.3	246.4	333.8	421.7	275.8	502.1	424.9	507.8
Official transfers	329.0	468.5	323.9	280.0	348.1	348.0	309.4	398.8	330.7	430.9
Capital account	**137.6**	**114.8**	**203.7**	**238.5**	**295.4**	**143.5**	**387.8**	**391.9**	**390.4**	**482.9**
Official medium and long-term (net)	167.6	144.1	166.2	201.0	196.3	117.3	247.1	197.2	216.1	227.2
− Inflows	...	...	247.1	302.8	274.8	189.8	310.1	271.0	291.7	309.4
− Outflows	...	...	−80.9	−101.8	−78.5	−72.5	−63.0	−73.8	−75.6	−81.8
Other capital (net)	31.0	−26.3	54.6	−88.2	121.2	121.0	175.0	210.0	222.1	254.4
Overall balance	**−31.7**	**24.2**	**80.0**	**105.9**	**97.5**	**4.77**	**84.0**	**42.3**	**−4.6**	**15.44**
Financing	...	...	**−80.0**	**−105.9**	**−97.5**	**−4.77**	**−84.0**	**−42.3**	**4.6**	**−15.44**
Of which reserves	−12.7	−50.7	−49.3	−166.9	−140.1	−68.9	−100.8	−92.3	−40.4	−43.8
Curr. account/GDP	...	...	−13.1	−8.5	−16.0	−18.0	−20.4	−23.5	12.65	−19.6
Trade/GDP	...	...	23.4	27.8	30.4	33.0	31.4	33.0	32.5	35.9
Exchange rate (Shs/$)	734.0	1133.8	1087.4	972.2	968.4	1046.1	1083.0	1240.3	1455.6	1644.5

Source: Background to the Budgets (various issues).

to both capital and labor, and these were enhanced in the first and third growth periods. Specifically, where market-based policies were pursued, a supportive environment for positive returns to education was created, also captured in the evolution of TFP. These developments fit neatly with the periodization of Uganda's growth phases based on the syndromes.

6.1 Transport bottlenecks

In the 1960s, when the East African Railways was still in existence, land-lockedness had only a slight impact on Uganda's development. In 1977, East African Railways was split into various sections which are now managed by the different East African countries. During the 1990s, this split, coupled with inefficiencies, led to a significant increase in the impact of Uganda's landlocked status on growth. Given the importance of transport costs to the competitiveness of a landlocked economy, a focus on transport costs and transport logistics within a regional setting is appropriate for Uganda.

Uganda's railways are in a state of collapse. Only two rail lines out of five are currently operating and there is need for significant rehabilitation. Rail links to the DRC, Sudan, and Rwanda have been considered as expansion possibilities. The high costs of road and rail freight to Mombasa, and long delays at the port, significantly disadvantage Uganda's export competitiveness for high-weight, low-value products.[8] Rail services from Kampala exhibit a pattern: inbound freight trains from Mombassa arrive full, but return largely empty, as exporters tend to choose more reliable but expensive road transportation.

There is a need to place rail and road transportation and port costs in a regional setting, because much of the transactions cost to Ugandan importers and exporters is incurred beyond Uganda's borders. There is hope, however, that a private investor may wish to buy both Uganda Railways and Kenya Railways and merge the two. This would improve the efficiency of the railway network and reduce the transactions costs incurred by Ugandans.

7. Concluding remarks and lessons

Of the four groups of syndromes that explain why Africa's economic performance has been dismal, three apply perfectly well in Uganda. These are the *regulatory, state breakdown,* and *redistributive* syndromes. With these three syndromes, three episodes of growth can be identified over the period

---

[8] World Bank (2004). Furthermore, Siggel and Ssemogerere (2004) estimate that due to the dilapidated roads and railways in Kenya, the transport costs faced in Uganda can be some 50 percent of the value of goods.

1961–2000 with the first phase stretching from 1962 to 1966, the second phase from 1967 to 1990, and the third from 1991 to 2000. The first post-independence Five-Year Development Plan pursued policies that promoted private sector-led growth while the second Five-Year Development Plan instituted some radical changes to promote the dominance of the public sector in economic development by introducing soft controls into the Ugandan economy. This was done through the implementation of the Nakivubo Pronouncements, which saw the nationalization of key industries, indigenization of labor, and emphasis on centralized planning. This set the stage for the deterioration of the Ugandan economy observed until 1987.

At the beginning of the 1970s the Amin regime continued with the efforts at nationalization through the declaration of Economic War, which culminated in the expulsion of the Asian community from Uganda. Here, a multiplicity of syndromes can be identified, including redistributive, regulatory, and looting regimes (the latter a sub-set of the redistributive syndrome), and state breakdown. The importance of the public sector in development and the goals of Ugandanization of the economy were strengthened. Unfortunately, state ownership of productive enterprises following the expulsion of Asians resulted in higher production inefficiencies and the collapse of public services. This, together with the pursuit of imprudent macroeconomic policies, breakdown of law and order, the deterioration in financial discipline, and misallocation of resources through price controls, was the main reason for continued contraction in economic activity. It is, therefore, not surprising that the actual economic performance continued to trend below the levels that had been witnessed in the immediate post-independence era.

On the other hand, the political economy in the post-1980 period was largely guided by the need to stabilize and restart economic growth following the decline witnessed in the pre-1980 period. Market-based policies in resource allocation, together with the increased role of the private sector in production, led to economic recovery. Pursuit of market-based policies and private sector-led growth could not be sustained, as peaceful mechanisms of conflict resolution were absent. Comprehensive reforms to support private sector-led growth were absent, and social capital formation to ensure that the growth process was deepened and integrated was not developed.

The absence of institutionalized mechanisms of peaceful conflict resolution in the first twenty-five years after independence increased both perceived and real risks and uncertainty, which in turn affected investment levels. On the other hand, the first two post-independence decades entrenched state ownership, which eroded confidence in the economy through control policies that were pursued. The policy environment was also poor and could not therefore sufficiently mitigate the exogenous shocks that affected economic performance.

In the period 1990–2000, we see concerted attempts to eliminate distortions in the microeconomic framework and strengthen or set up institutions of governance. Generally, the policy environment improved while political instability was reduced. This period has been characterized by outreach to different armed groups in order to disband and reconcile these groups with the government, or integrate them into the national army. Uganda has become more politically stable compared to SSA as a whole, as the combined effect of prolonged political stability and a good macroeconomic framework has increased the rate of return on investment and the productivity of factors of production. Significant structural transformation of the economy occurred during the period 1990–2000. Given that structural transformation is usually accompanied by new technologies, this could support the rise in labor productivity and return on education observed during the 1990s. In addition, the HIV/AIDS epidemic that had adversely affected the labor force and its productivity began to be addressed, with some effectiveness, through a participatory approach that involved all the stakeholders concerned.

The challenge for the future is sustaining political stability in order to guarantee a political economy that delivers sustained growth, as seen in the latter part of our growth process. Further improvements in social capital to deepen and integrate the growth process will not only sustain this growth but will also increase the opportunity cost of civil wars. In addition, continued strengthening of institutions to promote accountability, transparency, and peaceful conflict resolution is key to sustaining Uganda's economic performance. Transparent allocation of resources through a market-based mechanism supported by an enabling policy environment appears to be the way forward, judging from the experience of 1962–2000. Intervention by government should be limited only to the delivery of *public goods* and *services* rather than resources, as non-market allocation is easily subjected to abuse. There is also a need to raise domestic revenues and develop new export items that are resilient to weather changes and are less volatile in terms of international prices in order to reduce reliance on donor financing of the budget.

References

Atingi-Ego, M. and L. Kasekende (1998), "Uganda's Growth Experience and Prospects," *The Africa Competitiveness Report*, Harvard Institute for International Devlopment and the World Economic Forum, Cambridge, MA

Atingi-Ego, M. and R. Sebudde (2005), "Entrenching Peace in a Post-Conflict Economy: The Case of Uganda," in Augustin Kwasi Fosu and Paul Collier, eds., *Post Conflict Economies in Africa*. London: Palgrave Macmillan

Backgrounds to the Budget (various issues), Ministry of Finance, Republic of Uganda

Bigsten, A. and S. Kayizzi-Mugerwa (1992), "On Structural Adjustment in Uganda," *Canadian Journal of Development Studies* 13(1): 57–75

Collier, P. and J. W. Gunning (1997), *Explaining African Economic Performance*. Oxford: CSAE, University of Oxford

Collier, P. and S. A. O'Connell (2007), "Opportunities and Choices," chapter 2 in B. J. Ndulu, S. A. O'Connell, R. H. Bates, P. Collier, and C. C. Soludo, eds., *The Political Economy of Economic Growth in Africa, 1960–2000*, vol. 1. Cambridge: Cambridge University Press

Collins, S. and B. Bosworth (1996), "Economic Growth in East Asia: Accumulation Versus Assimilation," *Brookings Papers on Economic Activity* 2: 135–203

Deininger, K. and J. Okidi (2001), "Rural Households: Incomes, Productivity, and Nonfarm Enterprises," in R. Reinikka and P. Collier, eds., *Uganda's Recovery: The Role of Farms, Firms and Government*. Washington, DC: The World Bank: 125–76

Equity and Growth through Economic Research (EAGER) (2000), *Enhancing and Sustaining Growth in Africa: Uganda's Macroeconomic Management*. EAGER/PSGE Study, mimeo, Houndmills and New York: Palgrave, in association with the International Economic Association

Henstridge, M. and L. Kasekende (2001), "Exchange Reform, Stabilization, and Fiscal Management," in R. Reinikka and P. Collier, eds., *Uganda's Recovery: The Role of Farms, Firms and Government*. Washington, DC: The World Bank: 49–77

Hoeffler, A. E. (1999), "The Augmented Solow Model and the African Growth Debate," CID Working Papers 36

Holmgren, T., L. Kasekende, M. Atingi-Ego, and D. Ddamulira (2001), "Aid Reform: Uganda Country Case Study," World Bank Development Research Group, Washington, DC

Kasekende, L. and M. Atingi-Ego (1996), "Financial Liberalization and its Implications for the Domestic Financial System: The Case of Uganda," Paper submitted to the AERC workshop, Nairobi

Larson, D. and K. Deininger (2001), "Crop Markets and Household Participation," in R. Reinikka and P. Collier, eds., *Uganda's Recovery: The Role of Farms, Firms and Government*. Washington, DC: The World Bank: 177–203

Mamdani, M. (1983), *Imperialism and Fascism in Uganda*, 1st edn. London: Heinemann Educational Books

Mudoola, Dan M. (1993), *Ethnicity, Religion and Politics in Uganda*, 2nd edn. Kampala: Fountain Publishers

Museveni, Y. K. (1997), *Sowing the Mustard Seed*. Kampala: Macmillan

Ndulu, B. and S. A. O'Connell (2007), "Policy Plus: African Growth Performance, 1960–2000," chapter 1 in B. J. Ndulu, S. A. O'Connell, R. H. Bates, P. Collier, and C. C. Soludo, eds., *The Political Economy of Economic Growth in Africa, 1960–2000*, vol. 1. Cambridge: Cambridge University Press

Parliamentary Hansards (1964, 1965, 1966), Parliament of the Republic of Uganda

Reinikka, R. and P. Collier, eds. (2001), *Uganda's Recovery: The Role of Farms, Firms and Government*. Washington, DC: The World Bank

Sachs, J. D. and A. M. Warner (1997), "Sources of Slow Growth in African Economies," *Journal of African Economies* 6(3): 335–76

Siggel, E. and G. Ssemogerere (2004), "Uganda's Policy Reforms, Industry Competitiveness and Regional Integration: A Comparison with Kenya," *Journal of International Trade and Economic Development* 13(3) September: 325–57

World Bank (2007), "Competing in the Global Economy: An Investment Climate Assessment (ICA) for Uganda," The World Bank, Washington, DC

PART II

Coastal economies

9 | Economic growth in Ghana, 1960–2000

Ernest Aryeetey and Augustin Kwasi Fosu

1. Introduction

It was fairly common in the 1980s and early 1990s to read commendations of Ghana's economic growth achievements. Leechor (1994) described Ghana as a frontrunner in the economic reform process, and the Bretton Woods institutions regularly put Ghana forward as a showcase of economic success in Africa. But this occurred at a time when many Ghanaians showed little appreciation of that growth achievement (Aryeetey and Tarp 2000). The continuing fragility of the economy and the significant social costs of adjustment made it difficult to appreciate economic growth in a period of reforms. While there is no doubt that the economic growth record of the last two decades, following reforms, differed from that of the first two decades, it is also clear that the factors differentiating growth within shorter sub-periods show remarkable similarity. Any considerable capital injection into the economy has always been followed by significant growth. It is the difficulty in making those injections consistently in the absence of structural change that has left the economy still fragile after four decades of independence. However, the role of productivity has also been crucial.

The lack of public appreciation for the recent growth experience may reflect a certain sense of *déjà vu*: Ghana was widely admired for being the first African country to become independent from colonial rule in 1957 and for its rapid growth thereafter. Another possible reason, however, may be that measured growth figures have had little meaning for the livelihoods of people. This is a point that has been explored by Kanbur (2001). He asks the question: "How can people with seemingly the same ends disagree so much about means, and how can seemingly the same objective reality be interpreted so differently?" Obviously, aggregate growth in the economy does not necessarily imply income growth for the majority of the population, but should they not "feel" that there has been growth in the economy? Kanbur (2001) provides another twist to the puzzle when he wonders why "people are not dancing in the streets" if the economy has seen growth in the region of 4 percent–5.5 percent for almost two decades.

In 1993, Ghana set itself the target of becoming an upper-middle-income country by 2020, under its *Vision 2020* program. To achieve the targeted *per capita* income by that year, using a simple Harrod–Domar-type model, it was estimated that the economy needed to grow at an average of 8 percent annually for the period. Since then the economy has not shown a capacity to move towards the target. The performance of the economy and economic growth have been characterized by the non-attainment of macroeconomic targets: in particular, whereas GDP was expected to grow between 7.1 percent and 8.3 percent per year in the period 1996–2000, actual growth was between 4.2 percent and 5.0 percent. The significant deviation between targets and the actual was translated into low *per capita* GDP growth and poor sectoral growth.

We discuss in this chapter the factors behind the measured growth and then explain why the growth figures lead to questions in the minds of the people. Most of the growth has been driven by public investments of questionable productivity, the returns on which have been sometimes misallocated. Aryeetey and Tarp (2000) have argued that the growth of the 1980s came about as a result of the expansion of capital application, largely as a consequence of increased aid inflows, which was similar to the expansion that occurred in the 1960s financed largely by running down accumulated reserves from the 1950s. In both cases the increased use of capital was not always accompanied by significant improvements in TFP, largely because the role that significant economic agents should play alongside the state was overlooked, even in periods of reform. In both instances, the injection of capital came after long periods of relatively high capital depreciation. Again in both instances, the initial high growth rates could not be sustained in the medium term because the policies were not anchored in appropriate all-embracing development frameworks. The first attempt sought to deny the market its place while the second attempt was with weakened state structures that were unable to deliver outcomes in a timely and adequate manner.

The significance of structural change to economic growth may be derived from the findings that greater flexibility in economic structures leads to significant economic growth (Chenery and Syrquin 1986). In the Chenery–Syrquin analysis, the shift of resources from low-productivity to high-productivity areas was a major source of TFP growth, even within the same sector. The importance of changing structure in explaining economic growth in Ghana has been underscored by Killick (2000), who uses the above framework and observes: "It is no secret that Ghana's economy has not grown much since the early 1960s. Indeed it slipped from being classified (by the World Bank) as a middle-income country to a low-income country . . . If the fit between structural change and economic growth were perfect, the prediction for a non-growing economy would be that the structure would also remain unchanged." The absence of structural change is also suggested by the work of Powell and Round (2000).

As we seek to show that slow economic growth for most of the last four decades has been a consequence of the inadequate attention to structural change, we shall discuss in section 2 the Ghana growth experience in a cross-country perspective, focusing largely on two clear periods, 1960–82 and 1983–2000. The details of these sub-periods are associated with distinct political regimes. In section 3, we turn to the impact of government intervention on the structure and performance of key markets, focusing first on the markets for labor, credit, and land inputs and then on the market for goods and services. Affected economic growth at different times. In section 4, we discuss the political economy of growth, looking at the relative strengths of different groups and how they influenced economic decision-making and outcomes.

2. Ghana's growth experience

Historical discussions of Ghana's growth experience seem to have a common message. Indeed a feature of the Ghanaian economy that most analysts have agreed on over the years has been the absence of structural change. The oldest discussion is found in the study by Szereszewski (1965) on structural changes in 1891–1911. Rimmer (1992) provides a useful account of economic policies and outcomes for 1950–90, while a more detailed analysis of economic policies in Ghana in the years shortly before and soon after independence is provided by Killick (1978). Huq (1989) provides interesting and valuable material on the 1970s and the early part of the 1980s. For the period since the reforms began, there is a large volume of recent material, from the World Bank and from other independent sources. The most comprehensive collection of essays for the period, however, is provided in the volume edited by Aryeetey, Harrigan, and Nissanke (2000). In Szereszewski (1965) it is shown that even though the economy underwent significant structural shifts during 1891–1911, following the introduction of cocoa and gold mining and the associated development of the railway, "structural change lost its momentum after 1911, and after fifty years Ghana's economy retains a close affinity with [the] 1911 Gold Coast" (1965: 112). Killick (2000) notes that the influential *Report on Financial and Physical Problems of Development in the Gold Coast* that was commissioned by the colonial administration (Seers and Ross 1952), concludes: "If we were forced to sum up the Gold Coast economy in one word, the word we would choose would be 'Fragile'." Killick (2000) further notes that Seers and Ross "were particularly concerned with what they saw as an inflationary bias imparted to the economy by supply bottlenecks (of which a shortage of harbor capacity, as well as the more fundamental difficulty of low supply elasticities in agriculture, was at that time a preoccupation)."

Based on this identification of structural constraints to growth and development, a major part of colonial economic policies was devoted to tackling some of them, even if in obviously inadequate terms. Ghana's subsequent pioneering role in the political and economic transition in the region some four decades ago led to its being characterized as the beacon on the African continent. It was the first African country to gain political independence from colonial rule in March 1957, and under the leadership of its first President, Kwame Nkrumah, provided inspiration and critical material support to a number of African nationalist movements across the continent. The nation's early radical approach to development saw the repudiation of imperialism and neo-colonialism, while pan-African socialist ideas became the driving force in development thinking. Toye (1991) suggests that despite the pioneering role that Ghana has often played in African development, at various times it has also pursued economic policies that have proven self-destructive.

2.1 The growth record

The growth record of Ghana has been one of unevenness when the post-reform period is compared to the earlier period, as figure 9.1 clearly indicates. After reasonably high GDP growth in the 1950s and early 1960s, the Ghanaian economy began to experience a slowdown in GDP growth in 1964. Growth was turbulent during much of the period after the mid-1960s and began to stabilize only after 1984. In 1966, 1972, 1975–6, 1979, and 1980–3,

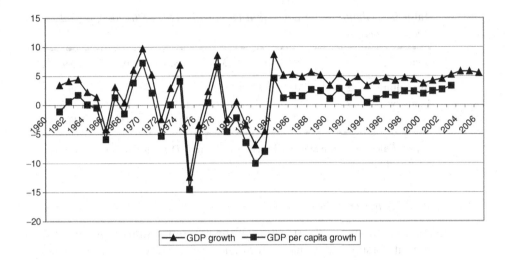

Figure 9.1 Ghana, trends in real GDP growth and real *per capita* GDP growth, 1960–2006

the growth rate was negative. The years with negative growth generally coincided with changes in government and sometimes with policy changes or reversals. Indeed negative growth was first recorded at the time of the first *coup d'état* in 1966, with a forceful transfer of authority from the dictatorial Nkrumah regime to the military. The lowest growth of –14 percent was experienced in 1975, coinciding with oil price shocks, as well as a policy reversal from a moderate market-oriented stance to an inward-looking protectionist regime. The period of turbulence, however, also had positive growth episodes, with the highest peak rate reaching 9 percent in 1970 and 1978.

The economy definitely responded positively to reforms[1] soon after inception, as figure 9.1 suggests. It recovered from its negative growth rate of about 5 percent in 1983 to a hefty positive rate of 8 percent in 1984. The favorable growth has continued since that time, with relatively little variance, even if there was a slight slowdown in the rate of growth after 1990. The fact that *per capita* GDP growth closely tracks that of GDP may suggest that population growth has been rather stable, though the larger gap between them since the 1980s may also suggest some acceleration in population growth over this period.

---

[1] The first phase of reform, marked by the adoption of a stabilization program dubbed the Economic Recovery Program (ERP), and with major support from the IMF and the World Bank, was instituted in April 1983, with implementation over 1983–6. Starting in 1986, the second phase of reform saw the ERP being supplemented with a Structural Adjustment Program (SAP).

Table 9.1 *Ghana, sectoral distribution of real GDP, 1970–2000, period averages, percent*

Sector	1970–5	1976–82	1983–6	1987–90	1991–5	1995–2000
Agriculture	52	51	52	46	42	39.5
Industry	19	17	12	14	14	27.5
Services	29	32	36	40	44	33.0

Source: Calculated from Statistical Services, *Quarterly Digest of Statistics*, various issues; see ISSER (1996).

2.2   Structure of the economy and growth

As table 9.1 shows, the structure of the economy through the early 1990s indicated a shift in dominance from agriculture to services, with little change in the share of industry. While a shift toward a higher-order service could be considered a positive sign for a possible take-off, this is generally seen as less of a structural change than an indication of the direction of new short-term capital flows to mark the end of stagnation. Indeed, much of the increase in services derives from the relatively low-order sector, "Wholesale, Retail, Restaurants and Hotels," whose share as a proportion of GDP increased from 13 percent in 1989 to 17 percent in 1996 (ISSER 1997). Meanwhile, the share of manufacturing remained about the same. Although the reforms seem to have halted the decline in the manufacturing sector, which reached a low of 7.4 percent of GDP in 1982, manufacturing growth appears to have fallen substantially during the latter part of the reform period. Indeed manufacturing experienced the slowest growth, at a rate of 1.3 percent annually during 1986–2000, compared with 4.3 percent for industry.

Despite the poor performance of manufacturing, in the last half of the 1990s the share of the industrial sector in GDP picked up considerably, as shown in table 9.1. It doubled its share from 14 percent of GDP in the first half of the decade to 27.5 percent in the second half. This is drawn largely from the expansion in the mining sector, but considering the weak link between mining and other sectors of the economy this can hardly be seen as evidence of structural change.

2.3   Accounting for Ghana's growth

We consider here the Collins and Bosworth (1996) growth-accounting results presented in O'Connell and Ndulu (2000) on the decomposition of *per capita* growth in Ghana during 1960–97. Table 9.2 reports these estimates, as well as those for SSA for purposes of comparison. During the entire 1960–97 period, output per worker declined by 0.12 percent annually

Table 9.2 *Ghana versus SSA, Collins–Bosworth growth-accounting-based decomposition of sources of growth, 1960–1997*

Period	Growth in real GDP per worker	Contribution of		
		Physical capital per worker	Education per worker	Residual
1960–4	1.56 [1.26]	3.02 [0.86]	0.49 [0.14]	−1.96 [0.26]
1965–9	−0.28 [1.60]	0.94 [1.03]	0.78 [0.18]	−2.01 [0.39]
1970–4	2.41 [2.29]	0.40 [1.22]	0.20 [0.20]	1.81 [0.87]
1975–9	−4.22 [−0.10]	−0.13 [0.81]	0.23 [0.27]	−4.32 [−1.18]
1980–4	−3.94 [−1.28]	−0.93 [0.41]	0.66 [0.30]	−3.66 [−1.99]
1985–9	2.32 [0.64]	−0.40 [0.06]	0.72 [0.30]	2.01 [0.28]
1990–7	1.27 [−1.55]	0.75 [−0.14]	0.41 [0.18]	0.11 [−1.59]
Total: 1960–97	**−0.12 [0.41]**	**0.52 [0.61]**	**0.50 [0.23]**	**−1.15 [−0.42]**

Note: Annual averages in percent. SSA averages in brackets.
Source: O'Connell and Ndulu (2000).

on average in Ghana. At the same time, growth in factor accumulation, measured by physical capital per worker, accounted for 0.52 percent, and education per worker for 0.50 percent; however, this positive contribution by physical and human capital was more than offset by the negative contribution of TFP, measured as the residual, of 1.15 percent. Thus, overall, the slow rate of *per capita* income growth in Ghana over 1960–97 seems largely attributable to productivity rather than to production inputs.

For SSA as a whole, output per worker over the 1960–97 period increased by 0.41 percent annually, of which physical capital and education contributed 0.61 percent and 0.23 percent, respectively, while TFP's contribution was negative at −0.42 percent. Thus, over the entire period, *per capita* growth was much smaller in Ghana than in SSA, the contribution to growth by physical capital slightly smaller, and productivity declines substantially larger. The only dimension where Ghana apparently out-performed SSA was, therefore, in the area of education, where the contribution to growth was about twice as large. This outcome may be attributable to the comparatively large investment in education made by Ghana after independence.

As table 9.2 further indicates, the half-decade decompositions suggest a non-uniform pattern over the period. While the periods of 1960–4, 1970–4, and 1985–97 show considerably positive growth rates, growth was substantially negative for 1975–84. This pattern differs somewhat for SSA as a whole, though, according to table 9.3. For example, in 1965–9, Ghana's growth was negative as compared with a positive rate for SSA; however, during the more recent 1990–7 period Ghana exhibits a positive growth rate, while SSA's growth is negative.

Table 9.3 *Ghana, savings and investment profile, 1991–2000*

Item/Year[a]	1991	1992	1993	1994	1995	1996	1997	1998	1999	2000
Gross investment	14.2	14.8	17.1	17.5	17.1	17.5	18.6	19.0	21.1	22.4
of which private	10.3	9.8	11.5	9.0	10.8					
Domestic savings	4.1	2.1	2.0	3.8	6.5	7.4	7.9	8.5	9.6	11.2
of which private	3.4	1.7	1.6	1.0	5.3					
Foreign savings	10.1	12.7	15.0	13.7	10.6	10.1	10.8	11.3	22.5	11.2
of which private	6.9	8.1	9.8	8.0	5.5					

Note: [a]Projected figures in the period 1996–2000.
Source: Ghana Vision 2020: The First Medium-term Development Plan (1997–2000)

The relatively strong growth in Ghana during the earlier 1960–4 period was explained mainly by physical capital accumulation, while that in 1970–4 was due to TFP. The decline in growth in 1975–84 was accounted for primarily by TFP; however, there was some disinvestment as well. When growth picked up during 1985–9, again the explanation was a positive TFP growth. The contribution of physical capital took over during the subsequent 1990–7 period, while the role of TFP, though still positive, waned substantially. Meanwhile, the role of education seems to be relatively uniform. Its contribution remains positive throughout the entire period, though it is rather low in 1970–9.

On the whole, Ghana appears to have performed worse than the SSA average during the earlier 1965–84 period, and better in the more recent 1984–97 period, in terms of output per worker growth, the contribution of physical capital per worker, and the contribution of TFP to that growth. The contribution of education per worker, on the other hand, was higher than the SSA average throughout 1960–97. These results also support the view that TFP contributed primarily to the observed pattern of economic growth in Ghana, and that a driving force of TFP might be the nature of the economic regime. For example, the periods 1970–4 and 1985–97, when *per capita* GDP growth was relatively robust, also corresponded roughly to the more liberalized economic periods.

2.4 Explaining growth performance across different periods

In this section we present a macroeconomic explanation of the growth trends presented above, looking at three distinct periods in the before-reform and after-reform periods. The story that emerges from the data is that Ghana has not invested enough over the years and that whatever investment has been made has not necessarily been the most productive. Figure 9.2 shows the nature of the dip in investments as a share of GDP throughout most of

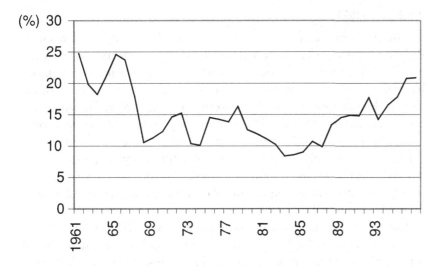

Figure 9.2 Ghana, the GDI:GDP ratio, 1961–1997.

the period under study. This began to climb up only slowly after 1984. A clearer picture is obtained from table 9.3 indicating the poor state of savings and investment. It is important, however, to underscore the major role that aid has played in revitalizing investment in the last two decades.

2.4.1 1960–1965

This period was characterized by the preparation and implementation of a Seven-Year Development Plan: 1963/4–1969/70 under the Nkrumah regime, and bold efforts to modernize the economy through industrialization. Physical capital accumulation over this period was the most significant contributor to output growth.

At the macroeconomic level, however, the economy was in decline. The investment–GDP ratio first declined from just under 25 percent in 1961 to 18 percent in 1963 before climbing again sharply after 1964 to almost 25 percent (see figure 9.2). The estimated decline in TFP of 1.96 percent in 1960–4 was a precursor to the economic decline; it suggests that the relatively high input growth was not efficiently allocated. Indeed, the external reserve position deteriorated significantly between 1957 when net reserves stood at US$269 million and 1966 when they were negative (–US$391 million). This reflected a deteriorating balance of payments position and also the poor credit rating accorded the country as it struggled to expand the economy rapidly. The country registered three consecutive years of negative growth in *per capita* GDP between 1964 and 1966 and inflation increased from 1 percent in 1957 to 22.7 percent in 1965.

2.4.2 1966–1971

The deteriorating economic situation and the fall in living standards were the stated reasons why a group of army and police officers overthrew the Nkrumah government in February 1966. The military regime subsequently handed over power in 1969 to the civilian government of Dr. K. A. Busia. The ideological stance of these two governments was pro-private capital and opposed to Nkrumah's "socialist" policies. They introduced IMF-sponsored monetary reforms, devalued the currency, and liberalized the external sector (Frimpong-Ansah 1991). Under the military, disinflationary policies aimed at stabilizing the macroeconomy were implemented. There was a reduction in domestic investment, tighter control over import licenses, and a devaluation of the cedi (Killick 1978).

The objective of stabilization was largely achieved. GDP growth increased from 0.2 percent in 1967 to 1.2 percent by 1969. The balance of trade moved into surplus and the current account and government budget deficits were also reduced. Inflation fell from 22.7 percent in 1965 to 6.9 percent by 1969; TFP nonetheless declined by 2.01 percent between 1965 and 1969. By the end of 1971, the economy was in the same position as it had been in 1965, with increasing fiscal and current account deficits. The government responded with a devaluation of the cedi at the end of that year. The devaluation, together with preceding economic difficulties, provided the reason for another *coup d'état* in January 1972, which ended Ghana's second democratic experiment. However the liberal stance did not significantly affect the structure of the economy and the relations among economic agents.

2.4.3 1972–1983

As observed earlier, the 1970s and early 1980s saw the most significant decline in GDP growth per worker, with the decline in TFP being the most significant contributory factor. This period was one of sustained deterioration in the economy under five "different" governments, and has been described by Aryeetey and Tarp (2000) as one of "muddling through." Under the different governments, mostly military, the policies of the period emphasized import substitution, underpinned by a restrictive foreign exchange regime, quantitative restrictions (QRs) on imports and price controls, with the state playing a major role as producer. The dramatic contraction between 1970 and 1983 entailed a decline in GDP *per capita* by more than 3 percent a year, in industrial output by 4.2 percent a year, and in agricultural output by 0.2 percent a year (Tabatabai 1986). The main foundations of the economy, cocoa, mineral, and timber production were being undermined. Cocoa exports fell from 382,000 metric tons in 1974 to 159,000 metric tons in 1983. Mineral exports declined from an index value of 100 in 1975 to 46 by 1983. Production of starchy staples fell from 7,988,000 tons in 1974 to 3,657,000 tons by 1983. Table 9.4 summarizes the macroeconomic conditions that emanated from those policies.

Although in 1983 food production was affected by the worst drought in Ghana's history, its decline was mainly due to the massive migration suffered by the rural sector. This exodus was partly a result of the deteriorating economic conditions and also of the 1973–4 oil boom in Nigeria (a crisis for Ghana), which induced more than 2 million Ghanaians to leave in search of better conditions in Nigeria. Inadequate food prices intensified the demand for food imports, and the diminishing capacity to import deprived agriculture as well as other sectors of inputs, the shortage of which hampered production still further. Particularly hard hit was the government's tax base, as those activities that provided it with the bulk of revenues shrank disproportionately. Central government revenues, which amounted to 21 percent of GDP in 1970, fell to only 5 percent of a smaller GDP in 1983 (Tabatabai 1986). The revenue collapse increased the reliance on the banking system to finance expenditures. Between 1974 and 1983 the monetary base expanded from 697 million to 11,440 million. The loss of monetary control accelerated inflation, which increased from 18.45 percent in 1974 to 116.5 percent by 1981 in the midst of a regime of controlled prices (table 9.4). The period of decline was also characterized by negative real interest rates, and domestic savings and investment decreased from 12 percent and 14 percent of GDP, respectively, to less than 4 percent.

Successive governments continued the policy of overvaluing the cedi, cognizant of the fate that had befallen the Busia government's attempt at devaluation in 1972. Between 1974 and 1983 the cedi was devalued only once in 1978 (from 1.15 to 2.75 to $US1) despite a hundred-fold increase in domestic prices. The current account deficit of US$2.7 million in 1975 increased to US$294 million by 1983. The current account deficits not only depleted gross official foreign reserves but also involved an accumulation of external debt. Arrears amounted to the equivalent of 90 percent of annual export earnings in 1982 (Kapur *et al.* 1991). Also, successive governments responded with import controls, which fell disproportionately on consumer goods. Consumer goods as a proportion of imports fell from 20.2 percent in 1975 to 17.1 percent in 1980. The continuing economic decline was, once again, the pretext under which Flight Lt. Jerry John Rawlings staged a *coup d'état* in December 1981, establishing the Provisional National Defense Council (PNDC).

2.4.4 1984–2000

The SAP was aimed at liberalizing the economy; exchange rate policy, fiscal and monetary policies, privatization, and trade policies all saw dramatic changes. The growth picture as shown in figure 9.1 suggests that there has been a marked contrast in the growth performance of the Ghanaian economy

Table 9.4 *Ghana, key macroeconomic indicators, 1970–1983*

	1970	1971	1972	1973	1974	1975	1976	1977	1978	1979	1980	1981	1982	1983
GDP current (cedi million)	2,259	2,501	2,815	3,502	4,666	5,283	6,526	11,163	20,986	28,231	42,853	72,626	86,451	1,84,038
Real GDP growth (%)	6.78	5.56	-2.50	15.3	3.39	-12.87	-3.52	2.29	8.48	-7.82	6.25	-3.50	-6.92	-4.56
Balance of payments (US$ million)														
Trade accounts	52.0	-34.0	161.0	213.0	-29.0	150.0	89.0	29.0	113.0	263.0	195.0	-243.0	18.3	-61.0
Current account	-68.0	-146.0	108.0	127.0	-172.0	17.0	-74.0	-80.0	-46.0	122.0	29.0	-421.0	-109.0	-174.0
Overall balance	NA	NA	NA	109.0	-142.0	106.0	137.0	-9.0	-46.0	36.0	-30.0	-289.0	-10.0	-173.0
Narrow fiscal deficit (cedi million)[a]	-31.0	-58.0	-122.0	-248.0	-190.0	-422.0	-592.0	-1212.0	-1678.0	-1875.0	-3041.0	-4606.0	-4364.0	-4514.0
% GDP	-1.4	-2.3	-4.3	-7.1	-4.1	-8.0	-9.1	-10.9	-8.0	-6.6	-7.1	-6.4	-5.1	-2.5
Money supply growth rate broad money M 2 (%)	22.2	27.3	33.1	12.2	33.9	22.4	25.7	37.3	54.4	25.6	47.7	40.3	38.9	12.4
Inflation CPI (%)	3.5	5.1	20.3	1.6	24.3	41.2	41.2	121.2	73.2	54.4	50.1	116.5	19.2	128.7
Exchange rate (cedi:US$)	1.020	1.030	1.330	1.149	1.149	1.149	1.149	1.149	2.750	2.750	2.750	2.750	2.750	30.00
Gross fixed capital formation/GDP (%)	12.0	12.4	8.7	7.6	11.9	11.6	9.8	9.4	6.5	6.7	6.1	4.7	3.5	3.8

Note: [a]Narrow fiscal deficit excludes expenditures financed by foreign loans and grants.

Source: IMF *Balance of Payments Yearbook*; Aryeetey, Harrigan, and Nissanke (2000).

since the reforms began. Obviously this is different from the question of whether this growth is enough. Indeed since 1983, GDP growth rates have averaged 5 percent per annum, with the output of cocoa, minerals, and timber recording significant increases. Inflation has fallen from the very high pre-reform levels (122 percent in 1983), declining to 10 percent in 1992. The inflation rate has not stayed low, however, increasing slightly from its 28 percent annual average in 1985–9 to 29 percent in the latter part of the reform period. Nor has private investment improved much, remaining at about 4.0 percent of GDP. The overall gross domestic investment rose from about 11 percent to 16 percent. However, all the improvement in investment during the latter part of the reform era was attributable to increases in public investment (see table 9.5).

While export growth rebounded strongly to show a growth of 11 percent in 1985–9 from a dismal decline in the pre-reform period of about 9 percent, it registered no growth in the latter 1990–6 period. Meanwhile, unlike the first two periods when the growth of imports paralleled that of exports, import growth was substantially positive at 5 percent despite no growth of exports in this latter period. Consequently, the current account balance worsened further to about 9 percent of GDP, from its earlier reform ratio of 5.0 percent. Furthermore, the fiscal condition of the economy reverted to its earlier condition of ill health in the 1990s. It registered a deficit of 11 percent of GDP (government deficits, excluding grants), nearly paralleling the 12 percent rate for the control period of 1975–84, and slightly more than twice the ratio during the earlier phase of the reform era. Much of this worsening in the government budget deficit could be attributed to substantial increases in government expenditures which, as percent of GDP, increased by 9.0 percentage points over the previous period, compared to only about a 3.0 percentage point increase in government revenues.

Cocoa has traditionally constituted a major source of export earnings and, presumably, of investment funds in Ghana. Earnings from cocoa exports in real terms rose to a peak of $495 million (real 1987 dollars) in 1987, from $426 million in 1986, and then started to decline. The dominance of this sector continued to decline as Ghana expanded its export base. Cocoa's share of export earnings steadily fell from 67 percent in 1986 to 26 percent in 1994, though it appears to have picked up somewhat to 35 percent in 1996 (table 9.6).

In contrast, contributions to export earnings by the minerals sector rose steadily through the 1986–95 period, taking over from cocoa as the principal foreign exchange earner. The mineral earnings share reached its peak in 1994 at 48 percent but declined to 41 percent in 1996. Unlike cocoa, there have been increases in contributions to total foreign exchange earnings by timber, minerals, and non-traditional exports since 1986. More recently (1995–6), however, the share of cocoa experienced an upward tick, while those of

Table 9.5 *Ghana, key macroeconomic indicators, 1985–1995*

	1985	1986	1987	1988	1989	1990	1991	1992	1993	1994est	1995est
GDP current (cedi million)	343	511	746	1,051	1,417	2,032	2,575	3,009	3,949	5,186	
Real GDP growth (%)	5.1	5.2	4.8	5.6	5.1	3.3	5.3	3.9	5.0	3.8	
Balance of payments (US$ million)											
Trade accounts	−185.0	−171.0	−300.0	−305.0	−399.0	−523.0	−554.0	−740.0	−964.0	−626.0	−235.7
Current account	−263.0	−204.0	−225.0	−264.0	−315.0	−432.0	−454.0	−592.0	−815.0	−466.0	
Overall balance (= change in net international reserves)	−115.5	−56.8	138.1	124.8	127.2	118.0	170.8	−124.3	−41.3	163.4	247.2
Narrow fiscal deficit (billion cedi)	−14.0	−28.3	−37.8	−56.1	−75.0	−98.0	−103.5	−321.7	−427.1	−352.2	
(% GDP)	−4.1	−5.5	−5.1	−5.3	−5.3	−4.8	−4.0	−10.7	−10.8	−6.8	
Broad fiscal deficit (% GDP)[a]	−1.6	0.6	1.2	0.9	1.3	0.6	2.0	−3.4	−2.5		
Money supply growth rate broad money (%)	65.0	66.5	57.1	50.0	60.6	22.6	69.2	50.0	23.0	46.0	
Inflation CPI (%)	10.4	24.6	39.8	31.4	25.2	37.2	18.0	10.1	25.0	24.9	60.0
Foreign debt outstanding and disbursed (%GDP)	35.5	57.1	71.4	59.2	64.4	58.5	59.3	61.8	78.6	92.3	
Real interest rate (%)	−2.4	−14.8	−12.5	−6.8	−10.7	14.1	18.9	6.1	3.3	1.0	
Exchange rate, annual average (cedi:US$)	54.4	106.4	162.4	202.4	270.0	330.0	375.0	437.0	649.0	956.6	1,200
Gross fixed capital formation (% GDP)	9.6	9.4	10.4	11.3	13.3	14.4	15.8	12.8	14.8	15.9	
Private investment (% GDP)	5.4	2.1	2.5	3.3	5.5	7.6	8.1	4.3	4.9	4.4	
Gross domestic savings (% GDP)	6.6	5.8	3.9	5.4	5.6	6.0	7.8	2.0	−1.0	4.4	

Note: [a]Broad fiscal deficit includes expenditures financed from foreign loans and grants, which are excluded from the narrow budget.

Source: Aryeetey, Harrigan, and Nissanke (2000).

Table 9.6 *Ghana, merchandise export earnings, by sector, 1986–1996 (real 1987 million US dollars)[a]*

Item	1986	1987	1988	1989	1990	1991	1992	1993	1994	1995	1996
Gross exports	634.5	826.6	908.2	865.0	882.7	921.2	970.8	1242.5	1641.5	1660.3	1863.6
of which:											
1. Cocoa total	426.2	495.4	476.3	436.6	354.9	319.9	297.7	334.0	424.7	451.9	654.6
% contribution	67.2	59.9	52.4	50.5	40.2	34.7	30.7	26.9	25.9	27.2	35.1
2. Minerals total	105.3	159.4	193.5	199.1	238.6	325.5	382.5	553.2	780.1	787.5	760.7
% contribution	16.6	19.3	21.3	23.0	27.0	35.3	39.4	44.5	47.5	47.4	40.8
3. Timber total	37.3	89.8	109.5	85.9	116.1	114.7	112.1	172.2	219.4	221.1	174.3
% contribution	5.9	10.9	12.1	9.9	13.2	12.4	11.5	13.9	13.4	13.3	9.4
4. Non-traditional products	20.2	27.9	43.6	37.2	61.3	53.6	63.9	83.8	114.9	116.0	172.0
% contribution	3.2	3.4	4.8	4.3	6.9	5.8	6.6	6.7	7.0	7.0	9.2
5. Others	45.5	54.1	85.3	106.2	117.4	107.5	114.6	99.4	102.5	83.9	102.0
% contribution	7.2	6.5	9.4	12.3	13.3	11.7	11.8	8.0	6.2	5.1	5.5

Note: [a]Real 1987 dollars; author's conversion using GDP deflator based on US dollar series.

Source: Bank of Ghana and Ghana Export Promotion Council.

timber and minerals fell. The share of non-traditional exports also showed an increase, from 3 percent in 1986 to 9 percent in 1996. Nevertheless, in 1996 minerals continued to be the major export earner for Ghana even though its contribution to total earnings fell from 47 percent in 1995 to 41 percent in 1996 (table 9.6).

During this latter period (1990–7), the Collins–Bosworth estimates show that growth of output per worker was 1.27 percent, compared to a growth rate of 2.32 percent in the 1985–9 period. Furthermore, the growth in physical capital and human capital accumulation were the most significant contributors to growth in this period, increasing by 0.75 percent and 0.41 percent, respectively. In 1985–9, on the other hand, the growth in TFP of 2.01 percent was the most significant factor contributing to growth.

What is interesting from these results is that 1985–9 was a period of intense structural adjustment in Ghana. At the onset of the SAP, Ghana's infrastructure had collapsed and an increased investment in physical capital was in order. Nonetheless, growth in this period was dominated by TFP. In 1990–7, on the other hand, when the rate of increase in physical capital accumulation ostensibly decreased, physical capital accumulation was the most significant contributor to growth. This suggests that the impact of increases in physical capital on growth, for example, may operate with a lag, while a change in the policy environment to one that is more conducive to higher productivity may have a more immediate effect.

3. Market structure and government intervention

In this section, we discuss the structure of markets and their performance under different regimes, focusing on capital, labor, land, and the goods markets under controlled and liberal regimes. The argument is that the state has always had a distinct role in the functioning of markets, even if this has been somewhat reduced in the last two decades, and that this role has always affected outcomes in a significant way.

3.1   The labor market and its performance

This market has been very difficult to study over the years in view of the paucity of data (Boateng and Fine 2000). The rural labor market is strongly influenced by local customs and traditions in employment and wage determination, and the process of settlements is largely informal. The agricultural and rural sector employs more than 60 percent of the total labor force, and much of that is employed in family farm holdings. This structure did not change under the system of controls.

Table 9.7 *Ghana, estimated annual growth of labor force, 1960–2000*

	Total	Males	Females
1960–5	1.92	2.18	1.57
1970–5	2.08	2.22	1.90
1980–5	2.66	2.94	2.26
1985–90	2.76	3.05	2.32
1990–5	2.99	3.14	2.76
1995–2000	3.10	3.25	2.87

Source: Boateng (1997).

The urban labor market has been dominated by informal labor exchanges in small enterprises, though it is not completely cut off from the formal sector. Indeed, the urban informal sector provides about 65 percent of the urban labor force, predominantly in self-employment. In the formal sector, which accounts for some 16 percent of the total labor force, employment contracts are generally written and subject to the general conditions of performance specified by the market. The primary institution of the formal labor market is the industrial relations system, comprising the system of laws, regulations and conventions, labor and employers' associations, regulators, and collective bargaining agreements. The labor market also seems to be segmented along gender lines, whereby females are predominantly engaged in the service and commercial sectors, or in the urban informal sector or as unpaid agricultural labor.

What is clear about the labor market in the pre-reform era is the extent to which different governments went to ensure that employment grew. Thus, the structure of the market (in terms of the regional and sectoral distribution of the labor force), extent of unemployment, and the level of real wages all experienced remarkable changes: from one of geographical immobility and shortage of all kinds of labor to one of great mobility and surplus of many types of labor. Some researchers have attributed the growing fiscal deficits in the 1960s and 1970s to considerable featherbedding of the formal sector (Boateng 1997). With this, formal sector employment grew significantly but with very little attention paid to productivity (table 9.7).

The main instrument used by government to control the supply and demand for labor has been the minimum wage policy. A minimum wage policy was first adopted in Ghana in 1963, the objective being to raise income levels of unskilled workers within a social policy context. The relatively rapid expansion of formal employment in the 1960s was a consequence of the expansion of the public sector itself. The creation of state enterprises of different sizes in almost every sector of the economy had the effect of

Table 9.8 *Ghana, distribution of economically active population, 1960–1992, percent*

	Agriculture	Industry	Services
1960	64	14	22
1970	58	17	25
1975	57	17	26
1980	56	18	26
1985	54	18	27
1990	53	19	28
1991	53	19	28
1992	52	19	29

Source: Boateng (1997).

attracting not only skilled labor into the modern sectors but also led to a major expansion of the informal and unskilled urban labor class to support the more formal sector. The public sector consequently became both the most significant employer and trend-setter in the determination of wages as well as regulator. This is a role that has not changed significantly despite the reforms of later years.

The movement of labor from rural areas to urban centers led to a decline of the share of the agricultural sector in the labor force from 64 percent to 52 percent, as shown in table 9.8. About 50 percent of the decline in the agricultural sector share in employment occurred in the period 1960–70 while the remaining 50 percent occurred in the period 1970–92. Boateng (1997) has reported that formal sector employment in 1991 was 44 percent less than in 1960, representing an average annual decrease of 1.4 percent compared with an average annual growth rate of the urban labor force of 5.3 percent between 1960 and 1990. The importance of the formal sector as a source of employment thus declined from 3.6 percent to 2.5 percent between 1981 and 1991. The period of mass employment in 1960–85 was the consequence of a policy of employment maximization supported by a broad-based regime of state controls on all major aspects of the economy, from price and exchange rate controls to state ownership of manufacturing and distributive trade centers. But this did not involve the private sector, where expansion has been slow (Boateng 1997).

Labor productivity (average value added per worker deflated by the manufactures' wholesale price index) in the manufacturing sector declined by about 43 percent between 1977 and 1981 (World Bank 1985). The downward trend in labor productivity was largely due to constraints in laying off redundant labor in spite of low rates of capacity utilization. The low wages, relative to the urban cost of living, provided little incentive to work. The

compressed wage structure offered little reward to greater skills and productivity, especially in the public sector. A point made by Collier and Gunning
(1999) is that while the productivity of Ghanaian workers is generally low,
it is matched by a relatively low wage packet. This is derived from a rapid
growth of the labor force and employment at a time when production hardly
grew at all. The rapid growth of the labor force and policy of rapidly absorb-
ing it through public sector employment while assuring labor a minimum
wage helped to achieve steady growth in the numbers until the reforms
began. The subsequent decline in employment in the face of rising output
implies that labor productivity has increased, at least in the formal sector.

3.2 The credit market and its performance

The early control regimes were an attempt to expand the credit market.
Thus, in dealing with a market failure that denied people access to credit
and other financial services, the interventionist approach began under "self-
rule" in 1953 with the establishment of the Ghana Commercial Bank for
both political and economic objectives. Subsequently, the financing needs
of specific sectors were addressed by establishing state-owned development
banks: the National Investment Bank (1963), the Agricultural Development
Bank (1965), and the Bank for Housing and Construction (1973). The Bank
of Ghana was established in 1957 to supervise all other banks (replacing
the role of the West African Currency Board). Government interest in small
clients during the 1970s fostered another generation of specialized banks –
the Co-operative Bank, the National Savings and Credit Bank, the Social
Security Bank, and unit rural banks – all charged to direct credit to specific
groups. Government intervention to overcome the perceived slow pace of
private banking also took the form of pressure on state-owned banks to
increase the number of branches. The total number of bank branches more
than doubled in the 1970s, reaching 466 (including rural banks) by 1985.
By 1983, there were eleven borrower categories for the distribution of loans
and advances identified for the purpose of directing credit. Using a mix of
interest rates and selective credit controls and ceilings, the Bank of Ghana
controlled the flow of credit to them. It adjusted interest rates periodically in
order to promote increases in the level of investment among different sectors.
For example, in 1983, the Bank of Ghana directed that commercial banks
should charge a preferential interest rate of 8 percent per annum (instead
of the general 9 percent at the time) on loans and advances to small-scale
farmers in order to boost agriculture.

The interventionist policies had the effect of reducing significantly the
size of the financial market, reducing competition in the financial system
and making the financial market respond more to the needs of the state
than to those of the productive agents. The negative impact of repressive

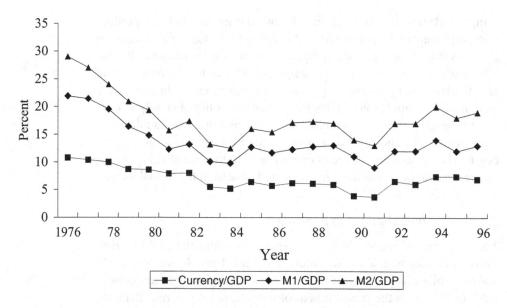

Figure 9.3 Ghana, indicators of financial deepening, 1976–1996.

policies on financial sector development was most clearly seen in the halving of financial depth, measured by the M2/GDP ratio, from over 25 percent in 1977 to only 12 percent in 1984 (see figure 9.3). Between 1977 and 1984, most other indicators of the development of the financial system declined in size (measured as a percentage of GDP); demand deposits fell from 11.6 percent to 4.6 percent; savings and time deposits fell from 7.1 percent to 2.6 percent; and domestic credit declined from 38.8 percent to 15.6 percent.

After two decades of reform and an expansion in the number of institutions, a number of problems persist in the banking system, including a widening spread in interest rates. The system is still characterized by a heavy concentration of assets in the short end of the market and the prevalence of non-performing term loans (Nissanke and Aryeetey 1998). The main malfunction of the banking system manifests itself in a lack of information production and facilitation of governance and control for the commercial sector. There is limited monitoring of the activities of borrowers, poor enforcement of collateral, and lack of enforcement of lenders' rights for fuller disclosure of financial information about borrowers. Efforts to strengthen the banking system through stricter portfolio quality requirements by the Bank of Ghana may have restricted the access of small- and medium-sized enterprises (SMEs) by leading to increased centralization of decision-making (at least initially) and greater risk aversion.

But the expected impact of a liberal interest rate regime on the monetary situation has been seldom achieved, as the ability of the monetary authorities to achieve set targets has often been compromised by an ineffective broader policy environment (Roe and Sowa 1997; Nissanke and Aryeetey 1998). In the presence of a shallow financial market and a poor development of the money market, rising interest rates have often led to a credit crunch, and to considerable excess liquidity – i.e. situations in which banks voluntarily increased their holdings of liquid assets on a large scale. Indirect monetary management has been difficult, with some improvements being observed only as late as 2005.

While it has always been known that the creation and development of active money and capital markets could considerably broaden the opportunities for diversification for both savers and investors and provide an avenue for active liquidity management by financial institutions and monetary control by the central banks, the process of erecting them has been fraught with numerous problems. Hence, despite the fact that the shift in monetary policy from direct credit control to indirect control required an operative money market to be effective, the development of such a market has not gained the same prominence as the other components of reform mentioned earlier. A major reason for the poor functioning of the money market is government financing approaches. The practice of government issuing large quantities of very high-yielding bills to meet fiscal requirements needs to be seen as a problem. Indeed, so long as banks have access to inexpensive and unlimited loans through central bank discount facilities, inter-bank borrowing and lending are unlikely to be attractive. Informal financial institutions flourished during the reform period (Aryeetey 1996). The increase in informal financial sector activity and competition was associated more with the increase in real sector activity during the adjustment period than with financial policy reforms *per se*. That is, increased activity in markets due to elimination of controls and increased foreign borrowing meant that traders had more money to save and to lend (either to business clients or to borrowers). There appears to be greater diversification in activity among some informal institutions in attempts to reach out to more borrowers than is observable among formal institutions after reforms.

3.3 The land market and its performance

There are major pieces of work that suggest that access to land is a problem; others suggest that such access has never been a major constraint to agricultural expansion and practices. Nukunya (1972) shows that the main constraint to expansion for shallot farming in the Anlo area (south eastern Ghana) is difficult access to land which is in short supply in view of the peculiar requirements of the crop. Shallot farmers are forced to use land more intensively than in other regions, but this does not necessarily lead to greater application of capital in view of the poverty of the area. The land tenure system in the area shows considerable variation in how one may obtain access to land, but in increasingly smaller portions and with rights that are becoming more and more diffused. Benneh's work (1972) in the savannah-forest contact zone of central Ghana showed that there were growing signs of pressure as a result of the introduction of cash crops. Where economic activity was gathering pace, communities were reluctant to permit the release of large tracts of land for commercial farming. The conclusion drawn from both pieces of work was that the land tenure system in Ghana was under considerable pressure, torn between social equity and efficient use of land.

In the changing environment for land acquisition, the state in the 1960s used its powers of acquisition to acquire land, largely for state farms and other public economic activities with only token (non-market) compensation paid to the communal/family owners. In using its authority to acquire land for various ventures, the state hardly affected the price of land as a land market never really existed. This was largely because the state implicitly discouraged the development of a commercial land market. In the case of corporate bodies seeking land for their ventures, the state sometimes acquired communal lands that were leased to the investors at non-market rates. The state also sometimes encouraged communal owners of land to make transfers of land directly to investors, a practice that Benneh (1972) saw as being problematic, often creating conflicts between public and private interests. The consequence has been that the land market is poorly developed and the use of land as an asset is often uneconomical.

3.4 The structure and performance of the goods and services markets

3.4.1 Industry

During the brief attempt at liberalization between 1966 and 1971, there was a slowdown in the establishment of state-owned enterprises (SOEs). With the adoption of the principle of self-reliance and the desire to capture the "commanding heights of the economy," however, the state-led import-substituting industrialization (ISI) strategy was revived in the 1970s. In addition to expansion in manufacturing production and capacity through ISI, policy statements also emphasized an expansion in manufactured exports. Export diversification was considered necessary if the foreign exchange constraint on the economy was to be reduced, but was never actively pursued. The choice of an inward-oriented trade strategy was motivated by export pessimism, in relation to the ability of primary exports to generate the necessary foreign exchange required for rapid growth. Unlike the East Asian tigers that were able to make the transition from an ISI strategy to an outward-oriented one, Ghana got stuck at the ISI stage. In pursuit of ISI, severe sectoral policy conflicts existed and there was a mismatch between policy objectives and implementation. It is today acknowledged that an expansion in manufactured exports could have occurred within the context of an ISI strategy only if measures had been introduced to counteract the anti-export bias inherent in the strategy. Unfortunately such a policy mix was not achieved in Ghana during the 1960s and 1970s. Steel (1972) indicated that "Ghana's industrialization and ISI policies were extremely unsuccessful in establishing a structure and level of manufacturing output which could efficiently reduce foreign exchange requirements and stimulate growth of GNP" (1972: 226–7). He suggested that massive capacity under-utilization was the consequence of inappropriate foreign exchange policies and high levels of effective protection which stimulated the domestic production of final-stage assembly, "non-essential" activities. Killick (1978) has also made similar arguments.

The reform program brought about change in the performance of the manufacturing sector. After years of steady decline, real manufacturing GDP saw positive growth rates from 1984, but at a decreasing rate after 1988 (Asante, Nixson, and Tsikata 2000). The initial growth was not sustained and came from a low base. The growth of manufacturing lagged behind that of GDP leading to a declining share of manufacturing in GDP and therefore a lack of inter-sectoral structural change of the type usually associated with development (Nixson 1990). The decline in the growth rate between 1988 and 1995 has been attributed to the fact that while competitive industries continued to grow, uncompetitive ones began to decline or fold up in the more liberalized environment. The slowdown in the growth of the manufacturing sector was reflected in the growth rate of the whole industrial sector, whose growth declined from 12.1 percent between 1984 and 1987 to 4.4 percent between 1988 and 1995; this picked up again after 1995.

Asante, Nixson, and Tsikata (2000) conducted statistical tests on the mean growth rates for the manufacturing and industrial sectors which showed that the growth rates were significantly higher for the reform period than for the earlier period. The shares of manufacturing GDP and industrial GDP in total GDP were significantly lower for the reform period as a result of the lagging growth rates of manufacturing and industry. A study by the World Bank (1984) showed that 40 percent of the firms in 1983 had negative value added at world prices. Closing them down would have yielded a net *real* benefit to the country, even though the loss of value added at (highly protected) domestic prices would look like "de-industrialization."

The slowdown in the growth of real manufacturing GDP after 1988 has been worrying. This has been interpreted to mean that appropriate trade and macroeconomic policies are by no means sufficient for sustained high performance in the environment of significant structural constraints. Output growth performance has, however, differed among sub-sectors of the manufacturing sector. The sub-sectors with significantly lower output include textiles, wearing apparel, and leather goods, where high-cost, over-protected firms have had difficulty competing with liberalized imports. Those whose output has increased significantly include sawmill and wood products, and beverages, which are domestic resource-based. The outstanding problems of the sector include:

- Inadequate finance for working capital, rehabilitation, and modernization.
- The large depreciation of the cedi, which has eroded the liquid resources which could have helped firms to undertake the necessary investments. In some cases, the depreciation has sharply inflated the cedi value of debts related to past imports of machinery and equipment.
- The tight monetary policy pursued, which has increased the cost of credit.
- Some of the enterprises operated under high protective barriers and found it difficult to cope with the liberalized and more competitive market environment.
- Macroeconomic instability.

Teal (1995) has also argued that labor regulations, price controls, and other obstacles to expansion have constrained output and export growth, especially in the case of wood products which is the major manufacturing export sub-sector. More generally, Teal (1995) argues that government-induced market failure explains the absence of progress in developing manufacturing exports. Structural adjustment and liberalization are not complete in Ghana and government policy continues to have an adverse effect on the output of firms, in the exportables sector in particular.

3.4.2 Agriculture

In agriculture, the pronounced role of the state was again exhibited in the immediate post-independence period. Policies placed emphasis on the modernization of agriculture and expansion through major capital investments controlled by the state. This led to the establishment of "state farms," covering large tracts of land in all regions and using huge amounts of labor to operate them. In the early 1970s, however, an attempt was made to accommodate the private sector. SOEs, machinery, and equipment were sold to private entrepreneurs and parts of the economy were returned to the market system. Experiments with import liberalization were carried out and small-scale agricultural development was emphasized *vis-à-vis* large state farms in the government's economic programs. Table 9.9 compares the performance of the agricultural sector with that of industry and services over the subsequent quarter-century.

Table 9.9 *Ghana, sectoral growth rates, 1972–1995, period averages, percent*

	1972–5	1976–82	1983–6	1987–90	1991–5
Agriculture	−2.3	1.4	1.5	1.3	2.7
Industry	1.9	−7.3	5.6	7.0	4.3
Services	0.2	1.2	5.7	7.9	6.1

Source: Calculated from Statistical Services, *Quarterly Digest of Statistics*, various issues; ISSER (1996).

Nyanteng and Seini (2000) have reported that another feature of agricultural policy in the early 1970s was the formation of single-product development boards such as cotton, bast fiber, grains, and cattle and meat development boards. Policy-makers believed that the ingenuity of the peasant farmer could be further exploited, as in the case of cocoa, by the establishment of development boards to offer advice and incentives, and oversee the production of agricultural raw materials that were vital to the newly established factories. So that farmers did not suffer income losses from over-production of these commodities, the government also instituted minimum guaranteed price schemes for them. Agricultural policies were supported by a massive rural development scheme, designed to provide the basic infrastructure of roads, water, and electricity that would encourage people to stay and farm in the rural areas. In the cocoa sub-sector, the multiple buying system, involving several companies, was re-established to replace the monopoly then enjoyed by the United Ghana Farmers Co-operative Council, which was subsequently dissolved.

The experiments of the early 1970s were short lived, however, as the military regimes after 1972 dismantled the policies. At the same time, there was considerable interest in raising agricultural production to self-sufficiency level. The military government instituted the Operation Feed Yourself (OFY) and the Operation Feed Your Industries (OFYI) programs after 1972. These were to spearhead the campaign to increase food and agricultural raw material production. Among the objectives of these programs was the increase in small-farm production through acreage expansion (Killick 1978). The OFY emphasized the production of cereals, mainly maize and rice, while the OFYI encouraged the production of cotton, kenaf, and sugarcane, among other agricultural raw materials.

In terms of outcomes throughout the control period, there was a complete lack of incentive to produce because the subsidized agricultural inputs of fertilizers and insecticides became primary targets for smuggling into the neighboring countries where high prices more than compensated for their loss of application in Ghana. Agricultural mechanization, which had been on the upturn, suffered, particularly as basic spare parts required to maintain machines were lacking. The cocoa sector also suffered from the unfavorable macroeconomic policy stance. The production of cocoa which reached its peak with an output of over 557,000 mt in 1965 declined to its lowest level in the 1983–4 season, with an output of about 158,000 mt, about 63 percent less than the output in 1980–1. The exchange rate policy made it impossible for the government to pursue a realistic cocoa-pricing policy. At the prevailing fixed exchange rate, an increase in nominal producer prices would have meant the government accepting a decline in cocoa revenues. The government was not willing to accept such a decline because of its heavy dependence on this source of revenue. Farmers responded to the decline in real producer prices by not replanting or maintaining the tree stock, and the quality of the tree stock was further eroded because of inadequate supply of insecticides and spraying cans even though they were heavily subsidized. The foreign exchange constraint limited the quantities of insecticides and spraying cans that could be imported for use in the cocoa industry.

Nyanteng and Seini (2000) have indicated that the fluctuations in agricultural growth primarily reflect fluctuations in the weather, particularly rainfall. The same trend is associated with cocoa, where the agricultural supply response has been weak. While exchange rate reforms and increases in producer price initially helped to increase earnings from cocoa, these have stagnated (Sowa 1996).

4.   The political economy of growth in Ghana

There have been a number of analyzes of why Ghana adopted the control regime of the 1960s, and continued with it in different forms into the 1980s before starting serious reform. The most detailed of the more recent analyzes have come from Leith and Lofchie (1993). The latter examined three theses that have explained the policy choices made. The first was the *urban bias* thesis generally associated with Bates (1981); the second was the *dominant development ethos* thesis that is supported by Killick (1978) and Aryeetey (1992); and finally the *transaction and agency costs thesis* derived from the New Institutional Economics on the premise that the government was aware of the institutional inadequacies and hence opted for policies whose implementation minimized transaction costs in the short run. There is some likelihood that elements of each of these played a role in specific policy choices. Just as we may wonder why the interventionist regime prevailed for so long, we may also consider why reform had to be designed the way it was, how the design affected different groups, and how they responded to it. Instead of examining each of the above theses in turn, the discussion in this section focuses on the roles played by the structure of political institutions in the determination of economic policy, looking out for those specific influences. This is weighed against other external influences such as the presence of pressure groups (captured, for example, by strikes), and the possibility of a direct assault on the state and government – as, for example, through a *coup d'état*. The role of corruption as a way of escaping from the legitimate influence of the state in the organization of economic activity is also discussed.

4.1 The structure of political institutions and economic policy

For both the control and liberal economic regimes there was no open system of decision-making. Both sets of policies were developed out of policy-making structures that were subject to different sets of influences and their own internal dynamics. For the earlier period Apter (1975) suggests that there was a basic difficulty in entrenching democratic institutions in Ghanaian political life in view of the social and political tensions that erupted soon after independence. These tensions had been brewing in the run-up to independence and the way that Nkrumah's government chose to deal with them led to the demise of democratic structures and their replacement by a single party that looked up to an individual for all guidance and inspiration. Faced with the development realities and difficulties of a young nation, and in order to hold on to power, the opposition had to be crushed, and this was done with relative ease. The ruling Convention People's Party (CPP) had to recreate itself in a manner that allowed it to dominate all social, economic, and political life, a process that made an ideology that emphasized the role of the new secular state paramount. That process also led to the removal of moderate thinking from the party machinery. With moderates and "capitalists" out of government in the first half of the 1960s, the stage was set for state control of all production processes.

This may be compared to the structures that led to the reform program thirty years later. Ironically, the decision to embrace liberal economic policies was taken by a government that had generally been perceived to be Marxist and significantly interested in a system of controls. The PNDC was a military regime that managed to develop a coalition of young radical ideologues who were more interested in the political outcomes of development issues than in economic outcomes. In that system, the issues of distribution were more important than production and growth. The coalition believed that the poor economic situation was a simple outcome of corruption related to incompetence and that, once the issues of equity were resolved through the institution of sanctions for wrong-doing, the situation could be resolved. In the interim, aid from sympathetic governments would ensure that the institutions to fight corruption would be erected and made functional, while taking care of Ghanaians' immediate material needs. While there is no doubt that the economic situation made it essential for solutions to be found, it is now generally acknowledged that the decision to embrace liberal economic reforms arose at that time because the leader of the military regime came to appreciate that no aid was coming. It is therefore fair to say that liberal reform was precipitated by the urgent need for assistance from donors in order to feed a hungry nation, just as the earlier modernization attempt had been prompted by the need to satisfy the hungry masses that had supported independence and were waiting to be rewarded.

In the pre-reform period, Apter (1975) noted: "The interest of the militants was in maintaining solidarity and cohesion in the society. They intended to make such cohesion a joint concern of party and state. The leaders of both were in effect political entrepreneurs using political power to mobilize and transform the conditions of material life, to develop the country, and to reach out to other African nations in some form of association" (1975: 356). For them, the state and party could do anything:

Political power was used also for economic ends. Emphasizing a kind of economic solidarity, Ghanaian socialism or Nkrumahism was a blend of moral values which emphasized many of the puritan qualities: thrift, hard work, honesty, sacrifice, devotion to duty. It was in addition a doctrine of state enterprise in which leaders used the state and the resources of the community both for development and in increasing measure, ownership. (1975: 356)

How was ownership seen in the reform program? Did the decision to embrace liberal reforms lead to Ghana developing a reform program that was intended to address the economic problems of the time? Aryeetey and Cox (1997), in a study of aid effectiveness in Ghana, note that the institutional structure for undertaking the negotiations with the Bretton Woods Institutions (BWI) was a rather ambiguous one, made up of a carefully crafted Economic Management Team that operated ostensibly from the Ministry of Finance without necessarily using the structure of the Ministry. The government insisted that it owned the reform program because it "took full responsibility for the preparation of the Economic Recovery Program and only received the endorsement of the World Bank and IMF when a finished document was already in place, in spite of the usual consultations along the process" (Aryeetey and Cox 1997). The issues of ownership and legitimacy of the regime have been addressed by Ninsin (1991), suggesting that the reform program did not embrace the interests of a larger cross-section of the people. While legitimacy might be disputed, the sense that the Ghanaian government was "not being pushed around" by donors prevailed. Whichever way one looks at the question of "ownership," Ghana gained a lot of respect internationally by being able to negotiate seemingly difficult points that other African governments had previously had to "acquiesce" on. This was used by Ghanaian officials as proof of ownership.

To pursue the control regime in the pre-reform period, most institutions associated with secular democracies were deliberately crushed in order to promote the party. The legal system was particularly weakened through the enactment of controversial laws that compromised the liberties of individuals and reduced the prospects for using the court system to resolve disputes in a transparent manner. The civil service was also partially weakened, largely through intimidation, while organized labor was highly politicized and made an appendage of the ruling party. Free enterprise could not be encouraged and the system for national economic management saw to that. Domestically a five-sector economy was called for which included: (a) state enterprises; (b) enterprises owned by foreign private interests; (c) enterprises jointly owned by the state and foreign private interests; (d) co-operatives; (e) small-scale Ghanaian private enterprises. Nkrumah's government was not in the mood for large private Ghanaian ventures and did everything to discourage them. Indeed, Nkrumah argued that there was no bourgeois class among Ghanaians to undertake large scale investments (Nkrumah 1965). What was remarkable about the institutional structure for the preparation of the Development Plan was the centralized nature of the whole process, very similar to the political process that emerged. The personal charisma of the leaders was vital to the adoption of the major economic endeavors of the two periods. Kwame Nkrumah and Jerry Rawlings both provided considerable personal support to make their programs take off.

Why did the structures eventually crumble? A centralized machinery needs accurate information from economic agents at all times in order to make meaningful economic projections and also determine their likely response to economic policies. Such information has been largely missing (Aryeetey 1985). The consequence was that hardly any private ventures materialized in the Nkrumah days. National economic management was reduced to government spending on state enterprises and little attention was paid to revenue mobilization, attraction of investments, savings mobilization, macroeconomic stability, etc. As Apter (1975) wrote: "Ghana proved to be neither a model of socialist endeavor nor a monument to African enterprise. Planning created an extremely grave organizational problem, which put unanticipated obstacles in the way of development. Ghana depleted her reserves in showpiece projects, public buildings and other costly endeavors, particularly in large towns" (1975: 359). One clear aspect of the failed plan and the economic policies of the time is the scant attention paid to agriculture, despite the growing number of state farms.

It was the lack of results of economic endeavors at a time when political repression had taken root in Ghanaian life that provided widespread support for the military overthrow of the Nkrumah government in 1966. While the change in government was popular, this did not lead to a restoration of democratic institutions in the country for a long time to come. The period from

1966 to 1983 saw a mixture of civilian and military governments that essentially worked with the same institutions, albeit with minor modifications in approach, which the Nkrumah government had erected. Democracy was seldom a feature of national governance, even under the elected government of Dr. K. A. Busia (1969–72). The absence of democracy may be regarded as having fueled the political instability that characterized Ghanaian political and economic life in the first three decades of its post-independence life.

It is important to underscore the fact that Ghana became a new democracy in 1992, almost a decade after the reforms began. This created new institutions, including a parliament and a strengthened civil service as well as the development of a new civil society. The government of the National Democratic Congress (NDC), again led by Jerry Rawlings, never stopped showing its disdain for the parliamentary processes that were supposed to oversee public expenditure programs and the raising of revenue from both domestic and foreign sources. Aryeetey and Cox (1997) noted that some donors believed that the process of reform had slowed down as a result of the introduction of democracy. But it is important to emphasize the fact that political reform did not come by chance, just as people failed to appreciate the growth outcomes, the perception that faster growth would take place in a politically liberal environment led to the pressures that eventually resulted in a democratic arrangement.

4.2   The role of pressure groups

In the absence of strong society organizations, organized labor and professional groups may be considered to be those that would offer alternative views to economic policy-making. It is crucial to note, however, that these have not until recently had major roles to play in Ghana. In the 1960s, the transformation of the labor movement into a party organ was singularly noteworthy in this regard. The fact that strikes were not a major cause of concern was remarkable; the most significant strike that took place was in 1961, organized by the railway workers of Sekondi-Takoradi, easily the best organized labor union at the time. While most of the labor movement had been absorbed by the government's party, the Railway and Harbour Workers Union at Sekondi-Takoradi saw itself as being threatened by the anti-trade stance of the government. Using the expected deterioration in their incomes and the growing instability in the economy to justify a strike, it was not difficult to develop an understanding with elements of the opposition party to organize one that had the potential to cripple both the government and the economy. When the strike was brought under control through the government's "divide and rule" tactics, every effort was made to compromise the leaders of the union politically. This effectively took away any resistance to the economic policy-making apparatus. Indeed, it was relatively easy to achieve this since most of the few academics had either been absorbed into the political struggles on the opposition side and been effectively sidelined or made to acquiesce through the edifice of patronage.

For the later reforms, even though Rawlings provided personal support, there was considerable difficulty with the political left, particularly since shares of social expenditures were expected to fall subsequently, suggesting that adjustment burdens would fall disproportionately on the poor. But supporters of the reforms responded that their early anticipation of these problems had led to the Programme of Action to Mitigate the Social Costs of Adjustment (PAMSCAD) (Aryeetey and Cox 1997). Most members of the government perceived "the left" to be "die-hards" who were not prepared to discuss compromise solutions. Following Batesian analysis, further resentment against the reform program came largely from urban populations who bore the costs of initially reduced real incomes, increased tax collection, an end to subsidies, etc. It is interesting, however, that in the period 1983–7, when opposition to reform was strongest, such opposition was hardly ever expressed in radical action, except for isolated cases of minor demonstrations. While a majority of the people were unclear about the likely outcomes of reform and therefore did not commit themselves to it, it was equally unclear what the other options were. A good description of people's attitudes to the Economic Recovery Program (ERP) would be "passive" at best. The Trades Union Congress (TUC) showed very little desire to fight the reform as it had itself been politicized earlier in helping to establish Rawlings' credentials as a supporter of workers' rights (Jeffries 1991).

4.3 Political instability

Aryeetey and Tarp (2000) have observed that "the distinct political instability that was aggravated by poor economic conditions throughout the 1960s and 1970s was reflected in high levels of corruption, policy reversals and a general lack of direction." As the growth in the role of the state became pervasive, it branched into many spheres of economic activity that yielded relatively little economic return and contributed significantly to macroeconomic instability. Indeed, one characteristic of the political economy of Ghana has been the high incidence of *coups d'états* and their association with economic conditions and sometimes with specific economic policies. Existing evidence suggests that among African countries, Ghana has had the largest indicator of this form of "elite" political instability, and that it may have contributed substantially to the observed dismal economic growth performance (see Fosu 1992, 2002).

There have been frequent discussions about the relationship between political instability and economic instability in Ghana (Frimpong-Ansah 1991), which may be growth-inhibiting as well (see Fosu 2001 for an analysis of the relative roles of export, investment, and import instabilities in growth). The consensus view is that they have over the years reinforced each other. Writing about the first coup, Apter (1975) wrote:

> The specific reasons for the coup are many. What is clear is that Nkrumah's political method of creating new alternatives without foreclosing others could not go on indefinitely. The restrictions of political opposition and personal freedom, rising prices, higher taxes, and other economic burdens, exaggerated by an inadequate administrative and inefficient managerial infrastructure (under the form of state capitalism which passed for socialism) all contributed. Everyone in the end was affected. (1975: 387)

Despite the unassailable evidence of foreign instigation of the coup, there is every indication that it was a generally popular occurrence in the aftermath of failed policies.

Most military take overs have led to poor experimentation with alternative policies. The worst example is associated with the second military regime of 1972–9, where economic policy-making could, at best, be described as an experiment in how to "muddle through." This was the period that was characterized by *kalabule*, a local expression for extortion and signifying "the survival of the fittest" in an economic jungle. It has also been referred to as *kleptocracy* in the political-science literature (Leith and Lofchie 1993). At the time that all attempts at sound economic analysis were suffering paralysis, the relative affluence of the army caused demonstrations, and brutal repression became the order of the day. The presentation of economic performance provided in section 2 illustrates the gravity of the vicious circle or state of collapse in which Ghana found itself in the late 1970s and early 1980s.

4.4 Corruption

To what extent did corruption contribute to the mismanagement that has characterized Ghana's economic history in the pre-reform era? The history of independent Ghana is replete with many cases of corruption in all the regimes, both civilian and military. Each new government in Ghana has accused the one it replaced of massive corruption. The famous "dawn broadcast" of Nkrumah in April 1961 signaled his disenchantment with corruption in the top echelon of the party, leading to the removal of some of the most trusted ministers from the government.

Gyimah-Boadi and Jeffries (2000) discuss why corruption became so pervasive in Ghana and the link between that corruption and the economic policies of the pre-reform years. Referring to the second military regime of 1972–9, they raise the question: "Why, then, did Acheampong and his colleagues in government become so corrupt?" They find the answer in "urban bias" arguments. In effect, as economic policies failed to yield desirable outcomes, they created an incentive for corruption because of the political instability that they generated. For many bureaucrats the only way to contain failed policy outcomes that had negative implications for their well-being was to be corrupt. Politicians had greater opportunity to be more corrupt, and seized the opportunity. Obviously this proposition suggests that corruption was not necessarily the cause of poor policies, but largely a consequence of it, and this naturally raises the question of how such corruption affects future policy-making. The suggestion is that a vicious circle is created: corruption creates its own dynamics, and becomes the most visible measure of failed policies. Since the public perception of high corruption is likely to lead to an active support for change in the political leadership that is what has always provided the immediate rationalization for forced changes in government. For every forced change of government, corruption has been listed as one of the major reasons (see also Collier 2000).

5. Conclusion

Policy improvements in Ghana in the 1980s helped to generate substantial growth. This growth came about as a result of the fact that the policy changes led to the availability of resources to the public sector which were invested in capital projects. But, indeed, whenever there has been a major investment in such capital projects, there has been some appreciable growth.

What has not accompanied the growth from capital injection has been a steady improvement in TFP. There are a number attributes and conditions of factor and product markets that impinge on the achievement of steady increases in TFP: for example the labor market remains constrained by weak human capacity, despite initial good education. But, more importantly, technological investments have not taken place adequately, and this is largely because the private sector has not been the main source of investment, while public investment is directed at the provision of basic infrastructure. The absence of technological investments can be linked to the weak credit market; it may to some extent also be associated with a land market that no one wants to reform, despite its ambiguities.

References

Apter, D. (1975), *Ghana in Transition*. Princeton, NJ: Princeton University Press
Aryeetey, E. (1985), *Decentralizing Regional Planning in Ghana*. Dortmund: Institut für Raumplanung, Universität Dortmund (IRPUD)
    (1992), 'Africa in Search of an Alternative Development Path,' in E. Aryeetey, ed., *Planning African Growth and Development: Some Current Issues*, Joint ISSER/UNDP publication, Accra

(1996), "The Formal Financial Sector in Ghana after the Reforms," Overseas Development Institute Working Paper 86

Aryeetey, E. and A. Cox (1997), "Aid Effectiveness in Ghana," in J. Carlsson, G. Somolekae, and N. van de Walle, eds., *Foreign Aid in Africa: Learning from Country Experiences.* Uppsala: Nordic Africa Institute

Aryeetey, E., J. Harrigan, and M. Nissanke, eds. (2000), *Economic Reforms in Ghana: The Miracle and the Mirage.* Oxford: James Currey and Accra: Woeli Publishing Services

Aryeetey, E. and F. Tarp (2000), "Structural Adjustment and After: Which Way Forward?," in E. Aryeetey, J. Harrigan, and M. Nissanke, eds., *Economic Reforms in Ghana: The Miracle and the Mirage.* Oxford: James Currey and Accra: Woeli Publishing Services: 344–65

Asante, Y., F. Nixson, and G. K. Tsikata (2000), "The Industrial Sector Policies and Economic Development," in E. Aryeetey, J. Harrigan, and M. Nissanke, eds., *Economic Reforms in Ghana: The Miracle and the Mirage.* Oxford: James Currey and Accra: Woeli Publishing Services: 246–66

Bates, R. H. (1981), *Markets and States in Tropical Africa: The Political Basis of Agricultural Policies.* Berkeley, CA, Los Angeles, CA, and London: University of California Press

Benneh, G. (1972), *Babaso: A Study of Land Tenure and Land Use,* Technical Publication Series 23. Institute of Statistical, Social, and Economic Research (ISSER), Legon: University of Ghana

Boateng, K. (1997), "Institutional Determinants of Labor Market Performance in Ghana," Research Paper, Accra: Center for Policy Analysis

Chenery, H. and M. Syrquin (1986), "Typical Patterns of Transformation," in H. Chenery, S. Robinson, and M. Syrquin, eds., *Industrialization and Growth: A Comparative Study.* Oxford: Oxford University Press

Collier, P. (2000), "How to Reduce Corruption," *African Development Review* 12(2): 191–205

Collier, P. and J. W. Gunning (1999), "Explaining African Economic Performance," *Journal of Economic Literature* 37: 64–111

Collins, S. and B. Bosworth (1996), "Economic Growth in East Asia: Accumulation versus Assimilation," *Brookings Papers on Economic Activity* 2: 135–203

Fine, B. and K. Boateng (2000), "Labor and Employment Under Structural Adjustment," in E. Aryeetey, J. Harrigan, and M. Nissanke, eds., *Economic Reforms in Ghana: The Miracle and the Mirage.* Oxford: James Currey and Accra: Woeli Publishing Services: 227–45

Fosu, A. K. (1992), "Political Instability and Economic Growth: Evidence from Sub-Saharan Africa," *Economic Development and Cultural Change* 40: 829–41

(2001), "Economic Fluctuations and Growth in Sub-Saharan Africa: The Importance of Import Instability," *Journal of Development Studies* 37(3): 71–84

(2002), "Political Instability and Economic Growth: Implications of Coup Events in Sub-Saharan Africa," *American Journal of Economics and Sociology* 61(1): 329–48

Frimpong-Ansah, J. (1991), *The Vampire State in Africa: The Political Economy of Decline.* Oxford: James Currey

Gyimah-Boadi, E. and R. Jeffries (2000), "The Political Economy of Reform," in E. Aryeetey, J. Harrigan, and M. Nissanke, eds., *Economic Reforms in Ghana: The Miracle and the Mirage*. Oxford: James Currey and Accra: Woeli Publishing Services: 32–50

Huq, M. (1989), *The Economy of Ghana: The First Twenty-Five Years Since Independence*. New York: St. Martin's Press

ISSER (Institute of Statistical, Social, and Economic Research) (1996), *The State of the Ghanaian Economy Report 1995*. Legon: University of Ghana

(1997), *State of the Ghanaian Economy in 1996*. Legon: University of Ghana

Jeffries, R. (1991), "Leadership, Commitment and Political Opposition to Structural Adjustment in Ghana," in D. Rothchild, ed., *Ghana: The Political Economy of Recovery*. Boulder, CO: Lynne Rienner

Kanbur, R. (2001), "Economic Policy, Distribution and Poverty: The Nature of Disagreements," *World Development* 29(6): 1083–94

Kapur I., M. T. Hadjimichael, P. L. C. Hilbers, J. A. Schiff, and P. Szymczak (1991), "Ghana: Adjustment and Growth 1983–1991," IMF Occasional Paper 86, Washington, DC: International Monetary Fund

Killick, T. (1978), *Development Economics in Action: A Study of Economic Policies in Ghana*. London: Heinemann Educational

(2000), "Fragile Still: The Structure of Ghana's Economy 1960–94," in E. Aryeetey, J. Harrigan, and M. Nissanke, eds., *Economic Reforms in Ghana: The Miracle and the Mirage*. Oxford: James Currey and Accra: Woeli Publishing Services: 51–67

Leechor, C. (1994), "Ghana: Frontrunner in Adjustment," in I. Husain and R. Faruque, eds., *Adjustment in Africa: Lessons from Case Studies*. Washington, DC: The World Bank

Leith, C. and M. Lofchie (1993), "The Political Economy of Structural Adjustment in Ghana," in R. H. Bates and A. O. Krueger, eds., *Political and Economic Interaction in Economic Policy Reform*. Oxford: Blackwell: 225–93

Ninsin, K. (1991), "The PNDC and the Problem of Legitimacy," in D. Rothchild, ed., *Ghana: The Political Economy of Recovery*. Boulder, CO: Lynne Rienner: 49–67

Nissanke, M. and E. Aryeetey (1998), *Financial Integration and Development in Sub-Saharan Africa*. London and New York: Routledge

Nixson, F. (1990), "Industrialization and Structural Change in Developing Countries," *Journal of International Development* 20(3): 310–33

Nkrumah, K. (1965), *Neo-Colonialism: The Last Stage of Imperialism*. New York: International Publishers

Nukunya, G. (1972), *Land Tenure and Inheritance in Anloga*, Technical Publication Series 30, ISSER, Legon: University of Ghana

Nyanteng, V. and A. W. Seini (2000), "Agricultural Policy and the Impact on Growth and Productivity 1970–95," in E. Aryeetey, J. Harrigan, and M. Nissanke, eds., *Economic Reforms in Ghana: The Miracle and the Mirage*. Oxford: James Currey and Accra: Woeli Publishing Services: 267–83

O'Connell, S. A. and B. Ndulu (2000), "Africa's Growth Experience: A Focus on the Sources of Growth," AERC Growth Working Paper No. 10. Nairobi: African Economic Research Consortium, April (downloadable: www.aercafrica.org)

Powell, M. and J. Round (2000), "Structure and Linkage in the Economy of Ghana: A SAM Approach," in E. Aryeetey, J. Harrigan, and M. Nissanke, eds., *Economic Reforms in Ghana: The Miracle and the Mirage.* Oxford: James Currey and Accra: Woeli Publishing Services: 267–83

Rimmer, D. (1992), *Staying Poor: Ghana's Political Economy, 1950–1990.* Oxford: Paragon Press

Roe, A. R. and N. K. Sowa (1997), "From Direct to Indirect Monetary Control in sub-Saharan Africa," *Journal of African Economics* 6(1), Supplement, Part 2, March: 212–64

Seers, D. and C. R. Ross (1952), *Report on Financial and Physical Problems of Development in the Gold Coast.* Accra: Office of Her Majesty's Governor

Sowa, N. (1996), *Adjustment in Africa: Lessons from Ghana,* Research Paper 32. Accra: Center for Policy Analysis

Steel, W. F. (1972), "Import Substitution and Excess Capacity in Ghana," *Oxford Economic Papers* 24(2): 212–40

Szereszewski, R. (1965), *Structural Changes in the Economy of Ghana, 1891–1911.* London: Weidenfeld & Nicolson

Tabatabai, H. (1986), *Economic Decline, Access to Food and Structural Adjustment in Ghana.* Geneva: International Labour Office

Teal, F. (1995), "Does "Getting Prices Right" Work? Micro Evidence from Ghana," Center for the Study of African Economies Working Paper 19

Toye, J. (1991), "Ghana," in P. Mosley, J. Harrigan, and J. Toye, *Aid and Power: The World Bank and Policy-Based Lending.* London: Routledge

World Bank (1984), "Ghana: Industrial Policy, Performance and Recovery," vol. 1. Washington, DC: The World Bank

  (1985), "Ghana: Towards Structural Adjustment," vol. 1, Report 5854-GH, October. Washington, DC: The World Bank

10 | Explaining African economic growth performance: the case of Kenya

Francis M. Mwega and Njuguna S. Ndung'u

1. Introduction

The objective of this chapter is to explain Kenya's economic growth performance from the 1960s to the 1990s, drawing mainly on growth-accounting decompositions and the cross-country endogenous growth literature. The chapter explains why the good economic performance in the 1960s and

Department of Economics, University of Nairobi; African Economic Research Consortium, Nairobi. Chapter prepared for the AERC Collaborative Project on Explaining African Economic Performance. We are grateful to Germano Mwabu, Benno Ndulu, and Steve O'Connell for helpful comments.

early 1970s was not sustained in the subsequent periods. The 1980s and 1990s were characterized by persistently low growth and limited economic transformation, despite the fact that the country was largely politically stable and pursued a fairly consistent development strategy. The introduction of competitive politics in the early 1990s, however, provoked ethnic tensions revolving around land ownership and control of the state. This tended to create uncertainty and to add to the poor growth performance. Kenya suffered from a regime shift towards redistribution for political expediency, destroying the policy environment and the incentive structure for economic agents and leading to the poor growth performance and rising poverty in the 1980s and 1990s.

The cross-country endogenous growth literature has been useful in identifying uniformities across countries and over time, and has helped to detect important associations in the growth performance of countries. However, studies on the robustness of these results typically find that they have limited predictive power (Syrquin and Kenny 1999). This lack of robustness is partly attributable to the incorrect assumption that growth processes across countries and over time are similar, while in fact growth processes differ across countries and over time. We therefore supplement the cross-country endogenous growth methodology with Kenya-specific analysis, with a focus on the role of markets, private agents, and political economy in the growth process.

A crude economic geography of Africa suggests a three-fold classification of countries into coastal, labor-surplus economies with high growth potential; mineral-rent economies with uncertain growth potential; and landlocked countries with relatively low growth potential. Kenya is clearly in the first category, and until the late 1970s the country out-performed SSA. Since the 1970s, however, Kenya has failed to achieve her potential. The story of this chapter is therefore one of missed opportunities in the 1980s and 1990s. Kenya, for example, did not exploit globalization to increase manufactured exports, given its coastal location, relatively cheap labor, and basically market-friendly orientation. The share of manufactured exports in manufacturing output remained quite low throughout the period (at less than 15 percent: 14.8 percent in 1980; 15.9 percent in 1985; 9.2 percent in 1990; 14.0 percent in 1995; 10.9 percent in 1997). Besides external market access barriers, including a lack of adequate information on markets abroad, this failure reflects a lack of political commitment to manufactured exports promotion. While the country opened its economy in the 1980s and 1990s, the trade liberalization policies were not credible and were often subject to reversals. Manufactured exports were also subject to serious supply constraints such as the unavailability and/or high cost of credit, infrastructural deficiencies, and an adverse regulatory framework, increasing transaction costs and undermining the country's competitiveness.

The rest of the chapter is organized as follows. Section 2 analyzes the growth experience in Kenya in a cross-country perspective. Sections 3 and 4 discuss the roles of markets and private agents, respectively, in the growth process. Section 5 examines the political economy of the Kenyan growth process, and Section 6 draws some conclusions.

2.   Kenya's growth experience in cross-country perspective

2.1   Periodization of Kenya's economic growth performance

Kenya's growth performance has varied substantially over time, and we first delineate the various economic performance episodes. We base our analysis mainly on Ndulu and O'Connell (2000) (henceforth, N&O). N & O simulate Kenya's growth performance (among other countries in Africa) using the cross-country studies by Collins and Bosworth (1996) (henceforth, C & B), Hoeffler (1999), and their own analysis, using half-decadal data to control for short-term influences. The periodization of Kenya's growth performance is based on residuals from the estimation equations generated by these three studies (see table 10.1). While the Collins–Bosworth (1996) study is based on direct growth decompositions from the Solow model, Hoeffler (1999) used an augmented Solow model to explain the factors that account for growth performance in eighty-five countries. Unlike many other studies, she found the Africa dummy to be non-significant, thereby validating her model. N&O (2000), on the other hand, estimated a typical endogenous growth model.

From table 10.1, we can identify four fairly distinct growth episodes (which conform with prior expectations): (1) 1960–74, a period of improving economic performance; (2) 1975–84, a period of poor performance; (3) 1985–9, a period of economic recovery; and (4) the 1990s, a period of poor performance. On the basis of the policy environment, we follow Azam and Daubreé (1997) and Takahashi (1997) and combine those episodes that fall in the 1960s and 1970s (with improving economic performance except for 1975–9 when growth deteriorated); and the 1980s and 1990s (poor performance except in 1985–9 when there was a growth turn-round).

These two broad episodes roughly coincide with the Kenyatta and Moi political regimes, respectively. Multi-party politics were introduced in 1991, with the subsequent period characterized by stalled political and economic reforms. The policy environments in the two broad episodes could therefore be seen as reflecting a choice of the political elites, reflecting the interests that they "served" and the forces acting upon them, and the investment and growth outcomes determined by microeconomic agents responding to

Table 10.1 *Kenya, growth decomposition and residuals, C & B (1996), Hoeffler (1999), and N & O (2000) models, 1960–1994*

Period	C & B model			Hoeffler model: GMM results			N & O model		
	Actual growth per worker	Predicted growth per worker	Residual	Actual growth per capita	Predicted growth per capita	Residual	Actual growth per capita	Predicted growth per capita	Residual
1960–4	0.38	0.31	0.07	−1.41	5.59	−7.01	0.71	0.307	−2.36
1965–9	3.67	1.37	2.31	−0.93	6.36	−7.29	3.82	2.05	1.77
1970–4	4.85	2.46	2.39	7.13	5.85	1.28	5.23	2.58	2.65
1975–9	1.62	2.21	−0.58	1.69	3.64	−1.94	1.63	1.29	0.33
1980–4	−0.76	1.45	−2.22	−2.75	1.18	−3.93	−0.88	−0.70	−0.19
1985–9	1.99	1.18	0.81	2.75	2.75	0.0	2.14	1.28	0.86
1990–4	−1.83	0.92	−2.76	0.08	2.53	−2.46	−0.52	2.29	−2.81
Total	**1.46**	**1.41**	**0.003**	**0.94**	**3.99**	**−3.05**	**1.73**	**1.31**	**1.14**

the policy environment and exogenous shocks.[1] Kenyatta represented the Kikuyu and allied groups whose interest (after an initial land distribution from Europeans) was in continuing a market-based economy which had benefited them as cash-crop exporters. Kenyatta's constituency also had a head start in human capital, and this helped to justify him in not using the state as a redistributive mechanism but as a mechanism for facilitating private capital accumulation by already relatively well-placed indigenous Kenyans. Kenyatta's politics ended up favoring a relatively market-friendly, growth-promoting regime.

Moi, on the other hand, represented groups that were disadvantaged under the Kenyatta regime and that sought to redistribute resources to themselves. The reversal of "trickle down" meant greater state intervention in the economy, with subsequent efficiency costs associated with the taxation of productive activity. It also meant the dismantling of various agencies of restraint with concomitant costs in terms of macroeconomic stability. Growth declined under the Moi regime, as it pursued redistribution and political power at the expense of private investment. The onset of democratization was largely exogenous (it happened all across Africa), and created a messy endgame throughout the 1990s as private investment was paralyzed by a combination of increased corruption (asset-stripping by a regime whose days were perceived to be numbered), policy uncertainty from ethnic polarization, and a deteriorating relationship with donors.

A stylized account shows that the economy performed relatively well in the Kenyatta era, with an average growth rate of about 6 percent during the first decade of independence (1964–73). Then came the oil shocks of 1973 and 1979 compounded by bad policies, especially the mismanagement of the 1976–7 coffee boom. The economy never fully recovered from these shocks and the redistributive policies of the Moi era, with each recovery from an exogenous shock weaker than the preceding one. This is despite the implementation of substantial donor-driven reforms in the 1980s and 1990s, covering nearly all sectors of the economy.

The poor performance was obviously aggravated by a number of exogenous shocks in the early 1980s, including a military coup attempt in 1982 and a severe drought in 1983–4. Growth rebounded in the second half of the 1980s (averaging 5 percent per annum) partly due to a mini-coffee boom in 1986, a decrease in oil prices, and good weather. Exogenous shocks in the 1990s included a drought in 1991–2, *El Niño* rains in 1997–8 followed by a major drought leading to power rationing in 2000, the oil price increase due to the Gulf War in 1991, the aid embargoes of 1991–3 and 1997–2000, and "ethnic clashes" in 1992 and after the 1997 elections. These shocks were

---

[1] Mwai Kibaki was elected President in December 2002 under the National Rainbow Coalition (NARC), and it is therefore too early to include his regime in the analysis.

Table 10.2 *Kenya, results from C & B data, 1960–1997*

	Growth in capital per worker, %	Growth in education per worker	Growth per worker
1960–4	−2.90	−0.03	0.38
1965–74	1.22	1.33	4.26
1975–9	0.29	1.14	1.62
1980–9	−1.51	1.05	0.61
1990–7	−2.06	0.43	−1.83

accompanied by increased macroeconomic instability arising from massive money printing to finance the 1992 elections (Ndung'u and Mwega 1999). The growth rate averaged about 2.2 percent in the 1990s. One broad observation regarding Kenya is that the downward shift in the growth trajectory is a widely shared experience in the world economy as a whole (save for the high-performing Asian economies, HPAEs). Data for SSA as a whole suggest a similar average experience – a sharp downward shift after 1978 that stays there except for the 1984–6 blip. Besides the political regime shift discussed above, this points to a significant influence of the external environment, such as growth in trading partners' economies in explaining the poor growth performance.

2.2   The macro-growth performance

2.2.1   The C & B model

As seen in table 10.2, this model shows that growth per worker roughly tracked growth in physical capital per worker and education per worker, although only the first variable is significant:[2] this conclusion is supported by a number of studies on the Kenyan growth process (e.g. Azam and Daubreé 1997; Glenday and Ryan 2000). Glenday and Ryan (2000), for example, conclude that private investment has been the "strongest and the most significant contributor to growth" in Kenya. Azam and Daubreé highlight the predominant role of insufficient private investment and its failure to match the progress of human capital accumulation as an important factor in slowing growth in Kenya during this period. Private investment lagged behind

---

[2] The estimated growth equation using C&B data (*t*-values in brackets) is: Growth per worker = 1.992 (1.97)+ 0.854 (2.03)* Growth in capital per worker + 0.146 (0.35)* Growth in education per worker, $R^2 = 0.10$. Empirical micro-evidence shows a large decline in returns to education in Kenya. Manda (1997), for example, shows that rates of return declined from 18.2 percent for primary education and 55.7 percent for secondary education in 1977–8 to 4.7 percent for primary education and 12.5 percent for secondary education in 1993–5 (based on unpublished RPED data).

accumulation of human capital, slowed by excessive competition from public investment in a context of financial repression.

There is also some evidence that the efficiency of capital use worsened over time, especially in the public sector activities, reducing the growth effects of investment. The three-year moving average ICOR, for example, increased from 2.4 in 1966 to 3.2 in 1972, due to the existence of excess capacity, the encouragement of capital-intensive production due to distortions in factor prices, and the possibility that the efficiency of investment fell as the "easier" opportunities were taken up (World Bank 1975). This study also argued that the various price distortions in the factor and product markets resulted in inefficient allocation of resources (with the ICOR increasing to about 6 by the 1990s).

In their study on Kenya, Matin and Wasow (1993) found the flow of real bank credit to the private sector (to capture credit rationing in a repressed financial system), the availability of foreign exchange reserves, and the real public sector infrastructure capital stock to be the main factors driving the private investment rate up to at least the 1980s.[3] The real exchange rate (RER) depreciation also significantly reduced private investment, reflecting the supply-side shock from the increased price of imports. These findings are supported by Fielding (1993), who found that the availability of finance (savings plus foreign aid) and foreign exchange were significant determinants of private investment in Kenya. He also found the price of capital goods and terms of trade to have adverse effects on private investment, at least in the short-run. According to Matin and Wasow (1992), reduced availability of credit and foreign exchange to the private sector (in the years following the coffee boom of 1976–7) and falling public infrastructure reduced private investment in the 1980s relative to the 1970s.[4] Simulations show that the private investment rate would have been 23 percent higher in the 1980s if these variables had remained at their 1978 level. The failure to implement adjustment policies following the collapse of the coffee boom and the East African Community (EAC) in 1977 undermined private investment. Though Kenya experienced greater macroeconomic stability than other SSA countries, her fiscal performance, both during and after the 1970s, was less acceptable. The failure to control current expenditure adversely affected public investment on infrastructure.

Similarly, in the 1980s, the low interest rate policy was changed and the rates were frequently adjusted upwards in an effort to maintain positive

---

[3] The results were from OLS and 2SLS (RER-instrumented) and covered the period 1968–88.
[4] The real investment: real GDP ratio fell by 6.4 percent in the 1980s (from 17.4 percent of GDP in the 1970s to an average of 11.0 percent in the 1980s). Private investment ratio fell by 4.2 percent in the 1980s relative to the 1970s, as compared to a fall of 2.2 percent for the public investment ratio (Matin and Wasow 1993).

Table 10.3 *Kenya, C & B decomposition of sources of economic growth, 1960–1997*

Period	Growth in real GDP per worker	Contribution of		
		Physical capital per worker	Education per worker	TFP growth
1960–4	0.38	−1.03	−0.02	1.43
1965–9	3.67	−0.12	0.12	3.67
1970–4	4.85	0.98	0.12	3.76
1975–9	1.62	0.10	0.74	0.78
1980–4	−0.76	−0.48	0.57	−0.85
1985–9	1.99	−0.66	0.48	2.17
1990–7	−1.83	−0.72	0.28	−1.39
Total	**1.42**	**−0.28**	**0.33**	**1.37**

rates in real terms. Rates were fully liberalized in July 1991 to allow them to vary with the demand and availability of loanable funds. A major concern through the 1990s was the high level of interest rates, which were pegged on the Treasury Bill rate, which remained high as the authorities implemented a tight monetary policy. This also reflects the oligopolistic nature of the banking system which was dominated by four banks that controlled four-fifths of total deposits. These banks focused on short-term lending to finance commerce, mainly foreign trade. As the 1997–2001 Development Plan (Kenya 1997–2001: 38) complained:

The short-term nature of their own corporate interests are in conflict with national interests which require longer term commitments and a better appreciation of the needs of the Kenya economy. Their policies of concentrating on a small corporate clientele have implied indifference or even hostility to small savers and borrowers.

During the 1980s and 1990s, growth of physical capital per worker was negative while human capital accumulation slowed, dragging down the performance of the economy. There was also a substantial decline in TFPG during this period (except in 1985–9, see table 10.3), attributable to a slowdown in accumulation of human capital and a turning inward of the Kenyan economy (Azam and Daubreé 1997).

2.2.2 The Hoeffler model

Table 10.4 shows the results from the Hoeffler model (Hoeffler 1999). This model extends the C&B model by adding initial income (to capture convergence) and population growth as determinants of *per capita* economic growth. Besides these two variables, the model shows the investment rate to be one of the most important variables in contributing to growth, and

Table 10.4 *Kenya versus other regions, Hoeffler (1999) model growth decomposition, 1960–1989*

Variable	Kenya	Kenya–SSA	Kenya–HPAEs	Kenya	Kenya–SSA	Kenya–HPAEs
		1960–4			1980–4	
$\ln(ynin)$	−0.982	0.016	0.109	−1.031	0.007	0.237
$\ln(hi6)$	0.690	0.170	0.011	0.650	0.163	−0.160
$\ln(ty15)$	0.005	0.003	−0.011	0.014	0.007	−0.006
$rpah$	1.050	−0.029	−0.004	1.011	−0.054	−0.111
Constant	−0.483			−0.483		
Explained	0.279	0.161	0.104	0.161	0.123	−0.041
Unexplained	−0.350	−0.300	−0.387	−0.298	−0.203	−0.280
Total ($gyso$)	**−0.071**	**−0.139**	**−0.284**	**−0.137**	**−0.080**	**−0.321**
		1965–74			1985–9	
$\ln(ynin)$	−0.968	0.051	0.182	−1.011	0.029	0.285
$\ln(hi6)$	0.729	0.193	−0.031	0.615	0.155	−0.183
$\ln(ty15)$	0.007	0.004	−0.010	0.014	0.005	−0.008
$rpah$	1.035	−0.039	−0.065	1.030	−0.036	−0.112
Constant	−0.483			−0.483		
Explained	0.321	0.209	0.075	0.165	0.153	−0.018
Unexplained	−0.166	−0.133	−0.238	−0.028	−0.010	−0.182
Total ($gyso$)	**0.155**	**0.076**	**−0.163**	**0.137**	**0.143**	**−0.200**
		1975–9				
$\ln(ynin)$	−1.019	0.016	0.201			
$\ln(hi6)$	0.675	0.154	−0.120			
$\ln(ty15)$	0.009	0.004	−0.010			
$rpah$	1.016	−0.051	−0.080			
Constant	−0.483					
Explained	0.198	0.123	−0.010			
Unexplained	−0.114	−0.066	−0.228			
Total ($gyso$)	**0.085**	**0.057**	**−0.238**			

Note: gyso = five-year growth in real GDP *per capita*, between initial year of current and subsequent half-decade, e.g. $\ln(ynin[1965]) - \ln(ynin[1960])$.

$\ln(ynin)$ = log of real GDP *per capita* in the initial year of the half-decade, 1985 international prices.

$\ln(hi6)$ = log of ratio of investment to GDP (%), 1985 international prices.

$rpah = \ln(0.05 + n)$ where n is the average log difference in population for the period (this is the replacement investment term used in Hoeffler 1999, with 0.05 a measure of the sum of technological progress and depreciation).

$\ln(ty15)$ = log of $ty15$, average total years of schooling in the population of age fifteen or higher, in the initial year of the period (only this variable was insignificant at the 5% level, although it was significant in OLS- and IV-level estimations. Hoeffler (1999) finds that, although insignificant, adding it to the instrument set strengthened it significantly).

HPAEs: Hong Kong, Indonesia, Korea, Singapore, Taiwan, Thailand.

Table 10.5 *Kenya versus HPAEs, Hoeffler (1999) half-decadal data, 1960–1989*

Country and period	Initial real GDP per capita, 1985 intl. prices, *ynin*	Initial av. yrs of educ. attained, popul. >=15 yrs, *ty15*	$(0.05 + n)$, from Hoeffler (1999), *rpah*	Ratio of investment to GDP(%), current intl. prices, *hi6*
Kenya				
1960–4	659.00	1.53	0.08	16.05
1965–9	614.00	1.67	0.08	18.31
1970–4	586.00	2.17	0.09	19.26
1975–9	837.00	2.20	0.09	15.08
1980–4	911.00	3.44	0.09	13.65
1985–9	794.00	3.35	0.09	11.88
HPAEs				
1960–4	1,351.55	4.11	0.08	15.37
1965–9	1,672.14	4.53	0.07	19.79
1970–4	2,371.47	4.79	0.07	22.84
1975–9	3,156.88	5.36	0.07	24.43
1980–4	4,359.03	6.01	0.07	25.97
1985–9	5,235.20	6.64	0.07	24.85
Total	**2,698.47**	**5.17**	**0.07**	**21.87**

suggests a positive but imprecisely estimated role for educational attainments.[5] As in the C & B model above, there is a close correlation between the investment rate and growth *per capita*, with the half-decadal Hoeffler data showing both increasing to a peak in 1970–4, and declining systematically thereafter. In the 1960–4 half-decade, the model predicts Kenya slightly out-performing the HPAEs[6] by about 0.10 percentage points, this declining to 0.075 the following decade (1965–74) and turning negative thereafter. While Kenya had a higher investment rate than the HPAEs in the early 1960s, it was disadvantaged by a more rapid population growth throughout the study period. Up to the 1980s, Kenya had one of the most rapid population growth rates in the world. The Hoeffler data (table 10.5) show the population growth rate increasing from 3 percent in the 1960s to 4 percent in the 1970s and 1980s, whereas that of the HPAEs declined from 3 percent in the early 1960s to 2 percent for the rest of the study period. Table 10.5 also shows Kenya lagging behind the HPAEs with respect to educational attainment throughout the study period. The average years of schooling increased from 1.53 in the early 1960s to 3.7 in the 1990s, while those of the HPAEs

---

[5] Indeed, educational attainments, measured by the average total years of schooling in the population of age fifteen or higher, in the initial year of the period, was insignificant at the 5 percent level in the GMM regression equation.

[6] Hong Kong, Indonesia, Korea, Singapore, Taiwan, Thailand.

increased from 4.11 in the early 1960s to 5.17 in the 1990s. Hence, while Kenya closed some of the gap with the HPAEs, it had not attained the level of education attainment prevailing in the HPAEs in the early 1960s.[7]

2.2.3 The N & O model

The N & O endogenous growth model (table 10.6) extends the other two models above by incorporating other variables. These are divided into (1) base variables (initial income, initial life expectancy, terms of trade shocks, landlockedness, dependency ratio, labor force growth, and trading partner growth); (2) policy variables (inflation, the black market premium, and the government expenditure ratio); and (3) political instability.

In general, the model shows Kenya benefiting, as in the Hoeffler model above, from the positive convergence effects of low income throughout the study period, with the Kenya–HPAEs gap increasing from 0.63 percent in 1960–4 to 2.6 percent in the 1990s (in table 10.7, which shows half-decadal means for all variables, the proportion of Kenya's initial *per capita* income declines from about 70 percent in the early 1960s to 23 percent in the 1990s). Due to a relatively low initial life expectancy relative to the HPAEs (the gap increased from about eight years in the early 1960s to 10.6 years in the 1990s), there was a relative *per capita* growth loss of 0.7 percent in the 1960s–1970s and 0.7–0.9 percent in the 1980s and 1990s. The high age dependency ratio relative to the HPAEs also caused a growth *per capita* loss that increased from 0.44 percent in 1960–4 to 2.30 percent in the 1990s. Similarly, the country suffered from a relatively low growth in potential labor force participation, resulting in a loss in *per capita* growth relative to the HPAEs of 0.05 percent in 1960–4, this increasing to 0.39 percent in the 1990s. The N&O results show that terms of trade shocks had a relatively small differential impact on growth. This variable was insignificant at the 5 percent level in the estimation model. The country was also disadvantaged by the poor performance of trading partners, even when compared to SSA (except in 1975–9). Relative to the HPAEs, Kenya experienced a growth per capita loss of about 1 percent in 1960–74, 0.34 percent in 1975–9, 0.9 percent in the 1980s, and 0.7 percent in the 1990s. Lastly, the country *per capita* growth benefited from access to sea compared to the HPAEs by a margin of 0.3–0.5 percent in the 1980s and 1990s. Overall, the combined effects of the base variables disadvantaged Kenya *vis-à-vis* the HPAEs by a margin of 1.53 percent in 1960–4, increasing to 2.18 percent in 1975–9, and 2.35 percent in the 1980s, but declining to 0.89 percent in the 1990s.

Among the policy variables, both inflation and the black market premium were relatively unimportant in explaining *per capita* growth in Kenya

---

[7] Kenya did better than SSA with respect to the investment rate and education attainments throughout the study period, but was disadvantaged with respect to population growth.

Table 10.6 *Kenya, growth decompositions, N & O pooled model, 1960–1989*

Variable	Estimated coefficient	Kenya	Kenya–SSA	Kenya–HPAEs	Kenya	Kenya–SSA	Kenya–HPAEs
		1960–4			1980–4		
ln($ynin$)	−1.765	−11.459	0.296	0.633	−12.031	0.092	1.705
$lxin$	0.089	4.077	0.525	−0.71	4.865	0.629	−0.728
$adep$	−0.052	−5.104	−0.716	−0.443	−5.939	−1.15	−2.155
$dlfp$	0.728	−0.554	−0.335	−0.046	0.105	0.160	−0.539
$tt1.c$	0.004	−0.001	0.003	0.000	−0.017	−0.01	−0.013
$dynt$	0.540	1.993	−0.018	−0.966	0.088	−0.25	−0.867
$lloc$	−0.912	0.000	0.249	0.000	0.000	0.397	0.000
Total – base variables		−11.047	0.004	−1.533	−12.929	−0.132	−2.597
$infL$	−0.004	−0.006	0.007	0.004	−0.057	0.017	−0.016
$bmpL$	−0.007	−0.011	0.052	0.005	−0.157	0.218	−0.152
$gxbx$	−0.113	−1.106	0.855	−0.344	−1.614	0.074	−1.041
Total – policy variables		−1.123	0.914	−0.335	−1.828	0.310	−1.209
pin	−0.975	−0.108	−0.049	−0.108	−0.065	0.025	−0.016
Constant	15.347	15.347			15.347		
Explained		3.068	0.869	−1.977	0.525	0.203	−3.822
Unexplained		−2.363	−2.405	−1.173	−1.409	−0.238	−1.357
Total		0.705	−1.536	−3.15	−0.884	−0.035	−5.179
		1965–74			1985–9		
ln($ynin$)	−1.765	−11.293	0.602	1.411	−11.788	0.258	2.289
$lxin$	0.089	4.310	0.499	−0.721	5.027	0.446	−0.78
$adep$	−0.052	−5.563	−0.972	−0.848	−5.862	−1.234	−2.453
$dlfp$	0.728	−0.203	−0.085	−0.586	0.350	0.218	−0.238
$tt1.c$	0.004	−0.005	−0.001	−0.004	−0.007	−0.014	0.004
$dynt$	0.540	1.694	−0.274	−1.045	0.904	−0.459	−0.896
$lloc$	−0.912	0.000	0.338	0.000	0.000	0.456	0.000
Total – base variables		−11.060	0.106	−1.793	−11.377	−0.329	−2.073
$infL$	−0.004	−0.021	0.008	0.015	−0.041	−0.022	−0.025
$bmpL$	−0.007	−0.190	−0.028	−0.131	−0.073	0.208	−0.044
$gxbx$	−0.113	−1.523	0.240	−0.854	−1.614	−0.402	−0.938
Total – policy variables		−1.734	0.220	−0.97	−1.729	−0.216	−1.007
pin	−0.975	−0.054	0.024	0.005	0.000	0.097	0.016
Constant	15.347	15.347			15.347		
Explained		2.499	0.349	−2.758	2.242	−0.447	−3.065
Unexplained		2.027	2.364	1.675	−0.102	1.691	−0.198
Total		4.526	2.713	−1.083	2.139	1.244	−3.262

(*cont.*)

Table 10.6 *(cont.)*

Variable	Estimated coefficient	Kenya	Kenya–SSA	Kenya–HPAEs	Kenya	Kenya–SSA	Kenya–HPAEs
			1975–79			1990–97	
ln(*ynin*)	−1.765	−11.881	0.435	1.327	−12.031	0.928	2.587
lxin	0.089	4.632	0.514	−0.67	5.067	0.063	−0.942
adep	−0.052	−5.783	−1.114	−1.531	−5.176	−0.99	−2.272
dlfp	0.728	−0.213	−0.113	−0.977	0.894	0.680	0.397
tt1.c	0.004	0.018	0.013	0.016	0.035	0.039	0.031
dynt	0.540	1.361	0.160	−0.341	0.839	−0.029	−0.692
lloc	−0.912	0.000	0.261	0.000	0.000	0.304	0.000
Total – base variables		−11.866	0.155	−2.176	−10.371	0.994	−0.891
infL	−0.004	−0.059	0.019	−0.014	−0.084	−0.057	−0.06
bmpL	−0.007	−0.065	0.278	−0.044	−0.141	−0.112	−0.12
gxbx	−0.113	−1.700	−0.052	−1.097	−1.614	−0.435	−1.091
Total – policy variables		−1.824	0.245	−1.156	−1.839	−0.604	−1.271
pin	−0.975	−0.065	0.009	0.130	−0.081	0.027	−0.041
Constant	15.347	15.347			15.347		
Explained		1.592	0.409	−3.201	3.056	0.417	−2.203
Unexplained		0.033	0.291	−0.772	−3.574	−1.484	−4.35
Total		1.625	0.700	−3.974	−0.519	−1.066	−6.553

Note: ln(*ynin*) = log of real GDP *per capita* in the initial year of the half-decade.

lxin = life expectancy at birth, interpolated to the initial year of the half-decade.

adep = age dependency ratio, given by ratio of population not 15–65 years to population 15–65.

dlfp = growth in potential labor force participation, given by the difference between growth of population of working age (15–65 years) and growth of total population.

tt1.c = terms of trade shock, given by initial share of exports to GDP, multiplied by the average % difference between the terms of trade in each year of the half-decade and the terms of trade in the initial year of the half-decade (only this variable was insignificant at the 5% level).

dynt = trading-partner growth rate, given by the average growth rate of real GDP *per capita* among trading partners, weighted by shares in total trade.

lloc = dummy equal to 1 for landlocked countries and 0 otherwise.

pin = political instability index (*Pin* + (*rev* + *stri* + *assa*)/3, i.e. average of revolutions, strikes, and assassinations).

infL = CPI inflation rate, if under 500% (otherwise entered as missing).

bmpL = black market premium, if under 500% (otherwise entered as missing).

gxbx = government spending exclusive of defense and education. This is a Barro–Lee (1993) variable extended to later periods using a proxy based on nominal data (the difference between current spending and total spending on defense and education, all as shares of GDP). The extension was done only if overlapping data existed for 1980.

Table 10.7 *Kenya, N & O (2000) model half-decadal data, 1960–1997*

	1960–4	1965–9	1970–4	1975–9	1980–4	1985–9	1990–7
Kenya							
ynin	659.00	614.00	586.00	837.00	911.00	794.00	911.00
lxin	45.95	47.2	49.95	52.2	54.83	56.65	57.11
adep	98.83	106.32	109.11	111.96	114.98	113.49	100.21
dlfp	−0.76	−0.27	−0.28	−0.29	0.14	0.48	1.22
tt1.c	−0.14	−0.43	−1.97	4.40	−4.16	−1.77	8.47
dynt	3.69	3.13	3.13	2.52	0.16	1.67	1.55
lloc	0.00	0.00	0.00	0.00	0.00	0.00	0.00
infL	1.54	2.11	7.77	14.06	13.56	9.91	20.17
bmpL	1.44	17.97	34.14	8.97	21.56	10.06	19.39
gxbx	9.81	12.67	14.35	15.07	14.31		
pin		0.11	0.00	0.06	0.06	0.00	0.08
HPAEs							
dyn	3.85	5.85	5.36	5.59	4.29	5.40	6.03
ynin	943.00	1261.00	1409.00	1774.00	2392.00	2903.00	3942.00
lxin	53.95	56.43	56.95	59.74	63.03	65.44	67.72
adep	90.24	93.77	88.81	82.32	73.25	66.00	56.22
dlfp	−0.69	0.32	0.72	1.04	0.88	0.80	0.68
tt1.c	−0.03	−0.90	0.27	0.58	−0.92	−2.71	0.90
dynt	5.47	5.87	4.26	3.15	1.76	3.33	2.83
lloc	0.00	0.00	0.00	0.00	0.00	0.00	0.00
pin	0.00	0.02	0.10	0.2	0.05	0.01	0.04
infL	2.57	4.79	12.15	10.65	9.84	3.90	5.87
bmpL	2.06	2.43	13.67	2.90	0.67	3.97	2.90
gxbx	6.75	6.52	5.35	5.34	5.07	5.99	4.63

vis-à-vis the HPAEs. When compared to the HPAEs in the 1960s and 1970s, the largest inflation effect was a *per capita* growth loss of 0.014 percent in 1975–9, 0.020 percent in the 1980s, and 0.060 percent in the 1990s. Similarly, the largest black market premium effect in the 1960s and 1970s was in 1965–74, resulting in a loss of 0.131 percent, declining to 0.098 percent in the 1980s, and 0.120 percent in the 1990s. The Achilles heel of the economy has been the country's fiscal policy. Inadequate control of government consumption expenditures, for example, reflected in over-establishment of the public sector (and inability to target these expenditures to achieve policy objectives) has been an important part of the budgetary problem in Kenya, for total government spending has risen relative to economic activity, with serious budget financing difficulties emerging from policies of the late 1970s. While Kenya did better than SSA in 1960–74, the relatively large government expenditure ratio *vis-à-vis* the HPAEs resulted in a *per capita* growth loss that increased from 0.344 percent in 1960–4 to about 1 percent in 1990s. High

government consumption expenditures have undermined public investment and its crowd-in effects on private investment while "hoarding" skilled
workers who could otherwise be more productive in the private sector. This
is consistent with the political-economy story, with the public employment
in the 1980s and 1990s mainly utilized for patronage and ethnic affirmative
action. Lastly, political instability was relatively unimportant in explaining
the differential growth. Compared to the HPAEs, the largest effects are a
per capita growth loss of 0.108 percent in 1960–4, offset by a gain of 0.130
percent in 1975–9, zero effects in the 1980s, and 0.041 percent in the 1990s.

The N&O model shows the HPAEs outperforming Kenya throughout the
period, with the margin increasing from 1.98 percent in early 1960s to 3.44
percent in the 1980s, but declining to 2.02 percent in the 1990s. Kenya's
overall performance in the 1980s and 1990s was quite poor, so that the
country under-performed even SSA.[8]

3. The role of markets in Kenya's growth process

After independence Kenya, like most African countries, tended to emulate
the development strategies of the western industrialized countries, which
stressed entrepreneurship and capital accumulation. The emphasis was laid
on massive injection of capital into the economy to accelerate the formation
of strong product and financial markets. In Kenya, government institutions
played an important role in the transformation and development of markets
in the post-colonial period. We briefly analyze below the development of
key markets in the study period.

3.1 Product markets

The agricultural policies were based on policies outlined in the *Sessional
Paper 10* (Kenya 1965) which emphasized political equality, social justice,
and human dignity. In the 1960s and 1970s, therefore, much of the agricultural policies decision-making depended heavily on the state. Although
farmers had their own institutions such as the national Kenya Farmers'
Association (KFA), Kenya National Farmers' Union (KNFU), and farmer

---

[8] The three models utilized in the growth analysis did not incorporate the impact of income
inequality on economic growth. Ali and Elbadawi (1999), for example, estimated an
endogenous growth model that controlled for feedback Kuznets effects and found income
inequality to be negatively associated with *per capita* real economic growth. The estimated
Gini coefficient parameter was stable at −0.075, consistent with other estimates in the
literature. From their estimates, Ali and Elbadawi (1999) postulate that about 22 percent
of the decline in economic growth in Kenya between 1965–74 and 1975–96 was caused by
increased inequality during that period.

Table 10.8 *Kenya, share of agricultural production in GDP at current prices, 1958–1973 (%)*

Sector	1958	1963	1970	1973
Non-monetary agriculture	24.0	22.3	17.7	15.8
Monetary agriculture	15.9	16.1	13.9	14.2
Total agriculture production	39.9	38.4	31.6	30.0
Total GDP	**100.0**	**100.0**	**100.0**	**100.0**

Source: Kenya, *Economic Survey* (various issues).

co-operative societies for various commodities, in reality the state heavily influenced what was to be grown and the way it was marketed. For example, agricultural production of major crops such as maize and wheat depended on the level of producer prices set before the planting season. This guaranteed prices for the farmers and led to less land being cultivated if the pre-set prices were not conducive. In order to ensure that these prices prevailed, there were controls on the marketing channels and inter-district cereals movements between the surplus and deficit regions. In addition to the emphasis on state control and the market development through the co-operative movement, the nature of production exhibited dualism, where subsistence production dominated. Even by the early 1970s, subsistence production was still higher than marketed agricultural production (see table 10.8). The presence and strength of the non-monetary sector reflected a large component in the economy that was not integrated in the market system, and so the product market was weak. Thus from the onset, production and pricing policies were controlled and did not evolve as envisaged because market developments were constrained by the policies in place as well as by regulations.

The manufacturing sector grew rapidly in the 1960s and 1970s. The policy prescription at this time was import substitution. This was aimed at improving and increasing the domestic capacity to produce those goods which could be produced with the locally available resources and reduce the imports of such commodities. But the manufacturing production was skewed toward consumer goods: beverages, electrical appliances, machinery, paper products, printing, confectionery, and petroleum products. Helped by high import-protection, import-substitution manufacturing was initially successful. However, the scope for such substitution was eventually exhausted. There was a rising demand for manufactured goods within the domestic market and a significant increase in exports of manufactures to the other partner states of the EAC, especially Uganda. In addition to those factors, substantial new capacity for certain types of manufactured goods was brought on stream. Given this early success, what slowed the growth of this sector in later years? Part of the problem was the policy of import substitution, which failed to proceed beyond the first phase but, more importantly, the system of controls did not allow the development of a product market. Final goods prices were controlled so that the price system that emerged did not reflect production efficiency and sectoral profitability. Thus the steam soon went out of the sector's growth engine.

The second decade after independence began with escalating import price increases and falling growth rates, as witnessed in most world economies as a result of the first oil price shock. Consequently, the value of Kenya's export of goods and services, in terms of the volume of imports of goods and services they could be exchanged for, was markedly lower. Indeed, GDP in real terms is estimated to have declined by approximately 2.2 percent in 1974, after allowing for the deterioration in terms of trade. Since population increased by 3.3 percent a year, real *per capita* income is estimated to have fallen by 5.5 percent in 1974 in constant prices. This is the first time since independence that a decline in *per capita* income had been recorded.

It is difficult to map out specific policies for each of the markets but the general trend was that major controls were introduced in this period. The controls introduced in this period included: (1) selective controls on bank lending; (2) licensing of foreign exchange transactions; (3) quota restrictions on most imports; (4) direct price controls on goods; and (5) controls on interest rates. These controls transcended all markets and acted as an easier response in controlling balance of payments and inflationary pressures as far as the policy-makers were concerned. But these administrative controls produced major distortions and the discretionary powers gave room to pervasive rent-seeking activities in the public sector that have been difficult to reverse and formed the basis of painful adjustment in the 1990s. In a sense, these controls prevented the development of markets and constrained resource movements and efficient allocations and thus growth. Researchers and most policy-makers regard the 1980s as a lost decade for growth. This is because the easy reaction to the crises in the early 1970s prevented the policy-makers from formulating and adopting stabilization and adjustment measures and policies in the financial sector, money market and foreign exchange transactions that could reorient the economy in the phase of severe internal and external shocks. The 1980s were characterized by economic reforms to aid markets work better, the SAPs. But the controversy surrounding these policies has tended to mask the broad goals and benefits, mostly due to the conditionalities that were attached. In the end, due to slow implementation and at times reversals, they did not achieve their intended goals.

To put the policy environment in perspective, we review the broad spectrum of SAPs and their intended effects on key markets. There were policies geared towards enhancing competition in the economy and others that were aimed at institutional reforms. Whereas the market reforms started slowly in the 1980s and then accelerated in the 1990s, institutional reforms were a phenomenon of the 1990s.

3.2 Foreign exchange market liberalization

The reforms related to foreign exchange in the early 1990s included the introduction of Foreign Exchange Bearer Certificates (Forex Cs) in October 1991, introduction of export earnings retention schemes for exporters in 1992, merging of the official exchange rate with the inter-bank foreign exchange rate, removal of exchange controls on current account transactions and capital account transactions in 1993. In the 1994 Budget Speech, all regulations pertaining to the Exchange Control Act were suspended, before parliament finally repealed the Foreign Exchange Act in December 1995. An important reform in the foreign exchange market was to allow legislation for a foreign exchange bureau in 1995, and in later years individuals were allowed to hold foreign exchange accounts. Removal of foreign exchange controls and liberalization of the exchange rate considerably eased the constraints hitherto imposed on the country's productive sectors, especially manufacturing and agriculture, caused by acute shortages of imported inputs due to the non-availability of foreign exchange when required. This had resulted not only in highly frequent interruptions in many firms' production schedules but also in chronic under-utilization of installed capacity. One of the beliefs in Kenya was that industrial growth was hampered by foreign exchange availability (see Coughlin and Ikiara 1988; Mwega 1993). In as far as controls on foreign exchange persisted, available imported inputs were a function of available foreign exchange allocations. But once this constraint was removed through liberalization, the determination of import demand reverted to its fundamentals with foreign exchange availability no longer being a significant determinant, although it may have helped to improve the transactions costs. In addition, in order to hedge against future foreign allocation shortfalls and their own supplies of inputs, firms engaged in two practices: first they had multiple applications for foreign exchange, which led to a large inventory of inputs as well as finished goods, with unit cost implications; secondly, for exporting firms, transfer pricing was pervasive.

3.3 External trade liberalization

Liberalization of Kenya's external trade was one of the areas that received greater attention in Kenya's three phases of the reform program. Trade liberalization included removing QRs, reducing tariff levels, and adopting a more flexible exchange rate regime. Import liberalization made considerable progress. Between 1980 and 1985 the share of items that could be imported without any restrictions rose from 24 to 48 percent of the total value of imported items. The average tariff rate was also reduced by about 8 percent over the same period. An improved import licensing system that had restricted and unrestricted schedules was established. In 1988, import liberalization was taken a step further when the import licensing system underwent significant improvements. By July 1991, import licenses were required almost solely on health, security, or environmental grounds.

3.4   Domestic trade liberalization

Price controls had extended to most manufactured and agricultural products by the end of 1970s. Beginning in 1983 and continuing until 1995, domestic price controls for virtually all commodities were dismantled. Between 1983 and 1991, the number of commodities whose prices were controlled under the general order dropped from fifty-six to six, while those controlled under the specific order fell from eighty-seven to twenty-nine. By September 1993, only petroleum products and some pharmaceutical products remained under price controls under the general order while under the specific order only three items remained. By July 1995, the maize market, hitherto the most resistant to reform and the central focus of donors, as well as the petroleum/oil sector, had been completely liberalized.

3.5   Financial sector reforms

At independence in 1963, Kenya inherited a financial system that lacked monetary and financial independence (Nasibi 1992). This prevented the authorities from controlling inflation and generating tax revenue. In 1966, the Central Bank of Kenya was established, allowing the country to formulate and operate an independent monetary policy. The Central Bank was given supervisory powers over commercial banks and financial institutions, while an interest rate policy was adopted where the government set maximum and minimum rates for lending and savings deposit rates. The aim was to encourage investment and protect the small borrowers. Interest rates were, however, too low to attract savings with negative real returns.

Three important outcomes stemmed from these financial sector policies. First, the firms invested in huge capacities in the hope that future demand for their goods would not constrain production. Second, even though labor was abundant this pattern of investment did not encourage absorption of the abundant labor, and thus the labor market, even though it had its own regulation, did not benefit as the capital market did from these policies. Finally, these heavy investment capacities led to low capacity utilization constrained by the size of the market. The average capacity utilization in some sub-sectors was below 50 percent. Under the blanket of protection, production costs pushed prices higher and thus the product market suffered.

With these factors, even though growth accelerated in the 1960s and 1970s, it did not have a firm base and thus slowed down later.

In the 1960s and 1970s also, the government invested heavily in the financial sector, by establishing a commercial bank and owning majority share holding in another bank. It also established Development Financial Institutions (DFIs) to alleviate perceived market failures in the provision of long-term capital investment. The DFIs provided equity and term loans to industrial enterprises and long-term agricultural investment loans. However their position was weak, as they concentrated on funding state enterprises which were often unable to service their loans due to poor management, lack of effective statutory powers to raise funds independently, failure to sell out the equities, and vulnerability to political patronage and abuse.

Kenya's financial sector reform program started in the 1990s, but in an attempt to remove distortions in the credit market in the 1980s it had focused on both market and institutional reforms. Positive real interest rates, the target of the market reforms, were aimed at enhancing efficient utilization of available credit resources. Institutional reforms related to the financial sector focused on strengthening the Central Bank to enable it to undertake its inspection and regulatory roles more effectively; the Banking Act was amended in 1989 to facilitate this. In addition to strengthening the Central Bank's regulatory and supervisory roles, other areas affected by the amendments included: introduction of stricter licensing requirements on financial institutions, raising of the minimum capital requirements, the establishment of the Deposit Insurance Fund, new guidelines for granting loans and disclosure requirements, and increasing the penalties for non-compliance. Enforcement of the banking regulations even after the amendment of the Banking Act continued to be hampered by political forces, leading to a new banking crisis in 1986 when two banks and twenty NBFIs had liquidity problems. Financial sector reforms in the latter part of the 1980s and the early 1990s emphasized tight credit control to suppress inflationary tendencies, especially through adjustments of the cash ratio requirements for the commercial banks and raising interest rates. The political factors seem to have persisted, in 1998, several banks and financial institutions were in financial crisis and placed under statutory management while others were liquidated. In the 1990s, a series of reform measures were implemented aimed at creating a dynamic and growing financial sector. For example, with economic liberalization, the central bank moved away from using direct instruments of monetary control such as credit ceilings and guidelines, interest controls and ceilings on lending rates, and a fixed exchange rate, to more indirect instruments such as open market operations (OMOs), flexible exchange rates, and market-determined interest rates.

There were complaints from the business community that the tight monetary policy had contractionary effects on their operations due to reduced lending by commercial banks. For instance, the cash ratio was increased from 10 percent in October 1993 to 20 percent in March 1994 and subsequently reduced, following successful reduction of the money supply through limits on Central Bank of Kenya (CBK) credit and OMOs, to 18 percent in September 1994 and to 13 percent in 1998. The problem was aggravated by the high interest rate on Treasury Bills that the government had used to mop up excess liquidity. This deprived the private sector of credit facilities as resources for investment were increasingly put in Treasury Bills at a time when there was no secondary market for government securities. The financial sector reforms and, in particular, the amendment of the Capital Markets Authority (CMA) Act further eased restraints on foreign ownership. The CMA, established in 1990, attempted to liberalize the financial and capital markets. As a result of these efforts, trading at the Nairobi Stock Exchange (NSE) opened up, on a limited scale, to foreign investors in January 1995. In June 1995, the limit on portfolio investment in Kenyan companies quoted on the NSE by foreigners was raised from 20 to 40 percent for the corporate group of investors and from 2.5 to 5 percent for individual portfolio holdings.

3.6   Labor market reforms

The Kenyan labor market was for many years highly regulated, with wage guidelines, approval mechanisms for redundancies by the Ministry for Labor, and government involvement in the election of trade unions leaders. There was a widespread belief by the Kenyan authorities for most of the post-independence period that the regulation of the labor market was indispensable for rapid economic development and improvement of the workers' welfare. It was argued, for instance, that wage guidelines were essential to ensure that labor costs remained low not only to attract foreign investment but also to encourage firms to use labor-intensive technologies to help create more employment opportunities. Government intervention in fixing minimum wages was also regarded as an important way of protecting the workers' interests. It was argued that high levels of unemployment created a facilitative environment for employers to exploit unskilled workers through under-payment. However, as we have argued earlier, the rate of interest was maintained low and incentives for investors made capital even cheaper than labor, so that this goal of encouraging the utilization of labor-intensive technologies was not achieved.

The labor market underwent considerable liberalization in the 1990s. In July 1994, the Industrial Court allowed trade unions to seek full compensation for price increases without hindrance through wage guidelines. As a result of this liberalization, various laws have been amended to allow firms to discharge redundant workers more easily when necessary. Due to relaxation of the redundancy declaration procedures in 1994, enterprises could declare workers redundant without having to seek the approval of the Ministry for Labor; the enterprises were required to simply notify regional or district labor officers of their intention. The removal of wage guidelines made it possible for firms to negotiate and change the level of wages on the basis of productivity and performance rather than on the basis of cost of living indices, as had hitherto been the case.

3.7   Growth performance: lessons from market reforms

Although the country was in a deep recession for much of the 1990s and beyond, there are several important stylized facts about Kenya's economic performance and market reforms since the 1980s.

First, economic recovery has been rather disappointing and real *per capita* GDP growth only marginally improved. Second, economic management has tended to be extremely short term, with conflicting goals and outcomes characteristic of a policy dilemma. For example, the liberalization period 1993–7 entailed short-run speculative capital flows responding to interest rate differentials. In this period, the authorities encountered a policy dilemma through the conflicting goals and objectives pursued in exchange rate management and accompanying policies. The policy dilemma relates to targeting a competitive exchange rate and low inflation in a floating exchange rate regime, with a high interest rate regime and open capital account. In order to pursue these goals, the authorities have on occasion intervened in the foreign exchange market to stabilize (and sometimes defend) the exchange rate due to volatile capital flows and then have had to follow this action with sterilization of these capital flows in the money market, thereby raising domestic interest rates. The result has been that the exchange rate was stabilized in the short-run but at high interest rates, thus, jeopardizing the goals of increased domestic investment and the chances of economic recovery. In 1998, the government realized that its own borrowing was keeping interest rates artificially high. The government, through the Central Bank, decided to sell fewer Treasury Bills than demanded by the financial sector (the main dealers) at auction. Due to excess liquidity in the financial sector and low investment, the weaker banks started to suffer, with their profit margins squeezed. The result was a banking crisis, which further depressed private investment.

One of the key factors behind this rather poor performance or precarious recovery is the slow response of private investment to macroeconomic stabilization and realignment of prices. This has further been worsened by high domestic interest rates and a shift into trading in lucrative financial instruments, government commercial paper. Even when interest rates on commercial paper have come down, alternative investments have been lacking, given the uncertainty in the social–political environment. Investors have tended to hold back investment plans in fixed irreversible assets, they are facing pervasive risks, which are both policy- and politically-induced. In this case, a co-ordination problem has emerged where the would-be investors exercise a waiting option until the front-loading of investment returns is sufficient to compensate them from the risk of investing or repatriating capital. When investments have come, they have tended to be of a short-term nature, mainly in financial instruments and in commercial activities, rather than in fixed investment. This ensures that the recession gripping the economy will linger.

Moreover, a large external and domestic debt has given rise to a debt overhang problem that has adverse effects on investment and growth. This is because investors expect current and future taxes to be increased to bring about the transfer of resources abroad, or to pay for domestic debt. In addition, there are the usual crowding-out and liquidity arguments. The problem is that private investors exercise a waiting option in their investment decisions just as in the risky environment argued above. Moreover, the domestic debt has affected the domestic interest rate structure, enlarged the fiscal deficit, and thus affected financial development, investment, and savings responses, and hence negatively affected output growth

4.   Private agents in Kenya's growth process

In discussing the incentives and constraints facing key agents in the economy, we focus on two types of agents that are very important in Kenya. These are rural households, mostly composed of smallholder peasants, and the firms that are mainly in manufacturing and commerce. By virtue of being in Africa, these agents face a distinctive environment: adverse climatic and geographical conditions, high risk, high transport costs, trade barriers, poor infrastructure, low levels of education, limited financial markets, and a high regulatory environment. How do these agents adapt themselves to this environment? How have the conditions they face constrained growth in Kenya?

4.1 Smallholders

Kenya gained independence in 1963, but already in the 1950s the peasants had been allowed to grow cash crops, the "White Highlands" had been opened up and extension services expanded for the peasant smallholders. This commercialization of smallholder agriculture led to a rapid increase of agricultural production. After independence, agricultural growth increased. Most of the remaining restrictions on smallholder agriculture were lifted; substantial amounts of previously European lands were transferred to

Table 10.9 *Kenya, average net household monthly incomes, by source and size of holding, 1988, Kshs*

Size of holding (acres)	Farm enterprise	Non-farm enterprise	Salary and wages	Other sources	Total
No. holding	305	63	359	6	733
0.1–0.9	171	88	298	76	634
1.0–1.9	255	89	145	101	590
2.0–2.9	295	102	118	101	616
3.0–3.9	341	149	129	123	742
4.0–4.9	371	162	128	156	817
5.0–6.9	416	174	126	147	861
7.0–9.9	462	195	152	158	966
10.0–19.9	633	202	185	142	1,162
20 and over	1,100	265	219	185	1,770
Average income	399	140	177	114	829

Source: Bigsten and Ndung'u (1991: table 10.10).

Kenyan farmers and large amounts of resources were devoted to land registration and adjudication. High-yielding cereals were introduced and there was a push to increase the shares of high-value crops in smallholder production.

4.1.1   Access to land

At independence, there were considerable areas of unused agricultural land in Kenya. The impressive performance of agricultural production after independence was largely based on an increase in the hectarage and making land access easier through the co-operative movement to purchase the former "White Highlands." But the land surplus was soon exhausted and so the future for agricultural production had to rely on increased production of existing land. This can be achieved only through investment in productivity, specialization, and public investment to support smallholder production.

There is a strong correlation between holding size and household income, as shown in table 10.9 using 1988 data that may not be radically different from that of the 1960s and 1970s. The group with no holding at all is seen on average to be worse off than those with a little land; it also comprises people with good jobs in the rural areas. Table 10.9 shows that, in rural Kenya, land is a major differentiating factor, but that, on average, income from non-farm enterprises and remittances follows the same pattern. This implies that households with larger holdings diversify their activities and thus are able to minimize risk and raise household incomes. Access to productive assets varies with the household's location in relation to major towns and with the level of agricultural development. For example, the purchase and use of agricultural inputs are heavily dependent on the potential of an area. In the high potential areas such as Central and Rift Valley Provinces, large quantities of inputs go into agricultural production.

4.1.2 The rural institutional structure: agricultural prices

Price regulation was a central ingredient in agricultural policy. The Ministry of Agriculture undertook annual price reviews for major agricultural products, and on the basis of this the government fixed prices at all points in the marketing chain. The Fourth Development Plan of 1979–84 was the first government document to explicitly recognize the importance of agricultural prices as incentives. The need to use the parity pricing principle was argued in the document, as well as the importance of considering the long-run development of world market prices. In the 1984–9 Development Plan, the need for prices to guide resource allocation in the appropriate direction and the use of export or import parity-pricing principles was explicitly recognized. This improved the government's methods of setting prices to reflect export and import parity levels. Official producer prices were thus set closer to import parity prices plus transport costs. This was a drastic change since previously producer prices had been kept low and so production held back. For example, in 1980, weighted producer prices (except for sugar) were 24 percent below the import parity price, and this meant that farm incomes were 7 percent below what they would have been with import parity prices. This income loss accrued to consumers in the form of low prices and to the government in the form of reduced subsidies to agricultural parastatals. However, by 1986, weighted producer prices (with the exception of sugar) were only 7 percent below import parity prices, which implied that there had been a real shift in policy to benefit farmers.

Studies on agricultural production in this period, especially in the 1970s and early 1980s, show that agriculture had a modest growth of 3.1 percent per year on average, but that the main driving factors were land expansion which contributed 2.4 percent of this increase and increases and higher producer prices, which accounted for an increase of 1 percent. Estimates also show that the price distortions in this period reduced farmers' share in GDP by 2.4 percent in 1980, but by 1986 this loss was down to 0.5 percent so that a drastic effort had been made to reduce price distortions. These figures seem to suggest that price-setting was a major factor that checked the growth of smallholder agriculture, and that were it not for smallholder land expansion little growth would have been registered. Price incentives are an important signal for production in the smallholder economy and most agriculture production growth was driven by price signals. This was even more important when prices for agricultural cereals were set before the planting season. For example, in the 1975–7 coffee boom, coffee estates produced more coffee than the smallholders, but ten years later the supply response from smallholders was such that smallholders were producing two-thirds of the coffee output. Smallholders thus reacted to the boom (the price incentive) with increased planting, which in turn raised their production significantly by 1980–1. But coffee prices came down drastically, and so since then there has been no trend towards increased output.

4.1.3   Marketing

Where food crops are concerned, the most important market outlets for smallholder output have been the local markets or small-scale traders. For major cash crops, only the official marketing channels are available. Some fifteen parastatals have been involved in the marketing of agricultural output. There are also cooperatives and private traders. The systems of control that existed in the 1970s and 1980s were criticized for their operational inefficiency and distortions in resource allocation: efficiency problems were particularly acute with regard to the internal food marketing system and the distribution of inputs. The distribution for export produce, especially through the cooperatives, was easier to operate and was more efficient than that of food crops under the parastatals. The marketing boards had different roles for different crops. In some markets – for example, coffee, tea, cotton, pyrethrum, tobacco, and wheat – the marketing boards acted (and in some cases still act today) as monopolies in processing and/or resale. The typical pattern where boards were involved was to take delivery from traders, cooperatives or large farms, and then deliver to processors and wholesalers.

One major element in the government's strategy to improve smallholder agriculture was the development of the cooperative system for marketing and provision of credit and inputs. In the 1960s and early 1970s, cooperatives were concentrated in the more productive areas. Cooperatives in poorer regions had considerable problems, and only in those regions with good agro-ecological environments and a developed infrastructure did cooperatives survive. In addition, cooperatives with a monopsony standard, such as the coffee unions, performed much better than those that faced competition, coffee made up as much as 75 percent of smallholder production delivered through the cooperatives. Cooperatives were successful only in regions where the environment favored high productivity, and where the rural economy was sufficiently differentiated to keep transaction costs low, especially where road networks were on average good. However, organizing cooperatives did not generate agricultural development. The cooperatives could not be substituted for other measures such as land redistribution, investment in rural infrastructure, and more efficient markets, the main factors that checked smallholder production in the 1990s.

4.1.4   Risk and uncertainty facing smallholders in the 1990s

Post-independence Kenya has been marked by a state of relative political stability and peace. Unlike most of the countries in SSA, Kenya has neither been under military dictatorship nor experienced any major internal strife that could be classified as a civil war. Until the early 1990s, internal conflict was virtually non-existent, save for the banditry activities in the North-Eastern Province and near the Somali border. During the 1990s, Kenya experienced a number of what have come to be referred to as "ethnic clashes"; these have not translated into civil wars nor have they lasted for extended lengths of time. They affected smallholder farmers and small businesses and helped to swell the informal sector in urban centers.

To a large extent, ethnic clashes were localized in limited geographical areas and did not significantly impact life in other parts of the country. Furthermore, the clashes did not involve rebel groups fighting to dislodge the government (see Kimenyi and Ndung'u 2002). Conflicts are a thus recent phenomenon in Kenya. During the 1990s, and coinciding with the introduction of competitive politics, sporadic incidences of violence were experienced that targeted certain ethnic groups. Starting in September 1991, organized bands of arsonists calling themselves "Kalenjin warriors" unleashed terror on Luo, Luhyia, Kikuyu, and Kisii in the Rift Valley region, targeting farms populated by these ethnic communities, looting and destroying homes, driving the occupants away and killing indiscriminately. The violence resulted in the displacement of thousands of people from their farms. Similar incidences erupted in Mombasa and Kwale districts in the Coastal Region in August 1997. The violence in the Rift Valley and Coastal Region is of particular significance because it was widely viewed as constituting a serious threat to the existence of a united Kenyan nation, the rule of law, the institutions of private property, contracts and the market economy. We look at the factors behind these clashes and how they affected economic agents and overall growth.

Ethnicity

The most commonly cited cause of the violence in Kenya is ethnic cleavage. The country is ethnically quite diverse with at least forty-two distinct tribal groups. It has been established that ethnic identification in Africa is very strong (Kimenyi and Ndung'u 2002). Collier (2001), for example, observes that the tribe and kin groups are the most powerful levels of social identity. Tribal identification has been demonstrated to be an important way of solving collective action problems, in particular, ethnic-based institutions have a comparative advantage in solving prisoner's dilemma problems (Kimenyi 1998). On the other hand, ethnic groups can impose costs on non-members. The implication is that ethnic clashes in Kenya were purely the result of "ethnic hatred." Such hatred has its origin in fears that non-indigenous groups that have come to dominate a geographical area through migration and land ownership will thereby dominate voter patterns in that area. The outcome of these fears was to distort smallholder production and settlement patterns. The smallholder production boom in the 1960s and 1970s was mostly spearheaded by settlement schemes in the Rift Valley. Along with their impact in widening the distribution of rights to land, these schemes created uncertainties in smallholder production that were driven by polities rather than the market forces.

Land

Kenya has a "land question," perhaps the most controversial issue in the country, and there is a general consensus that this land question lies at the heart of the ethnic clashes (Kimenyi and Ndung'u 2002). It has been observed that the violence resulted from the elite's appropriation of the land issue to fight those opposed to them by reactivating demands for territorial land claims in the Rift Valley and the Coast.

Land reform policies in Kenya have been based on free-market models emphasizing individualized freehold rights over customary tenure in the belief that this would encourage investments in farm productivity, encourage the emergence of land markets that would transfer land to more efficient farmers, and provide farmers with collateral for raising credit (Kimenyi and Ndung'u 2002). There is mounting evidence that the economic and social benefits of such programs are doubtful; they may also stir up dormant conflicts. The dynamics of land ownership in Kenya, as investigated under a theory of conflict based on grievance arising from land alienation, show that Kenya's land is categorized as government land, freehold land or trust land. "Government land" refers to all land that was vested in the crown during the colonial period (Kimenyi and Ndung'u 2002). At independence, the land was vested in the government of Kenya. The Government Lands Act (cap. 280) empowers the President to make grants of unalienated government land to any person and spells out how the government can dispose of this land. One of the three ways in which this can happen is through offering land for agricultural purposes. The Commissioner of Lands may under the direction of the President cause land available for alienation for agricultural purposes to be surveyed and divided into farms and that the leases of such farms shall be sold at auction. Local communities are often disadvantaged by such sales, as most cannot afford the purchase price. The disposal therefore dispossesses some communities of land that was previously under their occupation or use. This has historically given rise to strong resentment.

Given such resentment, a theory of conflict based on land grievances would find support in a positive correlation between the incidence of violence and the amount of government and trust land that has been alienated.

But the most important contribution to this discussion is to show the risk and uncertainty revolving around the main (and mostly the only) productive asset for the smallholders and the loss of productive means by smallholders in the 1990s and beyond.

State capture

It is doubtful that land and inter-ethnic hostilities singularly or together could have led to the kind of atrocities visited on the smallholders in the Rift Valley. The central dynamics of the violence appears to have been to maintain the political and economic status quo (Kimenyi and Ndung'u 2002). It is the political space that was and continues to be the object of contestation in the various areas rocked by violence. This explains the outbreak of violence in the run-up to the general elections in 1992 and 1997. Public-choice scholars have attributed ethnic conflicts in Africa to the failure of political institutions to accommodate diverse interests, arguing that the lack of political models to effectively deal with diversity in centralized states where competition for resources and power is prevalent leads to conflicts (Kimenyi and Ndung'u 2002). Kimenyi and Ndung'u (2002) further argue that the violence was part of a struggle for the capture of the state: the political elite mobilized to maintain a comparative advantage in the control of the structures of government and in the competition for resources. Whether these explanations are adequate or not, the outcome of the political and ethnic violence affected the smallholders negatively and scared existing and potential investors, and this explains the outcome of the growth process and profile in the 1990s–early 2000s. The immediate effect was on food security since most of the smallholders were in food-surplus regions. The second and most pervasive aspect was to destroy investment in land and perhaps the land market, destroying the basis of competitive production in smallholder agriculture which has been responsible for agricultural growth in Kenya.

4.2   Manufacturing firms

The modern manufacturing sector in Kenya had its beginning in the colonial period when an economic infrastructure linking Kenya to the world market emerged. Import–export houses were established in Kenya as early as 1905, but these were mainly exports of primary commodities and imports of consumer goods for the settler population (Bigsten 2002). Before the Second World War, only basic manufacturing firms had been established and only for producing consumer goods for the small domestic market. Most of these firms were agro-industries in nature. But there were others that were processing primary products such as soda and cement and producing power as subsidiaries of multinational corporations (MNCs). This was also the basis for an Asian community, excluded from farming, to move into the urban centers to establish small-scale industries and trading companies; these firms did not have direct support from the state. After the Second World War, the colonial government introduced tariffs in Kenya to protect colonial markets from foreign competition. This marked the beginning of British firms investing in East Africa, but the market was limited so that enterprise development was severely hampered.

4.2.1 Import-substitution policy

The introduction of tariffs was a slow start to the deliberate policy of import substitution as a strategy for industrialization. But during the struggle for independence in the 1950s and early 1960s there was a slowdown in industrial investment and substantial capital flight took place. In order to halt capital flight and establish confidence in an independent Kenya, the government passed the Foreign Investment Protection Act in 1964. On the basis of this Act, foreign firms were given the right to repatriate profits, loans, and interest on their loans and part of the proceeds from sale of assets. The government also guaranteed not to nationalize industries. In 1965, the government published the *Sessional Paper 10 on African Socialism and its Application to Planning in Kenya* (Kenya 1965). In this, the government spelled out its ambition to develop a free-market economy where foreign investors were welcome. This was a major deviation from its partners in the EAC, who were more inclined to socialism. This had the effect of making Kenya a more attractive location for MNCs wishing to invest in Kenya and to take advantage of the EAC market. The paper marked the roots of an effort to deepen an import-substitution industrialization policy, which was the industrialization strategy that was being popularized in most developing countries at the time. An International Industrial Protection Committee was set up to consider applications from potential investors and committee considered applications from firms seeking modifications of the structure of tariffs, quotas, duty drawbacks, and import licensing. A Foreign Exchange Allocation Committee was also set up to consider all foreign exchange allocation applications and to administer quotas on imports for which limited quotas had been established. The quotas were typically set equal to the difference between predicted local production and local demand. The pattern of quotas was made more restrictive in the 1970s when the foreign exchange squeeze became more formidable, during the first balance of payments crisis in 1970–1, and the oil price shocks of 1974 and 1979 compounded the problems.

The balance of payments crisis in 1970–1 led the government to tighten administrative controls in the economy. In 1971, the Capital Issues Committee was set up to vet stock issues in order to cut down on capital outflows and encourage local ownership; this committee also controlled the amount of loans firms could borrow from the commercial banks. Tariffs went up and import licensing became more restrictive, but this had to spill over to domestic prices and so the government had also to tighten price controls. The price controls also served as a basis for an incomes policy and wage guidelines which were set up in 1973. In 1972, the government also set up a sales tax, but domestic producers did not pay their dues and so they fell heavily on imports and became an implicit form of protection. In the early 1970s, the government also introduced a highly protective policy for domestic producers in the form of No-objection Certificates. This ensured that importers would not face competition since they would import only those goods not produced in Kenya and, likewise, domestic producers would not face competition from imports. This also implied that a firm wishing to enter the Kenyan market had to seek a 'No-Objection Certificate' from its potential competitor already established in Kenya! These sequences of policy interventions in the 1970s had the undesirable outcome of reducing domestic competition and competitiveness and shifting incentives against export production. It also ensured a large subsidy to manufacturing at the expense of the rest of the economy, and particularly against agriculture.

There were other policies in the regulatory environment that made the operations of firms expensive, and checked their growth. They included price controls on their final products, interest rate controls, regulations regarding foreign and domestic loans, foreign exchange transactions, and work permits for expatriates, to mention just the major ones. The system of foreign exchange control was so pervasive that firms had to apply for foreign exchange allocation from the Foreign Exchange Allocation Committee of the Ministry of Commerce and Industry (including the Ministry of Finance and Central Bank) for their imports and travel. Firms had to lodge multiple applications to cushion themselves against future shortfalls and at the same time were forced to keep large stocks of finished goods as well as inputs. They also had to apply for price adjustments detailing reasons why prices for their goods should be adjusted at the factory level and that would be followed through the supply chain to the retail level. Importing firms had to surrender their foreign exchange earnings to the Central Bank ninety days after the export shipment. This encouraged transfer pricing and made domestic production very unattractive to local entrepreneurs without the international network and support of the MNCs.

By the end of the 1970s, it was clear that the scope for further import substitution based on simple assembly – the easy phase – had been exhausted. Demand had slowed down, the competitiveness of Kenyan exports to regional markets had been severely eroded, and the break-up of the EAC reduced the remaining larger East African market. There were thus firms in Kenya that had been originally established to take advantage of a wider

EAC market that was now not accessible. The outcome was low capacity utilization and high unit costs which compounded the erosion of competitiveness. In the Regional Program on Enterprise Development (RPED) surveys of 1993–5 conducted by the World Bank, it was common to find firms with below 50 percent operating capacity that had positive profits. Even the Export Compensation Scheme introduced in 1975 was too weak to reverse the trend of the incentive structure for non-traditional exports. So the decade ended with serious disequilibria in the economy, but also firms relatively weak in competitiveness, and also checked demand for their products. An outcome was the proliferation of an informal sector that catered for the basic needs of the low-income households at more affordable prices.

4.2.2   Firms in the 1980s and 1990s: the structural adjustment phase

This phase represents a turning point for industrial policy and economic management in Kenya. There were several policy changes, focusing on tariff reforms, dismantling price controls, privatization and reform of parastatals, stepping up export promotion measures, improving the environment for investors, and also focusing on the informal sector. But there were also tensions with donors that produced policy reversals, which increased the risk for domestic firms. The situation continued in the 1990s and the results were a decline in investments and, in the middle of the 1990s, massive capital flight. The survey evidence from RPED shows how firms responded to adjustment and the impact of adjustment policies on manufacturing firms (Levin and Ndung'u 2002).

Export opportunities improved for domestic firms with structural adjustment and liberalization, but the firms were not competitive enough to take advantage of this environment so most of the SMEs closed down and turned to trading. Access to foreign exchange had improved with the liberalization of foreign exchange transactions but the cost of foreign exchange was a handicap and the exchange rate was unstable, introducing a risk dimension. This was further complicated by a lack of futures market and the fact that firms used the spot rate and no forward rate in the foreign exchange market. Competition from imports was a serious problem to most firms, but the biggest problem was unfair competition from local firms and from the evasion of import duties by importers. The economy was becoming more commercialized, rather than production-oriented, and corruption in the way that duties were applied to commercial imports that competed with domestic firms was increasing. A majority of the firms in the RPED survey indicated that escalating utility prices had increased their costs of operation. The problem cited by most firms was a combination of high utility prices and poor services, which did not encourage competitive production. Firms' responses indicated that access to credit was by far the most severe problem in the 1990s, mainly emanating from policies implemented to stabilize the economy. These had a negative impact on the operations of the private sector, and the effects of these policies trickled down quite fast to the firm level. These and other factors discussed above, and the lingering effects of a control regime, had negative consequences on firm growth, and added to the factors that led to the contraction of the manufacturing sector, in line with the declining growth and protracted recession in Kenya. These frustrations were translated by politicians into a call for price controls, with the interest rate and petroleum prices as key targets.

5. The political economy of Kenya's growth process

5.1 The Kenyatta era

At independence in 1963, Kenya inherited an economy whose structure and direction of development had been shaped by British colonialism. During this period, social and economic policies heavily favored British interests, with the country mainly managed as a source of raw materials for British industries and a market for their products (Brett 1973). After independence, the African elites took over the large farms owned by European settlers. The post-independence government also implemented schemes of settlement and registration (initiated during the colonial period) for the smallholders.

To explain Kenya's relatively good performance in the 1960s and 1970s, analysts have emphasized the role of the new Kenyan landed elites in securing policy conditions favorable to agriculture, in the context of strong linkages between urban and rural areas – the so-called "economy of affection" (Bates 1989). During the Kenyatta regime, resources for rural development projects were allocated through competition among different groups which were internally knitted together by tight patron–client relationships so that the system was to a large extent meritocratic (Barkan 1984). Through this political competition for resources, ethnic groups and their coalitions evolved as interest groups.[9]

The Kenyan agricultural sector did not experience much discrimination in resource allocation in the 1960s and 1970s. In this period, smallholders played a substantial role in agricultural growth; their marketed production grew rapidly and surpassed that of large farmers in the 1970s in all but a few major crops. While small and large farmers had different marketing arrangements, there is no evidence that the small farms were discriminated against in terms of pricing. Except for cotton and sugarcane, private traders sold all major cash crops through auctions where state intervention was limited. As a result, policy-based regional discrimination through pricing was largely

---

[9] The discussion in much of this section is influenced by Takahashi (1997).

non-existent for most cash crops.[10] Food crops were more regulated, justified as protection for farmers and provision of food security. Farmers were
better remunerated than in the typical SSA country; agriculture was thus a
leading growth sector, accounting for 25.5 percent of total annual growth
between 1966 and 1979, compared to 17.5 percent for manufacturing. The
relatively good performance of agriculture had favorable knock-on effects on
the industrial sector; discouraged rural–urban migration and urbanization;
and contributed directly and indirectly to tax revenues and enhancement of
food security, hence ensuring macroeconomic stability.

The agricultural sector, however, received minimal explicit government
subsidies and transfers, accounting for less than 2 percent of government
expenditure in the mid-1970s. Government loans to, and investment in,
agricultural enterprises were only 2.5 percent of the development (capital)
budget compared to 7 percent for commercial and industrial enterprises.
Public investment was quite favorable to the rural sector in the 1960s and
1970s; public expenditure for capital formation directed to the agricultural
sector was far larger than that for the industrial sector. The government and
public marketing agencies also supported agricultural production through
research and extension, construction of roads, and other facilities. This was
in addition to a *Harambee* (self-help) system through which many public projects (rural roads, schools, etc.) were implemented. However, much
of the benefits of the good agricultural performance accrued to the Central Province, whose farmers not only benefited from a close vicinity to
the market (Nairobi) and suitability of natural conditions but also benefited from a better socio-economic infrastructure. The last factor, especially
public investment in the 1960s and 1970s, was no doubt due to the political power held by people from the province, even though it had been also
endowed with a better socio-economic infrastructure at independence. On
the other hand, regional disparities widened, with Nyanza and Western
Provinces largely discriminated against and the most disadvantaged areas
neglected.

Kenya's manufacturing sector also grew rapidly, at over 9 percent per
annum in the first decade after independence (see table 10.10), reflecting
the availability of a large market within the EAC (which collapsed in 1977).
The sector, however, was not too protected and therefore did not unduly
tax agriculture. The use of tariffs for protective purposes or to raise revenue was constrained by membership of the EAC; there was therefore no

---

[10] Sugar, on the other hand, was mainly produced by parastatals, with the government
setting the prices of raw materials and final output. Similarly, cotton was mainly utilized
as input into parastatal textile firms. Both crops were therefore adversely affected by the
politics of the time, as they were mainly produced in Nyanza Province. With the fall of
Oginga and Mboya in the 1960s, Nyanza Province became antagonistic towards the
Kenyatta regime, leading to an undermining of the producer margins paid for these
products.

Table 10.10 *Kenya, average annual growth rates,*
real GDP, 1964–1979, percent

Sector	1964–73	1974–9
Agriculture	4.6	3.9
Manufacturing	9.1	10.0
Finance, real estate, etc.	9.8	12.4
Government services	16.9	6.5
GDP	6.6	5.2

Source: Kenya, *National Development Plan* (1997–2001).

tendency to escalate tariffs in the 1970s. Kenya also did not depend unduly on import revenues, and hence had less need to depend on import duties. In 1970s, the import-weighted tariff rate was quite low by African standards (at 16.5 percent). Politically, this was facilitated by the fact that private firms were largely dominated by non-Africans, with limited political power, even though it is possible that the Kenyatta administration was more urban or industry-biased than that of Moi. NBFIs, however, were quite active in the industrial sector, with the proliferation of parastatals in the later years increasing the government's interest in the sector. Government loans to, and investment in, commercial and industrial corporations, for example, accounted for 7 percent of the central government's development (capital) expenditure in the mid-1970s.

In general, the exchange rate was relatively well managed. This was partly due to the relatively low inflation rates, at least before the first oil price shock. The over-valuation of the Kenyan shilling was therefore rather limited when compared with other Anglophone African countries in the 1970s. In Kenya, the black market premium was kept around 20 percent and never exceeded 40 percent before 1990, except in 1972–3 during the forced exodus of Asians from Uganda, and 1982 (Azam and Daubrée 1997). The premiums were quite low when compared to those of other Anglophone SSA countries about the same period (1975–9): Tanzania 224 percent, Uganda 853 percent; Ghana 335 percent; Nigeria 161 percent; and Zambia 226 percent. Taking 1970 as an year when Kenya had both internal and external balances, Mwega (2002) shows that the country registered average misalignment of 7.2 percent in the 1970s, 6.8 percent in the 1980s, and 8.9 percent in the first half of the 1990s, supporting the contention that Kenya on average maintained a fairly good foreign exchange rate policy. Ndung'u (1999) explains the low premium and low misalignment by the fact that, during the crawling-peg regime in the 1980s, the Central Bank determined the crawl taking into account the parallel market rate, a process of backward indexation.

Kenya's tax base was also comparatively broad by African standards due to the relatively large industrial sector. Direct taxes accounted for

Table 10.11 *Kenya, evolution of income inequality and poverty, 1964–2000*

Year	Gini coefficient	% Population below poverty line
1964	63.00	38
1967	66.00	40
1969	68.00	40
1971	70.00	42
1974	69.00	40
1976	68.00	40
1977	59.00	n.a.
1981	57.30	48
1992	54.39	45
1994	44.50	40
1997	n.a.	52
2000	n.a.	56[a]

Sources: Bigsten (1986); van Ginneken and Park (1984); Kenya, Central Bureau of Statistics, *Welfare Monitoring Surveys* (various issues), Government of Kenya (2000)
[a] Central Bureau of Statistics. This is the poverty level incorporated in the Kenyan Poverty Reduction Strategy Paper (PRSP).
Notes: There were no nationally representative surveys before the 1980s and the observations in table pre-dating 1977, as compiled by Bigsten (1986), were based on tax accounts and poverty rates on wage data, with a poverty line of Kshs 1,000 per worker per month. The Gini coefficient for 1977 was derived from a Social Accounting Matrix (SAM) by van Ginneken and Park (1984).

33 percent of the central government's total recurrent revenue in the 1970s, unlike a typical African country which is more dependent on indirect taxes, especially on international trade. Direct taxes are less discriminatory against agriculture due to the difficulties in tax collection and the low level of incomes. Revenue from agricultural activities accounted for 3.4 percent of total tax revenue in the mid-1970s. The smallholders were, however, subject to the agricultural "cess" (the term refers to an assessment of a tax), a tax levied on marketed agricultural commodities. However, this was at a minimal rate of 3 percent until 1987, and was earmarked for infrastructural investments such as rural roads.

It is probably therefore true that the government succeeded in achieving relatively rapid economic growth in the 1960s and 1970s articulated in *The Sessional Paper 10* of 1965 (Kenya 1965). This may, however, have been achieved at the cost of increased income and regional inequalities. As seen in table 10.11, income inequality increased to a peak in 1971, but declined over the rest of the 1970s, while poverty levels remained fairly constant.

5.2 The Moi era

Analysts have attributed the poor economic performance in the 1980s and 1990s at least partially to a change in the political regime from Kenyatta to Moi. With the ascension of Moi to the presidency in 1978, the public resource allocation game became more regulated to ensure that the ruling groups won. The Moi regime changed the rules of the game from growth to regional and ethnic redistribution. His attempts to address the imbalances in Kenyan society marked a significant change in policy, entailing a trade-off between equity and productivity. This policy of redistribution led to complaints that Moi had merely switched resources from the Central Province to the Rift Valley, which was a significant if not central contribution to the social upheavals of the 1990s centered on multi-partyism (Morton 1998). It would seem that the distribution policies did not reach out to smallholders in the high-potential areas, the driving force of Kenya's previous agricultural growth.

A good example is the creation of National Cereal and Produce Board (NCPB) – from a merger of the Wheat Board and Maize and Produce Board in 1979 – which mainly benefited the Rift Valley, the political base of Moi's administration, and which contributed to macroeconomic instability in the 1980s. This new institution was given monopolistic power to engage in both inter-district and international trade in maize and was closely attached to the public administration system. The NCPB expanded in a rapid manner in the 1980s – for example, increasing the number of its employees by seven times by 1987. In response to the food crisis of 1980 and 1984 producer prices increased, causing a stockpile of surplus maize. This caused a massive deficit (which accounted for 25 percent of the public sector's budget deficits in 1987). The government also had to step in to take over the NCPB's massive debt (about 5 percent of GDP) in the latter half of the 1980s. There was also increased intervention by the state in the management of parastatals. In addition, ethnic-based quotas were introduced for higher official posts in the public sector as well as for secondary school places. The latter policy made it a requirement that 85 percent of provincial secondary school places should be allocated to the local community. As a result of the redistribution policies, the advantages that the Central Province previously enjoyed in roads and education before the 1980s were reduced by the 1990s. This led the Central Region to opt for the opposition politics in the competitive environment of the 1990s. Rural infrastructure was generally neglected; while new roads and pavements were constructed, repair and maintenance of existing paved roads was not kept up (Swamy 1994). The infrastructural projects, which were more politically appealing, were also mainly constructed in the relatively under-developed areas and therefore had lower rates of return than repair and maintenance of the existing infrastructure.

The government also tried to introduce export crops to the marginal areas – for example, the Nyayo Tea Zones – but the trials generally were not successful.

According to Morton:

The thinking was that these zones would protect the forests from destruction by local people, preserve the environment, stop oil erosion, earn much needed foreign currency and create jobs. By the end of the 1980s there were zones in fifteen districts, administered by the Nyayo Tea Development, a parastatal which Moi founded in 1987.

Unfortunately . . . the reality did not match the dream. These narrow strips of tea skirting the forests created problems with grazing . . . and, most important, undercut the prices of local tea farmers, who burnt their tea crops in protest at the government sponsored newcomer. It was a similar story at the Nyayo Bus Corporation, which foundered on the rocks of nepotism, vandalism, corruption and inefficiency. (1998: 207)

However, discrimination against the Nyanza and Western Provinces continued – with, for example, the lack of significant correlation between agricultural potential and the paved proportion of total roads remaining unchanged between the 1970s and the 1990s. The returns to sugarcane production also continued to be low. As seen in table 10.12, these are the areas (together with the Coast Province) that are generally the most afflicted by poverty.

Urbanization intensified (with migrants mainly from Nyanza, Western, and even Central Provinces) and the urban unemployment situation worsened. The rate of unemployment in Kenya's urban areas was about 16 percent in the 1980s, increasing to 17–23 percent in the 1990s (Manda 1997). The increase in unemployment reflected the low level of economic activities and public sector restrictive employment policies, including civil service reforms, which caused urban poverty to increase faster than rural poverty (see table 10.12). The urbanization and unemployment problems eventually became impossible to ignore: the informal housing areas and the informal sector in Nairobi were rapidly expanding due to an inflow of immigrants, which was a source of social and political instability. This induced an expansion in employment in the lower strata of the public sector, undermining the government's goals of improving efficiency in the public sector and reducing fiscal imbalances.

It is difficult to determine whether these policies improved incomes and regional equity. Household surveys suggest that the Rift Valley surpassed Central Province in *per capita* income through the 1980s. There was an apparently sharp decline in inequality, as measured by the Gini coefficient,

Table 10.12 *Kenya, trend and regional differences in poverty rates, 1980s and 1990s*

	Percentage of overall poverty			
	1982	1992	1994	1997
Rural areas: Province				
Central	25.69	35.89	31.93	31.39
Coast	54.55	43.50	55.63	62.10
Eastern	47.73	42.16	57.75	58.56
Nyanza	57.88	47.41	42.21	63.05
Rift Valley	51.05	51.51	42.87	50.10
Western	53.79	54.81	53.83	58.75
N. Eastern	–	–	58.00	–
Total rural	47.89	46.33	46.75	52.93
Total urban	–	29.29	28.95	49.20

Source: Kenya, Central Bureau of Statistics, *Welfare Monitoring Surveys* (various issues).
Note: – Areas not covered in the Surveys.

in the 1980s and 1990s, though the incidence of poverty appeared to have increased over the 1990s (see table 10.11).

6. Conclusion

Explaining growth performance in Kenya has been the main objective of this chapter, which has covered the period 1960–2000 and drawn some empirical evidence from growth-accounting decompositions and the cross-country endogenous growth literature. The chapter has divided growth episodes into the 1960s–1970s and 1980s–1990s. This helps to explain why there was a strong economic performance in the 1960s and early 1970s, and why this performance was never replicated in the later periods. In each period, the chapter has attempted to trace the role of markets, private agents, and political economy in Kenya's growth process.

In the 1960s and 1970s, for example, the empirical analysis shows a mixed picture. While the Ndulu and O'Connell (2000) model shows the HPAEs outperforming Kenya throughout the period, with the margin increasing from 1.98 percent in the early 1960s to 3.44 percent in the 1980s but declining to 2.02 percent in the 1990s, the Hoeffler (1999) model predicts Kenya slightly out-performing the HPAEs by about 0.10 percentage points in the 1960–4 half-decade, declining to 0.075 in the following decade (1965–74), and turning negative thereafter. Both models are therefore agreed that, in the 1980s and 1990s, the economy poorly under-performed the stellar performance of HPAEs and even the average performance of SSA.

The performance of markets in the 1960s and 1970s was mainly driven by the public sector. Economic policy stressed the role of entrepreneurship and capital accumulation, where the markets mechanism would effectively work. In addition, there was greater emphasis on capital injection into the economy in order to form strong market links in both the product and financial market in the hope that these would accelerate the pace of development. But these ambitions were checked by various factors. First, in the financial market, the regulated interest rate structure did not encourage savings but encouraged capital-intensive production. The outcome was low capacity utilization checked by the size of the market and high prices, and thus hampering the growth of firms and the product market. These factors continued to be important even in later decades. Second, even though the manufacturing sector grew rapidly, the driving force being import substitution, it was constrained after the initial easy phase and the growth process was not sustainable. Finally, the decade also witnessed some policy backlash in the form of controls, which at first worked to control the balance of payments and inflationary pressures but later created distortions in the economy and thus checked expansion of both firms and smallholder farms and overall economic growth. The system of controls continued into the 1980s and was gradually eliminated in the early 1990s. Growth performance therefore seems to revolve around the constraints of the control regime and the response to liberalization in the 1990s. This system of controls prevented and checked the growth of product and financial markets and created room for a rent-seeking environment. It is argued in the chapter that the slow process of adjustment, the emergence of policy reversals, and the reluctance to liberalize had serious consequences for the development of markets and agents' response and reactions, and explains the protracted recession in the 1990s and beyond. One interesting outcome of the legacies of the control regime is the struggle to control and capture the state. Control of the structures of government implies controlling resources and resource flows from the state, an explanation used in the chapter to account for the sporadic ethnic conflicts and tension in the 1990s. It strengthens the political-economy story and it can be argued that political cycles have created risk and uncertainty and destroyed the investment base, and hence dashed hopes for sustained future growth.

It appears that initial conditions and regime changes have been important, but have changed roles. Initial conditions promoted growth in the initial phases reinforced by regime changes, but in later decades regime changes took over and explained most of the growth failures. The first phase is where the favorable initial conditions seem to exist in the 1960s and 1970s and there is policy continuity soon after independence. These initial conditions relate to resource endowments, economic structure, economic policy, and national political institutions. These initial conditions are arguably supported by two important developments. First, *The Sessional Paper No. 10 on African Socialism and its Application to Planning in Kenya* (Kenya 1965) laid the foundations of a market economy and this enhanced the flow of FDI supported by an import-substitution policy started before independence. *The Sessional Paper* thus deepened the import-substitution policy of industrialization. Second, as Bates (1989) argues, by annexing the White Highlands, the colonial government indirectly increased access to land even though they limited access to land rights. When independence was won, power was seized by the conservative faction of Kenya rural society who had a commitment to accumulation, investment, and private property. These two factors thus combined to enhance productive capacity in agriculture as well as producing a class of entrepreneurs in the industrial sector via joint ventures (JVs) with foreign investors. But even though this was a vibrant period, coinciding with Kenyatta's reign, high and perhaps satisfactory economic growth was achieved in the 1960s and 1970s at the cost of increased regional inequality.

The second phase starts in the late 1970s and begins with a change in the political regime to the Moi era and also with the policy to address regional disparities. The policy of redistribution seems to have started in the 1980s. Such a policy change was combined with a weaker budget discipline, with the budget used as a redistributive tool. These factors thus produced lower growth performance, save for a few episodes of temporary recovery. It therefore appears that the role of initial conditions was dislodged by a changing regime, associated with a lower growth trajectory. But what explains this lower growth performance? There seems to be a combination of factors, but the most compelling ones come from political-economy issues and the destruction of the incentive structure. First, there was the political capture of both institutions and bureaucrats. Second, risk and uncertainty took center stage and policies became extremely short term. Third, there were policy-induced risks, and policy reversals were more prevalent in the 1980s and 1990s, thus compounding the problem of short-term response rather than long-term planning. Fourth, the collapse of the EAC in 1977 substantially reduced Kenya's market, and firms established under the import-substitution policy with large installed capacity started to suffer. Fifth, the "Dutch disease" effect from the 1976–7 coffee boom had two contributions – namely, expanded fiscal expenditures and appreciation of the exchange rate. The former reduced long-run growth while the latter was a disincentive to exporters and hence checked growth. Finally, all these factors added to governance problems, and weak economic management led to severe tensions with donors.

In summary, even though these two phases do seem to explain broadly the growth experience with initial conditions and regime shifts, there appear to have been intermediating factors coming through internal and external shocks. First, the commodity boom of 1976–7 ushered in the familiar "Dutch disease" symptoms, but above all triggered an unsustainable fiscal position. In addition, this boom may have been the one single factor that led to a switch in regime towards redistribution. The "aid embargo" in the 1990s was also a strong factor both to speed up reforms but also negatively to signal non-credibility of government policies. Finally, the ethnic tensions coming with competitive politics seem to have driven poverty and growth far from their targets in the 1990s.

References

Ali, A. A. and I. E. Elbadawi (1999), "Inequality and the Dynamics of Poverty and Growth," mimeo

Azam, J.-P. and C. Daubreé (1997), "Bypassing the State: Economic Growth in Kenya, 1964–90," Paris: OECD

Barkan, J. D. (1984), "Legislators, Elections and Political Linkage," in J. D. Barkan, ed., *Politics and Public Policy in Kenya and Tanzania*. New York: Praeger

Barro, R. and J.-W. Lee (1993), "International Comparisons of Educational Attainment," *Journal of Monetary Economics* 32(3), December: 363–94

Bates, R. H. (1989), *Beyond the Miracle of the Market: The Political Economy of Agrarian Development in Kenya*. Cambridge: Cambridge University Press

Bigsten, A. (1986), "Welfare and Economic Growth in Kenya, 1974–76," *World Development* 14(19), September: 1151–60

    (2002), "History and Policy of Manufacturing in Kenya," in A. Bigsten and P. Kimuyu, eds., *Structure and Performance of Manufacturing in Kenya*. New York: Palgrave

Bigsten, A. and N. S. Ndung'u (1991), "Structural Adjustment and the African Farmer: Kenya Case Study," in A. Duncan and J. Howell, eds., *Structural Adjustment & the African Farmer*. London: ODI

Brett, E. A. (1973), *Colonialism and Underdevelopment in East Africa*. New York: NOK Publishers

Collier, P. (2001), "Ethnic Diversity: An Economic Analysis of Its Implications," *Economic Policy* 32: 129–66

Collins, S. and B. Bosworth (1996), "Economic Growth in East Asia: Accumulation versus Assimilation," *Brookings Papers on Economic Activity* 2: 135–203

Coughlin, P. (1988), "Towards a New Industrialization Strategy in Kenya," in P. Coughlin and G. K. Ikiara, *Industrialization in Kenya: In Search of a Strategy*. Nairobi: Heinemann Kenya in association with James Currey

Fielding, D. (1993), "Determinants of Investment in Kenya and Côte d"Ivoire," *Journal of African Economies* 3(3): 299–328

Glenday, G. and T. Ryan (2000), "Trade Liberalization and Growth in Kenya," Equity and Growth through Economic Research (EAGER) Project, Policy Brief 43, June

Government of Kenya (2000), *Poverty Reduction Strategy Paper 2000–2003*. Nairobi: Government Printer

Hoeffler, A. E. (1999), "The Augmented Solow Model and the African Growth Debate," CSAE Working Paper, University of Oxford

Kenya (1965), *The Sessional Paper 10 on African Socialism and its Application to Planning in Kenya*. Nairobi: Government of Kenya

Kenya, Central Bureau of Statistics (various issues), *Welfare Monitoring Surveys*. Nairobi: Government Printer

Kenya (1979–84; 1984–9; 1997–2001), *National Development Plan*. Nairobi: Government Printer

Kenya (various years), *Economic Survey*. Nairobi: Government Printer

Kimenyi, M. (1998), "Harmonizing Ethnic Claims in Africa: A Proposal for Ethnic Based Federalism," *Cato Journal* 18(1): 43–63

Kimenyi, M. and N. S. Ndung'u (2002), "Sporadic Ethnic Violence: Why has Kenya not Experienced a Full Blown Civil War," Paper Presented at the World Bank Conference on the Economics of Political and Criminal Violence, Yale University, April 12–14

Levin, J. and N. S. Ndung'u (2002), "The Impact of Structural Adjustment Policies on Manufacturing," in A. Bigsten and P. Kimuyu, eds., *Structure and Performance of Manufacturing in Kenya*. New York: Palgrave

Manda, D. K. (1997), "Labor Supply, Returns to Education, and the Effect of Firm Size on Wages: The Case of Kenya," Ekonomiska Studier Utgivna av Nationalekonomiska Institutionen Handlshögskolan vid Göteborg Universitet 75

Matin, K. M. and B. Wasow (1992), "Adjustment and Private Investment in Kenya," World Bank Policy Research Working Papers WPS878, March

Morton, A. (1998), *Moi: The Making of An African Statesman*. London: Michael O'Mara Books

Mwega, F. M. (1993), "Import Demand Elasticities and Stability during Trade Liberalization: A Case Study of Kenya," *Journal of African Economics* 2(3), December: 381–46

  (2002), "Promotion of Non-traditional Exports in Kenya, 1980–96," in G. K. Helleiner, ed., *Non-traditional Export Promotion in Africa: Experience and Issues*. New York: Palgrave

Nasibi, R. I. (1992), "Financial Institutions and Monetary Policy in Post-Independent Kenya," in W. R. Ochieng and R. M. Maxon, eds., *An Economic History of Kenya*. Nairobi: East African Educational Publishers

Ndulu, B. J. and S. A. O'Connell (2000), "Background Information on Economic Growth," Paper prepared for the Explaining Economic Growth Project. Nairobi: African Economic Research Consortium (downloadable: www.aercafrica.org)

Ndung'u, N. S. (1999), "Monetary and Exchange Rate Policy in Kenya," AERC Research Paper 94

Ndung'u, N. S. and F. M. Mwega (1999), "Macroeconomic Policies and Real Exchange Rate Behavior in Kenya: 1975–1995," in J. de Brun and R. Luders, eds., *Macroeconomic Policy and the Exchange Rate*. Stockton, CA: International Center for Economic Growth

Swamy, G. (1994), "Kenya: Structural Adjustment in the 1980s," *World Bank Policy Research Working Paper* 1238

Syrquin, M. and C. Kenny (1999), "Growth and Transformation in East Africa," in S. Yusuf *et al.*, Tanzania: *Peri-urban Development in the African Mirror, World Bank Report* 19526 TA, June

Takahashi, M. (1997), "Changing Rules of the Game in a Multi-ethnic Sub-Saharan African Country: Economic Resource Mechanism in Kenya," Paper presented at a World Bank Workshop on the Political Economy of Rural Development Strategy, May 5–6

van Ginneken, W. and J. Park (1984), *Generating International Comparable Income Distribution Estimates.* Geneva: International Labour Organization

World Bank (1975), *Kenya into the Second Decade.* Baltimore, MD: John Hopkins University Press

11 | A shared growth story of economic success: the case of Mauritius

Shyam Nath and Yeti Nisha Madhoo

1. Introduction

Mauritius is unique because of its small size, location, and international dependence. It is an island in the Indian Ocean, 2,000 km off the east coast of Africa. It is a city-state of 1.2 million inhabitants with an area of 1,853 km². It has several island dependencies; the largest is Rodrigues, which is located about 560 km further east.

Mauritius inherited all the features of a backward economy – surplus labor, lack of natural resources, high commodity trade dependence (sugar), distance from present-day sea lanes resulting in high transport costs, a small domestic market, and a division of population on ethnic and religious lines. Its tropical climate suggested a high exposure to diseases capable of undermining labor productivity. Nevertheless, Mauritius witnessed remarkable

Department of Economics, University of Mauritius, Le Reduit, Mauritius.

growth despite the global slowdown that took place after the first oil shock in the early 1970s. The country's cumulative growth raised its *per capita* income from US$1,000 in 1982 to more than US$3,000 in 1995, putting Mauritius in the category of upper-middle-income countries. The country attained near-full employment by 1990 (about 1.5 percent unemployment rate), with *per capita* real income growing at an average of 5 percent in recent years.

Whereas during 1960–1990 economic growth can be attributed mainly to the use of traditional inputs, namely labor and capital, the significance of TFP rose remarkably after 1990, contributing to about 25 percent of the growth rate (IMF 2001). This compares favorably with the East Asian Tigers, but it is in contrast with African experience, which witnessed a decline in the rate of TFP growth (Collins and Bosworth 1996). Mauritius also fared well in terms of the Human Development Index (HDI), primary and secondary school enrollment rates, life expectancy, and income distribution.

On the fiscal front, Mauritius has maintained a moderate tax to GDP ratio (less than 20 percent) and fiscal deficits of less than 5 percent of GDP. The inflation rate has not crossed 8 percentage points. The ratio of government expenditure to GDP has fallen drastically, from 33.5 percent in 1975 to 24 percent in 1995, releasing more resources for social sectors (Nath 2001). Thus, the role of government has been drastically reduced in economic sectors giving way to the private sector. Savings rates increased from 17 percent of GDP in 1982 to about 24 percent of GDP in 1995. Current account deficits were scaled down over time, to –0.6 percent of GDP in 1995, from –7.0 percent in 1982.

These developments converted a mono-crop economy based on cane sugar into a newly industrializing and increasingly diversified modern economy. The success story of Mauritius has attracted many researchers; indeed, the country is considered a model of economic development. It was not always so, however. In the early 1960s, Meade's predictions for Mauritius were strikingly gloomy (Meade *et al.* 1961). Meade believed that the colonial heritage would have an adverse effect on growth prospects, and that the tropical climate would also create a drag on growth. It is evident from table 11.1 that Mauritius was not favorably endowed with initial conditions, which apparently guided Meade to take a defensive position and to recommend the traditional package of policies favoring import-substituting industrialization (ISI). In fact, he recommended welfare assistance to Mauritius from overseas.

We shall revisit this success story in this chapter, which is organized as follows. Section 2 outlines the contributions of this study to the existing literature. Section 3 attempts to analyze the growth process over different periods, utilizing the concepts of syndromes and episodes. Section 4 employs benchmarking and counterfactual analysis to examine missed growth opportunities. A brief analysis is presented, keeping in view the spectacular growth performance of East Asian countries which could have been replicated in

Table 11.1 *Inheritance, Mauritius versus the rest of the world*[a]

	Mauritius	Africa	Fast-growing economies	All other developing economies
Inheritance				
Catch-up[b]	8.72	7.29	7.90	7.85
Life expectancy in years (c. 1970) (human capital)	60.40	41.60	57.10	51.90
Ethno-linguistic fractionalization[c]	0.58	0.68	0.42	0.32
Population growth[d]	0.97	−0.09	0.82	0.33
Share of primary exports in total exports	0.29	0.18	0.09	0.12
Geography				
Fraction of area in tropical climate	1.00	0.89	0.69	0.59
Landlocked[e]	0.00	0.33	0.00	0.11
Remoteness from economic center of the world (km)[f]	11,249	9,183	9,464	8,633

[a] The fast-growing countries include China, Hong Kong SAR, Indonesia, Malaysia, Singapore and Thailand.
[b] Log of real GDP per economically active population, 1965.
[c] Probability that two randomly selected people from a country will not belong to the same ethnic or linguistic group.
[d] Growth of working-age population minus growth of total population between 1965 and 1990.
[e] 1 if landlocked, 0 if not. For a group it depicts the fraction of countries landlocked.
[f] Remoteness of a country is its average distance to trading partners, weighted by their share in world GDP.
Sources: Sachs and Warner (1997); Subramanian and Roy (2001).

Mauritius. Section 5 is devoted to expanding the analytical framework to capture growth dynamics by moving away from initial conditions and traditional determinants. Three major sources of growth – geography, globalization, and institutions – are examined in section 6 with a view to identifying the factors pertinent to economic success in Mauritius. A synthesis of these three stylized sources of growth is presented by laying emphasis on improved income distribution and shared growth as major sources of success. These resulted from the strategy of economic diversification and from political-economy factors. The final section 7 summarizes the main findings of the research.

2. Revisiting the economic success story

The spectacular growth accomplished in Mauritius presents a challenge of interpretation, in terms of both the main determinants of growth and of policy implications for other emerging economies. Below, we consider two leading alternatives, one a partial story dominated by EPZs and FDI, and the other a broader account integrating a variety of other factors including geography and institutions. In the partial story, the Mauritian economic miracle is driven almost exclusively by EPZs, FDI, and cheap labor (Romer 1992; Rodrik 1999). Even within its own terms, this approach under-emphasizes two additional features that were critical to the success of export-oriented manufacturing in Mauritius: the international political economy factor, in the form of preferential access to developed-country markets, and the substantial participation of local investors.

Our main contribution, however, is in synthesizing this still-partial account with the one in which geography, globalization, and institutions – factors that feature importantly in the broader literature on economic growth (Easterly and Levine 2003; Subramanian and Roy 2003; Rodrik, Subramanian, and Trebbi 2004) – play prominent roles. Our central contention is that the Mauritian success story can be understood in terms of improved income distribution and shared growth. The mechanisms of shared growth were various. The decline of sugar, for example, was not driven by a deteriorating terms of trade for this commodity; rather, the government aggressively exploited sugar preferences in European markets, with the result that this sector prospered, generating a substantial surplus for investment in other sectors of the economy. The export-promotion policy, in turn, was designed to avoid spatial concentration of benefits: the EPZs were legal rather than geographical entities, encouraging the regional diversification of production and employment. Political-economy factors also contributed; policies were implemented that produced growth with redistribution. Coalitional politics, together with a tendency for ethnic groups to specialize in different economic sectors and a strong presence of the Indo-Mauritian population in political management, helped to generate a wide distribution of growth proceeds. The political majority was able to transfer to itself a portion of the sugar surplus that had accrued largely to the Franco-Mauritian economic elite. The instruments of this sharing mechanism included the maintenance of a large and relatively well-paid civil service (of predominantly Indian origin) and a generous system of social security, mostly in the form of old-age pensions.

A social consensus in favor of shared growth has the potential to improve incentive mechanisms by motivating both political and economic agents to choose policies that encourage investment and saving. In the case of Mauritius, such a consensus played a central role in translating the opportunities

represented by international trade and globalization, institutional development, and geography into an effective platform for sustained rapid growth.

3. Periodization: episodes and syndromes

Mauritius is one of only two African countries to have enjoyed sustained
rapid growth over the last forty years (Botswana being the other). However,
there were significant differences across growth episodes, particularly during
the first two decades – the 1960s and 1970s – corresponding to a shift away
from the sugar-dominated and state-led import-substitution strategy to
one that focused on a policy-guided and private sector-led diversification
strategy based on market principles. The country's success originated in
turning away from a potentially disastrous path that had dogged many other
countries in SSA since 1982, preventing them from achieving sustained
growth.

During 1960–71, a development strategy dominated by import substitution was implemented, based on the 1960 Meade Report (Meade *et al.* 1961)
and similar in many ways to strategies adopted elsewhere in the continent.
The aim was to diversify away from dependence on sugar by subsidizing
manufacturing (via long-term loans from the Development Bank of Mauritius, DBM) and protecting industry (behind tariff walls and import quotas) based on the infant-industry argument. The result was a poor growth
performance (an average *per capita* growth of 0.7 percent) coupled with
an unemployment rate of 20 percent. The island was still under imperial
domination; what emerged as development strategy was the conventional
wisdom.

During the second period, 1971–81, after achieving independence in 1968,
a strong parliamentary democratic political regime was created. Certain
major political decisions were taken in order to move away from the existing development strategy. Rapid growth of 8.2 percent annually was accomplished as a result of the introduction of export enclaves (EPZs) and entry
into the Lomé Convention in 1972, which provided preferential arrangements for Mauritian sugar exports to Europe. The world sugar price boom
of 1972–5, in which prices rose three-fold, added to the investible resource
base of local entrepreneurs, who dominated investment in the early phase
of EPZ development, though often in partnership with foreign investors.

A part of this surplus in the sugar sector was mopped up by the government
through a sugar export tax. While this provided valuable public revenues
it also served to discourage aggressive reinvestment in the sugar industry.
Other aspects of the policy environment, including exchange controls and a
prohibition on investment abroad, also favored the diversion of private sugar
surpluses into domestic investment in export-promoting industrialization.

These developments can be compared with the policy of agriculture taxation in Japan during the Meiji Restoration, which was designed to finance state-led industrialization. In the Mauritian context, however, the government's sugar tax policy helped divert the agricultural surpluses to EPZs and the hotel industry.

It is noteworthy that the ruling coalition of Labor and the Mauritian Social Democratic Party (PMSD) turned its development strategy more to the right and away from Fabian socialism, granting a greater role to the private sector and foreign investors. The bulk of the sugar surplus therefore remained in private hands, and both savings and investment rates rose sharply. During the period of this boom, macroeconomic policy, though relatively prudent, came under severe populist pressures as political competition intensified around welfare concerns. The growth performance witnessed signs of severe strain whereby a meager average growth rate of 1.7 percent was produced, and the inflation rate rose to 42 percent due to a spending boom arising from populist pressures during 1978–83. It was a period of potential democratic failure that threatened the growth path of the economy. Between 1976 and 1983, the country went through three general elections (1976, 1982, and 1983) with fluid political coalitions, before settling down to a broad-spectrum coalition with a durable interest in growth. Sharp and decisive macroeconomic reform measures were undertaken towards the end of the period under an IMF/World Bank program – a major devaluation, a removal of subsidies, and a reduction of the fiscal deficit.

A phenomenal revival of growth took place during 1983–7, with a rapid expansion of EPZs and international tourism, followed by a consolidation phase based on an FDI- and export-led diversification strategy that focused on improved competitiveness and skill formation. The marked expansion in FDI was spurred on by two factors: an inflow of foreign capital fleeing from potential expropriation as Hong Kong was returned to China, and the availability of preferential access to the USA and European Community (EC) markets, particularly with East Asian exporters coming up against quota limitations under the Multi-Fiber Agreement (MFA). With the predominantly labor-intensive technology in use, the availability of human capital due to unemployment, combined with a policy of wage restraint, served as an advantage for attracting East Asian FDI.

Mauritius relied on selected controls throughout the period of analysis; the process of liberalization started in a phased manner only by the end of the century. As analyzed by Rodrik (1999), Mauritius had an unusual, restrictive trade regime, which effectively segmented its export sector from the rest of the economy. High tariff walls provided protection to the import-competing sectors but their import of inputs was also taxed. The export sector enjoyed fiscal concessions, including inputs that were exempted from import taxes. Restrictions also existed in labor and capital markets, with a significant effect in both. The restrictive nature of trade policy is revealed by the IMF's trade policy index, which ranked Mauritius among the most restrictive countries in the early 1990s, with an index value of 10. The IMF index had fallen only to 7 by the end of the 1990s (IMF 2001).

In their taxonomy of recurring policy regimes in SSA, Collier and O'Connell (2007) classify Mauritius as subject to "soft controls" during 1960–70 and as "syndrome-free" for the remainder of the 1971–2000 period. The latter classification is consistent with our view that after the early 1970s, the manufacturing export sector was insulated from the distorting effects of protection elsewhere in the economy. Where high rates of effective protection persisted, they served primarily as a growth-sharing mechanism, rather than as an industrial policy. For similar reasons, although redistribution was a feature of the Mauritian strategy, the country clearly avoided the negative-sum "redistributive syndrome," in which politically powerful groups undermine growth in order to divert a larger share of the economy's output to themselves (Collier and O'Connell 2007; Fosu 2007). In Mauritius, the bulk of redistribution was achieved through a diversified pattern of growth and, in turn, reinforced growth prospects further.

4. Benchmarking and counterfactual analysis

The various sources of growth have been identified in the literature generally using three approaches – parsimonious structural models like Hoeffler's (2002) augmented Solow model, more loosely specified regression models like the pooled conditional model of O'Connell and Ndulu (2000), and finally growth accounting, as in Collins and Bosworth (1996). Table 11.2 provides the growth decomposition by half-decades as calculated by Collins and Bosworth (1996). Mauritius seems to be midway between the East Asia and Pacific region and SSA in terms of growth in real GDP per worker. However a slight difference prevails. The disparity between Mauritius and East Asia and Pacific is 82 percent, in contrast to SSA, which is 70 percent. The results further suggest that the contribution of physical capital to growth in Mauritius is the lowest: 0.18 compared to the Asian and SSA countries, which are 0.5 and 0.23, respectively. But physical capital's contribution to growth started to pick up in the post-1985 period, becoming significantly higher after 1990. The contribution of physical capital per worker thus compared favorably with East Asia and Pacific. In the case of the contribution of education per worker, once again the East Asia and Pacific countries take the lead with 0.5, followed by Mauritius and the SSA countries with 0.38 and 0.23, respectively. These results further indicate the importance of the contribution of the residuals – that is, TFP growth – towards growth in Mauritius in contrast to SSA and East Asia and Pacific.

Table 11.2 *Mauritius, East Asia and Pacific, and SSA, growth-accounting decompositions, 1960–1997*

| | Mauritius | | | | East Asia and Pacific | | | | SSA | | | |
| | | Contribution of | | | | Contribution of | | | | Contribution of | | |
Period	Growth in real GDP per worker	Physical capital per worker	Education per worker	TFP growth residual	Growth in real GDP per worker	Physical capital per worker	Education per worker	TFP growth residual	Growth in real GDP per worker	Physical capital per worker	Education per worker	TFP growth residual
1960–4	3.82	−0.3	0.48	3.64	1.81	1.84	0.4	−0.43	1.26	0.86	0.14	0.26
1965–9	−2.31	−0.68	0.42	−2.04	4.29	2.27	0.51	1.51	1.6	1.03	0.18	0.39
1970–4	4.57	0.27	0.42	3.88	4.55	2.51	0.4	1.64	2.29	1.22	0.2	0.87
1975–9	3.04	0.64	0.62	1.78	4.39	2.43	0.47	1.49	−0.1	0.81	0.27	−1.18
1980–4	−2.33	−0.65	0.33	−2.01	3.54	2.4	0.67	0.47	−1.28	0.41	0.3	−1.99
1985–9	4.9	0.56	0.24	4.1	3.52	1.69	0.69	1.15	0.64	0.06	0.3	0.28
1990–7	3.04	1.39	0.14	1.51	4.94	2.29	0.39	2.26	−1.55	−0.14	0.18	−1.59
Total	**2.1**	**0.18**	**0.38**	**1.55**	**3.86**	**2.2**	**0.5**	**1.15**	**0.44**	**0.61**	**0.23**	**−0.42**

Source: Collins and Bosworth (1996).

It can be argued that some countries in East Asia, particularly Singapore and Hong Kong, served as a benchmark for the growth opportunities that were open to Mauritius. These countries are relatively similar to Mauritius in terms of size, tropical climate, export orientation, and lack of natural resources. Nevertheless, they have succeeded in attracting foreign capital on a significantly higher scale and reaching higher educational standards. Since the average growth rates of these countries have far exceeded that of Mauritius, these experiences can be utilized in constructing counterfactuals for missed growth opportunities.

5. Beyond the initial conditions and traditional determinants

From the preceding description it is evident that this economic success has several dimensions, which would take us much beyond the typical contributions from labor and capital and beyond the initial conditions that Mauritius inherited. There are three groups of economists, who have taken distinct positions to explain the clearly visible differences in the economic performance of Africa, Mauritius, and the East Asia and Pacific region. A first group attributes this success to the globalization route – that is, to an FDI-led and export-driven growth strategy supported by complementary domestic policies. A second group stresses variations in the quality of domestic institutions across countries. A third group lays the emphasis on physical geography, stressing location and climate as key determining factors (Easterly and Levine 2003; Rodrik, Subramanian, and Trebbi 2004).

5.1   Geography

It has been discussed in the literature that economic growth rates have some relationship with coastal, tropical, and temperate climates. Tropical countries produce lower growth rates than non-tropical countries. Nearly all countries in the geographic tropics are poor, due to higher disease burdens and limitations on agricultural productivity. Almost all countries in the mid- and high latitudes are rich. Moreover, coastal countries generally have higher incomes than landlocked countries, and countries in which the bulk of the population is coastal – with access to oceans or ocean-navigable rivers – grow more rapidly than countries with largely interior populations (Gallup and Sachs with Mellinger 1999). Geographical remoteness also reduces growth by increasing the transport costs associated with international trade (Limão and Venables 2001).

The size, location, and climate of Mauritius should have major consequences for its economic growth. Among 148 countries listed in the World Bank's *World Development Indicators*, Mauritius is ranked 146th in terms of area (bigger than only Singapore and Hong Kong) and 148th in terms of population, along with Estonia, Gabon, The Gambia, and Trinidad and Tobago. Size can affect policy choices: for instance, the size of the country may explain why Mauritius opted for external trade dependence. Small domestic markets, for example, limit the scope for achieving economies of scale in manufacturing based on the domestic market alone (Briguglio 1998). There may be disadvantages to small size even if export markets are used to break the scale constraint; Porter (1990), for example, places a strong emphasis on the role of competition for the domestic market in improving international competitiveness. Contrary to the Porter model, however, competition for the domestic market does not appear to have played an important role as a training ground for export-oriented firms in Mauritius.

As documented by Wellisz and Saw (1993), Mauritius' resource endowment – particularly its subtropical climate and rich volcanic soil – is favorable for a diversified agriculture. Due to the mountainous terrain, regional ecologies differ and there exist a variety of sub-climates. However, since Mauritius is in the strong cyclone belt, the threat of serious cyclones exists, which has implications for domestic agriculture. Much of the water supply depends on rainfall, which is brought by clouds associated with these cyclones. During 1960–2000, four or five cyclones had devastating effects on agriculture and infrastructure: Cyclone Hollanda in 1994, in particular, caused a sharp reduction in the growth rate of real GDP *per capita*.

Mauritius has no contiguous neighbors and is therefore insulated from the direct "neighborhood effects" emphasized in the growth literature, including spillovers from economic growth and/or civil conflict (Easterly and Levine 1998). Mauritius has nonetheless been an active supporter of regional trade integration, in an effort to expand its economic space. Its integration with the global economy is of course well established through its trade links with developed-country markets; Srinivasan (1986) argues that such integration is particularly important for small countries, where it can overcome the restrictions on specialization and exchange that would otherwise prevail in local markets.

Lack of mineral natural resources and its extreme vulnerability to the whims and caprices of a tropical climate may have a dampening impact on growth prospects. But nature has favored Mauritius with extraordinary beaches, extensive marine resources, and beautiful landscape, which attract tourists from the rest of the world. On a global basis, international tourism is one of the most important tradable sectors, with expenditure on tourist goods and services representing about 8 percent of total world export receipts. Lanza and Pigliaru (1999) used a two-sector endogenous growth model to demonstrate that many tourist countries have grown faster compared to other countries. They argued that manufacturing and international tourism are complementary and tend to reinforce each other. In the Mauritian growth context, the tourist sector can be viewed as a balancing factor in the process of economic transformation. Whereas sugar-based agriculture and the textile sector contributed to rapidly expanding export proceeds for investment, international tourism provided a cushion of steady foreign exchange earnings, gradually establishing itself as the third pillar of the economy after sugar and the EPZ. Tourist arrivals increased steadily over time, from only 10,000 in the early 1960s to 6,56,450 in 2000 (CSO, various years, a). Between 1990 and 1998, the tourism sector experienced an annual average real growth rate of 9.8 percent, while manufacturing and agriculture grew by 5.6 percent and 0.6 percent, respectively. As a percentage of total exports, earnings from tourism increased from 5.9 percent in 1975 to 14.9 percent in 1990 and to 19 percent in 1998. The influence of tourism on the economy depends in part on the retention of foreign currency in the country. In Mauritius, leakage of foreign currency earnings has been relatively low, with the bulk of industry financing generated locally and management mainly in the hands of Mauritian nationals (World Bank 1989).

5.2   Globalization

Given geography, colonial heritage, and dependence on sugar exports and international tourism, there were two options available to Mauritius: to maintain the status quo in terms of development policy or to diversify and expand its limited economic base through further opening the economy. The trade-in-goods to GDP ratio increased from 70 to 100 percent during the decade 1980–90, which is much higher in comparison to the 45 percent (approximately) for SSA. Even though this ratio is considerably lower than what was obtained in the East Asian economies, which increased from 85 percent to 180 percent during 1973–2000, Mauritius possessed quite a diversified export and import structure (see table 11.3). It is therefore expected that its external dependence is very high.

5.2.1   Export-oriented FDI

Apparently, the real story of economic success started in 1983 when the newly elected government introduced an economic policy to foster economic transformation by diversifying into manufacturing for exports. The alternatives included: (a) the purchase of new machinery and equipment and hiring consultants, (b) FDI, (c) the purchase of new technology licenses for domestic production of new products or the use of new processes. The adopted strategy was a mixture, with a view to encouraging international best practice technology for the production of textiles and clothing, for which an EPZ was created. The open door policy consisted of unrestricted tariff-free imports of machinery and materials, no restrictions on ownership or repatriation of profits, a ten-year income tax holiday, and a policy

Table 11.3 *Mauritius, international trade and tourism earnings, 1976–1995*

Year	Exports % of GDP			Imports % of GDP		
	Manufacturing	Sugar	Tourism	Intermediate consumption goods	Final consumption goods	Capital goods
1976	6.57	28.10	3.91	25.17	15.64	5.95
1980	10.28	24.93	4.15	29.43	13.84	5.25
1981	10.65	15.92	4.12	26.25	12.03	4.03
1985	19.69	17.25	5.08	29.75	9.33	3.94
1986	25.31	18.04	6.04	32.94	7.32	5.24
1990	29.22	13.27	8.91	36.44	9.99	9.49
1991	27.37	11.95	8.89	32.40	10.11	7.95
1995	26.38	9.16	10.14	28.82	9.46	6.75

Source: Computed from the *National Accounts Statistics,* CSO, Government of Mauritius.

of centralized wage setting to enlist moderate wage increases and industrial peace. Thus, the tax-free zone was designed not as a geographical area, but rather as an economic activity, textile and clothing manufacturing.

This package of EPZs generated a major foreign direct investment response from Hong Kong and a few other countries. An international technology transfer took place and local investors also joined in the process. EPZ textiles and clothing firms were largely owned by local investors (55 percent), which was followed by joint ventures (35 percent) and fully foreign owned (15 percent) (Fowdar 1991). The local investment was financed from the surpluses of the sugar sector, derived from the series of sugar booms beginning in the 1970s.[1]

There are two additional factors that contributed significantly to the massive manufacturing growth in Mauritius. First, the threat of expropriation by the mainland Chinese government in the case of investors from Hong Kong is considered to be decisive in explaining the arrival of FDI in Mauritius. Nevertheless, there was a second factor, seemingly the more important one, which placed Mauritius as a country of origin that would not be subject to quota limits set by the European Economic Community (EEC) and the USA. Mauritius has been the beneficiary of trade agreements, such as the Lomé/Cotonou conventions (which gave preferential access to Mauritius exports to the European market) and the MFA, which allowed Mauritius to build up its export-oriented garment industry.

Thus, whereas EPZ growth can be explained in terms of policies governing the Zone (as described above), a major source of strength came from preferential access to industrialized countries' markets. The origin of

[1] For a good discussion of sugar booms in Mauritius, see Blake *et al.* (1994).

Table 11.4 *Mauritius, growth accounting for the EPZ, 1982–1999*

| Period | Output growth | Contribution from growth in | | |
		Capital formation	Labor force	TFP
1982–90	19.0	24.1	17.5	−0.8
1991–9	5.7	0.7	0.0	5.4
1982–99	10.2	9.5	5.4	3.5

Source: IMF (2001).

this preferential treatment from these countries emanated from designing restrictions on exports from Hong Kong to their markets; they used quota allocations under MFA arrangements in an attempt to break the monopoly of low-cost countries such as Hong Kong. Countries with a relatively higher cost of production were allocated import quotas, which benefited Mauritius as well. This policy was guided by the contention that if more countries had preferential treatment, world production would increase.

The financial implications of these preferential treatments have been considerable. According to Subramanian and Roy (2003), the financial benefits – in conjunction with the direct benefits under the EPZ scheme – outweighed the disincentive effects of an anti-export bias in the form of protection offered to import-competing sectors. FDI inflows to EPZ firms can also be explained in terms of these preferences.

It may be pertinent to note here that developing-country MNCs tend to differ from western MNCs in that the former have derived their comparative advantage from smallness of scale, labor-intensive technology, and flexible product lines (Lecraw 1977; Lall 1983; Wells 1983). In other words, their competitive edge depended to a greater extent on relatively lower cost of production than on superior technology. However, in the Mauritian context, superior technology is also important because of the location of its export markets in those parts of the world where western MNCs also operated. Although most of the manufacturing exports have been governed by protected markets and conventions, the existence of developing-country MNCs along with western MNCs in the western markets ensured international, best-practice technology.

The expansion of value added through upgrading technology and/or diversifying the product range was vital. According to the IMF's calculations (IMF 2001), EPZ growth performance, unlike the aggregate growth rate, has been underpinned not just by rapid factor accumulation but also by a very high rate of TFP growth (table 11.4). During the period 1991–9, value added produced within EPZs grew at the rate of 5.7 percent per annum, out of which 5.4 percent could be explained by TFP growth. In

Table 11.5 *Mauritius, trade policies*

Sector	Main Form of Assistance
Import-substituting manufacturing	
Large new activities (e.g. foodstuffs, assembly of color televisions)	Development certificates scheme, tariff and import and quota protection
Other	Import licensing and tariff protection
Export-oriented manufacturing	
Wholly (e.g. knitwear)	Export Enterprise certificate scheme
Partially (e.g. furniture)	Tax rebate based on export growth
Agriculture	
Sugar: large growers	Tax of 23.6% on gross export receipts
Sugar: small growers	–
Rice	Subsidized exchange rate and subsidy payments on rice
Other agriculture	–

Source: Dabee and Milner (1999).
Note: – refers to the absence of a major trade policy intervention.

other words, capital accumulation has played a greater role in the economy as a whole but TFP growth contributed more to EPZ growth. It has been argued in the literature that the impact of FDI flows is significantly positive in economies which pursue an export-promotion strategy and not significant in countries which are characterized by an import-substitution policy (Balasubramanyam, Salisu, and Sabsford 1996).

5.2.2   Trade policy and liberalization

Besides FDI, trade policies seem to have been crucial in promoting the growth of the Mauritian economy. These policies comprised measures of import substitution, export-promotion assistance for manufactured goods and non-traditional agriculture, and export taxation of traditional export (such as sugar; see table 11.5). Signs of trade liberalization were seen only after 1979–83, the period of macroeconomic stabilization and exchange rate adjustment. Reforms before 1985 were limited mainly to liberalization of foreign exchange and import-licensing restrictions and reform of the border taxation of imports. The main phase of import liberalization and reduction of protection for local firms came in the period 1985–7, with the progressive dismantling of quantitative import restrictions. In 1987, the government reduced the maximum tariff rate to 110 percent, except for petroleum, tobacco products, and alcoholic beverages. Major tariff reductions took place in 1988, when fiscal and custom duties on a large number of commodities were abolished.

The process of trade liberalization was made credible through the availability of information. The government kept informing economic agents about the reform process – for example, the rising level of foreign exchange reserves was frequently advertised to increase confidence in the economy. Nevertheless, the government was cautious about the liberalization process; it was not fully submissive to the World Bank, which was expecting a reform of the tariff structure to follow the removal of QRs. The government argued that any further liberalization would be unsustainable as it would destabilize the balance of payments and the fiscal deficit. Liberalization resurfaced in July 1994 when a major revamping of the tariff structure was introduced. That year, the fiscal duty, the customs duty, and the import levy were merged into one customs duty. The maximum rate of the former three tariffs, which averaged 600 percent before the reform, was reduced to about 80 percent with the customs duty.

In assessing the effects of import protection on resource allocation in Mauritius, an important distinction should be made between revenue-generating and protective tariffs. Since Mauritius is a small country, there is no local production of many imported commodities. The case of motor vehicles serves as an illustration: there is no local automobile industry, so high tariffs on motor vehicle imports are motivated by revenue rather than by industrial policy. They restrict the demand for imported vehicles but not the competitive environment for (non-existent) domestic firms.

Levels of effective protection have nonetheless been comparatively high in Mauritius, as documented in tables 11.6 and 11.7, and they increased during the 1980s. Mauritius exceeded the African average on various indicators, suggesting that it cannot be classified as a strong reformer of restrictive trade policies. We noted earlier that the IMF's index of trade policy, which placed Mauritius at a level of 10 in the early 1990s (and therefore among the most restrictive countries) had declined only to 7 by the end of the decade.

The tendency on the part of researchers embarking on any research on trade and growth is to assume that trade restrictions are harmful for growth. Attempts have been made to establish this relationship. Nevertheless, Rodriguez and Rodrik (1999) have shown, after reviewing the extensive literature in terms of methodological limitations, that little evidence has been produced to confirm that open trade policies are significantly associated with economic growth. Against this background, the policy of mixed regimes, as adopted by Mauritius (favoring both export- and import-competing sectors) can be termed a blessing in disguise. Import restrictions to provide protection to import-competing sectors, however, did not act as a tax on exporting firms. This was made possible by maintaining two trade policy regimes with few linkages. This gave a boost to import substitution and export promotion at the same time, with positive implications for the

Table 11.6 *Mauritius, estimates of effective
protection, 1980 and 1990, percent*

Sector	1980	1990
Beverages and tobacco	123	182
Textile yarn/fabrics	77	11
Apparel	99	4
Leather products	269	8
Footwear	158	88
Wood products	191	38
Furniture	130	241
Paper products	131	57
Printing/publishing	75	7
Chemical products	38	21
Rubber products	125	144
Plastic products	89	59
Non-metallic products	77	48
Iron/steel	154	73
Fabricated metal products	156	48
Machinery	62	3
Electrical machinery	179	181
Transport equipment	23	4
Optical goods, etc.	266	9
Average	127	65
Memorandum item:		
Share of imports under licenses	57	–

Source: Milner and McKay (1996).

balance of payments. These impacts can be largely attributed to trade policy
with selective interventions.

5.2.3   Labor market trends

Figure 11.1 tracks employment, real wages, and productivity in the manufacturing sector during and after the trade liberalization period. Employment
rose by a remarkable 150 percent between 1983 and 1989 before stabilizing during the 1990s. Real wages were initially flat but began to trend
upwards in the mid-1980s, a process that continued through the 1990s, well
after employment had stopped rising. The average product of labor fell by
20 percent during the period of rapid labor absorption, but then stabilized
and rose gradually during the 1990s.

The persistence of low real wages during a period of rapid employment expansion suggests that the manufacturing sector faced a highly elastic overall supply of labor. Milner and Wright (1998) analyzed wage and

Table 11.7 *Mauritius and Africa, openness*

Criterion	Mauritius	Africa average
Parallel market (index of foreign exchange restrictions) (1996)	4.0	2.8
Discrimination against imports excise taxes (average rate of taxation) (1996)	219.0	27.4
Maximum trade taxes on imports (includes statutory tariff rates plus surtaxes and the *ad valorem* equivalents of specific duties)	80.0	78.3
Exemptions as percentage of dutiable imports	13.2	18.9
Unweighted average tariff rate	26.4	17.2
Import weighted average tariff rate	20.3	12.4
Tariff collections as percent of GDP	6.0	2.6
Import weighted average tariff on consumer goods	25.2	19.7
Unweighted average import tariff on inputs	19.3	11.0
Unweighted average import tariff on capital goods	15.9	7.7
Indicators of effective protection in agriculture	19.5	18.2
Indicators of effective protection in manufacturing	150.2	82.7

Source: Hinkle and Herrou-Aragon (2001).

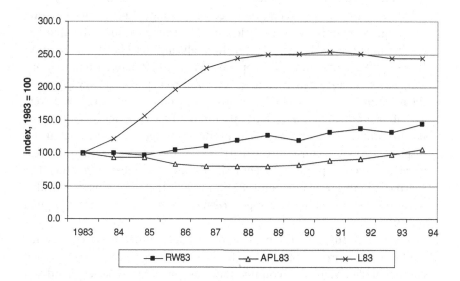

Figure 11.1 Mauritius, wage, productivity, and employment in manufacturing, 1983–1994
Notes: Data are from table 11.11, with all variables converted to index values of 100 in 1983. RW83 is the real wage: APL83 is the average product of labor; and L83 is employment.

employment dynamics in import-oriented and export-oriented manufacturing sectors in the Mauritian context using panel estimation techniques. From a standard two-sector perspective, *a priori* expectations were that wages and employment would rise in the exportable sectors but fall in the importable sectors due to the shifting structure of output. However, the results only partially supported these expectations. Employment in the exportable sectors did rise in response to trade liberalization, but real wage growth unexpectedly fell. More strikingly perhaps, employment and real wages actually expanded in the importable sectors following liberalization. Milner and Wright (1998) concluded that the most likely explanation for these results was that labor supply into manufacturing was not fixed. A very large increase in the labor supply occurred as females who had been under-employed or out of the labor force found employment in the EPZ. The elastic supply of female labor kept real wages low, while also allowing employment in the importable sector to be maintained as the exportable sector expanded. Employment in agriculture also fell during this period, providing a more traditional impetus to employment in the manufacturing sector. Investment figures document the central role of the EPZ in employment creation during this period: by 1985, the share of EPZ investment in total manufacturing investment had risen to 45 percent, from only 12 percent in 1982.

A comparison of wages across selected developing countries indeed shows that wages were initially relatively low in Mauritius as compared with other destinations (tables 11.8 and 11.9). In analyzing the Mauritian situation Romer (1992) argues that firms operating in the EPZ actually had monopsony power, at least initially, and so were able to pay workers a wage below the marginal product of labor. The divergent trends of real wages and average labor productivity in the latter part of the 1980s provide some support for this proposition. If the aggregate production function in manufacturing displays a roughly constant elasticity with respect to labor, then the real wage and average product of labor should move together over time. The sharp rise in this ratio between 1985 and 1990 is therefore consistent with a situation in which labor's real wage is rising over time relative to its marginal product.[2]

Table 11.10 suggests that physical capital accumulation played a dominant role in the growth response to trade liberalization in Mauritius. When compared with Mauritius, countries such as Korea, Malaysia, Thailand and

---

[2] The elasticity of output with respect to labor input is defined as $\varepsilon \equiv (\partial Y / \partial L)(L/Y)$. This is equal to the ratio MPL/APL, where MPL is the marginal product of labor and APL is the average product of labor. If this elasticity is approximately constant and labor is paid its marginal product, then the ratio w/APL should be constant over time. From this perspective, the sharp rise of w/APL in figure 11.1 between 1983 and 1989 is consistent with a situation in which w is rising relative to the marginal product, as firms' initial monopsony power is undermined by competition from new entrants to the EPZ.

Table 11.8 *Mauritius and other countries, relative annual wages in manufacturing, 1985–1993*

	Wages (US$ p.a.)			Mauritian wages as percent of others
	1985	1990	1993	1993
Mauritius	1,063	1,904	2,998	–
Sri Lanka	529	604	738	406.2
India	1,298	1,592	1,230	243.7
Pakistan	1,323	1,769	2,030	147.7
Bangladesh	557	854	905	331.3
Malaysia	3,375	3,240	4,148	72.3
Thailand	2,422	3,523	4,661	64.3
Indonesia	921	925	1,128	265.8
Philippines	1,257	1,968	2,433	123.2
China	384	500	656	457.0
Singapore	7,290	10,800	15,393	19.5
Hong Kong	4,808	9,161	13,220	22.7
Korea	3,476	9,353	12,269	24.4
Thailand	3,867	10,168	14,017	21.4

Note: Figures for Mauritius and other countries, being taken from different sources, may not be precisely comparable. However, broad indicative comparisons can be made.

Sources: CSO, *Annual Digest of Statistics* (1995); UNIDO, (1994, 1995).

Taiwan, achieved higher growth rates of total output during 1987–91, for lower or equal rates of physical investment. The comparison suggests that increases in human capital and/or TFP featured more importantly in these other countries than in Mauritius, at least over this period.[3] This is consistent with the lagging performance of average labor productivity in Mauritius during the period of rapid employment absorption. By the same token,

[3] If the production function takes the Cobb–Douglas form

$$Y = AK^{\alpha} H^{\beta} L^{1-\alpha-\beta},$$

where H is the stock of human capital, K is the physical capital stock, and A is the level of TFP, then the ratio of the growth rate of GDP to the net investment rate (see column (3) in table 11.10, which uses gross rather than net investment) is

$$g_Y/i = [(g_A + \beta g_H)/i] + (1 - \alpha - \beta)g_L/i + \alpha(Y/K),$$

where g_j denotes the growth rate of variable j. Since employment almost certainly grew faster in Mauritius than in these other countries over the period in question their sharply higher values for g_Y/i suggest higher values for the growth rates of TFP and/or human capital. An alternative possibility (considering the final term above) is that the *level* of total factor productivity is higher in these other countries, which would raise Y/K and produce a higher growth payoff from each unit of net investment.

Table 11.9 *Mauritius, international comparison of hourly labor cost, textile industry, 1998*

Country	Hourly labor cost (US$)
Indonesia	0.24
Pakistan	0.40
Madagascar	0.41
Bangladesh	0.43
Kenya	0.46
Zambia	0.48
Sri Lanka	0.49
India	0.60
China	0.62
Thailand	1.09
Philippines	1.12
Mauritius	**1.41**
Tunisia	1.76
South Africa	2.05
Chile	3.16
Venezuela	3.30
South Korea	3.63
Brazil	4.05

Source: Werner International (1998).

Table 11.10 *Mauritius, growth rate and investment efficiency, 1987–1991, percent*

Country (1)	Growth rate (2)	Investment rate (3)	Inverse of ICOR (4)
Mauritius[a]	5.8	29.9	19.4
Korea	9.7	33.3	29.1
Malaysia	8.1	29.3	27.6
Taiwan	7.9	22.3	35.4
Thailand	11.5	32.2	35.7

Notes: The inverse of the incremental capital–output ratio (ICOR) is given by the ratio of column (1) to column (2). This provides an approximation to the increment to output per unit of investment.
Source: NEDC (1994).
[a] 1988–92.

Table 11.11 *Mauritius, real wage, productivity, and export price,*
manufacturing sector, 1983–1994, base 1982

Year	Real wage index	Labor productivity index	Employment index	Export price index
1983	101	96	104	107
1984	101	90	126	119
1985	98	90	163	136
1986	105	80	205	144
1987	111	77	238	161
1988	120	77	254	173
1989	128	77	259	192
1990	120	79	261	216
1991	133	85	264	230
1992	138	87	261	246
1993	133	94	254	268
1994	145	101	254	276

Sources: Bank of Mauritius, (various years); CSO (various years, b).

increases in employment, rather than increases in real wages or productivity,
appear to have played the dominant role in generating favorable distributional outcomes in Mauritius (table 11.11).

5.2.4   The upshot

The discussion above suggests the following observations. First, while
Mauritius decisively re-oriented its trade policy after independence, it did
not abandon import protection. Second, its success in promoting exports
was due in substantial part to international political-economy factors, in
the form of trade preferences, rather than to domestic policy alone. Third,
favorable distributional effects were in part a result of the geographically
dispersed nature of employment gains; these, in turn, resulted from the
activity-based rather than geographically confined nature of EPZs.

  With regard to factors attracting domestic investment and FDI into manufacturing, labor market trends and trade policy suggest a mixed bag. Wages
were initially low but then rose significantly, and average labor productivity
rose only slowly after an initial decline. This suggests that factors other than
labor cost may have played an important role in attracting FDI to EPZs in
Mauritius. One may conjecture that the symptoms of political and social
stability due to the emergence of strong institutions made Mauritius an
attractive destination for FDI. The significance of political instability for
the African economic growth debacle is well documented in the literature
(see, for instance, Fosu 1992). This brings us to examine the significance of
institutions for accelerating the growth process.

5.3   Institutional development and quality

The economic-growth literature has come to place increasing emphasis on the political, social, and economic institutions that support the functioning of markets (see Ndulu and O'Connell 2007). Dismal African growth performance, the East Asian financial crisis, and the disintegration of the former Soviet Union (FSU) have magnified the importance of well-defined property rights, the rule of law, and economic policies that provide a stable and efficient environment for private economic activity. Institutions contribute significantly to both macroeconomic and microeconomic decision-making. For instance, production decisions in agriculture may depend strongly on the prevailing forms of land tenancy.

The economy of Mauritius reflects the country's colonial heritage, including a labor market historically dominated by slavery and indentured labor. The country's institutions may also have deep historical roots. Acemoglu, Johnson, and Rohinson (2001) argue that settler mortality guided the nature of institution-building in the colonies of the European powers. Colonies exposed to few health hazards, such as Mauritius, attracted the attention of early settlers, who brought with them the institutions necessary to secure property rights and establish the rule of law. Contemporary political institutions in Mauritius also reflect the British influence dating from the early nineteenth century – expressed, among other things, in the establishment of a parliamentary system. Mauritius enjoys multi-party democracy and its population, which is divided by ethnicity and class, participates actively in political and economic management. The country's geographical location and size, moreover, have increased its external dependence and integration with the world economy. Links with France and the EU, America's interest in Africa, and ethnic links with India and China have provided Mauritius with a distinct status. Different, vibrant institutions have been created for the effective political, economic, and social functioning of the island. Its ranking in quality of institutions is high compared to both African and fast-growing East Asian developing countries.

Comparative cross-country data on institutional quality, as presented in table 11.12, reveal the existence of high-quality institutions in Mauritius. The index of institutional quality is not only much higher than the average for Africa and other developing regions, but on average it is comparable to the fast-growing East Asian economies.

The quality of Mauritian institutions is expressed in a variety of arenas. Gulhati and Nallari (1990) attribute a large share of the country's success in adjusting to macroeconomic shocks to domestic institutions. Despite government change in the early 1980s, a commitment was shown to this program, which was made possible by the politics of consensus, much-needed transparency, and feedback mechanisms. The success of the EPZ

Table 11.12 *Mauritius and other countries, quality of institutions*

Institutional quality index	Mauritius	Africa	Fast-growing developing countries	Other developing countries
ICRG[a]	7.23	4.54	6.86	4.29
Protection against expropriation Index[b]	8.06	5.75	8.54	6.47
Democracy[c]	0.75	0.25	0.47	0.51
Participation Index[c]	0.80	0.30	0.49	0.44

[a]The ICRG Index is a measure of the quality of government institutions that affect property rights or the ability to conduct business. It is published by a private firm that provides consulting services to international investors.

[b]For the ICRG Index and the Index of protection against the risk of expropriation, Mauritius has fitted values. The scale is from 0 to 10, with higher values indicating better institutional investors.

[c]The Participation Index measures the extent to which non-elites are able to access institutional structures for political expression. This Index, like that for democracy, ranges from 0 to 1, with higher values denoting better quality.

Sources: International Country Risk Guide (ICRG) Index, the PRS Group; Jaggers and Gurr 1995; Inter-University Consortium for Political and Social Research, distributor, 1996 (Ann Arbor, MI).

provides a second example of institutional quality, particularly in limiting the rent-seeking and corruption that have undermined the success of targeted interventions in other countries. The management of the declining sugar sector provides a third example; the restructuring of this sector recognized the interests of incumbent workers and producers by allowing a phased reduction of the labor force in sugar mills.

Different political parties and coalitions have practiced the politics of consensus, which is reflected in the continuity of policies and programs despite regular elections and changing power-sharing strategies. This has been made possible by the nature of Mauritian society. Firstly, there is a separation of political and economic power. Secondly, political competition has promoted a culture of sharing the fruits of development widely in order to increase political prospects and retain political power. Thirdly, various groups have tended to co-exist by developing an attitude of compromise on major issues, allowing the political leadership to evolve more acceptable mechanisms to share benefits of development with citizens. The strategy of economic diversification plays an important role in improving income distribution and reducing social tensions, on the one hand, and ensuring political stability, on the other. The success story can thus be explained by economic diversification and shared growth. Whereas geography, trade policy, and institutions are important, shared growth provides a common denominator to help explain the success story. We develop this point in the following section.

6. A synthesis of the three stylized sources of growth

This section presents a synthesis of the three channels – geography, trade policy, and institutions – as a basis for an integrated account of growth success in Mauritius. We argue that the contribution of each of these channels to growth depends in large part on its contribution to the sharing of growth benefits among various groups.

6.1 Structural change and economic diversification

There are two important dimensions of resource allocation during the process of economic transformation (table 11.13). The first is a tendency towards agglomeration of economic activity, as labor and capital migrate to geographical areas of concentrated growth. The second dimension is a movement of resources from one activity to another, a process that may or may not involve spatial agglomeration. Spatial agglomeration is less likely to accompany the transformation of activity when an economy depends heavily on external markets for imported inputs and export markets.

In a small and relatively resource-scarce island country like Mauritius the forces pushing towards spatial agglomeration are weaker than in larger and more self-sufficient economies. In addition to the weaker natural forces of agglomeration, the decentralized availability of infrastructure facilities (in a very small country) limits the localization economies facing investment activities. The government of Mauritius arguably faced an unusually powerful opportunity to achieve economic transformation without creating a sharp concentration of activity. It seized this opportunity by using an activity-based criterion to define the EPZs – manufacturing of textiles and apparel – rather than a geographically-based criterion.

In the more typical developing-country case, spatial and sectoral concentration of economic activities go hand in hand and cause substantial economic and social distress (Bairoch 1988). In the Mauritian case, the common problem of urban densification was avoided even in the face of a rapid structural shift in the structure of GDP. The growth of manufacturing value added and employment was concentrated in a low-skill-intensive textile sector, but it was geographically dispersed. The benefits of rapid economic growth were shared by individuals, groups, and regions, with little evidence of the economic and social distress witnessed in many developing countries. The size of the island therefore contributed immensely to the success of the EPZs, with major implications for income distribution.

During the period of structural transformation and resource reallocation, traditional sectors such as agriculture faced a relative decline in their shares of GDP. But this decline was occasioned by factors atypical to developing

Table 11.13 *Mauritius, structural transformation of the economy,*
1970–1989

Period	Agriculture's share in GDP	Industry's share in GDP	Services' share in GDP	Manufacturing's share in GDP
1970–4	38.84	20.99	40.16	15.22
1975–9	22.44	24.32	53.24	15.76
1980–4	17.58	24.83	57.59	17.34
1985–9	15.52	30.46	54.03	22.40

Source: O'Connell and Ndulu (2000).

countries. The agricultural decline hypothesis is generally explained in terms of Engel's law and diminishing marginal returns in agriculture. The story of the decline of sugarcane and sugar-export-dominated agriculture in Mauritius is entirely different. Under the Sugar Protocol, Mauritius enjoys a quota for sugar exports at a guaranteed price, which has been above the market price in the EU. The Mauritian government chose access at a lower preference margin over the EU price but with higher guaranteed quotas, as against access at the then-high world price with limited quotas. This proved a propitious choice during the sugar boom of the early 1970s. Between 1972 and 1975, global sugar prices rose more than three-fold, and gross earnings of the sugar sector in Mauritius rose from 15.2 percent of GDP in 1971–2 to 34.2 percent in 1974–5. Preference margins in European markets resembled a foreign aid transfer from the EU to Mauritian sugar-exporting firms, the benefits of which were shared with the government in the form of an export tax on sugar exports. Although separate estimates are not available for sugar exports, rents in Mauritius from preferential access to sugar and clothing together amounted to about 7 percent of GDP in the 1980s and 5 percent in the 1990s (Subramanian and Roy 2003). Thus, the problem did not lie in a declining terms of trade for agriculture; in fact, the sugar sector generated substantial surpluses for investment in other sectors of the economy. These developments contributed to the diversification of both production and employment, resulting in improved income distribution.

The foregoing points are supported by table 11.14, which shows that during the period of most marked structural transformation in Mauritius, wage disparities fell, both between sectors and within the manufacturing sector.

6.2 The political economy of growth

Mauritius' growth success has been driven by three major factors: (1) a long tradition of competitive democracy that emphasized political stability and avoided ethnic–religious conflict by adopting fluid cross-party coalitions in

Table 11.14 *Mauritius, disparities in wage rates,*
1980–1993, standard deviation of log of earnings

Year	Intersectoral	Intrasectoral (Manufacturing)
1980	0.418	0.267
1984	0.232	0.305
1988	0.250	0.261
1992	0.247	0.221
1993	0.252	–

Source: Computed on the basis of data from Bank of
Mauritius (various years) and ILO (various years).

support of shared growth; (2) avoidance of the "Dutch disease" effects of booms and busts in sugar prices, through prudent macroeconomic management and, in the early 1980s, hard decisions that might not have been in line with popular opinion; and (3) the adoption of private-sector led, FDI-friendly policies and an export-led growth strategy for diversification away from dependence on sugar.

Political competition in Mauritius ensured that the interests of the narrow elites were encompassing and that regime changes tended to reflect the major concerns of the majority. The Mauritian story seems to fit quite well with the claims of Humphreys and Bates (2001), who argue that policy-makers who need to satisfy larger constituencies, who face checks and balances within the decision-making process, who are subject to electoral review, and who function in stable institutional environments, are more likely to produce good policies.

Fabian socialism characterized the early phase of policy in Mauritius, dominating political discourse throughout the 1960s, in the run-up to independence, and in the immediate post-independence period. Under the leading political faction, the Mauritian Labor Party (MLP), intervention was the main modality for managing development programs – a strategy employed by other regimes with comparable political posturing. A new political outlook followed during 1971–7, a period of sugar boom and intense political activity during which concerns about poverty gave rise to populist pressures on spending (stirred up particularly by the militant trade unionist party, the Mauritius Militant Movement (MMM)). Although the coalition government of Labor and the Mauritian Social Democrat Party (PMSD) retained power in the 1976 elections, the MMM established itself as a major political voice and a force behind populist pressures for spending. Despite a spurt of high growth with the initial adoption of EPZs and the sugar price boom, the underlying pressures favoring redistribution over growth appears to have characterized much of the policy discourse in the 1970s. A coalition that included the MMM (after purging the party of its radical activists) and the PSM (Mauritian Socialist Party) came into power in 1982. The coalition focused on macroeconomic management and growth. In 1983, a coalition that consisted of the Mauritius Socialist Movement (MSM: MMM minus its radical contingent) and the Labor and PMSD parties won another election and represented a wide spectrum of political opinion that emphasized rapid sustained growth and successful diversification of the economy as a means for an effective exit from poverty.

The various episodes of shift from more restrictive policies to gradual liberalization have been guided by general global trends, the policies of international institutions (the World Bank, IMF, and World Trade Organization, WTO), and domestic political consensus. As discussed by Lal (1987), in explaining policy shifts a major motivation for liberalization may lie in an attempt to regain control over the economy, which becomes less and less amenable to the usual means of government control. During and after the period of structural adjustment, the first attempts were made to reduce unsustainable public expenditure commitments. Further, a long tradition of competitive democracy produced political stability and avoided ethnic–religious conflict by adopting growth and welfare strategies that appealed to broad constituencies. Mauritian ethnic diversity, which is higher than that of East Asian countries, may not have produced undesirable consequences for growth because of strong democratic roots. Collier (1998) argued that highly fractionalized societies must be democratic if they are not to suffer high economic costs. Political competition ensured that regime changes by and large reflected the major concerns of the majority.

Unlike many African countries, as discussed earlier, Mauritius chose a package of a lower domestic EU price with higher guaranteed quotas as against an alternative package of the then-high world price with limited quotas for its sugar. World sugar prices increased later, giving the advantage of a higher quota to be sold at higher prices. A part of this surplus in the sugar sector was mopped up by levying a sugar export tax, rendering investment in the sugar sector unattractive. Exchange controls prohibited repatriation of sugar profits and resulted in the plowing back of abnormal profits into EPZs and the hotel industry. This started the first major wave of economic diversification.

Fine-tuning of policy response helped to take advantage of the international political economy by capturing developed-country textile markets. A cautious approach to trade liberalization and maintaining the tax haven status of the island stimulated both export- and import-competing sectors. Despite not being a strong reformer, intentions were made credible by accompanying policies and measures. Whereas economic power remained vested in the minority French community, the majority of Indian-origin

Table 11.15 *Mauritius, comparative picture of Gini coefficient over regions, 1965–1990*

		Gini		
Region	No of countries	Lowest	Highest	Mean
SSA	19	35.21	61.93	49.77
East Asian countries	6	34.90	49.30	41.51
East Asian countries (excluding Malaysia)	5	34.90	44.51	39.99
Mauritius	1			**40.67**

Note: Gini coefficients in our sample have been averaged over the period 1965–90.
Source: Computed from UNDP/UNU WIDER Income Inequality Database.

communities participated in politics and then the civil service as against economic activities as source of income generation. The civil service remained relatively well paid and a generous system of social security further reinforced rent-sharing between economic and non-economic elites. These well-thought-out, planned transfer regimes contributed to improved income distribution.

6.3   Evidence on improved income distribution

The distribution of land, wealth, and income across income and social groups helps to determine the consumption and savings potential of a population, with consequences for the evolution of social inequalities over time. Since information on the wealth and land distribution in Mauritius is not available, we focus on differentials in income and wages. Table 11.15 shows a comparison of average Gini coefficients for SSA, East Asian countries, and Mauritius over the period 1965–90; inequality is much lower in Mauritius than in SSA and compares favorably with that of the East Asia countries. While Gini coefficients are not available on a systematic basis through this period, inter-period estimates by the Central Statistical Office (CSO) show a very substantial improvement between the early 1960s and the mid-1980s, with the Gini coefficient falling from 0.50 in 1962 to 0.40 in 1986–7, followed by much slower improvements that produced a cumulative decline to 0.37 by 2000–1.

The income-share method provides corroborating information on developments after the mid-1980s. On average, the share of the lowest 20 percent of households during the 1986/7–1996/7 period was around 6 percent, whereas it was about 45 percent for the highest 20 percent of households (CSO Household Budget Surveys). (See table 11.16.) While both shares are

Table 11.16 *Mauritius, income share of top and bottom 20 percent of households, 1986–2002*

	1986/7	1991/2	1996/7	2001/2
Income share (% of total)				
Lowest 20% of households	5.6	6.4	5.9	6.2
Highest 20% of households	44.2	43.5	46.2	44.8
Ratio of highest 20% to lowest 20%	7.9	6.8	7.8	7.2
Gini	0.396	0.379	0.387	0.371

Source: CSO (1986/7) and subsequent budget surveys.

quite stable over the decade, the ratio of the highest-quintile share to the lowest-quintile share shows a modest decline.

7. Conclusions

We have argued in this chapter that narrow explanations of the Mauritian economic miracle based on export orientation and FDI-led industrialization are incomplete. We have put forward a broader explanation in which geography, globalization, and institutions all play important roles, and in which a broad sharing of the benefits of growth is central to the political sustainability of the overall strategy.

The Mauritian strategy exploited a set of opportunities open to a small-island economy with under-employed female labor and a comparative advantage in sugar, While the special features of Mauritius limit the precise replication of this strategy elsewhere in Africa, there may nonetheless be important lessons for larger countries with more diversified agricultures. For labor-surplus economies, the Mauritian experience suggests that strategies to attract foreign capital into labor-intensive manufacturing hold promise, and that EPZs offer a potentially powerful channel for policy support. However, there are two crucial preconditions for attracting international capital: political stability and appropriate government policies. On the latter score, we have emphasized the role of labor-market policies and institutions in obtaining labor-friendly outcomes in employment and wages.

The increasing cost of labor in Mauritius, however, presents a formidable challenge that will require a reorientation of domestic policies. Continued success will depend on the productivity-enhancing component of development policy. The experience of small East Asian countries, particularly Singapore and Hong Kong, may be particularly useful in identifying the growth opportunities now open to Mauritius. These countries are relatively similar to Mauritius in terms of size, tropical climate, export orientation, and lack of natural resources, but have succeeded in attracting foreign capital on a much higher scale and in reaching significantly higher educational standards. The experience of these countries may also help in confronting a particularly Mauritian conundrum – the demise of the manufacturing export preferences that have played such an important role in Mauritius' success, and in the protected access of commodity exports like sugar. In the context of the WTO, even though small-island countries may still mobilize some support mechanisms and safety nets, the consequences of globalization and economic liberalization will continue to exert pressures for structural transformation.

References

Acemoglu, D., S. Johnson, and J. A. Robinson (2001), "The Colonial Origins of Comparative Development: An Empirical Investigation," *American Economic Review* 91(5): 1369–1401

Bairoch, P. (1988), *Cities and Economic Development*. Chicago, IL: Chicago University Press

Balasubramanyam, V., M. Salisu, and D. Sabsford (1996), "Foreign Direct Investment and Growth in EP and IS countries," *Economic Journal* 106: 92–105

Bank of Mauritius (various years), *Annual Report*. Port Louis: Bank of Mauritius

Blake, A., C. Milner, G. Reed, and T. Westaway (1994), "Trade Shocks and Model Dimensionality: A CGE Analysis for Mauritius," Discussion Papers 95/11, CREDIT, University of Nottingham

Briguglio, L. (1998), "Small Country Size and Returns to Scale Manufacturing," *World Development* 26(3): 507–15

Central Statistical Office (CSO) (1986/7), *Household Budget Survey*. Port Louis: Government of Mauritius

(various years, a), *Annual Digest of Statistics*. Port Louis: Ministry of Finance and Economic Development

(various years, b), *Annual Digest of Industrial Statistics*. Port Louis: Ministry of Finance and Economic Development

Collier, P. (1998), "The Political Economy of Ethnicity," *Annual World Bank Conference on Development Economics*. Washington, DC: The World Bank: 367–99

Collier, P. and S. A. O'Connell (2007), "Opportunities and Choices," chapter 2 in Benno J. Ndulu, Stephen A. O'Connell, Robert H. Bates, Paul Collier, and Chukwuma C. Soludo, eds., *The Political Economy of Economic Growth in Africa, 1960–2000*, vol. 1. Cambridge: Cambridge University Press

Collins, S. and B. Bosworth (1996), "Economic Growth in East Asia: Accumulation versus Assimilation," *Brookings Papers on Economic Activity 2*: 135–203

Dabee, B. and C. Milner (1999), "Evaluating Trade Liberalization in Mauritius," in A. Oyejide, B. Ndulu, and J. Gunning, eds., *Regional Integration and Trade Liberalization in Sub-Saharan Africa, vol. 2, Country Case Studies*. New York: St. Martin's Press

Easterly, W. and R. Levine (1998), "Trouble with the Neighbours: Africa's Problem, Africa's Opportunity," *Journal of African Economies* 7(1), March: 120–42

(2003), "Tropics, Germs and Crops: How Endowments Influence Economic Development," *Journal of Monetary Economics* 50(1): 3–39

Fosu, A. K. (1992), "Political Instability and Economic Growth: Evidence from Sub-Saharan Africa," *Economic Development and Cultural Change* 40(4): 829–41

(2007), "Anti-growth Syndromes in Africa: A Synthesis of the Case Studies," chapter 3 in Benno J. Ndulu, Stephen A. O'Connell, Robert H. Bates, Paul Collier, and Chukwuma C. Soludo, eds., *The Political Economy of Economic Growth in Africa, 1960–2000*, vol. 1. Cambridge: Cambridge University Press

Fowdar, N. (1991), "Textiles and Clothing in Mauritius," *Textile Outlook International*, November: 68–86

Gallup, J. and J. Sachs, with A. Mellinger (1999), "Geography and Economic Development," NBER Working Papers 6849, National Bureau of Economic Research

Gulhati, R. and R. Nallari (1990), "Successful Stabilization and Recovery in Mauritius," EDI, Policy Case Series, The World Bank, Washington, DC

Hinckle, L. E. and A. Herrou-Aragon (2001), "How Far Did Africa's First Generation Trade Reforms Go?," World Bank, mimeo

Hoeffler, A. (2002), "The Augmented Solow Model and the African Growth Debate," *Oxford Bulletin of Economics & Statistics* 64(2): 135–58.

Humphreys, M. and R. Bates (2001), "Economic Policies in Africa: The Good, the Bad, and the Ugly," Paper prepared for delivery at the 2001 Annual Meeting of the American Political Science Association, San Francisco, August 30–September 2

International Labour Organization (ILO) (various years), *Yearbook of Labour Statistics*. Geneva: International Labor Organization

International Monetary Fund (IMF) (2001), *Mauritius: 2001 Article IV Consultation*, Washington, DC: IMF

Jaggers, K. and Gurr, T. R. (1995), *Polity III: Regime Type Political Authority, 1800–1994* (Computer file). Boulder, CO: Keith Jaggers/College Park, Maryland

Lal, D. (1987), "Political Economy of Economic Liberalization," *World Bank Economic Review* 1(2): 281–5

Lall, S. (1983), *The New Multinationals: The Speed of Third World Enterprises*. New York: Wiley

Lanza, A. and F. Pigliaru (1999), "Why are Tourism Countries Small and Fast Growing?," Department of Economics SOAS, University of London, mimeo

Lecraw, D. (1977), "Direct Investment from Firms in Less Developed Countries," *Oxford Economic Papers* 29: 442–57

Limão, N. and A. Venables (2001), "Infrastructure, Geographical Disadvantage, Transport Costs, and Trade," *The World Bank Economic Review* 15(3): 451–79

Meade, J. *et al.* (1961), *The Economic and Social Structure of Mauritius*. London: Methuen

Milner, C. and A. McKay (1996), "Real Exchange Rate Measures of Trade Liberalisation: Some Evidence for Mauritius," *Journal of African Economies* 5(1), March: 69–91.

Milner, C. and P. Wright (1998), "Modeling Labor Market Adjustment to Trade Liberalization in an Industrialization Economy," *Economic Journal* 108: 509–28

Nath, S. (2001), "Government Expenditure and Economic Development," in R. Dabee and D. Greenaway, eds., *The Mauritian Economy: A Reader*. London: Palgrave: 150–65

National Economic Development Council (NEDC) (1994), *Improving Efficiency in the Financial Sector in Mauritius*. Port Louis: NEDC, mimeo

Ndulu, B. and S. A. O'Connell (1999), "Governance and Growth in Sub-Saharan Africa," *Journal of Economic Perspective* 13(3): 41–66.

(2007), "Policy Plus: African Growth Performance, 1960–2000," chapter 1 in B. J. Ndulu, S. A. O'Connell, R. H. Bates, P. Collier, and C. C. Soludo, eds., *The Political Economy of Economic Growth in Africa, 1960–2000*, vol. 1. Cambridge. Cambridge University Press

O'Connell, S. A. and B. Ndulu (2000), "Africa's Growth Experience: A Focus on the Source of Growth," AERC Growth Working Paper No. 10. Nairobi: African Economic Research Consortium, April (downloadable: www.aercafrica.org)

Porter, M. (1990), *The Competitive Advantages of Nations*. London: Macmillan

Rodriguez, F. and D. Rodrik (1999), "Trade Policy and Economic Growth: A Skeptic's Guide to the Cross-national Evidence," Electronic Working Papers rodriguez9901, Department of Economics, University of Maryland

Rodrik, D. (1999), *The New Global Economy and Developing Countries: Making Openness Work*. London: Overseas Development Council

Rodrik, D., A. Subramanian, and F. Trebbi (2004), "Institutions Rule: The Primacy of Institutions over Integration and Geography in Economic Development," *Journal of Economic Growth* 9: 131–65.

Romer, P. (1992), "Two Strategies for Economic Development: Using Ideas and Producing Ideas," Proceedings of the Annual Conference on Development Economics, Washington, DC

Sachs, J. and A. Warner (1997), "Sources of Slow Growth in African Economies," *Journal of African Economies* 6: 335–76

Srinivasan, T. (1986), "The Costs and Benefits of Being a Small, Remote, Island Landlocked or Mini-state Economy," Discussion Paper, Development Policy Issues Series, The World Bank, Washington, DC

Subramanian, A. and D. Roy (2003), *Who Can Explain the Mauritian Miracle: Meade, Romer, Sachs, or Rodrik?*, in D. Rodrik, ed., *In Search of Prosperity: Analytic Narratives on Economic Growth*. Princeton and Oxford: Princeton Unversity Press: 205–43

UNIDO (1994, 1995). *Industrial Development Global Report*.

Wellisz, S. and P. Saw (1993), "Mauritius," in R. Findlay, and S. Wellisz, eds., *Five Small Open Economies*. New York: Oxford University Press

Wells, L. (1983), *Third World Multinationals*. Cambridge, MA: MIT Press

Werner International (1998), *Spinning and Weaving Labour Cost Comparisons*. New York: Werner International, Inc., Spring: 1–3

World Bank (1989), *Mauritius, Managing Success*. Washington, DC: The World Bank

12 | State control and poor economic growth performance in Senegal

Mansour Ndiaye

1. Introduction

Senegal is a coastal, resource-scarce economy. As such, it had the opportunity to follow the development path of Mauritius, which integrated into the world economy through labor-intensive manufactured exports. Indeed, Senegal enjoys a strategic coastal position with good maritime service connections, combined with relatively stable and democratic political institutions. At independence, the country benefited from a capital city endowed with infrastructure and an extensive industrial and commercial base. Membership in

BCEAO, Dakar. The bulk of this chapter was written while the author was an economist at the IMF. Financial assistance from the AERC is gratefully acknowledged, as are the comments of Shantayanan Devarajan, Steve O'Connell, and Jean-Paul Azam. However, the usual disclaimer applies.

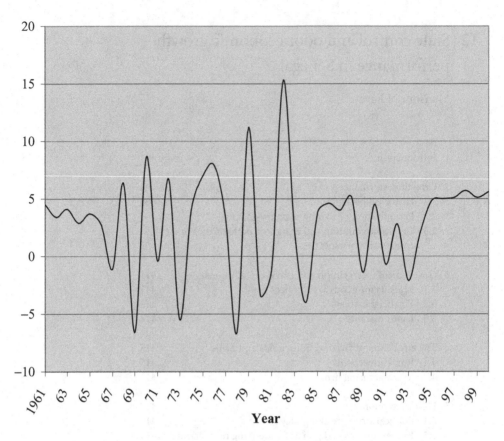

Figure 12.1 Senegal, real GDP growth, 1961–2000, percent
Source: Senegalese authorities (Direction de la Prévision et de la Statistique).

the West African Monetary Union (WAMU) provided the advantages of a convertible currency and access to imports. In short, Senegal's economic and institutional endowment appears to favor a growth strategy based on trade, tourism, and transportation activities. As we shall see, however, Senegal missed out on the transformation experienced by similar economies. Despite its favorable initial conditions, Senegal stagnated over much of the first four decades of political independence.

On a *per capita* basis, Senegal's economy contracted between 1960 and 2000. Real GDP grew at an annual average of 2.9 percent over the period (figure 12.1), while population grew by 3 percent. Export performance during 1960–90 compared unfavorably with most other West African countries, averaging only 2.4 percent growth per annum (World Bank 1994). A study of Senegal's growth record between 1960 and 1993 reveals the dramatic impact of poor policy choices – notably a "soft" control syndrome and an episode of unsustainable spending – that resulted in heavy market control, a poor investment environment, a large and inefficient government sector, a high level of trade protection, and an unsustainable debt strategy. To make matters worse, economic performance was badly hit by adverse climatic conditions, especially droughts, and declining world prices for the country's main exports.

These features support the findings of Sachs and Warner (1997) which attributed Africa's growth shortfall to economic policy failures and an institutional environment that failed to support market mechanisms. Indeed, the recent limits to growth in Senegal included: (1) market structures that preserved the pre-independence order (urban power and bias) and set limits upon structural change; (2) peanuts, the main source of revenue and most important tax base, was used as an infrastructure for constructing patronage-based political machines; (3) there was no competition in the industrial sector due to widespread government intervention; (4) the rent-seeking system ensured political stability by securing the allegiance of civil servants, modern sector enterprises, and religious leaders to the political regime; (5) interest groups made sure that inappropriate policies persisted due, in part, to a lack of commitment to reforms; and (6) favorable dispositions from the donor community eased the need for adjustment until 1993 when the devaluation and accompanying measures put the economy back on track.

Since the 1994 devaluation of the CFA franc, the policies pursued have been more growth-oriented and mostly "syndrome-free" (in the terminology of Collier and O'Connell 2007) on account of restored competitiveness, donor community conditionalities, and political commitment at the West African Economic and Monetary Union (WAEMU) level.[1]

This chapter contributes to the literature on African economic growth experience in many respects. First, it revisits the findings of Berthélemy, Seck, and Vourc'h (1996), the only other comprehensive study of Senegal's growth experience that we are aware of, by providing a clearer picture in terms of growth accounting and intersectoral resource-transfer dynamics. Secondly, it locates Senegal's growth and its determinants in a cross-country perspective. Thirdly, it provides a unifying political economy analysis of Senegal's growth experience.

The chapter is organized as follows: section 2 discusses growth performance in a comparative perspective; sections 3 and 4 present the microeconomic factors underlying the macroeconomic picture, namely market institutions and the response of households and firms; section 5 presents developments in the political economy; and section 6 concludes this accounting of Senegal's growth.

---

[1] WAEMU is the 1994 successor to the West African Monetary Union (WAMU).

2.   Growth performance

2.1   Historical background

Senegal's colonial legacy carried both advantages and disadvantages. On the one hand, with Dakar as the former administrative capital of French-speaking West Africa (Afrique Occidentale Française or AOF), Senegal was endowed with a well-educated elite, a relatively sophisticated infrastructure, and an extensive industrial and commercial base, centered on fish products, groundnut oil, and other food industries as well as textiles. Senegal also benefited from a strategic coastal position, with good maritime service connections combined with relatively stable and democratic political institutions. Because of these advantages, Senegal was able to build up a large industrial sector and become the dominant supplier of the regional West African market. At the time of independence, Dakar already represented the largest concentration of industrial activity in francophone Africa.

In addition, the country's membership in WAMU provided the advantages of a convertible currency and access to imports. Member countries share a common central bank, the BCEAO created in 1962, whose currency is pegged and fully convertible into the Euro (previously to the French franc). France guarantees the convertibility of the CFA franc through an operations account that the BCEAO holds at the French Treasury.

After independence and the gradual disappearance of the West African market bloc, as the other countries in the region tried to build up their own industries behind protectionist barriers, Senegal's large industrial sector became something of a liability. Its domestic market was far too small to sustain an industrial sector of this size, and its industries were not competitive enough to supply export markets on a sustained basis. Unlike Mauritius, another coastal, resource-scarce economy, Senegal did not benefit from trade, tourism, and transportation activities.

2.2   Periodization of economic policy-making

2.2.1   1960–1993: "soft-control" syndrome

The socialist government of President Léopold Sédar Senghor, the first President of the Republic of Senegal who came into power in 1960, made sure market structures preserved the pre-independence status favoring urban bias, which in return limited structural change. There was no competition in the industrial sector due to widespread political intervention. The monopolistic structure of the goods and services market explains both the low level of investment and the poor productivity in manufacturing relying on import-substitution industries protected by heavy tariff rates. Indeed, this particular structure gave rise to and ensured the viability of new investment in the sector. This structure of control over trade limited the extent to which reinvestment and the progressive deepening of capital would occur in the sector. This meant that the industry's greatest vulnerabilities lay at the political level, where decisions about import control were made and implemented. Labor market rigidities also contributed to the high cost of producing goods and services. The country thus missed the opportunity to integrate into the world economy through labor-intensive manufactured exports.

In the rural sector, government policies were counterproductive and were worsened by severe droughts, resulting in low investment and productivity. Agriculture, engaging about 70 percent of the labor force and whose leverage on the economy was considerable through its impact on exports and the size of the domestic demand for locally produced goods and services, was most adversely affected by the impact of the "soft control" regime. Peanuts, the main source of revenue and most important tax base, were used by the socialist government to organize and maintain its political support. Moreover, the economy remained strongly dependent on weather conditions, despite increasing diversification into regions less affected by drought such as Casamance and expansion of activities not dependent on weather such as manufacturing and tourism (figure 12.2). However, droughts were treated as exogenous shocks instead of being viewed as a structural problem (see Benson and Clay 1998).

As noted above, the rent-seeking system benefited civil servants, modern sector enterprises, and religious leaders, while ensuring political stability. Interest groups made sure that inappropriate policies persisted notably by encouraging a lack of commitment to reforms which was a major constraint for investment, thereby jeopardizing growth perspectives. Policies relied more on financing than on adjustment, as favorable dispositions from the donor community eased the need for major changes in policy. However, growing macroeconomic imbalances resulting from poor economic policy-making finally resulted in the 1994 devaluation and accompanying measures, which were intended to put the economy back on track.

2.2.2 1974–1978: unsustainable spending episode

The Government responded to a short-lived commodity boom of two of the country's main resources – phosphates and peanut oil – by using the temporary windfall in an unsustainable way. All-time-high fiscal surpluses were reached, and the government embarked on an expansionist phase. Senegal's current account deficit almost doubled, from an average of 4.5 percent of GDP in the first half of the 1970s to 8.5 percent in the second half. The rising deficit was financed by public sector foreign borrowing at market rates, which proved unsustainable. Total debt rose from 19 percent of GDP in 1971 to 35 percent of GDP in 1979 (IEO 2002). In 1978, the

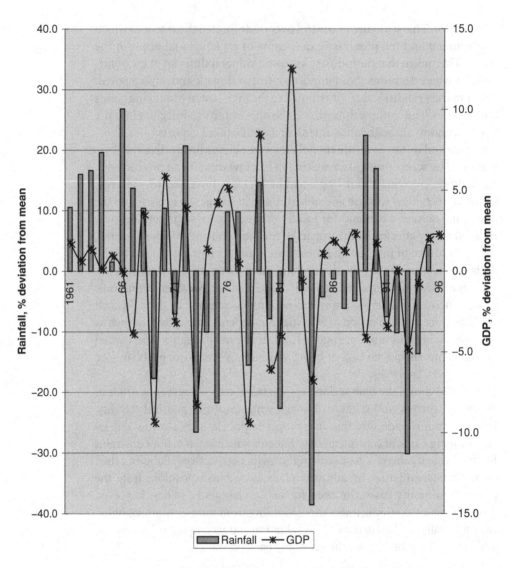

Figure 12.2 Senegal, economic performance and rainfall, 1961–1996
Source: Rainfall data derived from IMF (2001).

spectacular drop in prices of the main export commodities and the return of drought created a major financial crisis, revealing the phony nature of this short growth episode (see Azam and Chambas, 1992).

2.2.3   1994–2000: mostly syndrome-free

In January 1994, a bold and ambitious economic reform program was undertaken, through donor community conditionalities and peer pressure at the regional level. Indeed, the 1994 devaluation paved the way for renewed adjustment efforts, aiming to facilitate growth and development by reducing the role of the government in the economy, improving public sector management, enhancing incentives for the private sector, and reducing poverty. In addition, Senegal's participation in WAEMU has contributed to an improved macroeconomic environment through (1) a mechanism of fiscal policies convergence as of 1997, (2) the establishment of a customs union with a common external tariff (CET) starting in January 2000, and (3) the progressive harmonization of economic and sectoral policies.

Adjustment was achieved along with significant and sustained growth. After seeing its economy contract by 2.1 percent in 1993, Senegal experienced an important turnaround, with real GDP growth averaging over 5 percent annually during 1995–2000. Most of the real depreciation achieved in 1994 was maintained until 2000, as the real exchange rate was at about the same level as it had been at the end of 1994, implying a real depreciation of about 30 percent compared to its pre-devaluation level.

2.3 Growth accounting and economic performance in comparative perspective

Using Collins–Bosworth-type growth-accounting estimates to decompose *per capita* growth in Senegal during 1960–2000, we find the following: overall, average economic performance was low (output per worker declined by 0.1 percent per year: table 12.1). Low accumulation of physical capital – notably between 1960 and 1974 – was the key factor driving economic growth down (−0.2 percent per annum), while education made a significant contribution to observed growth (0.16 percent a year). Overall, TFP did not have a notable impact on real GDP *per capita* in Senegal, except during the 1965–84 and 1990–4 periods, when it adversely hit growth (see Collins and Bosworth 1996; O'Connell and Ndulu 2000).

The growth-accounting evidence is supported by the stylized facts. As mentioned above, the domestic market was far too small to sustain the large industrial sector of Senegal after independence, and the country's industries were not competitive enough to supply export markets on a sustained basis. Moreover, the structure of control over trade limited the extent to which reinvestment and the progressive deepening of capital control could occur in the sector. Senegal's industry also suffered considerable inefficiencies under the protection of high tariffs and oligopolistic situations created by the Investment Code.

In the years preceding the 1994 devaluation, Senegal faced growing macroeconomic imbalances, and its economic program with the IMF was off track. Structural reforms were not implemented in any sustained way and the over-valuation of the CFA franc adversely affected competitiveness, which explains the low TFP growth.

Table 12.1 *Senegal, Collins–Bosworth growth-accounting decomposition,*
1960–2000

Period	Observed real GDP growth per worker	Contribution of physical capital per worker	Contribution of education per worker	Residual
Growth decomposition, by period:				
1960–4	−0.24	−0.46	0.00	0.22
1965–9	−2.04	−0.79	0.04	−1.29
1970–4	−0.03	−0.26	0.33	−0.10
1975–9	0.67	−0.21	0.16	−0.73
1980–4	−0.96	−0.25	0.14	−0.84
1985–9	0.61	−0.01	0.17	0.44
1990–4	−1.18	0.06	0.19	−1.43
1995–2000	2.38	0.17	0.20	2.00
All periods	−0.03	−0.20	0.16	0.01
Deviations from sample mean, by period:				
1960–4	−3.05	−1.44	−0.21	−1.40
1965–9	−4.98	−1.99	−0.28	−2.71
1970–4	−2.67	−1.50	0.01	−1.18
1975–9	−2.31	−1.43	−0.26	−0.62
1980–4	−0.81	−1.00	−0.21	0.40
1985–9	−0.31	−0.30	−0.22	0.21
1990–4	−1.86	−0.33	−0.16	−1.52
1995–2000	0.78	−0.36	−0.10	1.24
All periods	−1.66	−1.03	−0.18	−0.46
Deviations from SSA mean, by period:				
1960–4	−1.57	−0.99	−0.12	−0.46
1965–9	−3.78	−1.59	−0.16	−2.03
1970–4	−2.36	−1.31	0.11	−1.16
1975–9	0.48	−0.95	−0.08	1.51
1980–4	0.74	−0.41	−0.15	1.30
1985–9	0.16	0.21	−0.17	−0.22
1990–4	0.56	0.14	−0.11	0.31
1995–2000	0.87	0.29	−0.04	0.54
All periods	−0.54	−0.56	−0.09	0.10

Our results depart from those of Berthélemy, Seck, and Vourc'h (1996).
Using a Cobb–Douglas production function with constant returns, they estimate the contribution of physical capital accumulation, labor, and improvement in TFP to growth during 1960–90 at 22, 58, and 20 percent, respectively.
They also claim that expenditure on education did not really bear fruit.

The evolution of Senegal's growth performance is atypical. Whereas most
African economies were growing in the period following independence,

Table 12.2 *Senegal, sectoral shares, 1960–1999, percent of GDP*

	1960–7	1968–73	1974–8	1979–83	1984–8	1989–93	1994–9
Primary	28.9	26.9	31.3	25.0	23.6	22.0	22.1
Secondary	22.5	24.3	26.4	18.5	20.5	20.7	20.3
Tertiary	48.6	48.8	42.2	56.5	56.0	57.3	57.6

Source: Senegalese authorities.

Table 12.3 *Senegal, sectoral shares' residuals, 1960–1997*

Periods	Agri./GDP	Ind./GDP	Serv./GDP	Manuf./GDP	Agri./LF	ALPD
1960–4	−4.95	−8.46	13.40	–	21.96	6.43
1965–9	−1.75	−8.24	9.98	–	24.22	5.29
1970–4	−1.90	−6.70	8.60	3.47	26.00	6.03
1975–9	−0.88	−5.42	6.31	4.25	27.50	5.56
1980–4	−4.21	−3.93	8.15	5.87	28.73	8.18
1985–9	−3.25	−3.35	6.60	6.43	29.40	7.24
1990–7	−3.70	−1.84	5.55	6.51	29.59	7.15
All periods	−2.95	−5.42	8.37	5.31	26.77	6.55

Source: O'Connell and Ndulu (2000).

Senegal was declining on account of the "soft control" syndrome. Senegal's per-worker growth performance was below the SSA mean by an annual average of 1.66 percent. Low levels of capital accumulation resulted in an annual negative *per capita* growth differential of over a full percentage point, while TFP growth was, on average, half a percentage point under the SSA mean. It is only since 1975 that the Senegalese economy began to grow faster that the African average.

These sectoral patterns suggest a policy and external sector environment ill suited to the challenge of rapid growth. The evidence based on a Chenery–Syrquin-type model, taking into account initial income and population characteristics, suggests that some transformation has taken place and appears to have favored services relative to agriculture (tables 12.2 and 12.3). At the same time, though the industrial sector as a whole did not benefit from this sectoral redistribution and the share of manufacturing increased, implying that the utility sector was squeezed. In turn, this contributes to explaining why TFP was so low.

Overall, the country experience depicted here departs from cross-country norms which seem to have favored industry relative to agriculture. It also departs from the findings of Berthélemy, Seck, and Vourc'h (1996) that "a large part, if not all, of the increase of TFP was due not to real technological

Table 12.4 *Senegal, fits and residuals from pooled conditional growth model, 1960–1997*

Periods	Actual growth deviation from sample mean	Contribution to predicted growth deviation				Breakdown of policy contribution by variable		
		Base variables.	Political instability	Policy	Resid.	Inflation	Black mkt prem.	Gov. spend./GDP
1960–4	−2.60	−0.22	0.20	−1.43	−1.15	0.06	0.13	−1.62
1965–9	−4.30	−0.26	0.00	−0.85	−3.19	0.06	0.10	−1.01
1970–4	−2.39	−0.47	0.20	−0.22	−1.90	0.03	0.16	−0.42
1975–9	−1.70	−0.98	0.20	−0.34	−0.58	0.02	0.14	−0.50
1980–4	−3.18	−1.83	0.20	−0.49	−1.06	0.02	0.15	−0.66
1985–9	−1.81	−0.61	0.20	–	–	0.05	0.15	–
1990–7	−2.09	−0.67	0.20	–	–	0.04	0.15	–
All periods	−2.58	−0.72	0.17	−0.67	−1.36	0.04	0.14	−0.84

Source: O'Connell and Ndulu (2000).

progress, or rationalization of production, but to the simple effect of labor migration from the primary sector to the secondary and tertiary sectors (mainly services)."

Our analysis confirms the importance of traditional economic variables in explaining growth. It also highlights the impact of economic policies, which was dramatic during the 1960s, reducing growth by an average of 1.2 percentage points, with a particular effect attributed to "unproductive" government spending (table 12.4).

3.   Government intervention and market institutions

3.1   Markets for goods and services

3.1.1   The manufacturing sector: heavy intervention with monopoly rights

After independence, the government found it difficult to adjust to the new economic environment produced by the break-up of French-speaking West Africa. The strategy adopted favored protectionist methods over market-forces. Boone (1993) argues that this strategy was designed to give firms a high level of protection, allowing them to survive under non-competitive market conditions.

Until the early 1970s, firms benefited from import controls, domestic market monopolies, and guaranteed market shares that were granted and enforced by the state. Under such conditions, competition was largely absent, allowing manufacturers to make large profits.

Furthermore, and in order to attract foreign capital, exemptions from the Investment Code under the regime of *conventions spéciales* – i.e. special long-term concessions that provided import protection, guaranteed prices and/or profit margins, and fiscal exemptions and subsidies – were widespread. In some cases (e.g. sugar and cement) the *conventions* went as far as to provide a legal monopoly of production and importation.

By the mid-1980s, this system dominated the market and the largest industries benefited from it. As much as 75 percent of value added in agro-industry (excluding fishing), 68 percent of textiles and leather, and 90 percent of construction material came from firms under this regime (World Bank 1994). However, these arrangements imposed a large cost on the economy in terms of lost revenues, distortions in resource allocation, and high input costs in a number of strategic areas including petroleum refining and cement. The costs of fuel and electricity were much higher in Senegal than in other SSA countries, partly because of the inefficiencies of petroleum refining and partly because of high taxation.

The government applied the same interventionist strategy in the textile sector, where industries were created throughout the former AOF in the

Table 12.5 *Senegal, ownership structure in the ten largest firms, 1991, percent*

Company	Sector	Private Senegalese	Foreign	Public Senegalese
SAR	Petrol refining	0	90	10
SONACOS	Vegetable oil	0	13	87
SENELEC	Electricity	0	0	100
CSPT	Phosphates	0	49	51
ICS	Fertilizers	8	69	23
CSS	Sugar	6	94	0
AFRICAMER	Fish processing	50	50	0
SOCOCIM	Cement	100	0	0
GMD	Four mill	3	97	0
MTOA	Tobacco	5	95	0

Source: World Bank (1992).

1960s by the trading houses and major French textile manufacturers. Amin (1973) stressed that, in the long run, this strategy compromised the possibilities for the expansion and deepening of capital in the West African textile industry as a whole. Following the fragmentation of the regional market, the Senegalese textile industry went into a recession that lasted until 1965. Import bans were imposed between 1960 and 1962 to cushion the shock of the break-up of the AOF, and were gradually replaced by import licensing. By 1970, the importation of nearly all textile goods that could compete directly with local products was subject to licensing.

The monopolistic structure of market control, relying on heavy state intervention, collapsed starting in 1975 because of growing smuggling of imports. Subsidies and state grants were required to keep the sector afloat from the late 1970s to the mid-1980s. Therefore, the import-substitution strategy failed both to maintain the existing firms and to create new ones.

It must also be emphasized that government policies ensured that most large-scale, private sector economic activity remained in the hands of either the parastatal sector or the foreign-owned – primarily French – private sector. Most large firms belonged to foreigners (table 12.5).

Learning from the failure of import substitution, Senegal progressively changed its strategy. To create employment and develop exports, Senegal established the first free-trade zone (FTZ) in SSA in 1974. A generous package of tax incentives was offered to investors, including exemption from most direct and indirect taxes. The new industrial policy (NPI) reforms of 1984 added measures to enhance the business environment for the private sector. A revised investment code and a one-stop investment approval window (*Guichet Unique*) were established in 1987 and 1988, respectively.

Despite all these measures, however, results have been below expectations. In particular, the array of support institutions developed to assist the private sector, including chambers of commerce and investment and export promotion agencies, proved inefficient.

However, against this background, the establishment of the WAMU in January 1994 offered new possibilities for expanding Senegalese exports particularly in the area of light manufacturing.

3.1.2   The agricultural sector

As it did in the manufacturing sector, the government intervened heavily in the rural economy. Marketing boards controlled the purchase and sale of the country's major cash crops. These agencies established a legally guaranteed monopoly on the provision of commercial services to peanut producers (supply of credit, seed, fertilizer, tools), and on the marketing of the crop at a producer price annually decreed by the government marketing agency Office National pour la Commercialisation Agricole au Développement (ONCAD). Extensive price controls were imposed in the food crops market, offering farmers a low domestic price in order to collect rents and provide urban consumers with inexpensive food. As a result, agricultural performance was not sustained and the sector, notably groundnuts, badly needed a restructuring. However, as argued by IEO (2002), the groundnuts sector still suffers from a lack of clarity on the aims of its restructuring – expansion of production, diversification of agricultural output, or stabilization of farmers' incomes – and this has further limited the resurgence of output.

The sector is also a focus of socio-political sensitivities as it remains a source of income for the majority of the population in the rural areas. As a result, attempts to privatize the groundnut milling and marketing company SONACOS have been protracted because the conditions imposed by the government, notably the provision of seeds and fertilizers to farmers on credit, have proved unattractive to potential investors.

After adhering to a producer-pricing policy based on world prices for about four years, the government returned to a more interventionist policy in 2000. In 2001, SONAGRAINES, a wholly-owned subsidiary of SONACOS, withdrew from the collection and transportation of groundnuts but this did not lead to the envisaged liberalization of the sector as the authorities continued to set indicative margins rather than allow the market to determine transport and collection costs.

3.2   Financial markets

The regional Central Bank defines and implements monetary policy. For its part, the financial sector has traditionally been dominated by a group of commercial banks controlled by French financial institutions. In the early

1970s, the BCEAO pursued a policy of credit restriction, with ceilings on the discount window until 1975. As development strategies sought to champion sectoral policies, a sectoral-credit policy favoring key priority development sectors – notably manufacturing, agriculture, and tourism – was implemented between 1975 and 1988. There were two Central Bank discount rates, with a 2-point differential between the normal and the privileged rate.

The government targeted privileged projects and sectors and subsidized investments by imposing low interest rates and by creating development banks to offer low-cost loans. Credit benefited mostly influential interest groups and was not necessarily used in profitable investments. As a result of the constrained lending practices of commercial banks (e.g. bank-by-bank credit ceiling constraints), there was no competition. The absence of market-based interest rates distorted key prices in the economy. Since 1989, monetary policy instruments – notably, interest rates – have increasingly relied on market mechanisms.

Despite the reforms of the early 1990s in the financial sector following the liquidity crisis, the cost, access, and availability of credit is still a constraint on the growth of the private sector cited by private entrepreneurs (World Bank 1994). Banks continue to be significantly more likely to engage in short-term trade-related lending than in longer-term finance.

Access to credit is also problematic for smaller enterprises due to the conservative bias against them and in favor of public enterprises (PEs). More recently, the crowding out of private credit appears to have abated somewhat as a result of the privatization process. At the same time, the health of the banking sector improved somewhat as confidence was restored and the economic situation has become more buoyant.

3.3   Labor markets

Labor market rigidities have been a key factor responsible for the high costs of producing goods and services. The Labor Code imposed heavy constraints on the hiring and firing of workers, resulting in high labor costs and low productivity. These labor market rigidities, in concert with a gradual real appreciation of the CFA franc starting in the early 1980s, sharply increased labor costs in Senegal relative to those in competing countries until the 1994 devaluation.

The government took steps during the second half of the 1980s to introduce more flexibility in the labor market. However, fear of political and social repercussions resulted in slow progress. In 1989, the use of temporary contract workers for up to five years was allowed. It was not until 1997, however, that a revised Labor Code was adopted. The current Code incorporates a number of major changes including a removal of prior government authorization for layoffs, the elimination of references to the minimum wage in wage negotiations, and encouragements to move such negotiations to the enterprise level rather than the national level.

4. The environment faced by households and firms

4.1 Rural households

Government policies were biased against the agricultural sector – as evidenced by the lack of appropriate incentives and support. In concert with adverse climatic conditions, the hostile policy environment constrained the development of the rural economy. Input supply was subject to commercial speculation on the part of co-operative officials, resulting in high costs, while producer prices were set to maximize state revenues in the short run. Agriculture depended heavily on one crop, groundnuts, whose prices were subject to marked fluctuations on the world market. As of 1968, producer prices for farmers became even lower as the result of an application of EEC rules that ended the preferential rate, 17 percent above world market prices, at which France had purchased groundnut harvests.

Moreover, agricultural production in Senegal is strongly affected by climatic and soil conditions. Rainfall is marginal in many parts of the country, and – even more importantly – subject to large annual fluctuations, while Senegal's soils are generally poor and their fertility is in a critical equilibrium. A final limiting factor was over-population in the groundnut basin, though there was no shortage of cultivable land in Senegal as a whole.

This adverse environment constrained the capacity and the willingness of producers to adopt more intensive farming practices. Though groundnut production increased over the 1960s, most of this expansion did not come from the growing use of fertilizers, tools, or new agricultural techniques, but rather from an expansion of cultivated land. Productivity per ha stagnated or even declined, and farmers switched to food crops such as millet.

Steps were taken to cope with the problem of the over-populated groundnut basin, by introducing modern labor-saving production methods for groundnuts and millet, and by stimulating and organizing rural migration toward the low-density regions in the southeast. For instance, the major challenge of the new agricultural policy introduced in 1984 was to ensure the institutional support services necessary for raising productivity. These included credit, input distribution, extension advice, and product marketing.

However, the unreliability of these services discouraged farmers and investment in agriculture. Even worse, Delgado and Jammeh (1991) show that favorable producer prices provided neither an adequate nor a sustainable foundation for growth in agricultural productivity.

4.2   Manufacturing firms

Although Senegal enjoyed tariff advantages for exports to the EC, which countries like Mauritius did not have, obstacles in terms of quality and price competitiveness of goods and services made transition from African-oriented to world-oriented exports difficult.

Indeed, most industries operated relatively inefficiently, protected by high tariffs and market-sharing arrangements. The principal policy-related constraint on the development of the private manufacturing sector in Senegal stemmed from the rigidities imposed by the country's inward-looking and highly monopolistic economic structure. The profitability of capital invested in the sector depended upon the ability of the state to restrict competition on the local market. These policies implied large inefficiencies and high profits in manufacturing, as the absence of internal and external competition allowed enterprises to set their prices at very high levels, independent of their costs. As a result, the sector recorded significant levels of investment and production between 1965 and 1975, but new investment occurred only when new import barriers were set up. At stressed by Boone (1993), this policy proved counter-productive in the long run, as it did little to stimulate investment in the renovation of the capital stock.

The overall competitiveness of the economy was further constrained by high freight rates because of the lack of competition in transportation, high electricity and petroleum costs due to market rigidities in the energy sector, and heavy taxation.

The impact of such an uncompetitive position can be illustrated with reference to Senegal's canned tuna exports. In 1976, Senegal was the second largest exporter of canned tuna in the world, accounting for 12 percent of world exports. A decade later, it accounted for only 6 percent of world exports and had fallen to the fifth place. Exports from Senegal to all countries of the EC, except for France, had been replaced by Thai exports, despite the fact that Thai exporters did not receive the export subsidy of 25 percent of value added which their Senegalese counterparts did, and that they had to pay a 24 percent import tariff while exports from Senegal could enter Europe free of duty. The main reasons for the poor competitive stance of the Senegalese economy were the growing over-valuation of the real exchange rate and the high utility costs which further deteriorated the competitiveness of the economy (Devarajan 1997). As a result, labor costs per kg of tuna processed were double those in Thailand and, though Dakar is closer to Europe than Bangkok, shipping costs were up to 70 percent higher. The incentive structure was consequently distorted with a high-cost production and consumption structure propped up through high effective rates of protection (exceeding 300 percent for flour and sugar, for example). Golub and Mbaye (2003) also show that, before the 1994 devaluation, the Senegalese competitive stance was very weak, as relative wages were too high to be justified by relative productivity. Rama (2000) also found misaligned labor costs in Senegal.

These observations help explain why, despite an attractive package of tax incentives, the Dakar Industrial Free Zone (DIFZ) has not been a success. The DIFZ's failure to attract significant foreign investment and to create jobs is due to the lack of competitiveness and rigid regulation. Production and transportation costs were much higher in Senegal than in competing countries in the African region. The World Bank (1994) argues that while labor regulations were more liberal within the DIFZ than outside, they were nonetheless too rigid to sustain an internationally competitive manufacturing sector.

Thereafter, adjustment measures met with a degree of success in stabilizing macroeconomic conditions and in partially liberalizing the economy. In 1986, a series of liberalization measures, including the removal of quantitative import restrictions and price controls on manufactures, were introduced under the NPI. Notwithstanding these measures, the supply response of the private sector remained weak, particularly in terms of new investments and exports. In 1990, further adjustment efforts focused on the removal of labor market rigidities, the reduction of government subsidies, and the implementation of a more aggressive privatization program. Overall, the investment climate has suffered from the long period of anticipation leading up to the devaluation and the lack of transparency in the implementation of the various investment regimes, especially the awarding of exemption packages like the *conventions spéciales* which have limited competition and productivity.

With the price competitiveness of exports improving markedly after the 1994 devaluation, a window of opportunity to embark on comprehensive price liberalization, trade reform, and the promotion of private sector activity opened. Government price controls and subsidies were steadily dismantled. However, it was only in the context of the regional initiative to establish a customs union among member countries of the WAEMU that trade reform took a prominent place on Senegal's policy agenda. Indeed, the rationale was to exploit comparative advantages, deepen economic linkages, and improve growth prospects for the region as a whole. Quantitative barriers were reduced and restrictions on payments for current transactions lifted, as Senegal accepted Article VIII of the IMF's Articles of Agreement in 1996. Furthermore, the authorities took steps to reduce administrative costs and limit the scope for discretionary treatment by promoting the services of Trade Point Senegal (trade facilitation services). In January 1999, the CET of the WAEMU was put in place. At the beginning of 2000, an improvement in Senegal's trade restrictiveness rating of about 3 points (5 instead of 8) was noted, as measured by the IMF's trade restrictiveness index, thanks to the lowering of average tariff rates to 12.1 percent, against 24 percent in 1997.

Notable progress was also achieved in the area of governance. The authorities have implemented a comprehensive program to promote good governance by strengthening the rule of law, increasing transparency, and fighting corruption. Measures were also taken to improve the legal and judicial environment. In order to further enhance the business environment, the government approved most of the recommendations of a survey by the Foreign Investment Advisory Services (FIAS) of the World Bank completed in 1998 to identify the bottlenecks faced by private investors.

5. Political economy

5.1 Political structure and policy reforms

In January 1959, Senegal joined French Soudan (now Mali) to form the Federation of Mali. The federation achieved full independence from France in April 1960 but broke up in August of the same year, and Senegal became a republic with Senghor as its first president. The *Parti Socialiste* (PS) governed Senegal from independence in 1960 until March 2000, when President Abdou Diouf was defeated by the veteran opposition leader, Abdoulaye Wade.

In the mid-1960s, Senegal became a *de facto* one-party state under the ruling *Union Progressiste Sénégalaise* (UPS) as all legal opposition parties were incorporated into it. Though the 1974 constitutional revisions provided for multi-party democratic politics, there was no electoral competition until 1983. Bates (2007) argues that politics abided by the logic of collective action and policy choices resulted from the interplay of organized interests, in which urban based-interests enjoyed significant advantages. Indeed, from independence to the mid-1970s, there was a clear pattern of urban bias. The government placed little weight on the interests of farmers, choosing instead to adopt policies favorable to the coalitions that kept them in power. This attitude brings into focus the fact that political interests have driven policy preferences the post-independence era. However, in the long run, even the initial beneficiaries suffered losses, as the distortions generated by the control regime destabilized the economy.

In 1981, President Senghor retired and was replaced by his prime minister, Abdou Diouf, who won the 1983, 1988, and 1993 presidential elections. However, the results sparked off violent rioting in the capital, Dakar, amid allegations of electoral fraud. Pressured by the international community, President Diouf formed several governments of national unity and gave ministerial posts to opposition leaders.

Until the mid-1990s, the PS could count on the support from the most powerful Islamic brotherhoods, but with the decline of the groundnut industry and the rise of other credible parties, this support waned. Therefore, political reforms and policy reforms went together.

Labor discontent was a factor in undercutting electoral support for the PS. For instance, in August 1993, the authorities announced a package of measures implying a 15 percent cut in most public sector nominal wages, but could not implement it following strong protests by trade unions whose membership was widespread in the urban formal sector.

Economic growth also suffered from developments in the southern Casamance region. After independence, regional leaders were absorbed into the government but, because of their lack of political influence, state investment in infrastructure and development projects in the region were neglected. This resulted in the formation of an armed resistance movement, the *Mouvement des Forces Démocratiques de la Casamance* (MFDC). Growing violence led to an impoverishment of a potentially wealthy region of the country. However, though adverse developments in Casamance have depressed growth in Senegal, it must be stressed that the roots of the poor growth performance lie primarily in the economic policies implemented.

5.2 Interest groups and policies underlying rent-sharing

5.2.1 Peanuts as a source of rents for constructing political machines

Policies adopted tended to lower the well-being of the peasantry, which is a highly undesirable equilibrium. Cruise O'Brien (1979) argues that the state set prices in order to maximize its short-run revenues, and that this strategy proved counter-productive both for smallholder production and for revenues over time. For many years, however, ONCAD generated a substantial financial surplus that supported the ongoing fiscal demands of the administration.

The regime allowed the government to mobilize an economic surplus from farmers through the mediation of Islamic religious leaders. Boone (1993) underlines that the political elite relied upon the Muslim leaders – the *marabouts* – to harness groundnut producers to state-controlled markets while limiting farmers' access to the political arena. In turn, the development of the groundnut economy benefited the Islamic leaders as credit, agricultural inputs, equipment, and land channeled through the co-operatives went in large shares to them. Cruise O'Brien (1979) argues that this well-managed government patronage system prevented any major antagonism from materializing.

However, as underlined by Cruise O'Brien (1971), the rurally based Mouride brotherhoods also provided some degree of defense of peasants' interests. That Muslim structure provided the framework for a peasants' trade union which threatened to withdraw from peanut production in favor of millet. That stance forced the government to virtually double the producer price in 1974, having held it almost constant for over a decade after independence.

5.2.2 Public employment and parastatals as sources of rents

The government depended on rents collected from the agricultural sector to pay the salaries of an ever-growing administrative staff. From 10,000 employees at independence, the number of civil servants increased to 34,900 in 1965 and 61,000 in 1973. Cruise O'Brien (1979) argues that Dakar's vast administrative building designed to house the whole AOF government could by the mid-1970s accommodate no more than four ministries. Until the launching of the privatization program in 1987, parastatals were also a source of rents. According to the World Bank (1994), the sector accounted for around one-third of total investment in the economy, but only 7 percent of GDP.

Not surprisingly, the effect of state ownership and control was to perpetuate inefficiencies, raise costs of goods and services, and constrain growth prospects for the economy by making Senegalese industry increasingly uncompetitive in export markets.

An important consequence of the poor financial performance of the public companies was a growing burden on the government budget. Many of these companies survived thanks to state subsidies. An estimated budgetary burden of CFAF 33 billion was reached in 1987 (World Bank 1994). Public enterprise deficits also placed acute pressures on the banking system. Over the period 1985–7, the share of the public sector in total credit to public and private enterprises was far in excess of the sector's contribution to GDP.

While public administration expanded during the 1970s and 1980s, this process was altimately reversed and the administration declined steadily in size during the 1990s. By 2000, most public enterprises had been sold or liquidated, as a direct consequence of the adjustment policies which tightened control over the public sector wage bill and the size of the civil service.

5.2.3 Import-substituting industrialization as a source of rents

Import-substituting industrialization (ISI) served the interests of French industrialists who were already established in the country. Industrial growth and diversification were promoted by protecting the domestic market and subsidizing foreign capital. The industrial sector, therefore, exhibited a non-competitive stance and the economy benefited from little investment during the 1960s and the 1970s while the capital stock became rapidly obsolete. The impact of the control regime was to divert productive resouces into rent-seeking activity.

In the textiles sector, Boone (1993) argues that by the mid-1960s local textile activities were in the hands of a few firms and large commercial houses that had market-sharing arrangements which allowed them to collect high profits. The industrial sector grew during the 1960s, but on a corporatist model that protected these incumbents through collusive price-setting arrangements, exclusive buyer contracts between local producers and the French firms that purchased the bulk of Senegalese textile output, and other devices. Reference prices were used to deliver high rates of effective protection to final textile output; these protected profits but at the same time discouraged vertical integration in the sector. The expansion of the 1960s had within it the seeds of its own unsustainability, however. The fiscal burden of tax concessions virtually eliminated any net contribution of the industrial sector to government revenues, leaving the burden to consumers. As stressed by Boone (1993), rural producers lost on both sides of the ledger in the 1960s, as they had in the colonial period: government interventions lowered the price they received for groundnuts while raising the price they paid for manufactured goods.

5.3   Why did inappropriate policies persist?

Senegal got into a financial crisis in the late 1970s, when a combination of poor financial and investment policies, worsened terms of trade, and successive droughts made adjustment unavoidable. But the need for structural economic changes had become apparent earlier when Senegal lost its large French West African market and found itself with over-sized industries and an excess of highly paid civil servants. Being one of the few democratic systems in Africa,[2] Senegal was able to mobilize substantial external resources over the years, obviating the need for fundamental structural changes.

It was not until December 1979 that Senegal announced its medium-term program for economic and financial adjustment covering the period 1980–4. The major impetus was the availability of external financial resources that would help ease the payments pressures without any genuine understanding or desire to remove the underlying distortions. The belief was that the financial and economic imbalances faced by the country could be resolved with the aid of financial support from the IMF and the World Bank. In this setting, a rise in unconditional aid often increased transfers to favored groups (Adam and O'Connell 1999). Boye (1993) also pointed out that the permanent availability of funds made investment unresponsive not only to domestic savings but also to the capacity utilization rate and finally to external disequilibria. Since Senegal's membership in the CFA zone precluded the possibility of using one of the potent policy instruments – i.e. exchange rate – the adjustment policies could not have the desired impact, but the support

---

[2] Between 1979 and 2000, presidential elections were held in 1983, 1988, 1993, and 2000. Legislative elections were also held in 1988 and 2001.

by key bilateral donors also obviated the need for building the capacity to implement the desirable reforms.

Senegal was among the first countries to receive an adjustment loan from the IMF and the World Bank in 1979–80, but the response from the Senegalese leadership did not address the fundamentals behind the imbalances. Senegal's record of program implementation exhibited a stop–go pattern (IEO 2002), and implementation was generally weak during 1979–82. Because of policy slippages, the 1980 extended financing facility (EFF) and the 1982 stand-by arrangement (SBA) went off track soon after they were approved.

Conversely, from 1983 to 1987, the rigor applied to demand management led to satisfactory measures. A core team of influential technocrats was instrumental in the implementation of the reforms by neutralizing the weight of vested interests. But once this core group left the scene on account of the electoral cycle and the desire to contain social unrest,[3] the implementation record became much weaker. Game-playing between IFIs and Senegal became the order of the day, with Senegal wanting to maximize external resource flows by making sure that the form of the program rather than the spirit was adhered to. Program implementation was not sustained during 1988–93, as fiscal policy loosened and legislative and presidential elections in the first half of 1993 hampered policy implementation on account of the political cycle.

It should be noted that ownership was also an issue, as many Senegalese officials felt that the policies implemented had been "imposed" on the authorities (IEO 2002).

6. Conclusion

Senegal's economic performance during the first forty years since independence (1960–2000) has been quite disappointing, with declining real GDP *per capita*. Compared to the SSA mean, Senegal recorded an annual negative *per capita* growth differential of over half a percentage point. Despite quite favorable initial economic conditions (a capital city endowed with infrastructure and a productive base, relatively stable and democratic political institutions, a solid monetary framework, and a coastal location), Senegal did poorly relative to its growth opportunities.

The evidence shows that the industrial sector lost its market advantage after independence and had excess capacity and little need for new investments. The disappearance of the AOF left Senegal with an industrial base that was too large compared to its domestic market. A way out would have

---

[3] Governments of national unity with representation from opposition parties were formed in 1991 and 1994, in an effort to tackle rising social and political unrest in the country.

been to adopt outward-oriented policies so as to supply export markets on a sustained basis. Instead, the government's response was to adopt a regulatory regime, as evidenced by protectionist measures designed to deliver captive markets to local manufacturers and thereby ensure the survival of existing firms run by monopolies with little incentive for productivity enhancement. As a result, the industrial sector exhibited a poor competitive stance and the economy benefited from little investment during the 1960s and the 1970s, while capital became rapidly obsolete. Hence, the control regime diverted productive resources into rent-seeking activity.

Meanwhile, agriculture policies showcased a clear pattern of urban bias, shifting resources away from rural populations in a weaker bargaining position that the urban elites. Indeed, pricing policies were guided by the objective of maximizing state revenues in the short run, which was counter-productive in the medium and long run. Therefore, state marketing co-operatives that were given a legally guaranteed monopoly on the pro-vision of commercial services to the peanut producer – supply of credit, seed, fertilizer, and tools – reaped substantial profits that were absorbed by the running cost of the administration at the expense of investment and growth. Moreover, since the government was providing significant tax exemptions to manufacturing firms, it meant fewer resources to invest in agriculture, so agricultural performance also suffered from low investment.

Monopolistic market structures in both the industrial and agricultural sectors and rigid labor regulations imposed a large cost on the economy by generating unnecessarily high-cost inputs. The priority given to public com-panies resulted in chronic inefficiencies, raising costs of goods and services and constraining growth prospects for the economy by rendering Sene-galese industry increasingly uncompetitive in export markets. Compared to Mauritius, Senegal's persistent failure to promote investment geared towards exporting outside Africa definitely appears as a major loss in terms of growth opportunities.

Being one of the rare countries in SSA to have a relatively democratic polit-ical system, Senegal benefited from favorable dispositions from the donor community and secured significant levels of foreign aid, easing the need for adjustment. This allowed the government to maintain the rent-seeking system benefiting civil servants, modern sector enterprises, and religious leaders while the economy was still plagued by the crowding-out effect of public enterprises on investment, a growing over-valuation of the CFA franc, and a poor investment climate. In turn, interest groups made sure that these inappropriate policies persisted.

Since the initiation of adjustments efforts supported by the IFIs, microeconomic-related constraints have been progressively removed. The 1994 devaluation helped restore the country's competitiveness and launch a process of sustained economic performance, while affording an opportunity to enhance the business environment. As a matter of fact, *conventions spéciales* were gradually phased out, private sector activity promoted, and public enterprises privatized. At the regional level, trade regulations were simplified, business laws were harmonized, and a regional financial market was created. Given its strategic location as a coastal nation and its established industrial base, Senegal should exploit this opportunity, a regional market being a natural first step before Senegalese light industry is able potentially to compete on export markets.

However, regional economic integration has yet to translate into significant investment flows and trade creation. As the world is tougher now than in the 1970s and early 1980s, economic policy-making most definitely needs to go beyond avoiding policy syndromes to adopting a proactive stance aimed at addressing structural limitations affecting the country – e.g. through infrastructure and public goods to offset geographical disadvantages, human capital, and strong institutions for enhanced domestic accountability and governance.

References

Adam, C. and S. A. O'Connell (1999), "Aid, Taxation and Development in Sub-Saharan Africa," *Economics and Politics* 11(3): 225–54

Amin, S. (1973), *L'échange inégal et la loi de la valeur.* Paris: Anthropos

Azam, J.-P. and G. Chambas (1992), "The Groundnuts and Phosphates Boom in Senegal (1974–77)," Etudes et documents du CERDI, Clermont-Ferrand

Bates, R. H. (2007), "Domestic Interests and Control Regimes," chapter 4 in B. J. Ndulu, S. A. O'Connell, R. H. Bates, P. Collier, and C. C. Soludo, eds., *The Political Economy of Economic Growth in Africa, 1960–2000*, vol. 1. Cambridge: Cambridge University Press

Benson, C. and E. Clay (1998), "The Impact of Drought on Sub-Saharan African Economies: A Preliminary Examination," World Bank Technical Paper 401, The World Bank, Washington, DC

Berthélemy J. C., A. Seck, and A. Vourc'h (1996), *Growth in Senegal: A Lost Opportunity?*, Long-term Growth Series, Development Center, OECD, Paris

Boone, C. (1993), *Merchant Capital and the Roots of State Power in Senegal 1930–85*, Cambridge: Cambridge University Press

Boye, F. (1993), "Senegal," in L. Taylor, ed., *The Rocky Road to Reform.* Tokyo: UN University Press

Collier, P. and S. A. O'Connell (2007), "Opportunities and Choices," chapter 2 in B. J. Ndulu, S. A. O'Connell, R. H. Bates, P. Collier, and C. C. Soludo, eds., *The Political Economy of Economic Growth in Africa, 1960–2000*, vol. 1. Cambridge: Cambridge University Press

Collins, S. and B. Bosworth (1996), "Economic Growth in East Asia," *Brookings Papers on Economic Activity* 2: 135–203

Cruise O'Brien, D. B. (1971), *The Mourides of Senegal. The Political and Economic Organization of an Islamic Brotherhood.* Oxford: Clarendon Press

(1979), "The Ruling Class and the Peasantry, 1960–76," in R. O. Cruise, ed., *Political Economy of Underdevelopment: Dependence in Senegal.* Beverly Hills, CA: Sage

Delgado, C. and S. Jammeh, eds. (1991), *The Political Economy of Senegal under Structural Adjustment.* New York: Praeger

Devarajan, S. (1997), "Real Exchange Rate Misalignment in the CFA Zone," *Journal of African Economies* 6: 35–53

Golub, S. and A. Mbaye (2003), "Unit Labor Costs, International Competitiveness, and Exports: The Case of Senegal," *Journal of African Economies* 11: 219–48

Independent Evaluation Office (IEO) (2002), "Senegal," in *Evaluation of the Prolonged Use of Fund Resources in Senegal.* IMF, Washington, DC

O'Connell, S. and B. Ndulu (2000), "Africa's Growth Performance: A Focus on the Source of Growth," AERC Growth Working Paper No. 10. Nairobi: African Economic Growth Consortium, April (downloadable: www.aercafrica.org)

Rama, M. (2000), "Wage Misalignment in CFA Countries: Were Labor Market Policies to Blame?," *Journal of African Economies* 9(4): 475–511

Sachs, J. and A. Warner (1997), "Sources of Slow Growth in African Economies," *Journal of African Economies* 6(3): 335–76

(1994), *Senegal: Private Sector Assessment.* The World Bank, Washington, DC

World Bank (1992), *Small Enterprises Under Adjustment in Senegal.* The World Bank, Washington, DC

13 | Tanzania: explaining four decades of episodic growth

Nkunde Mwase and Benno J. Ndulu

1. Introduction

Tanzania's growth experience during the first three decades after independence can be characterized as unsustainable, with a sudden decline after early

IMF, Washington, DC; The World Bank, Washington, DC. An earlier version was presented
at the Weatherhead Center Workshop on Explaining African Economic Growth,
1960–2000, Harvard University, March 17–19, 2005. We are very grateful for comments and
suggestions from this Workshop and also for advice from Bob Bates, Paul Collier, and Steve

success during the first ten years of independence. In terms of long-term growth, a strong control regime (1970–85) based on socialist principles spawned high private investment risk, epitomized by nationalization and widespread controls of markets for products and resources; an injudicious public investment program that did not follow rigorous project appraisal; and an over-extended public sector that faced both capacity and revenue constraints to operating and maintaining an ambitious redistributive development program. The last decade-and-a-half has seen a very significant change of course from this paradigm to a market-oriented one accompanied by a strong revival of sustained growth which has averaged nearly 5 percent annually since 1995. One additional important change during this period is Tanzania's adoption of competitive democracy which, unlike the short-lived experience just before and after independence, seems to be taking deeper societal root.

Despite its coastal location, sustained donor support, and large labor force Tanzania's growth experience during the control regime period was low, largely on account of economic mismanagement. The egalitarian undertones in government policy-making resulted in the subordination of economic incentives to political objectives. Economic policy-making during the 1970s and early 1980s was designed to support the political goal of achieving equity at the interpersonal, inter-regional, and rural–urban levels. Weak governance and weak incentives from the "socialist-type" policy-making resulted in the sustenance of a large, loss-making public sector. Inefficient and loss-making state marketing agencies and parastatals, and heavy taxation of agriculture and exports, coupled with an expansionary government expenditure aimed at providing universal access to social services, resulted in unsustainable fiscal deficits, a sharp decline in foreign reserves, and shortages of consumer goods. Government policy was unable to address the economic and structural problems and as a result the economy stagnated during the late 1970s and early 1980s.

It is noteworthy that as early as 1981, President Julius Nyerere encouraged a home-grown review of Tanzania's economic model of development. As Muganda (2004) notes, the openness and inclusiveness of the consultative process of the internal debates in the 1980s, led by the University of Dar es Salaam, which brought together reformers and non-reformers, helped to clarify and broaden the understanding of issues, and legitimized the need for economic reforms. In combination with experimentation with home-grown programs – such as the National Economic Survival Programme (1980–1), Tanzania's own SAP (1982–5), and partial import liberalization via the Own Funded Import Scheme (1984) – it provided the government with space to test, learn from, and adapt reform measures to country circumstances; to

O'Connell. The views expressed in this chapter are those of the authors and do not necessarily reflect the views of the IMF or World Bank, or the policies of these institutions.

minimize alienation of support groups; and build confidence in the government to scale up the reform measures systematically (Muganda 2004: 6).

Although the initial process of liberalization of trade and prices in 1984 and 1985 occurred under Nyerere's regime, the entrance of a new political actor, President Ali Hassan Mwinyi, in 1985 enabled the government to carry forward the shift toward a market-based economy much more decisively. This period was marked by rapid easing of controls – in particular, price and trade liberalization. The policy environment improved significantly following the resumption of the adjustment programs during the period 1985–90. The government embarked on an intensified adjustment program, focusing on devaluation of the shilling, in order to improve external competitiveness and spur growth. In addition, measures were undertaken to address the incentive structure in order to stimulate growth by gradually increasing producer prices, reorganizing public enterprises, and removing subsidies.

A second aid boom occurred in response to this positive policy environment. Unlike the future aid booms, this essentially substituted for monetary financing of the deficits but retained the fundamentals behind them. The single most important success of this regime was the freeing-up of the key product and resource markets and removal of the rents associated with price and exchange controls.

After the initial wave of successful reforms, commitment to further change weakened, partly reflecting the vested interests involved in the second-order structural reforms being pushed from 1990 onwards in order to address both the incentive and fiscal-gap issues. In addition, institutional weaknesses emerged as key economic actors sought to obtain the "rents from sovereignty" arising from the escalating aid inflows. The increase in tax exemptions and laxity in public finance management was symptomatic of corruption and governance issues, and the implicit role of donors as adjudicators and monitors of the government's performance was demonstrated through the withdrawal of assistance in the mid-1990s.

The emergence of the third post-independence government in 1995, under President Mkapa provided a fresh platform to ground the economic reforms undertaken in the previous decade in fundamental institutional and legal changes. The government undertook fundamental changes to underpin macroeconomic stability by taking measures that directly reduced the fiscal deficit sharply and granting autonomy to the central bank, whose mission was reconstituted to focus primarily on ensuring price stability and prudent exchange management. These measures were accompanied by structural reforms emphasizing the importance of restricting the role of the state to providing an environment conducive to private sector growth. Reflecting the government's concerns about raising the welfare of the people, poverty alleviation programs were also implemented. However, the government underscored the importance of increasing the efficiency and effectiveness

of projects, providing targeted basic social services to the poor, and emphasizing the importance of growth for sustained delivery of social services.
This marked a departure from the over-expanded government model of the
1970s, which emphasized universal provision of all social services, which
were largely funded by aid. Owing to the strong track record of policy implementation, the country experienced a resumption of, and subsequently a
sharp increase in, aid and private FDI, both of which remained high throughout the period.

From the foregoing, three features stand out regarding Tanzania's development experience. The first is Tanzania's sharp swings across development
paradigms, starting with a market-oriented economic regime for the first
decade after independence; a sharp shift to a "hard" economic and political
control regime, based on socialist principles, for the next two decades; and
a sharp turn back to a market-oriented economy and a democratic political regime thereafter. The second feature is the process of intense internal
debate and consensus-building prior to the change from the "hard control"
regime to the market-oriented one, which helped to underpin a sustained
reform process after 1986. To a large extent, the debate was paralleled by
wide exercise of exit options from controls by economic agents, in the form
of mushrooming parallel markets and the underground economy, which
served to underscore the weaknesses of the failing regime. The third is the
strong donor support and role in all these stages, notwithstanding the sharp
swings in the approach to development.

The rest of this chapter is organized as follows. Section 2 describes the
macroeconomic performance of the economy, decomposing growth into
three periods: 1967–85, 1985–95, and 1995–present. It presents the growth
decompositions from the growth-accounting and regression estimates.
Section 3 describes the market system in operation, with a particular focus
on the goods, labor, and financial markets. It presents the market structure,
including the constraints and the performance in view of the opportunities
available. Section 4 examines the responses of household and firms to the
constraints, with a focus on the factors hindering an increase in income *per
capita* and growth, respectively. Section 5 discusses the politico-economic
dimension of growth experience highlighting the linkages between the pace
of the reform process and the politico-institutional framework. Section 6
draws some conclusions.

2.   Growth experience

Four features characterize the growth opportunities of Tanzania: (1) easy
access to the international market given its coastal location; (2) a rural
labor surplus and low productivity of agriculture; (3) political stability and

ethnic cohesion built around a common national language, Swahili, and as a result of an early and persistent effort to forge and sustain national unity; and (4) more recently, mineral wealth discovery, predominantly gold and gemstones, as well as natural resource-based tourism.[1]

By far the most dominant long-term growth potential relates to the combination of coastal location and labor surplus. The capital-intensive nature of the booming mining sector limits its importance in translating growth into high welfare for the Tanzanian population. Translating growth into higher employment is important in light of the large labor surplus in agriculture and can be achieved through the use of market-friendly policies to attract lucrative labor-intensive private sector activity. Though Tanzania is ethnically diverse, with 133 tribes, there is a high degree of ethnic cohesion and political stability. This created a environment conducive to the movement of labor and partly explained the relatively high degree of inter-regional labor mobility in Tanzania as well as absence of acrimonious political geography.

However, the wide dispersion of Tanzania's agricultural potential and natural resources made exploitation highly transaction cost-intensive. With a vast geographic area, high agriculture potential and mineral wealth are located around the rim of the country. Tanzania has a poor dendritic transportation network to the coast (access to the international market) and the main domestic market (Dar-es-Salaam) which accounts for more than 60 percent of the income (and hence demand) base. Transport infrastructure is therefore a major constraint to growth. Furthermore, the wide dispersion of agricultural potential and population rules out economies of agglomeration and partly accounts for the high unit infrastructure cost associated with dispersion of services.

With these opportunities in mind, this section aims to provide an overview of Tanzania's growth experience. Section 2.1 provides a brief historical background of Tanzania's post-independence development experience and the motivation behind the strong control regime and its subsequent abandonment. Section 2.2 defines the time pattern of growth and identifies the relevant periods of this process. Section 2.3 describes the growth models utilized to decompose actual growth into the main factors of production and compares Tanzania's growth performance relative to other countries. Section 2.4 presents the empirical results and evaluates the performance of the models.

2.1 Historical setting

The immediate post-independence period (1961–7) was largely characterized by a continuation of the inherited economic policies and relatively

---

[1] Tanzania is currently the third largest producer of gold in Africa.

strong income growth *per capita* (Muganda 2004). Capital formation increased steadily during the period 1963–7, and the economy remained on a positive growth trajectory with an income growth rate *per capita* of 4.1 percent during this period.[2] The rising trend in domestic investment in the early 1960s was supported by a high level of domestic savings. Grain exports exceeded imports and the overall rural development effort in place was quite successful.

The government was not content with the speed of industrial growth and the extent to which indigenous ordinary Tanzanians were benefiting from independence. It highlighted the dangers of becoming trapped in a dependent capitalist development which offered nothing but increased alienation for the peasant majority. The government was concerned about Tanzania's continued high external dependence, particularly in the light of evidence indicating increasing manufacturing capacity in neighboring countries.[3] It was argued that, following independence, a dependent but growing African capitalist class had emerged, creating a potential for a dynamic coalition of this elite group with foreign capitalists and hence perpetuating dependence on the former colonial powers.

Initially, the government encouraged "Africanization" of the public sector through covert policies designed to promote the local economic base and retain the capitalist policies in place. Industrial development was promoted by import-substitution policy within the context of a fairly open economy. Peasant agriculture was promoted using conventional methods that encouraged agricultural intensification through mechanization and the use of fertilizers and pesticides.

However, in 1967 the government enunciated its move to socialism. The 1967 Arusha Declaration charted a new course of development, with a focus on public ownership of major industries – in particular, heavy industry. The government noted that its two overarching aims – stimulating rapid economic growth and achieving self-reliance – could not be achieved without government intervention. Self-reliance and African socialism were thus enunciated as the means to speed up development under the Arusha Declaration. The Declaration was specific about ownership, noting in particular that foreign investment could not act as the principal agent of industrial investment. This was partly on account of the unreliability of foreign capital inflows – particularly in view of the very poor and frustrating response of FDI relative to the goals of Tanzania's First Five-Year Plan (1964–9) – and due

[2] The average income growth rate *per capita* during the period 1961–70 is lower at 3.0 percent, on account of bouts of negative growth rate following independence and in the initial years after the Arusha Declaration, reflecting the uncertainties of foreign private investors.

[3] The government noted that Tanzania was forced to import even basic manufacturing goods while her neighbors, Kenya and Uganda, consolidated their manufacturing base.

to the inconsistency of foreign-led industrial growth with the principles of socialism and self-reliance. Furthermore, the Arusha Declaration brought to the core the objective of equity – inter-personal, inter-regional, and rural – urban – with its implication for industrial location and pay structures. The principles of state ownership of rents and the objective of equity found deep resonance with Nyerere's own Fabian socialist beliefs, which were widely embraced by many of the first-generation leaders in Africa (Ndulu 2007). Income growth *per capita* declined in 1969 and 1970, as the negative effects of the onset of socialist policies kicked in (Bank of Tanzania 1994).

It is quite striking that even the "hard control" phase of Tanzania's development received quite strong endorsement by development partners, as evidenced by the large inflows of aid and official credit to fund the country's socialist programs. Despite the enunciation of African socialism as the basis for government policy-making, aid inflows increased significantly during the period 1967–77, in both absolute terms and relative to other SSA countries.[4] The "socialist" vision of Mwalimu Nyerere's presidency excited widespread admiration and support from academics and policy-makers in the capitalist West. As the global developmental paradigm *in vogue* turned against state-led planning, Tanzania's policies were increasingly criticized by donors. Despite the decrease in aid inflows during the early 1980s, however, Tanzania received higher inflows than most SSA countries, including Ghana, which at the time was considered the "star" performer (Bigsten *et al.* 1999). Tanzania's evolving relationship with donors illustrates the endogeneity of the perceived state of the policy environment to the prevailing global developmental paradigm. It also suggests that aid inflows may be subject to a high degree of inertia; once committed, they are difficult to terminate.

2.2 Growth episodes

Tanzania's average *per capita* income growth averaged 0.7 percent during the years 1960–2000. Tanzania's post-independence growth experience is almost in the middle of the group of African countries, but displays a high degree of variation over the period. Following the characterization of the growth experience in the first decade in section 2.1 the rest of the period can be sub-divided into three periods: a "hard control" regime period, from 1970 to 1985; a period of softening of controls, 1985–95; and a market-friendly and democratic period, from 1995 to date (see table 13.1a, p. 437). A brief discussion of each period follows.

[4] The World Bank, for example, doubled its lending program to Tanzania between 1973 and 1977 as Tanzania's development strategy was consistent with the policy of redistribution and growth spearheaded by Robert McNamara, then President of the World Bank.

2.2.1   1967–1985: strong control

Economic mismanagement resulted in low income growth rate *per capita*, averaging 1 percent during the period 1970–85. Early success in achieving an income growth rate of 3.4 percent is attributable to the establishment and expansion of the industrial sector. Public investment during the period 1970–85 averaged 9.6 percent of GDP. However, preponderant controls, disincentives to work and invest encompassed in the collective production schemes, and an import substitution strategy spawned a thriving underground parallel market. With this undercurrent, the adverse exogenous shocks the country experienced during the late 1970s – in particular, the end of the coffee boom in 1978, the oil price shock in 1979, and the costly war against Idi Amin's Uganda in 1979 – prompted a sudden decline in growth during the period 1979–85. The tightening of controls in the face of adverse exogenous shocks and dwindling reserves further fueled the thriving parallel markets and undermined the revenue base of government and officially recorded exports.

In the face of a balance of payments crisis the government increasingly utilized deficit financing to close the resource gap. This resulted in high inflation rates and sharp declines in real wages – further fueling withdrawal from the official economy by a wide range of economic agents. Economic policy mistakes by Mwalimu Nyerere's government in the face of shocks worsened what had already become a crisis. As a result, the economy was in recession during the period 1980–5, with income *per capita* declining at an annual (negative growth) rate of 1.8 percent. Despite this negative income growth, investment during the period was not curtailed as the government sustained its capacity expansion drive to stimulate growth and maintain the political patronage system. Public investment remained high during the period 1980–5, averaging 8.7 percent, nearly at the historical levels of the previous decade.

2.2.2   1985–1995: softening of controls

There was a sharp recovery in income growth *per capita* during the period 1985–9, averaging 3.0 percent, mainly due to the resurfacing of the underground economy as the stringent controls were relaxed. In addition, the large supply response to the increased availability of goods – ending nearly a decade of frustrated demand – had a positive effect on growth. Symptomatic of the improvement of the macroeconomic environment was a rise in reserves from an average of 0.9 months of imports of goods and factor services during the period 1976–85 to 3 months of imports by June 1993. This recovery was followed by a period of setback with low income growth *per capita*, averaging negative 0.2 percent during the period 1990–5, as adherence to the reform process waned. A key reason behind the slowdown of reforms was a near-abdication of the government from its reformist role as the first constitutional application of term limits was about to be applied under competitive politics. This period was marked by a rise in corruption, reaching the highest levels of government (Helleiner 2000). The reform process was relegated, as efforts were employed to accrue "rents to sovereignty" emanating from the second aid boom. The exodus of key donors providing balance of payments support resulted in a decrease in reserves to 1.5 months of imports by 1995.

2.2.3   1995 to date: market-oriented reforms

The deepening and persistence of the reforms has resulted in sustained economic growth, with high growth particularly since 1999. Tanzania posted an average income *per capita* growth of 2 percent during 1996–2004. Two important features characterized growth recovery during this period. First, the growth trajectory shifted upwards due to a more diversified economic base. The main growth drivers were the mining sector (mainly the discovery of gold) and tourism, posting average growth rates of 15 percent and 10 percent, respectively. A second feature is that growth is now much more export-oriented. There has been a large increase in the share of foreign exchange earnings in total production. Merchandise export earnings increased from an average of $350 million during the period 1985–95 to slightly more than $1,000 million in 2004 (with $200 million of these being traditional exports) and earnings from services rose more than three-fold, from about $200 million to the current $700 million during the same period. In combination with the resumption of aid, official reserves increased from 1.6 months of imports of goods and services in 1985 to 7.9 months in 2002 and about $1 billion in 2004. In contrast to the previous phase President Benjamin Mkapa adopted a good policy environment as a legacy, even as he faced a constitutional term limit. His focus on binding reform success in legal and institutional reforms augured well for the sustainability of the market system beyond the constitutional term (Muganda 2004).

2.3   The growth models

Two models are utilized to capture the sources of growth in Tanzania: (1) standard Collins–Bosworth (1996) growth accounting, and (2) regression-based decompositions that tie down growth differences across SSA, picking up the "contributions" of various explanatory variables on growth. In essence, the regression-based decompositions explore the idiosyncratic determinants of growth in Tanzania after accounting for growth in SSA.

2.3.1 Collins–Bosworth growth-accounting exercise

The standard growth accounting exercise, draws on the Collins–Bosworth (1996) framework to estimate contribution to growth of capital, labor, and TFP. A Cobb–Douglas production function using a three-factor model with physical capital (K), human capital adjusted labor ($h.L$) is estimated. TFP (A) is obtained as a residual in the growth accounting framework,

$$Y_t = A_t \cdot f(K^{0.35}t, (h_t \cdot L_t)^{0.65}) \tag{1}$$

The model is based on two underlying assumptions: constant returns to scale with capital share of 0.35.[5] The capital stock series is generated using the perpetual inventory method where the depreciation rate of 0.04 is assumed.[6] Human capital is generated from average years of schooling data under the assumption that each year of additional educational attainment raises marginal product by 7 percent.[7]

2.3.2 Regression-based decompositions

Regression-based decompositions provide an indication of the variables that are likely to be important at the country level. These are based on a panel regression framework in which growth is estimated conditional on a list of plausible determinants of growth. Regression-based decompositions therefore overcome the limitations of the growth-accounting exercises in identifying the contribution of country specific variables,

$$\ln y_{it} - \ln y_{it-1} = -\alpha \ln y_{it-1} + x'_{it}\beta + z'_i\gamma + e_{it} \tag{2}$$

where x'_{it} is a vector of time-varying growth determinants; z'_i is a vector of fixed-effects determinants, and the lagged income variables ($\ln y_{it-1}$) allows for conditional convergence. Two different approaches are taken: the augmented Solow model using the general method of moments (GMM) and the pooled policy model.

The augmented Solow model decomposes growth to capture the "contributions" of initial income,[8] investment, human capital (proxied by education), replacement requirements, and a residual. The replacement

---

[5] The factor shares are based on the assumption that factors are paid their marginal value. Collins and Bosworth (2003) note that the higher capital share values reported in developing countries was partly a result of incorrect estimates of self-employed income in national accounts data.

[6] The capital stock series is taken from Nehru and Dhaervasal (1993).

[7] The returns to education are based on Mincerian coefficients. $H = (1 + \varphi)^s$, where H is human capital, φ is returns to education, and s is average years of schooling. Though microeconomic studies suggest that the return to education is highest in SSA at 0.13, evidence from macroeconomic studies shows lower returns. Hence, Collins and Bosworth (1996, 2003) generated human capital under the assumption of a 7 percent return to scale.

[8] Lag of GDP *per capita* is used as a proxy.

requirements variable is a composite variable comprising a linear combination of rate of population growth, technological progress, and the rate of capital depreciation.[9] The augmented Solow model utilizes the systems–general method of moments (SYS–GMM) approach in order to eliminate the potential biases arising from correlation of the estimated country-specific characteristics with other unobserved effects. A two-step procedure is utilized: the first step involves estimation without the measured country-specific characteristics. Having obtained consistent estimates, residuals are estimated and then regressed on the country-specific variables using the SYS–GMM approach. However, the model treats technological progress as exogenous and does not model the effects of changes in policy regime on the variables. The endogenous growth literature has shown that there are various channels through which changes in the policy environment can affect the rate of accumulation and/or the efficiency of factor utilization.[10]

The pooled policy model incorporates the impact of policy variables to growth, enabling it to capture the tragedy of the strong economic control regime, which sacrifices growth in favor of rents to the narrow political and managerial elite and the unsustainable redistributive strategy pursued by government. The black market premium, representing policy distortions related to the control regime, and institutional soundness are the key variables in the pooled policy model. In addition, country-specific variables, such as geography and initial growth, are included. The approach is based on the Chenery–Syrquin model and utilizes a panel OLS-based approach in which the baseline regression is first estimated, enabling growth to be characterized conditional on country-specific variables. This is followed by an examination of the partial correlations of growth with policy variables conditional on the baseline determinants. Finally, the "full" specification is estimated with both baseline and policy variables.

2.4 Empirical results

Based on the Collins–Bosworth model, for the forty-year period 49 percent of the growth is due to the contribution of growth in capital per worker, 6 percent is due to the contribution from education per worker, and 45 percent is due to productivity (the residual). The contribution of capital per worker declined from over 80 percent to 20 percent during the period 1975–85, reflecting the negative impact of the government's import-substitution program, particularly its focus on capital accumulation. The

---

[9] As is conventional, it is based on the assumption that the rates of technological progress and capital depreciation are constant across countries and sum to 0.05. The replacement requirements variable is therefore the sum of population growth augmented by 0.05. For a detailed discussion of the augmented Solow model see Hoeffler (2002).

[10] Barro and Lee (1993); Easterly (1996); Elbadawi and Ndulu (1996); Sachs and Warner (1997).

Table 13.1 *Tanzania and SSA, contributions to growth, 1960–1997*

	Contribution per worker of		
	Physical capital	Education	Residual
a Tanzania			
1960–4	−0.19	0.46	1.89
1965–9	0.60	0.13	2.61
1970–4	0.27	−0.13	1.27
1975–9	0.81	0.24	−1.57
1980–4	0.21	−0.02	−2.00
1985–9	0.20	−0.12	2.09
1990–7	0.79	−0.07	−0.89
Total	**0.53**	**0.07**	**0.49**
b SSA			
1960–4	0.86	0.14	0.26
1965–9	1.03	0.18	0.39
1970–4	1.22	0.2	0.87
1975–9	0.81	0.27	−1.18
1980–4	0.41	0.3	−1.99
1985–9	0.06	0.3	0.28
1990–7	−0.14	0.18	−1.59
Total	**0.61**	**0.23**	**−0.42**

Source: Collins and Bosworth (1996).

TFP decreased during the period, turning negative between 1975 and 1984. This period was characterized by a tragic collapse in investment productivity, decreasing foreign reserves, and capital controls. As the public investment projects had been largely financed through external borrowing the sharp rise in interest rates and scaling down of support from the multilateral institutions had a negative impact on growth, precipitating a balance of payments crisis. The rebound of the economy during the period 1985–90 was associated with a sharp rise in the residual. However, in essence this is mainly attributable to the resurfacing of underground activity, as opposed to an improvement in productivity. During the period 1990–7 TFP turned negative as a result of delays in the implementation of structural reforms – in particular, privatization during the early 1990s and the lagged effect of the benefits from privatization when it was eventually undertaken. However, capital productivity increased significantly during the period, reflecting the impact of increased capacity utilization particularly in the late 1990s. Tables 13.1a and 13.1b illustrate the results from the growth exercise by half-decade for Tanzania and SSA, respectively.

Table 13.2 *Tanzania, augmented Solow model*
a *The estimated model*

Growth in real GDP *per capita* (dependent variable)	Empirical results for full sample	Contributions to fitted-growth deviation for SSA
Initial income	−0.151 (−2.874)	3.08
Investment rate	0.249 (6.408)	−2.99
Replacement investment term	−0.419 (−2.897)	−0.86
Schooling attainment	0.011 (0.310)	−0.17
Fixed-period effects		−0.03

Source: Hoeffler (2002).
Note: The regression contains a full set of half-decade dummy variables. The replacement investment term is the average population growth rate during the period augmented by 0.05 (to capture technological progress and depreciation). *t*-statistics are in parentheses.

Table 13.2 *Tanzania, augmented Solow model*
b *Contribution to growth based on fitted growth from the augmented Solow model, 1960–1997*

	Estimated contribution of				
	Initial income	Investment rate	Initial schooling attainment	Replacement investment term	Time dummies
1960–4	6.14	−3.12	0.01	−1.02	0.60
1965–9	5.68	−1.4	−0.03	−1.22	0.63
1970–4	5.28	−0.69	−0.05	−0.69	−0.06
1975–9	4.73	−1.06	−0.07	−1.4	0.26
1980–4	4.9	−1.2	−0.07	−1.27	−1.44
1985–9	4.95	−0.93	−0.05	−1.29	0.10
1990–7	4.49		−0.05	−1.09	0.6
Total	**5.17**	**−1.4**	**−0.04**	**−1.14**	**0.1**

Source: Hoeffler (2002).

The Growth Projections from the augmented Solow model, developed using the SY–GMM approach, are broadly consistent with the actual pattern of growth and the findings from the growth accounting exercise. Table 13.2a presents the results from the augmented Solow model for SSA, which indicate that there is conditional convergence, as reflected in the negative coefficient on the initial income variable. This is particularly important since Tanzania's initial income *per capita* growth was lower than other countries. Consistent with results from other empirical studies, the human capital

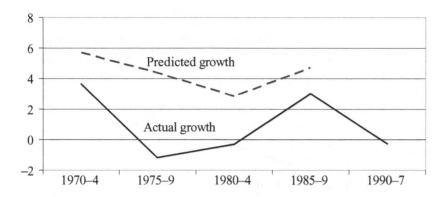

Figure 13.1 Tanzania, augmented Solow model, actual and predicted real GDP
per capita, 1970–1997, percent
Source: Hoeffler (2002).

variable does not affect income growth *per capita*.[11] There is an inverse relationship between population growth and income growth *per capita*; though investment is positively related to income growth *per capita* for the full sample, investment has a negative contribution to growth in Tanzania (table 13.2b), for the reasons discussed above.

However, the augmented Solow model over-predicts Tanzania's growth throughout the period. It indicates that Tanzania should have grown faster, necessitating an explanation of the large overall residual (figure 13.1), particularly large during 1975–85. A strong explanatory candidate here is the tragedy of collapsing investment productivity since the mid-1970s. A notable feature from the periodization is the sharp decline in the contributions of capital per worker and TFP, despite a major public investment drive during the period 1975–85. This can be attributed to poor investment decisions, including "white elephant" projects, resource misallocation resulting from capital subsidization, and constraints to capacity utilization as import capacity weakened.

The pooled policy model under-predicts growth during the control regime period in which poor economic policy dominated and over-predicts it during the positive policy reform period (Figures 13.2 and 13.3). Thus, despite the incorporation of policy effects, the residuals from the policy model are on average of similar size to those in the augmented Solow model. Tables 13.3a and 13.3b provide the baseline results from the pooled policy model and the estimated contributions to growth based on the fitted growth rate.

---

[11] The insignificance of the human capital variable in macroeconomic models has been attributed to poor measurement of the years of schooling and decreases in quality of education over time.

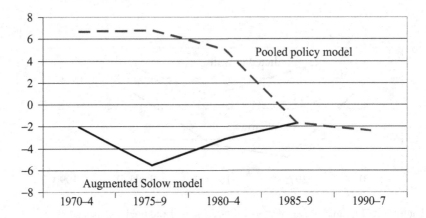

Figure 13.2 Tanzania, residuals from augmented Solow and pooled policy models, 1970–1997
Sources: Residuals from the augmented Solow model taken from Hoeffler (2002); pooled policy model residuals are based on Ndulu and O'Connell (2000).

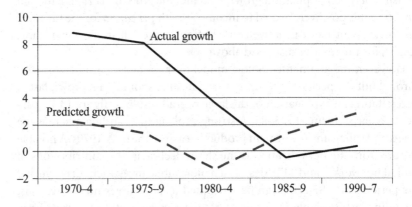

Figure 13.3 Tanzania, pooled policy model, actual and predicted real GDP *per capita*, 1970–1997, percent
Source: Based on Ndulu and O'Connell (2000).

The under-prediction of growth by the pooled policy model during the period 1970–84 suggests that there were other factors that bolstered growth. The focus on equity and poverty alleviation attracted financial support from numerous development partners despite the weak policy environment.[12] Tanzania's dependency on foreign assistance increased in spite of its

---

[12] In the model, the quality of policy environment is defined independent of the changes in the global development paradigm, which to a large extent influenced the quantity of aid a country received. As Ndulu (2005), for example shows, Tanzania's CPIA rating was relatively high during the 1970s, consistent with the ruling global development paradigm, which emphasized equity and universal access to basic needs.

Table 13.3 *Tanzania, contributions to growth*
a Baseline pooled regressions

Growth in real GDP *per capita*	Baseline pooled regression from full sample	Contributions to fitted-growth deviation for SSA
Initial conditions		−0.07
Initial income	−1.765 (−6.104)	
Initial life expectancy	0.089 (2.872)	
Demographics		−0.85
Age dependency ratio	−0.052 (−4.222)	
Growth in labor force participation	0.728 (2.711)	
External shocks		−0.05
Terms of trade shock	0.004 (0.146)	
Trading partner growth	0.540 (2.759)	
Geography		
Landlocked	−0.912 (−2.759)	
Political instability		
Political instability index	−0.975 (−4.220)	
Policy variables		−0.04
Inflation (<500 percent)	−0.004 (−1.830)	
Black market premium (<500 percent)	−0.007 (−2.403)	
Government non-productive consumption	−0.113 (−4.555)	
R^2	0.407	
Root MSE	2.186	

Source: Ndulu and O'Connell (2002).
Note: t-statistics are in parentheses.

rhetoric about the policy of self-reliance, with foreign aid excluding technical assistance rising from 0.5 percent in 1970 to 5.2 percent of GDP in 1984 (Helleiner 2000). The foreign assistance cushioned the adverse impact of adjustment measures on the economy, enabling Tanzania to maintain relatively higher import levels than would have been possible without the aid given the steep collapse of exports and foreign reserves. Drawing on the Hansen–Tarp (1999) findings that aid has a positive impact on growth even in economies characterized by weak policy environment, it can be argued that the higher-than-projected growth was partly supported by the sustained aid inflows. However, it must be emphasized that the donor inflows merely delayed the adjustment process and induced a decrease in external competitiveness as inflation soared. In addition, Tanzania's legacy of low

Table 13.3 b *Contribution to growth from pooled model, 1960–1997*

Contributions to fitted-growth deviation for Tanzania	1960–4	1965–9	1970–4	1975–9	1980–4	1985–9	1990–7
Initial conditions							
Initial income	1.58	1.33	1.34	1.31	1.22	1.17	1.82
Initial life expectancy	0.14	0.06	0.16	0.12	0.2	−0.07	−0.56
Demographics							
Age dependency ratio	−0.40	−0.26	−0.40	−0.53	−0.36	−0.44	−0.71
Growth in labor force participation	0.12	−0.09	−0.18	0.17	0.18	0.06	−0.11
External shocks							
Terms of trade shock			−0.07	−0.02	−0.02	−0.01	0.00
Trading partner growth	0.18	−0.15	0.04	0.15	0.21	0.17	0.20
Geography							
Landlocked	0.25	0.35	0.32	0.26	0.4	0.46	0.30
Political instability							
Political instability index		0.10	−0.01	0.07	0.03	0.10	0.11
Policy variables							
Inflation (<500 percent)		−0.03	0.00	0.02	−0.05	−0.11	−0.08
Black market premium (<500 percent)	0.05	0.04	−0.52	−0.47	−1.38	−0.89	−0.17
Government non-productive consumption	−0.19	−0.24	−0.57	−0.60	−0.90	−0.91	−0.13

investment productivity in comparison to other SSA countries can largely be attributed to the over-extended public sector and high capital accumulation.

However, the pooled policy model over-predicts income growth *per capita* during the period 1985–9. Though the policy initiatives had some positive effects, the achievement of sustainable growth remained constrained, with growth in income *per capita* being lower than the average for SSA. For example, though the reforms succeeded in reviving agricultural production, structural bottlenecks such as poor transportation and marketing of agricultural commodities and weak inter-sectoral linkages were not addressed. As a result, agricultural exports remained stagnant. In addition, inflation remained high, as the distribution of food across the country was poor. The delays in unification of the exchange rates (in the official and parallel markets) had severe fiscal and monetary ramifications, reinforcing inflationary pressures. The burden of external adjustment was placed on exchange rate controls and concessional financing as opposed to realignment of the exchange rate or aggregate demand management (Kaufmann and O'Connell 1999).

The pooled policy model over-predicts growth performance during the period 1990–7. The poor performance of the model in tracking growth *per capita* during this period is linked to limitations in the model with respect to capturing policy reversals and exogenous shocks. The black market exchange rate premium, a key measure of policy in the model, continued to fall (indicating continued improvement) as the process of unification of the foreign exchange market proceeded, with substantial amounts of aid continuing to flow into the country during 1990–3. The government's waning commitment to reforms, particularly after 1992, reflected its laxity in public finance management, as illustrated by the massive tax evasions, and resulted in a re-emergence of serious macroeconomic imbalances – a soaring inflation rate and large and widening fiscal imbalances. This led to negative growth in 1992 and had a dampening effect on growth in the ensuing years before its resurgence after 1996 as the third-phase government returned to a durable reform path.

The impact of exogenous shocks resulting from the *El Niño* rains in 1997 was possibly larger than that captured in the model. The rains had a detrimental effect on inflation and aggregate industrial production through their negative effect on the transport infrastructure, electricity generation, and food crop production. Reflecting these negative developments, actual GDP *per capita* turned negative in 1997. As a result, despite the prudent fiscal policy inflation remained double-digit and the period 1996–8 was characterized by periods of negative *per capita* growth.

The productivity effects of structural reforms, resulting from foreign capital injection and know-how, were felt towards the end of the 1990s and early 2000s. Moreover, as Moshi and Kilindo (1999) note, the response of investors to these policies differed. Thus, while there was a swift positive reaction from private investors to the trade liberalization policies, the response to privatization was more gradual. These factors reinforced the low growth rate in the mid-1990s.

3. Government intervention and market structure

Tanzania made a remarkable "U-turn" from strong government intervention in the late 1960s and 1970s to market-orientation by the 1990s. This section reviews the changing market structure and explains the underlying motivation of government intervention in the goods, financing, and labor markets. It also describes the performance of the market, with a particular focus on the incentives in place.

3.1   Goods market

3.1.1   1967–1985: The strong control regime

International and private trade was confined to state agencies with co-operatives and marketing boards officially dissolved in 1976 and replaced with crop authorities. The government felt that the co-operatives in operation following independence were dominated by petty capitalist farmers. Furthermore, they were seen as corrupt and inefficient (Hyden and Mwase 1976). In addition, the government regarded the co-operatives in place as competitive political forces (Lele, van de Walle, and Gbetibouo 1989).[13] The dismantling of the larger co-operative unions, such as the Nyanza Co-operative Union that covered several regions, was seen as part of a strategy to weaken their political force and that of its leaders. The government therefore set out to mold these agencies into "*Ujama'a*" villages managed and controlled by the indigenous farmers (peasants) in a new co-operation that embodied socialist egalitarian principles.[14] In practice, this involved the government appointing managers to run the crop authorities and represent farmers' interests. Maize, beans, and coffee trading were officially confined to state-controlled marketing institutions with the scope of issues handled expanded significantly to include loans and management in addition to the marketing of crops.[15]

Central to the government's policy was the creation of "*Ujama'a*" villages modeled along the lines of Mao Tse Tung's Chinese communes. *Ujama'a* villages were established in areas with scattered homesteads with the objective of replacing the individual farms with a network of village communities in which land could be collectively owned and production collectively organized. This resulted in an increase in the population residing in settled villages from 5 percent of the rural population at the start of the program to 60 percent by the end of 1975 (Lofchie 1989).

Production in remote areas was heavily subsidized by the government directly (through inputs subsidies) and indirectly (through the system of pan-territorial prices). The latter involved the setting of the same prices in

---

[13] These member-based co-operatives were established prior to independence in order to market cotton and coffee and protect producers' profit margins. However, over time, their control had increased with one in particular having a monopoly over all the handling of rice, sisal, and maize (McLoughlin 1967).

[14] This was part of the idea of the *Ujama'a* village spelled out in "Socialism and Rural Development," a document which explained the process of implementing the policy of socialism (McHenry 1994).

[15] However, maize sales at the local market through private channels were allowed.

all regions with the transportation costs absorbed by the state. Pan-territorial prices were introduced in the early 1970s and adjusted upwards several times in mid-decade. This encouraged production in potentially productive but remote areas (Amani, van der Brink, and Maro 1992; Sundet 1995).

The government intervened significantly in setting of food prices, as this was considered a captive market.[16] Stringent price controls were increasingly applied from the early 1970s as inflation increased in order to encourage production of domestic food crops and support the low wages paid to the civil service. Producer prices were announced before the start of the season and were designed to induce production, while ensuring equitable distribution of welfare across all the regions. In order to stimulate domestic production of maize, higher producer prices were offered in the ten most important maize-growing areas; however, consumer prices were also subsidized with little regard to the actual costs of marketing maize.

The cost of the "Villagization Program," coupled with weak state marketing agencies, loss-making parastatals, and an unsustainable attempt at providing universal access to social services, resulted in a sharp decline in foreign reserves and a shortage of goods. The villagization program, which was based on collective production with farmers sharing the profits of their labor, provided a strong disincentive to work particularly as output was divided without due regard to effort. The food crisis of 1974–5 was linked to drought, but also to the collectivization policy. The villagization program was eventually quietly abandoned as the costs entailed in relocating families escalated and production in the newly established villages remained low.

A state marketing and import controls strategy spawned a large underground economy, with thriving parallel markets. The pan-territorial pricing system penalized the producers near the major urban centers by cross-subsidizing distant producers who faced higher transportation costs of getting their products to the market (Jayne and Jones 1997).[17] Maize shortages emerged as inefficiencies in the marketing system and distribution costs of inputs increased

In response to the food shortages the government introduced dual producer and consumer prices in 1982–3 for some major and minor crops to provide an incentive to growers in designated regions for producing a crop in which it was felt the area had a comparative advantage. Consumer prices were also varied, depending on whether or not the region was a major producer of the predominant staple food. Subsidies on maize, as mentioned above, bore little relation to the actual marketing costs.

---

[16] Since food crop production was predominantly for the domestic market, the government utilized pricing policy extensively during the 1970s with the aim of achieving desired production and consumption.

[17] Smuggling was rampant, with only farmers in the remote Southern Highlands selling their surplus maize through official channels.

In order to increase ownership of industry, government policy focused on expansion of the public industrial sector and consolidated these initiatives with institutional foundations for socialist development. In addition, reflecting the equity objective, the link between industrial development and rural development was emphasized. To achieve this, the government encouraged the development of small-scale industries and adopted a decentralization policy, identifying nine towns where industries would be located.[18] The government emphasized the importance of structural transformation of the economy in terms of product mix; it also sought to increase the manufactured value added in exports and widen the range of manufactured products to include not only consumer goods but also intermediate and capital goods.

Industrial growth remained high in the first few years after the Arusha Declaration, reflecting the effect of the creation and expansion of the sector. The sector grew from some forty entities in 1966 to about 450 entities by the mid-1980s. Though backward and forward linkages were strong, when compared to other African countries the industries remained loss-making and were characterized by low productivity. The sector benefited from protection and transfers from the government; moreover, though the investment program was driven by the public sector, most of the investment undertaken was donor-funded.

The industrial sector was vulnerable to the external position of the country due to its reliance on state subventions for foreign exchange. The sharp decline in foreign reserves following the external shocks of the late 1970s had an adverse impact on the industrial sector since it depended on imports for its capital goods and more critical intermediate goods and relied heavily on state support for its financing. The shortage in foreign exchange resulted in an abortive import liberalization in 1978.

In the face of the adverse exogenous shocks, the government did not realign the exchange rate, partly because it felt that devaluation would hinder the development of the parastatals. Instead import restrictions supported by donor inflows were employed to maintain the over-valued exchange rate in the face of the balance of payments crisis. This had a sharp adverse impact on the very sector it was designed in part to protect; the industrial sector recorded negative growth rates towards the end of the 1970s and the early 1980s on account of sharp cuts in raw materials, intermediate inputs, and capital goods. The government argued that it was not microeconomic inefficiencies but macroeconomic weaknesses that needed to be resolved, stressing that the high costs of basic intermediates' substitutes were a key

---

[18] Dar-es-Salaam, the major city formerly the nation's capital, was not one of the identified cities.

factor behind the poor performance of the parastatals. It favored supporting the parastatals through the maintenance of a strong currency.

3.1.2 1985–1995: Softening the control regime and modest recovery of growth

The period was characterized by government withdrawal from direct involvement in production, processing, and marketing activities, retaining only its role in setting policies. The large losses incurred by the state agencies coupled with the food shortages and rampant smuggling forced the government to reform the food-crop sector (Bank of Tanzania 1981; Putterman 1995). These reforms gained momentum after the government expedited the implementation of a SAP emphasizing current account liberalization. Initially producer prices were increased and tariffs were reduced. There was a gradual move towards liberalization of the marketing of food and cash crops, removal of the monopoly export powers of crop export marketing boards, and restructuring of several parastatals (World Bank 1994). In addition, the government increasingly phased out the implicit subsidy on mineral fertilizers, which moved from 80 percent in 1988–9 to 70 percent in 1990–1 and was finally terminated in 1994–5.

Economic performance improved, albeit gradually, but the industrial sector did not recover. Though farmers responded positively to the increases in prices in the mid-1980s, weak marketing and a poor distribution chain hindered an increase in food supplies to urban areas and a sharp increase in cash crop exports between 1987 and 1989. In addition, though exchange controls were relaxed the underground economy reacted somewhat slowly, reflecting concerns about the tax implications of resurfacing and uncertainties about possible policy reversals. The increased emphasis on removing structural impediments to growth in the late 1980s increased the responsiveness of output to the changing policy environment, and as a result growth in marketed output and export crops was strong. By 1990 the increased food availability had eliminated the need for food imports. In addition, the non-traditional agricultural exports sector increased five-fold between 1985 and 1991 (Mans 1994). The revival of the industrial sector was not achieved, however, mainly on account of delays in the implementation of structural reforms – in particular, privatization and divesture of the parastatals. Weak management and rent-seeking, particularly in the early 1990s, hindered the necessary adjustment needed to improve investment productivity.

3.1.3 1995 to date: Market-based economy

In order to develop capacity, improve overall efficiency, and develop a more competitive business environment, public enterprises were privatized and investment-friendly policies introduced to encourage FDI.[19] Reflecting the government's focus on providing a conducive environment for investment, fiscal and legal frameworks governing mining activities were created to foster investment. A new Mining Code was introduced in 1998, following a five-year World Bank-financed sectoral reform project. Building on the institutional reforms in the public sector, the government established an investment promotion center with the aim of facilitating investment (a one-stop center) and amended a number of investment-related laws putting in place tax exemptions and tax holidays to attract investors: as a result, Tanzania currently has one of the most liberal investment regimes in Africa. The Land Act was prepared in consultation with various stakeholders with the aim of ensuring transparent, timely, and secure access to property titles with mortgage and transfer rights.

The reform process has succeeded in attracting FDI and, through this, changing the structure of exports. The share of exports has increasingly shifted from traditional exports (cotton, coffee, tea, and tobacco) to other exports, in particular mining and marine exports. Tanzania is currently one of the highest recipients of FDI in Africa. According to UNCTAD (2004), investors rank Tanzania as the most attractive destination for investment in Africa (excluding South Africa).[20]

3.2   Labor market

Government policy focused on developing a diverse and competent labor force for the public sector and achieving full employment. Active planning was undertaken to ensure against potentially divisive forces such as tribal and religious inequity which could result in internal factions within the country and distract from nation-building. The planning system was intended to ensure that all persons with a given predetermined education level would secure public sector employment.[21]

Labor productivity remained low as there were no incentives to raise performance and competence. The hiring of cronies weakened the capacity for innovation and was exacerbated by the hierarchical organizational structures. The assurance of lifetime employment and seniority as basis for promotion further reduced the incentive to perform. The low wages aggravated the situation, encouraging petty corruption and "moonlighting."

---

[19] More than half of the 400 public sector entities identified for privatization in 1993 had been divested by 1999.

[20] UNCTAD (2004).

[21] The education policy, particularly at secondary level, was designed to provide a broad cultural experience, with students sent to study in different regions laying a foundation for a united nation.

The centralized manpower planning geared towards the public sector stifled the development of a skilled private sector. The sharp expansion of the public sector resulted in an increase in demand for high- and middle-level manpower; this was achieved through a major change in the allocation of graduates from government to parastatals in an attempt to speed up localization of top posts in the parastatals and the government employing a pool of professional trained workers. This instilled a perception, which one can argue still persists, that participating in private-owned entrepreneurial activities reflects a low skill base and career drive.

The focus on creating inter-personal equity created a culture of state dependence and free-riding. Punitive taxes were introduced to ensure that equity in the distribution of income was maintained: during the control regime period, income tax rates of over 80 percent were not uncommon. However, it must be stressed that without investment in creating a united nation out of diverse ethnic groups, Tanzania would probably have succumbed like some her neighbors to inter-ethnic squabbles leading to political and/or civil instability. Though Tanzania is ethnically diverse, political stability and harmony among all the ethnic groups have been maintained. Tanzania's legacy of peace and ethnic cohesion is therefore largely a result of early investment in creating national harmony and a strong focus on poverty reduction.

Over time, there has been an increasing emphasis on performance-based remuneration. The third regime government, in particular, through civil service reform, made significantly strides in raising salaries, wages, and other conditions in order to reduce petty corruption and increase efficiency.

3.3 Financial markets

3.3.1 1967–1985: The strong control regime

The financial system was entirely state-controlled, characterized by state-owned financial intermediaries geared towards the provision of finance to specific sectors – in particular, housing, agriculture, and industry. Banking was essentially a form of quasi-government financing for SOEs rather than genuine financial intermediation. Ceilings were imposed on nominal lending and borrowing, with the goal of discouraging private sector borrowing. The financial sector was repressed, as reflected in negative real interest rates, a low broad money–GDP ratio, and a high fiscal deficit–GDP ratio. The degree of financial deepening was low even compared to other SSA countries.

Mandatory credit ceilings coupled with administratively directed credit allocation to priority sectors undermined allocative efficiency, resulting in large non-performing loans. The negative real interest rates discouraged savings mobilization and their channeling through the financial system. In addition, the negative interest rates led to credit rationing by the banking system, with adverse impacts on the quantity and quality of investment (Mwega 1990). State control of financial institutions resulted in credit allocation on political rather than commercial criteria. Some 60–80 percent of the total non-performing loans in the state-owned banks emanated from political pressure on banks to lend to politically connected borrowers, albeit with a bad credit record. In addition, there was limited competition as the financial system was dominated by a virtual monopoly; the National Bank of Commerce (NBC) had 85 percent of the market share and the clientèle was limited to the government and parastatals.[22]

Monetary policy was subordinated to supporting government objectives, resulting in hyperinflation. The central bank was faced with multiple objectives, including full employment, high growth, and low inflation and it frequently subordinated the latter to support the government's expansionary program. As the economic performance and foreign reserves dwindled, the central bank increasingly resorted to seigniorage activities in order to bankroll the loss-making parastatals and financial institutions.

A cornerstone in government policy-making was a reluctance to devalue the currency. The government adopted a fixed exchange rate regime and did not realign the currency in the face of widening current account deficits excluding grants. The currency remained broadly stable against the dollar during the 1970s despite the imbalances in the foreign exchange rate market, a stability largely due to the massive donor inflows the country received. The central bank accommodated external terms of trade shocks and other adverse shocks through sales of foreign reserves and external borrowing. In the face of a balance of payment crisis in the late 1970s and dwindling donor support, the government relied on capital and current account controls to maintain the exchange rate, including administrative import controls and mandatory surrender of the proceeds from exports. Following the decrease in reserves to less than 1 percent of GDP during 1980–5, pressure on the exchange rate forced the government to devalue the currency. However the realignments undertaken were insufficient to address the misalignment of the currency and the foreign exchange was allocated administratively within a framework of heavy restrictions. As a result, the exchange rate premium increased, reaching a peak of over 200 percent in 1985 (Bank of Tanzania 1994; Kaufmann and O'Connell 1991).

3.3.2   1985–1995: Softening of controls

This period was marked by a wide-scale restructuring of the financial architecture. The adjustment program was designed to reduce the monetization

---

[22] Brownbridge and Gayi (2000)

of the deficit and reverse the crowding-out effects on the private sector. State intervention was restricted to the provision of a transparent regulatory environment. Specifically, the central bank was granted legislative powers to oversee the prudential soundness of the financial system; in 1992, controls on interest rates were removed and in 1993 the exchange rate market was liberalized. Treasury Bill auctions were introduced in 1993 to allow a role for market forces to influence rates and to facilitate the use of indirect techniques of monetary control. Restrictions on the entrance of private banks, both foreign and local, were removed. The removal of foreign exchange controls allowed residents to purchase and hold foreign currency legally. This, combined with the rapid exchange rate depreciation following the realignment of the currency, made the holding of foreign currency assets more attractive relative to domestic currency assets.

Financial sector reforms became subject to powerful vested interests. The reforms were not accompanied by the needed macroeconomic and structural changes: state-owned banks remained captive markets exposed to political interference. Tanzania suffered a sharp contraction of financial depth in the second half of the 1980s but recovered almost half of the fall in 1990–5. Regulatory and supervisory capacities were, however, inadequate on account of the delays in adopting structural reforms.

Exchange rate unification was delayed as attempts were made to maintain patron–client networks through monetary financing and exchange controls. Unification of the black market and official exchange rate initially involved a devaluation of the official exchange rate and the decontrol of commodity prices that faced foreign exchange rate controls in the late 1980s. Reflecting the realignment of the exchange rate in the late 1980s, the black market premium decreased in the early 1990s, and was less than 10 percent by 1992. During 1993, the remaining restrictions on current account foreign exchange transactions were removed and the government introduced weekly central bank auctions for registered foreign exchange dealers and banks. In late 1993, the weekly auctions were replaced with a daily inter-bank foreign exchange rate market, which provided a mechanism for determining the official exchange rate (Bank of Tanzania 1994). Kaufmann and O'Connell (1997) note that a faster unification of the exchange rates would have reduced monetary growth and inflationary pressures.

3.3.3 1995 to date: Market economy

Financial liberalization was one of the key pillars of the reform process. The reforms aimed at deepening the financial system, instituting an independent monetary policy, and increasing competition in the financial system. Noting that continued disintermediation and negative interest rates in real terms were particularly harmful to the efficient allocation of scarce financial resources, Treasury Bill auctions were streamlined. To prevent

crowding-out, a cash budget system was introduced and tight fiscal policies employed, demonstrating the commitment of the new government to
operating within the constraints of the budget framework and maintaining fiscal prudence. To address the problem of wide-scale tax evasion and
improve transparency in tax regulation, the government rationalized the tax
system and improved the tax administration. An integrated financial management system was developed to ensure that financial decisions were taken
with due regard to availability of financial resources. The Central Bank was
provided with legislative powers in 1995 to focus solely on low and stable
price stability as the overarching objective.

Fiscal restraint coupled with tight monetary policy had a dampening
effect on inflation, resulting in an improvement in the external competitiveness of the economy. Liberalization coupled with deregulation induced a
large depreciation of the currency and, coupled with sound economic management, resulted in a decrease in inflation and hence a real exchange rate
depreciation. Inflation fell to its lowest levels in twenty years in 1999, reflecting the government's adherence to a strictly restrained monetary policy in
the context of a market-determined exchange rate system. The government
deficit halved to an average of 9.3 percent of GDP during the period 1990–7
compared to the period 1985–90, and was lower than the 10.3 percent average in SSA. Fiscal restraint coupled with a tight monetary policy had a
dampening effect on inflation, enabling an improvement in the external
competitiveness of the economy and resulting in an improvement in the
competitiveness of the external sector.

Despite these positive reforms, financial sector intermediation remained
weak. Reforms to the financial sector did not succeed in mobilizing savings,
which remained low in absolute terms and relative to other SSA countries.
The low savings mobilization was mainly attributable to the decrease in
deposit rates during the period; despite the decrease in inflation, the return
on deposits did not increase – if anything, deposit rates declined in real
terms. In addition, the costs associated with maintaining a bank account
escalated. As a result, though the formal banking system dominates the
capital outlay it has very limited outreach to the population. Despite the
reduction in inflation, lending rates remained high, reflecting the continued
high-risk premiums associated with Tanzania's legacy of archaic legislation
and nationalization as well as the past rapid build-up of non-performing
assets in the banking system.

4. The response of economic agents

This section discusses the constraints that traders and households face, and
their responses. In general in the first and, to some extent, the second phase,

governments' support for private sector activities was lukewarm. However, during the third phase and particularly more recently, the domestic sector was given more latitude which increasingly fostered confidence, especially from the local business community, in the irreversibility of the current policy regime.

4.1 Firms' response

The tribulations and fortunes facing manufacturing, trading, and other firms changed in response to the different development paradigms. Firm behavior was influenced by (1) the political economy, (2) market size and opportunities, (3) supporting physical and social infrastructure, (4) availability of credit, and (5) the regulatory environment. For half the post-independence period government policies favored agricultural, manufacturing, and trading parastatals at the expense of private sector activity. While the establishment of parastatals may have been well intentioned, their operations were loss-making, and many could not break even and relied on state budgetary subventions. However Tanzania more recently fell in line with the world-wide paradigm shift in favor of private-led development. Thus, over 400 parastatals have been privatized; the emergent private entrepreneurs, energized by the incentives associated with private profits, are already making a mark in industry and commerce.

Investment productivity, while increasing, has been retarded by low-capacity utilization, transportation costs, and low-skilled labor. Low-capacity utilization is associated with poor delivery of services by the utilities such as water and electricity. The supply of these utilities has been irregular, forcing industries to run at sub-optimal levels or incur the additional cost of generators and water pumps. Utility costs seem to be higher in Tanzania than in other East African countries, with Tanzanian businesses paying twice as much for electricity and fuel than those in Kenya (IMF 2004).[23] Recent moves to improve management of these utilities are expected to result in an improvement in service delivery. Telecommunication costs in Tanzania are three times higher than in Kenya and two-thirds higher than in Uganda (IMF 2004). As a coastal state, Tanzania's transport costs would have been lower and its external competitiveness higher if transport and communication infrastructure had been not less dilipated. This is aggravated by the concentration of economic activity – in particular, agriculture, fishing, and mining – in outlying peripheral areas far from ports and major consumption centers. However, current account liberalization and improved technology – for example, cumbersome documentation procedures and bureaucratic

---

[23] These costs are lower than in Uganda, partly because of the higher transportation costs resulting from its landlocked geographic position.

hurdles – have eased the non-physical constraints on traffic and trade flows.

Labor productivity has been low and is falling, partly because of the impact of HIV and AIDS and the low skill base. In addition, the level of professionalism remains low as the legacy of socialism on work culture remains – specifically, it has not recovered from the lack of incentives to invest and work harder for individual improvement.

Despite the structural reforms, the external perception about investing in Tanzania remains fragile and expansion of local SMEs is hampered by financial disintermediation. Given decades of peace and security in an unstable region, Tanzania is generally associated with low political risk; more recently, the perception of economic risk seems to have declined and private sector activity continues to expand domestically. However, despite the relatively high FDI that Tanzania has received, the weakness of external perceptions is reflected by the large share accounted for by the mining sector (40 percent). In order to induce FDI in other sectors the legal and regulatory environment needs to be strengthened. Investors need assurance that they can without delay get justice before the law: the introduction of a Commercial Court in Tanzania is a step in the right direction. In addition, lending rates remain high and credit allocation remains limited to a narrow set of investors, hampering the development of SMEs. Ongoing measures to create a credit information bureau and improve the judicial process of loan recovery would reduce the costs associated with lending.

4.2   Households' response

Tanzania has made concerted efforts to design policies to stimulate agriculture and develop the rural economy. At independence, slightly over 90 percent of the population resided in rural homesteads and were engaged in subsistence agriculture. Government policy sought to raise the productivity of agricultural labor by altering production systems to take advantage of scale economies. Under the "*Ujama'a*" policy and its "Villagization" thrust, the "*Ujama'a*" villages would be linked to agricultural extension centers and receive information on the mechanization of agriculture and developments in agricultural research.

Despite these reforms, over 70 percent of the population are still engaged in smallholder agriculture. Rural household incomes have declined continuously while real prices of consumer goods have been rising, with the decrease in income partly attributable to the decrease in producer prices (particularly cash crops) and the increase in agricultural input costs following the decontrol of prices (Cromwell *et al.* 1996). However, low agricultural input prices do not increase farmers' supply response if agricultural inputs are unavailable. Reflecting this, the public debate on market reforms has focused on the provision of social services in a market economy as opposed to reversion to the era of market controls and food shortages (Ponte 1998, 2002a).

Rural livelihoods remain hampered by financial disintermediation, poor transportation, and low producer prices. Most of the population remains marginalized with no access to financial services. Micro-finance institutions have alleviated the situation, but these tend to be located in more accessible rural communities. Rural feeder roads are poor and often impassible during the rainy season, which has hampered the development of the rural economy. The elimination of price support and subsidies has been a major disincentive to production, particularly of export crops (Bienefeld, 1995). Low commodity prices – for example, for coffee and cotton – have led to a situation where smallholders have substituted such cash crops for food crops and dairy industry and led to a virtual collapse of cotton production (Ponte 1998, 2002a, 2002b).

Agricultural production was expected to grow within the framework of "*Ujama'a*" villages in which the traditional system of rural settlement dominated by individual plots was replaced with large communal villages managed by the peasants themselves for their own benefit. However, recent changes have led to a shift towards individually owned "*shambas*" (plots), more or less as it was before the 1967 Arusha Declaration. The challenge for agricultural transformation persists: in particular, peasants need to be encouraged to produce not only for their own consumption but also for export.

5. A synthesis: the political economy of Tanzania's growth experience

A narrow elite at independence promised growth and poverty reduction in exchange for development autocracy. The promise combined a sense of urgency in catching up with developed countries ("we must run while they walk": Nyerere), promoting economic nationalism through the public sector, and providing improved and equitable access to essential services to the poor as painlessly as possible through redistribution. Failure to engender the promised growth represented a breach of the contract, setting in motion both a grass-root response and an explicit political discourse that led to the demise of the model of development autocracy and a move back to more market-oriented and open polity regimes. In this section we synthesize and offer a political economic explanation for Tanzania's paradigmatic shifts in its development strategies and the implications for growth performance.

5.1   The origin and logic of development autocracy in Tanzania

The interventionist stance adopted by Tanzania, akin to most African governments at independence, had its logic in the development paradigm of the day, which emphasized addressing the preponderance of market failures and the nascence/fragility of institutional structures which hampered development. The predominantly peasant economy was considered not only technologically backward but also lacking the requisite dynamism for autonomous development. It was argued that the state needed to play a central role as the principal agent for modernizing the economy (Ndulu 1986). The role of the government was therefore to use its fiscal powers, the external resources channeled through it, and indirect controls on private sector resource allocation to this end. The government promised development in exchange for the right of the state to maintain a centralized somewhat authoritarian system of governance. The political legitimation of this paradigm drew on the liberal assumption that the state is a neutral, and even a benevolent, arbiter among the different interest groups and can therefore be used to further national interest in economic growth, efficiency, and social welfare (Sandbrook and Barker 1985). Donor support of all types was channeled through the state on the same understanding. A *social contract* was thus struck early in the post-independence period that traded the right to open governance structures for patronage and a promise of rapid growth in what has been referred to as "developmental autocracy" (Ndulu 1986; Gordon 1990).

It is also noteworthy that during the early post-independence period the prize to freedom fighters for successfully wresting power from the colonial masters, dubbed the "fruits of independence," was increasingly used to signal that it was now "our" turn. As in many other African countries, with Botswana as an important exception, the indigenization program was the main channel for rewarding those who had made the sacrifices, and the rewards were in various forms of rents – ranging from jobs to preferential access to productive assets.

The private sector in these economies was in essence part of the covenant with the state that granted it protection, access to subsidized resources, and significant rents derived from protection. In the early phase, the government put in place an investment promotion scheme offering primarily rents from protection measures to attract foreign firms to engage in light import substitution. In many cases, a strong symmetry of interests existed between the public and the private sectors as far as price distortions, protective measures, and access to subsidized resources were concerned (Ndulu 2004). After the initial success of this strategy, signified by the rapid growth of light manufacturing, the risks associated with the shift towards a socialist regime – expropriation being the most blatant – far outweighed the rents from the above-mentioned preferential treatment. Reflecting the higher risks associated with socialist regime, there was an exodus of foreign private capital in the early 1970s and a closing of doors to new capital. In response, economic nationalism was promoted through mainly state enterprise and the encouragement of a politically connected indigenous private sector.

Alas, under developmental autocracy, policy has tended to be captured by a narrow group of elites operating under relatively weak institutional constraints. The tendency, under a strong control regime, to over-tax potentially dynamic sectors and a heavy reliance on revenues to service patron–client networks created a vulnerable balance of payments and fiscal situation. Rents from the control regime were largely based on the induced scarcity of imports, which generated large rents on rationed import licenses; on under-priced capital, giving access to subsidized capital to those who were politically connected; and on the sustenance of a large public sector for serving political patronage through jobs. The persistence of macroeconomic policy distortions was sustained partly for the above reasons as the regime attempted to close the resource gaps exacerbated by shocks through applying more stringent controls.

What is striking about this model of Tanzania's early phase of development is its strong endorsement by development partners, as evidenced by the large inflows of aid and official credit to fund the program. The thrust of the redistributive strategy and diversification of the economy through deepening import substitution was then in tune with the global development paradigm of the day. The large role of the public sector was in line with the dominant view of the 1960s and 1970s concerning the preponderance of market failures – needing public sector interventions, though not necessarily in a socialist approach – before the swing of the pendulum in the early 1980s towards a development paradigm that emphasized government failure. As noted earlier, there was strong external support for the largely populist regime, which though clientelist in orientation, like a handful other populist African regimes, strived to serve the interest of the poor majority mainly through a redistributive program dubbed "African socialism."

Another striking feature of the control regime was the protracted failure to recover from external shocks. We can find an explanation in the inability of the control regime to undertake a prudent management of booms and bust. The institutional framework through which Tanzania encountered shocks to its commodity markets in the 1970s and to world financial markets in the early 1980s offered limited flexibility to make the required but difficult adjustments. A typical example of the pattern of response to shocks constrained by inflexibility is that in relation to the commodity price boom of the mid-1970s (1975–7) followed by the second oil crisis in the late 1970s and exacerbated by the huge costs from war with Idi Amin of Uganda (1978–9). Tanzania weathered the first oil crisis by tightening import and exchange controls, as well as drawing down automatic and quick-disbursing facilities such as the oil facility operated by the IMF. The tropical beverage (coffee) boom of 1976–7 seemed to validate this strategy and even led to renewed expansion of spending (Bevan, Collier, and Horsnell 1989; Bevan *et al.* 1990). When the prices of export commodities collapsed in 1978 and the second oil crisis erupted in 1979, the government expected a similar short-lived crisis and a quick reversal of fortunes. But resource shortfalls worsened with the recession in the world economy and the debt crisis of the early 1980s. Calls from donors, in particular from the multilaterals for the government to curtail aggregate demand, and in particular its unsustainable expenditures on providing universal access to social services, were ignored. The government, faced with pressure to close the resource gap and sustain the patronage system, undertook deficit financing.

A recourse to raiding the already fledgling private sector and more stringent controls on it heightened investment risk and led to a virtual collapse of private investment. The forced savings arising from frustrated demand as the domestic supply of basic goods declined sharply resulted in a disproportionate squeeze on consumer imports and reinforced the decrease in incentives to production. As the balance of payments crisis persisted and shortages became more acute, the government responded by increasing taxes and intensifying a wide range of market interventions including foreign exchange controls, import restrictions and mandatory surrender of export proceeds, food rationing by state agencies, and price controls. Meanwhile, deficit financing continued. These developments resulted in high inflation rates and a sharp decline in real wages – further fueling a withdrawal from the official economy by a wide range of economic agents which in turn undermined the revenue base of the government and officially recorded exports. Under-reporting of export proceeds and over-invoicing of import needs was high during this period; some estimates put the level of smuggled exports at 50 percent, reflecting the move from official exports to the underground economy (Adam *et al.* 1994).

The government noted that Tanzania's need for external resources did not imply a loss of independence in setting its economic goals. With support from sympathetic donors, Tanzania was able to forge a "home-grown" economic recovery program following the collapse of its relations with the World Bank and the IMF in the late 1970s. The government emphasized that it would not make any concessions – in particular, it vetoed privatization, arguing that this would imply renouncing socialism. In addition, it refused to adopt market incentives, as this would imply the repudiation of egalitarianism. The government also resolved to continue its national policy for economic integration at the expense of restructuring its export sector. It also resisted selective austerity in provision of social services and remained committed to providing universal benefits. The program failed to address the core economic weaknesses of the country, as evidenced by maintenance of a large budget deficit and a worsening current account.

5.2 1985–1995: Softening the control regime and modest recovery of growth

The strong socialist phase was followed by a period we characterize as involving "soft controls," during which the major price controls were dismantled but the institutional and legal remnants of the strong control regime sustained uncertainty and a high risk for private investors. Reforms ran ahead of the necessary institutional and legal infrastructure for effective signaling. The supply response was largely in the form of a move back towards the production frontier and seldom through irreversible investment to expand productive capacity. Both domestic and foreign private sector investment response was minuscule, with FDI averaging no more than $20 million annually.

It is valuable to elucidate the motivation of the change from strong to soft controls building on our previous discussions. An untold story is the internal dynamics for change, when the contract of promised development did not materialize and societal cynicism about this model of development set in. Within the logic of the weak autocracy framework of governance, there were two main underlying trends, that made the demise of the regime inevitable. First was the time-inconsistency of the system of rent extraction via growth-reducing distortionary taxation, which very soon got the system to the wrong side of the Laffer curve. Second there was an assumption that the multitude of the unorganized interest groups, including the peasantry was politically passive and acquiescent to the benevolence of the state, even if state actions were geared towards catering for the interests of favored and vocal groups. The government totally underestimated the potential of grass-root responses to frustrate predation.[24]

The revenue base and aid were the most important political resource for servicing patron–client networks. Their erosion through faltering revenue collection and the reduction of aid after 1981 undermined the capacity of the political patrons in Tanzania to service their networks of clients. Economic stagnation due to under-investment in productive capacity and the increased proportion of the economy that went underground, had a negative impact on the tax base. The steady preponderance of controls to create rents for the favored groups was the main reason behind the mushrooming of parallel markets and illegal cross-border trade to evade them. This development not only undermined the fiscal base of the state but also led to the collapse of

---

[24] Ndulu (2002) and (2004) develops this argument in greater detail.

exports, significantly reducing the rental incomes which hitherto had been available to service patron–client networks.

There was also the latent tension between grass-root interests and the purported national interests advanced through state policies. Traditional social structures are characterized by the dominance of relatively autonomous networks bound by kinship, tribe, religion, race, or community ties. These networks span rural–urban boundaries in what Hyden (1983) calls the "economy of affection," and the state is structurally superfluous and is acknowledged only to the extent that its actions are considered beneficial to the interests of these networks. Where government policy is deemed unbeneficial or a threat to their interests, these networks through their own communication systems have frustrated such policies through the use of a variety of "exit options" (Hyden 1986).[25] These included participation in parallel markets, illegal border trade, and even informal banking systems and have proved to be a potent force of frustrating predation when their own interests are ignored.

The roots of a shift away from a "hard control" and authoritarian regime to a more encompassing economic governance system lie in the above developments. Conditionality associated with adjustment finance to a large extent amplified these latent pressures for change and catalyzed the process. By the time the externally enforced adjustment had taken effect in Tanzania in late 1986, the traditional role of the state had become unsustainable. The government had over-extended itself relative to its financial and managerial resources and the society's cynicism at the effectiveness of development institutions and management had set in. Pressure for dismantling controls was being expressed by rampant evasion of controls. Removal of the failed controls and downsizing of government operations was essentially a forgone conclusion given the latent opposition to controls, emerging unsustainable resource gaps, and the rising fiscal burden of debt service. Meanwhile, the global change towards a minimalist government gathered momentum and was brought home through aid relationships and international governance. The advent of Reagan–Thatcher influences on economic policy throughout the world further darkened external views of Tanzania's policies (Helleiner 2000). Furthermore, with the advent of democracy, the threat of removal of a regime from power rather than the use of latent exit options presented an additional imperative for enforcing more encompassing behaviour.

The shift in ideology towards market-orientation and private sector development was gradual, involving consensus-building within the ruling party and across the party's spectrum. It relied on members accepting and perceiving the reforms as integral to the party's manifesto, as opposed to running contrary to the party's ethos. The political resistance to reforms was strong, since the liberalization of the economy represented a "U-turn" from the

[25] Hyden (1986) refers to the exit options taken by the "uncaptured peasant."

development strategy outlined in the Arusha Declaration. The openness and inclusiveness of the consultative process in the national debates led by the civil society, including academics, helped clarify and broaden the understanding of issues and legitimized the need for economic reforms (Bigsten *et al.* 1999). The government's use of national commissions as instruments for collecting views and building consensus on issues broadened the domestic constituency for reforms and reinforced internalization of the process, instilling an ownership of the reform process. Though the more gradualist approach had dangers, creating tensions with donors, in the end popular discussions of hard policy choices and their sequentialization reduced the dangers of policy reversals. The legacy of acrimonious debate with the Bretton Woods Institutions (BWI) and the country's commencement of initial reforms without their support provided the government with leverage with which to vocalize its socio-economic concerns within the country's own socio-political framework.

The return to an adjustment program resulted in a surge in aid, with foreign assistance excluding technical assistance rising from 4.2 percent in 1985 to 17.4 percent of GDP in 1990. The support was possibly instrumental in the success of the adjustment process. It is difficult to know how the adjustment could have been undertaken without the cushioning effect of donor aid (Bigsten and Danielson 1999).

However, the shifting fortunes of various stakeholders induced policy inconsistencies and reversals, particularly in the early 1990s. Two factions emerged: those supporting limited and guided liberalization ("nationalistic liberalizers") and those supporting a more open approach ("free-marketers"). A significant proportion of the political elite had perceived the shift to market-oriented policies in the late 1980s as a temporary setback in the face of crisis, which meant that support for the reforms was not always wholehearted (Bigsten and Danielson 1999). The decision as to which type of reform to undertake, its course and pace, was influenced by the state, societal interest groups, and donors (Rutasitara 2004). During the last years of Mwinyi's presidency, leadership weakened, derailing the economic program and seeing rent-seeking dominate the political and business environment. Government expenditure as a share of GDP was almost double that of SSA; this led to an erosion of donor confidence, resulting in a wide-scale exodus of donor aid in the mid-1990s and an impasse in donor–government relations. The increased uncertainty with regard to the government's stance resulted in a decrease in investment as a share of GDP, from its peak of 40 percent in 1990 to 26 percent in 1994.

Conditioning aid on policy measures was a source of tension between government and donors. The government perceived it as eroding its sovereignty in pursuing national development objectives, emphasizing the importance of ownership and space for internal dialog. In 1994, the Helleiner process was initiated to mediate between government and donors and provide an institutional framework for accountability within the context of government ownership of the reform process.[26] As a result, government–donor relations evolved from confrontation to partnership approaches. Direct dialog with development partners was an important catalyst in Tanzania's economic reform process, contributing indirectly to the development of home-grown programs (Muganda 2004). The Independent Monitoring Group (IMG), an outcome of the Helleiner process, now serves as an instrument of mutual accountability and a performance-monitoring tool.

Reflecting the policy inconsistencies during the period 1990–4, the government adopted important positive legislative reforms, providing freedom of political associations and preparing a framework for multi-partyism. There was a realization that an array of political and institutional issues could critically shape the outcomes of reform episodes and that there was therefore a need to put in place key complementary measures. The ruling party was separated from the government, trade unions, co-operatives and other mass organizations, and greater freedom of the press was provided. These measures were propelled by the government and the former President Mwalimu Nyerere (Helleiner 2000; Muganda 2004).

5.3 1995 to date: Sustained growth through market-orientation and a democratic process: rewriting the social contract

Against the backdrop of the faltering reforms of the mid-1990s, the emergence of the third-phase government in late 1995 provided a fresh platform with which to demonstrate Tanzania's unequivocal commitment to a strengthening and sustenance of sound macroeconomic and structural policies. This was essential to raising the confidence of investors and donors from a low level. Economic reforms which had been put on hold were adopted, drawing on the consensus-building which characterized Tanzania's decision-making process, and national ownership of reforms. To engender a sense of national ownership within the context of a democratic process, a series of country-wide awareness campaigns were undertaken by the new President in which the actual and potential benefits of the reforms were stressed. Brain-storming sessions with various stakeholders, including the private sector and other civil society organizations, strengthened their place and voice in participatory development management.

The credibility of the government, coupled with the open and direct discourse with donors, helped strengthen relations and partnerships, improved

---

[26] The Helleiner process was an initiative of the Danish government in agreement with the Tanzanian authorities to evaluate Tanzania–donor relations during 1994. It was led by Professor Jerry Helleiner of the University of Toronto and a team of independent advisers on development co-operation issues, including Tanzanians, Professors Benno Ndulu and Nguyuru Lipumba (Muganda 2004).

aid co-ordination, reinforced government ownership, and increased harmonization of donor practices with government processes. The government
established a solid track record of policy implementation, receiving endorsement from donors on its economic and institutional effort as evidenced by
the expanded level of donor support.

In addition, the government developed modalities for institutionalizing
the then ad hoc consultative process with the private sector, evolving appropriate and effective macro- and sectoral policies. Having put in place a
now largely market-led economy, the main thrust of the reform effort was
directed towards removing the remaining impediments to growth, ratio-
nalizing the structure of the government, and strengthening public–private
sector partnerships. In order to attract FDI the government identified mining as a pivotal sector, whose regulatory framework could be used as an
illustration of its change from nationalization policies.

Economic growth *per capita* accelerated significantly, particularly after
1999, as the benefits from reforms kicked in. Growth improved, reflecting the
rebound of the non-agricultural sector which currently accounts for more
than half of export earnings, and improvements in the country's external
competitiveness. Inflation declined from 8 percent in 1999 to less than 6 percent in the ensuing years, reflecting the government's adherence to a strictly
restrained monetary policy in the context of a market-determined exchange
rate system. In addition, improvements in governance and the strengthening of institutions resulted in an improvement in Tanzania's overall ranking
in the corruption index. In 1998, Tanzania was on the 95th percentile relative to other countries in the ranking; it is currently on the 60th percentile
and stands well, particularly when compared to other SSA countries (ICRG
2004).

The macroeconomic improvements were not matched by significant
progress in social welfare; the challenge was therefore to raise the effectiveness of public sector service delivery further. The booming capital-intensive
mining industry did not create a commensurate number of jobs. In addition,
the transition from an emphasis on macroeconomic stability to structural
reforms in the civil service and divesture of major parastatals was not easy.
There was latent distrust of the private sector activities, especially since
the booming non-traditional sector absorbed only a small share of the labor
force. The nostalgia for the socialist days, when social services were provided
"free," remained, coupled with political anxiety concerning the benefits from
reform. Specifically, there were concerns over the dualistic development of
the economy, with growth in urban centers and stagnation in rural areas.
As over 70 percent of the population resided in rural areas, the challenge
facing the government was to provide an environment conducive to rural
sector growth thereby translating macroeconomic stability into higher overall growth. The escalating costs of living, necessitated concerted efforts to

ensure that the introduction of user charges did not aggravate poverty. However, it must be emphasized that part of the strain on incomes reflected the impact of the AIDS epidemic which put the social fabric of society under severe pressure.

Reflecting the elevated status of poverty reduction in the government's objectives, policies were developed to reverse the deterioration of the social indicators and, in the face of tightening fiscal environment, improve the delivery of social services. The government initiated the process of devolution to boost the effectiveness and efficiency in the delivery of basic services, as well as to address issues of equity, participation, and accountability (Romeo 2003). Devolution was achieved through the transfer of significant powers and responsibilities to locally elected authorities. In order to develop the capacity of local government, the national government agreed to allocate 20 percent of its budget to the provision of basic social services; although this proportion is small, it represented 75 percent of local government funding. Priority sectors were identified for which budgetary allocations were protected. By redistributing power and extending the influence of the center over the periphery through patronage relationships, it solidified political stability.

The government's sustained commitment to economic reforms triggered its eligibility for debt relief under the enhanced Heavily Indebted Poor Countries (HIPC) initiative in 2000, making it one of the first countries to reach the completion point and to benefit from irrevocable and substantial debt reduction. Tanzania received one of the largest amounts of Paris Club debt relief in SSA during this period. Debt reduction, in turn, paved the way for additional aid inflows, allowing the government to increase budgetary expenditure allocations to social sectors and other priority sectors. This led to visible improvements in public service delivery – in particular, education and health.

In order to prevent aid dependence undermining the domestic control of the development agenda, institutional arrangements have been set that tie program aid within the multi-pronged national objectives since 2002.[27] This enables transparency and has fostered the strengthening of governance, contributing to the sustenance of donor support. In addition, by incorporating the national development strategy within this institutional arrangement, the government can focus on stimulating rural development within an overall framework that does not constrain the achievement of its other objectives, such as sustaining macroeconomic stability. However, the continued maintenance of low revenue as a share of GDP (which at 14 percent remains

---

[27] The government-led Tanzania Assistance Strategy (TAS) provided a framework for partnership and helped delineate the role of external resources for development, as stated in the National Planning Commission's *Vision 2025* (see *The Tanzania Development Vision 2025*, at www.tanzania.go.tz/vision.htm). It encompasses the National Poverty Eradication Strategy (NPES) and the Poverty Reduction Strategy Paper (PRSP).

the lowest in SSA) suggests that the government's growth objectives remain highly dependent on continued donor support. Therefore the reform process remains vulnerable to continued positive government–donor relations and exogenous factors, including geopolitical uncertainties. Moreover, the rise in aid dependence may eventually impinge on ownership of the reform process. Collier (1991) and Ndulu and O'Connell (1999) have noted that where donors pay for reforms, there is a danger that ownership by citizens will be sacrificed.

Sustaining the reform process beyond the current presidency remains to be seen. The Tanzanian leadership has played an important role in advancing the reform process with the work of each President serving as a building block for the next set of reforms. It remains to be seen whether political cohesion will be a sustained force in the context of a democratic process with various players. The legacy of consensus-building and participatory decision-making within the political process has reduced the scope for dramatic reform action by any incoming new leadership. However, ownership has been embedded in the politico-institutional framework with political parties at the helm. This suggests that the policy environment remains susceptible to the political process despite the institutionalization of the reforms within the policy-making system.

Nevertheless, Tanzania has managed to steer clear of political destabilization, introducing and effectively managing the transition to political pluralism and encouraging the proliferation of civil society organizations. The legacy of the one-party system and state-controlled economy has faded and new legislative and institutional frameworks have been established to ensure the continuity of multi-partyism. One of the most important political achievements in Tanzania is strict adherence to the stipulations of the Constitution, including that limiting presidential terms to two. This suggests that the legacy of a smooth transition of the reform process will be maintained.

6. Conclusion

Tanzania has undergone a dramatic change in its entire social and economic set-up. The pattern of economic growth in Tanzania over the past four decades has closely mirrored the country's political trajectory, and can be sub-divided into three main periods: a strong control regime (1967–85), softening control (1985–95), and market-orientation and democratic process (1995–present). Ownership of reforms by Tanzania's leadership has fostered sustainability of the reform process. The founding President's smooth transfer of power signaled a break from socialist policies, enabling a smooth, albeit gradual, transition to a market economy. The institutional and structural reforms ushered in by the incoming President resulted in a gradual sustained movement towards a market economy. The entrance of President Mkapa onto the political field in 1995 reinforced these changes, re-establishing credibility and placing Tanzania ahead of most African countries in terms of a strong macroeconomic environment.

Economic decline during the strong control regime was largely due to the negative effects of the *Ujama'a* policy on economic efficiency. Principal–agent problems emerged, undermining the efficiency and effectiveness of the state agencies and parastatals. Production costs were determined in an ad hoc manner by centralized planning agencies that did not have full information on costs. Managers had an incentive to inflate production costs and accrue rents from the subsidies provided. Low wages in the civil service encouraged collusion in the embezzlement of funds. The state-controlled marketing institutions and parastatals faced fierce competition from parallel market traders, who operated mostly at night and usually connived with government officials. Protection of the industrial sector from outside competition weakened the incentives to produce more efficiently. In addition, the restriction on imports induced smuggling from neighboring countries. The failure of government economic policy in the early 1980s was reflected in shortages of food and consumer goods, negative industrial sector growth, and a persistent balance of payments problem, despite high import tariffs and quantitative controls on imports.

The implementation of broad-based economic and structural reforms has resulted in a rebound of the economy. The period 1985–95 was marked by renewed growth following trade liberalization. However, weak governance, coupled with delays in structural reforms and decline in donor support, had an adverse effect on growth. The period from 1995 onwards has been marked by intensified reforms which have resulted in an overall rise in TFP and a rise in real GDP *per capita*. Inflation, which for over two decades was over 25 percent, has been reduced to single digits. However, with over 70 percent of Tanzanians residing in rural areas and engaged predominantly in subsistence agriculture, the remaining challenge is to translate the fruits of economic growth to the people. To realize this, the government has intensified its efforts to stimulate the traditional sector and transform the value added to agricultural produce.

Development partners have been, and continue to be, an important and integral part of the reform process. What is striking about Tanzania's development trajectory is its strong endorsement by its development partners, as evidenced by the large inflows of aid and official credit to fund the programs. External assistance supported the government during the socialist regime, as it sought to achieve growth through public sector delivery in an "essentially co-operative, arm's-length relationship."[28] As pressure

---

[28] Adam *et al.* (1994)

increased for a change in the orientation of the economy mounted, financial support was provided, though couched in confrontational terms, between 1980 and 1985. The renewed collaboration post-1986 enabled the government to aggressively reverse the socialist policies, resurrect the economy, and improve public sector service delivery. The implicit role of donors as partners and monitors of government performance was demonstrated through the withdrawal of assistance. The fatigued international donor community withdrew support when the government was reluctant to adopt economic reforms in response to economic crisis in the early 1980s, and also in the mid-1990s, when macroeconomic reforms faltered. Following the Helleiner process, and particularly after the emergence of the third-regime government in 1995, Tanzania has maintained a candid and cordial relationship with donors. This reflects its focus on improving governance and achieving a stable macroeconomic environment. Increasingly, some kind of balance is emerging, aided not least by a proactive civil society.

References

Adam, C., A. Bigsten, P. Collier, E. Julin, and S. A. O'Connell (1994), *Evaluation of Swedish Development Co-operation with Tanzania: A Report for the Secretariat for Analysis of Swedish Development.* Stockholm: Regeringskansliets Offsetcentral, July

Amani, H. K. R., R. van den Brink, and W. E. Maro (1992), "Tolerating the Private Sector: Grain Trade in Tanzania after Adjustment," Working Paper 32, Cornell Food and Nutrition Policy Program, Cornell University, Ithaca, NY

Bank of Tanzania (1981), *Tanzania: Twenty Years of Independence (1961–1981): A Review of Political and Economic Performance.* Bank of Tanzania, Dar-es-Salaam

(1994), *Annual Report.* Bank of Tanzania, Dar-es-Salaam

(various issues a), *Annual Report.* Bank of Tanzania, Dar-es-Salaam

(various issues b), *Economic Bulletin.* Bank of Tanzania, Dar-es-Salaam

Barro, R. J. and J. Lee (1993), "International Comparisons of Educational Attainment," *Journal of Monetary Economics* 32(3): 363–94

Bevan, D., A. Bigsten, P. Collier, P. Horsnell, and J. W. Gunning (1990), *Controlled Open Economies: A Neo-Classical Approach to Structuralism.* Oxford: Oxford University Press

Bevan, D., P. Collier, and P. Horsnell (1989), "Supply Response under Good Market Rationing in Tanzanian Peasant Agriculture," in J. Azam, T. Besley, J. Maton, D. Bevan, P. Collier, and P. Horsnell, eds., *The Supply of Manufactured Goods and Agricultural Development.* Paris: OECD

Bigsten, A. and A. Danielsson (1999), "Is Tanzania an Emerging Economy?," Paris: OECD

Bigsten, A., D. Mutalemwa, Y. Tsiaka, and S. Wangwe (1999), "Aid and Reform in Tanzania," The World Bank, Washington, DC, mimeo

Brenefeld, M. (1995), "Structural Adjustment and Tanzania's Peasantry: Assessing the Likely Long-term Impact," in V. Jamal, ed., *Structural Adjustment and*

Rural Labor Markets in Africa, Macmillan Series of ILO Studies. New York and London: St. Martin's Press and Macmillan: 85–130

Brownbridge, M. and S. K. Gayi (2000), "Progress, Constraints, and Limitations of Financial Sector Reforms in the Least Developed Countries," IDPM Finance and Development Research Program, Working Paper Series 7

Collier, P. (1991), "Africa's External Relations, 1960–1990," *African Affairs* 90: 339–56

Collins, S. M. and B. P. Bosworth (1996), "Economic Growth in East Asia: Accumulation versus Assimilation," *Brookings Papers on Economic Activity* 2: 135–91

(2003), "The Empirics of Growth: An Update," *Brookings Papers on Economic Activity* 2: 113–206

Cromwell, E., M. Bagachwa, F. Shechambo, H. Sosovele, K. Kulindwa, and A. Naho (1996), "Case Study for Tanzania," in D. Reed. ed., *Structural Adjustment, the Environment, and Sustainable Development.* London: Earthscan Publications: 107–27

Easterly, W. (1996), "When Is Stabilization Expansionary?," *Economic Policy* 22, April: 65–107

Elbadawi, I. A. and B. J. Ndulu (1996), "Long Term Development and Sustainable Growth in Sub-Saharan Africa," in M. Lundahl and B. J. Ndulu, eds., *New Directions in Development Economics: Growth, Environmental Concerns and Government in the 1990s.* Studies in Development Economics, 3. London and New York: Routledge: 67–103

Gordon, A. A. (1990), *Transforming Capitalization and Patriarchy.* London and Boulder, CO: Lynne Rienner

Hansen, H. and F. Tarp (1999), "The Effectiveness of Foreign Aid," Development Economics Research Group, University of Copenhagen, mimeo

Helleiner, G. (2000), "The Legacy of Julius Nyerere: An Economist's Reflections," CIS Working Paper 3, University of Toronto, Toronto

Hoeffler, A. (2002), "The Augmented Solow Model and the African Growth Debate," *Oxford Bulletin of Economics and Statistics* 64(2): 135–58

Hyden, G. (1983), *No Short Cut to Progress: African Development Management in Perspective.* London: Heinemann

(1986), "The Anomaly of African Peasantry," *Development and Change* 17(4): 677–704

Hyden, G. and N. Mwase (1976), *Co-operatives in Tanzania: Problems of Organization.* Dar-es-Salaam: Tanzania Publishing House

International Country Risk Guide (ICRG) (2004), *International Country Risk Guide (ICRG)* (online), The PRS Group, http://www.icrgonline.com

International Monetary Fund (IMF) (2004), *Tanzania: Selected Issues and Statistical Appendix,* IMF Country Report 04/284, International Monetary Fund, Washington, DC

Jayne, T. S. and S. Jones (1997), "Food Marketing and Pricing Policy in Eastern and Southern Africa: A Survey," *World Development* 25(9): 1505–27

Kaufmann, D. and S. A. O'Connell (1991), "The Macroeconomics of the Parallel Foreign Exchange Market in Tanzania," in A. Chhibber and S. Fischer, eds., *Economic Reform in Sub-Saharan Africa.* Washington, DC: The World Bank

(1997), "Fiscal and Monetary Effects of the Parallel Premium: Theory and the Tanzania Case," chapter 7 in M. Kiguel, J. Lizondo, and S. A. O'Connell, eds., *Parallel Exchange Rates in Developing Countries*, London: Macmillan: 247–90

(1999), "The Macroeconomics of Delayed Exchange Rate Unification: Theory and Evidence from Tanzania," World Bank Policy Paper 2060, The World Bank, Washington, DC

Lele, U., N. van de Walle, and M. Gbetibouo (1989), *Cotton in Africa: An Analysis of Differences in Performance*, MADIA Discussion Paper 7, The World Bank, Washington, DC

Lofchie, M. F. (1989), *The Policy Factor: Agricultural Performance in Kenya and Tanzania*. London and Boulder, CO: Lynne Rienner

Mans, D. (1994), "Tanzania: Resolute Action," in I. Husain and R. Faruqee, eds., *Adjustment in Africa: Lessons from Country Case Studies*. Washington, DC: The World Bank: 352–426

McHenry, D. E. (1994), *Limited Choices: The Political Struggle for Socialism in Tanzania*. London and Boulder, CO: Lynne Rienner

McLoughlin, P. F. M. (1967), "Agricultural Development in Sukumaland," in J. C. De Wilde assisted by P. F. M. McLoughlin *et al.*, *Experiences with Agricultural Development in Tropical Africa*. Baltimore, MD: Johns Hopkins University Press for the International Bank for Reconstruction and Development

Moshi, H. P. B. and A. A. L. Kilindo (1999), "The Impact of Government Policy on Macroeconomic Variables: A Case Study of Private Investment in Tanzania," AERC Research Paper 89, African Economic Research Consortium, Nairobi

Muganda, A. (2004), "Tanzania's Economic Reforms – And Lessons Learned," The International Bank for Reconstruction and Development, The World Bank, Washington, DC

Mwega, F. M. (1990), "Financial Sector Reforms in Eastern and Southern Africa" (online), *African Voices on Structural Adjustment*, chapter 10, IDRC Booksonline, http://www.idrc.ca/en/ev-56345-201-1-DO_TOPIC.html

Ndulu, B. J. (1986), "Investment, Output Growth and Capacity Utilization in an African Economy: The Case of Manufacturing Sector in Tanzania," *Eastern African Economic Review* 2(1): 14–30

(2002), "Partnership, Inclusiveness and Aid Effect in Africa," in V. FitzGerald, *Social Institutions and Economic Development: A Tribute to Kurt Martin*. Dordrecht, Boston, and London: Kluwer Academic: 143–67

(2004), "Inclusiveness, Accountability, and Effectiveness of Development Assistance in Sub-Saharan Africa," in F. Bourguignon and B. Pleskovic, eds., *Accelerating Development*, Annual World Bank Conference on Development Economics. Washington, DC: The World Bank and Oxford: Oxford University Press

(2007), "The Evolution of Global Development Paradigms and Their Influence on African Economic Growth," in B. J. Ndulu, S. A. O'Connell, R. H. Bates, P. Collier, and C. C. Soludo, eds., *The Political Economy of Economic Growth in Africa, 1960–2000*. Cambridge: Cambridge University Press: 315–47

Ndulu, B. J. and S. A. O'Connell (1999), "Governance and Growth in Sub-Saharan Africa," *Journal of Economic Perspectives* 13(3): 41–66

—— (2000), "Background Information on Economic Growth," Paper prepared for the Explaining African Economic Growth Project. Nairobi: African Economic Research Consortium (downloadable: www.aercafrica.org)

Nehru, V. and A. Dhaervasal (1993), "A New Database on Physical Capital Stock: Sources, Methodology and Results," *Revista de Analisis Economico* 8(1): 37–59

Ponte, S. (1998), "The Political Economy of Agricultural Input Distribution in Post Liberalization Tanzania," Paper presented at the African Studies Association Meeting, Chicago, mimeo

—— (2002a), *Farmers and Markets in Tanzania: How Policy Reforms Affect Rural Livelihoods in Africa.* Oxford: James Currey, Dar-es-Salaam: Mkuki na Nyota, Dar-es-salaam, and Portsmouth: Heinemann

—— (2002b), "The Politics of Ownership: Tanzanian Coffee Policy in the Age of Liberal Reformism," Paper presented to the African Studies Association of the UK Biennial Conference, University of Birmingham, September 9–11

Putterman, L. (1995), "Economic Reform and Smallholder Agriculture in Tanzania: A Discussion of Recent Market Liberalization, Road Rehabilitation, and Technology Dissemination Efforts," *World Development* 23(2): 311–26

Romeo, L. (2003), "The Road from Decentralization to Poverty Reduction and the Role of External Assistance," *Public Administration and Development* 23(1): 89–96

Rutasitara, L. (2004), "Exchange Rate Regimes and Inflation in Tanzania," AERC Research Paper 138, African Economic Research Consortium, Nairobi

Sachs, J. D. and A. M. Warner (1997), "Sources of Slow Growth in African Economies," *Journal of African Economies* 6(3): 335–76

Sandbrook, R. and J. Barker (1985), *The Politics of Africa's Economic Stagnation.* Cambridge: Cambridge University Press

Sundet, G. *The Politics of Land in Tanzania,* unpublished DPhil dissertation, University of Oxford

United Nations Conference on Trade and Development (UNCTAD) (2004), "FDI Survey," UNCTAD Press Report 5, April, fdisurvey@unctad.org

World Bank (1994), *Tanzania Agriculture: A Joint Study by the Government of Tanzania and the World Bank,* A World Bank Country Study, The World Bank, Washington, DC

14 | Togo: lost opportunities for growth

Tchabouré Aimé Gogué and Kodjo Evlo

1. Introduction

Economic growth has been quite poor in Togo over the past four decades. Real GDP *per capita* barely changed between 1960 and the end of the century, although sub-periods have shown better performance. Togo started at independence with a weak but stable economy. Performance was relatively good between 1960 and 1973, due principally to prudent and market-friendly economic policies and to a stable international environment. The situation deteriorated significantly since the middle of the 1970s, when real GDP

Université de Lomé, Lomé, Togo.

per capita started to decline and the country began to struggle with generalized macroeconomic problems. Since 1973, the growth performance worsened consistently, with growth rate of GDP *per capita* declining from 6.2 percent in the 1960s to 0.46 percent in the 1970s, to –0.3 percent in the 1980s and to –0.96 percent in the 1990s. The instability of the growth rate was particularly acute in the case of some components of aggregate demand, such as government consumption and investment. The ratio of public investment to GDP averaged 36.1 percent between 1975 and 1980, 18.5 percent in 1980s, and 35.6 percent in the 1990s.

In trying to compare the economic performance of countries with the same characteristics, Togo is best grouped with coastal countries (Collier 2003). In this group of countries, Mauritius is the highest-performing country, even though Togo has more opportunities for growth. Togo is not an insular country, it is nearer developed markets, and it has natural resources (phosphate rocks) which is not the case in Mauritius. Therefore, Togo should have had better economic performance than Mauritius. In fact, Togo has done poorly even compared to the average African country although it had clearly out-performed the latter in the 1960s (Ndulu and O'Connell 2000).

The objective of this chapter is to explain why Togo has not performed well. The macroeconomic performance of a country can be explained by many factors, such as history, geography, natural-resource endowment, accumulation of physical and human capital, international economic environment, political economy, and economic policies. The chapter is structured as follows. In section 2, the period of analysis (1960–99) will be sub-divided into four distinct sub-periods, each of which illustrates recurring features in the country's economic performance. The economic performance of the country will then be presented, using the growth-accounting model of Collins and Bosworth (1999), the cross-country regression suggested by Ndulu and O'Connell (2000), and Hoeffler's (2002) SYS-GMM model.[1] In the growth-accounting model, the respective contributions of physical capital, human capital, and TFP to growth will be analyzed. The role of economic policy and the base variables (demography, trade shocks, and initial endowment) will be considered in presenting the cross-country regression evidence.

In section 3 the study will show how market institutions impact growth performance, whereas in section 4 the role of microeconomic agents, mostly the government sector, in explaining economic growth will be the central focus. In section 5, political-economy (interest groups) will be used to explain the poor economic performance of the country, especially since 1973. Some concluding remarks will be drawn in section 6.

---

[1] Hoeffler's augmented Solow model was developed in a 1999 background paper for the Growth Project. The present discussion is based on the fits and residuals from that model as presented in O'Connell and Ndulu (2000).

The study shows that the downturn that began in the 1970s was due to a few intertwined factors relating to the instability of the international environment and mostly to the adoption of inappropriate macroeconomic policies by the government and the political crisis the country had undergone since 1990. Therefore if better economic policies were implemented and if the country had avoided the political crisis the economy would not have been out-performed by the average African country represented in the O'Connell and Ndulu (2000) sample.

This chapter will fill a gap in the economic literature of the country, as no study of this depth has ever been undertaken in the past. No study in the past has followed an approach as comprehensive as that used in the current study. In particular, the current study will use an innovative framework that sheds light on the anti-growth syndromes that plague most African economies.

2. Growth experience in cross-country perspective

2.1 Historical background

The period immediately preceding independence was characterized by a stable international environment and prudent macroeconomic policies. The colonial power had put in place an administrative structure that bonded the country to the metropolis while taking a rather low profile in economic activity. The share of the public sector in GDP was low. The economy was dominated by agriculture, accounting for more than half of GDP. The industrial sector was weak and dominated by the mining of phosphate rock. The service sector was fairly strong and growing, but dominated by informal traders.

Economic policy was market-friendly and geared toward the interests of the colonial power. The latter had introduced commercial policies in the 1950s with a view to giving French companies control over the economy. Exports were diversified little and included mainly agricultural products and phosphate rock. Trade and budget imbalances were negligible. Inflation was kept under control as the colonial currency was pegged to the metropolitan French franc and monetary policy was managed by the French. Saving and investment were not strong. However, the potential for growth was good, given the untapped natural resources of the country and the enabling policy environment. It is with this background that the country got its independence on April 27, 1960.

2.2 Distinct periods of growth history

Togo was out-performed by the average SSA country between 1960 and 1999. However, the economic performance of the country was not uniform over the forty-year period of the study. The high performance of the economy in the 1960s and early 1970s, when the country out-performed the average SSA country, is in contrast with the bad performance since the second half of the 1970s. Based on key macroeconomic indicators, four periods can be distinguished in the country's economic growth history: (a) 1960–73; (b) 1974–9; (c) 1980–90, and (d) 1991–7. Interestingly, average annual growth rate of GDP *per capita* fell consistently from one period to the next.

From an economic point of view, the post-independence period, *1960–73*, was the most stable of all and demonstrated great performance. It was characterized by a fairly rapid growth rate, warranted by prudent and market-friendly macroeconomic policies, with efforts to modernize the (economic) administration and to realign the economy from colonial to post-independence structures, and a stable international environment. GDP *per capita* grew by 4.5 percent per year on average. However, the growth rate varied substantially across the period. Part of this was due to (a) the young history of the country as a sovereign nation, and (b) the successive coup of 1963 and 1967 that almost immediately followed independence.

Concerning monetary policy, the most important development was the Olympio government's refusal to join the West African Monetary Union (UMOA), created in 1962. Olympio opted for relative monetary independence although he negotiated an individual arrangement with France. France agreed to provide the Togolese currency (to be created) with some support similar to that given to the CFA franc. After the 1963 coup, Togo joined the UMOA in November 1963 and benefited from the monetary stability this currency area gave its member countries.

1974–9 was the period of various international shocks (oil shocks and commodity booms), bad macroeconomic policies, and unsustainable growth. Even though the 1.9 percent *per capita* GDP growth rate during this sub-period was lower than that in the preceding sub-period, this growth rate was unsustainable as it was mainly driven by demand with no improvement in the production capacity of the country. In fact, the high increase in export revenues due to terms of trade improvement ended up creating rapid public sector expansion and generalized government intervention. The oil shocks of 1973 and 1975 surprised the country and caused the GDP growth rate to fall sharply. But the phosphate boom of 1974 and 1975, and the rise in coffee price in 1977, exerted the opposite effect on the economy. Overall there was a considerable increase in public sector revenues.[2] The temporary increase in income due to the external terms of trade improvement was thought to be permanent. More important, the country failed to transform this temporary increase into permanent income, and the policy-makers made a series of mistakes. The increase in

---

[2] Phosphate rocks, coffee, and cocoa were the main export crop of Togo in that period.

revenue was used to increase public investment and implement ill-conceived projects and expand the parastatal sector by creating publicly owned manufactures behind heavy import protection. Public investment rose to 47 percent of GDP in the late 1970s. Employment in the formal industrial (mainly public) sector increased from 8,288 in 1973 to 19,254 in 1979. The effective rate of protection for the SOEs was over 200 percent (Baniganti and Lawson 1994). In 1976, the SOEs accounted for 68.4 percent, 47.7 percent, and 100 percent of the value added of the mining, manufacturing, and energy industries, respectively. In 1979, 77 percent of firms in the industrial sector were state-owned or state-controlled. There was an unprecedented expansion of the public sector, with massive recruitment in the civil service leading to an increase in payroll that was difficult to reduce in periods of public resource shortages. Government expenditure rose sharply, leading to large budget deficits (from 13.4 percent of GDP in 1973 to 39.6 percent of GDP in 1979). Because of the increase in revenue, the government was able to borrow in international financial markets and the country therefore also experienced a rapidly growing public external debt, which grew from 15.1 percent in 1970 to 53.9 percent of GDP in 1977, and to 116.4 percent of GDP in 1978, whereas debt service increased from 58.8 percent in 1970 to 185.5 percent in 1977, and to 372.5 percent in 1978. Resources from short-term commercial loans were used to finance ill-conceived industrial projects.

1980–90 was marked by economic reforms but was under the control of a one-party system and an ethno-regional minority. The economic reforms began with an IMF-sponsored Financial Stabilization Program (FSP) in 1979 followed by IMF and World Bank-sponsored SAP after 1982. Togo was one of the first SSA countries to implement a SAP, which reduced the budget deficit and external public debt reduction to 3.8 percent and 74 percent of GDP by 1989, respectively. The budget deficit was reduced mostly through a decrease in public investment and suspension in recruitment in the civil service. However, the average annual growth rate of GDP *per capita* was −0.3 percent. This bad performance is the consequence of the unsustainable growth and economic mismanagement in the second half of the 1970s. The contraction of the public sector as a result of the reforms and the debt burden were the principal causes of the GDP decline. By the end of the period, however, the lag effects of the 1970s mismanagement had run out and the reforms led to a recovery in the mid-1980s, resulting in a positive growth rate of GDP *per capita* in the second half of the decade.

The main feature of the *1990s* was the fight for democracy. GDP *per capita* grew by an annual average of −0.9 percent, which was the worst of the four periods. As in most of the West African countries, the aspiration of the population to democracy increased during this period. The first half of 1990s was marked by socio-political crisis, which led to confrontations between the population and the government and ended with a substitution of the political elite. This change was, however, short-lived: 1991–3 was marked by an unstable economic environment, public authority dysfunction, and ended with a nine-month general strike. The incumbent regime resorted to violent means to suppress the public protests and to return to power. Even though the power was restored, the regime never achieved strong control of the country and the population still contested their authority. As a result, in the second half of the 1990s, due to anticipated regional redistribution, looting and widespread corruption occurred. Because the political elite in power was not sure that it would maintain power for long, it used its position to amass wealth as rapidly as possible. The economy was not managed with a development objective and the situation became a protracted political crisis, with damaging effects on the economy. The refusal of the government to accept democratic rules caused the international community to impose economic sanctions, which compounded the difficulties and caused further decline in economic activity. Government consumption remained high although it had declined after 1970 as a result of the SAPs. Private investment was weak and falling, primarily because of the instability of the political environment, the weak level of domestic saving, and the inability of the economy to attract FDI.

2.3   Analysis of Togo's economic growth performance

There is a rapidly growing body of literature that tries to explain the economic performance of developing countries (see, for example, Young 1992, 1993; Fischer 1993; Krugman 1994; World Bank 1994). One branch of such literature, which uses a growth-accounting framework and an extended Solow model, emphasizes the role of physical human capital and capital accumulation. Other models stress the role of structural features and economic policy.

2.3.1   Growth accounting

Human and physical capital accumulation is the main determinant of economic growth (Collins and Bosworth 1996). This growth-accounting model has been applied to a number of countries but the result of the study was not applied in the case of Togo. Following O'Connell and Ndulu (2000), the Collins–Bosworth coefficients are used to calculate the contribution to growth of capital per worker and education per worker.[3] Key variables have been defined as follows: (a) the capital stock has been constructed (Cohen 1993) as the sum of initial capital stock and accumulation of net investment flows per period, and (b) secondary education has been

---

[3] Education has been used as a proxy of human capital.

Table 14.1 *Togo, estimated residuals based on Collins–Bosworth coefficients, 1960–1997*

Period	Growth in real GDP *per capita*	Contribution of education per worker	Contribution of capital per worker	TFP growth residual
1960–4	7.26	2.09	1.51	3.66
1965–9	5.35	1.88	1.72	1.75
1970–4	0.93	1.93	1.57	−2.57
1975–9	0.00	1.35	0.90	−2.25
1980–4	−1.28	0.31	0.19	−1.75
1985–9	0.67	0.08	0.04	0.55
1990–7	−0.96	0.02	0.01	−0.99
1960–97	1.71	1.09	0.85	−0.23

used to represent the variable "education." The estimated equation is the following:

$$bgno = 0.35\ bcko + 0.65\ bcho + bcro,$$

where *bgno* is the growth rate of real GDP *per capita*, *bcko* is the growth rate of physical capital per worker, *bcho* is the growth rate of human capital per worker, and *bcro* is the TFP residual.

Based on the coefficients above, the residuals have been computed for the various sub-periods as shown in table 14.1. Growth performance in Togo between 1960 and 1997 was influenced by weak productivity, especially TFP, since the 1970s. During the forty-year period, output per worker grew by an annual average of 1.71 percent. The contributions of physical capital per worker and education per worker were positive (0.85 percent and 1.09 percent, respectively). However, TFP growth was negative – except in 1970–4 and 1985–9. The relatively good contribution of physical and human capital to growth in the 1960s and early 1970s was the result of appropriate macroeconomic policies and productive public investment in 1973–4. The contribution of both factors constantly declined from the mid-1970s as a result of inadequate investment and education policies. Both types of capital were influenced in the same way by government policies, and thus followed similar growth patterns. In the case of physical capital, considerable amounts of resources were spent on non-productive investment projects. The ambitious public investment program of the 1970s was not based on any carefully planned development strategy but was the result of increased revenue. Such a program did not help the economy grow but, instead, left the country with a large public external debt. Similarly, investment in human capital did not give satisfactory results. As explained earlier, in the 1970s the government pursued a policy that aimed at increasing enrollment in the education

Table 14.2 *Togo, fits and residuals from the SYS-GMM estimation of the augmented Solow model, 1960–1997*

| | | | | | | | Estimated contribution of | | | |
Period	Actual growth rate	Predicted growth rate	Residual	Actual deviation of growth from sample mean	Initial income	Investment rate	Initial education attainment	Replacement investment term	Time dummies	Residual
1960–4	5.74	7.32	−1.58	3.81	5.72	−0.96	−0.62	0.68	0.60	−1.60
1965–9	4.68	4.24	0.44	2.75	4.85	−0.28	−0.45	−2.42	0.63	0.42
1970–4	0.00	6.06	−6.06	−1.93	4.14	0.92	−0.33	−9.53	−0.06	−6.08
1975–9	3.36	8.06	−4.72	1.42	4.14	2.85	−0.24	−0.84	0.26	−4.74
1980–4	−2.75	3.24	−6.00	−4.69	3.63	0.36	−0.08	−1.14	−1.44	−6.02
1985–9	0.13	4.13	−4.00	−1.81	4.05	−0.14	−0.04	−1.75	0.10	−4.02
1990–7	−2.27	4.10	−6.36	−4.20	4.03	−1.24	−0.03	−1.18	0.60	−6.38
Total	**1.27**	**5.31**	**−4.04**	**−0.66**	**4.36**	**0.22**	**−0.26**	**−1.03**	**0.10**	**−4.06**

Source: Ndulu and O'Connell (2000), background information on economic growth.

system in order to increase the stock of a skilled work force. The number of high-school and university graduates increased sharply, but usually not in the fields most needed by the labor market. A growing structural gap between the products of the education system and the needs of the labor market resulted, causing a rapidly increasing unemployment of skilled labor.

2.3.2   Cross-country regression evidence

O'Connell and Ndulu (2000) and Hoeffler's (2002) SYS–GMM model provide convenient frameworks to trace the effects of geography, policy, politics, and the international environment on economic growth. The results of the application of these models to Togo are mixed.

Overview of estimation results

Based on the analysis of the contribution of initial income, investment, education, and population on growth, Togo's overall experience is reasonably well captured by the O'Connell and Ndulu regression model (O'Connell and Ndulu 2000). However, for the average of the period, the Hoeffler (2002) SYS–GMM results based on an augmented Solow model predicted a growth rate of 5.31 percent whereas the actual growth rate was only 1.27 percent. The residual was small in the 1960s but became large for the rest of the sample period. The terms of trade shocks of 1973–4 accounted for a great part of the residual in 1970–4. On the other hand, the political crisis was responsible for the large prediction errors in the 1990s. The decrease in aggregate demand due to the implementation of the SAP in the early 1980s justifies the size of the residual in that sub-period.

During the four decades, Togo under-performed the sample mean by 0.66 percent. This situation was the result of the combination of the effect of initial income (4.46) and investment (0.22), both of which were offset by the replacement investment term (−1.03) and initial education attainment (−0.26). The negative effect of population is due to a rapid demographic growth rate and a high dependency rate. Overall, however, the residual was high, suggesting that the variables in the model failed to explain the dependent variable satisfactorily.

Regression results reported in table 14.2 suggest that the Togolese economy performed better than the sample mean in the 1960s and in the second half of the 1970s. The growth rate was 3.81 and 2.75 points above that of the sample mean in the two half-decades of the 1960s. The poor performance in the first half of the 1970s could be explained by the fact that the (negative) effect of the oil crisis outweighed the (positive) effect of terms of trade improvement in the phosphate sector. The better-than-average performance in 1975–9 was mainly the result of a short-run Keynesian multiplier effect following the large increase in government spending in response to terms of trade improvements in 1973–4 and 1976–8. As we noted earlier,

Table 14.3 *Togo, fits and residuals from pooled conditional model, 1960–1997*

| | Fits and residuals | | | Actual and predicted growth rate deviation from sample mean | | | | Breakdown of policy contribution variables | | |
| | | | | Actual deviation from sample mean | Contribution to predicted deviation of | | | | | |
Period	Actual growth rate	Fitted growth rate	Residual		Base variables	Political instability	Policy	Inflation (<500%)	Black market premium (<500%)	Non-productive government spending/GDP
1960–4	7.26	3.58	3.68	5.06	1.67	0.13	−0.93	0.07	0.13	−1.13
1965–9	5.35	3.60	1.75	3.15	1.61	0.07	−0.32	0.06	0.10	−0.48
1970–4	0.93	3.48	−2.55	−1.27	0.92	0.13	−0.39	0.04	0.16	−0.59
1975–9	0.00	2.22	−2.22	−2.20	0.39	0.20	−0.78	0.02	0.14	−0.93
1980–4	−1.28	0.51	−1.79	−3.48	−0.70	0.20	−0.47	0.03	0.15	−0.65
1985–9	0.67			−1.52	0.83	0.13		0.07	0.15	
1990–7	−0.96			−3.15	0.57	−0.37		0.03	0.15	
Total	**1.71**	**2.68**	**−0.23**	**−0.49**	**0.76**	**0.07**	**−0.58**	**0.04**	**0.14**	**−0.76**

Source: Ndulu and O'Connell (2000), background information on economic growth.

this is unsustainable growth, and will explain the poor performance in the next half-decade. In fact, performance in 1980–4 is attributable in part to the effects of the Financial Stabilization Program (FSP) concluded with the IMF in 1979 and the SAPs (which started in 1982). These programs brought a sharp decrease in public spending; as a consequence, the public deficit shrank to 3.8 percent of GDP. The reduction of the deviation from the sample mean's growth rate in 1985–9 is attributable to improved economic policies arising from the implementation of the SAPs.

As table 14.2 shows, conditional convergence, as predicted by the Solow model, took place only in the 1960s and late 1970s.[4] These were the only sub-periods when Togo, which had a lower initial income than the sample mean, grew faster than the latter. Violation of the convergence principle in the rest of the sample period is warranted by the fact that predicted growth rates overestimate actual ones except in the 1960s. This finding is consistent with the negative and relatively large residuals, and underscores the fact that, during most of the period of the study, the Togolese economy was out-performed by the sample average. Several factors contributed to the situation. Although it played a positive role in the 1970s and early 1980s – when in fact there was an over-investment in the public sector – a lower-than-desirable investment rate had a negative effect on growth in most of the period. Likewise, the replacement investment term and initial education attainment, two factors for which the country is at a disadvantage compared to the sample mean, contributed to the relative under-performance of the economy.

The role of economic policy

The conditional model allows for a breakdown of the contribution of policy variables and economic environment. The residuals in the regression equation of the conditional model for Togo are reported in table 14.3 (O'Connell and Ndulu 2000). As table 14.3 indicates, the contribution of base variables (demography, trade shocks, and initial endowments) to growth was highest in the 1960s and 1970s, althrough this contribution weakened between 1960 and 1984. The contribution of political instability was weak but positive for most of the period because the country lived in a (seemingly) stable political environment during the first three decades of the study. Such an environment could be included among the factors that contributed to growth in the 1960s and 1970s. It also helped to reduce the growth rate deviation from the sample mean, as suggested by the estimation results reported in table 14.4.

---

[4] As already stated, the growth in the late 1970s was unsustainable.

Table 14.4 *Togo, effective rates of protection,*
1970–1979

Period	Effective rate of protection
1970	65.24
1971	74.24
1972	88.07
1973	87.56
1974	97.04
Average of period 1970–4	*82.43*
1975	109.70
1976	108.30
1977	147.99
1978	140.95
1979	113.61
Average of period 1975–9	*124.11*

Source: Baniganti and Lawson (1994).

3. Market institutions

The organization of market institutions impacts the economic growth of the country (Afeikhena and Olawade 1999; Oyejide 2000). Everything else being equal (factors and goods), a market-friendly economy, with moderate controls and less government intervention, has a positive effect on growth.

In the case of Togo, the structure and functioning of market institutions have changed considerably since the 1960s. There was a sharp contrast between the early 1960s, which were characterized by an undisturbed private sector operating in a market-friendly environment, and the mid-1970s, when there was extensive government intervention. The 1980s and 1990s were marked by a disengagement of the government from some sectors of the economy and a gradual re-empowerment of market institutions.

3.1 1960–1973 sub-period: a market-friendly economy

The first government led by Sylvanus Olympio, from 1960 to 1963, was the most conservative in Togo's history. Olympio favored small government and a free market in part because of (1) his background as former executive of an international trading company, and (2) the influence of the business community, which made up his support base. No particular price control mechanisms were put in place; the markets for goods and services continued to evolve without much government intervention and in a way that encouraged the development of internal and external trade. This period can be characterized as syndrome-free with very mild controls of the economy (Collier and O'Connell 2007).

The government had inherited agricultural products' export control policies put in place by the colonial power in the 1950s with a view to protecting French interests – i.e. aiming at giving French companies control over the exports sector. However, such policies had not affected regional trade significantly, partly because the customs administration was not large enough or adequately equipped to enforce the relevant regulatory measures. Overall, the export control policies of the 1960s were weaker, more flexible, and less constraining than those introduced in the second half of the 1970s.

Factor markets also continued to evolve within the framework established by the colonial power. The labor market was characterized by a relative scarcity of skilled labor; there were trade unions but their influence was limited to a tiny modern labor market (less than 5 percent of the labor force). The influence of government labor policies was hardly felt outside the modern labor market. The government pursued a strategy aimed at improving the quality of the labor force in the long run; it started by increasing and improving the network of public schools, while continuing to encourage the creation and operation of mission schools. There were no higher-education institutions in the country: qualified students were sent to Dakar, Europe, and North America for higher education, and the government tried to diversify the education system as much as possible by sending students to different countries and different education systems.

The capital market was weak because of limited savings and the underdeveloped state of financial institutions. However, the government did not try to influence the development of this market through public investment. Instead, it tried to encourage private investment, which was weak because of the lack of domestic saving. International trading companies, whose affiliates controlled most of the international trade sector, played a major role in private investment spending. The openness of the economy favored some FDI flows through the activities of these trading companies.

The government led by Nicolas Grunitzky, in the wake of the 1963 coup, made significant changes compared to the Olympio government. It began to introduce measures that gave the government more control over the markets for goods and services. In particular, it created a marketing board in 1964, the Office des Produits Agricoles du Togo (OPAT), to regulate the producer price of most agricultural export products. The commodities covered by OPAT, which included coffee and cocoa, accounted for more than two-thirds of Togo's export earnings.

However, these changes did not significantly hamper growth. In fact, OPAT did not significantly affect the output of agricultural export goods in the 1960s and early 1970s, because of low domestic inflation and a stable international environment. Producers did not show major signs of discontent about the prices set by OPAT, partly because they felt better off than they would be if they were to produce other agricultural goods. In addition, the prices set by OPAT were at times higher than those prevailing in neighboring Ghana – due in part to the instability of the Ghanaian currency, the cedi – which made producers pleased with what they were earning. OPAT was thus viewed as a price stabilizer: it did relatively well because of little political interference.

3.2 1974–1979 sub-period: a government-intervention economy

Market institutions took a more severe blow in the 1970s. With the increase of public resources from the control of the main export commodities, the government increased its grip on the economy after 1974. There was also the consolidation of the single-party system, the creation of public enterprises protected by high tariffs and non-tariff barriers (NTBs), and interest and price controls. Price controls were introduced in the consumer goods and export commodities markets. In addition, the public sector expanded at the expense of the private sector, which hurt competition, efficiency, and growth. Price control was administered either directly, through price-setting mechanisms, or indirectly, through public production or supply.

To directly regulate prices, three institutions were created or became more active. Following the 1975–6 food crisis, the government forbade the export of agricultural food starting in February 1976. To ease the adverse effect of the 1977 severe drought on the urban population, the government tried to control the marketing of cereals. Togograin was founded, with the objective of avoiding wide fluctuations in food prices by buying, storing, and selling grains and vegetables. This institution would operate a buffer stock, buying when food was plentiful and prices moving against the interests of producers, and selling when prices began to rise higher than consumers could afford. With the support of the armed forces, Togograin took control of the grain market. Nevertheless, due to lack of resources, inefficient management, and strong links between producers and traditional private traders, the institution was not able to successfully take advantage of its monopoly power. More specifically, it did not succeed in imposing its price policies on the sector and overall, its operations introduced serious distortions in the agricultural food production sector.

The Société Nationale de Commerce (SONACOM) was founded in 1973, with the objective of importing essential consumer goods. SONACOM soon became a monopoly, as it was the sole company granted the right to import these commodities. Its monopoly was later extended to other commodities, including cigarettes and alcohol.

The price control system set up for agricultural export commodities by OPAT from the mid-1960s continued, and was reinforced. OPAT consolidated its bases and increased its monopoly power, becoming a dominant force in the export sector and an invaluable source of non-fiscal revenue for the government. It became less and less efficient as a price stabilizer in the export sector because its price-fixing system failed to provide farmers with incentives to increase output. Added to these problems was the worsening management that the agency was experiencing by the end of the 1970s.

The government set up a host of public enterprises, most of which quickly became state monopolies that forced several private firms out of the market. A great number of these public enterprises never became profitable, but closed down after persistent accumulation of losses.

Finally, the government implemented a broad-based program of nationalization of private enterprises. The most publicized case was the government's takeover of the Compagnie Togolaise des Mines du Bénin (CTMB), which became the Office Togolais des Phosphates (OTP), the parastatal enterprise that produced and marketed phosphate rock, the country's number one export commodity. In the short run, the nationalization did not cause any significant change in output. However, it led to increased corruption, because it benefited party leaders.

The increase of government controls over the economy resulted in redistribution. The first type was vertical redistribution. With the growing influence of the one-party system, a disproportional part of the resources benefited the political elite: they had privileged access to imported goods via SONACOM and became the resellers of these goods; and also to employment in the enterprises owned or controlled by the government.

There was also redistribution from the rural to the urban population. First, the operation of Togograin resulted in redistribution from food crop producers to food crop consumers. Even though Togograin controlled less than 20 percent of the cereals market, its power allowed it to impose prices in the market. Second, in setting producer prices of agricultural export crops well below international prices, the government was able to extract large resources to finance its spending, which mostly benefited the urban population, and later the Kara region and the Kabye ethnic group.[5]

Regional redistribution was favored by the nationalization of the phosphate rock sector, which generated large rents for the government. The population of one of the districts where the phosphate rocks were located was one of the poorest of the country. The public sector and parastatal public enterprises – and mostly CTMB, the biggest enterprise in the country – were used to create jobs for the Kabye, the ethnic group of the President.

The detrimental effect on growth was high, mostly in the agricultural sector, as low producer prices did not provide incentives to production. The subsidy to inefficient parastatals was protected by high NTBs and tariff barriers, and maintained distortions in the economy.

---

[5] The President is from the Kara region and from the Kabye ethnic group.

The labor market experienced distortions as well. For political reasons, the government recruited college and university graduates into the civil service, where they contributed little to aggregate output. The recruitment system was highly distortionary because surplus civil servants were paid salaries that were higher than their marginal productivity. As a consequence, many youths were attracted to the cities, in particular the capital city. The recruitment program also blurred unemployment figures. This situation comforted the government in its demagogical rhetoric and spared it the social trouble that could come from the unemployed. The over-sized civil service resulted in wage bill problems that contributed to the overall government finance crisis of the late 1970s. Since 1983, the reforms imposed a test for recruitment in the civil service; however, the results of these tests were biased in favor of the Kabye. This bias disproportionately increased their representation in the civil service and may have had a negative impact on the efficiency of the public sector, which in turn impacted negatively on growth.

The increase of controls and these resource redistributions thus had a negative impact on growth.

3.3 1980–1990 sub-period: economic reform

Market institutions started to regain strength with the implementation of SAPs in the 1980s, when the IMF and World Bank-led reform programs portrayed broad-based liberalization as a key condition for sustained economic growth. These programs included measures to reduce the budget deficit, mainly through (1) control of government expenditure and (2) gradual disengagement of the government from some sectors of economic activity, a clear reversal of the policies adopted in the 1970s.

Spending controls and disengagement of the government caused a recession in the early 1980s because of both supply-side and demand-side effects. On the demand side, the reduced government expenditure produced a Keynesian-type decline in output in the short run. On the supply side, the disengagement left a vacuum that the private sector was not quite ready to fill. Fortunately, these problems faded with time, and a resumption of growth occurred in the second half of the decade.

In the market for consumer goods and services, the liberalization was symbolized by the dismantling of some state monopolies such as Togograin and SONACOM. The dissolution of Togograin and the subsequent price liberalization program were appreciated in the rural areas. In particular, price liberalization resulted in an increase in agricultural output and established new dynamics for internal trade of agricultural products. The abolition of SONACOM's monopoly power restored a competitive environment to the import sector and revived rival companies such as the Société Générale du Golf de Guinée (SGGG), the Société Commerciale de l'Ouest Africain (SCOA), and CICA-Togo, a distributor of vehicles.

In the agricultural export commodities markets, OPAT's monopoly power started to decline owing to several factors. First, the share in total export revenue of the main products exported through OPAT declined significantly. Second, a new agency, the Société Togolaise de Coton (SOTOCO) started making aggressive inroads in the cotton market. Cotton had become the country's number one agricultural export product. SOTOCO's policies toward producers were friendlier than OPAT's; in particular, the new agency gave technical assistance and provided producers with inputs (improved seeds, fertilizers, and pesticides) that contributed to the spectacular increase in production in the 1980s.

Phosphate remained the country's key export commodity although its share in total export revenue declined compared to the 1970s. OTP continued to be in charge of the production and marketing of this product; the government steadfastly resisted suggestions by donors to liberalize the sector. Lack of good governance and environmental concerns made OTP operations less and less popular, and the government feared that a liberalization of the sector would have political and financial consequences for the regime, as OTP was a great resource provider for the regime and its beneficiaries.

In the labor market, measures to rationalize recruitment in the civil service were introduced with the SAPs. Efforts to reduce public expenditure led the government to freeze recruitment in the civil service, and retired employees were not replaced by newly recruited ones. In addition, new laws were introduced that set the retirement age at fifty-five. However, civil servants who had served for thirty years (or more) were retired, even if they had not reached the age limit. Access to the civil service was filtered by a national recruitment exam, for which the rate of success was 7.2 percent in 1985, which caused a great deal of social discomfort. The size of the civil service shrank by 13 percent between 1985 and 1988; the population could not react or protest because any disagreement with the government was swiftly and severely repressed. The unemployment rate increased (although no official figures were available), since the civil service was the destination of most college and university graduates entering the labor market.

The effect of the reduction of civil service size on growth is complex to evaluate. Unsustainable growth (like that in the late 1970s) was followed by a decline in GDP (Collier and O'Connell, 2007). In fact, the economy experienced negative growth during the early years of the period. It could be argued that the reduction in government expenditure – in particular, in the wage bill of the civil service – had adverse demand-side effects on output. The direct supply-side effect was minimal. First, the reduction of numbers in the civil service did not cause a meaningful decline in output because over-staffing during preceding periods had resulted in under-employment. Second, the reduction of the size of the public enterprise sector was not detrimental to growth, given the inefficiency that characterized that sector.

The public sector's contraction – notably the decline in the government budget deficit – had positive effects on the current account, whose deficit fell from 25.4 percent of GDP in 1978 to 2.3 percent in 1989 while the budget deficit shrank from 31.1 percent to 3.2 percent of GDP. An important element of fiscal consolidation was the reduction in public expenditure: in particular, government investment spending was cut from 47 percent of GDP in the late 1970s to 20 percent of GDP in 1989. This decrease in public investment had an adverse effect on growth because of the lack of maintenance of the infrastructures built in the previous period.

In the money market, the BCEAO introduced a reform in 1989 that represented a timid but crucial step toward liberalization, including measures to consolidate the interest rate structure. The most important element of the new interest rate policy was the introduction of a single discount rate applicable to all private sector activities. The former policy, which had compelled banks to devote a minimum volume of credit to the so-called "priority sectors," had not worked: it was distortionary, and banks did not apply it.

The new interest rate policy was simpler and allowed banks to determine their own interest rates based on their desired mark-up over the official discount rate. Still, the system was rigid since (1) interest rates were not fully determined by market forces and (2) no individual member country had its own monetary policy. Money supply was particularly tight during this period, because the Central Bank was trying to resolve a bad-loans crisis that first erupted in Côte d'Ivoire and Senegal and then spilled over to other member countries of UMOA. Tight monetary policy was viewed as a virtue and was therefore recommended to several non-CFA zone countries in the region as one of the fundamental elements of the structural adjustment package, and the BCEAO was praised for its conservative policy. Nonetheless, this policy, which was too rigid at times and became rather deflationary during most of this sub-period, did not favor growth in Togo (Evlo 1997).

This sub-period was also characterized by a redistribution of resources along ethnic lines. The shrinkage in the civil service was not uniformly applied to all ethnic groups; even though the applicants had to pass a test before being recruited the Kabyes, the president's ethnic group, as we have seen were still favored in the process. The weak GDP growth in this sub-period can mainly be explained by the "lag effect" of the mismanagement of the economy during the previous sub-period.

3.4   1990–1999 sub-period: political crisis

The pace of economic liberalization accelerated in the 1990s, with reforms affecting both the markets for goods and services and the parastatal sector. In addition important events, such as the devaluation of the CFA franc, occurred in the area of monetary policy, boosting the efficiency of market institutions.

First, many public enterprises that the government had previously been reluctant to privatize were restructured or privatized. These included the Compagnie Energie Electrique du Togo (CEET) and SOTOTOLES a provider of building materials. The capital of the Office des Postes et Télécommunications du Togo (OPTT) and many other companies were opened to private shareholders: in many cases, the privatization did not bring about the change expected by the population, because the government continued to hold the majority of the shares in some of these new companies. The privatized companies essentially kept their monopoly power and continued to produce at sub-optimal levels: this was the case of the former CEET, which became Togo Electricité, and OPTT. The restructuring of the former OPTT has resulted in the separation of postal services from telecommunications. The government continued to have control over the telecommunications sector as it held the majority of the shares of Togo Télécom. In the beginning, Togo Télécom had a strong monopoly in the area of telecommunications, although the advent of the Internet brought a few changes into the sector. Provision of Internet services was liberalized, and Togo became one of the most developed countries in the region in terms of such services. The sector had opened up further by the end of the 1990s when a new company, Télécél, was given authorization to operate and supply mobile telecommunications services, and thus to compete with Togocell, the unit of Togo Télécom that was the sole supplier of these services. The competition produced favorable effects on the prices of telecommunications.

Second, the market for agricultural export commodities continued to undergo institutional changes. OPAT lost its monopoly power over agricultural products exports in 1996, and several private companies began to operate in the sector. The gradual liquidation of OPAT was made in a broad context of trade liberalization.

The redistribution of resources in favor of the Kabye can be seen, as noted earlier, in the regional distribution of public health provision and of civil servants. With 14 percent of the country's population, the Kara region has 22 percent and 23 percent of the health centers and personnel, respectively (see table 14.5). In 1995, public health expenditure per inhabitant was 1844 FCFA in the Kara region, compared to 784 FCFA in the poorest region of the country. There are 92 habitants per civil servant in the Kara region, compared to 109 in the rest of the country.[6]

---

[6] There is a concentration of the civil servants in Lomé, the capital of Togo. Therefore, the region where Lomé is located is not taken into account in the regional distribution of civil servants. The Kara region is the region mostly populated by the Kabye.

Table 14.5 *Togo, public health expenditure, by region, 1995*

	Personnel CFAF 000	Other CFAF 000	Total CFAF 000	FCFA *per capita*
Maritime region	1,184,897	1,650,004	2,834,901[a]	1,777
Plateaux region	694,816	155,742	850,558	883
Central region	375,998	166,422	542,420	1,212
Kara region	603,336	368,448	971,784	1,844
Savanes region	217,844	74,885	408,474	784

Note: [a] Includes an allocation of 1,005,000 CFAF to the two university teaching hospitals in Lomé.
Source: World Bank (1996: 79).

4. Microeconomic agents

The government is the microeconomic agent that has had the greatest influence on Togo's economic performance; it is responsible for events that have marked major transitions in the country's economic history. Its economic philosophy has changed considerably during the forty-year period, and such changes have had determinant effects on performance. Throughout most of the 1960s, the government played a positive role by keeping a low profile and refraining from intervening excessively in the economy. In particular, the Olympio government gave the market a leading role in the economy. The size of the public sector was small: in 1965, the civil service employed about 15,000, less than 2 percent of total labor force. Fiscal policy was conservative and the budget deficit insignificant, with government expenditure averaging one-tenth of GDP. Overall, the low level of government interference had a positive effect on efficiency and economic performance, but the situation changed in the mid-1960s when the government started to play a larger role in the economy.

4.1 Increased government intervention in the 1970s

In the second half of the 1970s, the government became the predominant economic agent and its policies contributed to the poor macroeconomic performance the country experienced throughout the rest of the period.

4.1.1 Fiscal policy

Following the international phosphate rock price increase of 1973, the government was haunted by a "grandeur" complex and it called itself a "government of big projects." It embarked on a bigger expenditure program than Togo had ever experienced before and behaved as if it could be financed indefinitely with windfall resources from the terms of trade improvement. The goal pursued through these expansionary policies was to bring about structural transformation in the economy so as to foster sustained growth. Particular emphasis was put on industry because this was the weakest sector of the economy and also because the government believed that development required rapid industrial development. Public investment increased dramatically, from 13.4 percent of GDP in 1973 to 39.6 percent of GDP in 1979. As a consequence, formal employment in the industrial (mainly public) sector increased from 8,288 in 1973 to 19,254 in 1979.

Institutionally, this strategy was supported by a favorable investment climate. The Investment Code drafted in 1968, and revised in 1973 and 1978, was intended to promote the creation of "big" industrial enterprises. Between 1976 and 1980, fifteen state-owned or funded enterprises accounted for more than half the investment in this sector; because of their high operating costs, these enterprises could not operate without tariff barriers and NTBs.

Most elements of this highly improvised development strategy were far-fetched, and the economy as a whole was not ready for them. They included the building of a petroleum refinery plant in the middle of the oil crisis of the 1970s. The plant was supposed to be supplied with crude oil through bilateral trade agreements, but the agreements were never signed and the plant had to close down. Other examples of bad projects included the building of a steel mill that closed down a couple of years after it began operation.

Some strategic mistakes can also be cited. First, most of the projects were highly capital-intensive but the government under-estimated subsequent financing needs. The government failed to adopt projects that could make judicious use of human capital, the factor of production it had striven to develop with an arguable degree of success. It continued to make the civil service the principal recipient of the qualified labor force.

Second, the government failed to associate the private sector in its development strategy. In fact, certain elements of the strategy discouraged the private sector as they caused the crowding out of some firms. In 1976, SOEs accounted for 68.4 percent, 47.7 percent, and 100 percent of the value added of the mining, manufacturing, and energy industries, respectively. In 1979, 77 percent of firms in the industrial sector were state-owned or state-controlled, and accounted for about half of the industrial sector payroll outside the civil service.

The development strategy was not accompanied by measures to create a generally enabling environment for industrial development. In particular, the government failed to build adequate development infrastructures such as transportation and communication networks. The strategy focused essentially on import-substitution activities, which were highly subsidized. Private firms, which produced or imported these commodities, were crowded out, as inefficient public or parastatal enterprises drove more efficient private firms out of the market.

4.1.2 Monetary policy

Monetary policy did not change much during this period. Overall, the monetary system worked fairly well, but it was too static and too passive in some respects. In particular, the monetary authority failed to adjust its policy to respond to the shocks that occurred during the period. First, continued and unrestricted use of the resources of the Operations Account did not encourage the government to work out a solution to the current account deficit problem. The Central Bank did not sanction member countries for behavior that could have detrimental effects on the UMOA as a whole or on the common currency. Member countries felt free to carry out practices that suited their individual interests, with no regard to potential effects on the community. Practices that contributed to the aggravation of the current account or the external debt positions of member countries were not sanctioned. On the contrary, the common reserve pool served as a factor that boosted creditworthiness, solvency, and liquidity of individual member countries; it therefore favored individual member countries' access to international financial resources and thus contributed to the debt crisis experienced by Togo and other member countries (Evlo, 1997).

Second, monetary policy lacked dynamism. The Central Bank did not introduce measures to help its credit allocation policy respond to economic difficulties. No action was devised to help reduce member governments' budget deficits. No measure was envisioned to foster fiscal discipline. Governments were free to run as large deficits as they desired, provided they could have them financed outside the monetary system. Togo's record-high deficits in the second half of the 1970s were condoned by the Central Bank: in fact, it made credit facilities available to member governments that were determined on the basis of factors that had nothing to do with the size of budget deficits. More importantly, most member governments, including Togo, never exhausted the resources allocated to them through these facilities, so they had the possibility of running even larger deficits.

4.1.3 Trade policy

The second half of the 1970s was also characterized by an increase in government control over the external trade sector and an aggressive import-substitution policy. By the end of the 1960–73 sub-period, the government had nationalized CTMB, the company that produced and marketed phosphate rocks. Through this move, the government controlled over 90 percent of export revenues.

The agricultural export products marketing agency, OPAT, created in 1964, did not really stabilize producer prices until the mid-1970s. However, it served as a mechanism through which financial resources were transferred from producers to the government. The differential between the domestic and international prices of cocoa and coffee increased during this sub-period, in particular between 1976 and 1978. The ratio of the domestic cocoa producer price to the international price fell from an average of 41 percent in the 1970–4 period to 24 percent in the 1974–8 period. Likewise, the ratio of the coffee producer price to the international price declined from an average of 31 percent in 1970–4, to 24 percent in 1974–8. The increase in exported quantities of coffee and cocoa during this sub-period was essentially due to smuggling from Ghana.[7]

The effective rate of protection (ERP) was generally high and the domestic resource cost coefficient also suggested that there were inefficiencies in the operation of most of the enterprises. The ERPs for SOEs, which in many cases exceeded 200 percent, were extremely high in some sectors (Baniganti and Lawson 1994). For example, the ERP for the Brasserie du Bénin was in the range 118.5–349 percent. The average rate of effective protection for textile and leather products was 354 percent compared to 216.7 percent for wood and wood products. The textile industry was also highly protected. The Balassa effective rate of protection index reached 614 percent for the textile industry and a record high of 673 percent for Togométal. One of the least protected industries was the Ciments du Togo, whose effective rate of protection did not exceed 175 percent in 1979. Table 14.4 shows (p. 482) the average effective rate of protection estimated by Baniganti and Lawson (1994).

4.2 Adjustment policies and economic reforms

Due to an unsustainable public finance deficit and the debt overhang, the government's behavior changed considerably in the 1980s. The government remained the most important economic agent because of its willingness to carry out economic reforms and also because the public sector remained large, it implemented most aspects of the SAPs, although certain measures were unpopular. Any reduction in the size of the civil service could be politically costly in a democratic regime. Likewise, liquidation or privatization of some non-performing public enterprises was not well received by the public, which was concerned not only about job losses but also the way these enterprises were sold. Nonetheless, the government felt no pressure from

---

[7] Such smuggling activities were not necessarily due to lower producer prices in Ghana. They were primarily motivated by the opportunity to earn CFA francs that these producers could use (in Togo or other neighboring countries) to buy imported consumer goods that were severely rationed in Ghana. So, inappropriate exchange rate policies (in Ghana) might have made Ghanaian cocoa producers contribute to the prosperity and wealth of OPAT.

the population; because of its authoritarian style, it implemented such programs without consultation. Togo was one of the few countries that accepted the structural adjustment aid package proposed by the IMF and the World Bank without any major amendment. In reality, it did not have much choice, given the severity of the government finance crisis it was experiencing.[8]

The current account deficit decreased throughout most of the sub-period. Positive growth resumed in the second half of the sub-period, but was quite weak: 15.5 percent cumulatively between 1985 and 1990. The recovery was caused principally by a 24 percent growth in the agricultural sector and a 47 percent growth in the mining sector. The recovery was hampered, on the one hand, by the weakness of the services sector, due in part to the continued contraction of the public sector, and by deteriorating terms of trade.

The budget deficit was lower in the sub-period than in the second half of the 1970s. Official Development Assistance (ODA) increased steadily from US$ 63 million in 1981 to US$ 260 million in 1990, which was its highest level ever (see figure 14.1, p. 495). In this sub-period Togo was also granted debt relief through the Paris and London Clubs. From 1984 to 1990, five countries cancelled Togo's bilateral debt partially or totally in compliance with the Toronto Plan, various aid initiatives for LDCs, or the resolution of the Third Francophone Summit held in Dakar in 1989.

Total debt relief was US$ 315.4 million. However, this debt relief effort proved inadequate to help the government to pay its debt service on time. Debt service payments were rescheduled eight times by the Paris Club, and the flow of financial resources from the IMF and the World Bank increased although the country did not satisfactorily implement the adjustment programs it agreed with these institutions. World Bank loans increased from US$ 47 million in 1980 to US$ 400 million in 1990 and IMF loans from US$ 33 million to US$ 87 million in 1990.

4.3   The socio-political crisis

In the 1990s, the government continued to implement IMF and World Bank-sponsored economic reforms despite the socio-political crisis (see section 5). The pace of the reforms accelerated, leading to an even higher degree of liberalization and privatization. However, the crisis caused a slowdown of economic activity in virtually all sectors and household savings and private investment decreased, causing a long-term reduction of the physical capital stock. The problem was aggravated by the economic sanctions imposed on the government by the donor community, which caused a reduction in the

---

[8] The fact that there were many such programs suggests that they were often not implemented.

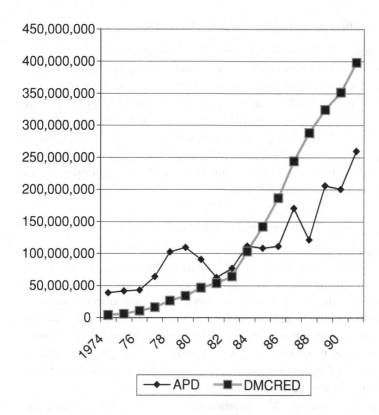

Figure 14.1 Togo, official development assistance and loans from the World Bank and IDA, 1974–1990, US$
Note: APD = Official development assistance; DMCRED = IBRD loans and IDA credit.

flow of FDI and ODA. ODA shrunk from 260 million CFAF in 1990 to 71 million CFAF in 1999.

5. Political economy

For an increasing number of economists, political economy is an important determinant of growth (Bates and Devarajan 1999). Togo has been one of the countries where political leadership has not changed much over the past forty years: three presidents have governed since 1960, and only one since 1967. For this reason, Togo has often been labeled as relatively politically stable among African countries. This stability ended in 1990, however, and the country has been going through a socio-political crisis since then. Moreover, as we shall see, interest groups and their role changed during the forty years of the study period.

5.1   The political environment and interest groups

The sub-period following independence was unstable because of covert interference by the former colonial power and inter-party rivalries carried over from the pre-independence period. These destabilizing factors contributed to the two military coup that rocked the country in the 1960s. The 1963 coup, in which the first elected President was assassinated, was the first military coup in SSA. The second coup occurred in 1967; it looked like a "palace revolution" in that it did not really affect the country's political stability. In spite of these two military coup, 1960–74 was the period in which the economy had its best performance.

5.1.1   The post-independence political instability of the 1960s

The struggle for independence was a concern of the majority of Togolese regardless of ethnic group or region of origin. The political environment in the pre-independence period and the early 1960s was characterized by a multi-party system. Some parties favored the continuation of colonial rule while others fought for independence. Usually, parties in weak political settings operate under the influence of foreign powers and do not always agree on the way to govern. Conflicts often erupt and cause the collapse of coalitions, leading to political crises like those that crippled most newly independent African countries.

In Togo, the coalition that assumed power after independence comprised two allied parties, the Comité de l'Unité Togolaise (CUT) of Sylvanus Olympio and the JUVENTO of Anani Santos. The only thing that united these two parties was their common desire to free the country from colonial rule as quickly as possible. Interestingly, however, the two parties were very different ideologically, as they came from opposite ends of the political spectrum. Conservative-minded, thriving businessmen and women made up the core ideological constituency of the CUT while the JUVENTO, led by middle-class intellectuals and trade unions, was influenced by Marxist–Leninist ideology. In particular, the JUVENTO did not favor the conservative and market-oriented philosophy embraced by Olympio. The JUVENTO preferred progressive, pro-labor, policies that would put agriculture and rural development at the center of the economic development strategy.

The ideological divide between the two parties persisted and widened quite rapidly, causing the break-up of the coalition. The atmosphere was not helped by Olympio's pro-Anglo-Saxon rhetoric, an emphasis that did not please France, the former colonial power, which lent its support to opposition parties and to some leaders of the JUVENTO. The political environment deteriorated rapidly, starting with public clashes between the parties. The coalition collapsed, leading to open hostilities, which intensified as opposition parties joined in, and resulted in arrests of political leaders. As early as 1961, the government crushed the opposition by jailing some political leaders.

In the process, the government made some fatal political mistakes by trying to reduce the influence of France. The President strengthened ties with West Germany,[9] at the expense of relations with France, snubbing the French to seek German financing for the construction of the Port of Lomé, the most important public infrastructure investment in the country.

The discontent of the French increased by the end of 1962, when the government requested all Togolese soldiers fighting under the flag of the former French colonial army against the Algerian independence army to withdraw from the war and from the colonial army. This prompted the French to increase their covert support not only to opposition parties, but also to the military; the latter believed that Olympio's plans, which called for their withdrawal from the French colonial army and aimed at reducing the size of the national armed forces, would marginalize their role in the country's affairs. Interestingly, the government did not perceive the discontent of the Algerian war veterans that the French only reluctantly released and that it did not itself intend to recruit into the national army.

The Olympio administration, in power from 1960 to 1963, was quite popular; it felt so confident about itself that it overlooked basic security matters. In particular, it did not imagine any other force than the will of the people that had elected the President could topple a government that was so popular. This was justified by the fact that there had been no previous case of violent change of executive authority in independent SSA countries. The President therefore ignored the military coup that was being plotted, and that eventually took place in January 1963.

The coup resulted in the death of President Olympio and the end of his regime. The first significant change that occurred following the coup was the improvement and strengthening of Togo's ties with France, which had backed the coup. France's involvement in Togo's politics increased, making France the most important political, economic, and military partner of the government.

Nicolas Grunitzky, who was put in power by the military junta, was the leader of the opposition party, the Parti Togolais du Progrès (PTP), which did not want independence in 1960, but instead advocated the continuation of colonial rule for a few more years in order to better prepare the country for self-rule. Grunitzky quickly made overtures toward France and the post-colonial institutions it supported in the West African region. These institutions included UMOA, which Grunitzky wasted no time in joining, abandoning Olympio's long-standing quest for monetary independence.

---

[9] Germany was the country that colonized Togo between 1884 and the end of the First World War.

The Grunitzky government was not popular, for at least two reasons. First, the PTP had not been a popular party, being viewed as a party that represented the extension of French colonial interests. Second, Grunitzky was not elected. His accession at the request of the military was not tolerated by the population, the majority of whom saw him as an accomplice in the coup that killed Olympio. Others viewed him as a weak leader who did not have an agenda of his own, or who was a puppet of the military.

Lack of popular support impaired Grunitzky's ability to carry out any well-defined program of government, and the new government's inability to improve the socio-economic situation gave the military an excuse to intervene again, to remove the President through a bloodless coup in 1967. Grunitzky's removal was not greatly regretted by most Togolese; the population was worried, however, that these successive military coup might result in the establishment of a dangerous trend in the country's political life, where military power and violence would have precedence over the rule of law and prohibit democracy.

The 1967 coup brought to power the military junta that had staged the 1963 coup. Gnassingbe Eaydema, who led the second coup, imposed himself as President. The military government quickly consolidated its power and Togo has since experienced one of the strongest, best-consolidated and most ruthless military dictatorships in Africa.

Political life was banned following the 1963 coup; it was only in 1969 that the military government founded the Rassemblement du Peuple Togolais (RPT), a single party, to give a political base to its rule. The true objective of the government was to make the population and the outside world believe that it was bringing back political life; in reality, the establishment of this single party was a move to outlaw any other political party and strengthen the long-existing ban on political activity.

Ethnic harmony was a positive feature of the new regime. The first two presidents came from the southern region of the country, while the soldiers of the Kabye ethnic group who led the military coup were from the North. However, there was no serious ethnic conflict.

Trade unions were silenced in most parts of the period, especially following the abolition of political and union activity in 1963. The military feared trade unions and other civil associations as they did political organizations.

5.1.2   The advent of the one-party system in the 1970s

The Eaydema government consolidated itself in the 1970s, during which the single-party regime established in 1969 campaigned for legitimacy. The President took advantage of the population's compassion when he survived a mysterious plane accident in January 1972 to quickly consolidate his power base, achieve his goals, and make the public idolize him through the party. The regime became more and more autocratic and repressive; through manipulation, persecution, and persuasion, the regime organized youth, women, and labor associations under the party's umbrella. Because of the prevailing Cold War climate the regime was quite popular internationally.

The main other feature of the end of this period was the five-fold increase in the price of phosphate between 1974 and 1975. There was a tendency toward bad economic management, a phenomenon facilitated by the windfall increase in revenue enjoyed by the government (McGuire and Olson 1996).

The political environment was unstable elsewhere in the sub-region, notably in Burkina Faso, Ghana, and Nigeria. Marxism–Leninism made progress and took hold in neighboring Benin. Such a situation was of concern to the West, given the Cold War context, and human rights abuse was apparently of no concern. In the sub-region, Côte d'Ivoire and Togo were the main defenders of western countries' interests, and their governments therefore enjoyed the support of the West. Capital and foreign aid flowed in and ACP–EEC conventions were signed in Lomé. Togo also enjoyed important inflows of foreign investment because of the over-liquidity of banks.

The legacy of the second half of the 1970s was the consolidation of a repressive regime, the institution of a predatory method of government, large budget deficits, and a record-high external public debt. All this happened with the blessing of France and the West in an international environment dominated by the Cold War.

5.1.3   The 1980s and the consolidation of the single-party regime

The government imposed a Constitution in 1981 to give the regime some institutional and legal bases and to reinforce the pre-eminence of single-party rule. This new situation put an end to the exceptional regime under which the country had been ruled since 1963; the political environment became very repressive as the government adopted a North Korean style of administration. In the first half of the 1980s, the political system was fairly stable; there were only two cabinet reshuffles. The regime in Lomé in 1985 and 1986 stood firm and appeared undisturbed despite the isolated bomb attacks and rebellions. The political leadership remained almost the same as in the 1970s. The 1985–6 political turmoil probably changed the attitude of the government, made the executive branch less secure, and shortened its time horizon. The President increasingly mistrusted citizens from ethnic groups other than his own. In addition to the interest groups of the previous period – i.e. the RPT leaders and the military – there was a third group, the ethnic group of the President. Ethnicity therefore became an increasingly disturbing phenomenon, as more and more people from the President's ethnic group held the most important senior management positions in the civil service and public enterprises.

5.1.4 The socio-political crisis of the 1990s

In the 1990s, the troubled political situation deeply affected economic performance. The highly unstable environment turned violent, as the unpopular dictatorial regime turned to the armed forces for swift repressions. These events caused a severe slowdown of economic activity and a sharp decline in *per capita* income. 1993 marked the climax of the economic downturn, with an 18 percent decline in GDP caused principally by a nine-month strike.

The fight for democracy produced some results, as it brought about perceptible changes in the country's political arena. Such changes were in part the result of strong pressure on the President from the international community, but they also reflected powerful social sources operating within the country. In particular, the civil strife that started on October 5, 1990 profoundly changed the socio-political environment. At the beginning, the regime resorted, as usual, to political manipulations to shackle the opposition. But this strategy failed. In the end, the regime was overwhelmed by events: it reluctantly yielded to the demands of the population and brought an end to the one-party political system in April 1991. Following a National Conference held that summer, a transitional government led by a Prime Minister was put in place; a parliamentary system of government was instituted to replace the one-man terror show run by the President.

But the new system of government never functioned properly because of permanent frictions between the President, who had the support of the armed forces, and the Prime Minister, who was supposed to be the choice of the people. These frictions resulted in a *putsch* in December 1991, through which the President gradually recovered his former power. The new political environment was characterized by increased insecurity, generalized violence, assassination of political leaders, and abuse of human rights. Faked elections were held periodically, through which the President imposed himself and his party. In the second half of the 1990s, the President's party was the only one that sat in Parliament.

The opposition continued to enjoy interest groups' support, which facilitated the process toward democracy. The government adopted a more clientelist behavior as the make-up of interest groups changed. Members of the President's party, who were predominantly from his own ethnic group, held most of the senior positions in the civil service and parastatal enterprises. Regional distribution of social services was biased towards the Kara region.

5.2 Economic policy

5.2.1 1960s and early 1970s

During this period, some 80 percent of the population lived in rural areas; industrial employment made up less than 15 percent of the labor force; bureaucracy and institutions were rather weak. Foreign trading companies (mostly French) dominated the private sector. The economic philosophy was conservative and market-oriented, reflecting the legacy of the first President fairly well. Increased involvement of the government through the introduction of price control measures in 1964 did not cause any major hindrance to growth because such measures were below the "harmful" level they reached in the mid-1970s.

The business community and the private sector supported the first President's political party. Before independence, private companies were in charge of the export sector. The government carefully cultivated their interests by resisting pressure to interfere with their activities. The situation in Togo contrasted with that in neighboring countries, such as Ghana and Côte d'Ivoire, where state-controlled marketing boards were established. Producer price stabilization measures were not introduced before 1964 despite the 45 percent decline in the price of coffee and cocoa between 1958 and 1962. It is still not clear what the net effect of such policy was on output and exports. Supporters of a price stabilization policy could argue that the uncompensated price decline discouraged production, a phenomenon undesirable for a country that had just attained independence. Because of their lack of political power or proper organization, farmers did not have means to put pressure on the government; proponents of a free market system would argue that, by behaving in this way, farmers avoided establishing dangerous precedents that could prejudice long-term growth. In fact, most of the JUVENTO leaders believed that the government could have done more for farmers: some went even further, advocating actions that would counterbalance the negative effects of the commodity price fall on farmers' welfare. The debate over agricultural policy put the JUVENTO at odds with the CUT and contributed to the tension between the two parties. Fortunately for the CUT, farmers did not get involved in the conflict, which minimized the potential adverse effects on the President's popularity.

In June 1964, the new government founded OPAT, which was granted the monopoly of marketing major agricultural export products, following the pattern established by other French colonies such as Côte d'Ivoire. OPAT soon became a stabilization fund with growing revenues, part of which the government used to finance development projects. The Eaydema government that assumed power after the 1967 coup was interested in regional economics because the Kabye ethnic group from the Kara region dominated the armed forces. Part of the revenue from taxes on coffee, cocoa, and cotton was channeled into development programs in the Kara region, the beginning of a strategy that tended to favor the north at the expense of the south, and that helped Eaydema consolidate his political base.

During this period, the Eaydema government did not introduce any major economic reform program – the President was more interested in consolidating his political base. Besides the port of Lomé, which was planned by Olympio and started by Grunitzky, the government did not undertake any major investment project. Fiscal policy was mostly prudent; both the budget deficit and public debt were negligible. Togo joined UMOA in 1963. The monetary regime in place since colonial times was unchanged until 1973 when it underwent minor reforms, and monetary policy was *de facto* designed and managed by the French Treasury. By convention, the French Treasury was responsible for the convertibility of the CFA franc, UMOA's currency. Because of this arrangement, and as a consequence of conservative fiscal policy, Togo had an adequate quantity of international reserves. Government claims on the banking system were positive and significant. Bank loans benefited mostly foreign-owned trading companies, which accounted for more than 90 percent of total bank deposits and loans. UMOA remained a low-inflation currency area: the inflation rate averaged 1.2 percent a year during the period, and the international economic environment was stable until the first oil shock in 1973.

5.2.2 Second half of the 1970s

Clientelistic management resulted in greater pressure on public resources with an impressive increase in the civil wage bill and in fiscal deficits. There was also an increase in social infrastructure (schools and health centers, water and sanitation). The government implemented policies with ethnic and urban biases. The increase in the size of the civil service was a sign of this policy change: the number of civil servants grew three-fold between 1965 and 1977 and increased further, from 30,000 in 1977 to 49,000 in 1980, with most of the newly recruited workers coming from the Kara region.

Economic policy was urban-biased largely because the potential opposition to the regime was represented by educated people who resided in the main cities. This bias was illustrated by the creation of Togograin and SONACOM (see p. 484) for the purpose of controlling the price of consumer goods in the cities. The operation of such companies only caused distortions and hurt overall economic performance.

The government nationalized the production and marketing of phosphate rocks in order to increase its control over the economy. The President and the party made this improvised nationalization a big political issue: to get the public involved (emotionally and otherwise), the party leadership claimed that the 1974 plane accident was plotted by the West as a pre-emptive reaction to the President's intention to nationalize the phosphate sector.

The country remained a member of UMOA and did not have an independent monetary policy; a reform in 1975 gave the Central Bank, the BCEAO, a more active role in monetary planning. The Central Bank was given more authority in the determination of interest rates and the allocation of credit, and a union-wide money market was created in 1977 with the objective of improving capital and credit mobility within the union. France continued to play a determinant role in the design of monetary policy, using the reform to increase its influence over the sub-region. Many aid programs were tied to membership in the Franc zone or to public support of French culture. The promotion of agencies such as the Agence pour la Coopération Culturelle et Technique (ACCT) and the institution of Francophone Summits were meant to develop special ties with France. France gave military and security assistance to loyal regimes in the sub-region and got privileged access to the national resources and markets of these countries in return.

5.2.3   1980s

The government continued to grant special privileges to its supporters through public enterprises such as SONACOM and OPAT, but the situation began to change with economic reforms sponsored by the Bretton Woods Institutions and bilateral donors. The international political environment was dominated by the Cold War, which helped the regime receive the support of the West – indeed the President portrayed himself to the outside world as an anti-communist champion. This situation weakened the position of the Bretton Woods institutions as power brokers and reduced the effectiveness of their role in influencing the pace of economic reforms. The degree of implementation of economic reforms depended to a great extent on the President's will and mood: trade liberalization and privatization programs were implemented with delays even though the government declared its commitment to them. Nonetheless, there was evidence of the government's disengagement from several sectors, and the effective rate of protection fell from 128.5 percent in 1980 to 72.6 percent in 1999.

Pressure continued on public expenditure, which decreased by an average of 14.2 percent between 1980 and 1987, and the financial situation of public and parastatal enterprises worsened. However, the budget deficit declined from 8.4 percent of GDP in 1979 to 2.9 percent of GDP in 1990, thanks to a fall in expenditure and an increase in external aid (see figure 14.1).

Economic reforms began to have adverse effects on the welfare of the population. Most social sector indicators worsened substantially: between 1980 and 1985, the primary school enrollment rate declined by 12.5 percent and the secondary school enrollment by 31 percent. The number of civil service employees dropped from 39,000 in 1981 to 34,000 in 1988. The population's discontent was overwhelming, the government reacted by introducing measures to improve the social situation. Such measures were a setback in the implementation of the SAPs and contributed to the increase in government expenditure during the late 1980s.

5.2.4   1990s

Important policy and institutional changes took place in the 1990s. In the area of monetary and exchange rate policy, the authorities of the CFA zone finally consented to effect the historic and long-awaited devaluation of the CFA franc in January 1994. Second, the monetary union, UMOA, was transformed into a new regional economic community, the Union Economique et Monétaire Ouest Africaine (UEMOA). The new arrangement had broader goals and objectives than the old; notably, it aims at achieving full (monetary and) economic integration among its member countries. In addition to monetary integration, which these countries had enjoyed since independence, UEMOA achieved a customs union in 2000 with the removal of tariff barriers and NTBs on intra-community trade and the application by all member countries of a common external tariff (CET). Overall, the creation of UEMOA brought about a profound change in the institutional framework within which macroeconomic policy was conducted. Participation in UEMOA is subject to respecting some specific conditions, including the convergence criteria discussed above, which impose new constraints on the government with regard to economic policy.

The governments of all member countries committed themselves to increased fiscal discipline and to avoiding the types of macroeconomic imbalances that they experienced in the 1970s. For example, they are required to keep their debt to GDP ratio at 70 percent, their budget has to be balanced, and their inflation rate cannot exceed 3 percent. In addition, no government is allowed to indulge in cheating practices that would accumulate payment arrears. All these measures are supposed to lend support to the common currency and contribute to the cohesion of the Union. However, it is still too early to evaluate their effect on growth in Togo.

The government kept its official commitment to economic reforms. However, the macroeconomic situation worsened due to the instability of the socio-political environment. The fiscal deficit increased to 6.2 percent in the 1990s; accumulation of arrears on civil servants' salaries and retired civil servants' pension payments, on the one hand, and reduction of public investment, on the other hand, caused a contraction of aggregate demand and output.

Partisan politics helped accelerate the public enterprise privatization program, which this regime had resisted in the 1980s when its time horizon was longer: RPT dignitaries were major shareholders in the newly privatized public enterprises. Politicization of the civil service and delays in salary payments affected the performance of the administration. Trade unions kept persistent pressure on the government through strikes that impaired the adminstration's ability to function.

The population's first concern was political liberties. The second main demand of interest groups essentially related to access to public resources. Each interest group had its own demands – student organizations sought improved social benefits (housing, transportation, food, health care, etc.), and trade unions increased salaries.

Non-respect for human rights had adverse effects on the economy, not least through its dampening effect on foreign aid, which in turn worsened the government's financial situation. World Bank financing did not decline outright, but its dissatisfaction (and that of the IMF) over the government's unwillingness to respect agreed-upon programs and to service its multilateral debts in a timely way led to a sharp decline in overall external aid during the 1980s (figure 14.1).

The resources devoted to partisan politics decreased because of poor economic performance and suspension of international co-operation. However, strong demands from interest groups contributed to increase government expenditure: the budget deficit rose from 2.84 percent of GDP in 1980–90 to 6.5 percent of GDP in 1991–8. The bulk of current government expenditure was allocated to salary payments and transfers. The civil service wage bill reached 51 percent of fiscal revenue in 1999, exceeding the UEMOA ceiling of 35 percent. Public investment fell from 25 percent of GDP in 1980–90 to 12.5 percent of GDP in 1991–8. There had been an increase in public investment during the period of political crisis, during which the time horizon of political leaders was supposed to be shortened. Rational behavior went against investment and other types of long-term commitment under such circumstances. However, in an environment characterized by bad governance, spending relating to investment supplied opportunities for corruption, so the corruption effect offset the time-horizon effect.

In conclusion, this sub-period was dominated by political factors that hampered economic performance. Changes in the domestic context and the international environment put unprecedented pressure on the government to move toward democracy. Throughout the 1990s, the population contested the regime openly, even though the latter succeeded in hanging on to power. Shortage of resources – in particular, reduced aid flows – made it difficult for the government to sustain its development policies. Social sectors were among the most affected by the situation: shortening of the political time horizon caused the political leadership to be less attentive to good economic management and governance issues.

6. Conclusions

The Togolese economy has gone through ups and downs since independence in 1960. Performance was satisfactory in the 1960s and early 1970s but worsened after the end of the 1970s. The difficulties began with the commodity shocks of the 1970s, which caused strong swings in the terms of trade. First, the 1973–4 oil shock contributed to the recession of the mid-1970s. Second, the 1974–5 phosphate boom had mixed effects on the economy. In particular, the unexpected increase in revenue that it caused induced the government into several policy mistakes, including a spectacular increase in expenditure and extensive government intervention. The increased size of the public sector hampered the functioning of market institutions and resulted in reduced efficiency; productivity dropped and overall economic performance began a downward trend that the implementation of SAPs was not able to reverse and that the socio-political crisis of the 1990s only helped to intensify.

The economic performance of Togo over the past forty years cannot be explained by a single factor. Accumulation of physical and human capital was not determinant in the performance of the economy, in part because of the inappropriateness of the underlying investment policy. Political factors and economic policies played determinant roles in the performance of the economy: stability of the economic and political environment is a prerequisite for good economic performance. In turn, the stability of the political environment requires a form of government that enjoys a broad-based support from the population and in which consensus, not conflict, is used to deal with the issues facing the nation. This study also shows that redistribution does impede growth. High growth rates were attained when no (weak) redistribution was taking place in the 1960s. The growth rate was weak at the start of redistribution in the late 1970s. The economy experienced stagnation with the improvement of regional- and ethnic-based redistribution in the 1980s. When the anticipated redistribution took place, due to the doubt that the actual political elite could maintain power the economy collapsed in the 1990s.

The prospects for the future are dependent on the way the government manages the ongoing political crisis and, as a member country, respects the convergence criteria of UEMOA. A suitable solution to the crisis will stabilize the political environment and reduce anticipated redistribution. This in turn will pave the way for the resumption of co-operation with the international community, increasing the opportunity for getting debt relief through the Highly Indebted Poor Countries (HIPC) initiatives. But as of now, the political crisis still remains.

The improvement of economic policies will depend on the ability of UEMOA to play the role of an agency of restraint. Since 2002 the member countries have had to respect the convergence criteria, which place limits on some economic aggregates. The criteria dictate that the budget has to be in equilibrium, the inflation rate no more than 3 percent, the debt to GDP ratio no more than 70 percent with no more arrears in debt servicing, the wage bill at most 35 percent of total public spending, and domestic funding no less than 20 percent of public investment. However, the budget deficit exceeded 10 percent of GDP in 2002 (if proper account was taken of the accumulation of arrears), which was a significant increase from 9.3 percent in 2001. As a result, the debt burden gets heavier and heavier; by early in the millennium it had exceeded 100 percent of GDP. Even though there were some improvements in 2003, the public finance situation is still fragile; apparent improvements were achieved through exceptional financing, (domestic arrears, bank financing, and advances from public enterprises) and an increase of 14.2 percent of current expenditures compared to a 16 percent decrease in public investment. Public investment, which fell by 17.4 percent, 16.9 percent, and 5.7 percent in 1999, 2000, and 2001, respectively, remains very low, at 17 percent of total public spending in the 1998–2002 period. Public investment from domestic sources is extremely low, at 3 percent of fiscal revenue, while civil servant salaries represent 40 percent of current public expenditures.

For UEMOA to be an agency of restraint, it must be able to implement some sanctions against member countries that do not respect their commitments. History shows that in the case of regional integration between developing countries, institutions such as UEMOA do not have the power to impose and implement such sanctions. In the short run, therefore, prospects for improvement in macroeconomic policies will not come from Togo's membership of UEMOA. The credibility of developing countries' policies increases when they are locked into agreements of which the developed countries are a part (Schiff and Winter 2003). One can therefore expect the country to improve its economic policies in the context of the Economic Partnership Agreement (EPA) which West African countries are negotiating with EU, and which may take effect as early as 2008.

References

Afeikhena, J. and O. Olawade (1999), "Characteristics and Behaviour of African Commodity/Product Markets Institutions and their Consequences for Economic Growth," Framework Paper for the Explaining African Growth Project. Nairobi: African Economic Research Consortium

Baniganti, K. R. and F. Lawson (1994), *Les indicateurs de protection, d'incitation et d'avantage comparatif: méthodologie pour l'étude de l'industrie manufacturière du Togo*. Université du Bénin, mimeo

Bates, R. H. and S. Devarajan (1999), "Political Economy of African Growth," Framework Paper for the Explaining African Economic Growth Project. Nairobi: African Economic Research Consortium

Cohen, D. (1993), "Two Notes on Economic Growth and the Solow Model," *Center for Economic Policy Research*, Discussion Paper 780

Collier, P. (1997), "La zone CFA et performance économique," *Annales de l'Université du Bénin*, Série Droit et Sciences Economiques 17: 81–122

Collier, P. and S. A. O'Connell (2007), "Opportunities and Choices," chapter 2 in B. J. Ndulu, S. A. O'Connell, R. H. Bates, P. Collier, and C. C. Soludo, eds., *The Political Economy of Economic Growth in Africa, 1960–2000*, vol. 1. Cambridge: Cambridge University Press

Collins, S. and B. Bosworth (1996), "Economic Growth in East Asia: Accumulation versus Assimilation," *Brookings Papers on Economic Activity* 2: 135–203

Evlo, K. (1996), "Capital humain et croissance economique au Togo: une extension du modèle de Solow," *Annales de l'Université du Bénin*, Série Droit et Sciences Economiques 16: 68–86

Fischer, S. (1993), "The Role of Macroeconomic Factors in Growth," *Journal of Monetary Economics* 32: 485–512

Hoeffler, A. (2002), "The Augmented Solow Model and the African Growth Debate," *Oxford Bulletin of Economics and Statistics* 64(2), May: 135–58

Krugman, P. (1994), "The Myth of Asia's Miracle," *Foreign Affairs* 73(6), November–December: 62–78

McGuire, M. and M. Olson (1996), "The Economics of Autocracy and Majority Rule: The Invisible Hand and the Use of Force," *Journal of Economic Literature* 34: 72–96

Ndulu, B. J. and S. A. O'Connell (2000), "Background Information on Economic Growth," Paper prepared for the Explaining African Economic Growth Project. Nairobi: African Economic Research Consortium (downloadable: www.aercafrica.org)

O'Connell, S. A. and B. J. Ndulu (2000), "Africa's Growth Experience: A Focus on Sources of Growth," AERC Growth Working Paper No. 10. Nairobi: African Economic Research Consortium, April (downloadable: www.aercafrica.org)

Oyejide, A. T. (2000), "Markets and Economic Growth in Africa," Framework Paper for the Explaining African Economic Growth Project. Nairobi: African Economic Research Consortium

Schiff, M. and L. A. Winters (2003), *2003 Regional Integration and Development*. Washington, DC: The World Bank

World Bank (1994), *Adjustment in Africa: Reforms, Results and the Road Ahead*. New York: Oxford University Press

(1996), "Togo: sortir de la crise, sortir de la pauvreté." Washington, DC: The World Bank

Young, A. (1992), "A Tale of Two Cities: Factor Accumulation and Technical Change in Hong Kong and Singapore," *NBER Macroeconomics Annual*: 13–54

(1993), "Substitution and Complementarity in Endogenous Innovation," *Quarterly Journal of Economics* 108(3): 775–807

PART III

Resource-rich economies

15 | The indigenous developmental state and growth in Botswana

Gervase S. Maipose and Thapelo C. Matsheka

1. Introduction and overview

At the time of independence in 1966, Botswana was one of the poorest countries in the world. The country has since sustained the world's highest growth rate in terms of GDP *per capita* and is now classified by the World Bank as a high-middle-income country. It also received some of the highest ratings in Africa in the UNDP Human Resource Development Index after 1992. In this chapter, Botswana is depicted as an "indigenous developmental state," in which a secure political elite (with electoral support since independence) has pursued growth-promoting policies and developed or modified and maintained viable inherited traditional and modern institutions of political, economic, and legal restraint. These institutions proved robust in the face of initial large aid inflows and spectacular mineral rents. With huge reserves of mineral wealth, especially diamonds, Botswana belongs to the group of "resource-based" African countries, but it is also a land-locked country whose development path has been largely "syndrome-free." We argue that Botswana managed to minimize the adverse consequences of resource wealth. The country has a long track record of good policies – pursued by a relatively strong and competent state that provided a visionary and

University of Botswana.

management role, operating under viable traditional and newly-constructed modern institutions of economic, political, and legal restraint. In this chapter we stress the "indigenous" nature of Botswana's developmental state and how this helped shape interest in growth and stability – leading to growth outcomes determined by microeconomic agents responding to the policy environment and external shocks. Botswana stands out as one of the few countries in Africa with both an impressive sustainable development and political stability record. The country is also the region's longest democracy, with a good governance and state management record. The role of the state in Botswana is, in many respects, similar to the development success story of the "East Asian miracle" where the state has been strategically interventionist rather than crisis-driven under a capitalist market economic development formula. But the institutional context of rapid growth in Botswana – that is, a multi-party democratic system of government – offers a sharp and refreshing contrast to authoritative and undemocratic regimes elsewhere (including China and the "East Asian miracle" economies) which have not had a history of democratic institutions until quite recently, if at all.

2. Growth experience in cross-country perspective

As already noted the growth record of independent Botswana has been quite impressive. Initially based on agriculture and heavily dependent on foreign aid, Botswana's growth was driven by the mining sector, particularly the diamond industry. Growth was been strategically led/influenced and managed by the state and decreasingly complemented by foreign aid, within an overall institutional context of a liberal market economy and a multi-party democratic system of government. Growth *per capita* averaged 6.3 percent for four decades (1960–2000), while real GDP average growth was almost 10 percent; Botswana has been Africa's lead performer in cross-country perspective (Ndulu and O'Connell 2003a).

We distinguish three periods. The first phase, from 1960 through independence to 1975, was described as a period of initial base-creating, a transitional phase starting with some degree of uncertainty about the nature of the Botswana state and ending with institutional transformation and development policy direction. Once the threat of incorporation into South Africa or Southern Rhodesia (now Zimbabwe) had receded, the new elite merged local interests into a broader commitment to build up a non-racial (reformist) and unitary state. This period was characterized by the end of colonial rule and integration of traditional institutional structures into modern institutions, underlined by a policy stance that sought to maximize the flow of foreign capital – aid and private investment – resulting in moderate growth and the introduction of a multi-party democratic system of government under the inherited market-based economy. At this time the thrust of development policy involved experimenting with or emphasis on state-led development in a mixed liberal economy. The institutional baselines were largely similar to those of many African countries at independence.

The second phase, from 1975 to 1989, saw the consolidation of both the market-based state-led development strategy and continuity with the multi-party system of government – avoiding the wave of one-party or military regimes and forms of socialist/communist ideologies cutting across the African continent. The policy thrust, as shaped by the interest and institutional context, was towards building a relatively strong and competent state that would provide visionary leadership and a management role without becoming excessively involved in the nuts and bolts of production. It is during this period that the mining sector clearly emerged and consolidated itself as the engine of growth. The phase turned out to be a period of rapid economic transformation, marked by rapid economic growth but limited structural diversification. It was also during this phase that the state emerged as a major saving agent and as a conduit for redistributing "rent" to the rest of the economy to enhance economic growth.

The third period, from 1990 to 2000 and beyond, marked the start of a new policy environment: the end of a state-led development strategy and a new reorientation towards private sector-led development, and realignment of the main interests arising from rapid urbanization and spread of education as Botswana strove towards new production ventures. During this period, the economy experienced a reduced rate of economic growth, explained by the complex political choices involved in the new dynamics in Botswana's new political-economy order.

Table 15.1 shows the growth and composition of GDP. This is complemented by figure 15.1 on foreign aid and figure 15.2 which shows domestic saving and investment patterns. From 1960 to 1997, real GDP average growth was almost 10 percent. It is noteworthy that Botswana's real GDP *per capita* growth was the world's fastest over these years (Harvey 1992; Leith 2001). Agriculture's share in GDP shrank significantly from over 40 percent in the 1960s to below 4 percent in 2000, whereas the share of mining rose from almost zero to nearly 50 percent for some years before sliding to 34 percent by 2000. The share of manufacturing remained almost constant at 4 percent.

While the rate of growth was exceptionally high there was an extreme shortage of skilled/educated manpower in Botswana and "Dutch disease" was avoided. Manpower constraints did not seriously affect economic growth partly because of the increased inflow of foreign aid in the form of technical assistance with a policy of allowing foreign operational experts to occupy line positions, and partly because Botswana also avoided rushing into "Africanization" (Stevens 1981; Maipose, Somolekae, and Johnston

Table 15.1 *Botswana, sectoral percentage share of GDP and annual growth rates, 1966–2000, constant 1993/4 prices*

	1966	1975/76	1977/78	1979/80	1982/83	1985/86	1987/88	1989/90	1991/92	1993/94	2000
Agriculture	39	25.4	21.3	13.1	8.9	5.5	7.2	4.8	4.4	4.4	3.2
	–	(1.3)	(–0.5)	(2.0)	(–12.5)	(10.8)	(65.5)	(3.6)	(2.0)	(–0.9)	–
Mining	0	12.5	15.2	31.2	32.0	47.2	45.5	51.2	37.7	35.7	33.7
	–	(64.5)	(86.1)	(41.8)	(46.3)	(3.1)	(2.8)	(–3.3)	(–0.5)	(5.4)	–
Manufacturing	8	6.9	5.8	3.7	6.7	5.2	5.1	5.0	5.0	4.6	6.0
	–	(28.2)	(–6.4)	(–35.1)	(–8.1)	(30.1)	(29.9)	(4.8)	(6.4)	(–0.6)	–
Water and electricity	2.8	3.8	2.5	2.0	2.6	2.4	2.9	2.0	2.0	2.2	2.2
	–	(51.1)	(9.9)	(–3.8)	(–1.3)	(33.6)	(14.4)	(2.2)	(5.7)	(14.9)	–
Construction	5	8.9	9.8	7.6	5.1	4.0	4.9	5.5	7.8	6.5	6.4
	–	(1.1)	(36.3)	(11.6)	(–18.4)	(–11.2)	(18.1)	(25.1)	(4.6)	(3.7)	–
Trade, hotels and restaurants	5	8.0	8.1	8.2	6.8	6.9	5.7	5.2	5.6	8.3	9.7
	–	(15.8)	(–1.5)	(9.3)	(–33.4)	(44.4)	(20.2)	(18.0)	(–8.7)	(65.1)	–
Transport	2	4.0	3.6	1.7	3.0	2.5	2.9	2.6	3.4	3.7	3.8
	–	(20.6)	(11.1)	(57.6)	(11.3)	(29.5)	(52.3)	(7.7)	(13.9)	(1.3)	–
Finance, real estate and bus. serv	2	6.4	6.9	7.7	6.3	6.0	5.1	6.1	7.8	10.1	10.8
	–	(8.3)	(–3.1)	(46.4)	(5.4)	(21.8)	(6.9)	(27.9)	(3.9)	(8.1)	–
General govt services	12.3	14.1	15.3	13.0	16.4	13.0	13.4	11.5	14.6	15.6	15.5
	–	(22.8)	(1.9)	(3.4)	(9.6)	(7.9)	(21.8)	(2.1)	(16.8)	(3.4)	–
Social and personal services	3.2	4.4	3.7	2.7	3.3	2.8	2.7	3.1	4.1	4.3	4.4
	–	(32.7)	(1.6)	(0.0)	(19.9)	(13.8)	(30.6)	(16.3)	(5.4)	(1.8)	–
+ Adjustments: Dummy sector	–	0.9	–1.7	–1.9	–2.1	–2.0	–2.0	–2.2	–2.2	–2.7	–2.8
	–	(50.0)	(–2.5)	(32.1)	(17.1)	(48.0)	(16.2)	(2.7)	(3.2)	(18.0)	–
Customs duties	–	6.6	9.5	11.1	11.1	6.5	6.6	5.4	9.9	7.3	6.1
	–	(5.8)	(26.9)	(28.3)	(8.2)	(–9.2)	(12.4)	(8.5)	(32.6)	(–25.5)	–
Total GDP (aggregate)	–	**(18.4)**	**(19.5)**	**(14.4)**	**(16.0)**	**(7.5)**	**(14.7)**	**(5.5)**	**(6.3)**	**(4.2)**	–
GDP excluding mining	–	(12.2)	(6.3)	(6.2)	(–3.2)	(11.7)	(25.1)	(11.5)	(10.3)	(3.5)	–

Source: National Accounts Statistics of Botswana, 1974/5 to 1994/5 (Central Statistics Office, Gaborone, March 2000).

Note: Annual growth rates are in parentheses.

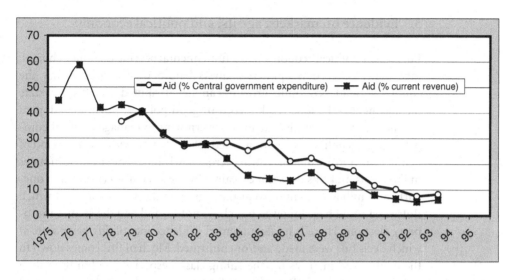

Figure 15.1 Botswana, government expenditure and foreign aid, 1975–1993

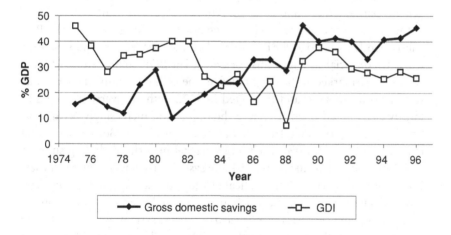

Figure 15.2 Botswana, GDI and gross domestic savings, 1975–1996, percent of GDP
Source: Calculated from Botswana "DAC data," 1998.

1996). "Dutch disease" was avoided mainly because the government took care not to spend more than the economy could absorb. Reserve accumulation during boom periods and rapid responses to adverse terms of trade shocks were two crucial facets of Botswana's super-prudent macroeconomic policy: diamond price increases were treated as temporary and declines as permanent.

3. Evidence on markets, agents, and political economy

Botswana's political economy had a fundamental bearing on policy choices. Like many other development analysts before us, we believe that the country's rapid economic growth can be attributed to effective state management – the long track record of good policies. Botswana adopted a multi-party democratic system of government to manage political competition. This policy choice conformed relatively well with the first wind of democratic transformation cutting across newly independent African states in the 1960s. But this does not explain why the system survived when one-party and military regimes swept the region by the 1970s – a trend which Botswana could have followed but chose not to, and had the second multi-party election. There is no documented evidence identifying key points at which decisions were made and/or confirmed. Much of this comes down to the quality and interests of "the ruling class," especially within the ruling Botswana Democratic Party (BDP) leadership. Moreover, democracy tied in relatively well with the consensus-seeking approach that had deep roots in the Tswana culture, as demonstrated later.

During this period, two main political parties participated in the two general parliamentary and local government elections – the BDP, known as the liberal/conservative party, and the Botswana Congress Party (BCP) – subsequently replaced by the Botswana National Front (BNF), known as radical leftist or socialist/communist-oriented. The BDP, led by Seretse Khama, who was earmarked to become chief of one of the prominent tribes, was put in power in 1966 and re-elected in 1972 with an overwhelming and largely rural-based majority, while the opposition increasingly became an urban-based party (table 15.2). It was inconceivable for Botswana's ruling elite, who enjoyed an overwhelming electoral majority including support from the traditional rulers, to break the system that was operating in their interest as compared with the radical ideology of the opposition. This issue has two inter-related points, which are elaborated later. First, the evolving political system was basically a *de facto* one-party system dominated by the conservative-led BDP government. Being reasonable and good leaders – a reputation they were building – they chose to retain the status quo and to avoid instability. The social background of the political leadership, particularly the founding father, Khama, and the "conservative" ideological orientation of the ruling party combined with other factors to determine regime performance. Although drawn from a small educated elite, Khama's social background was not confrontational with traditional authorities and the well-entrenched system of property rights. This was evident in agriculture, especially the cattle industry to which most leaders were tied, and in line with the capitalist development strategy the BDP-led government was advocating.

Table 15.2 *Botswana, electoral performance of major parties, 1965–2004*

Party	1965	1969	1974	1979	1984	1989	1994	1999	2004
BDP	28	24	27	29	28	31	27	33	44
BNF	–	3	2	2	5	3	13	6	12
BPP	3	3	2	1	1	0	0	–	–
BIP/IFP	0	1	1	0	0	0	0	–	–
BCP	–	–	–	–	–	–	–	1	1
BAM	–	–	–	–	–	–	0	0	–
Total no. of seats	**31**	**31**	**32**	**32**	**34**	**34**	**40**	**40**	**57**
% of popular vote									
BDP	80	68	77	75	68	65	55	54	53
BNF	–	14	12	13	20	27	37	25	23
BPP	14	12	6	8	7	4	4	–	–
BIP/IFP	5	6	4	4	3	2	4	–	–
BCP	–	–	–	–	–	–	–	11	18
BAM	–	–	–	–	–	–	–	5	1
Other	1	0	1	0	2	2	0	0	–
Rejected	–	–	–	–	–	–	–	5	5
Total	**100**	**100**	**100**	**100**	**100**	**100**	**100**	**100**	**100**
% of seats									
BDP	90	77	84	91	82	91	67	83	77
BNF	–	10	7	6	15	9	33	15	21
BPP	10	10	7	3	3	0	0	–	–
BIP/IFP	0	3	2	0	0	0	0	–	–
BCP	–	–	–	–	–	–	–	2	2
BAM	–	–	–	–	–	–	–	0	–
Total	**100**	**100**	**100**	**100**	**100**	**100**	**100**	**100**	**100**

Sources: Botswana Independent Electoral Commission (2002: 75); Botswana Independent Electoral Commission (2004).

Botswana's leaders adopted an open policy towards foreign investment and pursued a non-aligned foreign policy to maximize the volume and diversify the sources of foreign aid. These policies paid off – leading to the discovery and successful exploitation of copper, nickel, and diamonds, and increasing flows of aid from an increasingly wide range of donors, initially financing the whole development budget and about half of recurrent expenditure. Botswana also gained access to the EEC for beef exports, at prices above the world market under the special provisions of the Lomé Convention (initiated in 1975). They also adopted growth-promoting policies that were closely related to historical economic links with white-ruled South Africa – a clear demonstration of a pragmatic approach motivated by self/national interest while remaining opposed to racist regimes. One of these policy choices was membership in the Southern African Rand Monetary Area (RMA), thereby limiting the country's discretion over monetary policy at a time of implied temptation to use deficit financing given Botswana's limited financial and manpower resources. The government's pragmatism was similarly demonstrated by the decision to remain within the Southern African Customs Union (SACU) of 1910 and the renegotiation of the revenue-distribution formula in 1968, a policy choice which ensured a stream flow of revenue for necessary development projects (Harvey and Lewis 1990). Retrospectively, this policy limited the temptation to adopt the growth-retarding import-substitution industrialization policies which many African countries pursued. These examples illustrate how Botswana's membership in RMA and SACU provided external agencies of restraint in both crucial trade and monetary policies. When a policy decision was subsequently taken to get control over monetary and exchange rate policies – following a decision to move out of the monetary union in 1975 and the creation of the country's currency, the pula, in 1976, Botswana was well prepared (in terms of capacity) to undertake it. The decision was timely given that it was in Botswana's self-interest to pursue independent economic strategies and, with prospects of growing aid and mineral revenue, to have full control over macroeconomic management and manage strategic reserves, including foreign exchange reserves (Hudson 1978; Herman 1997: 181, 215).

Another important policy choice was the approach to national development, underlined by development planning and pragmatism, not "ideological dogma," for economic policies and the overall strategy of state-led development. As elaborated later, Botswana's development analysts acknowledged the significance of state strategic intervention, especially the idea of formulating and implementing a national development plan, a forerunner of development planning, as an instrument for resource mobilization and management in what was basically a market economy. Since then, each of the country's development plans sought to promote the four national principles of democracy, development, self-reliance, and unity – leading to the four overall national development objectives of rapid economic growth, social justice, economic independence, and sustainable development.

Botswana's economic development strategy has been to exploit the country's mineral wealth and invest the proceeds from mining in improving social and economic conditions and creating new economic opportunities, while at the same time encouraging the role of foreign aid and private (foreign) investment. This strategy of transforming the mineral endowment into physical and human endowment had the potential to achieve self-sustaining growth because physical and human capital was renewable whereas the mineral endowment was not (Bank of Botswana 1995: 5). State management capacity was enhanced by some early government policies, such as land policies and their management by Land Boards; vesting mineral rights (taken from local/traditional authorities) into central government; negotiated equity/business shares as opposed to nationalization of mines; and the policy of gradual localization by relying on foreign experts. These policies averted land and mineral right disputes which were the main source of tribal or regional conflicts in some countries. Of equal importance, private foreign investment was not threatened and reliance on foreign operational experts enhanced technical and management competency.

Botswana continued to have a multi-party system (Tordoff 1993: 4). By the early 1970s, few countries retained multi-party systems and, with the "odd exceptions" such as Botswana and The Gambia, political scientists talked in terms of competition within the single party rather than of competition between parties. The crucial question is: why did Botswana not follow the obvious trend in Africa? The answer has been briefly touched on and is elaborated below.

The institutional context of rapid growth and early sectoral transformation were vital for explaining the forces behind some crucial development changes and policy choices. The quality of democracy/governance was important in influencing policy choices and reconciling various interests. The country's performance with respect to each of the five political variables employed by Humphreys and Bates (2001) for cross-country comparison – democracy, strikes, demonstrations, coup, and guerrilla wars – was outstanding. By 1974, Botswana had had two competitive general parliamentary and local government elections won by the BDP, with overwhelming and largely rural-based majority support (table 15.2). The two main political parties had different ideological orientations, the main opposition party being regarded as "radical leftist" with socialist/communist ideals (Maundeni, 2002). But the interests of the Botswana elite were largely homogenous, based on cattle and land-owning; this made it relatively easier to reach a consensus on policies. The leadership in the ruling party had a considerable interest in promoting their own version of good governance: because the government knew that it must stand for election every five years, the ruling party pursued policies it believed would gain it the political support necessary to defeat its opponents, seeking "profit" in the form of "political income." The priorities of the key rural development programs, such as the Arable Land Development Programme and the Accelerated Rural Development Programme, initiated during this period, and the attention given to the cattle industry, were not biased against rural areas. Thus, neglect of rural interests, a widespread problem in SSA, was largely avoided in Botswana because the BDP-led government was representative, widely supported/elected by the rural majority, and the ruling elite had interests in rural development policies/programs.

As already noted, the survival of Botswana's liberal democracy can be partly explained by the country's tradition, because it is solidly based upon the inherited political culture. Viewed in another light, democracy was in the interest of Botswana leaders, seen as a "magic wand" with which to deliver a better public good by using it to attract foreign resources and manage internal politics. From their position in one of the poorest countries in the world, Botswana's leaders had clearly recognized how valuable "a commodity" democracy had become internationally, and they engaged in a conscious effort to project their country as a liberal political and economic model for the rest of Africa (Molutsi 1993). The international community viewed the choice of a multi-racial and multi-party democracy – in the context of the racially troubled Southern Africa of the 1960s and 1970s – with considerable sympathy, and this paid off in terms of aid inflows. In terms of managing national politics, democracy in Botswana operated in the ruling BDP interest. The opposition was not a threat to the dominance of the ruling party; the system operated more or less like a *de facto* one-party system in which the opposition was marginalized. This worked well to contain various interests, and ensured social and political stability. It was the most pragmatic option for rational/liberal leadership to take.

4. State resource mobilization and economic management

4.1 State resource mobilization

Co-existence of wealth and power is traditionally and culturally legiti-mate under the Tswana polity (Wylie 1990: 5–7; Parsons, Henderson, and Tlou 1995: 89), thereby providing a solid ideological orientation for the Botswanan leadership. Being basically pragmatic – following a capitalist development strategy – Khama listened to conservative and market-based advisors/economists. Whereas Kaunda and Nyerere were teachers, the BDP's founders, such as Khama and Ketumile Masire, were leading cattlemen and land-owners. Being historically associated with wealth accumulation and production, the Tswana elite had an interest in upholding a legal frame-work governing property rights and resolution of commercial disputes. Botswanan traditional rulers – the three principal tribal chiefs – "invited" a colonial power by proposing Bechuanaland protectorate status to the British government, and subsequently nationalists "negotiated" for independence and its timing (Maundeni 2002). Against this background it was not sur-prising that they pursued an open policy for foreign investment with which they negotiated for equity shares to work in partnership – not nationaliza-tion (Harvey and Lewis 1990). Thus, Botswana's leaders were not against FDI and the country's early opening to foreign investment was rewarded by large inflows, especially in the 1970s–1990s. FDI played a significant role in the country's development effort, and in "smart partnership" with the government as a shareholder, the government developed the mining sector, providing the resources critical for the first phase of economic diversification from purely agriculture to include mining.

Given the inherited shortage of trained and experienced manpower, the government avoided rushing into Africanization. Botswana's government leaders tended to respect the views of experts – largely liberal economists in line with their ideology. Botswana also had a long tradition of using and trusting friendly outsiders/foreigners according to their perceived national interest (Lewis 1993: 22; Maundeni 2002: 144). Because it was traditionally normal to work with and trust knowledgeable and qualified foreigners, Botswanan leaders pursued a slow but smooth localization policy, enabling nationals to acquire the necessary skills and experience – a wise policy that exploited legitimate ambitions to give progressive responsibility to persons who had the capacity for it. The Botswanan political leadership believed that an appeasement policy, which gave in too readily to pressures based on unreasonable ambitions, might start a process of progressive reductions in standards, which would be hard to arrest and difficult to remedy (Somolekae 1993, 1999).

The government worked to attract aid from a number of donors and built donors' confidence through ensuring proper allocation and efficient management of aid-supported projects and the government budget. Being the only liberal democracy with a liberal economic policy surrounded by racist and minority-ruled southern African states, Botswana attracted sympathy from the western donor agencies, leading to large inflows of aid; this might have motivated the Botswanan political leadership to keep the liberal democracy and economic system in place:

Botswana leaders took advantage of the geographical situation of their country to project their democratic experiment on the doorstep of apartheid. They appealed for support to the United Nations and its agencies, to foreign governments and to international humanitarian agencies. The message was fairly clear and simple: Botswana was a young poverty-stricken nation, but whose political success could contribute to racial harmony and peaceful transformation in Southern Africa. By the mid 1970s this democratic ideology and the country's geo-political situation had begun to pay dividends. (Molutsi 1993: 52)

Thus, in addition to using foreign aid effectively aid agencies were also motivated by the country's democratic attributes in the troubled southern African region. In fact, international aid was a crucial resource that the government initially used strategically to develop a physical and social infrastructure, which helped to diversify its economy. The government had a relatively open economic policy, as already noted. Private foreign capital

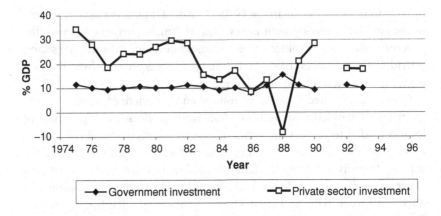

Figure 15.3 Botswana, government and private sector gross investment, 1975–1993, percent of GDP

was attracted by political stability, a relatively open liberal economic policy, and maintenance of an enabling environment, especially macroeconomic stability for foreign and private investment. The role of foreign capital – foreign aid and private investment – is shown in figures 15.1 and 15.3.

The role of foreign capital, including aid, has changed over time. In the early years, aid was essential in relaxing macroeconomic constraints – particularly the foreign exchange constraint and financing the development budget – and thus financed priority government projects. It may be seen from figure 15.3 that investment exceeded domestic savings before 1986, and the shortfall of domestic savings over investment was obviously financed by foreign savings. During this period, Botswana was a net recipient of capital flows and the country's rapid rate of economic growth, at least during the first two decades of independence, depended to a considerable degree on capital from abroad. The period of sustained and exceptionally high economic growth rates annually from 1966 to 1989 also coincided with sustained jerks or step-like increases in aid to Botswana (figure 15.1).

Aid helped finance much of the original public investment in infrastructure and mining – facilitating private capital inflows, especially for the mining sector (Maipose, Somolekae, and Johnston 1996). A well-functioning infrastructure is regarded as a precondition for economic development and sustained growth; on the basis of this argument it can be concluded that Botswana's development strategy of opening up to foreign investment and the donors' response to support infrastructural development during the early period of independence were in the right direction, and it was probably this combination which was lacking or not sustained in many other African countries.

Like many other open economies relying on one or two primary exports, Botswana's revenue can be volatile, and tended to grow in a series of discrete steps. The government tried to minimize such disruptions and to avoid a "boom and bust" cycle in the budget by taking a long-term view of revenue trends and attempting to stabilize expenditure around a sustainable growth rate. A number of measures were taken to achieve this, and these continued to be useful and instrumental for enhancing sustainable development during the budget deficit period when revenue lagged behind its trend level. Three funds were established to provide for stabilization reserves, public debt service, and local development opportunities (Faber 1997). These measures were taken after the first year of budgetary independence in 1973, anticipating that having achieved domestic responsibility for spending it was important to develop vehicles for prudent management. The Domestic Development Fund (DDF) was the key domestic source of funding for development projects; money intended for capital expenditure together with finance from external funding agencies was first paid into the DDF and then paid out to meet approved capital project expenditures. The DDF helped the government to avoid costly delays in project implementation by allowing donors' funded projects to go ahead on a reimbursement basis, and it was also effective in integrating foreign aid into annual budgets. The Revenue Stabilization Fund (RSF) helped to even out fluctuations in revenue trends and accumulate assets from the budget surplus. The idea was to run a budgetary surplus in good years to accumulate assets that would be run down in deficit periods. The Public Debt Service Fund (PDSF) was earmarked for debt servicing, thereby avoiding arrears as well as a debt crisis; the money from this fund was used to lend to public enterprises and combined with state-owned financial institutions to make the government almost as big a lender as the commercial banks. The high level of foreign exchange reserves was a result of a deliberate policy to accumulate as much as possible for unexpected changes in the balance of payments.

A related important strategic policy choice to note was that all these special funds (which could be seen as budget surplus funds), including the foreign exchange surplus, were invested to generate more financial resources. The significant increase in non-mineral revenue, especially since 1989, was primarily due to government investment revenue. Bank of Botswana profits (mainly profits from off-shore investments) have become one of the major sources of government revenue. Effective economic management was also reflected in progressive adjustments of the exchange rate to encourage other sources of foreign exchange earning. The government explicitly pursued a countercyclical policy in the management of foreign exchange reserves and government cash balances, basing year-to-year spending decisions on the intermediate-term forecasts of export earnings and government revenue and on a realistic view of spending capacity. Seen as a package, these measures enabled Botswana to moderate the inflationary pressure that would have followed massive government spending, and to avoid "Dutch disease," fluctuations in revenue trends, incomplete or under-staffed projects, and disproportionately large debt servicing obligations. Despite considerable political pressure (especially from the opposition who advocated more state spending on social services and employment creation) the temptation to spend reserves was avoided. The decision to adopt the principle of sustainable government budgeting demonstrates an effort to anticipate problems and opportunities and to take measures to deal with the situation rather than wait to be "forced" to do so by donors or economic crisis. Reserve funds enabled the country's development effort to proceed uninterrupted for many years, especially during the years of fiscal deficits.

4.2   Government as the main agent in savings and investment

Fiscal revenue and expenditure trends throughout the 1980s and 1990s reflected a coherent view of development and priorities in government policy, including how to facilitate the role of the private sector (tables 15.3 and 15.4). All the three main sources of income – the customs union, mineral revenues, and aid – grew rapidly, and the peak in aid inflows was attained before it declined in relative terms and was replaced by earnings from foreign exchange reserves. On the expenditure side, the government was rather cautious, despite its enormous revenue base, resulting in budget and trade surpluses throughout this period (table 15.5 and table 15.6). The government did relatively well in building socio-economic infrastructure and developing the human resources without which little growth could be achieved and sustained.

It is clear from figure 15.2 (p. 515) that the contribution of domestic savings to investment rose significantly during this period. Domestic savings financed almost all of gross fixed capital formation (GFCF) for the first time in 1984, even though capital inflows remained positive.

It is also clear that the country was prone to volatility in savings and investment trends, a pattern mainly associated with changes in the volume of activity in the mining sector – the main engine of growth – and this correlated with the GDP growth rate changes. However, the country's average savings rate was much higher than the African average and any other country in the world except Singapore (table 15.3 and figure 15.2), and savings have been dominated by the government.

A breakdown of sources of growth in savings and investment is shown in figures 15.2, 15.3, and 15.4. Interestingly, it is the government – not the

Table 15.3a Botswana, a Saving, 1975–1996, institutional gross savings at current market prices, 1975–1996, pula million

End-June	Govt[a] (1)	%	Household[b] (2)	%	Business[c] (3)	%	Private sector (4) = (2) + (3)	%	GDS[d] (5) = (4) + (1)	q %	ROW[e] (6)	%	GNS[f] (7) = (5) + (6)	%
1975	15.9	7.2	15.3	6.9	3.1	1.4	18.4	8.3	34.3	15.5	70.4	31.8	104.7	47.3
1976	31.1	10.3	7.9	2.6	16.9	5.6	24.8	8.3	55.9	18.6	52.0	17.3	107.9	35.9
1977	20.9	6.0	2.5	0.7	27.6	7.9	30.1	8.6	51.0	14.5	48.0	13.7	99.0	28.2
1978	32.4	7.9	−11.3	−2.7	28.5	6.9	17.2	4.2	49.6	12.0	88.6	21.5	138.2	33.5
1979	103.7	18.3	−31.9	−5.6	58.7	10.4	26.8	4.7	130.5	23.0	73.6	13.0	204.1	36.0
1980	181.9	23.6	−74.4	−9.6	114.6	14.9	40.2	5.2	222.1	28.8	71.1	9.2	293.2	38.0
1981	88.0	10.1	−38.5	−4.4	38.5	4.4	0.0	0.0	88.0	10.1	270.9	30.9	358.9	41.0
1982	49.9	5.5	−17.6	−2.0	109.4	12.2	91.8	10.2	141.7	15.7	252.2	28.0	393.9	43.8
1983	71.1	6.2	48.3	4.2	103.1	8.9	151.4	13.1	222.5	19.3	124.5	10.8	347.0	30.1
1984	96.8	7.0	96.5	6.9	137.1	9.9	233.6	16.8	330.4	23.8	34.7	2.5	365.1	26.2
1985	212.3	11.6	11.7	0.6	208.6	11.4	220.3	12.0	432.6	23.7	128.7	7.0	561.3	30.7
1986	717.5	29.6	90.2	3.7	−7.9	−0.3	82.3	3.4	799.8	33.0	−343.9	−14.2	455.9	18.8
1987	980.8	34.9	59.9	2.1	−112.2	−4.0	−52.3	−1.9	928.5	33.0	−203.8	−7.3	724.7	25.8
1988	1059.7	27.9	307.2	8.1	−277.7	−7.3	29.5	0.8	1089.2	28.7	−766.5	−20.2	322.7	8.5
1989	1310.9	22.5	466.3	8.0	931.6	16.0	1397.9	23.9	2708.8	46.4	−819.9	−14.0	1888.9	32.4
1990	1507.9	23.1	265.9	4.1	845.4	12.9	1111.3	17.0	2619.2	40.1	−153.8	−2.4	2465.4	37.7
1991	1838.5	24.6	..	..	..	..	1251.3	16.7	3089.8	41.3	379.7	5.1	3469.5	46.4
1992	2038.1	24.3	100.7	1.2	1212.1	14.5	1312.8	15.7	3350.9	40.0	−890.8	−10.6	2460.1	29.4
1993	1731.1	19.0	118.4	1.3	1176.1	12.9	1294.5	14.2	3025.6	33.2	−480.5	−5.3	2545.1	27.9
1994	2172.6	19.5	..	..	..	..	2367.3	21.3	4539.9	40.8	930.7	8.4	5470.6	49.2
1995	854.0	6.8	..	..	..	..	4336.8	34.6	5190.8	41.4	789.2	6.3	5980.0	47.7
1996	1230.8	8.4	..	..	..	..	5404.7	36.9	6635.5	45.4	1816.9	12.4	8452.4	57.8

Table 15.3b *Saving rates, 1975–1993, percent of GDP*

As at end of June	Industrial countries	South Africa	Singapore
1975	22.6	29.2	29.4
1976	23.0	28.1	32.6
1977	23.3	28.0	33.5
1978	24.2	30.4	34.5
1979	24.0	32.8	36.3
1980	23.0	36.5	37.5
1981	23.1	32.5	40.7
1982	21.2	29.3	43.5
1983	20.8	28.2	46.1
1984	21.8	27.6	45.7
1985	21.2	29.2	40.1
1986	21.4	27.5	38.9
1987	21.5	25.9	39.9
1988	22.3	25.7	42.3
1989	22.6	25.8	43.7
1990	22.0	23.1	45.7
1991	21.7	21.3	47.4
1992	21.3	18.8	38.8
1993	21.4	19.3	47.4

Notes: [a]Government savings include savings of both the local and central government.
[b]Household savings include savings of households and private non-profit institutions serving households.
[c]Business savings include savings of private non-financial enterprises and non-financial parastatal organizations.
[d]GDS = gross domestic savings.
[e]ROW = rest of the world (foreign) savings.
[f]GNS = gross national savings.
. . . = that data were not available from the source.
Source: Botswana data are from various National Accounts of Botswana published by the Central Statistics Office as reported in Bank of Botswana (1998). Data for industrial countries, South Africa and Singapore are from World Bank (1995), World Tables.

private sector – and until quite recently was the major source of investible funds in Botswana (figure 15.4).

With regard to investment rate, the role of government can be described as relatively consistent and stable to ensure the provision of basic services and infrastructure, and facilitative for the private sector as a source of investible funds. The government, which had been a major saver in the economy, had a fairly low investment rate as compared to the high and also widely fluctuating private sector rate of investment (figure 15.3 and table 15.3). It

Table 15.4 *Botswana, institutional gross investment at current market prices, 1975–1996, pula million*

End-June	Govt[a] (1)	%	Household[b] (2)	%	Business[c] (3)	%	Private sector (4)=(2)+(3)	%	Total (5)=(4)+(1)	%	Industrial countries	Developing countries	Asia
1975	25.7	11.6	15.7	7.1	60.3	27.3	76.0	34.4	101.7	46.0	22.9	25.5	21.5
1997	30.6	10.2	20.2	6.7	64.2	21.4	84.4	28.1	115.0	38.3	23.4	25.0	21.7
1977	33.1	9.4	18.4	5.2	47.2	13.5	65.6	18.7	98.7	28.1	23.7	25.5	21.7
1978	41.5	10.1	32.4	7.9	67.7	16.4	100.1	24.3	141.6	34.4	24.0	25.5	23.5
1979	61.2	10.8	21.6	3.8	114.9	20.3	136.5	24.1	197.7	34.9	24.4	25.2	24.5
1980	78.6	10.2	23.6	3.1	185.6	24.1	209.2	27.1	287.8	37.3	24.0	25.5	24.1
1981	90.1	10.3	19.2	2.2	240.8	27.5	260.0	29.7	350.2	40.0	24.0	26.4	26.8
1982	101.3	11.3	10.1	1.1	248.3	27.6	258.4	28.7	359.7	40.0	24.0	24.9	25.6
1983	123.4	10.7	-7.8	-0.7	187.7	16.3	179.9	15.6	303.3	26.3	22.4	22.9	25.2
1984	126.3	9.1	-1.6	-0.1	192.5	13.8	190.9	13.7	317.2	22.8	21.4	22.1	24.0
1985	184.3	10.1	-17.4	-1.0	332.3	18.2	314.9	17.2	499.2	27.3	21.9	22.3	24.2
1986	197.1	8.1	8.0	0.3	194.6	8.0	202.6	8.4	399.7	16.5	21.6	21.9	23.7
1987	312.5	11.1	12.0	0.4	364.0	13.0	376.0	13.4	688.5	24.5	21.3	22.5	24.3
1988	588.9	15.5	67.8	1.8	-379.2	-10.0	-311.4	-8.2	277.5	7.3	21.6	23.6	26.1
1989	660.1	11.3	86.8	1.5	1142.1	19.6	1228.9	21.1	1889.0	32.4	22.4	24.6	27.3
1990	605.3	9.3	118.8	1.8	1741.2	26.6	1860.0	28.5	2465.3	37.7	23.0	24.3	29.1
1991	...	...	...	...	...	...	...	...	2687.7	36.0	22.5	23.5	28.4
1992	946.5	11.3	-124.2	-1.5	1637.8	19.6	1513.6	18.1	2460.1	29.4	21.5	23.7	28.6
1993	910.5	10.0	171.8	1.9	1462.8	16.0	1634.6	17.9	2545.1	27.9	21.2	23.3	27.5
1994	...	...	...	...	...	...	...	...	2837.8	25.5	21.0	23.4	28.5
1995	...	...	...	...	...	...	...	...	3531.8	28.2	...	...	...
1996	...	...	...	...	...	...	...	...	3774.4	25.8	...	...	...

Notes: [a]Government investment includes investment by both the local and central government.

[b]Household investment includes investment by households as well as by private non-profit institutions serving households.

[c]Business investment includes investment by financial institutions, private non-financial enterprises and non-financial parastal organizations.

... = means that data were not available from source.

Source: Botswana data are from various National Accounts of Botswana published by the Central Statistics Office as reported in Bank of Botswana (1998). Data for industrial countries, developing countries, and Asia are from the International Monetary Fund (1996).

Table 15.5 *Botswana, external trade, direction of trade, imports, 1994–2001, pula 000*

	Total imports	Common custom area	Zimbabwe	Other Africa	UK	Other Europe	South Korea	USA	All other
				(%)					
1994	4,407,344	78.0	5.9	0.5	2.5	5.9	2.1	1.9	3.3
1995	5,307,073	74.0	5.5	0.3	2.5	6.0	7.1	2.0	2.5
1996	5,720,603	78.0	5.7	0.4	2.6	4.2	4.4	1.3	3.4
1997	8,255,755	72.4	4.5	0.5	2.0	7.0	9.5	1.1	3.0
1998	9,513,126	74.8	3.9	0.6	3.4	6.8	4.8	1.4	4.4
1999	10,164,384	76.6	3.9	0.3	2.7	6.5	2.6	1.8	5.6
2000	10,613,069 (P)	73.9	3.5	0.3	4.2	12.3	0.2	1.6	4.0
2001	2,334,704 (P)	75.6	3.3	0.4	5.3	8.0	0.2	2.8	4.5

Note: (P) = Provisional.
Source: CSO (2002).

Table 15.6 *Botswana, external trade, direction of trade, exports, 1994–2001, pula 000*

	Total exports	Exchange rate for exports	Common custom area	Zimbabwe	Other Africa	UK	Other Europe	USA	All other
					(%)				
1994	4,964,998	1.3243	13.9	2.7	1.0	25.1	56.4	0.7	0.2
1995	5,941,470	1.3197	21.5	3.1	0.8	37.4	36.1	0.9	0.2
1996	8,133,358	1.3194	18.3	3.1	0.6	54.3	22.5	1.0	0.3
1997	10,390,700	1.2948	14.3	3.7	1.1	56.2	23.5	1.0	0.2
1998	8,696,921	1.3373	17.2	2.9	1.3	55.5	21.5	1.0	0.6
1999	12,227,848	1.3645	10.4	2.4	1.1	66.5	18.2	0.7	0.7
2000	13,834,682 (P)	1.3980	6.7	3.9	0.9	69.7	17.5	0.6	0.7
2001	4,063,159 (P)	1.4988	6.1	1.9	1.0	86.8	3.0	0.2	0.1

Note: (P) = Provisional.

was basically this situation – an interventionist and facilitative role for the state – which put the Botswanan government in a dominant position in the economy, as a conduit through which the vast financial resources (released mainly through the mining sector) could be channeled into the general socio-economic development of the country. This strategy continued to be followed for much of the post-independence period until it was modified in the 1990s – a period of relatively slow growth. Government savings began to decline, while private sector savings increased significantly (figure 15.4).

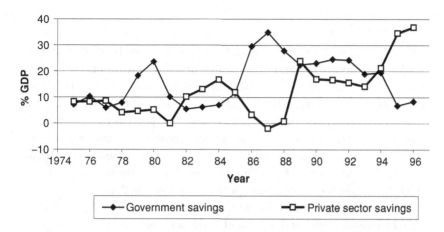

Figure 15.4 Botswana, government savings and private sector savings, 1975–1996, percent of GDP

4.3 Good management versus good luck

The explanation for Botswana's "success story," and the outlook for the country's future prosperity, tend to oscillate between emphasis on the "good luck" factors, on the one hand, and the "good management," on the other hand (Harvey and Lewis 1990: 6–7; Tordoff 1993: 282). The current President (when he was the Vice President) reasserted this observation in his address to the International Conference on Southern Africa and East Asia in Gaborone (January 1991). He observed that:

Indeed, while it is recognised that Botswana's development record reflects "good luck" to a substantial degree, we are also proud of the reputation that has been established for "good management" on part of the government . . . Although the national diamond endowment has for the past 15 years or so been the main element in the "good luck" factor, it is nevertheless recognised by those who are well acquainted with our country that we have striven with good effect to minimise adverse consequences of the "mineral led economy" syndrome. (Somolekae 1999: 29)

The achievements owed something to "good fortune," but more to careful or "good management" (Tordoff, 1993: 282). Some other countries which enjoyed a windfall of resources immediately after independence (such as Zambia and its copper, and Nigeria and its oil) did not perform nearly as well as Botswana (Harvey and Lewis 1990; Maipose, Somolekae, and Johnston 1996: 440–1). The important lessons and challenges for the region seem to be less about the "good fortune" factor than the elements of "good management," and these are analyzed in section 4.3.2.

4.3.1 Good luck

There are four elements of good luck: the national mineral endowment, particularly diamonds; the production and marketing of diamonds within the most durable and successful producer/marketing cartel run by De Beers, the Central Selling Organization (CSO); the inflow of foreign aid; and the small and basically homogenous population. The "good fortune" element in terms of the natural mineral endowment or exploitation of mineral wealth – such as copper, oil, gold, and also diamonds – applies to many other African countries as well. However, the diamonds marketing cartel under the control of De Beers has had continuous operation for over six decades; it is one of the most successful commodity buffer stock arrangements in the world and also the most durable producer cartel (Jefferis 1998a: 306–8). Botswana did not suffer an extended period of depressed demand or low diamond prices and enjoyed political stability since independence. This goes a long way to explain why "diamonds are forever" in Botswana, at least so far. Botswana has had "bad luck" too – serious profitability problems with regard to the BCL copper-nickel and soda ash mining, which commenced operation in 1973 and 1991, respectively. These projects have been a drain on government revenue during many years of their operation (Gaolathe 1997: 409).

With regard to foreign aid, Botswana, like all SSA countries, has been a long-term recipient of foreign development assistance. As an aspect of "good luck," the country has had the highest *per capita* aid in the region, and aid in the form of grants continued to flow long after Botswana attained middle-income status (Maipose, Somolekae, and Johnston 1996). But unlike the situation in most African countries, which have become increasingly dependent on aid with disappointing results, Botswana has managed its aid resources effectively and sustained economic growth with decreasing dependence on aid (Stevens 1981; Carlsson, Somolekae, and van de Walle 1997; Maipose and Somolekae 1999).

In terms of country size, Botswana is large – mainly arid, with drought a regular occurrence on the scarce arable land – making communication difficult and agriculture a precarious undertaking. The country's population is quite small and although there are different tribes (seemingly dominated by Tswana-speaking groups) the population looks largely homogenous, at least in the sense that "tribalism" and "sectionalism" are not automatically used to explain electoral behavior and leadership competition in Botswana. One can appreciate, to some degree, the advantages of the "small-country" effect in key macroeconomic indicators, and the managing of people is relatively easier than in the larger but ethnically divided populations in many other African countries. This partly explains the factors behind the high GDP *per capita* and frustrations regarding broad/agricultural-based poverty-reduction strategies; a multi-party political system and good macroeconomic management satisfied various interests, thereby managing not just the country's wealth but also the diversity of its people. The context of the "good natural fortune" is thus crucial.

Additional elements in the "good luck" factor relate to the benefits derived from the country's close economic ties with South Africa. Botswana has no debt burden for two main reasons. First, and foremost, this is due to diamond "windfalls" and how they have been managed. The second relates to how the economic status of the country changed during the post-independence period. Botswana progressed from being classified as a very poor country at independence to middle-income status in the mid-1990s with positive implications for the country's debt profile. When the country was classified as a less-developed country (LDC), nearly all of Botswana's foreign aid was in the form of grants complemented with concessional loans. This cash-strapped country could not have resorted to increasing trade taxes (even for import-substitution industrialization), because the country's membership in the SACU and the RMA restricted its discretion in trade and monetary policies, leading to no internal public debt. Following the country's gradu-ation to middle-income status, Botswana has had a very low external debt burden and the profile of the external debt was basically that of a poor coun-try. Fortunately, debt – servicing or choices to repay – arose when Botswana was a prosperous middle-income country. Given this situation, debt service costs did not impair the ability of the Botswanan government to operate normally and the country could even choose whether or not it made eco-nomic sense to pay off its external debt. Again, this may be contrasted with Zambia, which was a middle-income country in the 1960s and 1970s. Zam-bia could not qualify for concessional loans, and borrowed from commercial sources, including preferred creditors (such as the World Bank and the IMF) who until the late 1990s never rescheduled/canceled their debt. Much of the acquired debt was short term in addition to an increasing level of internal debt – all in the hope of copper prices recovering soon. As an aspect of "bad luck," copper prices remained depressed for a long time. Unfortunately, Zambia has the debt profile of a middle-income country and has to service or repay its external debt when it has, ironically, has been reclassified among the poor countries of the world. The point is that debt service costs can impair the ability of the borrower to operate normally.

4.3.2   Good management

There are many elements of "good management." The significance of tra-dition and history for post-colonial institutions and attitudes appears to be critical to understanding modern Botswanan institutions and some pol-icy choices. The pre-colonial Tswana culture regarded state leadership as crucial to the process of accumulating wealth, and the centrality of the state was promoted to facilitate economic accumulation and redistribution as a worthy function, thereby creating an interdependent relationship between the state and the asset-owning class (Maundeni 2001). The Tswana chieftaincy, according to Wylie (1990: 32), was "the trunk from which new leaves sprouted and was the 'wife,' milk-pail, and 'breast of the nation'." The point that has already been made, and bears repeating here, is that state-led development strategy appears to have blended well with pre-colonial Tswana political theory regarding the role of the state, leadership, and the intimacy of the political and economic elite. Political and economic powers were interdependent (Wylie 1990; Good 1993) and this is analytically evidenced "by the use of the term kgotsi for both Chief and rich man" (Wylie 1990: 23).

Similarly, the consultative process which underlines the Botswana policy making process, including the management of negotiations and contracts, was firmly established within the traditional institutions, such as the *kgotla* through which traditional leaders consultatively made and legitimized policies, where there was an opportunity to express one's view and a need to achieve a degree of consensus. We have also already noted that the use of expatriates with a relatively high degree of trust conforms, to some degree, with Botswana's "long tradition of using friendly outsiders to help cope" with problems (Lewis 1993; Maundeni 2002).

National development planning and its integration with the annual budgetary process was the foundation of Botswana's development management machinery and the basis for managing its windfall gains – mineral rent and foreign aid (Stevens 1981; Raphaeli, Roumani, and Mackella 1984; Maipose, Somolekae, and Johnston 1996). The country relied on a six-year planning cycle, with mid-term reviews to update the plans in response to changes in the economic and political context. National Development Plans (NDPs) are essentially plans for public spending and human resource use, and the Ministry of Finance and Development Planning (MFDP) plays a central role. On the basis of the projections underlying the Botswanan macroeconomic model (which includes forecasts for economic output and growth, employment, foreign trade, government revenue, etc.), the MFDP derives three main ceilings for the public sector. These are the skilled labor ceiling; the recurrent expenditure ceiling (which in recent years has had to be financed out of recurrent non-mineral revenue); and the development expenditure ceiling (Jefferis 1998b). Initially, the NDPs were constructed around the programs and a "shopping list" of projects for which finance was derived from own current income, mainly mineral rent, or sought from donors. For effective aid management and co-ordination, the donors were asked to support (and had flexibility to choose) projects that were already identified as national priorities in the plan. This increased national project ownership and avoided problems elsewhere in Africa where donors allegedly "imposed" or took over design of key policies/programs (Van de Walle and Johnston 1996). In Botswana, the plan and how it was enforced ensured that programs and projects addressed government priorities.

We do not have to go into details about how this system works, but it is a common view among donors and development analysts that it has performed relatively well in Botswana as opposed to many instances of failure in many developing countries (World Bank 1984; Harvey and Lewis 1990; Maipose, Somolekae, and Johnston 1996). A review of the literature on the nature of development planning and its institutional, operational, and procedural relations with budgeting suggests that a government's budget is a key instrument in converting a development plan into a program for action (Hermans 1962: 319; Waterston 1979: 201). In Botswana, this was structurally enforced by putting overall economic, financial/budgetary, and planning responsibilities for the government under a powerful Ministry of Finance and Development Planning (MFDP) with a considerable degree of career continuity for its largely merit-based staff. Planning in Botswana is not an academic exercise of little operational value, and is a means of enforcing accountability. It also explains why the government has done relatively well in redistributing mineral revenue to the wider society and economy, especially with regard to investment in physical and human capital and targeted subsidies without adverse consequences of the mineral-led economy syndrome. Further, "the government's commitment to planning is not intended to stifle private initiative but to create favorable conditions in which the private sector can contribute to national development . . . there would be no point in setting targets for variables that are not within government's control, or in imposing controls whose costs (in administrative resources or disruption to the economy) outweighed the benefits" (MFDP 1985: NDP6, paras. 2.2–3.4).

Another important aspect is that planning in Botswana is a more open process than in many other African countries, with the ruling party, interest groups, the private sector, and parliament involved in plan preparation. The resulting plan is above all not a "planner's plan" because many stakeholders, including politicians, feel committed to it and the government tries wherever possible to avoid the temptation of introducing major projects not in the original plan and can refuse if such projects do not meet national priorities. As already noted, the operational success of development planning in Botswana is partly explained by traditional and historical factors. Even in the early stages when plans were centrally conceived there is evidence to show that policies were, and continue to be, realistically rooted in the tradition of the people. A case in point is again the relevance of the *kgotla*, because it provided the community with a forum to express their views and a need to achieve a degree of consensus. Openness and consultation were always essential and this was a springboard for modern development planning and its legitimacy for support and implementation, though policy-making including planning is dominated by government officials (Somolekae 1993). It also explains why both the political leadership and planners worked together from the start to ensure that plans were correctly formulated and implemented. The Economic Committee of the Cabinet, made up of permanent secretaries and their ministers and created during the Transitional Plan, continues to function today. It is a forum where both sides deliberate on policy matters, ensuring that politicians and experts keep each other informed about what policies need to be implemented or reviewed, and why. Both sides learn in the process, thus keeping the political leadership in the picture of what is going on and bureaucrats learning what constraints and worries the political leadership might be having (Somolekae 1999: 33). Another important and related institutional development was the creation of a National Economic Advisory Council (NEAC) to ensure that the non-governmental sector was not left out of the planning process.

Another important institutional factor is that the MFDP in Botswana has always been politically and administratively powerful. Until quite recently, the ministry was politically headed by the Vice Presidents and heads of each of the four main divisions (known as Directors), who were of permanent secretary rank, while the permanent secretary in the ministry ranked above the rest of the permanent secretaries within the civil service structure. The practice of putting political and administrative leaders of unquestioned authority at the top of the ministry made it relatively easy to impose the discipline necessary to ensure that priorities were respected and targets vigorously pursued. Quett Masire, the Vice President until 1980 (when he became the President) had considerable political weight and enjoyed the respect of civil servants who, like the ministers, had career continuity, with some officers serving for over twenty years (Maipose, Somolekae, and Johnston 1996: 51). At the political level for example, the ministry has had only four ministers since independence – Masire, Mmusi, Mogae (elected President in 1998 and 2004), and as of this writing, Gaolathe. Whereas in many African countries donor representatives may see key ministry positions frequently changing hands, the Botswana civil servants watch heads of donor agencies come and go. Clearly, development planning has been successful in Botswana for many reasons – partly rooted in the country's tradition and history, in how competence was acquired through trial-and-error experience, and in the quality and commitment of the country's leadership.

The good governance record, underlined by the nature of Botswana's political system and the quality of its political leadership, is another important factor which explains good management. The development of a stable and relatively non-corrupt multi-party democratic system of government, coupled with sound leadership, entailed putting in place an administrative system that provided an enabling environment for development. It also reinforced the national vision in government plans and helped ensure accountability. Compared to rapid growth under authoritative regimes in China and in the "Asian Tigers" and the new fragile/emerging democracies in many African countries, multi-party democracy in Botswana seems to have been institutionalized. The ruling party, in power since independence, has had unimpeachable electoral legitimacy, the product of fair and honest regular elections (table 15.2). This, in our view, seems to be a continuing vote of confidence in the ruling party, its leadership, and policies. Some critical political observers, such as Ken Good (1997, 2000), have interpreted the continuation of one party in power as one of the main limitations of Botswana's democracy, since it has not been seriously tested. This critique is probably applicable to all liberal democracies where governments have not changed for a long time, such as Italy and Japan, but in Botswana this is probably one of the main reasons for the sustainability of political stability and good economic management. Moreover, the regional experiences of government changing hands peacefully in Zambia, Malawi, and Kenya prevented the ruling BDP from becoming complacent: the increasingly large popular vote of the combined opposition is a serious threat to the predominance of the ruling BDP (table 15.2).

Given the nature of the political context in Botswana, we are inclined to argue that the "national fortune" has not been mismanaged and the strategy of state-led development has worked well, partly because politics have been relatively free of the corruption and patronage common in many African countries. Botswana is often cited as the foremost example of a stable multi-party democracy in Africa that has maintained freedom of speech, press, and association – and, most importantly, property rights and rule-based governance. The judiciary is independent of both the legislative and executive branches, and Botswana has one of the best human rights records in Africa. A participatory and transparent political system has combined with good and disciplined political leadership to moderate/limit corruption and, most importantly, enhance public accountability. The question is: why have these factors evolved and worked so well in Botswana? Again part of the answer goes back to tradition and history. The country had a strong tradition of participation and consultation at all levels of public life from the village to central government, and this had strong roots in the *Tswana* custom of holding "town meetings" known as the *kgotla*, which is still part of the local consultative network (Lekorwe 1989: 217). Many analysts and Batswana themselves acknowledge the exemplary ethical leadership and political foundation created by Seretse Khama; he established a precedent for high ethical standards, a strong and relatively independent but accountable civil service, and a developmental orientation of the government. These attributes have been carried on and built upon by his successors (Tordoff 1993: 281). Although corruption is probably increasing (Good 1994, 2000), there have also been cases of suicides, resignations, or dismissals on matters of principle/accountability, and imprisonment involving politicians and government officers: state action remains a key player in ensuring public accountability.

The "checks" in place thus appear to have worked relatively well so far in Botswana. It must be added that the country has been lucky to have produced honest and committed leaders so far, which has fostered a general trust in the government or leadership to spearhead development and handle the "national fortune." There is a strong feeling among the Batswana that the country is rich, but they are also quick to note that wealth is in the hands of the government and to some extent foreigners, and not the Batswana. They point to the absence of indigenous business people outside the cattle industry, a disappointingly high level of unemployment, and noticeable poverty among the people. This perception has been partly translated into voters' choice and the size and shape of the budget, especially the government expenditure pattern. The 1990s marked an end of the economic boom, which may partially explain why the BDP relatively did not do so well in 1994 and the overall decline in the party's share of the popular vote since 1974 (table 15.2). It may also explain why government expenditure has been growing at a considerably faster rate than revenue, especially from 1998, leading to overwhelming electoral victories in 1999 and 2004. Over the five years from 1998/9 to 2002/3, for example, total revenue and grants grew by 73.6 percent, while expenditure grew by 124.7 percent, leading to budget deficits in three of these five years (Republic of Botswana 2003: 29). This illustrates the interests at work in line with the economic theory of democracy, explaining the victories and defeats, the compromises and the bargains; the ruling BDP wants to maintain its electoral dominance and managed to regain overwhelming support again in the 1999 and 2004 elections, and the leadership succession within the ruling party was smooth.

A point worth noting is that despite the disappointing performance of the ruling BDP in the 1994 election and the rise of electoral support for the opposition, the government did not impose new forms of central control or display authoritative tactics in order to regain its electoral support. Instead, it encouraged meaningful popular participation by introducing electoral reforms which could have worked against it, such as a re-demarcation of electoral constituencies in 1992, leading to an increase in seats in the urban areas where BDP support has been relatively low; a reduction in the voting age from twenty-one to eighteen years; the introduction of an Independent Electoral Commission; and a limitiation of the presidential terms of office to two terms (Molomo 2000). During the period from 1980 to 1996, government revenue (excluding grants) as a percentage of GDP averaged over 50 percent – reaching a peak of 64 percent in 1988 and a low of 44 percent in 1993 (World Bank 1995: 2000). Second, unlike most other African countries, aid represents a small portion of Botswana's national budget and is hardly significant in other key macroeconomic variables (Carlsson, Somolekae, and van de Walle 1997: 14; World Bank 1999). Financial aid as a percentage of public capital expenditure came down from nearly 100 percent in the 1960s (Stevens 1981) to 15 percent in 1992, and represented about 5 percent

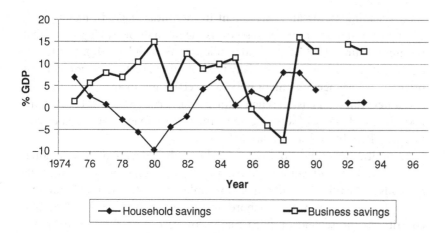

Figure 15.5 Botswana, household and business gross savings, 1975–1993, percent of GDP

of total government revenue in recent statistics (Maipose, Somolekae, and Johnston 1996; Maipose and Somolekae 1999). Moreover, foreign debt remains almost insignificant and the debt-service ratio is about 3 percent of export earnings. Recent developments in the flow of aid are, to a significant degree, a reflection of Botswana's position as a "phase-out country" for the key donors who have scaled down their programs or closed their missions with a sense of task completion; the country was at one time listed among the new donors for the International Development Association (IDA) (IDA 2000: 13).

Botswana is also unique in terms of the state's capacity to accumulate assets to finance development efforts. Unlike nearly all the recipients of aid in Africa Botswana, in relative terms, has had a substantial net inflow of foreign exchange in the form of mineral rents, complemented by development aid. Much of these inflows accrued to the government, and a significant proportion of public revenue in the form of annual budget surpluses and the foreign exchange reserves have been saved – constituting off-shore capital investment or savings abroad (Jefferis 1998b: 38). This situation has made Botswana unusual in three inter-related respects. First, the economy has excess liquidity *vis-à-vis* the absorptive capacity of the economy, with domestic savings exceeding domestic investment since 1986 (as illustrated in figure 15.2) and the government has been a net saver – not borrower, as is the case in many countries, while households have been net borrowers from the banking system (Motsomi 1997). The evidence for these observations is to some extent shown in figures 15.3, 15.4, and 15.5, respectively plotted from statistical data in tables 15.3 and 15.4. This is a moot feature; some people may argue that it is not a "conventional" practice and therefore not sustainable. Others see this as a good attribute for a developmental state – leading saving and investment in the initial stage. In many developed economies, the household sector is the main or net saving sector that releases resources for business and public sectors (Reinke 1997). To encourage private sector savings, especially the household sector, the government broadened coverage of Bank of Botswana certificates to attract small savers and a new funded pension scheme for public service was effected in April 2001 to afford public officers the opportunity to manage their own pension benefits (Republic of Botswana 2001: 3).

Secondly, Botswana holds one of the highest levels of international reserves in the world, equivalent to approximately forty months of imports of goods and services as at the end of December 2001 (Republic of Botswana, 2002: 7). Income from its off-shore investment/savings, as already noted, constituted the second or third major source of government income – a development which effectively makes Botswana an exporter of capital. Prospects of Botswana becoming one of the region's "financial centers" look good, and again, the government has taken a lead in facilitating this transformation.

The underlying fiscal problems, which are inter-related, are the vulnerability of the budget to external shocks and the over-dependence of government revenue on mineral rents. The other main concern is the government's overwhelming dependence on diamond revenue and the extent to which the dominance of diamond-related revenue sources may have retarded the development of other sources of income. This observation led some analysts, such as Wright (1997), to wonder whether or not Botswana suffers from a particular kind of "fiscal Dutch disease." In the 1995/6 budget, for example, mineral revenue contributed 47 percent of the total. Together with the revenues from the Bank of Botswana (earnings from off-shore cash investments) and SACU, which relies on diamond-based capacity to import, the contribution was 82 percent. In contrast, the non-mineral income tax and sales tax accounted for 6 percent and 4 percent of total revenue, respectively. In fact, one can observe more or less the same trend from the 1989 to the 2001 budgets. "Such a tendency," argues Wright (1997: 168), "can be characterised usefully in the same terms as the so-called Dutch disease problem of exchange rates."

This argument is persuasive, but it needs to be qualified. The well-known "Dutch disease" effect arises where the rapid development of one sector – in this case, the export mineral sector, with its substantial revenue to government – crowds-out all except the most robust activities, thereby serving to hamper/obstruct new industrial/export development elsewhere, possibly on a permanent basis. That government has been aware of this danger is not in doubt; economic diversification policies, if successful, entail the broadening of tax bases in the medium to long term. Botswana's exchange rate policy seeks to maintain a real effective exchange rate that is supportive of, and does not disadvantage, macroeconomic stability and productive activities in an economy that is highly dependent on imports. This is in line with the goals of sustainable economic diversification and employment creation and, therefore, sustainable sources of public income. It should also be acknowledged, as Wright (1997) to some extent implies, that the government in Botswana has not ignored the development of other alternative revenue sources, as demonstrated by the gradual extension of the scope of the sales tax since its introduction in 1982 and the more recent decision to introduce a broad-based value added tax (VAT) to replace the sales tax (Republic of Botswana 1997, 2001). To encourage savings and stimulate investment and growth in the economy, the government reviewed the structure of income taxation in 1994 and 1996. It reduced the top marginal rate of personal income taxation from 40 percent to 25 percent and set the rate for businesses, which qualify for the status of manufacturing operations, to only 15 percent. While this entailed losing some taxable income in the short run, low tax rates are known to induce people to declare their taxable income and to encourage savings and investment, and this will eventually widen the tax base and increase revenue. The tax reforms also gave Botswana a clear advantage within the Southern African region in having the potential for establishing itself as a low-tax jurisdiction, building on the country's long track record of political stability and prudent economic management.

Prudent macroeconomic management, including an emphasis on openness, macroeconomic stability, and recurrent funding, for which Botswana has acquired a good reputation, is regarded by many analysts as having played a key role in the country's success (Harvey and Lewis 1990; Hill and Knight 1999; Leith 2001). We can highlight just a few dimensions of sound economic management. First, Botswana's main economic development strategy has been to exploit the country's mineral wealth and invest the proceeds in improving social and economic conditions and creating new economic opportunities. Strikingly, the government has been able to maximize the domestic benefits of its mining development, increase its domestic savings and investment, and diversify (rather than suppress) the non-mining economy, while at the same time, as already noted, mitigating the potentially adverse effects of a mineral-led development syndrome. Second, the government has had a relatively good sense of priorities and a conscious policy of reviewing key policies and programs in the light of set targets with an appreciation of limits and opportunities consistent with expected revenue and the absorptive capacity of the economy. For example, when Botswana's economic and fiscal prospects were expected to improve dramatically, in the first year of budgetary independence in 1979 the government established the Public Debt Service Fund (PDSF) and the Revenue Stabilization Fund (RSF). These funds were conceived as mechanisms that would, respectively, enable the country to service its debt obligations and cope with any temporary revenue shortfalls that might arise from fluctuations in international mineral markets, drought, and other contingencies. These funds, as already noted, turned out to be good vehicles for prudent management – simultaneously working as a device for siphoning government surpluses away from the recurrent budget and as a source of funding for capital formation and public debt management.

Third, the management of inflation and the current account has been good over the years, consistent with a broad countercyclical policy of managing booms and slumps. Although the Botswana economy has, to some degree, experienced ups and downs, the latter have not been dramatic and the government has been relatively successful in avoiding extreme episodes of government-led inflation, which actually has been relatively low (Hill and Knight 1999). Indeed, the rate of inflation has until quite recently been moderate. This conscious and deliberate policy illustratively included bold decisions not to award salary/wage increases for public servants during the sensitive election years in 1994 and 1999 because of projected deficits, and yet they government could have easily done so and increased the deficit, financing it through past savings. This said, from a perspective focusing on interests and policy choices, the government has been fully aware of its dominance of the electoral space. The decisions to award or not to award wage/salary increases are recommended to the government by the National Employment, Manpower and Incomes Council (NEMIC) taking into account each year's macroeconomic and budgetary constraints. The decisions not to award salary/wages for public servants in elections years were "bold" because these policy choices were seemingly not based on gains and losses of votes. Electoral victory was probably taken for granted, at least in view of a perceived good performance record by the ruling party and its electoral dominance since independence, but the government chose to forgo an obvious opportunity to "buy off" the political opposition, especially during the 1994 elections, held against the background of general economic downturn. This was probably a miscalculation in the narrow sense, given the major electoral setback in terms of the parliamentary and local government seats and percentage of the popular vote that the ruling party lost (table 15.2).

Self-interest in growth and macroeconomic stability seems to be one plausible explanation. One can also argue that prudent macroeconomic management is perceived, at least by the ruling party, to be one of the ways of enhancing public confidence, and therefore the credibility and legitimacy of the ruling party. This, too, is a good device for "vote-buying." The government's self-imposed adoption of orthodox stabilization and adjustment policies is viewed by many development analysts as illustrative of strategic state intervention, in sharp contrast to the "forced adjustment reforms" in some other African countries.

Exchange rate policy has been quite consistent since the country moved from the RMA and created an independent currency in 1976 with a fixed exchange rate. Unlike a floating exchange rate regime, it is not easy to determine the appropriate level because of the danger of having an over-valued currency, which would hamper export diversification by crowding out all but the most robust exports. Botswana has deliberately set the pula at a level below the perceived equilibrium in spite of substantial foreign exchange reserves, currently equivalent to about three years' worth of imports requirement. This strategy was designed to avoid the "Dutch disease" effect and encourage non-traditional exports. The policy has also been in the interests of the cattle industry, the basic asset for a Batswana elite with relatively broad social linkages.

Another development related to the policy choice dilemma is about privatization and how competing interests might have stalled its implementation. The role of the government budget lies at the heart of Botswana's socioeconomic development, acting as conduit through which the rent earned from the extraction of diamonds or other dividends is transferred from surplus-generating sectors/enterprises to benefit the population at large. For this reason, the government has been under pressure not to sell its assets while a few rich Batswana advocate such a sale as a means of empowerment. The trade unions have resisted privatization because of perceived job losses and the fear of selling national assets to foreigners. Thus, although the government has a clear policy on privatization it has been under pressure not to privatize, or at least to stall such a policy, and this appears to have cost the country in terms of inflows of FDI as compared to other countries which have benefited because of privatization (Allan 2002).

5. Conclusions

To understand Botswana's development success story, we have looked backwards to create a retrospective view of the development experience. The perceived development strategy for Botswana, as laid out in the Transitional Plan and elaborated in subsequent NDPs such as those of 1968–73, was growth, based on the then known minerals – copper, nickel, and subsequently diamonds – and development was led by the government. It is important to note that the strategy of "state-led" development and national economic planning, which Botswana pursued successfully, was not unique. Many African countries adopted essentially the same strategy, but it worked very well in Botswana and the country prospered under a democratic system of government. The same strategy is, however, associated with, and now blamed for, the general economic crisis in many African countries, most of which have been under authoritative/one-party regimes.

There is one difference which seems to be the main explanation of this paradox. In Botswana, a secure political elite (with electoral support since independence) has pursued growth-promoting policies, and developed or modified and maintained viable inherited traditional and modern institutions of political, economic, and legal restraint. In an institutional context of restraint, self-interest in growth coincided with the interests of the Botswana ruling elite with roots in the cattle industry and in partnership with foreign investment. As illustrated by the state's mobilization of development resources – especially savings and investment – it has been shown that the Botswana developmental state managed the economy without getting excessively involved in the nuts and bolts of production.

The democratic system of governance appears to have enhanced good policies in Botswana; national policy has been contested through regular elections and a meaningful legislative system, both of which enforce a discipline of accountability that benefits the electorate more broadly. The long democratic tradition was built on a tradition of Tswana consensus, helped by virtual ethnic homogeneity and sustained traditional legitimacy of power. In contrast to other African countries, Botswana's traditional governance structure was not supplanted or manipulated by colonial governance systems and the modern state has integrated it into the legislative system, with a house of chiefs co-existing with the modern representative parliament.

The interest of the Botswana ruling elite has rural roots and caters for majority interests in the cattle industry and diamond areas. Self-interest in growth coincides with that of the rural majority, explaining their persistent victories over the urban-based opposition. Public investment in urban infrastructure and improved provision of urban social services also kept a potential opposition takeover at bay. This seems to be consistent with political economic models, in which policy-makers who need to satisfy larger constituencies; who face checks and balances within the decision-making process; who are subject to electoral review; and who function in stable institutional environments are more likely to produce good policies for growth (Humphreys and Bates, 2001, 2004). A more encompassing regime would choose to expand future productive capacity rather than maximize transfers to the narrow elite. The political stability and well-established democratic process of political transitions in Botswana also helped to reduce the perception of higher investment risks typically associated with violent regime change.

However, it has been suggested that although economic growth has been very rapid so far, there are grounds to think that it was probably less rapid and diversified than it might have been and that long-term self-sustaining growth may be uncertain in view of some crucial negative dimensions/constraints indicated above. The rate of real growth slowed down during the 1990s. Again, this was mainly due to reduced activities in the mining sector and mineral revenues. The problem was also partly caused by the fact that policy choices and timing became more complex given an increasing divergence in interests. Major macroeconomic problems are few, but significant. Negatively, a growth rate of Botswana's magnitude, sustained for a long period, has had a limited impact on structural economic diversification. The diamond industrial sub-sector continues to be the main engine of growth and foreign exchange earnings, while manufacturing remains insignificant. Second, Botswana's population, currently estimated at 1.7 million, is quite small relative to its geographical size and real GDP growth rate, but the level of unemployment and inequality in income have not been significantly reduced. A positive and remarkable puzzle of international credibility is that Botswana has avoided suffering from "Dutch disease" and rapid growth has been sustained, yet there has been an extreme shortage of skilled and educated manpower over the period – a resource that is currently under serious threat from HIV/AIDS. Since the quality of policies and individual actions have been crucial for the country's success so far, Botswana has a good legacy of experience to help it confront new challenges and sustain growth. Policy choices entail a regular review of some existing policies that have worked well in the past – such as the exchange rate and privatization policies – that may contribute to improving the performance of the external sector and enhance its role in achieving its broader development goals.

References

Allan, R. (2002), "Investment Policy Review: Botswana," Paper presented at the BOCCIM 7th Business Conference, Francistown, Botswana

Bank of Botswana (1996), *Annual Report 1995.* Gaborone: Bank of Botswana
  (1998), *Annual Report and Economic Review 1997.* Gaborone: Bank of Botswana

Botswana Independent Electoral Commission (2002), *Voter Apathy Report: An Abridged Version.* Gaborone: Government Printer
  (2007), "Elections 2004," at www.iec.gov.be

Carlsson, J., G. Somolekae, and N. van de Walle (1997), *Foreign Aid in Africa: Learning from Country Experiences.* Uppsala: Nordiska Afrikainstitute

Central Statistical Office (CSO) (2002), *Statistical Bulletin 2001*, 26(1). Gaborone: Government Printer, March

Faber, M. (1997), "Botswana's Somnolent Giant: The Public Debt Service Fund – Its Past, Present and Possible Future," in J. S. Salkin *et al.*, eds., *Aspects of the Botswana Economy: Selected Papers.* Oxford: James Currey

Gaolathe, B. (1997), "Development of Botswana's Mineral Sector," in J. S. Salkin *et al.*, eds., *Aspects of the Botswana Economy: Selected Papers.* Oxford: James Currey

Good, K. (2000), "Autocratic Elites and Enfeebled Masses: Africa and Botswana," Paper presented at Political & Administrative Studies Department, Seminar

Series, April 5; reprinted in K. Good, *Elites Against Democracy*. London: Palgrave

(1997), "Authoritarian Liberalism in Botswana," in K. Good, *Realising Democracy and Legitimacy in Southern Africa*. Pretoria: Africa Institute of South Africa

(1994), "Corruption and Mismanagement in Botswana: A Best Case Example," *Journal of Modern African Studies* 32(3): 499–521

(1993), "The End of the Ladder: Radical Inequalities in Botswana," *Journal of Modern African Studies* 31(2): 203–30

Harvey, C. (1992), "Botswana: Is the Economic Miracle Over?," *Journal of African Economies* 1(3): 335–468.

Harvey, C. and S. R. Lewis (1990), *Policy Choice and Development Performance in Botswana*. London: Macmillan

Herman, H. C. (1997), "Bank of Botswana: The First 21 Years," in J. S. Salkin *et al.*, eds., *Aspects of the Botswana Economy: Selected Papers*. Oxford: James Currey

Herman, R. S. (1962), "Two Aspects of Budgeting," *Indian Journal of Public Administration* 3

Hill, C. and J. Knight (1999), "The Diamond Boom, Expectations and Economic Management in Botswana," in P. Collier and J. W. Gunning, *Trade Shocks in Developing Countries Vol. I: Africa*. Oxford: Oxford University Press

Hudson, D. J. (1978), "The Establishment of Botswana's Central Bank and the Introduction of the New Currency," in *Botswana Notes and Records*, 10: 119–35.

Humphreys, M. and R. H. Bates (2001), "Political Institutions and Economic Policies: Lessons from Africa," Center for International Development, Harvard University, Cambridge, MA

(2004), "Political Institutions and Economic Policies," *British Journal of Political Science* 35: 403–38

International Development Agency (IDA) (2000), *IDA in Action: Improving Aid Effectiveness and Reaching the Poor*, Summer Report. Washington, DC: The World Bank

International Monetary Fund (IMF) (1996), *International Financial Statistics Yearbook*. Washington, DC: IMF

Jefferis, K. (1998a), "Botswana and Diamond-dependent Development," in W. Edge and M. H. Lekorwe, eds., *Botswana: Politics & Society*. Pretoria: J. L. Van Schaik Publishers

(1998b), "Botswana's Public Enterprises," in W. Edge and M. H. Lekorwe, eds., *Botswana: Politics & Society*. Pretoria: J. L. Van Schaik Publishers

Leith, J. C. (2001), "Why Botswana Prospered," Preliminary Draft for presentation at CSAE Seminar, November 14

Lekorwe, M. (1989), "The kgotla and Freedom Square: One-way or Two-way Communication?," in P. Holm and P. Molutsi, eds., *Democracy in Botswana: The Proceedings of a Symposium*. Gaborone: Macmillan

Lewis, S. (1993), "Policy Making and Economic Performance: Botswana in Comparative Perspective," in J. S. Stedman, ed., *Botswana: The Political Economy of Democratic Development*. Boulder, Co and London: Lynne Rienner

Maipose, G. S., G. M. Somolekae, and T. A. Johnston (1996), *Aid Effectiveness in Botswana: Botswana's' Management of External Assistance and Case Studies of the US/Botswana Bilateral Aid Relationship.* Washington, DC: Overseas Development Council (ODC)

Maipose, G. S. and G. M. Somolekae (1999), "Managing a Transition from Aid Dependence in Africa: The Case of Botswana," AERC Policy Working Paper. Nairobi: African Economic Research Consortium

Maundeni, Z. (2002), "State Culture and Development in Botswana and Zimbabwe," *Journal of Modern African Studies* 40(1): 105–32

Ministry of Development Planning (MFDP) (1985), *National Development Plan 6 – 1985–91.* Gaborone: Government Printer

Molomo, M. C. (2000), "Political Parties and Electoral Process in Botswana," Paper presented at a workshop for Members of Parliament and Councillors, Parliamentary Village, Gaborone, June 21–22

Molutsi, P. (1993), "International Influences on Botswana's Democracy," in J. S. Stedman, ed., *Botswana: The Political Economy of Democratic Development.* Boulder, CO. and London: Lynne Rienner

Motsomi, A. (1997), "Policy Options for Savings Mobilization in Botswana," in J. S. Salkin *et al.*, eds., *Aspects of the Botswana Economy: Selected Papers.* Oxford: James Currey

Ndulu, B. J. and S. A. O'Connell (2007), "Policy Plus: African Growth Performance, 1960–2000," chapter 1 in B. J. Ndulu, S. A. O'Connell, R. H. Bates, P. Collier, and C. C. Soludo, eds., *The Political Economy of Economic Growth in Africa, 1960–2000*, vol. 1. Cambridge: Cambridge University Press

Parsons, N., W. Henderson, and T. Tlou (1995), "Seretse Khama, 1921–1980," Gaborone, Botswana Society, and Braamfontein, Johannesburg, Macmillan Boleswa.

Raphaeli, N., J. Roumani, and A. C. Mackella (1984), "Public Sector Management in Botswana: Lessons in Pragmatism," World Bank Policy Research Working Papers 709

Reinke, J. (1997), "Savings Mobilization in the Household Sector: The Case of Botswana," in J. S. Salkin *et al.*, eds., *Aspects of the Botswana Economy: Selected Papers.* Oxford: James Currey

Republic of Botswana (1997), *Budget Speech*, Ministry of Finance and Development Planning. Gaborone: Government Printer

(2001), *Budget Speech*, Ministry of Finance and Development Planning. Gaborone: Government Printer

(2002), *Budget Speech*, Ministry of Finance and Development Planning. Gaborone: Government Printer

(2003), *Budget Speech*, Ministry of Finance and Development Planning. Gaborone: Government Printer

Somolekae, G. M. (1993), "Bureaucracy and Democracy in Botswana: What Type of a Relationship," in J. S. Stedman, ed., *Botswana: The Political Economy of Democratic Development.* Boulder, CO and London: Lynne Rienner

(1999), "The Nature and Evolution of Botswana's Development Planning System: Achievements and Challenges Ahead," in H. K. Nordas, G. Sekgoma, and G. M. Somolekae, *Managing Good Fortune: Macro-economic Management and the Role of Aid in Botswana – Evaluation Report.* Oslo: Royal Ministry of Foreign Affairs

Stevens, M. (1981), "Aid Management in Botswana: From One to Many Donors," in C. Harvey, ed., *Papers on the Economy of Botswana*. Gaborone and London: Heinemann

Tordoff, W. (1993), *Government and Politics in Africa*. London: Macmillan

Van de Walle, N. and T. Johnston (1996), *Improving Aid to Africa*. Washington, DC: Overseas Development Council

Waterston, A. (1979), *Development Planning: Lessons of Experience*. London: Johns Hopkins University Press

World Bank (1984), *World Development Report*. Washington DC: The World Bank (1995), *African Development Indicators 1995*. Washington, DC: The World Bank (2000), *African Development Indicators 2000*. Washington, DC: The World Bank

Wright, M. (1997), "Fiscal Policy in Botswana: Challenges for Public Sector Finance in the Mid 1990s," in J. S. Salkin *et al.*, eds., *Aspects of the Botswana Economy: Selected Papers*. Oxford: James Currey

Wylie, D. (1990), *A Little God: The Twilight Patriarchy in a Southern African Chiefdom*. Hanover, NH: Wesleyan University Press

16 | The political economy of Cameroon's post-independence growth experience

Georges Kobou, Dominique Njinkeu, and Bruno Powo Fosso

1. Introduction

The growth performance of Cameroon, as in other countries, reflects the interaction of factors such as labor and capital, productivity,[1] and structural characteristics. The structural characteristics can be considered from two perspectives: the role of new technologies in the growth process (Gordon 2001) and qualitative aspects such as the functioning of markets and the regulatory framework. These qualitative aspects assume center stage in Cameroon. Most markets are under-developed, partly due to the institutional rigidities that can be traced to alternative sources of foreign reserves, especially from agriculture and natural resources, including oil and wood.

Department of Economics, University of Yaoundé II; International Lawyers and Economists Against Poverty (ILEAP); Institute of Applied Economics, HEC Montréal.
[1] See Solow (1956, 1957).

As such, Cameroon's growth performance follows that of the resource-rich economies; however, the availability of more than one resource base has at times prevented Cameroon from feeling the full effect of shocks and so has enabled the government to take a lax macroeconomic management approach, with painful decisions postponed. This overall economic configuration, combined with potentially volatile social tensions, has prevented Cameroon from growing at its potential level.

For a resource-rich country sound policy is crucial, and in the case of Cameroon the franc zone institutional arrangements provide the ingredients for an acceptable macroeconomic framework. But performance has been below potential because of institutional rigidities that are particularly evident in the case of currency appreciation.

Ethnic and regional tensions also complicate policy-making, putting security concerns at the center of all successive governments' strategy. The 1960s were influenced by a pre-independence rebellion, with significant efforts allocated to peace-building and security and a considerable share of state resources devoted to security expenses. Only with the end of the rebellion beginning in the 1970s could the country really start putting in place its industrial development infrastructures. Public institutions were designed through a consolidation of the British and French cultures of public administration, with a tension between a strong central government and a center more evenly balanced with lower levels of governments. This also carried over to the legal framework which borrowed from the French civil code and British common law to produce a hybrid system that at times has led to different interpretations of the law and increasing uncertainty for investors.

Although Cameroon has not experienced open conflict, peace-building has been a permanent concern of the government and has led to some economically inefficient decisions which have not stimulated economic growth.

At least four regional groups need to be taken into account in major policy decisions: the North, the Center and South, the West, and the English-speaking provinces (North-West and South-West). Religion also plays a role; the country is almost equally divided among Christian, Muslim, and traditional believers, with Muslims primarily in the north of the country. Social cohesion obtained through specific management of these linguistic, geographic, and religious entities has driven all governments' policy-making.

Under each regime politicians have exploited these differences to their advantage, to the point that rent-seeking dominated business behavior (Yates 1996), particularly in recent periods. Cameroon shares the characteristics of resource-rich countries (Wunder 2005), compounded by the availability of agricultural export revenues to compensate for government revenue shocks induced by changes in the price of natural resources. The offsetting behavior of these two sectors has tended to reduce the overall variability of government revenues. From 1986 to 2003, for example, cocoa and coffee prices dropped, but the attendant revenue losses were compensated by an oil and wood boom.

Since independence, successive governments have primarily relied on this relatively rich economic set of opportunities to support social cohesion through redistributive policies. Lack of a sound governance structure has turned well-intentioned redistributive policies into rent-seeking and corruption. No sustainable long-term economic strategy was ever developed; the rich resource base and carefully designed macroeconomic institutions in fact retarded growth instead of setting the country on a sound economic growth path.

Post-independence economic growth performance in Cameroon was based on a combination of resource wealth with particular social and institutional characteristics. The objective of this chapter is to disentangle the process stimulated by abundance of natural resources over the period 1960–2000, in order to understand the contribution of each of these components of the growth process. The rest of the chapter is organized as follows. Section 2 presents the main resource-rich characteristics of the economy, and then section 3 we analyze the patterns and economic determinants of growth before assessing the role of social and institutional variables in section 4. Section 5 concludes with some lessons for future economic policy.

2. Natural resources and economic performance in Cameroon

Economic performance in the post-independence period was driven by the diversified primary export base, which included both natural resources and agricultural products. These sources of foreign reserves are analyzed before we consider their macroeconomic implications on the economy as a whole.

2.1 Analysis of data

Time-series annual data for the period 1960–2001 are used for the analysis. As described more completely in the appendix (p. 582), we use data from the Food and Agriculture Organization (FAO), the IMF, the World Bank, and the OPEC *Annual Statistical Bulletin*.

We divide the period of study into three sub-periods: 1961–77, 1978–85, and 1986–2001.[2] During the first phase, the government's priority was

---

[2] The breakdown adopted here is dictated by the focus on political-economy aspects. There is, however, some overlap with the breakdown followed in other studies. For example, Kobou, Fouda, and Njinkeu (2003) use a four-category periodization: (a) the organization phase of productive structures, from 1960 to 1975; (b) the phase of sustainable growth,

Table 16.1 *Cameroon, fraction of agricultural area to total area use, 1961–2001, percent*

Period	Agricultural area	Permanent crops area	Forestry area
1961–77	17.16	1.38	77.14
1978–85	19.29	2.37	77.14
1986–2001[a]	19.71	2.62	77.14
1961–2001[a]	18.60	2.07	77.14

Note: [a] Data for forestry area end in 1994.
Source: FAO.

peacebuilding following the pre-independence rebellion by the *Union des Populations du Cameroun* (UPC) and the early 1960s subversion of state security. This period was also characterized by early industrialization based on import substitution. The second phase is dominated by the initiation of oil production and exports from 1978. Two social and political events during this period are important: the constitutional change of political leadership in 1982 and the political leadership struggle that led to social tension and a failed military coup in 1984. This period was marked by major industrial and agro-industrial projects. The third phase, from 1986 to 2001, was characterized by a combination of social tensions in the post-1984 coup period, the introduction of press freedom and multi-party politics in 1990, and the devaluation of the national currency in 1994.

Cameroon has an area of 475,000 km². Table 16.1 shows that the agricultural area represents on average 19 percent of total area use. The forest area is constant over time, and represents 77 percent of total area use. These results can be explained by the fact that rapid urbanization due to the oil boom has been good for the conservation of the forest (Wunder and Sunderlin 2004). There was a modest evolution of the area used for permanent cultivation in the three sub-periods: 1.38 percent in 1961–77, 2.37 percent in 1978–85, and 2.62 percent in 1986–2001.

For a commodity-exporting country such as Cameroon, movements in the terms of trade (defined here as the ratio of export to import prices) are key determinants of economic performance. As depicted in figure 16.1, the evolution of the terms of trade of Cameroon has been very irregular. Fluctuations are driven primarily by shocks external to the country, including mainly variations in the international prices of primary agricultural and

from 1976 to 1985; (c) the phase of the economic crisis, from 1986 to 1994; and (d) the phase of return to growth, from 1995. Ghura (1997), in his study covering the 1963–96 period, also had four categories: (a) pre-oil, 1963–77; (b) oil boom, 1978–86; (c) recession, 1987–93; and (d) post-devaluation, 1994–6.

Table 16.2 *Cameroon, primary commodity exports, 1961–2003, million USD*

Period	Oil	Cocoa	Coffee	Banana	Cotton	Wood	Rubber	Tea	Tobacco	Groundnut	Palm oil	Total
1961–77	–	61.83	70.33	5.21	9.97	27.36	5.71	0.34	1.37	2.43	2.65	187.22
1978–85[a]	748.66	160.85	228.53	3.53	29.15	100.89	8.48	1.10	5.09	0.48	1.67	1288.43
1986–2003	842.52	133.46	138.08	39.18	70.71	284.16	28.22	0.47	1.23	0.08	0.26	1538.37
1961–2003[b]	819. 06	110.24	127.89	19.12	38.97	148.54	15.65	0.53	2.01	1.08	1.47	1282.55

Notes: [a] 1980–1985 for oil. [b] 1980–2003 for oil.
Sources: FAO, OPEC.

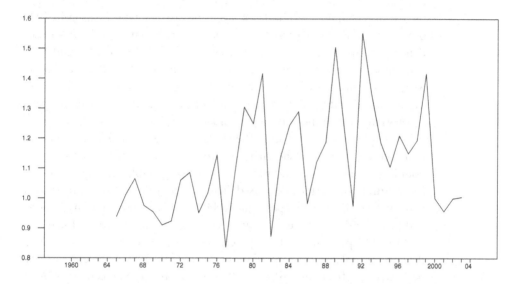

Figure 16.1 Cameroon, evolution of terms of trade, 1965–2003
Notes: Authors' calculations with WDI data. The terms of trade are defined as the ratio
of an implicit price deflator for exports to an implicit price deflator for imports, with
deflators computed as ratios of current-price exports and imports to base – year-price
exports and imports.

mineral products. In what follows, we focus mainly on developments
in the mineral sector, which since 1978 has been an important driver
of Cameroon's growth. As oil export volumes rose, Cameroon initially
benefited from record-high global oil prices. Real oil prices declined after
the early 1980s, however, and these developments exerted a significant
adverse impact on Cameroon's terms of trade, starting in 1986 and again in
1991.

As table 16.2 illustrates, exports of major agricultural commodities (coffee and cocoa) increased from the period 1961–77 to the period 1978–85.
After the beginning of the oil exploitation, exports of coffee and cocoa fell
drastically to USD 133 and USD 138 million in 1986–2003 from USD 161

and USD 229, respectively, in 1961–77. Exports of wood, cotton, and rubber increased in all sub-periods, even after the beginning of oil exports. These products, unlike coffee and cocoa, were not affected by oil exports. During 1961–77, the total value of commodities exports was USD 187 million; this jumped to USD 1,288 million in 1978–85 due to oil exports and reached USD 1,538 million in 1986–2003.

In figures 16.2 and 16.3 we compare the share of all export commodities with the share of oil exports in GDP. Figure 16.2 shows that between 1961 and 1978 exports of cocoa and coffee fluctuated around 5 percent of GDP. But after the beginning of oil exports in 1978 there was a significant fall in the exports of these commodities. Even the currency devaluation in 1994 did not improve their export performance. From figure 16.2, we can see that wood exports grew slowly until 1974 and fell between 1975 and 1987 whereas oil exports increased. Wunder and Sunderlin (2004) argue that oil wealth was not large enough to reverse forest loss and cause the forest area to expand. But after 1989, wood exports began to increase, reaching a peak in 1994, the year of the currency devaluation.

The exploitation of oil and other natural resources had social and economic consequences. As shown in table 16.3, the urban and non-agricultural populations increased rapidly after the discovery of oil, while the rural and agricultural populations decreased. The urban population rose from 20.4 percent in 1961–76 to 32.7 percent and 44.2 percent, respectively, in 1978–85 and 1986–2001, while the non-agriculture population rose from 19.86 percent to 32.81 percent and 41.68 percent over the three periods. Meanwhile, the agricultural and rural populations declined from 80.1 percent and 79.6 percent, respectively, in 1961–76 to 67.2 percent and 67.3 percent in 1978–85 and to 58.3 percent and 55.8 percent in 1986–2001. Rural–urban migration was spurred on by rising public sector employment and an increase in urban construction (Benjamin, Davarajan, and Weiner 1989; Devarajan 1999). The macroeconomics effects of natural resource exploitation are presented in the next sub-section.

2.2 Macroeconomic implications of natural resources: explicit and implicit "Dutch disease"[3]

In this sub-section, we analyse the effect of the oil boom and the management of other natural resource exports (e.g. wood) on income, consumption, savings, investment, and government expenditures. There are two complementary hypotheses about how domestic prices behave in the presence of a windfall (Devarajan 1999). One is the case of "Dutch disease," whereby

---

[3] See Corden and Neary (1982) and Corden (1984).

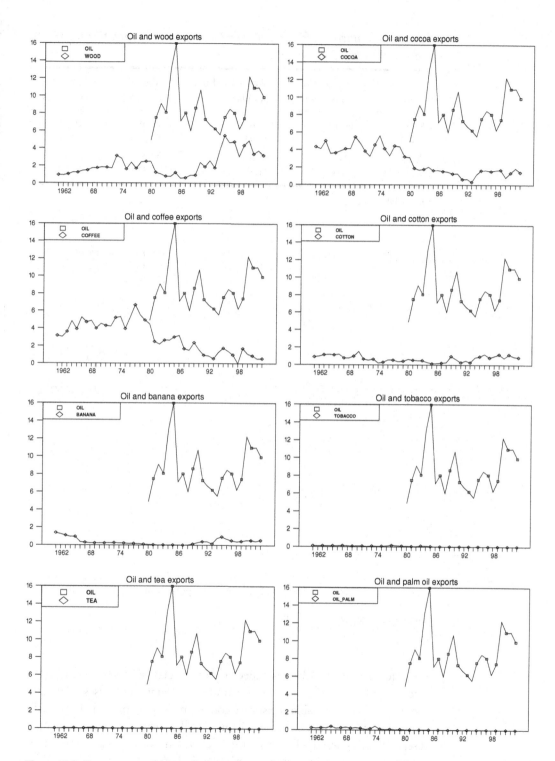

Figure 16.2 Cameroon, evolution of commodity exports relative to GDP: 1, 1962–2000, percent of GDP
Sources: OPEC, FAO, and WDI.

Table 16.3 *Cameroon, fraction of different segments of population to total population, 1961–2001, percent*

Period	Agricultural population	Non-agricultural population	Rural population	Urban population
1961–77	80.14	19.86	79.59	20.41
1978–85	67.19	32.81	67.29	32.71
1986–2001	58.32	41.68	55.81	44.19
1961–2001	68.60	31.40	67.35	32.65

Source: FAO.

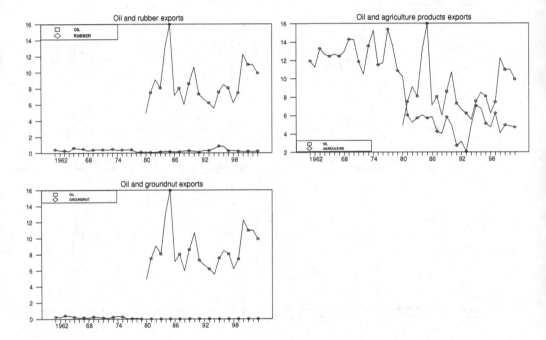

Figure 16.3 Cameroon, evolution of commodity exports relative to GDP:2, 1960–2001, percent of GDP
Sources: OPEC, FAO, and WDI.

the price of non-tradables is expected to rise relative to that of tradables. The second is that the price of non-tradable capital goods rises relative to the price of non-tradable consumer goods. In the case of Cameroon, with many natural resources, we can distinguish the case of an explicit "Dutch disease" (the oil windfall) and an implicit "Dutch disease" (exports of other resources such as wood when the price of oil declines).

Table 16.4 *Cameroon, growth of GDP, inflation, and real interest rate, 1961–2001, percent*

Period	GDP	GDP per capita	Inflation	Real deposit rate	Real lending rate
1961–77[a]	4.61	2.11	8.97	NA	NA
1978–85	6.88	4.05	9.99	−3.15	2.74
1986–2001	0.53	−2.06	4.20	2.26	13.98
1961–2001[b]	3.39	0.79	6.97	0.62	10.56

Notes: [a] 1968–77 for inflation. [b] 1968–2001 for inflation; 1978–2001 for deposit and lending rates.
NA = Not available.
Source: WDI, IFS.

The macroeconomic analysis of Cameroon offers a good opportunity to study the link between external economic changes and forests. We know that oil economies often fluctuate due to their heavy reliance on a single export commodity with an unstable world market price. Wunder and Sunderlin (2004) assume that "on average oil- and mineral-exporting tropical countries have more forest left and lose them at a slower rate than non mineral-exporting countries." In the case of Cameroon, the forest area remained constant over time, and in fact wood exports have provided a cyclical buffer against fluctuations in oil revenues.

As illustrated in figure 16.2, exports of wood have tended to fall during periods of oil boom and to rise during periods of oil revenue collapse. This suggests that the government used wood exports revenues to offset losses in oil revenues. For this reason we can say that the wood exports can be an implicit source of "Dutch disease."

Economic growth in Cameroon was irregular from 1960–2000, and this can be seen at both the overall macroeconomic level and at the sectoral level. Table 16.4 and Figure 16.4 show that during the first phase, from 1960 to 1977, the economy grew at an annual average rate of 4.6 percent; this period was also characterized by early industrialization based on import substitution. The end of this period coincided with the beginning of oil exploitation and exports, and fits with a "soft control" classification in the terminology of Collier and O'Connell (2007).[4]

The second phase started with oil production and exports in 1978, and was characterized by exceptional growth: the economy grew by 6.9 percent

---

[4] Within this framework, cooperative unions were created, and they played a role in supervising and guiding farmers: encouraging them to increase production either by distributing inputs to them at subsidized rates, or by providing them with modern techniques of production.

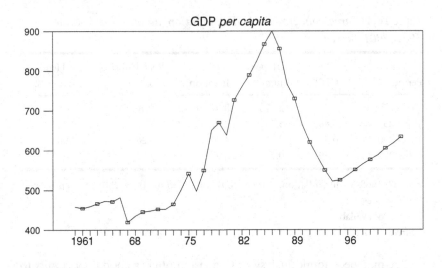

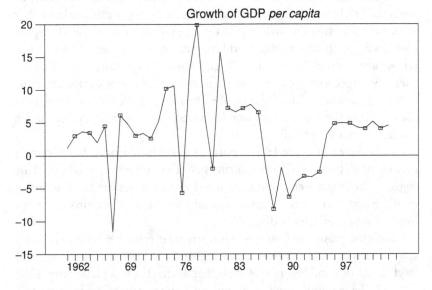

Figure 16.4 Cameroon, evolution of GDP *per capita*, constant 2000 dollars, and growth of GDP *per capita*, 1960–2003
Source: WDI, World Bank.

per annum. The shares of investment, consumption, and saving in GDP increased during this period, while the share of government expenditures decreased (see table 16.5 and figure 16.5). GDP *per capita* reached a peak of US$900 in 1985 (figure 16.4).

Rapid growth during the second period was stimulated by the peace dividend from the first period, combined with favorable exchange rates and other macroeconomic policies. In particular, when Cameroon formally

Table 16.5 *Cameroon, macroeconomic aggregates relative to GDP, 1961–2001, percent*

Period	Govt exp.	Investment	Final consumption	Gross domestic savings
1961–77	8.13	18.84	82.68	14.72
1978–85	7.31	29.73	68.86	25.19
1986–2001	9.89	18.74	75.22	19.50
1961–2001	8.72	21.78	76.98	19.07

Source: WDI.

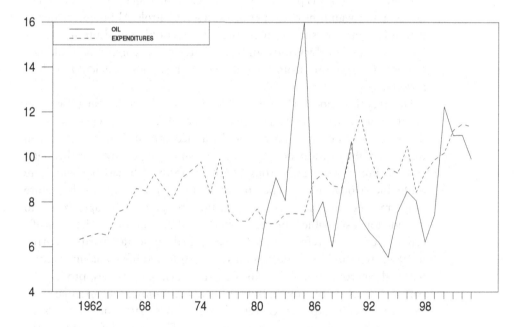

Figure 16.5 Cameroon, evolution of oil exports and government spending, 1961–2003, percent of GDP
Sources: OPEC; WDI.

announced the discovery and exploitation of important oil wells, the government decided to avoid the "Dutch disease" by ensuring that the focus of economic operators was kept on the pursuit of the Green Revolution. This was done by removing oil revenues from the normal budget process and creating a special account managed directly by the Presidency. Mismanagement of oil revenues, however, can be considered one of the main reasons for the subsequent decline in growth observed during the 1980s. Policy during the mid-1980s was inconsistent with sustainable growth. The period was marked by major industrial and agro-industrial projects as the state prioritized industrial activity and massively subsidized it across a range of sub-sectors.

The 1986–2001 period was characterized at the outset by a combination of social tensions following the coup in 1984 and the introduction of press freedom and multi-party politics in 1990. These socio-political events, combined with an appreciating exchange rate and other external shocks (e.g. the fluctuations in the international price of primary agricultural and mineral exports) led to an unprecedented collapse in growth early in the period. Economic growth was then reignited via exchange rate adjustments and the reform of trade and fiscal policy in 1994. In the terminology of Collier and O'Connell (2007) this period displayed a combination of near state breakdown (at the beginning of the period) and soft controls. Although the devaluation facilitated positive growth rates, ill-functioning institutions (manifested, for example, by Cameroon's position in global corruption rankings) prevented the country from generating growth at rates sufficient to reduce poverty.

During this period, GDP grew at 0.53 percent. The decline in growth can be attributed to a generalized fall in the prices of cash crops, which reduced the purchasing power of farmers and was accompanied by an increase in the costs of their production. Farmers responded in part by diverting agricultural inputs from cash crops to food crops, which had become more profitable (Douya 1995). The growth decline was also due to the failure of the macroeconomic institutions set up through the CFA agreements to provide for sustainable long-term growth and development. The intensification of economic reforms and the change in the monetary parity occurred in 1994:[5] the combined effect of the devaluation and of an enabling[6] international environment, thanks to the rise in cash crop prices, produced a partial restoration of growth. But the overall economy, and particularly the industrial sector, experienced very difficult times, partly because of state involvement and exposure to external shocks. The industrial sector was the hardest hit by the adjustment program.[7]

In the face of government resistance to pro-democracy movements, protracted civil disobedience paralyzed the country for a period starting in the late 1980s. The most virulent episode was "Operation Ghost Towns," an opposition campaign of demonstrations, voluntary business closures, and mass revolt that lasted eight months in 1990. The economic

---

[5] On January 12, 1994, the CFA franc was devalued by 50 percent in terms of the French franc (FF).

[6] The international context was particularly favorable for crops such as bananas, timber, and cotton.

[7] With regard to liberalization in particular, the program exposed the poor competitiveness of the sector, which had previously survived thanks to diverse protective measures and massive subventions.

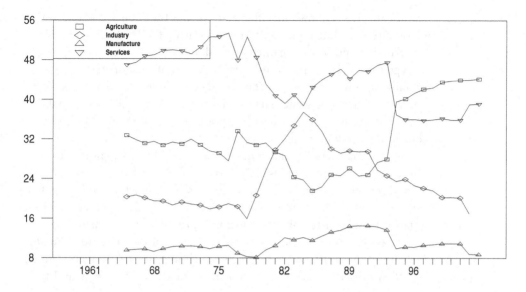

Figure 16.6 Cameroon, contribution of sectors, 1965–2003, percent of GDP
Sources: WDI; World Bank.

and social loss was significant and security concerns became even more important.

The political and social forces operating during this period were configured on largely ethnic and linguistic lines. By the 1992 Presidential election, three main political groups stood out. English-speaking Cameroon and the Bamileke-dominated provinces were primarily members of the Social Democratic Front (SDF). The North comprised primarily the late President Ahidjo's loyalists; while the Center, South, and Eastern Provinces were primarily in favor of the ruling party. The main cleavage, however, operated between the "Anglo-Bami" alliance of anglophones and Bamileke business interests and the Biya and Ahidjo loyalists, who saw the Anglo-Bami coalition as threatening their exclusive right to rule.

Turning briefly to the structural transformation of Cameroon's economy, an important question was whether the economy was characterized by a reallocation of factors of production from low-productivity traditional sectors to high-productivity modern sectors, a process that should contribute to economic growth by equalizing the marginal productivity of labor between them. The ratio of labor productivity in the non-agricultural sectors to that in the agricultural sector was 6.8 throughout the entire period, suggesting a dramatic productivity disadvantage in agriculture.

Figure 16.6, however, suggests that while there have been dramatic short-term developments in the sectoral structure of output the growth process in Cameroon did not produce a major long-term reallocation of factors of production from low-productivity to high-productivity sectors. Thus

Devarajan (1999) shows that the share of the traditional tradable sector (agriculture) declined quite substantially during the 1978–85 period while construction and services gained ground, but in figure 16.6, this apparent passage from agriculture to industry lasts for only a short time, notwithstanding the substantial support received by the industrial sector. Such supports and oil revenue seem to have restricted the structural transformations of the industrial sector, as well as the possibility for it to make a significant contribution to long-term development.

For Devarajan (1999), the "Dutch disease" and construction boom are both associated with windfalls in Cameroon. The "Dutch disease" was milder than observed in other countries because a sizeable portion of the windfall was saved abroad. Similarly, the construction boom did not translate into a sharp rise in non-tradable capital goods prices *vis-à-vis* consumer goods prices because import prices were rising rapidly at the same time. Finally, the path of the construction boom was such that construction accelerated and then slowed, while imports of capital goods started slowly and then speeded up.

Studying Cameroon, Benjamin, Devarajan, and Weiner (1989) provide another explanation for the expansion of the manufacturing sector during the boom period, by relaxing the assumption of perfect substitutability between domestically produced and imported manufactured goods. Their modification in the basic model renders domestic manufactured goods semi-traded. The increased national income then expands domestic manufactured output by raising its relative price and therefore its profitability.

3. Economic determinants of growth performance

We turn now to consider economic explanations of growth performance focusing first on the macroeconomic and then on the microeconomic determinants of growth.

3.1 *Macroeconomic determinants of growth*

To provide a proximate analysis of sources of growth in Cameroon, we rely on two methodological approaches: growth accounting (Solow 1957; Denison 1967) and regression analysis. Growth accounting proceeds by decomposing the observed growth into portions attributable to physical and human capital accumulation and to the growth in total factor productivity (TFP).[8]

---

[8] The growth in TFP is an important indicator of the nature of the growth process in the economy. It captures all of the factors that influence the amount of output generated by a given supply of labor and capital, including institutional and sociological variables.

Table 16.6 *Cameroon, contribution of factors to growth,*
1960–2000

Sub-period	bgno	bcko	bcho	bcro
1960–77	1.41	1.40	0.22	−0.22
1978–85	7.66	3.17	0.47	4.01
1986–2000	−2.58	1.00	0.28	−3.86
Mean	1.16	1.61	0.29	−0.74

Note: bgno represents the real GDP per worker; *bcko* represents the
contribution of physical capital accumulation per worker; *bcho* is
the contribution of human capital acummulation per worker; and
bcro is the contribution of TFP growth (the residual).
Source: Authors' construction from data provided by O'Connell
and Ndulu (2000).

The results obtained by applying this methodology (see table 16.6) show
that during the last four decades economic growth in Cameroon was fundamentally driven by physical capital deepening. Thus, for an annual average
growth rate of 1.16 percent of GDP per worker, the physical capital stock per
worker registered an annual average growth rate of 1.6 percent, as against
0.29 percent for the stock of human capital per worker. These results are
similar to those of Amin (2002) who shows that capital input was more
important than labor input in terms of contribution to economic growth
during the period 1961–98. The annual average growth rate of TFP is negative, at −0.74 percent. This suggests that the productivity of factors declined
on average over the full period, an observation reflected today by the continuing lethargy of the Cameroonian economy.

This long-run picture, however, conceals the contrasts that appear within
the various sub-periods of the study. In fact, during the first two periods,
from 1960 to 1985, capital accumulation (physical and human) accounted
for two-thirds of the observed GDP growth *per capita*, with productivity
growth contributing the remaining third. The mobilization of factors during
these first two periods can be linked to the deliberate action of policy-makers
whose goal was to provide Cameroon with an appropriate infrastructure
and production units that would fit into a large-scale industrialization process. The final period, however, presents a different picture. Between 1986
and 2000 the contribution of capital accumulation fell to an annual rate of
1.28 percent. Declining productivity, meanwhile, weighed heavily on the
growth process, with TFP evolving at an annual rate of −3.86 percent during the period. We should be careful with the latter figure, however: in a
context of structural adjustment, the productivity residual reflects all of the
dislocations associated with the economic reforms that ultimately condition
the return to growth that began after 1994.

Growth accounting, despite the possibility it offers for an explanation of growth, is not fully satisfactory because it does not make it possible to measure the intensity of the relationships between *per capita* GDP and other macroeconomic variables. We have therefore combined this with a regression model to give a fuller picture.

To define the influence of a number of variables on economic growth in Cameroon, we have analyzed the role played by the macroeconomic framework, then investment and human capital. In previous empirical studies on Cameroon economic growth, Amin (2002) shows that the capital and labor inputs are the main significant factors. Mbaku (1993) and Most and Van Den Berg (1996) show that domestic saving had a stronger impact on economic growth in Cameroon than foreign aid. Ghura (1997) finds that private investment and government investment had positive and significant effects on economic growth during the period 1963–96.

We shall focus on variables that have featured prominently in "new" growth theories (see Easterly *et al.* 1991; Renelt 1991; Levine and Renelt 1992). The growth rate of GDP *per capita* in Cameroon stood at 1.37 points below the world average over the whole period. Using the regression model developed by O'Connell and Ndulu (2000), macroeconomic policy variables including inflation (*inf*),[9] the black market premium (*bmpl*), and unproductive government expenditure (*gxbx*), together reduced the growth rate by 0.16 points as compared to the average (see table 16.7 and figure 16.7). The contribution of inflation is slightly positive (0.04), and this also holds for the black market premium, which shows a relatively more substantial contribution (0.14). The favorable contributions of these variables reflect Cameroon's membership in the *Banque des Etats de l'Afrique Centrale* (BEAC), a six-member monetary union with its currency pegged to the French franc (and later to the European Currency Unit, ECU). BEAC members, like those of the West African Monetary Union (UMOA), experienced lower inflation than global averages, as well as very low black market premia, reflecting the convertibility guarantee extended to both unions by the French treasury.

The evolution of predicted growth in the O'Connell–Ndulu model is roughly consistent with the actual growth of *per capita* GDP in Cameroon. But it is important to highlight the relative importance of each of the variables. Though the inflation rate did not drop during the 1990s (pushed upwards by the CFAF devaluation of 1994), its contribution does not vary significantly during the various sub-periods. Its weakest contribution is during the 1976–85 period, confirming some sort of laxity in the implementation of fiscal policy during this period. The low black market premium contributed positively over the whole period. A relatively high ratio of

---

[9] Table 16.4 and figure 16.7 describe the evolution of the inflation rate.

Table 16.7 *Cameroon, contribution of macroeconomic variables to deviation vis-à-vis average real GDP per capita, 1960–2000*

| Sub-period | Growth deviation vis-à-vis average of sample | Macroeconomic framework | | | | Total contribution |
		pin	*infl*	*bmpl*	*gxbx*	
1960–77	0.03	0.18	0.04	0.13	−0.37	−0.20
1978–85	0.75	0.18	0.03	0.15	−0.34	−0.17
1986–2000	−4.45	0.13	0.04	0.15	−0.33	−0.14
Average	−1.37	0.15	0.04	0.14	−0.34	−0.16

Note: pin is the political instability index, *infl* the inflation rate, *bmpl* the black market premium, and *gxbx* the unproductive government expenditure as a ratio to GDP. The entries for political instability and the macroeconomic framework are the associated regression coefficients from the O'Connell and Ndulu (2000) pooled conditional model, multiplied by the deviation of each variable from the sample mean for that variable. The Total contribution is just the horizontal sum of the preceding four columns.
Source: Authors' construction from data provided by O'Connell and Ndulu (2000).

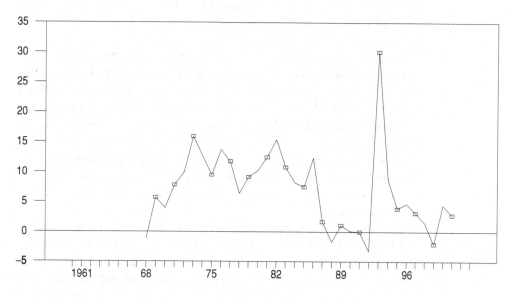

Figure 16.7 Cameroon, inflation rate, 1968–2001
Sources: WDI; World Bank.

unproductive government expenditure to GDP, in contrast, contributes −0.34 points to the growth rate deviation. This expenditure variable therefore plays the dominant role in the reduction of growth imputable to economic policy variables.

It was during the 1978–85 period that Cameroon's *per capita* GDP came closest to the global average. Investment was very strong over this period, a result both of the oil boom and of a liberalized investment code which made it possible to remove certain obstacles to foreign investment. The subsequent slackening in growth relative to the global average is imputable to the economic crisis, which was accompanied by a deterioration in several macroeconomic variables. In particular, the drop in investment from 27 percent in 1985 to less than 11 percent in 1993 had a negative impact on growth. Similarly, the share of public investment in total investments, which had exceeded 50 percent over the preceding periods, dropped to about 20 percent during the last period.

3.2   Microeconomic determinants of growth

We consider two microeconomic growth determinants: the functioning of markets and the behavior of households and firms.

3.2.1   Commodity and labor markets

In Cameroon, markets for goods and services do not operate properly as a result of numerous government interventions, which constitute the main source of inefficiency in these markets.

Looking first at product markets, government intervention in agriculture was relatively high during the first three decades after independence. In this period the government fixed producer prices for basic products, regulated markets, and decided on distribution and profit margins. An export tax was levied on most agricultural products and a number of import substitutes were subjected to import duties. For cocoa, coffee, and cotton, prices were fixed each year by Presidential decree, on the recommendations of the National Produce Marketing Board (NPMB). In the cocoa and coffee sectors, the NPMB established a scale that fixed margins at each stage of the marketing process.[10]

In this way, the NPMB secured a stable price for producers and exporters and bore all the risks involved in price fluctuations on world markets.[11] However, the pricing system taxed farmers heavily. The assessment base for cocoa ranged from 24 percent to 76 percent between 1970 and 1985, and from 35 percent to 76 percent for coffee during the same period. Between

---

[10] This scale used is based on the "equilibrium price," which then serves to determine the deductions to be made on agricultural products. Whenever world prices exceeded the equilibrium price, the NPMB levied a tax on exporters equal to that difference. Also, whenever world prices fell below the equilibrium price, the NPMB subsidized exporters by drawing from the Stabilization Fund set up during the years of plenty.

[11] There is no set scale for cotton, because the monopoly of SODECOTON over exports guaranteed that cotton costs were deducted from the export price.

Table 16.8 *Cameroon, evolution of international and national prices of certain cash crops, 1973–1993, per kg*

Period	cpint	cpnat	rpint	rpnat	apint	apnat
1973–77	500.10	182.80	528.02	201.00	632.34	210.20
1978–85	768.30	277.00	884.60	300.00	1045.80	315.50
1986–1993	469.00	316.20	514.00	293.10	752.00	356.20

Note: cpint, rpint and *apint* represent the international prices of cocoa, Robusta coffee, and Arabica coffee, respectively; *cpnat, rpnat* and *apnat* represent the national prices of the same crops.
Source: Authors' construction from data provided by the Ministry of Planning.

the 1970s and the first half of the 1990s, the average international price of cash crops stood at CFAF 618.6, 698.1, and 885.4 per kg, for cocoa, Robusta coffee, and Arabica coffee, respectively, while the corresponding farm prices for the same products stood at averages of CFAF 285.3, 288.4, and 323.4, respectively (see table 16.8). Though this difference represents 17 percent of market prices for cocoa, it is very high for Arabica coffee, representing 74 percent. Only a small portion of the international price of coffee was passed on to the farmer.

Such practices as a whole were ineffective, and did not permit producers to make any profit whatsoever. In stabilizing its prices at a low level Cameroon encouraged farmers to invest less in the production of export commodities compared, for example, to Côte d'Ivoire, where production tripled over the same period thanks to the payment of high producer prices (World Bank 1989). Price stabilization is often motivated as a mechanism to protect producers against the fluctuations of an unstable market. In the context of Cameroon, however, it prevented them from making profits during the price increases. Whenever prices dropped, moreover, the stabilization of producer prices at a fixed level eliminated the signal that would have been sent by the price drop to growers, spurring them to reduce production of the crops affected and raising the production of other crops whose prices increased.[12]

These interventions and associated inefficiencies applied equally to the labor market, which did not undergo any significant changes from the 1960s. This means that the labor market is still to this day characterized by significant structural and institutional rigidities that constrain the growth process (Kobou 1993). The origins of these institutional rigidities, apparent also in other African countries, appear to derive from the influence of powerful

---

[12] Between 1981/2 and 1985/6, the operating costs of the NPMB increased by 300 percent while export commodities stagnated at 200,000 tons, a sign of the adverse impact of state structures on farmers, and their consequent disillusionment with the system.

trade unions and the promulgation of progressive labor regulations by post-colonial governments (Lindauer and Roemer 1994).

Institutional rigidities in the labor market included codification of the salary scale and the linkage of wages to the educational levels attained in the conventional training system.[13] But, as in other SSA countries, the labor movement was not particularly strong in Cameroon, and while the country has had two labor regulation codes they have typically not been uniformly complied with or actively enforced. Access to employment is one of the major components of these norms: employment opportunities are concentrated in the public sector and in informal activities, with a poor regional and sector-specific allocation.

3.2.2   The behavior of economic agents

The main microeconomic agents considered here are firms and households. In Africa these agents face a very risky environment, partly because of natural causes (climate) and commodity prices, and partly because of the difficulty of enforcing contracts (Collier and Gunning 1999b).

From an agricultural perspective, Cameroon is characterized by regional diversity and dominated by small-scale farming. As of the late 1980s, about 1.1 million small-scale farmers used an average of 1.8 hectares of land. At least 70 percent of farms were 2 ha or smaller, and these occupied some 40 percent of the cultivated area; only 5 percent exceeded 5 ha and these accounted for only 10 percent of the land. These traditional farms contributed 90 percent of agricultural production from independence through the late 1980s (World Bank 1989). In parallel to the traditional sector, there exists a modern agricultural sector run by both the state and the private sector and accounting for approximately 10 percent of the farmed area and 20 percent of marketed produce. This structure of production and the risky environment affect farmers, who employ a variety of coping strategies including the survival strategy, the withdrawal strategy, the risk-reduction strategy, the extensive-accumulation strategy, and the intensification strategy (Herbel, Bamou, and Mkouonga 2002).

The survival strategy was conceived by producers faced by a risk of destitution. This category includes a large majority of farms in Cameroon, which are too primitive and under-capitalized to ensure their survival. In such cases, producers economized on the use of purchased inputs and so there was over-exploitation of the ecosystem and consequently a fall in production capacity. The withdrawal strategy, in contrast, is practiced by farmers who previously cultivated cash crops such as cocoa, coffee, and cotton, but whose positions became vulnerable due to collapses in the prices of these crops.

---

[13] This is the situation that prevailed prior to the 1992 Labor Code reform.

Lacking sufficient income to sustain and revive their plantations, they withdrew from cash crop cultivation. The same response is also widely observed among older farmers who were also pressured to decrease production by out-migration of family members.[14]

Well-endowed farmers, having land, can achieve some degree of protection from adverse outcomes through their access to credit markets. Small producers, in contrast, may be forced to reduce their *ex ante* exposure to risk by diversifying. For example, small cocoa and coffee growers combined their usual activities with other crops. Most agricultural households of the Center and Western provinces – where mixed farming of cash crops and food crops (cereals and tubers) was already being practiced – implemented this strategy. The same was true in the Northern provinces for millet production and cotton production (Douya 2001).[15] This pattern of diversification is different from the shift in modern agriculture world-wide towards large, capital-intensive farms.

Farmers faced by scarcity of labor on large farmlands, primarily in regions of low population density, apply the extensive-accumulation strategy. The intensification strategy, finally, is common in a situation where there is abundant labor and demographic pressure (the West or certain areas of the Center); here, intensive farming can take the form of monoculture or diversification of crops.[16]

In manufacturing activities, the policy environment has influenced the production process, which has been dominated by low productivity. In particular, legislation remained quite restrictive until the end of the 1980s; firms were highly protected, and this weakened their internal and external competitiveness. Thus Collier and Gunning (1999a) argue that trade liberalization is a necessary but not sufficient reform to make African manufacture competitive. The level of protection in Cameroon is estimated to be over 75 percent, and this penalized the export sectors (Milner 1990). This protection was provided through special regimes; in Cameroon by 1993 firms enjoying one or more special tax regimes accounted for 99 percent of total sales. The grant of licenses and the completion of fiscal and customs procedures often necessitated payments, which added to already high transactions costs (Tybout *et al.* 1996). In combination with the problems created by rent-seeking (see section 4.1), the overall impact of the policy environment was to create an environment hostile to business.

[14] Where it exists, this population may be mobilized in substitution activities likely to compensate for their diminishing income.
[15] An acceptable explanation is that farmers seek to diversify their sources of income; in this case, millet was destined for the market rather than for self-consumption.
[16] The case of the small-scale farmers of Robusta coffee- and cocoa-producing areas, who diversified their sources of revenue by creating palm oil plantations, is worth noting.

It is useful to distinguish between two types of manufacturing firms: small businesses and large firms. The challenges facing small firms are the result of interest-group dynamics. They struggle for survival and growth; most of them never reach the minimum size required and remain in the informal sector. They operate in a rather hostile environment, facing such barriers to entry and growth as credit and insurance market imperfections, rent-seeking by private rackets, predatory regulation, and taxation by government officials. They also face risks that cannot be handled by the informal insurance markets since the latter are usually locally based and therefore unable to diversify against region-wide risks. The problem is aggravated by infrastructures that keep small businesses very specialized and therefore highly vulnerable to risk.

Predatory regulation is also an important barrier. Given that small businesses, moreover, are dispersed and weak politically, public policy is more supportive of large firms. The surviving businesses, moreover, do not enjoy their monopoly power, because rents are taxed away in bribes. Rent-seeking distorts the incentives for the adoption of new technologies and compromises the growth process.

Credit markets also operate differentially by firm size. Large firms are predominantly foreign- or state-owned, operate with a relatively large capital base, and have access to national and international production and distribution networks. Their main concern is the ability to restructure in response to changing external conditions. Existing credit markets have primarily targeted these firms. Small firms can sometimes satisfy their own credit needs through the informal credit markets and institutions of micro-credit, and credit may be available from family networks, which are relatively extensive and often include family members working abroad. But the firm size that can be supported by such schemes is low. As such, informal markets have not proved sufficient to create a fast-growing manufacturing sector.

We shall turn next to socio-institutional aspects, which also condition the economic growth process in Cameroon in the period under study.

4. Social and institutional determinants of growth performance

The political-economy literature studies the role of collective action processes in resource allocation and rent distribution. The main concern in our study is the extent to which the collective action process hinders or promotes growth. Our focus is therefore on the collective action of ethnic-based interest groups or policy-making institutions, and whether the incentives of economic agents in the long run are to invest and to improve productivity. Attention will be paid to the role of institutions, and how they hinder or deter growth-promoting policies. A commitment agreement that constrains the policy-maker and avoids time-inconsistency is, in theory, available within the CFA zone Accords, which incorporate the main elements for ensuring fiscal and monetary discipline.[17]

Two points – the social and institutional aspects of growth performance – will now be analyzed.

4.1 Social aspects of growth performance

In Cameroon, social aspects of growth are related to the desire of ethnic and other social coalitions to divert resources toward their private interests. From this perspective, we focus on (1) the role of interest groups, rent-seeking, and coalition-building and (2) the management of regional equilibrium.

4.1.1 Interest groups, rent-seeking, and coalition-building

To analyze these issues we use the framework of Castanheira and Esfahani (2003), who identify three groups of agents – the public, lobbying groups, and politicians – and three broad elements that influence their incentives and interactions. These include the sources of rents, the heterogeneity of interests across socio-economic groups, and the institutional structure within which they interact. This framework can best be illustrated by the following example, assuming an economy in which the government seeks to allocate a rent (R) to two groups X and Y.[18] Each group is composed of identical, risk-neutral participants; groups X and Y comprise, respectively, n and m members, with $n < m$. The two groups compete in a two-stage game to appropriate the rent R held by the government. In the first round, both groups determine the probability of obtaining the public good. In this round, each member of each group is fighting to appropriate the rent for his group, and the rent-seeking effort depends on the value of R and on the number of persons in each group. As the larger of the two groups gets bigger, the small group spends less on rent-seeking. In the second round of the game, members of the group now compete to appropriate the now private but indivisible good won by the group. The member of the group that wins keeps all the rent. This group competition for rents, in which the winner-takes-all principle holds, fits the political game played in the name of the tribe in Cameroon (Nitzan 1994).[19]

---

[17] See Allechi and Niamkey (1994), Devarajan and de Melo (1987), and Guillaumont, Guillaumont, and Plane (1988) for the costs and benefits of participating in CFA monetary unions.

[18] See Katz and Tokatlidu (1996) and their analysis of group competition for rents.

[19] Rents may be redistributed within each group according to a mixed rule, with a proportion of the rent distributed on an egalitarian basis and the remainder allocated according to each member's relative efforts (Nitzan 1991, 1994).

In such a game, asymmetry in group sizes tends to reduce the waste in rent-seeking. Effort in rent-seeking increases with the size of group X, reaching a maximum when $n = m$ and then decreasing with further increases in n. Uncertainty with respect to the net benefits of rent-seeking can also limit the effort on rent-seeking (Nitzan 1991, 1994); consistent with this, when groups are risk-averse, the waste due to rent-seeking is relatively limited compared to a case with risk-neutrality (Nitzan 1991, 1994).

Lobbies and interest groups seeking to influence public choices strongly characterize the group structure of political economy in Cameroon. The pattern has changed focus from Ahidjo to Biya, but overall almost the same tactics have been used. For Bayart (1985), contemporary dynamics of group interactions in Cameroon can be considered as a "process of reciprocal assimilation and fusion of dominant groups, old and new elites born from colonization and de-colonization." Hegemonic alliances have emerged through the multi-ethnic coalitions that gave birth to the country's public service, and that still serves as its base in the post-independence period. Such coalitions became the framework for the redistribution of rents. Peace and security were also an important policy objective given that a rebellion started prior to independence, paralyzing a major part of the territory. The first President, Ahmadou Ahidjo "voluntarily" decided to retire in 1982. After serious disagreement with his successor, Paul Biya, loyalists of Ahidjo, primarily but not exclusively from his regional and ethnic base, attempted a coup in April 1984. The failed coup provoked a change in Biya's approach to government, which increasingly focused on building an ethnically based political alliance. Biya's original political message of improving morality of public life, equity, honesty, and professionalism in public service was increasingly downplayed.

This framework suggests that rent-seeking interactions may have contributed both positively and negatively to Cameroon's growth, depending on the period. A public choice framework can help understand the political economy of the growth outcomes that emerged. According to McGuire and Olson (1996), redistributive democracies tend to enhance economic performance more effectively than is possible under a stationary bandit. The reason, in part, is that a policy-maker driven by rent extraction is more vulnerable than a democratically elected one. In order to secure his status against overthrow by competing forces, he is forced to create a power base; this is done by ensuring support within his ethnic or tribal group through the distribution of rents – sometimes in the form of direct subsidies but often through complex and costly networks of economic regulation. The policy-maker will consolidate this loyalty base by limiting access to rents to groups whose support helps him stay in power. As a result, he will not tolerate rent-seeking outlays by groups that do not constitute his core support. Recognizing this, outside groups rationally will not seek rents from the incumbent leader, choosing instead to contend his claim on political power. To the extent that such anti-establishment activity is effective, the stationary bandit is transformed into a roving bandit who is no longer capable of (or interested in) protecting the private economic activity that is crucial for development.

Both Ahidjo and Biya sustained a monopoly on political power by looting the country's resources. Ahidjo in five years subverted pre-independence democracies into autocracies and consolidated this with policies of overt rent extraction. Centrifugal forces threatened the political viability of the government and provided ingredients for building political support that in turn contributed to reducing the incentives for long-term development. Ahidjo sought to improve productive capacity in order to raise the stock of wealth available to support his regime. He limited looting in order to create an environment in which some economic growth would take place. He created a controlled economy, with minimalist laws designed to protect property rights. These provided the ingredients of growth, but never created the social infrastructure of public goods necessary to increase productivity and foster long-term sustainable growth and development.

Given the pre-independence rebellion, the main objective of the government after independence was to obtain a consensus on maintaining social order in a situation characterized by a strong central government co-existing with peripheral and centrifugal units. Ethnic, religious, or other interest groups could represent such centrifugal units with significant influence over their members. Mouiche (1997) dubbed this a "fragmented state." From this perspective, there was a need to scale down ethnic identities: Ahidjo had to consolidate central authority through a policy of zero-tolerance of demonstrations of autonomy or of ethnic (regional) solidarity. However, the "policy of national unity" was more than words as it allowed him to accumulate political capital.

The pre-independence political scene was dominated by numerous political parties and associations, headed by individuals from Beti tribes in French-speaking Cameroon. This ethnic group also dominated the civil service and so constituted a real threat to President Ahidjo's authority. He solved the problem by wooing the Beti parties and associations into his own party, the "Union Camerounaise,"[20] through appointments to administrative and ministerial positions. Ahidjo's hand-picked successor, a Beti, retained the hegemony of this tribe in public administration (see table 16.9); the Beti account for nearly 40 percent of general managers (GMs)

---

[20] That was how the one-party state came into being and helped monopolize the political scene. This party was exclusively a support machinery for the regime and was a structure to stabilize and consolidate state hegemony (Sindjoun 2002).

Table 16.9 *Cameroon, distribution of managers of public enterprises and SOEs, by ethnic group, percent*

Region or ethnic group	General managers	Deputy general managers	Total	Influence of ethnic groups[a]
Beti	39.2	46.2	39.6	24.1
Sawa	7.8	15.5	10.8	14.0
Northerners	6.1	3.3	5.4	29.7
Anglophones	12.1	7.4	10.5	19.6
Bamileke	16.7	20.2	18.3	12.6
Expatriates	18.2	7.4	15.5	
Total	100.0	100.0	100.0	100.0

Note: [a] There are no data on the influence of the various ethnic groups. We have made a gross approximation of the influence of each group by supposing that each group's influence corresponds, in relation to its total population, to its regional representation (by so doing, we relied on the fact that the administrative break-up of Cameroon conformed with the ethnic reality of the country) (see the collective statement Collectif Changer le Cameroun: 1990).
Source: IMPACT Tribune (1993).

or deputy general managers (DGMs) in public enterprises and SOEs.[21] The number of Beti holding these positions is twice that of the Bamileke and eight times that of the Northerners, highly represented in the total population (29.7 percent), but holding only 5.4 percent of the positions of responsibility.

The Bamileke (in the West) in May 1955 initiated a guerilla war against the colonial powers alongside the Bassa (in the Littoral and Center). Ahidjo first resorted to force, and when this failed he developed a strategy based on assimilation and manipulation. Because of their business acumen, Ahidjo encouraged the Bamileke to engage in business activities. As a result, they had a dominant position, to the point that some suggested that national cohesion would be threatened if they also had a prominent role on the political scene. Under Ahidjo, unwritten rules recognized a tripartite distribution of roles: the Beti controlling the public administration and the State apparatus; the Bamileke running the economy; and the Northerners (Ahidjo's ethnic group) controlling the political arena in coalition with the Beti in public

---

[21] The distribution here highlights ethnic lobbies counted since the democratic opening in 1990. The Beti group is made up of people of the South, East, and Center provinces, excluding the Bassa associated with the Sawa, in the Littoral province; the Bamileke comprise people of the West province to whom the Bamoun people should be added. The anglophone group include people of English culture, the people of the South West and North West provinces, while the Northerners consist of people of the three Northern provinces, notably the North, Adamawa, and Far North Provinces.

administration and with Bamileke business interests. To ensure peaceful cohesion, Ahidjo avoided excessive pressures on the village structures of the West, but in return for not having a bourgeoisie independent of the state he opted for economic independence from the world (Bayart 1985), combined with a liberal system behind closed doors to ensure that he controlled everybody. Economic development at all costs was not the overarching objective. The relatively good economic performance in our first period is partially related to this three-way "distribution" system, which is thought to have had a neutralizing effect on the centrifugal forces and in turn had a positive impact on growth.

When Biya came to power in 1982, the status quo left by Ahidjo was maintained for some time. Although Biya entered with the declared intention of opening up the country, the same centrifugal forces produced a regime not significantly different from Ahidjo's. Biya's regime is closer to that of roving bandit in an environment of anarchy. For McGuire and Olson (1996), the roving bandit does not exhibit a stable and encompassing interest in the domain over which he rules and there is little incentive to invest in improving future productive capacity. The main difference between the two regimes is that Ahidjo did have a set of policies for wealth accumulation and redistribution, whereas Biya's regime had no apparent long-term planning.

Meanwhile, through incremental but important changes, Biya modified the power structure in favor of his ethnic group. The transformation has serious consequences for growth. Ahidjo had retired (some said temporarily)[22] from administrative control of the country but remained the Chair of the party. His sympathizers staged a military coup in April 1984, which failed. The failed coup pushed Biya to steadily retreat from the public sphere and to focus more narrowly on ethnic identity, abandoning a variety of interest groups under the pressure of his clansmen, who believed it was their own time to control the country's resources. This power reallocation meant taking away from the Northerners some of the control of the public administration while the grip of the Bamileke on the economy was a source of worry. The unease of the Beti was also motivated by the fact that the Bamileke had also become the dominant group in higher education and among candidates for public service jobs. The structure used by Ahidjo to control the centrifugal forces became increasingly loose.

Biya employed a wide variety of tactics. These included directed credits in commercial banks, with the result that the ratio of delinquent claims to bank assets increased sharply. At the time of Ahidjo's resignation, the insolvent

---

[22] The fact that Ahmadou Ahidjo preserved his control over the single party added more pressure to the political atmosphere and placed doubt on his desire to retire from active political life (Bandolo 1986).

debt ratio stood at 5.6 percent; it reached 13.7 percent in 1985 and 37.7 percent in 1988 (Tchamanbe 2001).[23]

In the early 1990s pressure mounted for political opening; the climate carefully crafted and controlled by Ahidjo had become conflict-prone. This affected the efficiency of public administration and the state had to freeze hiring and wages in the public sector. Given the importance of the parastatal sector in the economy, the limited state resources had spillovers for the rest of the economy and led to a contraction, further adding to social tension with growing unemployment and in turn pushing the economy further into recession.

4.1.2 Management of the equilibrium between regional entities

Ahidjo initiated the policy of regional balance, and used it to build a new power base. Revenue derived from oil was kept outside the regular budget process and extensively used for discretionary allocation of major projects and rents. The economy was organized around liberal principles, but balanced development and social justice also played a role. Social justice was pursued under the objective of equitably redistributing the fruits of development among the various interest groups and therefore giving each citizen an equal chance within the framework of national solidarity.[24] The doctrine of balanced development means that the same attention should be given to the different sectors of economic activity, to the different regions and towns, and to men and to women. Erected into a norm to legitimate the state by Ahidjo, this policy would be pursued by his successor with few variations, as is evident from a comparison of the main characteristics of the various governments under Ahidjo and Biya.

A regional dimension in economic and social policies was also introduced by the Ahidjo regime as a useful mechanism of peace and social cohesion that would provide for long-term economic development. While the government in many ways constituted the ideal structure for the realization of regional balance, this role was abused by both regimes. Since the country experienced sustained growth under Ahidjo, the policy was largely accepted. The policy has not formally been continued by Biya, but there is substantial evidence that the second President, used and abused the regional dimension. Cabinet reshuffles, for example, have been frequent, and have increasingly become a mechanism for rewarding clansmen and friends. Biya used an average of 40.8 ministers between 1983 and 2002, compared to an average of 26.9

---

[23] An examination of the real situation of some banks shows that this category of credits represented at least 62 percent of bank credits undergoing liquidation in 1988, including the Cameroon Bank, the Cameroon Development Bank, the Société Camerounaise de Banque, and the Banque de Paris et des Pays-Bas.

[24] This is more a question of distributive justice than commutative justice, which presupposes the putting in place of a set of reforms.

Table 16.10 *Cameroon, ministerial positions, by ethnic group, 1960–2002*

Region or ethnic group	Ahidjo (1970–82)	Biya (1983–2002)
Beti	8.7	14.1
Sawa	1.9	5.8
Northerner	5.6	8.7
Anglophone	5.9	6.7
Bamileke	4.9	5.6
Average ministerial team	26.9	40.8
Average group per ministerial team	5.4	8.2

Source: Table compiled by authors from data collected at the Ministry of Territorial Administration.

between 1960 and 1982; the Beti remain dominant (see table 16.10). Though the Sawa were relatively under-represented in the population, they obtained nine ministerial positions under Ahidjo, a figure tripled under Biya. This can largely be explained by the fact that the multi-party politics era saw a multitude of opposition parties in the Littoral province, the region of origin of the Sawa people and the country's main industrial base. Simultaneously not much was done to stimulate economic activity in that region, as it was felt that it would primarily benefit the opposition power base.

The argument for social cohesion was really a *quid pro quo* for power- and resource-sharing between the ruling elites and representatives of the various interest groups. Its aim was not economic development but rather the consolidation of political power. The number of ministerial positions increased over time even though the ministers did not fulfil any specific function. The democratic process initiated at the beginning of the 1990s further strengthened the link between the title of minister and the ethnic origin of the holder: this minister spoke for his region of origin, even if his nomination ignored the fact that he or she did not necessarily embody the aspirations of the local population concerned. Thus, in the absence of legitimacy in a particular region, an individual was propelled into being the spokesperson of the region. In a system where politics was conceived and lived as a competition between the various segments of the society for the allocation of national resources (Moukoko Mbonjo 1993), the distribution of political positions becomes a primary means of controlling civil society. Biya resorted to substantive law, notably Decree 7/9/83, for example, to institute quotas per province in competitive entrance examinations. Such a policy stance was not without its own problems, including the non-optimal allocation of resources. This is illustrated, for example, through access to employment in the public service, where the opacity that characterized this process followed the patrimonial logic (Médart 1991)[25] on which the Cameroonian state was founded. As in many other developing countries, the public sector was the dominant formal sector employer. But in Cameroon, the public sector payroll was used to create employment rather than to deliver services, through a process that creates political support for senior officials of the central administration by distributing less qualified jobs at guaranteed incomes (Mbembe 1995). Each minister was thus able to recruit people from his village or his ethnic group; in some cases, he used his influence to identity plausible candidates for appointment through the mediation of the networks to which he/she belonged (Kobou 1999). During the 1980s some 30,000 low-skilled public sector jobs were created through this process (Hugon 1999). The proliferation of unnecessary positions created the problem of disguised unemployment within the administration, thereby undermining efficiency within the public sector and creating an important impediment to growth.

These practices were also evident in the political system. Especially during the first three decades after independence, there was a strong overlap between the single party and the state and osmosis among the officials of the party and those of the administration. Access to resources was conditioned by membership in one and/or the other of these two spheres, and membership in the ruling party could at times be an important asset for social status.[26] These practices annihilated the state's capacity to anticipate problems, as it was obliged to manage the economy solely to preserve social peace. Though the quest for social peace was important to growth, it needed to be sought rationally so as not to lead to a massive diversion of productive activity and to the malfunctioning of the state. In particular, politicking constituted a dominant factor in the economy, and the propensity not to consider competence in filling job vacancies increased; the individual's capacity to mobilize support in a given region became the prime factor. This practice served to perpetuate the reign of the incumbent powers.

Our argument here has been that management of social cohesion was a constraint that exerted some influence over Cameroonian growth.[27] We turn now to assessing the influence of key macroeconomic policy institutions.

---

[25] Social institutions (families, friends, clans, tribes) also play a major role, so that positions are not always occupied by those with the requisite skills and experience.

[26] The contract between the individual and the party is based on the search for an ideal about which we are convinced and on which we have strong convictions. It is a game of calculations, at the center of which are mainly material interests.

[27] The quest for social cohesion has been of major concern to the Cameroonian authorities since independence. Social cohesion delivered a growth dividend because it led to political stability, which enhanced growth. In table 16.7, the political instability index contributed an average of 0.15 percentage points to Cameroon's growth deviation relative to the sample mean over the full post-independence period. This contribution was as high as 0.20 between the mid-1960s and mid-1980s, a period of social peace and relative stability reinforced by the iron hand of the ruling political regime.

4.2 Institutional aspects of growth performance

The institutional framework in the macroeconomic sphere constituted another constraint that the authorities had to contend with at the same time as they developed growth strategies. This was particularly important with respect to monetary and exchange rate policies and fiscal discipline. The impact of financial markets on growth comes through savings processes, the interface between savers and borrowers, and the reallocation of resources when their current uses were no longer the most profitable. In particular the interface between savers and borrowers was important and depended on the level of development of the banking sector and other financial intermediaries. The main functions of this interface included the screening of firms, identification of profitable investment opportunities, and monitoring of borrowers. Contract enforcement, disclosure of business information to outside investors, and property rights were the main elements of efficient financial markets.

4.2.1 Financial repression

In the early post-independence years, funds derived from former colonial institutions were exclusively allotted to business companies as well as to mining enterprises owned by foreign financial interests. Given that this posed serious problems for the financing of the economy as a whole, the government deemed establishing state control of financial activities to be necessary. The government considered that in the absence of any intervention the country's financial systems were not in a position to provide the necessary support to the process of industrialization, the implementation of which required the availability of low-cost capital. From the beginning of the 1970s there was excessive intervention by the state in banks, accompanied by financial repression in the form of administered interest rates and a sector-specific orientation sustained by credits at preferential interest rates. Throughout the 1970s and 1980s the state maintained controlled interest rates at very low levels. Interest rates were modified only once over that period, increasing from 4 percent to 4.5 percent. Likewise, the preferential discount rates that were applied to prioritized sectors over this period were modified only once every three years; the normal discount rates could be changed only every two years. Control of these different rates obviously had consequences for the process of growth, since the offering of low or negative interest rates provoked the flight of financial assets from the banking system and the country (see table 16.4 and figure 16.8). On this last point, a World Bank report (1986) on the Cameroon banking system revealed that the large differential between interest rates in Cameroon and in external markets, particularly Paris, considerably hindered the domestic mobilization of savings

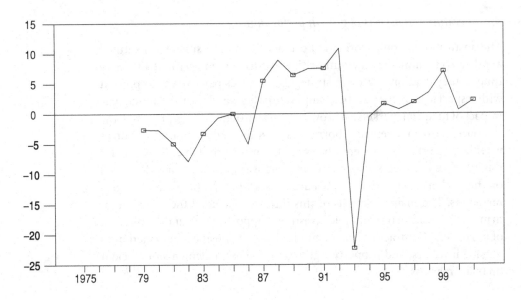

Figure 16.8 Cameroon, evolution of real deposit rate, 1975–2000
Sources: IFS; IMF.

by attracting available funds, such as those of large firms, into the more profitable foreign financial markets.

With regard to the sectoral distribution of bank credit the policy adopted by the government was characterized by the fixing of global rediscount ceilings for commercial banks and individual ceilings for enterprises. Through the rediscount operations mechanism, banks were required to grant some assistance at preferential rates and to assure the funding of priority sectors[28] without any consideration for profit. Thus policy provoked distortions in the allocation of resources and favored an increase in unsound lending. In the short run, ironically, these two policies may have had a positive effect on Cameroon's economic growth, particularly during 1978–85. During this period of growth, four new banks were created[29] with a substantial increase in the capacity to allocate credit in the economy. But their long-run impact was adverse. Credit contracted during the period of economic crisis, reflecting in part an absence of worthy projects, but also reflecting the exhaustion of banking resources. Banks had remained the tributary of public deposits and foreign transfers, their position undermined by the unfavorable world environment and the slowdown in growth.

[28] The priority sectors were agriculture, SMEs, public enterprises, small and medium industries (SMIs), housing, and others.
[29] The four banks are Banque de Paris et des Pays-Bas, Boston Bank Cameroon, Bank of Credit and Commerce Cameroon, Bank of America.

The policy of financial and economic liberalization initiated on October 16, 1990 involved a liberalization of administered interest rates. With the 1994 devaluation, the lending rates of the BEAC increased to contain inflationary pressures, before dropping rapidly (this rate stood at 14 percent in March 1994 and reached 7.75 in December 1994). The borrowing rates of commercial banks remained very high, however, due to their high operational costs; reliable borrowers were discouraged by high interest rates which further undermined the growth process.

Cameroon continued to influence monetary policy particularly through two channels: one relating to its relations with the BEAC, the other concerning the funding of elections. In connection to its relations with the BEAC, Cameroon's monetary policy deviated considerably from the policy promulgated by the supervisory authority of the BEAC. The latter had very little independence in relation to the government,[30] as demonstrated by Cameroon's frequent indifference to or outright rejection of its demands (Stasavage 1996). Medhora (1995) notes that in the BEAC region the Cameroonian share of seigniorage greatly increased. From the beginning of the 1970s, the governors of the BEAC were always plagued by tense relations with Cameroon, and during the 1994–5 period President Biya even refused to grant audience to the BEAC's governor. Cameroon's partners in BEAC had little recourse with respect to the country's behavior since the uneven distribution of seats at the Board of Governors gave Cameroon the undeniable advantage[31] of being able to block important decisions. Fouda (1997) illustrates the existence of a political/monetary cycle in Cameroon, showing that macroeconomic aggregates were manipulated by successive governments to ensure a prolonged stay in power. There was an increase in liquidity prior to every election (seven–eight months before parliamentary elections and eight months before Presidential elections) and a downturn in liquidity five months after elections (whether parliamentary or Presidential). The main causes were the need to gain national popularity and to satisfy the international community. The existence of the monetary/political cycle highlighted the lack of independence of the Central Bank.

A third form of intervention originated from the privileged political relationship with France that in particular undermined the fiscal discipline built into the CFA Accords. For example, in 1987, when the French Treasury was hoping that credit restrictions would oblige Cameroon to redress its budgetary balance, the government went directly through the French President to secure an increase in assistance that postponed budget stabilization. The

---

[30] In a multi-country analysis of monetary policy in Africa, Savvides (1998) finds that only Cameroon was unable to pursue an independent monetary policy.

[31] The BEAC has a Board of Governors, with the seats distributed as follows: Cameroon (four seats); France (three seats); Gabon (two seats); and the other states (one seat each).

government of Cameroon also gained from the pressure exerted by France at the level of the Bretton Woods institutions, the end result being that a group of French political and civil service officials worked against the interest of their own government agency charged with implementing the aid conditionality (Stasavage 1996).

4.2.2 Financial discipline and the inefficient macroeconomic framework

The CFA franc is a fixed exchange rate *per excellence*, its convertibility into the French franc guaranteed by the French treasury. As such, its role as an anchor for inflation dominates any role it might have as an instrument for maintaining competitiveness. The RER in turn (defined as the relative price of traded to non-traded goods) is strongly influenced by multilateral movements of the French franc against other currencies, as well as by macroeconomic developments within Cameroon. An appropriately valued RER facilitates optimal resource allocation given adequate institutional arrangements and other factors such as competitive and rent-free economies, sound financial institutions, strengthened trade policies, and human capital accumulation are in place. The specific arrangements of the CFA Accords assured currency convertibility, to the point that the CFA became the reserve currency for neighboring countries in the 1980s and early 1990s. During the first period the built-in restraints on fiscal and monetary policies, coupled with currency convertibility, were the driving forces behind the growth outcomes achieved. Unfortunately, these were due to factors external to the zone: for example, until the late 1970s the French franc was relatively weak, and was frequently devalued *vis-à-vis* the US dollar. Because of this depreciation, the RER of the CFAF was not over-valued despite the worsening terms of trade. All in all, the country performed well.

Beginning in 1985, however, the French franc started to appreciate *vis-à-vis* the US dollar while the deterioration of the terms of trade continued, particularly among the oil producers of the CFA zone. To make things worse, the currencies of neighboring countries, including Nigeria, were also depreciating. This further eroded competitiveness. Cameroon's growth collapse from the mid-1980s is therefore in part the result of an accumulated real over-valuation associated with the inability to implement a nominal devaluation: the inertia of the CFA Accords prevented the adjustment required to restore competitiveness (Elbadawi and Madj 1996).

The CFA Accords at the same time improved the investment climate, by lending long-run stability to inflation. With respect to exchange rate management, therefore, these Accords embody a trade-off: while useful for long-run growth they may exert sharp short-run costs in the form of maladjustment to economic shocks. Counterfactual analysis by Devarajan and Rodrik (1992) suggests that maintenance of the fixed parity and low inflation in the period after 1980 (and before the devaluation of 1994) was highly costly in terms of employment and growth, and that allowing for some flexibility and a higher level of inflation would have produced a significantly stronger growth performance.

The BEAC is a monetary union, and the joint determination of monetary policy introduces a new set of considerations. On the one hand, shifting monetary and exchange rate policy decisions to the supranational level increase the likelihood of spillover effects of national conditions. Coordination failure in an environment with multiple decision-makers may lead to externalities that deterred rather than promoted long-term growth. One area where this is possible is fiscal policy and its inflationary effects and, consistent with this, the CFA Accords restrict the use of deficit financing in the form of a 20 percent ceiling rule aimed at preventing the monetization of member-country fiscal deficits. On the other hand, growth may be over-constrained by the inertia of a system that led to too great a focus on monetary stability at the cost of serving as an agent of overall economic development. As noted by Elbadawi and Majd (1996):[32]

Notwithstanding the increasing demand pressure for central bank refinancing of the commercial banks' meagre portfolios and the pressing need for monetary financing of the government deficit, the two central banks appear to have opted for their commitment to financial stability at the expense of their responsibilities as lenders of last resort.

In practice, the independence of Central Bank governors from political interference in the BEAC was constrained by the decision-making process and the effective power of the governor in setting and/or implementing policy. Key management positions at the BEAC, from the Governor to departmental heads, were allocated to country members and France. National considerations prevailed in the daily management of the bank and this undermined the bank's operation. The BEAC was only nominally independent; it operated as an agent of fiscal authorities with substantial refinancing of politically directed or government-inspired bank lending. The confusion of ownership and control responsibilities implied that the central banking aspects of the Indispensable Institutional Framework (IIF) were lacking in the BEAC. The CFA Accords also provided for prudent deficit financing, but the rigidity of the institutional framework established for monetary and banking arrangements gave policy-makers a false sense of security. These rules did not guarantee an IIF: the rigidities in fact induced an evolution of banking practice, which violated the IIF by subordinating both commercial and central banking to fiscal pressures.

Despite their superficially modern and competitive structure, then, the Franc zone in general, and the BEAC in particular, lacks flexibility (Honohan and Vittas 1996). For this reason, the Franc zone demonstrates

---

[32] The quotation refers to two central banks; the Francophone West African countries share the BCEAO, a similar arrangement to BEAC.

both the benefits and the costs of external restraint (Collier and Gunning 1999). The growth collapse of the post-1985 period, in particular, was in substantial part due to the rigidity of Cameroon's institutional setting for macroeconomic policy.

5. Conclusions

We have argued that the weak growth outcomes observed in Cameroon can be traced to contracting problems among the players in the economy. Inefficiency was primarily due to the fact that policy-makers represented only narrow interests, which were pursued in the name of a larger group. The centrifugal forces among the three main groups of the country prevented the formulation and implementation of policies that could have secured long-term economic growth.

Cameroon suffered from a variety of shocks, but its growth experience cannot be attributed to a single major negative shock or a sequence of smaller ones. The key problem was a weak capacity for policy formulation. The authorities failed to adequately appraise the nature of the shocks it faced and, therefore, chose inappropriate directions for policy. Cameroon's current performance is partly the legacy of these past policy failures (Blandford et al. 1994). Moreover, where policy appeared to diagnose and respond correctly, the deeper constraints to which it responded undermined economic performance. The authorities displayed considerable prudence, for example, in responding to the oil boom of the late 1970s: to avoid the "Dutch Disease," President Ahidjo and his successor kept most of the oil revenues in a special foreign account not directly included in public finance accounting. Our analysis suggests that the macroeconomic benefits of such prudence were overwhelmed by the opportunities it created for state patronage and the creation of a culture of rent-seeking and political coruption.

Finally, we have emphasized the role of macroeconomic instability in Cameroon's long-run growth performance. A pegged exchange rate regime is consistent with low exchange rate inflation, but Cameroon's experience suggests that this objective can produce major macroeconomic costs when the appropriate response to economic shocks requires a substantial RER depreciation.

Appendix: Data definitions and sources

In this appendix we describe our data sources and the key steps in the analysis of our data. The sources of the data are the Food and Agriculture Organization (FAO: see www.faostat.fao.org); the IMF's *International Financial Statistics* (IFS: CD ROM 2003), the World Bank's World Development

Indicators (WDI: CD ROM 2005); and the OPEC *Annual Statistical Bulletin* (see www.opec.org).

(1)   Cocoa, coffee, wood, banana, cotton, rubber, tea, tobacco, groundnut, and oil palm

Cocoa is exports of cocoa beans; Coffee is green coffee; Wood is forest products; Cotton is cotton lint; Rubber is natural dry rubber; Tobacco is tobacco leaves; and Oil palm is palm kernels. Data for these products are from the FAO in thousand US dollars.

(2)   Oil exports and price

Oil exports in thousand barrels per day are from OPEC.

(3)   GDP, Government expenditures, investment, exports, imports, and saving

GDP is the gross domestic product in US dollars (source: WDI). Government expenditures is general government final consumption expenditure. Investment is gross fixed capital formation. Consumption is the final consumption expenditure and exports and imports are, respectively, exports and imports of goods and services, all in US dollars. Savings is gross domestic savings as a percent of GDP. These variables are all from the World Bank's WDI.

(4)   Terms of trade

The terms of trade are defined as the ratio of implicit price deflator for exports to the implicit price deflator for imports, with deflators computed as ratios of current-price exports and imports to base-year-price imports and exports (*Source*: WDI).

(5)   Contributions of sectors to GDP

The contribution of sectors to GDP is manufacturing value added, services value added, industry value added, and agriculture value added as percents of GDP (*Source*: WDI).

(6)   Real deposit interest rate

The real deposit interest rate is the nominal deposit interest rate (*Source*: IFS) minus the inflation rate. The inflation rate is calculated using the consumption price index (*Source*: WDI).

(7) Land use

The data for total land area, agricultural area, permanent crops area, and forest and woodland area are taken from the FAO database. The data are in 1,000 ha.

(8) Population

The data for total population, agricultural population, non-agricultural population, rural population, and urban population are taken from the FAO database.

References

Allechi, M'bet and M. Niamkey (1994), "Evaluating the Net Gains from the CFA Franc Zone Membership: A Different Perspective," *World Development* 22: 1147–60

Amin, A. A. (2002), "An Examination of the Sources of Economic Growth in Cameroon," Research Paper 116 for the Explaining African Economic Growth Project. Nairobi: African Economic Research Consortium

Bandolo, H. (1986), *La flamme et la fumée.* Yaoundé: SOPECAM

Bayart, J. F. (1985), *L'état au Cameroun.* Paris: Presse de la Fondation Nationale des Sciences Politiques

Benjamin, N. C., S. Devarajan, and R. J. Weiner (1989), "The Dutch Disease in a Developing Country: Oil Reserves in Cameroon," *Journal of Development Economics* 30: 71–92

Blandford, D., D. Friedman, S. Lynch, N. Mukerjee, and D. E. Sahn (1994), "Oil Boom and Bust: The Harsh Realities of Adjustment in Cameroon," in D. E. Sahn, *Adjusting to Policy Failure in African Economies.* Ithaca, NY: Cornell University Press

Cashin, P. and C. Pattillo (2000), "Terms of Trade Shocks in Africa: Are They Short-Lived or Long-Lived?," IMF Working Paper WP/00/72

Castanheira, M. and H. S. Esfahani (2003), "Political Economy of Growth: Lessons Learned and Challenges Ahead," Global Development Network, mimeo

Chenery, H., S. Robinson, and M. Syrquin, eds. (1986), *Industrialization and Growth: A Comparative Study.* Oxford: Oxford University Press for the World Bank

Collectif Changer le Cameroun (1990), *Pourquoi pas? Livre blanc par un groupe d'intellectuels.* Yaoundé: ESF

Collier, P. and J. W. Gunning (1999a), "Explaining African Economic Performance," *Journal of Economic Literature* 37: 64–111

(1999b), "The Microeconomics of African Growth, 1950–2000," Framework paper for the Explaining African Economic Growth Project. Nairobi: African Economic Research Consortium

(2007), "Sacrificing the Future: Intertemporal Strategies and their Implications for Growth," chapter 5 in B. J. Ndulu, S. A. O'Connell, R. H. Bates, P. Collier, and C. C. Soludo, eds., *The Political Economy of Economic Growth in Africa, 1960–2000*, vol. 1. Cambridge: Cambridge University Press

eds. (1999), *Trade Shocks in Developing Countries, Volume 1: Africa.* New York: Oxford University Press

Collier, P. and S. A. O'Connell (2007), "Opportunities and Choices," chapter 2 in B. J. Ndulu, S. A. O'Connell, R. H. Bates, P. Collier, and C. C. Soludo, eds., *The Political Economy of Economic Growth in Africa, 1960–2000*, vol. 1. Cambridge: Cambridge University Press

Corden, W. M. (1984), "Booming Sector and Dutch Disease Economics: Survey and Consolidation," *Oxford Economic Papers* 36: 359–80

Corden, W. M. and J. P. Neary (1982), "Booming Sector and De-industrialization in Small Open Economy," *Economic Journal* 82: 825–48

Denison, E. (1967), *Why Growth Rates Differ.* Washington, DC: The Brookings Institution

Devarajan, S. (1999), "Cameroon," in P. Collier and J. W. Gunning, eds., *Trade Shocks in Developing Countries, Volume 1: Africa.* New York: Oxford University Press: 399–419

Devarajan, S. and J. de Melo (1987), "Evaluating Participation in Africa Monetary Unions: A Statistical Analysis of the CFA Zones," *World Development* 15: 483–96

Devarajan, S. and D. Rodrik (1992), "Do the Benefits of Fixed Exchange Rate Outweigh their Costs? The Franc Zone in Africa," World Bank Policy, Research, and External Affairs Working Paper 777, October

Douya, E. (1995), "Impact de la dévaluation sur la production agricole et la sécurité alimentaire au Cameroun," *Rapport de synthèse, FAO*: 1–56

(2001), "Accès aux marchés des produits pérennes camerounais: cas de la filière cacao," *Colloque International*, November 4–9: 1–21

Easterly, W., R. King, R. Levine and S. Rebelo (1991), "How do National Policies Affect Long-run Growth? A Research Agenda," World Bank Policy, Research, and External Affairs Working Papers 794, October

Elbadawi, I. and N. Madj (1996), "Adjustment and Economic Performances under a Fixed-exchange Rate Regime: A Comparative Analysis of the Franc Zone," *World Development* 24: 939–51

Fouda, S. M. (1997), "Cycles politico monétaires et indépendance de la banque centrale dans une union monétaire: une vérification empirique," *Revue d'Economie du Développement* 4: 121–43

Ghura, D. (1997), "Private Investment and Endogenous Growth: Evidence from Cameroon," IMF Working Paper WP/97/165

Gordon, R. J. (2001), "La technologie et les succès de l'économie américaine," in R. Solow, ed., *Institutions et Croissance.* Paris: Albin Michel Economie

Guillaumont, P., S. Guillaumont, and P. Plane (1988), "Participating in African Monetary Unions: An Alternative Evaluation," *World Development* 16: 569–76

Herbel D., E. Bamou, and H. F. Mkouonga (2002), *Elaboration et évaluation des politiques agricoles.* Yaoundé: Ministère de l'Agriculture, Division des Etudes et Projets

Honohan, P. and V. Vittas (1996), "Bank Regulation and the Network Paradigm: Policy Implications for Developing and Transition Economies," World Bank Policy Research Working Paper WPS 1631

Hugon, P. (1999), *La zone franc à l'heure de l'euro*. Paris: Karthala

IMPACT Tribune (1993), *La démocratie africaine, otage du tribalisme?* Yaoundé: Publication IMPACT

Katz, E. and J. Tokatlidu (1996), "Group Competition for Rents," *European Journal of Political Economy* 12: 599–607

Kobou, G. (1993), "Dysfonctionnement du marché du travail au Cameroun: quelles alternatives pour une politique de l'emploi?," Paper presented to the Colloquium on the Methodology of Creating Employment Policies, Ministère du Travail et de la Prévoyance Sociale, September 22–26: 1–27

(1999), "Ajustement structurel et exclusion sociale au Cameroun. une analyze fondée sur le marché du travail," in L. Sindjoun, ed., *La révolution passive au Cameroun: état, société et changement*. Série de livre du CODESRIA, December: 101–55

Kobou, G., S. M. Fouda, and D. Njinkeu (2003), *Explaining African Economic Growth: 1960–2000: The Cameroon Case Study*, Report submitted to AERC, Nairobi

Levine, R. and D. Renelt (1992), "A Sensitivity Analysis of Cross-country Growth Regression," *American Economic Review* 82: 942–63

Lindauer, D. L. and M. Roemer, eds. (1994), *Asia and Africa: Legacies and Opportunities in Development*. San Francisco, CA: Institute for Contemporary Studies

Mbaku, J. M. (1993), "Foreign Aid and Economic Growth in Cameroon," *Applied Economics* 25: 1309–14

Mbembe, Achille (1995), "Les projets socio-culturels des nouvelles démocraties Africaines," Colloquium IAD-UNESCO, October 4–6, Dakar, Sénégal

McGuire, M. and M. J. Olson (1996), "The Economics of Autocracy and Majority Rule: The Invisible Hand and the Use of Force," *Journal of Economic Literature* 34: 72–96

Médart, J. F. (1991), *Etats d'Afrique noire, formations, mécanismes et crise*. Paris: Karthala

Medhora, R. (1995), "The Allocation of Seigniorage in the Franc Zone: The BEAC and the BCEAO Regions Compared," *World Development* 23: 1781–93

Milner, C. (1990), "Identifying and Quantifying Anti-exports Bias: The Case of Cameroon," *Weltwirtschaftliches Archiv* 126: 321–40

Most, S. J. and H. Van Den Berg (1996), "Growth in Africa: Does the Sources of Investment Financing Matter?," *Applied Economics* 28: 1427–33

Mouiche, I. (1997), "L'ethnicité, l'état et la question nationale en Afrique," in D. Zognong and I. Mouiche, eds., *Démocratization et rivalités éthniques au Cameroun*. Yaoundé, CIREPE: 201–28

Moukoko Mbonjo, P. (1993), "Le retour au multipartisme au Cameroun," in G. Cognac, ed., *L'Afrique en transition vers le pluralisme politique*. Paris: Economica

Nitzan, S. (1991), "Collective Rent Dissipation," *Economic Journal* 101: 1522–34

(1994), "Modelling Rent-seeking Contests," *European Journal of Political Economy* 10: 41–60

O'Connell, S. A. and B. Ndulu (2000), "Background Information on Economic Growth," Paper prepared for the Explaining African Economic Growth Project. Nairobi: African Economic Research Consortium (downloadable: www.aercafrica.org)

Persson, T. and G. Tabellini (1990), *Macroeconomic Policy, Credibility and Politics.* Chur: Harwood Academic Publishers

Renelt, D. (1991), "Economic Growth: A Review of the Theoretical and Empirical Literature," World Bank Working Papers WPS 678

Savvides, A. (1998), "Inflation and Monetary Policy in Selected West and Central African Countries," *World Development* 26: 809–27

Sindjoun, L. (2002), *L'état ailleurs: entre noyau dur et cas vide.* Paris: Economica

Solow, R. (1956), "Une contribution à la croissance économique," reprinted in G. Abraham-Frois, ed., *Problématiques de la croissance.* Paris: Economica, 1974
    (1957), "Technical Change and the Aggregate Production Function," *Review of Economics and Statistics* 39: 65–94

Stasavage, D. (1996), "La zone franc et l'équilibre budgétaire," *Revue d'Economie du Développement* 4: 145–79

Tchamanbe L. (2001), *Crise et faillites bancaires en Afrique Subsaharienne: le cas du Cameroun.* Doctoral thesis, Université de Yaoundé II

Tybout, J., B. Gauthier, G. B. Navaretti, and J. de Melo (1996), "Réponse des entreprises Camerounaises à la dévaluation du franc CFA," *Revue d'Economie du Développement* 4: 5–39

World Bank (1986), "Cameroun: étude du secteur financier," Rapport 6028-CM
    (1989), "Cameroun: rapport sur le secteur de l'agriculture," I: 7486-CM

Wunder, S. (2005), "Macroeconomics Change, Competitiveness and Timber Production: A Five-Country Comparison," *World Development* 33: 65–86

Wunder, S. and W. D. Sunderlin (2004), "Oil, Macroeconomics, and Forests: Assessing the Linkages," *World Bank Research Observer* 19: 231–57

Yates, D. A. (1996), *The Rentier State in Africa: Oil Rent Dependency and Neo-colonialism in the Republic of Gabon.* Asmare: Africa World Press, Inc.

17 | Explaining economic growth in Africa: the case of Guinea

Sékou F. Doumbouya and Fodé Camara

1. Introduction

Guinea is a coastal country in West Africa, situated to the south of Senegal, to the north of Sierra Leone, and to the west of Côte d'Ivoire. Its total surface area is 250,000 km² and its population is around 7.2 million (1996). With an

Groupe de Recherche et d'Analysé de la Pauvreté et des Politiques Economiques en Guinée.

average *per capita* income of $540 (1998), Guinea belongs to the low-income group of countries. On the UNDP's Human Development Index (HDI), it ranks 162nd of 174 countries in the world (République de Guinée 2001); 40 percent of Guinea's population is reckoned to live below the poverty line ($300 per year).

Given its massive natural potential in terms of agriculture, mineral deposits, and hydroelectric power, the case of Guinea repays close study. The country is the world's leading exporter of bauxite, being responsible for 40 percent of the quantity traded world-wide. Guinea also possesses substantial unexploited reserves of other minerals, including iron and diamonds. In addition, valuable lessons can be learned from the quarter-century of socialist experimentation applied in the wake of Guinea's abrupt rupture with France, and from the subsequent process of economic liberalization, a process that remained, fifteen years after its inception in 1985, far from complete.

By global standards, Guinea's economic performance since independence (1958) has been mediocre at best. With an annual growth rate of PPP-adjusted real GDP *per capita* of just 1.3 percent, one would have to wait another fifty-three years to see average income double. Weak though it may be, this level of performance is superior to that of the majority of African countries: a study conducted by the IMF classed Guinea among the nine African economies whose growth was fastest over the 1965–95 period (IMF 1999).

Our aim in this chapter is, on the one hand, to analyze the growth opportunities and constraints that confronted Guinea over time and, on the other, to account for the country's successes and failures in grasping such opportunities. Section 2 begins with the main economic and political developments prior to independence. Section 3 then divides the post-independence period into a sequence of distinct policy regimes, providing a periodization that will structure the remainder of our analysis. Section 4 analyzes the stylized facts of aggregate growth in Guinea, using growth accounting to highlight the roles of factor accumulation and productivity growth, and global regression models to track the main determinants of growth over time. Our analysis then turns to the sectoral and microeconomic levels to document, in sections 5 and 6, the evolving policy environment and the responses of key economic agents. Finally, in section 7 we turn to political economy considerations to explain the economic policy choices. Section 8 draws some conclusions.

2. Changes during the years before independence

Before independence, Guinea's institutions and economic trajectories were heavily influenced both by colonization and by the basic features of the country. During the colonial period Guinea was subsumed into French

West Africa (Afrique Occidentale Française, or AOF), a larger political entity which was created in 1895 and received its definitive organization in 1905. The capital of French West Africa was in Dakar, where the Governor-General resided.

The setting-up of a colonial authority did not fundamentally alter traditional economic and social structures in Guinea, which were based upon subsistence farming. The country's colonial status did have an impact, however, on the sectors integrated into the global economy. The latter passed through several distinct cycles (Goerg 1986). In an initial phase, the colonial authority attempted to suppress the slave trade, finally banning it by a decree of December 1905. While this trade never completely disappeared from French West Africa, it declined in economic importance as liana rubber replaced slaves as the main export: by 1909, rubber accounted for two-thirds of the value of the country's exports.

The high demand for rubber was linked to the advent of the bicycle and the motor car, but competition from plantations in the Far East led to a fall in the value of the Guinean product, to which plantation rubber – being higher quality and cheaper to process – was preferred. The steep drop in prices led to a slump in rubber exports in 1913, and to their definitive disappearance in Guinea by 1945.

The third major economic cycle involved the great banana plantations. The rise of this new form of production occurred during the crisis of the 1930s, owing to the colonizers' tastes and to changes in modes of transportation, and it represented the introduction of a modern sector into the colony's economy. European colonial society had almost exclusive control of the larger plantations, with native cultivation accounting for no more than a tenth of total production. The modern sector also extended to the mining industry, where it registered its most spectacular development. Gold and diamonds came first, followed by bauxite (1952) and iron (1953). At formal decolonization in 1958, a number of major mining projects were already under way (among them the Boké bauxite deposits).

Several factors favored decolonization, most of them involving circumstances beyond Guinea's control. The latter included the *loi-cadre*[1] of June 1956, which granted semi-autonomous status to the overseas territories of France, and the return to power in May of 1958 of General de Gaulle, who favored a rapid transition to political independence in France's Sub-Saharan territories, within a framework that would guarantee continued close integration with – and control by – France. In 1957, with the enactment of the

---

[1] Fearing that the waves of unrest affecting countries colonized by France, such as Indochina (Dien Bien Phu in 1954) or Algeria (the start of the Algerian War of Independence) might spread, the Minister of Overseas France, Gaston Deferre, introduced a draft law granting semi-autonomous status to the overseas territories, until such a time as the Constitution could be reformed.

loi-cadre, the Parti Démocratique de Guinée (PDG) was officially granted a share in the running of local affairs. Sékou Touré, Secretary-General of the PDG and leading light of the Groupement d'Etudes Communistes (GEC) in Conakry, became Vice President of the Government Council. Between 1957 and 1958, the PDG proceeded to launch a number of institutional reforms, including the abolition of the customary chiefdoms, an increase in the minimum wage, a reduction in personal taxes, the freedom to sell or to trade in rice, and the granting to Africans of the legal right to mine diamonds. Touré won a number of political victories. In the referendum of September 28, 1958, over 95 percent of the Guinean electorate chose the complete independence advocated by the PDG, over the draft constitution that was backed by de Gaulle and entailed the creation of the Communauté française.[2]

3. Policy episodes since independence

The most striking feature of economic governance in Guinea in the period since independence has been the oscillation of the state between dramatically different levels of control over markets. Between 1958 and 1963, state regulation of the economy was "soft," in the terminology of Collier and O'Connell (2007). The period from 1964 to 1977 was one of "hard" controls, in which the state attempted to replace the market with state planning. 1978–84 saw a modest retreat from state interventionism, with a perceptible degree of tolerance of the market. Since 1984, the lifting of controls on markets has been more or less effective, producing a "syndrome-free" period through 2000 (see table17.1).

At the time of Guinea's independence, communist and socialist development strategies were in fashion. After a period, extending from 1958 to 1964, during which market institutions inherited from colonial times continued to exist, with the state exerting a loose form of control, Guinea adopted a socialist strategy from 1964 to 1984. However, Guinea's mineral resources, notably bauxite, influenced the general direction of economic policy during the period 1973–84. The opening-up of the bauxite deposits of Boké (CBG) and Kindia (OBK) in 1973–74 earned the state temporary export revenues of some importance between 1973 and 1977, and the economic growth recorded during this brief phase was never again equaled in the post-independence history of the country (6.98 percent annual growth in real GDP *per capita*). In an example of the "unsustainable spending" syndrome analyzed by Collier and Gunning (2007), the state treated temporary bauxite revenues as permanent, using them for public consumption rather than

---

[2] This draft Constitution, backed by General de Gaulle, envisaged the setting up of independent African republics, under France's control but with the right to associate with each other.

Table 17.1 *Guinea's growth episodes, growth rates of GDP per capita, 1960–1997*

Growth episode	Trend growth rate per year (%)	Average growth rate (%) per year	Std dev.	Coefficient of variation	No. of negative growth years (total # years)
1960–72	−0.98	−0.64	(8.70)	13.54	7 (12)
1973–7	7.25	6.98	(3.86)	0.55	0 (5)
1978–84	−1.29	−1.01	(5.01)	4.97	4 (7)
1985–97	1.05	1.47	(2.30)	1.52	3 (13)
1960–97	1.29	1.29	(6.05)	4.70	14 (37)

Source: Authors' calculation. The tendential growth rates are based on regressions of the form $\ln y = a + bt$, where y is *per capita* income in constant 1985 dollars at international prices and t is a time trend. Data are unavailable for the first two years after independence (1958–60).

investment. Booming revenues were spent on public sector salaries and employment guarantees for all secondary school graduates, and on the subsidizing of consumption including the direct supply of consumer goods to the urban population. Mining revenues began to fall in 1978, following a drop in the price of aluminum and operational problems within OBK and, due in part to the second oil crisis, the country experienced negative economic growth (at −1.01 percent per annum) between 1978 and 1984. With Guinea being buffeted by outside forces, the opening up to the West preached by political leaders and the free trade championed by private companies was in part realized. The first structural adjustment measures backed by the IMF and the World Bank date from 1982.

The First Republic collapsed in 1984, a week after the death of Guinea's Sékou Touré. Since 1985, economic policy choices have departed systematically from the previous socialist framework and have been designed to guarantee the free functioning of markets. From 1984 to 1992 there was a transitional military regime, and the move towards the democratic process began in 1992–3. The average rate of *per capita* growth observed between 1985 and 2000 was 1.47 percent per year.

4. The determinants of Guinean growth: a macroeconomic approach

Over the full 1958–2000 period, the average rate of growth of the real per capita GDP (at 1985 international prices) was 1.29 percent per year.[3] At

---

[3] Rate calculated by the authors on the basis of the data to be found in Penn World Tables (Summers and Heston 1991).

Table 17.2 *Guinea, growth accounting, 1960–1990, percentage points per year*

| | | Contribution of | | |
Period	Average growth of GDP per worker (1)	Physical capital accumulation per worker (2)	Increased education per worker (3)	TFP growth (4)
1960–5	−0.17	0.72	−0.89	
1965–70	−2.90	0.57	−3.47	
1970–5	7.96	1.43	0.03	6.50
1975–80	3.69	0.16	0.06	3.47
1980–5	2.10	1.29	0.06	0.76
1985–90	0.14	−0.99	0.07	1.06
1970–1990	3.47	0.47	0.05	2.95

Source: Authors' calculation on the basis of data from Easterly and Sewadeh (2002).
Notes: The contribution of physical capital per worker is given by its rate of growth multiplied by the marginal productivity of capital (0.35). The contribution of education per worker is given by the growth of the index of quality of labor, multiplied by the marginal productivity of labor (0.65). The growth of the index of human capital is measured by the growth of the average number of years of schooling of the working population, u, multiplied by 0.07. We assume, as in Collins and Bosworth (1996) that each year of schooling implies a salary increment of 7%. TFP growth is given by the difference between column (1) and the sum of columns (2) and (3). For the 1960s, the increase in education per worker is unavailable, so we show the sum of this component and the growth in TFP, given by the difference between GDP growth per worker and the contribution of physical capital accumulation (column (4)).

this pace, one would have to wait, as we have seen, for over fifty years to see average Guinean income double. By comparison, the doubling time for income among the high-performing Asian economies – growing at over 5 percent *per capita* for the last three–four decades – has been barely above a decade. Weak economic growth has important implications for employment growth and poverty reduction. Opinions vary as to the underlying causes of this low rate of growth and the policies best suited to improving it. We shall survey here a number of different approaches to Guinea's aggregate growth performance.

A simple growth-accounting exercise applied to Guinean data (cf. table 17.2) suggests that the behavior of total factor productivity (TFP) holds the key to Guinean growth outcomes. According to this model, a marked fall in TFP largely explains the negative growth recorded for 1960–72,[4]

---

[4] Because we do not have data on educational attainments during the 1960s, the contribution of human capital accumulation cannot be calculated for that period.

while a combination of physical capital accumulation and productivity growth accounts for the strong growth recorded during the 1970s, and particularly between 1973 and 1978. A deeper understanding of Guinean growth will therefore require particular attention to the determinants of TFP growth.

Hoeffler's (2002) growth model, which permits an historical, international, and cross-country analysis, shows that the relative weakness of Guinean growth in the long term was mainly due to the low levels of capital accumulation, and to a lesser extent to the weakness of human capital and to the pressure exerted by population growth. Our analysis of Hoeffler's panel of eighty-five countries (table 17.3) shows that *per capita* growth in Guinea was 0.84 points per year lower than that of the average in the panel over the period 1960–97, and that this long-run discrepancy is attributable to the relative preponderance of determinants that are weaker on average in Guinea than in the full sample (4.35 points due to relatively low investment; 0.34 points due to low educational attainment; and 0.10 points due to fast population growth), over determinants that boost predicted growth in Guinea relative to the sample (in particular, 4.04 points due to low initial income). Over the full sample, Guinea's average residual is close to zero, but this masks very large fluctuations from one five-year period to the next. Given the high variance attributed to unexplained factors, the Hoeffler model is of limited relevance for explaining turning points in Guinea's growth.

The Ndulu–O'Connell model (Ndulu and O'Connell 2000; O'Connell and Ndulu 2000) provides us with another diagnostic tool for analyzing Guinean growth, and one that focuses more squarely on economic policy. As was the case with the Hoeffler model, our analysis follows a cross-country and historical perspective. Taking the high-performing countries of East Asia as a reference point, our analysis suggests that Guinea, when compared with the latter, benefited from a "catch-up effect" because its initial income was much lower. Since this income discrepancy in relation to Asia increased over time, the potential for accelerating growth in Guinea likewise increased, going from 0.92 percent in 1960–4 to 2.89 percent in 1990–7. As with the Hoeffler model, however, the Ndulu–O'Connell (2000) model displays conditional convergence rather than absolute convergence. The advantages due to low income can therefore readily be offset by other factors that reduce growth by lowering steady-state income or reducing the rate of technological progress. Among these, we observe the conjunction of several adverse factors.

Table 17.2 therefore shows the only the sum of the contribution of human capital accumulation and TFP growth for the 1960s. This figure is dominated by TFP growth, because increases in human capital per worker can be accumulated only slowly over time as workers with higher educational attainments reach working age.

Table 17.3 *Guinea, fits and residuals from Hoeffler's SYS–GMM estimation of the augmented Solow model, 1960–1997*

| Period | Observed growth | Predicted growth | Residual | Actual deviation of growth from sample mean | Estimated contribution of | | | | | |
					Initial income	Investment rate	Initial educational attainment	Replacement investment term	Time dummies	Residual
1960–4	−0.51	–		−2.44	4.44	−4.00	–	−0.13	0.60	–
1965–9	−3.09	–		−5.02	4.52	−3.35	–	−0.34	0.63	–
1970–4	7.69	4.15	3.54	5.76	4.99	−3.25	−0.35	0.92	−0.06	3.52
1975–9	3.50	1.81	1.69	1.56	3.82	−4.60	−0.35	0.76	0.26	1.67
1980–4	−2.75	−2.00	−0.75	−4.69	3.29	−5.24	−0.33	−0.19	−1.44	−0.77
1985–9	1.49	−0.95	2.44	−0.45	3.71	−5.24	−0.32	−0.97	0.10	2.42
1990–7	1.35	0.16	1.19	−0.58	3.49	−4.79	−0.30	−0.74	0.60	1.77
Total	**1.10**	**1.24**	**−0.14**	**−0.84**	**4.04**	**−4.35**	**−0.34**	**−0.10**	**0.10**	**−0.16**

Source: Ndulu and O'Connell (2000: 44, appendix B) and authors' calculation.

First, the accumulation of human capital, measured in terms of life expectancy at birth, yielded growth dividends in East Asian countries on the order of 1.74–2.13 percent (depending upon the period in question) *vis-à-vis* Guinea. This variable's contribution to growth increased over time to the advantage of East Asia.

Second, East Asia benefited from a demographic transition that has not yet occurred in Guinea. The dependency ratio – the ratio of non-working-age to working-age population – in East Asia went from 90.2 in 1960–4 to 56.2 in 1990–7, whereas in Guinea during these same years the dependency ratio went from 88.2 to 96.1 percent. A low dependency ratio boosts economic growth through the increase in participation in the labor market and in saving. In 1990–7, the difference in dependency ratios accounted for 2 percentage points of predicted growth differential between East Asia and Guinea.

Finally, the economic policy climate, as measured by a set of macroecomic policy variables, brought dividends to East Asia as against Guinea over the full period. During the 1990s, however, Guinean values for the key variables – the Ndulu–O'Connell (2000) model features the inflation rate, the black market premium, and the ratio of unproductive government spending to GDP – displayed a tendency to converge towards those of the the East Asian economies.

5. Determinants linked to market institutions

In this section we examine the determinants of capital accumulation and productivity growth from a qualitative perspective, through an analysis of government interventions in key markets. It is important to note that the years from 1964 to 1977 represented a period in which the state attempted to replace the market as a mechanism for resource allocation, and that it continued to intervene forcefully during from 1978 to 1984. The state also played an important role in fixing the prices of numerous goods and services, whether imported or produced locally. We focus in turn on two key markets: the market for agricultural products and the labor market.

5.1 The market for agricultural products

We consider here the nature of the incentives offered to producers during the periods before and after 1984.

5.1.1 Incentives under the First Republic

State marketing was practiced under the First Republic (1958–84) and took place in a context in which the surrender of commodities was compulsory.

In the mid-1970s the government had introduced a system of compulsory deliveries, or *livraisons obligatoires*, whereby each farmer had no choice but to market a part of his agricultural production in state shops. These official marketing quotas were set by a national commission and applied to the crop grown most widely in each zone of production.[5]

The prices of many agricultural products were also set administratively by the government, initially with a view to encouraging production. But nominal producer prices were kept largely stable, against a background of monetary expansion and inflationary pressure. According to the World Bank, official purchase prices for coffee producers rose just once over the period 1975–82, while the average annual rise in palm kernel prices was only 6 percent (World Bank 1984).

Official producer prices were adjusted more aggressively after the tentative liberalization of 1981, rising by 19 percent per year for rice, 21 percent per year for palm oil and Robusta coffee, and 33 percent for groundnuts between 1982 and 1985. But these increases proved inadequate to revitalise the state network. Indeed, the 54 percent depreciation per year in the exchange rates for Guinean currency (the syli) on the parallel exchange market between 1982 and 1985 shows that in real terms producers faced a declining incentive to produce for the state network.[6]

This picture is reinforced by the data collected by Arulpragasam and Sahn (1997) on production costs (table 17.4). In 1981–2, these authors reckon, the production costs for rice grown using the traditional (manual) technology were approximately three times the official price paid to producers by the state. The cost of improved manual technology was more than twice the producer price.

Exchange rate misalignment undermined production incentives during the First Republic, through a mechanism of indirect taxation. Arulpragasam and Sahn (1997) underscore this point by calculating the crop-by-crop nominal protection coefficients (NPC), defined as the ratio of the official producer price to what producers could have received, net of transportation and marketing costs, if they had sold their crop at the world price. When world prices are converted at the official exchange rate, the impression is one of substantial protection: for the period from 1975–85, the average NPC exceeded 2 for rice and equaled 1.99 for groundnuts, 1.76 for palm kernels, and 1.24 for Robusta coffee (table 17.5). But this impression disappears when sales to the world market are converted at the parallel exchange rate.

[5] At the beginning of the 1980s, a reform abolished the official marketing quotas for products save for those associated with stockbreeding.

[6] The syli was the currency of Guinea during most of the control period. It replaced the Guinean franc (FG) at a rate of 10 FG per syli in 1971. The FG was then restored in 1985, at a 1:1 exchange rate with the syli.

Table 17.4 *Guinea, estimated costs of production, by crop and production method, compared with official and parallel market prices, 1981–1982, syli per kg*

Crop	Traditional (manual)	Production cost — Improved labor Manual	Animal traction	Motorized	Price — Official Producer	Official Market	Parallel Market
Rice	—	—	—	—	9.0	20.0	40–70
Mangrove	28.7	—	—	—	—	—	—
Upland	30.2	21.2	—	—	—	—	—
Inland swamp	29.4	22.6	—	—	—	—	—
Flooded rice							
Uncontrolled	—	—	23.7	25.2	—	—	—
Controlled	—	—	14.8	—	—	—	—
Maize	26.6	17.3	11.3	11.9	10.0	—	—
Groundnuts	31.0	19.1	12.8	—	7.5	18.0	50–110
Tobacco	—	43.1	—	—	44.0	—	—
Coffee	62.1	58.3	—	—	45.0	—	240–280
Cocoa	75.7	46.1	—	—	—	—	—
Cotton	—	25.1	16.8	16.8	20.0	—	—
Pineapples							
Industrial	—	8.7	—	—	9.0	—	—
Village	—	8.4	—	—	9.0	—	15
Palm oil	—	—	—	—	28.0	—	—
Cassava	—	—	—	—	5.0	—	—

Source: Drawn from Arulpragasam and Sahn (1997).

The average NPC for coffee fell to roughly a third; the NPCs for groundnuts and palm kernels fell to 0.5 and 0.6. While nominal producer prices began to be adjusted starting in 1982, we saw above that the rate of adjustment was inadequate. By 1984, Sékou Touré's last year in power, the NPCs at the parallel exchange rate had fallen to 0.12 for coffee, 0.22 for groundnuts, and 0.11 for palm kernels.

The NPC figures at the parallel exchange rate give a better indication of the nature of the incentives induced by producer prices, in at least two important senses. First, given the excess demand for foreign exchange at the official exchange rate, the exchange rate in the parallel market provides a better indicator than the official rate of what the equilibrium exchange rate would have been in a unified official foreign exchange market. The world price converted at the parallel exchange rate, minus transport and marketing costs per unit, therefore provides a reasonably good indication of the value added price producers would have faced in the absence of exchange controls and administrative pricing. Second, the large and growing gap between the

Table 17.5 *Guinea, nominal protection coefficients (NPCs), 1975–1992*

	At the official exchange rate					At the parallel exchange rate				
Year	Rice	Robusta coffee	Arabica coffee	Groundnut	Palm kernels	Rice	Robusta coffee	Arabica coffee	Groundnut	Palm kernels
1975	1.77	–	–	1.15	2.69	0.63	–	–	0.41	0.96
1976	2.12	–	–	1.32	2.18	0.71	–	–	0.44	0.73
1977	2.68	0.77	0.62	1.15	1.48	0.90	0.26	0.21	0.39	0.50
1978	2.14	0.67	0.54	1.12	1.32	1.43	0.45	0.36	0.75	0.89
1979	1.96	1.06	0.97	1.27	0.95	1.31	0.71	0.65	0.85	0.64
1980	1.65	0.88	0.74	1.57	1.54	0.81	0.43	0.36	0.77	0.75
1981	1.47	1.10	1.26	1.21	1.75	0.41	0.31	0.35	0.34	0.49
1982	1.75	1.72	1.31	2.08	2.48	0.36	0.36	0.27	0.43	0.52
1983	3.59	1.49	2.14	2.97	1.63	0.57	0.24	0.34	0.48	0.26
1984	3.86	1.65	1.64	2.99	1.57	0.28	0.12	0.12	0.22	0.11
1985	5.03	1.86	1.85	5.02	–	0.33	0.12	0.12	0.33	–
1986	1.04	0.58	0.36	–	–	0.96	0.53	0.33	–	–
1987	1.09	0.46	0.86	–	1.00	1.05	0.44	0.83	–	0.97
1988	0.80	0.77	0.61	–	–	0.73	0.70	0.55	–	–
1989	0.57	0.42	–	–	–	0.52	0.39	–	–	–
1990	0.62	0.52	–	–	–	0.58	0.49	–	–	–
1991	–	0.58	–	–	–	–	0.55	–	–	–
1992	0.98	–	–	–	0.96	0.90	–	–	–	0.88

Source: Drawn from Arulpragasam and Sahn (1997).

parallel and official exchange rate provides a strong indicator of the incentive to smuggle export crops rather than sell them through official channels.

5.1.2 The reform of agricultural markets (1985–)

With the death of President Sékou Touré in 1984, the center of gravity of political power shifted. The context of agricultural crisis and the new military rulers' quest for legitimacy provided a strong motive for a change in incentives. Policy reforms began in 1984 and continued within the formal framework of the SAPs adopted after 1986. The aim was to have market mechanisms play a larger role in the functioning of the economy.

As Arulpragasam and Sahn (1997) emphasize, several policy measures associated with the new incentives were implemented in advance of the programs supported by Guinea's multilateral and bilateral donors (World Bank, USAID, etc.). To begin with, in 1984 the government abolished the state farms and liberalized marketing by repealing measures requiring the compulsory delivery of agricultural products to the state and lifting restrictions on the internal circulation of goods. In 1985, the government deregulated producer prices. Since 1986, with the lifting of the monopoly exercised by public enterprises, private traders have participated at every level of domestic and foreign trade. For example, in 1985, several public enterprises lost their monopoly status, among them SEMAPE and AGRIMA, which had been responsible for the marketing of fertilizers and of agricultural implements, respectively. Entry barriers were also lifted in the traditional market of public enterprises such as FRUITEX and PROSECO, which had been responsible for exporting fruit and coffee, respectively.[7]

Prices for all consumer goods were liberalized in 1986, with the exception of petroleum products and rice imported as food aid; the rationing system for goods sold at official prices was abolished in 1985. All imported goods, including non-rice food aid, were assessed at market prices with a minimum of 10 percent for customs duties.

These reforms in the system of prices, in marketing, and in the institutional framework were accompanied by a liberalization, in 1986, of the exchange rate and trade regime. In 1988, taxes on the turnover of imported and domestic products were harmonized at 10 percent. These taxes were replaced by VAT at a rate of 18 percent in 1996. The tax on exported products, which stood initially at 2 percent, was scrapped in 1991. These reforms had a profound impact upon the volume of trade, particularly that of imported rice. In 1991, the government endorsed a Policy Letter on agricultural development (or *Lettre de politique de développement agricole*, LPDA), a document serving as a point of reference for any interventions in this sector.[8]

Bearing in mind Guinea's earlier history of state interventionism and of discrimination against the agricultural sector, one can well understand why these reforms represented a profound change to the institutional framework of the country.

5.2   The labor market

A defining feature of the working population in Guinea is its low level of education. Based on survey data from the Planning Ministry, 85 percent of the employed workforce had no formal education at all in 1994–5, 7.3 percent had had a primary education, 4.5 percent had had a secondary education, 1.4 percent had benefited from professional training, and 1.1 percent had received a higher education.[9] These figures confirm the view

---

[7] SEMAPE is the Entreprise Nationale de Semence des Produits Agricoles et d'Engrais, AGRIMA is the Entreprise Nationale d'Importation de Materiels Agricoles, FRUITEX is the Entreprise Nationale de Fruits d'Exportations, and PROSECO is the Entreprise Nationale de Commercialization de Produits Secs et Oléagineux.

[8] A document presenting a balance-sheet for the LPDA, denoted LPDA2, was endorsed in 1998. LPDA2 was meant to reinforce the role of agriculture in the Guinean economy.

[9] Ministère du Plan et de la Coopération (1996).

that investment in human capital has been particularly low in Guinea, and it is reasonable to suppose that the low educational attainment of the working population has had a negative effect on growth.

The same data source reports the distribution of work activity by occupational status. Wage earners accounted for only 4.5 percent of the surveyed working-age population, and employers accounted for only 0.3 percent. The vast bulk of activity was accounted for by self-employed individuals and "*aides familiaux*" (subsistence workers not receiving wages), at 38.5 and 52.6 percent, respectively; a final 4 percent were apprentices/trainees. The context is therefore one of very limited wage labor. Of the 4.5 percent receiving wages, moreover, only 29.6 percent had signed a contract with their employers. The distribution of wage employment across sectors reveals a heavy preponderance of public employment: 48.2 percent in the private sector, 37 percent in the public sector, 12 percent in the parastatal sector, and 2.7 percent not accounted for.

The policy framework for the labor market differed considerably between the First and Second Republics. The predominance of the public sector in wage employment was a legacy of Guinea's long socialist experiment; as we have emphasized, the First Republic set up a state apparatus which controlled every aspect of economic and political life, including in the villages, during the twenty-six years following independence. The state sought to eliminate all activity in the formal private sector and to become the source of employment for virtually the entire formal sector. The state's guarantee that it would employ all graduates caused the public sector workforce to grow at the rate of 7 percent during the 1970s, a period in which the government continued to allocate a high proportion of its resources to extending the sector. This was particularly true at the beginning of the 1980s, when the government financed large deficits in the balance of payments by drawing upon its foreign exchange reserves and by accumulating large arrears in payments.

During the 1960s and 1970s, serious administrative inefficiencies restricted the public sector's capacity to provide essential goods and services which, before independence, had been supplied by the private sector. As a consequence a wide range of parallel markets emerged, bringing relief to the majority of citizens who had no access to the state's distribution channels for goods and services. At the same time, the institutional inefficiencies occasioned by the rapid growth in the public sector led to a deterioration in the legal and educational systems. The formation of human capital was retarded and the perceived legitimacy of public sector institutions and of the civil service was diminished.

A deterioration in the conditions governing public sector employment during the First Republic led to rent-seeking, with the attendant corruption of public officials. Nominal salaries were frozen between 1965 and 1980, so that by 1985 the average monthly wage of a Guinean civil servant was FG 5,500, or only $US 18 at the black market exchange rate. In place of a regular salary, civil servants were entitled to a number of in-kind transfers – more particularly, access to ration shops, which sold goods at a much lower price than applied on the parallel market. Nonetheless, public sector workers had to create new sources of income in order to survive. Given the lack of any obligation to account for what they did, and the potentially adverse consequences of deviating from prevailing practice, civil servants were reluctant to do more than the bare minimum. Instead, they opted for rent-seeking behavior and used the public resources at their disposal.

To summarize, at the end of the First Republic, fiscal deficits associated with supporting the largely imported consumption of the urban-based civil service were a driving force behind balance of payments deficits. Public employees caused losses to the economy through their rent-seeking behavior and boosted private sector transaction costs by imposing opportunist regulations on market activities. Institutional constraints on the functioning of the labor market in the huge public sector were therefore among the main obstacles to economic growth in Guinea.

A military faction founded the Second Republic after seizing power through a coup a week after Sékou Touré's death in April 1984. In 1986, the new ruling faction embarked upon a wide-ranging series of liberal reforms. The new economic and political philosophy took the form of a reduction in the public sector work force. Various mechanisms were used: a campaign promoting early retirement, voluntary redundancies and special leaves of absence; liquidation and restructuring of parastatal enterprises and of banks whose employees were also civil servants; the suppression of automatic hiring; and a freeze on the recruitment of young graduates. Out of a total of 104,000 civil servants, including military personnel, recorded at the end of 1985, only 71,000 remained in place at the end of 1989 (World Bank 1990).

Public sector retrenchment created slack in labor markets and by the mid-1990s the probability of being unemployed in Guinea increased with one's level of education: 1.3 percent for individuals without any education, 19.9 percent for individuals with a secondary, technical, or professional education, and 16.7 percent for university graduates (data for 1995; Ministère du Plan et de la Coopération 1996). During the 1990s the authorities reacted to the unemployment problem with a variety of employment-promotion programs, among them the Programme d'Aide à l'Emploi (PAE), the Programme de Création de Micro-Entreprises (PCME), the Programme Spécial de Création d'Emploi (PSCE), and the Programme Spécial d'Insertion des Femmes (PSIF).

Table 17.6 *Guinea, official marketing of agricultural products,*
1974–1980, 000 tonnes

Production	1974/5	1977	1980	As percentage of production in 1980
Rice (paddy)	28.3	32.5	7.5	1.8
Rice (net)	–	20.6	8.8	3.6
Fonio (paddy)	–	5.5	0.9	1.1
Fonio (net)	2.8	7.3	2.7	5.5
Maize	8.3	8.1	5.9	7.9
Millet	4.9	3.9	1.9	–
Dry manioc	0.7	–	1.9	0.7
Groundnuts in shells	–	4.8	0.7	0.8
Groundnut oilcake	–	0.4	0.0	0.0
Palm kernels	–	13.2	13.7	–
Coffee	–	2.2	3.5	22.6
Bananas	0.6	0.1	0.0	0.0
Pineapples	6.5	2.4	1.3	–
Mangoes	1.3	1.5	1.0	–

6. Determinants linked to the behavior of economic agents

The lack of any sustained dynamic in capital accumulation and the stagnation and outright decline of TFP are also due to the responses of economic
agents to the negative incentives mentioned above, and to structural constraints on the supply and productivity of key factors of production. We
begin with the responses of firms and households to economic controls,
before turning briefly to the characteristics of agricultural enterprises and
to some of the structural constraints on factor accumulation and productivity in Guinea.

6.1 Avoidance of state marketing channels

Given the weakness of official producer prices in relation to production
costs, private cultivators began to bypass marketing channels in the state
network during the socialist period (table 17.6). Between 1977 and 1980,
purchases of agricultural produce by state marketing institutions fell by
46 percent for pineapples, 57 percent for rice, 63 percent for fonio (a leading
cereal crop), and 85 percent for shelled groundnuts. As a consequence, only
1.8 percent of the rice grown in Guinea was sold on the state network in
1980. The corresponding percentages for fonio and groundnuts were 5.5
and 0.8 percent, respectively.

6.2   Pressure on foreign exchange reserves

Due to the limited quantity of foodstuffs supplied to the state network by cultivators, the government began to import large amounts of foodstuffs in the 1970s to satisfy domestic demand, particularly in urban areas. Between 1974 and 1977, the volume of cereal imports climbed sharply, reaching 62,000 mt per year, a figure that subsequently continued to increase.

Guinea's increasing dependence on imported foodstuffs became a political preoccupation during the control period. In 1984, 80,000 tons of rice were imported; the figure in 1974 had been 30,000. As a percentage of domestic production, rice imports more than doubled between 1973–5 and 1983–5, rising from 13.4 percent to 27 percent. The share of food aid in total imports rose very sharply over the same period, from around 4.5 percent in 1973–5 to around 41 percent in 1983–5.

The tendency of agricultural producers to stop selling on the official markets (the state network) led to a two-fold loss in foreign exchange reserves – first through increased dependence on imported foodstuffs and second through declines in cash crop exports. Between 1966–70 and 1980–5, the officially recorded exports of the traditional export crops underwent a catastrophic decline: 58 percent for palm kernels, 92 percent in the case of pineapples, and a complete collapse for bananas. The ensuing loss of currency was in part to blame for a further over-valuation of the syli, which served to curb incentives for export-oriented production still further.

It is worth noting that the lowering of import restrictions after 1985, during the period of market liberalization, probably played a part in increasing Guinea's dependence on imported rice.

6.3   Development of barter in rural areas

The development of barter in rural Guinea under the First Republic has been described in an anecdotal fashion by Wilhelm (1988). Through barter, the peasants avoided the loss of income caused by the policy of low producer prices imposed by the government. Wilhelm describes the triangular trade as follows: "salt was purchased in Lower Guinea and exchanged for cola and palm oil in the Forest Region. The latter were then transported as far away as Fouta Djallon, Senegal and Gambia and exchanged for goods that were scarce in Guinea, such as clothes" (Wilhelm 1988: 24).

6.4   Development of smuggling

Export smuggling arose in the context of commercial relations with neighboring countries. Smuggling of export crops allowed peasants to avoid the loss of income caused by the over-valuation of the official exchange rate.

Using the black market exchange rate of the syli against the CFA franc, a kg of coffee was worth only CFA 49 if sold at the Guinean producer price, by comparison with roughly CFA 175 per kg if sold into West African markets. Guinean peasants living in regions adjoining neighboring countries therefore found it increasingly profitable to sell their produce to traders involved in smuggling. Border markets also gave the peasants access to imported goods not available on the official markets. The rapid growth of the informal market in consumer goods contrasts with the state of the official market.

6.5 Rationing of consumption

The crisis in the balance of payments necessitated restrictions on imports. The official trade circuits proved less and less able to satisfy the demand for consumer goods, and consequently a parallel market developed (World Bank 1984). The government set up a rationing system for essential products, which to a certain extent allowed wage earners in the towns to buy provisions at the official prices; but in the smaller towns and in the rural areas demand could be satisfied only at prices far higher than the official prices.

6.6 Stagnation of production

State interventionism did not succeed in persuading economic agents to boost their production (table 17.7). Production levels for groundnuts, tobacco, coffee, bananas, manioc, yams, maize, and rice all rose only very slightly in the 1970s and therefore fell significantly in *per capita* terms. The legacy of the full control period was that total agricultural output *per capita* fell very substantially relative to levels at independence. Performance in the export sector was particularly poor, with banana exports falling from 100,000 tons in 1955 to zero in 1984 and pineapple exports falling by nearly 80 percent (table 17.8). The single largest agricultural export, coffee, was dramatically affected by the control regime, with coffee exports declining by 80 percent relative to their 1960 levels. As indicated in table 17.8, the coffee network appears to have responded favorably to the incentives offered by the new, more liberal policies instituted after 1985.

6.7 The means of production

6.7.1 Agricultural enterprises

The total surface area of Guinea under cultivation is estimated to be 979,000 km^2.[10] Nearly half is devoted to rice, with the remainder used for groundnuts (16 percent), fonio (13 percent), manioc (12 percent), and maize

---

[10] Ministère de l'Agriculture, des Eaux et Fôrets (2000).

Table 17.7 *Guinea, estimates for production per crop, 1970–1998, 000 tonnes*

Year	Paddy rice	Maize	Manioc	Banana	Pineapple	Green coffee	Cocoa	Tobacco	Groundnut	Mangoes
1970	350	68	480	85	23	12	2	1	75	24
1971	375	68	495	80	23	13	2	1	76	24
1972	375	67	505	70	25	13	2	1	76	24
1973	413	66	598	93	18	14	2	1	77	24
1974	417	68	604	94	17	14	2	1	78	24
1975	422	68	610	95	16	14	3	1	79	24
1976	426	68	616	96	15	14	4	1	80	24
1977	418	70	622	97	15	14	4	1	81	24
1978	366	70	629	98	16	14	4	1	82	24
1979	348	80	475	99	16	14	4	1	82	24
1980	480	90	480	100	17	14	4	2	84	24
1981	485	90	485	101	17	14	4	2	84	28
1982	490	90	490	102	18	15	4	2	85	28
1983	396	90	494	103	18	15	4	2	77	32
1984	403	100	496	104	30	15	4	2	82	32
1985	437	100	520	105	40	15	4	2	74	36
1986	510	100	550	106	50	7	3	2	70	36
1987	515	90	570	107	60	7	3	2	60	40
1988	525	71	594	119	72	20	1	2	81	40
1989	560	71	642	110	76	28	1	2	78	40
1990	616	78	658	121	83	30	2	2	78	50
1991	688	85	658	113	92	30	2	2	78	70
1992	757	94	781	125	91	29	2	2	102	93
1993	833	95	781	115	87	29	2	2	105	77
1994	650	79	620							
1995	651	79	640							
1996	662	79	646							
1997	696	81								
1998	715	85								

(9 percent). Rice is therefore the main crop grown in Guinea and as with all the other agricultural products, is mainly produced for home consumption. The government's 1994/5 survey into household budgets and consumption patterns (Ministère du Plan et de la Coopération 1996) shows that the entire harvest was consumed at home for 65 percent of the fields cultivated during the season preceding the survey (the percentage may be as high as 77 percent in certain regions, such as Middle Guinea). Ministry of Agriculture data confirm that some three-quarters of agricultural added value was consumed at home or bartered (Ministère de l'Agriculture des Eaux et Forêts, 1990). The agricultural sector is crucially important for livelihood in Guinea:

Table 17.8 *Guinea, volume of agricultural exports, 1960–1999, 000 metric tons*

Year	Coffee	Palm kernels	Pineapples	Bananas
1960–5	10.38	19.73	4.12	43.00
1966–70	8.46	14.64	7.40	31.40
1971–5	4.79	12.06	8.64	9.12
1976–80	1.84	12.33	2.06	0.05
1980–5	0.58	6.08	0.62	0.00
1992	5.36	...	1.38	...
1993	...	...	1.18	...
1994	...	...	1.04	...
1995	18.00	...	2.48	...
1996	...	...	1.16	...
1997	...	...	0.24	...
1998	26.00	...	0.56	...
1999	...	...	0.62	...

Sources: World Bank (1984); Ministère de l'Agriculture des Eaux et Forêts (1998); Ministère du Commerce de l'Industrie et des PME (2001).
Note: ... = Not available.

43 percent of the income of Guinean households derives from agriculture, which employs perhaps four out of five of all persons in work.

A potentially serious bottleneck in agricultural production comes from the difficulty families experience in gaining access to land, and from uncertainties over rights to land. The traditional system tends to exclude women from land ownership; they cannot be left it as an inheritance, and have only the right to cultivate it. The 1994/5 survey into budgets and consumption shows that only 2 percent of those in charge of agricultural enterprises were women.

6.7.2 Physical and human capital

A low equipment rate

Modern agricultural equipment, as well as other sophisticated inputs, is crucial to achieving sustained increases in TFP, and therefore growth. The Guinean authorities recognized this early in the post-independence period, as is borne out by the various attempts at agricultural mechanization carried out by the state between 1975 and 1977, including the introduction of mechanised production brigades (2,098 in number) and agricultural cultivation brigades (2,211).

These experiments ended in failure, however, due to poor management, a lack of spare parts, and a failure to maintain machines (World Bank 1984). Furthermore, the strategy adopted was itself ill conceived, in that the attempt at modernization was not combined with an improvement in agricultural methods. Even today Guinean agriculture remains virtually unmechanized, and the use of fertilizers and improved seeds is still very limited. The state's withdrawal from this sector since 1984 made significant subsequent advances in mechanization unlikely, as confirmed by the Planning Ministry's study of household budgets and consumption in the mid-1990s (Ministère du Plan et de la Coopération 1996; see table 17.4).

The demographic context: a young population

Population growth increased over the post-independence period in Guinea, from 2.3 percent between 1960 and 1980 to 2.7 percent in the 1990s. As a consequence, the population became younger. The share of the working-age population (fifteen–sixty years old) in the total population fell from 54 percent as late as the 1980s to roughly 47 percent in 2000.

According to the life-cycle theory of saving, an increase in the size of the dependent population relative to the working-age population tends to reduce capital accumulation and growth, by lowering national saving. A younger population, moreover, implies that larger expenditures on education and health are required to maintain or increase the level of human capital per worker. The growth impacts of such spending are not immediate, and to the degree that social spending competes with investments that pay off more quickly, there may be a reduction in the growth rate, at least in the short run. Barro and Sala-i-Martin (1996) emphasize a final, mechanical channel through which high fertility rates reduce real income growth: for any given growth rate of real GDP per worker, a fall in the ratio of workers to population reduces the growth rate of real GDP *per capita*.

6.7.3   Essential infrastructure

Guinea's infrastructure is for the most part failing. Only 10 percent of the country's 19,215 km of road is surfaced (Guinée, 2001). While there are also 5,620 km of rural roads, the passability of these roads varies seasonally, and even the surfaced roads are subject to rapid deterioration for climatic reasons. The railway network no longer exists, although a rail line is in use to transport bauxite and alumina from mines to the port. The public rail system that made it possible to attract produce from the central basin of the river Niger fell into disuse, succumbing to management failure by the public enterprise in charge of it; the system had largely been abandoned by 1986. The telephone service is poor; in 1996, there were reckoned to be only 0.21 trunk lines per 100 inhabitants, as against 0.87 and 1.1 lines per 100 inhabitants in Côte d'Ivoire and Senegal, respectively (World Bank 1999). In 1995 only 3.5 percent of households had access to a telephone, and each subscriber suffered on average two power cuts a year. Finally, the availability of electricity remains extremely limited; only 0.8 percent of the rural population has access to it. The high cost, limited availability, and low quality of infrastructure seriously undermine the economy's productivity.

6.8 Climatic factors

When the climatic factor is considered in terms of rainfall levels, one discovers that precipitation has tended to decline over time in every region of Guinea, but most markedly in Conakry. The fall was at its most pronounced at the beginning of the 1970s, when there was a major drought in the Sahel. What matters for agriculture, however, is not so much the level of rainfall as its distribution over time. Taking the vicissitudes of cereal production as a yardstick, the climatic factor appears to have become more unstable over time in Guinea. Random shifts in climate, as reflected in variations in production and therefore in income, represent potentially negative determinants of growth.

6.9 The financial sector

Inadequate credit to the production sectors is another constraint on growth in Guinea. As much in quantity as in quality, credit extended by the formal financial sector made little contribution to growth. Interest rates remained very high, creating a discouragingly high profitability threshold for bankable projects. Maturities also tended to be short; over 50 percent of loans extended by the financial sector were short-term. Finally, the volume of credit was small, at 5 percent of GDP as against 15 percent in the WAMU countries. In this context, Guinean peasants, lacking the collateral to secure bank loans, are rationed out of the credit market. The 1995 agricultural survey indicated that in 87 percent of farms, no one benefited from a loan for agricultural activities.

7. Determinants linked to political economy

The economic difficulties experienced by Guinea on the eve of the 1980s were a legacy of earlier policy decisions, including the country's too-abrupt breach with the colonial power; its departure from the CFA zone soon thereafter, with the attendant subordination of monetary policy to domestic political pressures; and its adoption of a *dirigiste* development strategy in 1964.

The consequences of these developments were highly damaging. In addition to the fall in official exports and the emergence of export smuggling, they included an increasing dependence of public revenues on the mining sector (to the tune of 33 percent in 1984, as against 0 in 1966), an increase in the share of government consumption in GDP from 6.9 percent in 1960 to 13.9 percent in 1985 at international prices, and a major increase in the quantity of money in circulation, from 12 percent to 46 percent of GDP between 1960 and 1975.

Several reasons may be adduced to account for these decisions, chief among them the desire to cultivate political support at home when the breach with western countries had been consummated.

Guinea was reduced to an impoverished state by this strategy, which was not sustainable in the long term and which stood in need of urgent reforms, made possible by the change of regime in 1984. The new regime swiftly embarked upon wide-ranging and ambitious reforms under the aegis of the donor community (World Bank, IMF, etc.).

However, reforms, no matter how ambitious, are not automatically backed by the local population, especially in the cities. For example, how was one to explain to the 100,000 civil servants, and to the thousands of new graduates arriving each year on the labor market, that the state was no longer able to guarantee their jobs?

7.1 The analytic framework

The analysis presented here takes its inspiration from the theory of government based upon rent-seeking (Posner 1975; Buchanan, Tollison, and Tullock 1980; Pedersen 1995, 1997; Clark 1997). This theory enables us to explain the impact of interest groups on government policy. Six pressure groups are considered here, namely, the so-called "economic operators" or important actors in the private business sector; the army; formal interest groups (for example, civil servants and students); informal interest groups (for example, community groups); donors; and political parties.

- The *economic operators* control the rice trade and their influence is therefore exercised through the greater or lesser availability of rice in the market. Rice is in fact regarded as a "strategic" product, politically speaking, as the peoples of Guinea consume up to 91 kg *per capita* per year. Its income elasticity, at 0.33, is the lowest of all the products in the household's shopping basket (Del Ninno 1993).
- The *army's* influence is highly visible. While the economic crisis caused the number of civil service personnel to fall by 65 percent early in the reform period, the number of soldiers rose by 25 percent (World Bank 1990). The need to intervene in regional conflicts, including those in Sierra Leone and Liberia, increased its influence in the country still further.

- *Formal interest groups* consist of unionized workers, secondary school pupils, and university students. Such groups may easily exert pressure because they exist as organized structures and are very often located close to sites of power. Their political influence is often wielded through strikes or demonstrations capable of disrupting routine activities.

- *Informal interest groups* consist of indigenous ethnic groups based in the capital, and religious organizations. Owing to their geographical location close to sites of power, indigenous ethnic groups represent an obvious source of political pressure. They played a significant part in the PDG's success in organizing support for the referenda over independence. Muslim religious organizations also exert a high degree of political influence, drawing as they do from all levels of society; 95 percent of the population is Muslim.

- After the change of regime and the democratization of 1984, two additional political groups emerged into prominence: the *donor community* and *domestic political parties*. The donors may use conditionality criteria to exert pressure for economic reforms on governments in need of loans. A democratic system, because it presupposes the existence of a countervailing political power, allows opposition parties to exert pressure on the party in government. The influence of these last two groups has not always prevailed in the post-1984 period, however. The influence of donors tends to be undermined by the possibility of self-financing through mining revenues; that of opposition parties, by the army's backing of incumbent governments (the head of state is head of the army). Political liberalization has therefore been somewhat slow to assume a concrete form.

7.2 Interactions with macroeconomic and sectoral policies

How do these different interests impinge on government policy choices? Table 17.9 allows us to summarize what is at issue. Table 17.9 distinguishes between the policy changes a government may consider and the "forces" likely to influence its choices. The signs used in table 17.9 indicate whether the reform program listed in the given row met with a positive ($+$), negative ($-$), or neutral (.) response on the part of the forces represented in the columns. In what follows we develop the analysis underlying this table.

7.2.1 Commercial policy

Commercial policy typically elicits sharply divergent responses from domestic interest groups. Import liberalization is favorable to importing firms, but it removes protection from firms producing substitute goods and threatens the very survival of firms that depend on excessively high customs barriers. In the case of Guinea the formal import-substituting sector was dominated by public enterprises.

Table 17.9 *Guinea, policy choices and their political determinants*

Reform policies	(Case 1) Economic operators	(Case 2) Army	(Case 3) Civil society	(Case 4) Socialist regime	(Case 5) Liberal regime
				Political determinants	
Commercial policy	(+/−)	(.)	(+/−)	(−)	(+)
Exchange rate policy (devaluation)	(exp +) (imp −)	(.)	(−)	(−)	(+)
Public spending (−)	(+)	(−)	(−)	(−)	(+)
Monetary policy (−)	(+)	(−)	(−)	(−)	(+)
Financial restraint (+)	(+)	(+)	(+)	(−)	(+)
Public infrastructure	(+)	(+)	(+)	(+)	(+)
				Period I	Period II

Source: The authors.

Under the old regime (prior to 1984), trade policy tended to be protectionist. The actual level of protection was highly variable across sectors and even firms, making it impossible to link investment decisions (whether public or private) to the underlying relative costs of production. To rectify this situation, a reform of the customs regime was effected in January 1986. Tariff rates were fixed to a base of 10 percent, with essential goods and agricultural imports entering at 5 percent and luxury goods at 20–30 percent. Controls on official marketing agencies were reduced, though important exceptions prevailed, including the maintenance of price controls on rice and the fact that the prices fixed for certain public enterprises remained short of real costs of production (including fuel, electricity, water, and urban transport). The import license regime was also modified, abolishing the state's exclusive access to official foreign exchange; in the new allocation system, importers could apply for foreign exchange from the Central Bank by presenting a "Description of imports" that indicated the type and quantity of products they wished to import.

Logically enough, local merchants backed these measures, which on the one hand meant that their activities would be authorized and recognized by the authorities rather than being banned, as in the previous regime, and on the other, meant that they would have access to foreign exchange from the Central Bank and would benefit from favorable customs duties. City-dwellers had no cause to oppose such measures either, since the prices of the principal goods and services consumed by them did not alter markedly. The public enterprise sector faced new competition but otherwise remained outside of the spheres affected by the initial reforms; drastic reductions in public employment and privatization began later and were implemented more gradually. Was it fear of the city-dwellers' reaction that prompted the decision to shield this sector from the initial reforms?

7.2.2 Exchange rate policy

After independence in 1958, one of the new government's first measures was to quit the CFA sub-regional monetary zone, which enabled it to cast off the monetary constraints associated with participation in a multi-country currency union. The introduction of an independent national currency was followed, however, as we have seen, by a long period of exchange controls and over-valuation.

In the 1986 reforms, depreciation was sought by means of a currency devaluation of 1,500 percent (to FG 300 to the US dollar, from FG 25). This reduced the premium in the parallel foreign exchange market from 1,600 percent to less than 16 percent. The corresponding adjustment in official prices for imported goods meant that the government was able to satisfy a much larger share of shopkeepers' import requests, notably in foodstuffs. Urban consumption was no longer subsidized, but it was hoped that the removal of shortages would satisfy city-dwellers, who had until then been used to the heavily subsidized but shortage-prone "provisioning system,"[11] and win their support for the program. It was hoped in any case, and justifiably so, that the abundance of goods in the shopkeepers' displays might stop prices rising too high. In the newly introduced foreign exchange auctions, sales to finance imports of consumption goods, destined mainly for the population of Conakry, were thus fixed at 99 percent of total sales in 1986 and at 89 percent in 1988.

In order to balance the currency market, the decision was taken to let the Guinean Franc depreciate further. Between 1986 and 1987, the exchange rate slid from FG 300 to FG 428.5 to the US dollar.

The exchange rate policy implemented in 1986 did therefore have some influence upon the urban population and shopkeepers. On the one hand, the government could count on the support of the urban population, despite the abolition of the provisioning system, because the reformed system allowed the supplying of the market (through the shopkeepers) with heavily used foodstuffs such as rice. On the other hand, all risks of shortages should have been avoided by ensuring a sizeable quantity of products on the market. The actor through which this objective was to be attained was the importer–shopkeeper, who benefited from an exceptional combination of favorable circumstances. On the one hand, he was granted favorable customs duties and on the other he was given privileged access to foreign exchange through the auction system.

---

[11] The appendix (pp. 618–19) explains how the provisioning system worked.

Table 17.10 *Guinea, state finance 1974–1984, percent of GDP*

Budgetary category	1974	1977	1980	1984
Revenue and aid	3.33	7.98	10.77	11.10
Expenditure	4.57	6.82	10.89	13.30
Current expenditure	3.01	4.34	7.19	11.20
Capital expenditure	1.56	2.48	3.70	2.10
Deficit	−0.25	0.17	−0.12	−0.22

Source: Arulpragasam and Sahn (1997).

7.2.3 Public spending policy

Budgetary policy is viewed nowadays as a crucial variable in a country's economic growth. The structure of public spending during the period preceding 1984 did not favor growth, reflecting the populism of the government in power, and of a civil society aligned with it. We should bear in mind that this regime had drawn its support, ever since the electoral campaigns of the 1950s, from the popular masses and from the trade union movement. In order to maintain its own stability, the regime privileged forms of spending which directly or indirectly favored urban interest groups, particularly those in the capital. The main part of the budget was therefore devoted to current expenditure, which financed automatic employment in the civil service for all new graduates of tertiary or professional secondary schools, as well as subsidies to parastatal enterprises and subsidized food imports for the population of Conakry. Current expenditure accounted for 84 percent of the state's budget in 1984. Between 1981 and 1984, almost 40 percent of the public budget was spent on civil servants' salaries; another 28 percent went to subsidies to public enterprises. The resulting deficit was financed in large part by Central Bank credit to the government, thus undermining monetary equilibrium.

Conversely, little attention was paid to capital expenditure, much of which was on behalf of the poorer sectors of the population (the building of schools and hospitals, hydraulic schemes at the village level). In 1984, capital expenditure accounted for only 16 percent of total expenditure, as against 24 percent in 1974 (see table 17.10).

In order to rectify this situation, a series of measures adopted in 1986 set in train reforms which were both bold and difficult to implement. These included the privatization of parastatals and a shrinkage of the civil service by 40 percent, the latter requiring the laying off of almost 12,000 civil servants.

7.2.4 Monetary policy

The various interest groups viewed monetary policy in much the same fashion as they did public spending. Thus, when it was restrictive, urban groups, and in particular civil society and the army, were liable to respond negatively in the short term.

In Guinea, the introduction of the SAP and currency reform in 1986 signaled a more restrictive monetary policy, which entailed limiting the potential sources of excessive monetary growth. Reforms included the introduction of credit ceilings for the state and the economy, a permanent mopping-up of the excess liquidity in commercial banks through the introduction of a system of compulsory bank reserves, and a reinforcement of the monitoring of banks' prudential criteria.

7.3 Political economy: conclusions

The aim of this section was to give a structured explanation of the interactions between policies and interest groups. We set out to discover how government policies were influenced by pressure groups, and whether these groups were liable to curb, or even to defeat, attempts at economic reform. Basing our argument upon interest group theory, we identified the key interest groups, the stakes they had in various policies, and the channels through which they acted.

During the period before 1984, the party-state appears to have invested actively in interest groups, using them to bolster the regime in power. The political support of key groups was rewarded through the distribution of foodstuffs via import subsidies and the "provisioning" system. In the post-1984 period, this system as originally constituted certainly disappeared. It nonetheless continued to function in other guises; in particular, the new regime used shopkeepers to import foodstuffs, especially rice, and granted them access to foreign exchange. Rice constitutes a politically strategic product, being by far the most widely consumed food in Guinea and a preoccupation of all the urban groups in Conakry. A more extended study of the issues surrounding this product, in terms of its socio-economic and political impact, would shed light upon the complex inter-relationship between rice, government policy, and interest groups.

8. General conclusions

A case study analyzing economic growth performance might be expected to answer the following questions:

- How did the determinants of growth evolve over time?
- What explains the associated choices by households, firms, and government?
- How did these choices affect growth outcomes?

On the basis of the foregoing analysis, a series of answers to these questions may now be given. These answers may be ordered in terms of the two major episodes in the political economy of Guinea.

A longitudinal growth-accounting analysis for Guinea since the 1970s enabled us to bring out the crucial roles of physical capital accumulation and TFP growth. Fluctuations in TFP growth played a dominant role in the medium-term growth story, while low levels of investment played a preponderant role in the slowing down of growth, especially after the mining boom of 1973–9.

Comparison with the experience of other countries through cross-country econometric analyzes proved useful for the case study of Guinea. Hoeffler's (2002) panel estimates of the augmented Solow model suggest that the low levels of growth in Guinea may in large part be explained by its poor rate of investment. A broader growth model estimated by O'Connell and Ndulu suggests that the low level of life expectancy at birth and the high dependency ratio in Guinea had a significantly negative effect on growth. Determinants influencing Guinean growth favorably included the country's low initial income, its coastal location, and its relative political stability.

We have sought to account for Guinea's position in relation to other countries by surveying the various phases of its development. After independence in 1958, significant changes were made to the policies adopted by the colonial power. The structure of the Guinean economy traditionally rested on small-scale individual enterprises, particularly in agriculture, and on a relative openness to international trade. The new government, instead, placed the emphasis on central planning and collective production, and on achieving a degree of autonomy on the external plane. To achieve these goals the new regime distanced itself from the majority of constraining agencies inherited from the colonial period, quitting the Franc zone in order to adopt an independent monetary policy and refusing to join the General Agreement on Tariffs and Trade (GATT) in order to pursue an independent commercial policy.

On the internal plane, the government created a complex system of state enterprises controlling all key sectors of the economy, including production, the financial system, commerce, and transportation. In general, this strategy was also designed to weaken countervailing centers of power, in Collier's (1995) sense, in economic life. At the same time, the foreign exchange market, prices, and wages were all subject to centralized controls. Only by explaining the reasons underlying such a choice can we solve the enigma of Guinean economic growth in this period. We argued in section 7 that the explanation rested on the government's desire to transfer resources to politically strong urban groups in order to muster political support in the domestic arena. Our analysis of market institutions showed that agriculture was very heavily taxed in the process, and that this led to the stagnation of the agricultural sector and a decline in agricultural exports.

The period from 1973 to 1978 seemed to inaugurate an era of prosperity. The mining sector emerged as a prominent feature of the economy, growing at a rate of nearly 20 percent in real terms and rising from 4 percent of GDP in 1973 to 15 percent in 1977 (World Bank 1984). Real GDP increased by 6 percent per year between 1973 and 1977. But clouds were gathering: outside of the mining sector, real GDP contracted in *per capita* terms, growing at only 2.6 percent per year. The mining boom then turned out to be short-lived, as is the case with most booms. Mining activity peaked in 1977, and the sector went through serious difficulties over the period 1978–84 due to declining demand in foreign markets. Economic growth was also curbed by the second oil crisis of 1979–80. The party-state applied its own reform programs which in the last analysis were half-hearted and failed to address the key questions of exchange rate over-valuation and the reform of agricultural marketing. A segment of the economy, including a large part of the export sector, became entirely clandestine. Production fell, for lack of imported inputs. So grave was the crisis that the seizure of power by the military in 1984, a week after Sékou Touré's death, was greeted with a degree of popular support.

The period of more liberal reforms began in late 1985. The Guinean authorities implemented the essence of the reform agenda recommended by the donors, an agenda based in turn on the Washington Consensus. The change in political regime in 1984, together with the negative growth outcomes after 1978, played a part in ensuring that these reforms were adopted. The planning institutions inherited from earlier periods were almost entirely dismantled. However, variations in the reforms adopted, or retreats from them, frequently occurred. We have observed that the reform process was not sustained during periods of severe macroeconomic difficulty. Thus, in 1990, social unrest forced the government to double civil servants' wages and to increase family allowances by 50 percent. The fall in the price of bauxite in the 1990s led the government on several occasions to relax its budgetary policy and to have recourse to massive loans from the Central Bank (the reinforced facilities for structural adjustment (FASR) granted by the IMF in 1991 and in 1994 were not followed up). Furthermore, several privatized enterprises were taken over by the state (among them, in 2001, the services distributing water and electricity).

This chapter thus clearly illustrates the problematic nature of economic growth in a changing political environment. A pertinent datum to take into consideration was the political redistribution of revenues. This redistribution, which some might describe as corruption, was designed to buy political support and enable the government to stay in power. Those in power will pursue the goal of growth so long as their political stability is guaranteed, but they will not hesitate to sacrifice it once their political stability is threatened. Sustaining growth-promoting policies in Guinea would thus seem to require a stage at which some guarantees of political stability are provided. This could be done by, for example, holding democratic elections through which a government reflecting a majority vote was elected.

Appendix: The provisioning system

The *Système de Revitaillement* was an ambitous project aimed at meeting the demand for food, and particularly rice, of the urban population of Conakry. At a monthly consumption of 8kg of rice per person, the required total was estimated at 70,000 tonnes per month. Since domestic production was weak, this was satisfied by imports. The state had its own channels for distributing these products to the population of Conakry, with priority to the military and the civil service.

To benefit from the distribution system, each family had to present a card listing the members of the family in two categories – Category *A* consisting of the head of the family, spouses, and children, and Category *B* consisting of all other family members. Individuals in Category *A* received larger allocations than those in Category *B*. The price of rice within the system was 20 sylis per kg in 1984, a price that at the official exchange rate did not appear to convey a major subsidy; but the parallel exchange rate by that time was 250 sylis per dollar. The system therefore provided a subsidy close to ten times the official price.

In reality, the provisioning system permitted those in power to exercise a degree of control over the population of Conakry. The provisioning cards were sometimes distributed by labor unions at political information meetings at the workplace. The urban population supported the party and participated in demonstrations organized by it, partly in the expectation that at the end of each month the provisioning stores would be re-stocked with staple foods and manufactured goods.

The system was undermined from the start, however, by the "nomenklatura" that it itself created. Household heads had an incentive to declare fictitious persons in order to obtain larger allocations, a phenomenon that with the collaboration of those in charge led to an abnormally rapid growth in demands on the system. The system was used to support contraband and the black market, which grew rapidly.

The evidence suggests that the provisioning system was not sustainable in the long term. It began to flag in the late 1970s when debt service on the government's external borrowing began to fall due. The number of products on offer in the provisioning stores fell sharply, leaving only a few essential commodities: rice, groundnut oil, and tomato concentrate. Distributions became irregular and insufficient, and were finally transferred to workplaces and military barracks. The system as such was completely abandoned a few months after the initiation of the Second Republic on April 3, 1984.

References

Arulpragasam, J. and D. E. Sahn (1997), *Economic Transition in Guinea: Implications for Growth and Poverty*. New York: New York University Press

Barro R. J. and X. Sala-i-Martin (1996), *La croissance économique*. Paris: Ediscience

Buchanan, J.M., R. D. Tollison, and G. Tullock, eds. (1980), *Toward a Theory of the Rent Seeking Society*. College Station, TX: Texas A & M

Clark, D. J. (1997), "Pressure and the Division of a Public Budget," *Public Choice* 93: 179–95

Collier, P. (1995), "The Marginalization of Africa," *International Labor Review* 134 (4–5): 541–57

Collier, P. and J. W. Gunning (2007), "Sacrificing the Future: Intertemporal Strategies and their Implications for Growth," chapter 5 in B. J. Ndulu, S. A. O'Connell, R. H. Bates, P. Collier, and C. C. Soludo, eds., *The Political Economy of Economic Growth in Africa, 1960–2000*, vol. 1. Cambridge: Cambridge University Press

Collier, P. and S. A. O'Connell, (2007), "Opportunities and Choices," chapter 2 in B. J. Ndulu, S. A. O'Connell, R. H. Bates, P. Collier, and C. C. Soludo, eds., *The Political Economy of Economic Growth in Africa, 1960–2000*, vol. 1. Cambridge: Cambridge University Press

Collins, S. and B. Bosworth (1996), "Economic Growth in East Asia: Accumulation versus Assimilation," *Brookings Papers on Economic Activity* 2: 135–203

Del Ninno, C. (1993), "Welfare and Poverty in Conakry: Assessments and Determinants," Washington, DC: Cornell University Food and Nutrition Policy Program

Easterly, W. and M. Sewadeh (2002), "Global Development Network Growth Database," www.worldbank.org

Goerg, O. (1986), *Commerce et colonisation en Guinée, 1850–1913*. Paris: Harmattan

Guinée (2001), *Rapport National sur le développement humain*. Conakry: Secrétariat d'Etat au Plan et Mission Résidente du PNUD

Hoeffler, A. (2002), "The Augmented Solow Model and the African Growth Debate," *Oxford Bulletin of Economics and Statistics* 64(2): 135–58

International Monetary Fund (IMF) (1999), "Perspectives de l'économie mondiale," October: 148–64

Ministère de l'Agriculture des Eaux et Forêts (1990), *Recensement National de l'Agriculture 1987/1988*. Conakry, mimeo

(1998), *Bilan du secteur agricole 1984–1997*. Conakry

(2000), *Enquête agricole de 1997/98*. Conakry, Mimeo

Ministère du Commerce de l'Industrie et des PME (2001), *Rapport pour la Table Ronde sur le Secteur Privé*. Conakry

Ministère du Plan et de la Coopération (MPC) (1996), *Enquête Intégrale sur les Conditions de Vie des Ménages avec Module Budget et Consommation 1994–1995*. Conakry

Ndulu, B. J. and S. A. O'Connell (2000), "Background Information on Economic Growth," Paper prepared for the Explaining African Economic Growth Project. Nairobi: African Economic Research Consortium, April

O'Connell, S. A. and B. J. Ndulu, (2000), "Africa's Growth Experience: A focus on Sources of Growth," AERC Growth Working Paper No. 10. Nairobi: African Economic Research Consortium, April (downloadable: www.aercafrica.org)

Pedersen, K. R. (1995), "Rent-seeking, Political Influence and Inequality: A Simple Analytical Example," *Public Choice* 82: 281–305

(1997), "The Political Economy of Distribution in Developing Countries: A Rent-seeking Approach," *Public Choice* 91: 351–73

Posner, R. (1975), "The Social Costs of Monopoly and Regulation," *Journal of Political Economy* 83: 807–28

République de Guinée (2001), *Rapport National sur le développement humain*. Conakry: Secrétariat d'Etat au Plan et Mission Résidente du PNUD

Summers, R. and A. Heston (1991), "The Penn World Table (Mark 5): An Expanded Set of International Comparisons, 1950–1988," *Quarterly Journal of Economics* 106: 327–68

Wilhelm, L. (1988), *Circuits de Commercialisation et de Distribution en Guinée*. Vol. 1. Conakry: UNCTAD/UNDP

World Bank (1984), *Guinea: The Conditions for Economic Growth: A Country Economic Memorandum*. Washington, DC: The World Bank

(1990), *Republic of Guinea: Country Economic Memorandum*, 2 vols. Washington, DC: The World Bank

(1999), *World Tables*. Washington, DC: The World Bank

18 | Explaining African economic growth performance: the case of Nigeria

Professor Milton A. Iyoha and Dickson E. Oriakhi

1. Introduction and overview

Nigeria's economic performance since independence in 1960 has been decidedly unimpressive. It is estimated that Nigeria received over US$228 billion from oil exports between 1981 and 1999 (Udeh 2000), and yet the number of Nigerians living in abject poverty – subsisting on less than $1 a day – more than doubled between 1970 and 2000, and the proportion of the population living in poverty rose from 36 percent to 70 percent over the same period. At official exchange rates, Nigeria's *per capita* income of US$260 in 2000 was precisely one-third of its level in 1980 (see World Bank 2005). Meanwhile,

Department of Economics, University of Benin, Nigeria.

Nigeria's external debt rose almost continuously, as did the share of its GDP owed annually in debt service.

Nigeria's story is one of missed opportunities and, more specifically, of misspent natural-resource rents. Corruption is an important part of the story, as is a pervasive lack of transparency and accountability in governance. Above all, serious mistakes have been made in macroeconomic management, notably including a "Dutch disease"-generating syndrome in which policy-makers erroneously treated favorable but transitory oil shocks as permanent. We argue in this chapter that Nigeria's failure to harness its resource rents resulted mainly from distributional struggles between ethno-regional interests, and that imprudent macroeconomic policies in particular were motivated by the single-minded attempt by political leaders to transfer resources from the Southern to the Northern part of the country. We begin with a brief political overview before turning to an analysis of policy regimes and growth performance.

1.1 Political background

The Protectorate of Northern Nigeria was formed in 1900, with Lord Lugard as High Commissioner. Six years later the British Colonial Office combined the colony and Protectorate of Southern Nigeria as a separate Protectorate. According to Bevan, Collier, and Gunning (1999: 10), Lord Lugard favored the aristocratic society of the North, to the degree that the British became not only agents of development but also defenders of a stagnant feudal structure there. Amalgamation of the two Protectorates took place in 1914 and was driven in part by the British desire to create a single, economically viable political entity. The Northern and Southern regions continued to be administered separately but, from an early date, British colonial policy presumed that resources would flow from the more advantaged coastal regions to the poorer Northern interior.

The construction of Nigeria culminated, late in the colonial period, in a three-way federation of Northern, Western, and Eastern regions, under the 1954 Lytelton constitution. While the federal structure accommodated what were by that time undeniable ethno-regional political divisions, these in turn were largely a creation of British colonialism: people saw themselves in ethnic terms because the British had insisted on seeing them in that way. As noted by Suberu (2001: 2) "British-created Nigeria was and remains one of the most ethnically diverse countries in the world and perhaps the most deeply divided of all the countries in the course of the European occupation of Africa." Regional polarization gave rise to distributional conflict well before the transition to independence, and a focus on redistribution rather than production was later to intensify as the country's state governments multiplied in number and ethnic nationalities struggled for the center's abundant resources and power.

The major ethno-regional groups united as independence approached, spurred on by a common desire to get the colonialists out of the country. But sharp lines of polarization were apparent, especially between the Hausa–Fulani, Yoruba, and Igbo ethnic groups that dominated the Northern, Western, and Eastern regions, respectively. These rivalries crystalized into bitter political struggles under the combined impact of economic competition and electoral mobilization. The adoption of a federal structure at independence therefore represented an institutional response both to the administrative autonomy and political salience of Nigeria's existing regions and to their explosive demographic configuration, which pitted three major nationalities in fierce competition over economic resources and political power (Suberu 2001).

During the first six years of independence (1960–6), regional tensions pushed the country into chaos. Political stability was undermined when the federal government, dominated by the numerically superior North, intervened in elections in the West, and then again when the North and West formed an alliance to benefit from the oil-rich Eastern region. The latter development led to two military coup in 1966 and culminated in the secession of the Eastern region in 1967 and its forcible reintegration after three years of civil war (Bevan, Collier and Gunning 1992: 7).

Perhaps the most dramatic expression of regional conflict in Nigeria was the domination of non-elected Northern military officers, who held the Presidency for nearly 90 percent of the period between 1967 and 2000 (table 18.1 shows the history of executive transitions in Nigeria). The country's 1993 transition to multi-party democracy was aborted by the ruling military government when Moshood Abiola, a Yoruba politician, clearly won national multi-party elections. Chief Ernest Shonekan, a Yoruba, was installed as the head of the Interim National Government, but before this government could establish itself another Northerner, General Sani Abacha, took over as the head of a new military administration. Only with the death of Abacha in 1998 and the accession to power of General Abdulsalami Abubakar, another Northerner, was the groundwork laid for the transition, in May 1999, to an elected civilian administration headed by Chief Olusegun Obasanjo, a Yoruba and retired General.

Relying on the communiqué of a major national conference on Nigerian Federalism, Suberu (2001: 9) concluded that Nigeria's federal system was perched precariously on a "weak productive base" due to the preoccupation of local, religious, and ethno-regional interests with redistributing a shrinking national cake rather than producing a bigger one. Ethno-regional conflict continues to express itself in a wide variety of ways, including ongoing debates over the rules for intergovernmental sharing of revenues;

Table 18.1 *Nigeria, executive transitions, 1960–2003*

Year	Leader	Mode of assumption of office
1960	Sir Abubakar Tafawa Balewa	Elected
1963	Nnamdi Azikiwe	Establishment of Republic with Azikiwe as President
1966	Johnson Aguiyi-Ironsi	January 1966 coup
1966	Yakubu Gowon	July 1966 coup
1975	Murtala Muhammed	coup
1976	Olusegun Obasanjo	coup
1979	Alhaji Shehu Shagari	Elected
1983	Muhammadu Buhari	coup
1985	Ibrahim Babangida	coup
1993	Ernest Shonekan	Selected Head of Interim National Government in August 1993
1993	Sani Abacha	Palace coup in November 1993 due to the declaration as unconstitutional of Interim National Government by a Federal High Court
1998	Abdulsalam Abubakar	Selected due mainly to unexpected demise of the former leader, Sani Abacha
1999	Olusegun Obasanjo	Elected
2003	Olusegun Obasanjo	Elected

Source: Compiled by the authors (2006).

calls for further subdivision (or amalgamation) of the thirty-six state structure;[1] popular repudiation of population census figures which appear to favor particular sections of the country; and debates over the "federal character principle" which constitutionally mandates the equitable representation of states in federal public services and institutions. A common feature of these struggles is the tension they bring out between politically motivated redistribution and economic efficiency. Several reasons have been adduced, for example, for requiring roughly proportional representation of states in some important political positions and in recruitment into the senior echelons of the federal civil service: a leading one is the relative educational backwardness of the northern part of the Nigerian federation.[2]

---

[1] In an effort to defuse regional tensions, the military government sub-divided the original three regions into twelve states in 1967. Further sub-divisions were implemented after 1976, culminating in 1996 in the present thirty-six-state structure. Suberu (2001) argues that the sub-divisions of 1967 and 1976 probably enhanced the stability of the Federation, by making region-wide collective action more difficult to sustain, but that subsequent sub-divisions were one of many forms of zero-sum competition for federal resources and patronage (among other benefits, new states received large subventions to construct state capitals).

[2] Bevan, Collier, and Gunning (1999: 22) point out that "out of 944 students enrolled at the university college in Ibadan in 1959, Yoruba was listed as the tribal classification for 408, Ibo for 333, Fulani for 6, and Hausa for 3."

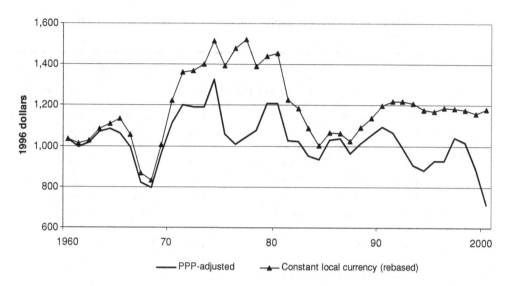

Figure 18.1 Nigeria, real GDP *per capita*, 1960–2000
Source: World Bank, *World Development Indicators 2005.*

However, while this imbalance provided an equity rationale for educational investment in the North, the argument for proportional recruitment seems clearly weaker given its potentially discouraging effect on both bureaucratic efficiency and on educational investment within Nigeria as a whole. As this example suggests, distributional conflict has acted over time to reduce the drive for growth and development of the Nigerian economy, both directly (via the misallocation of existing resources, and their wastage via court cases, work stoppages, and ethnic clashes) and indirectly (via the undermining of incentives for productive new investment).

1.2 Economic outcomes

Nigeria's long-run growth performance has been extremely poor. For the full 1960–2000 period, real income *per capita* grew at only 0.43 percent per annum at constant domestic prices, and in PPP-adjusted terms average income actually fell (figure 18.1). The importance of economic growth for poverty reduction has been established by numerous empirical studies and has recently been underscored by the phenomenal progress of China and other countries in East Asia and Pacific region.[3] In Nigeria, the consequence of long-run stagnation in average income was a sharp cumulative increase

---

[3] Lal (1999) summarizes a large empirical literature by stating that "*per capita* growth of over 3 percent a year indisputably reduces the headcount index of poverty" (1999: 1). China's growth exceeded 6 percent per annum between 1970 and 1988 and 5 percent in the 1990s. This cut the proportion of people living in poverty in half (World Bank 2001: 3).

Table 18.2 *Nigeria,* per capita *real income, dollars, and its growth rate,*
1965–2000

Pre-liberalization era			Economic liberalization era		
Year	Level	Growth rate (%)	Year	Level	Growth rate (%)
1965	318.60	–	1987	287.70	−3.59
1966	297.00	−6.78	1988	307.20	6.78
1967	243.60	−17.98	1989	320.02	4.17
1968	234.20	−3.86	1990	336.50	5.15
1969	283.05	20.86	1991	342.64	1.82
1970	344.30	21.64	1992	342.60	−0.01
1971	382.60	11.12	1993	340.10	−0.73
1972	384.70	0.55	1994	330.60	−2.79
1973	394.20	2.47	1995	328.90	−0.51
1974	425.95	8.05	1996	333.40	1.37
1975	392.20	−7.92	1997	333.20	−0.06
1976	415.45	5.93	1998	330.60	−0.78
1977	427.67	2.94	1999	325.90	−1.42
1978	391.10	−8.55	2000	331.60	1.75
1979	404.99	3.55			
1980	409.18	1.03			
1981	344.51	−15.80			
1982	332.96	−3.35			
1983	305.50	−8.25			
1984	281.83	−7.75			
1985	299.90	6.41			
1986	298.40	−0.50			

Source: World Bank (2005) and author's calculations.

in poverty, in terms of both absolute numbers and as a share of the overall population.

As indicated in figure 18.1 and table 18.2, Nigeria's long-run stagnation occurred in a context of acute short-to-medium-run volatility. Nigeria was a poor country at independence in 1960, with a per capita income in constant 2000 US dollars of less than $250 at official exchange rates (about $1,000 in PPP-adjusted terms). Real *per capita* income rose impressively between 1960 and the mid-1970s, with the exception of a brief but sharp interruption immediately before and during the civil war of 1967–70. In the mid-1970s, income fluctuated with little overall trend, but then it plummeted in 1981 with the onset of an acute economic crisis. Between 1981 and 1984, real output fell at an annual average rate of nearly 6 percent. The SAP adopted in 1986 brought about temporary relief, with real growth averaging over 5 percent per annum between 1988 and 1990. The 1990s, however, witnessed

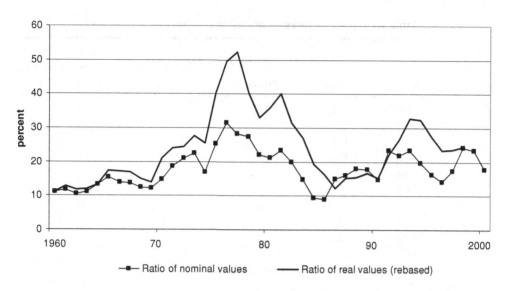

Figure 18.2 Nigeria, investment as a share of GDP, 1960–2000
Source: World Bank, *World Development Indicators 2005.*

almost complete stagnation, with average income growing at a rate of less than half a percentage point per annum.[4]

1.2.1 Aggregate investment

Figure 18.2 shows the ratio of investment to GDP in Nigeria, and in table 18.2 we also provide a public sector/private sector breakdown for available years. A comparison of figures 18.1 and 18.2 shows a distinct co-movement of real GDP *per capita* with the aggregate investment share. Both variables fall sharply during the civil war and again, after a protracted boom, during the economic crisis of the early 1980s. Consistent with the dominant share of the public sector in total investment (table 18.3), revenues from oil exports serve as an extremely powerful driver of the overall investment rate. This is apparent in a comparison of figure 18.2 with figure 18.3, which shows the real world price of oil over time. Since investment has a domestically produced component, changes in the investment share affect growth from both the demand side and from the supply side. Short-run aggregate demand effects of oil-financed investment are readily apparent in figure 18.1. Sustained impacts on productive capacity, in contrast, are less evident, consistent with severe inefficiencies in the allocation of domestic investment, documented below.

---

[4] World Bank data show a revival following the democratic transition in 1999, with average growth for 2000–3 at 2.4 percent.

Table 18.3 *Nigeria, investment and its components, 1960–2000*

Year	Total	Private	Government	Ratio of private to government investment
	Investment as a share of GDP (percent)			
1960	11.0	–	–	–
1961	12.0	–	–	–
1962	11.0	–	–	–
1963	11.0	–	–	–
1964	13.0	–	–	–
1965	15.0	–	–	–
1966	14.0	–	–	–
1967	14.0	–	–	–
1968	12.0	–	–	–
1969	12.0	–	–	–
1970	15.0	–	–	–
1971	19.0	–	–	–
1972	21.0	–	–	–
1973	22.4	14.6	7.8	–
1974	17.0	7.0	10.0	–
1975	25.2	7.0	18.2	38.5
1976	31.5	7.1	24.4	29.1
1977	29.0	9.9	19.1	51.7
1978	27.6	10.8	16.8	64.4
1979	22.0	8.0	14.0	57.3
1980	22.2	6.9	15.3	46.0
1981	23.3	6.8	16.5	41.2
1982	20.1	5.5	14.6	37.7
1983	14.8	4.0	10.8	37.2
1984	9.5	2.4	7.1	33.7
1985	9.0	2.3	6.7	34.5
1986	15.1	3.1	12.0	26.0
1987	13.7	4.8	8.9	54.0
1988	13.5	4.5	9.0	50.2
1989	14.4	4.6	9.8	46.8
1990	16.0	6.5	9.5	68.3
1991	17.0	5.9	11.1	53.0
1992	17.5	5.7	11.8	48.2
1993	15.0	–	–	–
1994	10.0	–	–	–
1995	16.0	–	–	–
1996	14.0	–	–	–
1997	17.0	–	–	–
1998	24.0	–	–	–
1999	23.0	–	–	–
2000	18.0	–	–	–

Sources: Author's computation based on (1) CBN, *Statistical Bulletin*, various issues; (2) Miller and Sumlinski (1994); World Bank (2005).

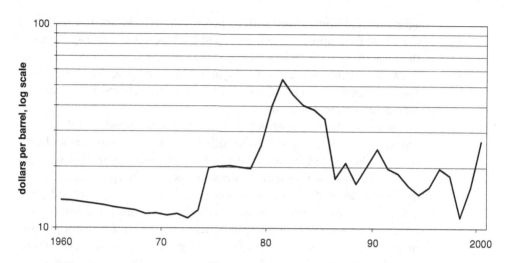

Figure 18.3 Nigeria, real first-purchase price of crude oil, USA, 1960–2000, deflated by US GDP deflator, 2000: 0.1
Source: US Energy Information Administration, *Annual Energy Review*, www.eia.doe.gov/emeu/aer/txt/stb0518.xls.

The performance of private investment since the initiation of structural adjustment has been particularly disappointing. Progress in macroeconomic adjustment was expected to trigger a significant resurgence of private investment, financed by increases in domestic savings and an acceleration of foreign capital inflows. Serven and Solimano (1992: 96) document the failure of private investment to respond strongly to structural adjustment in a number of Heavily Indebted Poor Countries (HIPCs) during the 1980s and make the following observations that we shall argue below are relevant in Nigeria's case:

First, the decline in the availability of foreign savings has not been matched by a corresponding increase in domestic savings. Second, the deterioration of fiscal conditions due to cuts in foreign lending, higher domestic interest rates, and the acceleration of inflation in several countries forced a fiscal adjustment that in many cases took the form of a contraction in public investment. Third, the macroeconomic instability associated with external shocks has hampered private investment. And fourth, the debt overhang has discouraged investors through its implied tax on future output and the ensuing credit constraints in international capital markets.

1.2.2 Structural transformation

The sectoral structure of output in Nigeria changed substantially over time, reflecting the emergence of the oil sector starting in the early 1970s. Agriculture's share in total output fell from approximately 64 percent in 1960 to 33 percent in the 1990s. By 1990, only 43 percent of the population remained in agriculture, by comparison with 73 percent in 1960. Meanwhile industry's share rose from approximately 8 percent to 50 percent. While agriculture's share was in line with the SSA average in the 1990s, the contribution of industry, at 50 percent, exceeded even the non-SSA developing-country average. The contribution of manufacturing, by contrast, was well below the SSA average, at a mere 5 percent.[5]

The reallocation of labor out of agriculture contributed to real GDP *per capita*, given the labor-productivity differential between industry and agriculture, which stood at nearly 3.5:1 in the early 1970s. Nonetheless, Nigeria does not display productivity-driven growth of the type emphasized in dynamic models of the dual economy (e.g. Jorgensen 1961; Fei and Ranis 1964; Matsuyama 1992). There is no evidence of ongoing labor productivity improvements in either industry or agriculture. Agricultural labor productivity fluctuated over time, reflecting the vagaries of a rain-fed agriculture, but advanced only marginally between 1973 and 1996 (real value added per worker rose from 2.49 to 2.54). Industrial labor productivity declined outright over the same period, with the result that the industry/agriculture ratio of labor productivities fell to 2.5:1. Labor productivity in services, the third-largest sector at nearly 30 percent of GDP in the 1990s, also fell. In agriculture, persistently low productivity growth reflected a host of factors, including inconsistent government policies towards the sector, inadequate use of modern inputs such as fertilizer and modern machinery, and low level of education and skills of farmers. Industrial labor productivity growth was held back by a hostile and uncertain policy environment for private investment, as well as by low capacity utilization, inadequate infrastructure (especially – and ironically – affecting domestic energy supplies), and the continued low skill level of workers.

1.2.3   Oil rents and regional distributional struggles

Figure 18.4 shows the ratio of natural resource rents to gross national income (GNI) in Nigeria, by comparison with the same ratio among resource-rich countries in SSA and the rest of the developing world. Rents are calculated here as the difference between the world price of energy, mineral, or forest resources and their marginal cost of extraction, multiplied by the volume of the corresponding category of commodity exports. GNI is converted to dollars at official exchange rates. Two striking observations emerge. First, Nigeria *became* a resource-rich country during the 1970s, and a strikingly resource-rich one. Before the first OPEC oil shock in 1973, Nigeria's resource rents were well below global norms for resource-rich countries; by the early 1980s, Nigeria's rents exceeded average rents among other resource-rich

---

[5] O'Connell and Ndulu (2001) provide the regional data on which this paragraph is based.

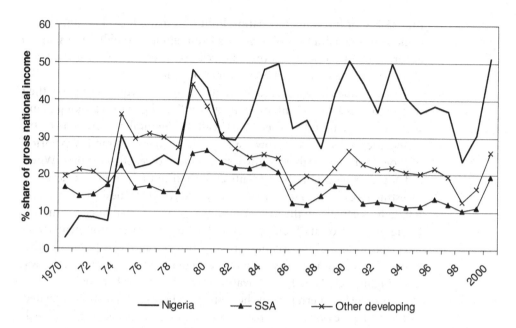

Figure 18.4 Nigeria, SSA, and Other developing countries, resource rents in resource-rich countries, 1970–2000
Source: World Bank. The figures show the sum of rents from energy, minerals, and forest resources, as a share of GNI. Rents are calculated as the difference between world prices and domestic marginal costs of extraction. Resource-rich countries are all those characterized as resource-rich by Collier and O'Connell (2007) for at least ten years over the 1960–2000 period.

countries globally, and by a considerable margin. Second, Nigeria *remained* resource-rich to a striking degree: the ratio of rents to GNI showed no trend in Nigeria after the late 1970s, by comparison with the distinct downward trend among other resource-rich countries.

Fluctuations in the ratio of rents to GNI are driven primarily by (1) changes in world commodity prices, (2) changes in commodity export volumes as a share of GDP, and (3) changes in real official bilateral exchange rates against the US dollar. In Nigeria, the remarkable explosion of oil rents during the 1970s reflects the first two of these influences, in the form of the OPEC oil price increases (figure 18.3) and a sustained increase in the volume of Nigerian oil exports. The third influence, by contrast, operated in the other direction during the 1970s: a very sharp real appreciation of the naira meant that the ratio of dollar oil rents to naira GDP rose less rapidly than it would have done had the real exchange rate been stable. The continued weight of commodity rents in Nigeria after the early 1980s reflects similar considerations, operating in reverse: a lack of diversification out of energy production, on the one hand, and a gradual unwinding, starting in the mid-1980s, of the real appreciation built up during the oil boom. Depreciations of the naira kept oil revenues from falling as rapidly, as a share of Nigeria's naira economy, as they did relative to industrial country prices (figure 18.3 deflates by the US consumer price index).

The continued importance of oil rents in Nigeria's economy mirrors their importance as a flash point for political conflict. Nigeria is a striking example of what Sachs and Warner (2001) call the "natural-resource curse': the systematic tendency for narrowly specialized primary commodity exporters to grow more slowly than countries with more diversified exports. Where did Nigeria's natural resource rents end up, if not as productive domestic investments capable of supporting economic growth? One answer is in capital flight: virtually all the former military rulers amassed huge fortunes in foreign bank accounts. We argue below that the political environment of military rule rewarded rent-seeking activities, bribery, and corruption. Another answer is that domestic investment, particularly by the public sector, was often highly inefficient. Ethnic rivalries encouraged Northern political elites to ignore the Southern part of the country, where oil resources originated, in favor of developing the North. In pursuance of this goal, many costly mistakes were made regarding the siting of investment projects.

Given Nigeria's federal structure, the allocation of revenue and spending authority both vertically – between the federal government and the state and local governments – and horizontally – mainly across state governments – was a focal point for distributional struggles since before independence. Ekpo (1994) and Ekpo and Ubok-Udom (2003) document the repeated attempts to establish a widely acceptable revenue-sharing arrangement at the constitutional level. In the very early post-independence period, when the mainstay of the nation's economy was agriculture, fiscal rules were characterized by substantial revenue and expenditure decentralization. The principal of derivation was unquestionably accepted, implying that states retained the bulk of tax revenues derived from local economic activity. This arrangement was reversed from the mid-1960s, however, as oil became a major revenue-earner. The twin principles governing all subsequent arrangements – the bulk of which were developed under northern military governments – were that oil revenues would accrue in the first instance to the federal government, and that a major component of these revenues would flow to the states via block grants allocated with reference mainly to equality across states and population (Suberu 2001). These criteria guaranteed a massive redistribution of oil revenues to the northern part of the country.[6] Regional distributional struggles were exacerbated over time by the neglect

---

[6] These two principles accounted for 100 percent of horizontal revenue allocation in 1970–81, 80 percent in 1981–90, and 70 percent in 1970–2000. As the weight given to these principles declined starting in 1981, a small weight was placed on the level of social

of infrastructural deficiencies and environmental damage (air and water pollution and agricultural land degradation) in the oil-producing areas of the country.

In table 18.4 we document the regional bias in revenue-allocation policies, emphasizing the vertical allocation of oil revenues between the states of derivation and the federal government and providing examples of public investment decisions with a clear regional character.

1.2.4 Periodization

In what follows we split the 1960–2000 period into two sub-periods, with the line of demarcation given by the initiation of major economic reforms under the aegis of the 1987 SAP. We refer to these periods as the *pre-liberalization era* (1960–86) and the *economic liberalization era* (1987–2000). Overall economic growth differed only marginally between the two periods, at 0.18 percent during the period of economic controls and 0.80 percent during the liberalization era. But as indicated in figure 18.1 and table 18.1, the intertemporal pattern of growth differed markedly, with the first period characterized by a massive "boom and bust" cycle and the second by protracted stagnation following an initial burst of growth. As we will see, while 1986/7 marks the outset of a cumulatively substantial reorientation of economic policy in Nigeria, the legacies of the earlier period, combined with the continued realities of political conflict in Nigeria, prevented any fundamental transformation of the growth environment through the end of the century.

In section 2 we provide an overview of macroeconomic and debt-management policies over the entire 1960–2000 period. Sections 3 and 4 contain the bulk of our analysis. For each of the two major sub-periods, we undertake a detailed study of the determinants of growth performance, focusing in turn on economic policies and outcomes at the macroeconomic and sectoral levels, the changing institutional organization of key markets, the response of microeconomic agents to the policy environment, and the political economy of policy and governance. Some concluding remarks are made in section 5.

2. Macroeconomic policy, debt management, and growth, 1960–2000

This section presents a comprehensive analysis of macroeconomic and debt management policies in Nigeria in 1960–2000.

development, another criterion distinctly favoring the North, with its lower income and educational attainments (Suberu 2001: 59, table 2).

Table 18.4 *Nigeria, regional bias in oil revenue allocation, 1957–*

Leaders	Notable actions on oil revenue-sharing
Abubakar Tafawa Balewa (1957–66)	Supported the construction of the first Port Harcourt Refinery by Shell BP in 1965. Established several industries in the Northern part of Nigeria: Funtua Seed Cotton Mill, Arewa Textile Mill, etc.
Major-General Johnson Aguiyi-Ironsi (1966)	No notable action.
General Yakubu Gowon (1966–75)	Initiated the construction of the Yakubu Gowon Dam in Kano. Established the Volkswagen and Peugeot Plants in Lagos and Kaduna. Responsible for the construction of dual road network across the country. Built the National Stadium and the National Arts Theater in Lagos. Carved out twelve States from the original four regions in 1967. Established the Nigerian Agricultural Bank with headquarters in the North. Seized offshore oil as federal property and, in 1971, assigned all revenues from offshore oil to the federal government, without regard to state of location.
General Murtala Muhammed (1975–6)	Created additional seven states out of the existing twelve, to make nineteen in 1976. Set up the machinery for the movement of the Federal Capital Territory from Lagos to Abuja. Completed the Fertilizer Plant in Kaduna.
General Olusegun Obasanjo (1976–9)	Initiated the construction of the Ajaokuta Steel Company, Delta Steel Company, Aladja, and established the Oshogbo Steel Rolling Mill, Nigerian Machine Tools Limited, Oshogbo, and the Katsina and Jos Steel Rolling Mills. Ensured the take-off of the Warri Refinery in 1978. Reduced the 50 percent non-off-shore oil royalties and rents due to state of origin from 50 percent to 30 percent.
Alhaji Shehu Shagari (1979–83)	Established the Aluminum Smelter Company of Nigeria at Ikot Abasi in 1983 to make up for several industries located in the North by his administration, including the Kaduna refinery, which started operation in 1980. Completed an additional steel plant and three rolling mills at Ajaokuta. Reduced the share of oil royalties and rents to state of origin from 30 percent to 2 percent.

General Muhammadu Buhari (1983–5)	Probed and detained several corrupt military governors and ministers. Reduced the share of oil royalties and rents to state of origin from 2 percent to 1.5 percent.
General Ibrahim Babangida (1985–93)	Increased the share of oil royalties and rents to state of origin from 1.5 percent to 3 percent. Established the Oil Mineral Producing Area Development Commission (OMPADEC) in 1992. Established the Federal Environmental Protection Agency (FEPA) in 1985, with headquarters at Abuja. Created two additional states (Akwa Ibom and Katsina) and several local government councils. Built the Toja Bridge in Kebbi, established the Jibia Water Treatment plant and the Challawa Cenga Dam in Kano. Moved the seat of the Federal Government to Abuja on December 12, 1991. Annulled June 12 election results. Commissioned Ajaokuta Steel Company. Introduced the SAP in 1986. Created eleven more states with a bias towards the North.
Chief Ernest Shonekan (August–November 1993)	No notable action.
General Sani Abacha (1993–8)	Created six new states and 181 new local government councils with a heavy bias towards the north on December 5, 1996. Looted the Nigerian Treasury; initiated the Vision 2010 economic blueprint for Nigeria; promulgated Decree 18 in 1994 to facilitate the trial of the executives of failed banks.
General Abdusalam Abubakar (1998–9)	Granted autonomy to the Central Bank of Nigeria in the formulation and implementation of monetary policies. Established the Independent Electoral Commission (INEC) and facilitated the hand-over of power to a Civilian Administration in 1999.
Chief Olusegun Obasanjo (1999–)	Established the Niger Delta Development Commission (NDDC) and increased the 3 percent for oil producing states from the Federation account to 13 percent to enhance development and solve ecological problems. Introduced the Universal Basic Education Program (UBE) to enhance the literacy level of Nigerians. Introduced the Independent Corrupt Practices Commission (ICPC) to check fraudulent financial activities of Nigerians. Resuscitated the National Fertilizer Company (NAFCOM) in Kaduna and Onne–Port Harcourt.

Source: Compiled by the authors (2006).

2.1 Macroeconomic policy, 1960–2000

Given the prevailing orthodoxy that industrialization was a prerequisite for rapid economic growth, the aim of government at independence was to promote industry and manufacturing – then accounting for less than 8 and 4 percent of GDP, respectively (Iyoha 2003) – through development planning. During 1962–85, the country used the approach of fixed medium-term plans. Four Development Plans were adopted and implemented in succession.[7]

During the era of development programming, fiscal, monetary, and commercial policies were used as the key tools for achieving plan objectives. While these objectives included attention to both industry and agriculture, the discovery of oil and its predominant position after 1974 led to the relative neglect of agriculture.

With the end of the oil boom in 1982, Nigeria found itself in an economic crisis. Internal problems included economic contraction, high unemployment, inflation, and rising fiscal deficits; external problems included chronic current account and balance of payments deficits, an escalating external debt stock, and a rising debt-service burden. There was also ample evidence of sectoral disequilibrium, as demonstrated by the emasculation of the agricultural sector, the stunted development of the industrial sector, a lop-sided dependence on the oil sector, and the repression of the financial sector. Between 1982 and 1986, the government made a valiant attempt to combat the economic crisis, adopting a variety of austerity measures as reflected particularly in the Economic Stabilization Act of 1982 and the National Economic Emergency Act of 1985. However, because of the fundamental nature of the economic and financial disequilibria, the government found that mere austerity without structural adjustment constituted an inadequate response to the economic crisis. Matters came to a head in early 1986 when the world oil market collapsed and the price of oil fell by over 50 percent. With Nigeria's earnings from petroleum exports tumbling from approximately US$25 billion in 1980 to US$6.4 billion in 1986, trade arrears piling up, and international credit lines disappearing, the nation was on the verge of economic collapse. Accordingly, in July 1986, the government adopted a SAP in order to bring about a fundamental restructuring of the economy to ensure its long-term survival.

The origins of the SAP can be traced to the oil boom of the 1970s, and the structural maladjustments engendered by the associated macroeconomic policy response. The quadrupling of oil prices (consequent on the Arab–Israeli War) in November 1973 and their renewed sharp increase in 1979

---

[7] These were the First National Development Plan (NDP), 1962–8, the Second NDP, 1970–4, the Third NDP, 1975–80, and the Fourth NDP, 1981–5.

resulted in an unprecedented transfer of wealth to Nigeria. Export revenues skyrocketed, producing major increases in foreign exchange reserves, imports, and domestic incomes. The oil boom came to an end with the collapse of oil prices in 1982 and the rise in real interest rates on a world-wide basis. Revenues from oil exports dropped precipitously, balance of payments deficits emerged, international reserves fell to precariously low levels, and the debt crisis appeared.

In retrospect, Nigeria clearly showed more flexibility in adapting to the short-run possibilities generated by the oil boom than it did in adjusting to the end of the boom. During the boom, government expenditures rose to mop up the phenomenal inflow of foreign exchange. As noted earlier, real wage rates increased and the real exchange rate appreciated sharply. The spending effect of the commodity boom resulted in a classic case of the "Dutch disease," in the form of a decline in the non-booming traded-goods sectors, most notably agriculture. On the eve of the oil price collapses of the 1980s (1982, 1986), the Nigerian economy was precariously dependent on oil. Petroleum production accounted for nearly a quarter of total GDP, for 90 percent of foreign exchange earnings, and for 70 percent of budgetary revenues.

While sharp increases in aggregate spending, imports, real wages, and real exchange rates are consistent with an efficient macroeconomic adjustment to a highly persistent boom, they rely on an implausible level of downward flexibility if the boom in question is known with reasonable probability to be temporary. Sharp reductions in government spending, imported inputs and capital goods, real wages, and real exchange rates are all politically difficult, as is a reversal of real exchange rate movements that have favored a booming non-traded-goods sector. In Nigeria, such adjustments did not take place. Instead government spending, imports, and the real exchange rate were all kept at unrealistically high levels as oil prices fell. The consequence of these macroeconomic policy mistakes was the emergence of current account and balance of payments deficits, which in turn implied an escalating external debt stock and a falling reserve:import ratio. A more prudent response to the original boom would have relied more heavily on accumulating foreign assets, to support a more moderate but more sustained increase in domestic spending (Gavin 1993). From this perspective it was the inability of the Nigerian economy to adjust to post-oil boom realities, and the associated policy inadequacies during the boom period, that produced the economic crisis of the early 1980s.

The central objective of Nigeria's SAP was to restructure and diversify the productive base of the economy in order to reduce dependence on the oil sector and on imports. The main SAP measures included (1) deregulation of the exchange rate, (2) trade liberalization, (3) deregulation of the financial sector, (4) rationalization and privatization of public sector enterprises, and

(5) adoption of appropriate domestic pricing policies (by eliminating subsidies) especially for petroleum products (Federal Government of Nigeria
1986). Originally planned to last for only two years (July 1986–June 1988),
the SAP was extended several times to allow for the phased introduction of
the requisite policy reforms and provide a period within which results could
come to fruition – in policy analysis, therefore, the SAP epoch is now generally taken to cover the period from 1987 to 1992. Unfortunately, the SAP
did not deliver all its protagonists promised. Deregulation and liberalization
improved conditions for agriculture and led to positive developments in the
financial sector, as we shall see; and overall economic growth rebounded
during the SAP period. But as of the early 1990s there was little evidence
that reforms had transformed the overall climate for growth.

Nigeria abandoned fixed-term development planning and embraced Perspective Planning in 1990. In the post-1990 period, Perspective Planning was
intended to provide a fifteen–twenty-year-ahead framework within which
medium-term planning could take place and an annual budget be developed.
However, lack of focus, policy inconsistency, corruption, fiscal profligacy,
and deficit financing combined to weaken Perspective Planning and reduce
its gains. Assessing the long-term impact of planning in Nigeria, Okojie
(2003) concludes that:

After four decades of planning, the aspirations of Nigerians at Independence for a
prosperous economy and stable polity are yet to be realized. If anything, the quality
of life of majority of Nigerians is worse than it was at Independence. (2003: 369)

2.2   Debt management, 1960–2000

By the 1990s, Nigeria was among the fifteen most heavily indebted poor
countries of the world. Despite its oil wealth, Nigeria was at the end of the
century one of thirty officially designated "severely indebted low-income
countries" (a group including twenty-four other countries in SSA) and one
of thirty "debt-distressed" countries in SSA (Onah 1994). In 1999, Nigeria's external public debt amounted to over US$28 billion, equivalent to 87
percent of GDP. Excluding arrears, annual debt service obligations totaled
US$4.14 billion, or 30 percent of exports of goods and non-factor services;
and since actual debt service payments in 1999 amounted to only US$1.7
billion, arrears were continuing to accumulate. By the end of 1997 outstanding arrears had already reached the astronomical level of US$15 billion,
equivalent to 52 percent of the total debt stock (Central Bank of Nigeria
2002).

Nigeria's debt stock at the end of the century was a legacy of borrowing that
began in the late 1970s and accelerated with the rise in international interest
rates and the collapse of oil export earnings in the early 1980s. Arguably

"under-borrowed" before the second OPEC oil shock (the external debt stock amounted to a mere US$1 billion, equivalent to 8 percent of income, in 1977), Nigeria became, by the early 1990s, one of the most heavily indebted countries in the world. External debt peaked at over US$33 billion in 1991; in 1993, external debt *per capita* amounted to US$300, considerably more than Nigeria's income *per capita* at official exchange rates. Accompanying the escalating external debt was a crushing debt-service burden and a sequence of debt-rescheduling exercises. After peaking at about 40 percent in 1986, the actual debt-service ratio (the ratio of debt-service payments to export earnings) showed a declining trend, reaching 22 percent in 1990 and 14 percent in 1996. Reductions in debt service paid during the 1990s were strongly influenced by Nigeria's unilateral decision in 1993 to limit debt-service payments to no more than 30 percent of net oil revenues – a decision that led to the non-servicing of much of the Paris Club debt and, therefore, to the steady growth of arrears.

A direct consequence of Nigeria's high debt-service burden was insufficient foreign exchange to finance the importation of the raw materials, intermediate goods, and capital goods needed for rapid economic development. Nigeria was thus in the invidious position of having to allocate increasingly rising amounts of its dwindling foreign exchange earnings to debt service. The deleterious effect of the escalating external debt was aggravated by domestic macroeconomic policy deficiencies which resulted in declining GNP *per capita*, uneven growth of real GDP, mounting fiscal deficits, and rising inflation.

Debt-management policies included: commercial debt restructurings and reschedulings; debt buy-backs at a discount with interested bilateral creditors; interest rate options; and debt-conversion schemes such as the debt–equity swap. In the second half of the 1980s, Nigeria's primary instrument for managing the external debt problem was commercial debt restructuring and debt rescheduling. However, as Ogbe (1992) and others have demonstrated, this tool fails to address the underlying problem of an unsustainably high debt stock: indeed, the recapitalization of interest and arrears leads to an increase in it. Frequent debt rescheduling exercises in London and Paris also entail sizeable administrative and financial costs for the borrowing country. An analysis of the records also shows that the practical impact of debt buy-backs and debt conversion-schemes was minuscule. Proceeds from the debt-conversion program (including the debt–equity swap) were small, amounting to US$1.276 billion during the ten years between July 1988 and December 1997. This is not surprising given that Nigeria's capital market is under-developed, thin, and shallow. Until late in the 1990s, moreover, creditors may have been deterred by over-valued official exchange rates which made naira assets over-priced. A substantial reduction was, however, achieved through the debt buy-back deal closed in 1992. Under this arrangement, 62 percent of the London Club debt of $5.8 billion was bought back, with the remaining $2.1 billion converted into par bonds.

3. Explaining growth performance, 1960–1986

The pre-economic liberalization period was characterized by what Collier and O'Connell (2006) call "soft controls," reflecting direct government intervention in prices and often quantities in key markets throughout the economy. National planning was in the ascendancy, with rapid economic development to be brought about through a series of fixed-term National Development Plans (NDPs). During the pre-civil war period, growth in *per capita* income was moderate, driven by agricultural exports (mainly cocoa, groundnuts, palm oil, and rubber) and the massive draw-down of foreign exchange reserves and Marketing Board surpluses accumulated during the Korean War agricultural export boom of the 1950s. Growth accelerated sharply after the civil war, driven mainly by petroleum exports, but then, as we have seen, collapsed under the weight of falling oil prices during the first half of the 1980s.

Oil already accounted for 57.5 percent of total exports in 1970 but by 1977 it accounted for 93.3 percent (Iyoha 1995). During the boom, balance of payments surpluses and buoyant government revenues led to a major expansion in government expenditures, including capital expenditures. Commendably, much of the federal government's recurrent spending during the 1970s went into educational expansion. The Western and Eastern Regions had already introduced Universal Primary Education (UPE) to the Southern parts of the country, but during this period the Northern Region introduced free primary and secondary education and even adopted a program of awarding overseas scholarships to its indigenes. The percentage of the federal government budget devoted to education was between 5 percent and 10 percent in the 1970s, as compared to less than 1 percent committed by the colonial government (Central Bank of Nigeria 2002). The number of federally-owned universities expanded from one to six during the period.

Investment, and particularly public investment, rose very sharply during this period: in 1976, the aggregate investment: income ratio was an impressive 31.5 percent while the public investment: income ratio amounted to 24.4 percent. The absence of sustained growth in the Nigerian economy, despite these high investment rates, is partly traceable to the inefficiency of the public sector's investment response. As Bevan, Collier, and Gunning (1992: 2) observe, the public investment response was intertemporally inefficient in terms of both its ultimate magnitude and in terms of the domestic investments undertaken. The ideal response to an export price boom is to invest the proceeds in income-earning assets abroad and to repatriate them only as the economy develops domestic investment projects with a social rate of return at least as high as that of the nation's overseas portfolio. Nigerian policy-makers succeeded initially in accumulating international reserves, but public investment programs were then pushed rapidly and with little concern for efficiency. Policy-makers fell prey to a vision of import-substituting indus-trialization that was already discredited at the time, allocating vast sums to public sector mega-projects (including two steel mills built at a cost of some US$11 billion) that were never able to compete in world markets.

While this period was dominated (from the civil war onwards) by military rule, the brief interregnum of civilian rule in between 1979 and 1983 did not bring greater coherence to economic policy in Nigeria. Instead, while military administrators had depended heavily on the civil service to initiate and implement economic policies, the civilian administration of President Alhaji Shehu Shagari saw a drastic reduction in the powers of the civil service and an increase in rent-seeking activity. Maximization of political support through patronage became the order of the day; patronage was made easier by increasing the number of states and by failing to enforce legal rules against corruption. Kickbacks appear to have increased the costs of investment projects spectacularly: the contract for the construction of a dam, for example, which had been concluded by the military government for US$120 million, was renegotiated by the civilian government for US$600 million (Bevan, Collier, and Gunning 1992: 8).

Over the full period of the oil boom, the excessive and highly inefficient public investment response is consistent with successive governments hav-ing viewed the boom as effectively permanent. Bevan, Collier, and Gunning (1992) observe that it was not until after the fall of oil revenues in 1980–1 that the Nigerian government recognized the transitory nature of the shock. But during the period of military government, the public investment strat-egy reflects in addition the capital-accumulation dogma of the civil service, while during the civilian period public investment became a focal point for patronage and corruption. Throughout the period, the oil-financed invest-ment boom contributed little to the underlying growth process of the econ-omy.

Having reviewed the basic macroeconomic management of the oil boom and bust, we now turn to sectoral policies affecting trade and agricultural.

3.1   Trade and commercial policy

Nigeria's trade policy between 1960 and 1970 was basically a continuation of colonial trade policies, with their heavy use of quantitative import controls, licensing systems, and prohibitions. Over the full 1960–87 period the thrust of trade policy was inward-oriented, aimed at developing a local techno-logical base in industrial production and achieving self-sufficiency in food and raw materials. Under this strategy of import-substituting industrialization (ISI), "infant" manufacturing industries were protected using the whole range of tariff barriers and NTBs. Trade policy was at times adjusted endogenously to balance of payments pressure; the policy of export promotion and market penetration through bilateral arrangements, for example, was adopted to offset emerging balance of payments problems. For much of the 1960–87 period, foreign exchange was available for the purchase of capital goods and there was orderly and steady supply of both durable and semi-durable consumer goods. More importantly, expansion was stimulated in local primary production for both exports and internal consumption. In order to harness these positive contributions, tariffs were altered from time to time.

The trade and industrial policies pursued during this period resulted in a rapid increase in manufacturing production and employment from its very low initial base, particularly during the era of the oil boom (1975–80). The share of manufacturing in GDP rose from 5.6 percent in 1962/3 to 8.7 percent in 1986. Yet, *ex post*, Nigeria's ISI policy must be viewed as largely unsuccessful. As the ISI period drew to a close, manufacturing sector remained tiny as a share of GDP as well as of exports. Protected industries continued to have high import content. Perhaps most fundamentally, firms with a prior interest in the market accounted for the major part of Nigeria's ISI, suggesting that the tools of trade policy had mainly rewarded incumbents rather than creating new entry (Bevan, Collier, and Gunning 1999: 31).

3.2 Agriculture and agricultural policy

At independence in 1960, Nigeria was an agricultural country and agriculture was the most dynamic sector of its economy. The country was self-sufficient in the production of staple foods. The oil boom of the 1970s, however, led to a severe disruption of the agricultural economy. In a classic case of "Dutch disease," labor and other resources were drawn out of agriculture and into the cities and industrial locations producing non-traded goods.[8] Between 1970 and 1982, the annual production of the country's major cash crops – cocoa, rubber, cotton, and groundnuts – fell by 43 percent, 29 percent, 65 percent, and 64 percent, respectively. Nigeria's share in the world

---

[8] Sachs and Warner (2001: 833) outline the "Dutch disease" as follows:

> Positive wealth shocks from the natural resource sector create excess demand for non-traded products and drive up non-traded prices, including particularly non-traded input costs and wages. This, in turn, squeezes profits in traded activities such as manufacturing that use those non-traded products as inputs, yet sell their products on international markets at relatively fixed international prices.

> This has made the export products of resource-rich economies less competitive on international markets.

production of cocoa fell from about 16 percent to roughly 8 percent. The share of agricultural imports in the total import bill meanwhile rose, from roughly 3 percent in the late 1960s to some 7 percent in the late 1970s and then over 10 percent in the early 1980s. By the early 1980s, Nigeria – once a net agricultural exporter – spent more on agricultural imports than it earned from agricultural exports.

The "natural-resource curse" goes beyond standard "Dutch disease" effects and may involve a general de-emphasis of growth-oriented economic activities such as agriculture and manufacturing when the contribution of a specific natural resource seems to meet current expenditure requirements (Sachs and Warner 2001). In Nigeria, the precipitous decline in agriculture was exacerbated by erratic import policies and counter-productive government pricing policies for both food crops and cash crops. In the absence of the oil boom, it is likely that agriculture and manufacturing would have received more serious attention in the localities or regions that made up the Nigerian federation and such attention could have initiated a sustainable growth process. Additional and highly debilitating effects can operate through the impetus to rent-seeking that a major and highly concentrated natural resource can create (Sachs and Warner 2001). In the case of Nigeria, rent-seeking and corruption often diverted oil earnings into private hands, with a huge part of these earnings then leaving the country as capital flight rather than being deployed to fuel economic growth and development at home.

While the effect of the oil boom on the cash crop sector was severe, its effect on the production of staple food crops was disastrous. Within a short period of time Nigeria went from being a food exporter to being a food-import-dependent economy. Between 1960 and 1966 Nigeria was self-sufficient in basic food items. Staple food production expanded *pari passu* with population growth, and staple foods were not imported. The small amount of food imports – never exceeding 11 percent of total imports – consisted mainly of sugar, fruits, milk, fish, beverages, and beer, items purchased mainly by high-income-earners in urban areas. The country remained self-sufficient in food production during the civil war (1967–70). However, the situation changed dramatically as a result of the oil boom. In 1971, maize and rice became imported food items for the first time. This was a harbinger of things to come: by 1975, Nigeria had become a net importer of food, with food imports exceeding food exports for the first time.

It may be asked whether Nigeria's loss of food self-sufficiency status from 1975 onward was due to the oil boom or to an agricultural policy failure. The answer is that it was due to both. Although government reacted to the loss of food self-sufficiency with various programs and policies (discussed below), its response was clearly inadequate. The agricultural policy of the government, at both the macro and micro levels, tended to boost the effect of the oil-boom-induced "Dutch disease," leading to further marginalization of agriculture.

At the macro level, only 3 percent of government (federal and state) disbursements were allocated to agricultural investments in the 1970s. The bulk of Nigeria's increased public expenditure went instead into transport, primary education, construction, and some high-profile industrial projects such as the Ajaokuta Steel Complex. Focusing on federal government policy, Bevan, Collier, and Gunning (1999: 171) point out that:

in the 1970s the share of agriculture in Federal expenditure declined to 5 percent (1970–74) and 2.5 percent (1975–79). This occurred although the Federal government took over many agricultural responsibilities from the regions – an act probably motivated by the desire to emasculate the regions rather than to stimulate agriculture.

The same authors point to a policy reversal in the late 1970s that permitted foreign companies to acquire large-scale interests in agriculture. In a context of general government antagonism to foreign investment, they interpret this reversal as confirmation of policy-makers' low regard for agriculture. The sector was not important enough to warrant an increased allocation of domestic resources; its travails therefore led, instead, to its re-opening to foreign investment (Bevan, Collier, and Gunning 1999).

At the microeconomic level, Nigerian agricultural policy in the 1970s can be criticized for its deficiencies in three key areas: (1) failure to encourage private price-setting and marketing channels; (2) failure to ensure a workable agricultural credit system; and (3) failure to provide necessary infrastructure and thus an enabling economic environment to support provision of key services such as machinery maintenance, repairs, and the supply of spare parts to farmers. Most damaging of all were the Commodity Boards, which taxed farmers heavily by setting low producer prices.

Before independence, government support to agriculture focused on the major export crops. The government's interest in cocoa, palm produce, rubber, cotton, and groundnuts derived from the fact that during the 1946–60 period these cash crops had accounted for between 83 percent and 92 percent of the total export revenue (although constituting only about 17 percent of total agricultural produce). The government seemed content to leave the issue of self-sufficiency in the production of food crops and raw materials to private initiative. The critical issue of employment-generating investment in agriculture was also left to the private sector. The relative neglect of agriculture during this period seems surprising given the fact that agriculture contributed roughly 65 percent of GDP and nearly 80 percent of adult employment and exports in the early 1960s.

Agricultural policies underwent a set of fundamental changes after independence. These reflected changes in government philosophy as much as changes in governments themselves. The 1960s were characterized by a decentralized approach to agriculture, major policy initiatives were left to the states, with the federal government playing only a supporting role. Before the end of the decade, however, production shortfalls led to increasing prices for foodstuffs and staples and decreasing shares in world exports. These outcomes were largely attributable to declining productivity in the agricultural sector. The unsustainability of this situation, particularly with respect to food shortages, galvanized the government into action during the next major phase. With the creation of a twelve-state structure in 1967 by the Gowon administration, attention was directed towards improved production in the agricultural sector and efforts were directed at the processing of export crops with a view to expanding and diversifying the country's foreign exchange earnings. Planning objectives included an increase in agricultural employment sufficient to absorb the growing rural population. Price incentives were to play a prominent role in improving agricultural performance: reasonable producer prices were introduced and kept under constant review, and the administration of these prices was improved.

The 1971–86 period was characterized by a greater involvement of government in agricultural development as a result of the belief that only a more pronounced intervention could arrest the decline in agriculture. Initiatives included the setting up of specialized institutions and the launching of special program and projects. In 1973, the National Accelerated Food Production Program (NAFPP) was launched, with the objective of accelerating the production of food crops such as maize, cassava, sorghum, rice, wheat, and millet. The 1970s also witnessed the setting up of the Integrated Agriculture Development Projects (ADPs), the River Basin Development Authorities (RBDAs), the National Seeds Services (NSS), and the Commodity Boards. The ADPs concentrated on providing inputs (fertilizer, agro-chemicals, and farm machinery), extension services and training in the use of improved farm methods, and credit facilities to enable farmers to purchase required inputs. Nigeria had become a food-deficit country in 1975; during the 1975–80 period, the estimated total expenditure by the government on its various food programs amounted to over N1.5 billion.

The setting up of two new Commodity Boards in 1976 – the Nigerian Grains Board and the Nigerian Tuber and Root Crops Board – signaled the advent of government intervention in the marketing and distribution of staple food in the Nigerian economy. Existing Commodity Boards, such as the Nigerian Cocoa Marketing Board (NCMB), had been charged only with the marketing of cash crops.

Two programs, Operation Feed the Nation (OFN) (1976–9) and the Green Revolution Program (1979–83), were also launched during this period. The OFN campaign, which was launched by both federal and state military governments in 1976, had three objectives: (1) mobilizing the country towards self-sufficiency and self-reliance in food through increased food production; (2) encouraging citizens who had hitherto relied on buying food to grow their own, thereby increasing total food production and reducing food prices; and (3) encouraging balanced nutrition as a way of producing a healthy nation. The OFN program was later integrated into the Green Revolution Program launched by the civilian government in 1979. Two important initiatives that were part of these programs were the setting up of the Nigerian Agricultural and Co-operative Bank (NACB) and the Agricultural Credit Guarantee Scheme Fund (ACGSF). The main objective of the NACB was the provision of adequate finance to farmers at affordable terms.

In spite of these initiatives, however, this period was ultimately one of agricultural decline. What spelled doom for Nigerian agriculture was the oil boom and its aftermath. Rising urban wages and the over-valued naira made domestic production of food unviable; agricultural output grew at an annual rate of only 1 percent over the period, while population increased at the rate of 3 percent. Food imports increased as the gap between food supply and food demand widened. The capacity of agriculture to absorb the growing labor force weakened, leading to an exodus from the land. Whereas about 75 percent of the labor force was engaged in agriculture in 1960, this percentage had fallen to 52 percent in 1985. The share of agriculture in GDP had meanwhile fallen to 24 percent and the share of agricultural products in total exports to 2 percent. The quantity exported of virtually every cash crop declined in the 1970s.

3.3   Market institutions

Most market institutions were highly regulated during the pre-liberalization period, a phenomenon we witnessed in the case of agricultural markets. We turn briefly now to developments in the financial, labor, and foreign exchange markets.

3.3.1   The financial market

The Central Bank of Nigeria (CBN), established in 1959, is at the apex of the financial market in Nigeria. It is empowered to supervise and regulate the activities of banks and other financial institutions in the country. The Securities and Exchange Commission (SEC), which is the regulating body in the capital market, was established in 1961. Of the seventeen banks in Nigerian in 1964, only six were foreign-owned and controlled. In spite of the large number of indigenous banks, these banks controlled less than 15 percent of total deposits of the banking system. The three largest banks – all foreign-owed – accounted for over 70 percent of total deposits. One important feature of the financial market between 1960 and 1977 was the introduction of rural banking.

3.3.2 The labor market

Before the outbreak of the civil war in 1967, the unemployment rate in the Nigerian economy was very low. Immediately after the civil war, however, the labor market became flooded with unskilled rural workers, young school leavers, artisans, and technical workers from trade schools. Efforts made to solve the unemployment problem during this era included the introduction of farm settlement schemes and the National Youth Service Corps (NYSC) scheme. Though plausible, these efforts were not equal to the task they were given. The unemployment problem was partly attributable to inappropriate education and training, which over-emphasized paper qualifications to the detriment of needed technical training. The majority of highly technical jobs were handled by foreigners.

Industrial relations were seriously disturbed in 1975. A total of 766 trade disputes were reported between January and December, 345 of them resulting in work stoppages involving about 117,089 workers and a loss of 435,492 man-days. In 1974, 338 trade disputes were reported, involving 129 work stoppages and 62,565 workers and a loss of 144,881 man-days. Yet, the overall position during the second half of the 1960–87 period showed a loose labor market where unemployment was rising and job openings scarce, owing to the general decline in economic activities precipitated by the declining oil revenues.

3.3.3 The land market

To the Nigerian peasant farmer, land is not a commodity to be traded for its exchange value. It is considered as nature's gift to man, to be used for his benefit and to be passed on to succeeding generations. In the decade immediately after independence this philosophy increased the impetus behind land acquisition and led inevitably to land fragmentation. However, the acquisition and use of land were subject to different land tenure systems in the different communities. In the North, the Emirs had authority to distribute land to their subjects in the emirate. Peasant farmers who occupied land paid tithe and tax in cash and kind to the Emir or members of his immediate family. The well-to-do people in the community also owned land and recruited laborers to work on these holdings. In the East, among the Ibo, communal land was inherited through the head of the family, and family members were often encouraged to use the land for food crops. Those who succeeded in acquiring virgin land automatically became the rightful owners of such land. Individuals also acquired land through purchase. Among the Yoruba of the Southwest, the village chief acted as a trustee of the community land; he could authorize the redistribution of land and prevent alienation, and leases could be granted to non-indigenes as tenants with the approval of the owners of the land. Among the Bini in the Southwest, before the Land Use

Decree of 1978, the Oba was the sole trustee of land in the community. The power of allocation to end-users resided in the land-allocation committees set up by him (Central Bank of Nigeria 2000).

The estimated land area *per capita* in Nigeria declined from 1.9 ha in 1961 to 1.1 ha in 1986, while the available cultivable land area *per capita* declined from 1.4 ha to 1.1 ha. Traditional systems were not well suited to handling this population pressure, tending instead to aggravate the fragmentation of land and arrest the introduction of land-use planning and improved farming systems. Acquiring land for farming in Nigeria remained an arduous task, resulting in the over-use of marginal lands and the perpetuation of low farm productivities and incomes.

3.3.4 The foreign exchange market

Before the enactment of the Foreign Exchange Control Act in 1962, foreign exchange was earned by the private sector and held in balances abroad by commercial banks on behalf of local exporters. The establishment of the CBN shortly before independence facilitated the development of a local foreign exchange market, as the authority to manage Nigeria's foreign exchange was centralized in the Central Bank. Between 1960 and 1987, the CBN operated a fixed exchange rate regime and several policies were introduced to ensure a viable balance of payments position. These included: trade and exchange controls, export promotion, external reserves diversification, and the introduction of formal administrative mechanisms for external debt management and exchange rate administration. For most of the period, the authorization of foreign exchange disbursements was shared by the Federal Ministry of Finance and the CBN, with the Ministry of Finance handling public sector applications and the CBN allocating foreign exchange to the private sector.

Starting with the civil war, balance of payments pressures are apparent in figure 18.5, in the sharply rising trend of the black market premium, a trend interrupted but not reversed by the favorable oil shocks of 1973/4 and 1978/9. Official exchange rate policy nonetheless paid relatively little attention to the parallel market, especially during the oil boom period. In February 1973, the Nigerian currency was devalued by 10 percent, in sympathy with the devaluation of the dollar that year; the intention was simply to safeguard external competitiveness, since the level of reserves was relatively comfortable. When the balance of payments came under acute pressure in the early 1980s, however, the decision to tighten exchange controls rather than devaluing the naira produced an exploding black market premium. Maxi-devaluations in 1986, and especially 1987, then brought the premium down, and an active exchange rate policy then kept it below 100 percent until the military coup of 1993 (see p. 624).

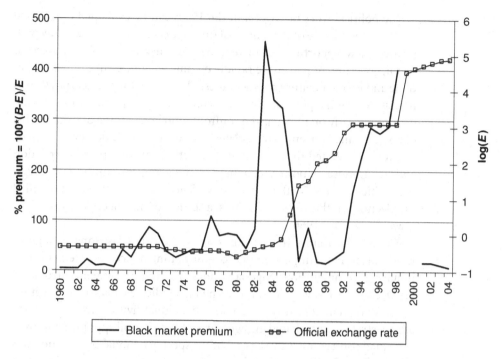

Figure 18.5 Nigeria, official exchange rate and black market premium, 1960–2004
Source: Until 1998, the black market exchange rate *B* is from the GDN, based on data
from the *World Currency Yearbook*. For 2001–4, *B* comes from *Africa Confidential*. The
official exchange rate *E* is from the IMF, *International Financial Statistics*. Both are in
naira per dollar.

3.4 Political economy and governance

The period 1960–87 had only two democratically elected governments: the
parliamentary government of Sir Abubakar Tafawa Balewa (1960–6) and
the presidential government of Alhaji Shehu Shagari (1979–83). There were
six military regimes, headed in turn by Major-General Johnson Aguiyi-
Ironsi (January/July 1966), General Yakubu Gowon (1966–75), General
Murtala Mohammed (1975–6), General Olusegun Obasanjo (1976–9), General Muhammadu Buhari (1983–5), and General Ibrahim Babangida (1985–
93). The rapid executive turnover characteristic of this period did not augur
well for economic growth and development. In spite of some scholars' contention that the organizational characteristics of coercion which the military
possessed could be used in mobilizing resources and achieving a break-
through in national economic development (e.g. Bello-Imam and Obadan
2004), the fragmentation of the military elites along ethnic lines and their
ineptitude in political and economic administration led only to retardation
of economic growth and development.

The political woes of Nigeria in the 1960s can be explained only if one takes full cognizance of the avarice of the political class. In an economy with relatively few opportunities for remunerative investment in the industrial sector, government patronage rapidly became a major source of benefits in trade and in other commercial activities. The contest for political power was re-cast by regional political elites as a contest for group economic survival, developing early on into a naked confrontation bereft of the outward forms of restraint and convention associated with western-style democracy. Leaders were discredited through public perceptions of widespread corruption and fraud, abuses of power, sectionalism, and nepotism; citizens lost faith in the political system. With the wave of violence and arson that accompanied the elections in the Western Regions, a section of the Nigerian army seized power in January 1966.

Though the Aguiyi-Ironsi administration did not last long enough to have a meaningful impact on the economy, it introduced the elements of a unitary government into Nigeria politics. The unitary system, introduced via Decree 34 of May 1966, was designed to eradicate tribalism and regionalism. To this end it provided for a unified national civil service and a strong administrative center based in Lagos. From the center, all appointments were to be made on a competitive basis. The prospect of national competition was perceived by Northern political elites, however, as placing the region at an acute disadvantage in accessing the executive cadres of the civil service. The Decree led to the outbreak of severe rioting in the North. This marked the beginning of bitter ethno-regional rivalries in resource allocation, recruitment, and the control of executive power, and contributed directly to the outbreak of the civil war in 1967.

The Gowon administration's approach to economic management and development was laid down in the Second NDP (1970–4), which focused on the post-war reconstruction and the promotion of economic and social development. With the oil price hikes of 1973 and thereafter, the administration enjoyed huge revenue receipts which they utilized in providing infrastructure in the form of road construction and building of new airports and refineries.

The Murtala Mohammed–Obasanjo administrations' management of the economy was anchored on the Third NDP (1975–80), launched in March 1976 by Gowon but modified after he was overthrown. The NDP provided for the expansion of agriculture, the oil and petrochemical industries, infrastructure, housing, and education. On the whole, it was projected that the national economy should be able to achieve a growth rate of 9.6 percent per annum during the NDP's implementation.

The civilian administration of Alhaji Shehu Shagari (1979–83) confronted a period of massively adverse external shocks and proved unable to reverse the political malpractices of the 1966–79 era. Instead, corruption deepened and the economy entered a downward slide characterized by sharp increases in poverty. In spite of the Green Revolution Program, the importation of food, including even such traditional staples as palm oil and rice, rose to alarming levels, constituting a serious drain on foreign earnings and reserves. The introduction of austerity measures such as the Economic Stabilization Act of 1982 did not improve the situation. The civilian regime was overthrown on December 31, 1982 by a clique of military officers led by Major-General Muhammadu Buhari. The Buhari regime (1983–5) was widely believed to be well intentioned. The administration froze wages, reduced government spending, and clamped down on "economic saboteurs" with the Miscellaneous Offences Decree 20 of 1984. The tough stabilization measures of the administration resulted in large-scale retrenchment of public workers and resulted in student protests against the re-introduction of school fees in higher institutions. On the whole, the well-intended measures of the Buhari regime were derailed by the dwindling revenues from oil exports and the tremendous burden of huge internal and external debts. The regime of General Buhari was overthrown in August 1985, in the wake of growing public criticism resulting from the increasing alienation of the civilian population. The Babangida administration took over and within a year had implemented the SAP.

4. Explaining growth performance, 1987–2000

The SAP and post-SAP periods were marked by deregulation and economic liberalization. However, the success of market liberalization was constrained throughout by haphazard implementation, frequent policy reversals, weak institutions, and the regional redistribution syndrome. Thus, in spite of a determined effort to deregulate and liberalize both the real and financial sectors of the economy, economic growth barely improved.

4.1 Performance of the manufacturing sector

The performance of the manufacturing sector was extremely poor during this sub-period. While weak growth in domestic aggregate demand may play some role, the more fundamental problem appears to be a consistent failure to meet price and quality competition from imports at the more modest levels of protection afforded by post-liberalization policies. The high price of domestic manufactures reflects, among other influences, inordinately high energy costs, inefficient and old equipment, and inadequate infrastructure. Other constraints which have been identified as militating against output growth are the incidents of civil and religious disturbances in some parts of the country, as well as the general insecurity of lives and property arising from banditry and armed robbery (Central Bank of Nigeria 2002). The issue of poor infrastructure, however, bears particular emphasis. Electricity was erratic and unreliable, with frequent power outages, load-shedding, and power rationing. The erratic nature of power supply forced high-income households and businesses to purchase generators at prohibitive initial and operating costs. The failure of infrastructural services extended to the areas of water supply and telecommunications. All these had implications for the cost of producing manufactured goods and, by extension, the competitiveness of domestic industry.

4.2   Trade and commercial policy

The SAP introduced in 1986 constituted the institutional framework for the design and application of trade and commercial policies for a substantial part of the 1987–2000 period. The government abolished Commodity Boards and deregulated the pricing and marketing of agricultural commodities. The import and export licensing system was also abolished and the number of import-prohibited items reduced. In 1988, the desire to provide a more stable and predictable tariff regime prompted the introduction of tariff reform. A tariff structure expected to last seven years was initiated, and variety of incentives were introduced to promote non-oil exports and FDI, including duty and tax concessions.

Towards the end of the 1980s, the continuation of economic distress led to the introduction of a new set of reform-oriented measures, some of which were a direct reversal of measures introduced under the SAP. Selected crops and their derivatives were placed under an export-prohibition list, in order to lower food prices and stimulate the output of agro-allied industries. The 1988 tariff reform was reversed before its seven-year expiration period, through amendments implemented in 1989, 1990, and 1991. In 1994, the Abacha government pegged the exchange rate at N22 to $1, a direct reversal of the move to a market-determined exchange rate. These policy reversals, and the conflicting policy objectives that produced them, acted over time to undermine the supply response to economic reforms.

4.3   Agricultural policy

From the early 1980s to the inception of the SAP in 1986, it became obvious that the agricultural sector could not keep up with domestic demands for food and raw materials. In addition to the creation of the Directorate for Foods, Roads, and Rural Infrastructure (DFRRI) in 1986, the government developed an agricultural policy as a part of a sectoral perspective plan up to the year 2005. The perspective plan stressed the introduction of financial policy measures to improve credit allocation to the agricultural sector, and in pursuance of this objective new financial institutions were established, including Community Banks and the People's Bank of Nigeria (PBN). The removal of price distortions under the SAP, however, probably had the greatest responsibility for the revival of agricultural production after 1986. Aggregate output of the agricultural sector grew by 7.5 percent per annum between 1986 and 1996, a rate significantly higher than during the pre-SAP period.

In targeting the reversal of "government failures" in the agricultural sector, the structure of the SAP paid less attention than was perhaps appropriate to the possibility of market failures. Thus although SAP reforms greatly reduced the output price distortions facing Nigeria's farmers, they also removed government input subsidies to the sector – subsidies that might have been justifiable as a means of encouraging the adoption and diffusion of yield-enhancing technologies (e.g. fertilizer-intensive seed varieties).

4.4 Market institutions

4.4.1 The financial market

The SAP introduced broad-based regulatory and institutional reforms in the financial sector with a view to deregulating the system and creating a level playing field for the growth and development of financial institutions, markets, and instruments. In 1992, bank-by-bank credit ceilings were lifted and replaced by open market operations (OMO) as the primary method of monetary management. Interest rates, which had previously been adminis-tratively fixed, were left to market forces through the removal of all controls on bank deposit and lending rates. Though controls were re-introduced in 1991 and between 1994 and 1996, interest rates on deposit and lending were de-controlled again in October 1996. In 1997, the CBN was vested with the control and supervision of all commercial, merchant, and commu-nity banks; the People's Bank; finance companies; discount houses; primary mortgage institutions; bureaus de change; and all development banks. In 1988, the Nigerian Deposit Insurance Corporation (NDIC) was established to complement the regulatory and supervisory role of the CBN, to provide deposit insurance and related services for banks, in order to promote confi-dence in the banking industry. The SEC, which had been established in 1979, was strengthened by the SEC Decree of 1988 to perform a role of effective promotion of an orderly and active capital market.

Other major changes in the Nigerian financial system during the 1987–2000 period include the promulgation of the Failed Banks (Recovery of Debt) and Financial Malpractices in Banks Decree 18 of 1994, aimed at prosecuting those who contributed to the failure of banks and to recover the debt owed to them. In 1994, the CBN inaugurated the Financial Services

Regulatory Co-ordinating Committee (FSRCC) to co-ordinate and standardize the regulatory policies of all financial institutions in the system and create some co-operation among regulatory agencies. In 1995, three decrees to further regulate the financial system were promulgated. These were the Money Laundering Decree 3; the Nigerian Investment Promotion Commission Decree 16, and the Foreign Exchange (Monitoring and Miscellaneous Provisions) Decree 17, which established an autonomous foreign exchange market.

Financial sector reforms during this period led to the expansion of the number of banks and financial institutions; they also significantly reduced government domination of the capital market and enhanced its capitalization. The value of new issues of securities rose steadily, from N399.9 million in 1988 to N10,813.6 million in 1997, giving an average annual rate of growth of 36.6 percent in nominal terms. However, given that the average annual rate of inflation was 36.9 percent during the sub-period, there was hardly any growth in the value of the new issues in real terms. Also, the number of listed securities increased from 180 in 1985 to 264 in 1997. In spite of the increase in the number of banks in the economy, however, the ratio of savings:GDP declined steadily over much of the liberalization period, from 16.0 percent in 1988 to 7.8 percent in 1997. At least through the early 1990s (table 18.3), as we saw earlier, private investment remained below its levels in the early 1970s. The basic structure of the financial system changed very little, as commercial banks continued to dominate institutionalized savings, providing about 80 percent of total savings. Despite some progress, the overall performance of the Nigerian financial system was not impressive, especially with the many cases of bank distress reported between 1989 and 1996. The number of banks classified as distressed increased from eight to fifty-two and the licenses of five banks were revoked. The CBN also took over the management of seventeen distressed banks in 1995 and one in 1996.

4.4.2 The labor market

In 1988, unemployment rate stood at 5.3 percent but decreased to 4.5 percent in 1989. Though there was a decrease in the number of trade disputes from 156 in 1988 to 144 in 1989, the number of workers involved rose from 55,620 to 157,342. As a result, the man-days lost rose from 230,613 in 1988 to 579,968 in 1989. The disputes were due, among other things, to the agitation for an upward review of fringe benefits and better conditions of service. Other reasons included non-implementation of the SAP relief package announced by the federal government in June 1989, and the fear of job displacements arising from the prospective privatization and commercialization of some public enterprises. In recognition of the lack of access to credit by many who sought to be self-employed, the federal government introduced a policy to liberalize access to credit. The People's Bank was established in October 1989 while the Community Banks were established in 1990. Other programs introduced to boost employment included the National Directorate of Employment (NDE), and Mass Agricultural Projects (MAP) in seven states of the Federation in 1993. The Family Economic Advancement Programs (FEAP) was introduced in 1997 to empower locally based producers of goods and services and potential entrepreneurs in cottage industries through the provision of loans, training, and the acquisition of skills.

4.4.3 Traded goods markets

In the public sector, the federally-run Commodity Boards and state-run bulk-purchasing companies, hitherto involved in the distribution of primary and manufactured products, were scrapped at the inception of the SAP in 1986.

4.4.4 The foreign exchange market

With the adoption of SAP, the foreign exchange market was completely liberalized and the exchange rate left largely to market forces. To enhance the smooth operation of the market, bureau de change offices were introduced in 1989 to handle small-scale foreign exchange transactions based on funds from unofficial sources. The Abacha government in 1994, however, reversed the exchange rate reforms and pegged the naira for a wide range of transactions. In 1995, the government formalized its reversal by adopting a policy of "guided deregulation." Given ongoing Nigerian inflation, foreign exchange available at the pegged rate was increasingly over-valued, and the black market premium skyrocketed (figure 18.5). The exchange rate remained effectively pegged until 1998, although restrictions on external payments began to be lifted even in advance of the maxi-devaluation of 1999.

4.5 Political economy and governance

The Babangida administration introduced the SAP in 1986 and was responsible for its initial implementation. The administration's efforts were hampered by continuous declines in oil revenues and increases in external debt, but also by its commitment to an unending program of political transition. The quality and consistency of economic policy management declined sharply: the government yielded to domestic political pressures, and despite repeated official pronouncements that it would continue with reforms, could not sustain the original objectives of the SAP. Ad hoc policies were implemented instead, to meet short-term expediencies. The most serious issue was irresponsible fiscal behavior, primarily in the form of excessive spending. The early 1990s were characterized by rising fiscal deficits, increasing poverty, and mounting discontent, a situation that resulted in several anti-SAP protests, riots, and strikes. The SAP led to a major decline in expenditure on the social sector (Obadan 1996) and created a new class of the poor. It forced down capacity utilization in industry, from an average annual rate of 53.1 percent between 1981 and 1985 to 39.8 percent between 1986 and 1993. It may also have contributed to the widespread distress among banks which destroyed the confidence of the public in the financial system and caused hardship to bank customers (Iyoha 1996).

Of all the election results since Nigeria gained independence in 1960, the 1993 result is believed to have been the fairest, but because it did not allow the Northerners to remain in control of power it was annulled and the winner of the Presidential election, Chief M. K. Abiola, a Yoruba from the South, was arrested and detained. The interim administration of Chief Ernest Shonekan (another Yoruba), who was invited to take over after President Babangida was forced to step aside, was removed from power after only three months by a military *putsch* led by Sani Abacha, another Northerner, in 1993. The desire of the North to remain in perpetual control of power can be explained by their quest to receive the lion's share of earnings from Nigeria's crude oil.

In his first budget speech to the nation, General Abacha noted that the nation's economic foundations had been badly shaken and rightly observed that a viable political system could not stand on a fragile economic base. The intention of his administration was to place the economy on a sound footing, emphasizing the need to ensure fiscal discipline through the eradication of deficit financing; to mobilize new sources of revenue; to stabilize the exchange rate; and to attract foreign investment. With the exception of the exchange rate, on which we have commented, these intentions were not actualized and the economy stagnated. Industrial production was retarded by power outages resulting from the failure of the National Electric Power Authority (NEPA) – starved of funds – to maintain its facilities. Lack of maintenance of Nigerian refineries resulted in petrol shortages and the massive importation of refined petroleum products. As with the Babangida regime, the Abacha government's economic policies were inconsistent and unstable, with contradictory fiscal and monetary policies.

One important feature noted in virtually all the administrations in Nigeria during this period is the quest for power for the sole purpose of enriching government functionaries, their families, and their close associates, to the detriment of national economy growth. Nigeria has suffered from a lack of leaders genuinely interested in public welfare and the development of the national economy; it is therefore not surprising that the policies, programs, and projects they pursued failed to support a sustainable development of the economy. Almost all the administrations in Nigeria during this sub-period were unsuccessful because they failed to effect changes in the basic structure of the economy, which had historically relied heavily on export-driven primitive agriculture, small-to-medium-scale manufacturing, and petty trading. With crude oil becoming the dominant product in Nigeria's exports, political elites and their administrations failed to harness the receipts from oil for a proper diversification of the export base of the economy. Instead they engaged in capital flight and massive importation of consumer goods, to the detriment of the balance of payments position. Ethnic affiliations and nepotism acted over time to constrain the growth process: the majority of leaders directed their attention to the diversion of state resources – public investments, infrastructure improvements, public sector employment – to the regions that constituted their political base. This phenomenon is central to the political instability that has been a permanent feature in Nigeria since the 1960s, with dire consequences, including the discouragement of foreign investment and the encouragement of capital flight and brain drain.

5. Conclusions

We conclude this study of Nigeria's growth experience by referring briefly to a resource-rich African country at the other end of the growth tables. Botswana reported an average real GDP growth rate of 11 percent between 1982 and 1989 and 7.5 percent between 1990 and 2000. Nigeria grew at 3.7 percent between 1960 and 2000. Nigeria's average real GDP growth rate was thus one-third that of Botswana in the 1980s and one-half that of Botswana in the 1990s. Given Nigeria's abundant human and natural resources, its average growth rate could have approximated that of Botswana if good macroeconomic policies had been consistently implemented.

Why, then, did Nigeria fail to develop in spite of the huge amount of petrodollars it received from the early 1970s? The simple answer is that Nigeria's petrodollars were misused, misspent, and mislaid. As proximate causes for these outcomes, we have stressed in particular poor leadership and governance, on the one hand, and ineffective macroeconomic policies, on the other.

The issue of poor leadership and governance should not be under-emphasized. Nigeria has been governed by leaders excessively motivated by narrow ethnic and sectional loyalties and lacking the conceptual scope required to develop viable strategies for sustained growth and development. In short, Nigeria has not had a pro-development leadership in its forty-odd years of existence.

It is now accepted in the development orthodoxy that policies can matter profoundly for development. We have argued that, by and large, Nigeria's policy choices were poor, and the reforms that sought to correct them starting, in the mid-1980s, were plagued by inconsistencies, reversals, and a general lack of policy coherence.

During the past two decades, uncertainty in the Nigerian economy has been brought about as much by social and political instability as by macroeconomic policy errors. A case in point was the early 1990s, when the nullification of Presidential election results brought about an acute political crisis and proved a harbinger of major policy reversals. Deeper institutional problems of governance also remain acute, including a lack of grass-roots participation in politics, malfunctioning formal political institutions, and inadequacy of democratic structures. Resolution of these stubborn social and political problems will go a long way to reducing perceived uncertainty and increasing confidence in the stability of the Nigerian economy. In turn, this will clear the way for a return of flight capital and an increase in both domestic and foreign investment in Nigeria.

References

Bello-Imam, I. B. and M. I. Obadan (2004), *Democratic Governance and Development Management in Nigeria's Fourth Republic, 1999–2003*. Ibadan: Centre for Local Government and Rural Development Studies

Bevan, D., P. Collier, and J. W. Gunning (1992), *Nigeria, Policy Responses to Shocks, 1970–1990*. San Francisco, CA: ICS Press

(1999), *Nigeria and Indonesia*, World Bank Comparative Studies. The Political Economy of Poverty, Equity, and Growth Series. Oxford and New York: Oxford University Press for the World Bank

Central Bank of Nigeria (CBN) (2000), *The Changing Structure of the Nigerian Economy and Implications for Development*. Abuja: CBN

(2002), *Annual Report and Statement of Accounts*. Abuja: CBN

Collier, P. and S. A. O'Connell (2006), "Opportunities and Choices," Paper prepared for the Explaining African Economic Growth Project. Nairobi: African Economic Research Consortium, June

Ekpo, A. H. (1994), "Fiscal Federalism: Nigeria's Post-Independence Experience, 1960–1990," *World Development* 22(8): 1129–46

Ekpo, A. H. and E. U. Ubok-Udom (2003), *Issues in Fiscal Federalism and Revenue Allocation in Nigeria*. Uyo State, Nigeria: University of Uyo

Federal Government of Nigeria (1986), *Structural Adjustment Program for Nigeria, July 1986–June 1988*, Lagos

Fei, J. and G. Ranis (1964), *Development of the Labor Surplus Economy*. Homewood, IL: Irwin

Gavin, M. (1993), "Adjusting to a Terms of Trade Shock: Nigeria, 1972–88," in R. Dornbusch, ed., *Policymaking in the Open Economy*. Oxford: Oxford University Press: 172–219

Iyoha, M. A. (1995), "Economic Liberalization and the External Sector," in A. Iwayemi, ed., *Macroeconomic Policy Issues in an Open Developing Economy*. Ibadan: NCEMA

(1996), "Macroeconomic Policy Management of Nigeria's External Sector in the post-SAP period," *Nigerian Journal of Economic and Social Studies* 38 (1), March: 1–18

(2003), "Assessment of Nigeria's Economic Performance since 1960," in M. A. Iyoha and C. O. Itsede, eds., *Nigerian Economy: Structure, Growth and Development*. Benin City: Mindex Publishing Company

Jorgensen, D. (1961), "The Development of the Dual Economy," *Economic Journal* 71, June: 309–34

Lal, D. (1999), *Financial Times*, October

Matsuyama, K. (1992), "Agricultural Productivity, Comparative Advantage, and Economic Growth," *Journal of Economic Theory* 58, December: 317–22

Miller, R. and M. Sumlinski (1994), "Trends in Private Investment in Developing Countries 1994: Statistics for 1970–92," IFC Discussion Paper 20, International Finance Corporation and the World Bank, February

Obadan, M. I. (1996), "The Macroeconomic Framework of Economic Management," in A. H. Ekpo, ed., *Beyond Adjustment: Management of the Nigerian Economy*. Ibadan: Nigerian Economic Society

O'Connell, S. A. and B. J. Ndulu (2001), "Africa's Growth Experience: A Focus on Sources of Growth," AERC Growth Working Paper No. 10. Nairobi: African Economic Research Consortium, April (downloadable: www.aercafrica.org)

Ogbe, N. E. (1992), "Evaluation of Nigeria's Debt-relief Experience (1985–1990)," Technical Paper 55. Paris: Organization for Economic Co-operation and Development

Okojie, C. E. E. (2003), "Development Planning in Nigeria since Independence," in M. A. Iyoha and C. O. Itsede, eds., *Nigeria's Economy: Structure, Growth and Development*. Benin City: Mindex Publishing Company

Onah, F. E. (1994), "External Debt and Economic Growth," in F. E. Onah, ed., *African Debt Burden and Economic Development*. Ibadan: Nigerian Economic Society

Sachs, J. and A. Warner (2001), "Natural Resources and Economic Development: The Curse of Natural Resources," *European Economic Review* 45: 827–38

Serven, L. and A. Solimano (1992), "Private Investment and Macroeconomic Adjustment: A Survey," *The World Bank Research Observer* 7(1), January: 95–114

Suberu, R. T. (2001), *Federalism and Ethnic Conflict in Nigeria*. Washington, DC: United States Institute of Peace Press

Udeh, J. (2000), "Petroleum Revenue Management: The Nigerian Perspective," Paper presented at World Bank/IFC Petroleum Revenue Management Workshop, Washington, DC, October 23–24

World Bank (2001), *World Bank Policy and Research Bulletin* 12(2), April–June

(2005), *World Bank Africa Database CD-ROM 2004*. Washington, DC: The World Bank

19 | Sierra Leone's economic growth performance, 1961–2000

Victor A. B. Davies

1. Introduction

Sierra Leone is a striking case of growth failure in Africa. At independence, Sierra Leone's substantial growth opportunities included a rich endowment of diamonds and other minerals, a long coastline, a developed educational system boasting the first university in SSA, and a seemingly stable political system. However, Sierra Leone ended the twentieth century a growth

Department of Economics, University of Oxford.

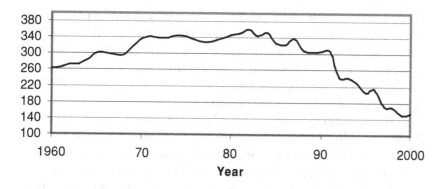

Figure 19.1 Sierra Leone, *per capita* GDP, 1960–2000, 1995 US$
Source: World Bank, *World Development Indicators 2003.*

tragedy. Per capita GDP growth for 1961–2000 averaged −1.2 percent per annum, compared with about 1 percent for SSA. *Per capita* GDP in constant 1995 dollars nearly halved between 1961 and 2000, from US$260 to US$150 (figure 19.1). Worse still, civil war raged from 1991 to 2001.

What explains Sierra Leone's growth tragedy? The literature lacks a comprehensive attempt to answer this question. Much of the focus has been on the civil war: Richards (1996); Abdullah (1997); Abdullah and Muana (1998); Davies (2000); Smillie, Gberie, and Hazleton (2000). Saylor (1967) analyzes the economy in the 1960s; Clapham (1976) and Reno (1995, 1998) the political economy; and van der Laan (1965) and Zack-Williams (1995) diamond mining. This chapter fills the gap in the literature with a comprehensive analysis of Sierra Leone's post-independence growth performance from 1961 to 2000.

The analysis is laid out in the following blocks: cross-country econometric analysis, markets, private agents, and political economy. To set the stage we provide a historical context in section 2, highlighting the role of the divisive, growth-inhibiting ethno-regional rivalries pre-dating independence. We delineate Sierra Leone's growth history in three episodes. Macroeconomic stability characterized 1961–72, the first episode. At the start of the second episode, 1973–90, the oil shocks prompted extensive market intervention, aggravating macroeconomic imbalances. After consolidating power, the ruling All People's Congress (APC) transformed the government into a kleptocracy, precipitating state collapse by the late 1980s. Civil war defined the final episode, 1991–2000.

Section 3 contains the cross-country econometric analysis, divided into growth-accounting and prediction analyzes. In the growth accounting only education per worker contributed positively to the growth of real GDP per worker in 1960–2000. Capital per worker and TFP contributed negatively. In the growth-prediction exercise the Hoeffler (2000) and O'Connell and

Ndulu (2000) models under-predict Sierra Leone's growth. A possible reason is under-estimation of investment in the Hoeffler model. Second, the Barro–Lee (2000) ratio of unproductive government expenditure, the main driver of growth under-prediction in O'Connell and Ndulu (2000), may be conceptually inappropriate for a country like Sierra Leone, with huge differences in domestic and international prices.

Section 4, focusing on key factor and product markets, argues that policy distortions induced market dysfunction while diamonds have been mixed blessings, fueling the civil war and exerting a corrupting and destabilizing political and economic influence. Section 5 focuses on two key agents – rural households with about 70–90 percent of the national population, and manufacturing firms. An inauspicious environment facing rural households encourages subsistence and informal economic activity. Manufacturing firms face severe infrastructural constraints, resulting in a minuscule manufacturing sector accounting for only about 5 percent of GDP and virtually no exports.

Section 6, the political economy block, identifies the following key culprits for growth collapse and the 1991–2001 civil war: diamonds, kleptocracy, ethno-regional rivalries, and external actors. Ethno-regional rivalries aided a kleptocracy that sowed the seeds of self-destruction and state collapse by informalizing and controlling access to diamonds and other markets and undermining any institutions that posed a threat. The ensuing collapse of fiscal revenues, infrastructure, and government services induced growth collapse. This produced suitable conditions for rebellion – extreme poverty, widespread youth unemployment and disillusionment, and government dysfunction. Libya trained some of the first rebels while the civil war was triggered from neighboring Liberia. Diamonds sustained the war. Section 7 compares diamond-resource management, and the political economy of growth in Sierra Leone and Botswana. Section 8 draws some conclusions.

2. The context

2.1 History

The period leading to independence on April 27, 1961 featured a major divide between the Creoles, with 2 percent of the population, and "indigenous," ethnic groups. The Creoles are descendants of former African slaves from Europe and North America, or recaptured in Africa, who were resettled by Britain in the Freetown peninsular area around 1800. In 1808 Freetown became the British crown colony of Sierra Leone; in 1896, the hinterland became a British Protectorate. The British ruled the Protectorate indirectly, through traditional rulers, and the colony directly. This divide limited interactions between the two regions. Incipient rivalries intensified in the run-up to independence, with the Protectorate-based Sierra Leone People's Party (SLPP) emerging dominant. After independence, the Protectorate's electoral supremacy bridged the Creole–Protectorate rivalry with the Creoles realizing that they must join a Protectorate-led party to exert any political influence (Clapham 1976).

A new divide emerged. In 1960 Siaka Stevens formed the APC, which "soon attracted a large following, particularly from the north" (Alie 1990). After independence, the APC became the main opposition party to the ruling SLPP. Incipient rivalries deepened between the pro-APC northern regions dominated by the Temne, and the pro-SLPP south-eastern regions dominated by the Mende. The Temne and Mende each account for 30 percent of the population, and together with their affiliates they split the national population roughly in half, a demographic characteristic fostering ethno-regional polarity. The two political parties, the SLPP and the APC, ruled between them throughout the post-independence period, except during periods of military rule.

2.2 Periodization

Three episodes in the domestic environment for growth are discernible in Sierra Leone's 1961–2000 growth history: 1961–72, 1973–90, and 1991–2000. Although growth outcomes differ markedly by episode, the criterion for identifying episodes is the environment for growth, not outcomes. In 1961–72, the macroeconomic environment was relatively stable, with single-digit inflation (table 19.1) and the leone, the national currency, pegged to the pound sterling. Three military coup occurred between March 1967 and the restoration of democracy in 1968. However, these coup did not fundamentally change the environment for growth.

The next episode was 1973–90. The oil price shocks precipitated a tightening of price controls and larger subsidies for imported rice and fuel, aggravating macroeconomic distortions and fostering black markets. Meanwhile the APC, which ruled from 1968 to 1992, consolidated power and transformed the government into a kleptocracy. Government services and infrastructure gradually collapsed in the 1980s, *per capita* income went into long-term decline around the mid-decade. Civil war consummated the economic and political implosion in 1991–2000, the final episode.

3. Cross-country econometric perspective

This section ties in Sierra Leone's economic growth performance with the general empirical cross-country growth literature through a growth-accounting and prediction analysis.

Table 19.1 *Sierra Leone, macroeconomic indicators, 1961–2000*

Period	GDP per capita (constant 1995 US$)	Growth in real GDP per capita (national accounts data) (%)	Investment (% GDP)	Inflation (%)	Black market spread (%)	Real exchange rate over-val. index	External debt (% GDP)	Budget deficit after grants (% GDP)
1961–6	283	2.3	–	4.1	0	193	–	–
1967–72	321	2.0	12.8	3.4	0	179	–	–
1973–5	342	0.5	12.1	13.3	2	171	30	7.0
1976–80	336	0.3	12.3	14.0	12	173	42	8.9
1981–5	347	–2.6	13.1	52.0	224	229	50	8.3
1986–90	316	0.0	8.5	93.0	50	171	111	5.0
1991–5	245	–7.1	6.9	48.0	8	153	183	4.8
1996–2000	171	–6.0	6.1	22.0	18	157	162	6.8

Notes: – indicates missing data. Black market spread (%) = [1 – (black market rate/official exchange rate)] × 100. Real exchange rate over-valuation index: a value above (below) 100 indicates over-valuation (under-valuation).

Sources: Black market spread: Bank of Sierra Leone; all others: World Bank (2003).

Table 19.2 *Sierra Leone, growth accounting, 1960–2000*

Period	Growth in real GDP per worker (%)	Percentage point contribution to growth in real GDP per worker		
		Physical capital per worker	Education per worker	Residual
1960–4	2.71	−0.09	0.09	2.71
1965–9	2.75	1.02	0.12	1.60
1970–4	2.17	0.39	0.40	1.38
1975–9	0.03	−0.18	0.28	−0.07
1980–4	0.49	−0.07	0.28	0.27
1985–9	−0.36	−0.85	0.30	0.19
1990–4	−3.69	−0.33	0.24	−3.6
1995–2000	−7.37	−1.08	0.22	−6.51
Average 1960–2000	−0.66	−0.17	0.24	−0.73

Source: Generated by Susan M. Collins based on Collins and Bosworth (1996).

3.1 Growth accounting

Growth accounting decomposes growth among its proximate sources, indicating the contribution of productivity gains and physical and human capital accumulation. Our growth-accounting results are based on Collins and Bosworth (1996) using the following production function[1]:

$$\ln y = 0.35 \ln k + 0.65 \ln h + \ln A,$$

where y is real GDP per worker, k is physical capital per worker, h is a labor quality index, and 0.35 and 0.65 are the assumed capital and labor elasticities, respectively. A is TFP capturing technological progress but it could also capture other factors such as capacity utilization. Data on growth in physical capital per worker were generated by applying the perpetual inventory method to national accounts investment data, using initial 1950 capital stocks, with a depreciation rate of 0.05. The labor quality index imputes a return of 7 percent to an additional year of schooling that the adult population attains. Educational attainment data are from Barro and Lee (2000) and Cohen and Soto (2001). Typically both series are available, and then the average is used; otherwise, the available series is used.

Table 19.2 shows a negative growth in real GDP per worker in Sierra Leone of −0.66 percent for the overall 1960–2000 period. Only education per worker generated positive growth, 0.24 percentage points, about the same as SSA's 0.25 percentage points and slightly lower than Latin America and

[1] The growth-accounting results were generated by Susan Collins, one of the authors. We would like to thank her for making available the results for Sierra Leone.

the Caribbean's 0.33. By default, the contribution of education per worker tends to be low: one additional year of average schooling increases human capital by only 7 percent. The contribution of physical capital per worker and TFP over 1960–2000 was −0.17 and −0.73 percentage points, respectively. In 1960–74 productivity was the main source of growth, accounting for well over half of the (positive) growth in output per worker. Thus, investment has contributed negatively to the growth of real GDP per worker in Sierra Leone, while education per worker's contribution has been positive but low. However, negative TFP during the 1991–2000 civil war period has been the main source of negative growth in real GDP per worker.

3.2   Growth prediction

The drawback of growth accounting is that it cannot identify the fundamental causes of growth. Growth regression, to which we now turn, is more informative in this regard. To determine the extent to which growth-regression norms explain Sierra Leone's growth performance, we predict Sierra Leone's growth using empirical estimates from two standard cross-country growth models: Hoeffler's (2000) System–GMM estimates of the augmented Solow model of Mankiw, Roemer, and Weil (1992), and O'Connell and Ndulu's (2000) reduced-form OLS model.[2]

The two models were estimated using half-decadal data for a panel of eighty-five countries, of which forty-three were developing and twenty-three were in SSA. The estimation period is 1960–1990 for the Hoeffler model and 1960–97 for the O'Connell–Ndulu model. The regressors in the Hoeffler model are (1) initial income; (2) the national saving rate as proxied by the ratio of investment: GDP, both at constant international prices; (3) replacement investment, given by 0.05 plus the population growth rate; (4) a measure of saving for human capital accumulation, using average years of schooling achieved by the population aged fifteen or more; and (5) time dummies. The dependent variable is growth in real GDP *per capita* at 1985 international prices.

O'Connell and Ndulu (2000) follow Barro (1991) to assess the relative contributions to growth of initial conditions, structural features, institutional characteristics, and the policy environment. The dependent variable is the average growth rate of real GDP *per capita*, from national accounts data. Real GDP *per capita* in international dollars and life expectancy at birth, both measured at the beginning of the relevant half-decade, capture initial conditions. Demography is captured by the age-dependency ratio – the ratio of the non-working age (outside the fifteen–sixty-four age range) to the working-age (15–64) population; and growth in potential labor force

---

[2] We would like to thank Stephen O'Connell, Benno Ndulu, and Anke Hoeffler for providing the empirical estimates and underlying data.

participation – the average difference between the growth rate of the population fifteen–sixty-four and growth rate of total population. Terms of trade shocks are captured by the initial share of exports to GDP, multiplied by the average percentage difference between the terms of trade in each year of the half-decade and the terms of trade in the initial year of the half-decade. The average growth rate of real GDP *per capita* among trading partners, weighted by shares in total trade, captures trading partner growth. A dummy variable taking a value of one for landlocked countries and zero otherwise, captures landlockedness. The inflation rate, the black market premium, and the Barro–Lee unproductive government spending:GDP ratio (government spending net of expenditure on education and defense), capture policy. The "Barro–Lee" ratio is the ratio of real government consumption: real GDP, both at 1985 international prices, minus the ratio of the sum of nominal government spending on defense and non-capital education expenditures: nominal GDP. Due to data constraints, Barro and Lee use nominal, rather than real, values for the ratio of spending on education and defense to GDP. For Barro and Lee (2000) (1994) all government spending must be financed by distortionary taxes that tend to undermine growth, so that the net effect of the government budget on growth depends on the supply-side contribution of the spending. Barro and Lee (2000) assume that defense and education spending have direct positive effects on productivity or the security of property rights and therefore impact on growth differently from other categories of expenditure. Thus the Barro–Lee ratio is expected to be negatively correlated with growth. An index based on the number of coup per year, the average number of revolutions, assassinations, and strikes per year, capture political instability. The index is expected to affect growth negatively.

Generally speaking, the evolution of the growth determinants used in the two regression models was unfavorable for Sierra Leone, by comparison even with SSA (see table 19.3). Between 1960 and 2000, life expectancy in Sierra Leone, reflecting health conditions, increased only modestly, from thirty-two to thirty-five years, compared with forty–forty-eight years for SSA. Average years of schooling attained by the population aged fifteen or more in Sierra Leone was 0.66 in 1960 and 1.34 in 1960–90, compared with 1.13 and 1.53, respectively, for SSA. Sierra Leone's real GDP *per capita* (1985 international prices) was US$876 in 1960 and US$905 in 1985, compared with US$733 and US$963 for SSA. On the whole, real GDP *per capita* over 1960–97 was higher in Sierra Leone: US$996, than in SSA: US$876. An already high age-dependency ratio of 77 percent in 1960–4 for Sierra Leone increased to 93 percent in 1990–7. Such a high age-dependency ratio could lead to low financial savings, and undermine human capital accumulation by spreading educational resources more thinly. Sierra Leone's relatively low population growth rate of 2 percent compared with SSA's 2.8 percent in 1960–97 suggests that population pressure might not account for much of

Table 19.3 *Sierra Leone, variables in the regression models, 1960–1997*

Variable	Sierra Leone 1960–97	SSA 1960–97	Full sample 1960–97
Age-dependency ratio (%)	84.0	89.0	77.0
Barro–Lee unproductive government expenditure (% GDP)	28.0	15.0	9.1
Black market spread (%)	36.0	33.0	23.0
Growth in real GDP *per capita* (1985 international prices)[a]	−0.05	0.03	0.1
Growth in real GDP *per capita* (national accounts)	−0.46	0.96	2.2
Inflation (%)	29.0	11.3	15.8
Average years of schooling: population aged 15 or more[a]	1.34	1.53	3.3
Life expectancy	34.0	45.0	61.0
Real GDP *per capita* (1985 international prices)[a]	996.0	876.0	2,426.0
Investment (% GDP) (constant international prices)[a]	1.3	7.8	14.2
Landlockness dummy	0.0	0.36	0.14
Population growth rate[a]	2.0	2.8	
Political instability	0.12		0.2

Notes: [a] Variables feature in the Hoeffler model.
Sources: Age-dependency ratio and population growth rate: World Bank 2003; Barro–Lee unproductive government expenditure, black market spread, growth in real GDP *per capita* (national accounts), inflation, life expectancy, landlockness, and average years of schooling: Global Development Network (www.gonet.org); real GDP *per capita* (1985 international prices) and its growth rate, investment (% GDP) (constant international prices): Heston, Summers, and Aten (2002).

Table 19.4 *Sierra Leone, Hoeffler augmented Solow model*
a Estimation results

	Log of initial income	Log of investment	Log of (0.05 + population growth)	Log of schooling	Constant term
Parameter	−0.151	0.249	−0.419	0.011	−0.483
t-statistic	−2.9	6.4	−2.9	0.3	−1.78

Note: Root mean square error: 2.94.
Source: generated by Anke Hoeffler, based on Hoeffler (2000).

Sierra Leone's poor growth performance. Investment measured in constant international prices was extremely low in Sierra Leone, 1.3 percent of GDP for 1960–97, compared with 7.8 percent for SSA. A black market spread of 116 percent in the 1980s, and an inflation rate of 63 percent suggest an inauspicious policy environment for growth in the 1980s. Finally, the Barro–Lee unproductive government spending ratio was very high for Sierra Leone, 28 percent of GDP in 1960–84, compared with 15 percent for SSA (for 1960–97).

Tables 19.4a and 19.5a present the parameter estimates of the two models, and tables 19.4b and 19.5b the corresponding predictions. Both models

Table 19.4 *b Fits and residuals*

Period	Actual growth (%)	Predicted growth (%)	Residual	Deviation of actual growth from sample mean	Estimated contribution to deviation of predicted growth from sample mean				
					Initial income	Investment rate	Initial educational attainment	Replacement investment term	Time dummy
1960–4	4.81	−5.23	10.03	2.87	3.08	−10.93	0.37	0.48	0.60
1965–9	5.06	−4.65	9.71	3.13	2.36	−9.44	−0.35	0.24	0.63
1970–4	−3.58	−8.39	4.81	−5.51	1.59	−11.53	−0.31	0.02	−0.06
1975–9	−1.04	−8.16	7.12	−2.98	2.13	−12.10	−0.18	−0.19	0.26
1980–4	−4.60	−9.03	4.43	−6.53	2.29	−11.30	−0.16	−0.33	−1.44
1985–9	−0.09	−8.0	7.92	−2.02	2.98	−12.30	−0.13	−0.57	0.10
1990–7	−8.21	−6.91	−1.30	−10.15	3.00	−11.78	−0.10	−0.54	0.60

Source: Derived using parameter estimates from table 19.4a.

Table 19.5 *Sierra Leone, O'Connell–Ndulu model*

a Estimation results

Variable	Base variables							Policy variables				
	Initial income	Life expectancy	Age-dependency ratio	Growth of potential labor force participation	Terms of trade shock	Trading partner growth	Landlockedness	Inflation	Black market premium	Barrro–Lee govt non-productive consumption (% GDP)	Political instability	Constant
Coefficient	−1.77	0.089	−0.052	0.728	0.004	0.540	−0.912	−0.004	−0.007	−0.113	−0.975	15.35
t-statistics	−6.1	3.85	−4.99	2.69	0.14	2.82	−2.72	−1.24	−3.14	−4.90	−4.22	5.37

Note: Root mean square error: 2.186.
Source: O'Connell and Ndulu (2000).

Table 19.5 *b Fits and residuals*

Period	Fits and residuals			Deviation of actual growth from sample mean	Contribution to deviation of predicted growth from Sample mean				Breakdown of policy contribution to deviation of predicted growth from sample mean		
	Actual growth	Fitted growth	Residual		Base variables	Political instability	Policy	Time dummy	Inflation (%)	Black market premium (%)	Barro–Lee govt spending/GDP (%)
1960–4	2.06	–	–	−0.14	–	–	−2.08	0.00	0.05	0.17	−2.30
1965–9	2.11	−0.4	2.51	−0.09	−0.88	−0.13	−1.65	−0.50	0.05	0.17	−1.87
1970–4	1.77	−0.7	2.47	−0.43	−1.44	0.07	−2.15	0.10	0.04	0.16	−2.35
1975–9	−0.33	−1.18	0.85	−2.53	−1.57	0.20	−2.22	−0.30	0.00	0.16	−2.38
1980–4	−0.30	−4.26	3.96	−2.50	−3.01	0.07	−2.81	−1.22	−0.10	−0.81	−1.9
1985–9	−1.56	–	–	−3.76	−0.56	0.13	–	−0.96	−0.29	−0.12	–
1990–7	−6.97	–	–	−9.17	−1.91	0.12	–	−0.76	−0.14	0.097	–

Source: Derived using parameter estimates from table 19.5.

Note: – = .

under-predict Sierra Leone's pre-1990 growth, implying that for the observed values of the regressors, *per capita* GDP growth should have been worse than observed. The O'Connell and Ndulu (2000) model, with smaller residuals, gives better predictions. Its under-prediction is less than 2 standard errors of the residuals, ranging from 3.96 percentage points in 1980–4 to 0.85 percentage points in 1975–9. The Hoeffler model's under-prediction ranges from 10 percentage points in 1960–4 to 4.4 percentage points in 1980–4, well over 2 standard errors of the residuals. Neither models conditions on civil war, and predictions for this period are in any case unavailable from the O'Connell–Ndulu model due to missing values for the included variables. Unsurprisingly, however, the Hoeffler model over-predicts growth during this period (1990–7) by 1.3 percentage points.[3]

The tendency of these models to under-predict Sierra Leone's pre-war growth is in contrast with their tendency to over-prediction for Africa in general. Measurement error is a possible explanation. Notably, prior to 2001 GDP estimates excluded informal sector services, suggesting that pre-2001 GDP *per capita* would be under-estimated. Low measured investment at international prices may be driving under-prediction by the Hoeffler (2000) model, given the leverage of this variable in the model: its 1968–89 average for Sierra Leone is only 1.3 percent of GDP, as compared with 7.8 percent for SSA Africa and 14.2 percent for other developing countries. This low figure may be due to valuation problems as a result of informal or black market activities. Also, for Sierra Leone, investment measured in domestic prices, relative to GDP, is much higher, 12.6 percent for 1968–89, than at constant international prices, 1.4 percent. One explanation for the difference is that capital goods are much more expensive domestically than internationally.

The Barro–Lee ratio of government unproductive expenditure (percent GDP) appears to be driving under-prediction by the O'Connell and Ndulu model (2000). Its coefficient of -0.113 is statistically significant at the 1 percent level (table 19.5), justifying its inclusion in the model. In the original paper, Barro and Leo (1994), the coefficient was -0.17 and also statistically significant at the 1 percent level. However, the Barro–Lee ratio for Sierra Leone (used in O'Connell and Ndulu 2000) is very high: 28 percent for 1960–84 compared with a mean of 9 percent for the sample countries. At domestic prices, total government expenditures (inclusive of defense and education) averaged 21 percent of GDP for Sierra Leone in 1960–84. Nominal government expenditures (net of defense and education) – unproductive government expenditures in the Barro–Lee sense – were 18 percent of GDP for Sierra Leone in 1960–84. The ratio of unproductive government expenditures therefore rises very sharply when converted from current domestic to

---

[3] The Hoeffler model was estimated through 1990, so this is based on out-of-sample prediction.

1985 international prices *à la* Barro–Lee. This raises the question of the relevance of the Barro–Lee ratio for a country like Sierra Leone, with seemingly huge differences in domestic and international prices.

In conclusion, the key insights from the preceding analysis are first, that the low value of the standard growth determinants in Sierra Leone lead to low growth predictions. Second, although Sierra Leone's growth has been low, it has been much higher than the two growth models predict. The standard growth determinants in the models do not explain much of Sierra Leone's growth performance. In the rest of the chapter, we focus on a question that the above insights raise: Why have standard growth determinants performed so poorly in Sierra Leone? Furthermore, we look beyond the standard growth determinants and models, focusing on the specificity of the Sierra Leone situation for additional insights into the country's growth experience.

4. Markets

In this section we examine the role of the diamond, financial, and labor markets in the growth process. Diamonds have played a primordial role in the economic and political life of Sierra Leone. The literature highlights the importance of the other two markets for economic growth. In section 4.1 we focus on agriculture, which employs 70–90 percent of Sierra Leone's labor force.

4.1   The diamonds sector

The "natural-resource curse" thesis articulated by Lewis (1984, 1989), Gelb (1988), Auty (1993), and others holds that natural resources constrain, rather than promote, economic development through problems such as rent-seeking and civil conflict. Rent-seeking in turn breeds corruption in business and government, distorting resource allocation and undermining economic efficiency, growth, and social equity (Gylfason 2001; Sachs and Warner 2001; Torvik 2002). Gylfason (2001) argues that resource-rich nations can live well off their natural resources over extended periods with poor economic policies. The analysis here and in the political-economy section (section 6) suggests that Sierra Leone has faced many of these problems, failing to capture any substantial portion of diamond rents for productive investment. Worse still, diamonds helped sustain the 1991–2001 civil war.

Sierra Leone's alluvial diamonds have two key features that differentiate them from the capital-intensive 'point' resources – like oil, copper, and deep-pit diamonds – that dominate the resource-curse literature. First, the deposits are widely dispersed, appearing within a 7,700 mile^2 area that lies, mainly in the eastern regions of the country and covers about a quarter of its total area. Only 1 percent of this area is actual diamond-bearing soil. The geographically dispersed nature of the resource dramatically increases the cost of effective policing. Second, the deposits can be mined using simple tools like picks and shovels, facilitating illicit mining and smuggling.

Diamond production started in Sierra Leone in the mid-1930s and was initially restricted to the corporate Sierra Leone Selection Trust (SLST) which held a monopoly concession. However, growing illicit artisanal mining forced the authorization of small-scale mining in 1956, and the SLST concession areas were reduced. Legitimate diamond production accounted for 15 percent of GDP and 70 percent of exports during the peak late 1960s and early 1970s. In 1970 the government nationalized SLST, acquiring a 51 percent interest and renaming it the National Diamond Mining Company (NDMC). Total taxes on the NDMC amounted to 70 percent of net profits (income tax, surtax, and diamond industry profits tax). Furthermore the government received 51 percent of the balance in dividends. Corporate mining thus made substantial fiscal contributions, amounting in 1974 to US$60 million (in constant 1995 dollars), or 3.6 percent of GDP. Although statistics are unavailable, fiscal revenues from the artisanal sector were thought to be negligible. This is hardly surprising, given the difficulty of policing artisanal mining activities.

NDMC production decreased from 1 million carats in 1970 to 18,000 carats in 1988, lowering total recorded diamond production from about 2 million carats to 24,000 carats over the same period (table 19.6). The NDMC's profits had given way to losses by the early 1980s, and the NDMC was liquidated in the early 1990s. Even before then, however, artisanal mining had become virtually ubiquitous. The political-economy analysis of section 6 suggests the underlying motivation for the universalization of artisanal mining.

From the mid-1970s, diamond resources appeared to be gradually depleting. Recorded output from the 1960s up to the early 1970s ranged from about 1.5 to 2 million carats. The figure dropped to about 460,000 carats in 1980–3 and continued to fall subsequently. Total exports (recorded plus smuggled) in the 1990s were less than recorded exports in the 1961–76 period alone. Correspondingly, recorded export revenues fell massively in real terms. Real recorded export revenues in the 1961–76 period exceeded US$200 million a year (in 1995 dollars) compared with less than US$50 million since 1984. Falling fiscal revenues were a corollary: fiscal revenues, mainly from corporate diamonds taxes, were around US$60 million (in 1995 dollars) a year in the early 1970s, about 3–4 percent of GDP. They were less than 0.1 percent of GDP by the mid-1980s.

The fall in recorded output was not entirely due to resource depletion. Artisanal mining expanded from the 1970s, eclipsing the corporate sector.

Table 19.6 *Sierra Leone, diamond production and exports, 1965–2000*

Period	Recorded output (000 carats)	Recorded exports (current US$ million)	Smuggled diamonds (000 carats)	Smuggled diamonds (US$ million)	Total exports: recorded + smuggled (000 carats)	Total exports: recorded + smuggled (US$ million)	Real recorded export revenues (constant 1995 US$)	Real total exports: recorded + smuggled (constant 1995$)
1965–9	1,566	54					241	
1970–2	1,998	64					242	
1973–6	1,469	77					233	
1980–3	457	53					88	
1984–5	226	29					41	
1986–7	354	21					28	
1988	24	9					11	
1989	127	22					28	
1990	90	13	331		421		15	
1991	250	32	534		784		36	
1992	313	31	831		1,144		34	
1993	156.0	20	344		500.0		21.0	
1994	221	30	526		747		31	
1995	214	22	455		669		22	
1996	270	28	566	58	836	86.5	27	84
1997	104	8	803	71	907	78.5	7	75
1998	9	2	770	58	778.5	60.2	2	56
1999	9	2		69		70	1	64
2000	77	10					9	

Note: We computed real diamond exports (US$) from nominal exports using the US consumer price index.

Sources: Recorded diamond output: Saylor (1967); IMF (2001 and other issues); Smillie, Gberie, and Hazleton (2000). Recorded diamond export (US$): IMF (2001 and other issues); World Bank (1993, 1994, 2002). Smuggled diamonds (quantity): Smillie, Gberie, and Hazleton (2000). Smuggled diamonds (US$): IMF (2001, 2005); Smillie, Gberie, and Hazleton (2000).

This coincided with a rise in the proportion of smuggled diamond output. In the 1960s and early 1970s the estimated proportion was less than 20 percent of total output; in the 1990s, the subsequent period with available statistics, about 95 percent of total output was smuggled. Outside of the 1991–2001 war period, recorded output increased from less than 25,000 carats in 1986–90 to 500,000 carats in 2003. The increase in recorded output since 2000 may be due to the termination of war, to initiation of the Kimberley certification process set up to counter the trade in conflict diamonds and, more generally, to increased attention to problems relating to Sierra Leone's diamonds.[4]

Diamonds have induced economic and social dislocation. The 1950s "diamond rush" saw large-scale migration from farms to diamond mining, turning Sierra Leone from a net exporter to a net importer of rice (Saylor 1967). Between 1953 and 1957 the number of illicit diggers grew from 5,000 to 75,000, or 10 percent of the labor force (Smillie, Gberie, and Hazleton 2000), fostering crime and violence. Kono District and other diamond mining areas "verged on anarchy, with armed bands of as many as 400 to 500 men raiding SLST . . . areas, and on occasions doing battle with the police" (Cartwright 1970). Future illicit miners were among the first rebels in the civil war.

Growing informalization and criminalization of the diamond industry from the 1970s, and increasing government intervention in economic activity more generally, aided state collapse. Scarce essential imports of rice, petroleum, and other goods, subject to price control, were purchased abroad with proceeds from smuggled diamonds, gold, and agricultural produce, and sold on black markets to finance the purchase of exports for further smuggling (Davies and Fofana 2002). By the mid-1980s, the Sierra Leone economy was largely underground; the dollar black market premium exceeded 200 percent in 1981–5.

Lastly, using evidence from Sierra Leone, my own research provides micro-foundations for an aggregate resource curse under conditions of dispersed alluvial diamond mining and low income. In Davies (2006), I argue that open access attracts excessive labor, dissipating diamond rents through two sources of market failure: the lottery problem and desperation.

The lottery problem is due to diminishing returns to diamond extraction and the lottery nature of the activity. Open access usually spawns uncoordinated and speculative artisanal diamond searches, making diamond finds a matter of chance. With roughly equal chances for everyone, private entry into mining sets the marginal private return equal to the average

---

[4] The Kimberley Process groups sixty-seven countries (including EU countries) accounting for 98 percent of world trade – production, export, and import – in rough diamonds. It replaced the UN diamond certification scheme designed to prevent the trade in conflict diamonds from Angola and Sierra Leone.

social return (i.e. to the total returns divided by the total labor input). Given diminishing returns due to resource endowment constraints, this means that, in equilibrium, the marginal private return to extraction exceeds the marginal social return. Market failure ensues as labor input, driven by the marginal private return, exceeds the socially optimal level.

Desperation, in turn, is defined as an observed preference for diamond digging unwarranted by returns. Evidence of a desperation effect comes from the co-existence of unemployment among diggers and labor shortage in agriculture, the main alternative activity, in the face of lower average earnings from diamond digging.

Putting the lottery problem and the desperation effect together, I find that the net social benefit from artisanal diamond production may even be negative in equilibrium, and that the conditions consistent with this outcome have prevailed in Sierra Leone. The theory helps to account for the propensity for civil war in certain alluvial diamond-rich African countries, including Sierra Leone: desperation induces "excessive" war enlistment. It also helps account for low income levels in Sierra Leone relative to certain other African diamond producers. Sierra Leone failed to avoid the lottery and desperation problems by allowing open access to its alluvial diamond deposits. Namibia avoided them by imposing monopoly production. As analyzed further in section 7, nature resolved that issue for Botswana, by endowing that country with Kimberlite, and not alluvial, diamond deposits.

4.2   The financial sector

Financial markets can facilitate economic growth by mobilizing savings for investment and reducing transactions costs. North (1987) argues that the cost of transacting is the key to the performance of economies. Industrial countries successfully developed the elaborate institutional structures needed for complex and impersonal exchanges to take place at minimum cost. Without this institutional development, economic growth would have been thwarted.

Sierra Leone's financial sector was unable to mobilize large-scale savings. Total bank deposits were only 6.8 percent of GDP in 1964–9, 10.3 percent in the 1970s, 14.7 percent in the 1980s, and 7.3 percent in 1990–2000 (table 19.7). From about 12 percent in the 1960s, the M2:GDP ratio – a common measure of financial depth – peaked at 25–28 percent in the mid-1980s, falling to less than 15 percent in the late 1990s. The financial sector is fragmented, with a small formal sector and a large informal sector. The formal sector is urban-based and oligopolistic, dominated by the three–seven commercial banks. (The war claimed the five–eight rural banks set up around 1985–92.) Five–eight insurance companies have operated over the years. Informal institutions – traditional moneylenders, and savings and

Table 19.7 *Sierra Leone, financial indicators, 1965–2000*

Year	M2 (% GDP)	Total deposits (% GDP)	Inflation tax (total) (% GDP)	Inflation tax on bank reserves (% GDP)	Domestic credit to govt (% total)	Black market spread (%)	Interest rate spread	Real saving interest rate
1965–9	12.0	6.8	0.26	0.06	29.0	–	–	–
1970–4	13.0	8.8	0.46	0.1	38.0	–	–	–
1975–9	16.0	11.8	1.16	0.26	69.0	4.4	3.9	−5.4
1980	20.6	15.0	1.6	0.8	78.0	34.9	1.8	−3.3
1981	20.4	13.8	2.4	0.9	82.0	46.9	5.0	−10.8
1982	21.4	18.3	2.3	0.8	84.6	140.0	5.0	−13.3
1983	25.9	18.6	9.2	4.8	85.6	140.0	6.3	−34.1
1984	23.1	16.3	7.7	2.9	90.5	178.9	6.0	−32.8
1985	22.0	17.6	7.9	3.3	94.8	202.0	5.7	−36.9
1986	22.2	16.1	7.1	2.6	88.7	279.8	3.0	−36.9
1987	13.4	10.5	11.3	3.3	88.3	20.9	15.9	−59.6
1988	14.0	10.4	2.4	1.0	84.4	65.7	11.7	−13.4
1989	14.4	10.9	4.7	2.2	77.1	47.5	9.7	−25.4
1990	14.3	9.5	8.4	3.8	91.0	50.5	12.0	−33.4
1991	10.7	6.8	5.5	1.8	81.6	74.6	8.5	−27.1
1992	10.8	6.9	3.9	0.9	74.5	7.2	8.2	−6.5
1993	10.6	6.6	1.2	0.3	63.4	4.0	23.5	3.9
1994	9.1	5.9	1.1	0.1	96.5	−0.85	15.7	−10.1
1995	8.7	5.5	1.2	0.3	95.9	12.9	21.8	−15.0
1996	8.8	5.6	0.9	0.1	95.0	3.9	18.2	−7.5
1997	12.7	8.1	0.8	0.1	94.5	24.4	14.0	−4.4
1998	12.7	7.3	3.1	1.1	94.3	17.0	16.7	−21.0
1999	13.9	8.9	2.0	0.3	95.5	35.4	17.3	−18.3
2000	15.5	9.5	−0.1	0.0	94.5	10.6	17.0	10.2

Notes: Total deposits comprise demand, time, saving, and foreign currency deposits. The real saving interest rate is computed as $100 \times (r - i)/(100 + i)$, where r is the interest rate (%) and i is the rate of inflation (%). Inflation tax is computed as $i/(1 + i) \times$ inflation tax base, where i is the inflation rate and the tax base is total high-powered money or bank reserves, as appropriate.

Sources: Black market spread: Bank of Sierra Leone; all others: directly from or computed using variables from IMF (various years).

Note: – = Unavailable.

rotating credit societies – are ubiquitous. Such a rudimentary financial system's potential to reduce transactions costs is limited. This situation constrains portfolio and risk diversification and savings mobilization.

The financial sector was repressed prior to the liberalization measures of the early 1990s. Real saving interest rates were negative from 1977 (the earliest year with available statistics) to 1992; and as low as −34 percent–60 percent in 1983–7 (see table 19.7). Large interest rate spreads normally reflect lack of competition, the government received over 80 percent of domestic credit in the 1980s. The inflation tax on bank reserves ranged from 1 percent to 4.8 percent of GDP in the 1980s, and the literature suggests that such financial repression and high inflation hurt financial development. Real lending rates turned positive after the liberalization measures while real deposit rates often remained negative. Interest rate spreads increased from 7 percent in the 1980s to 18 percent in 1995–2000.

Exchange rate policy was fickle in the 1980s, unlike the 1960s and 1970s. The leone was pegged to the pound sterling in 1964 and then to the IMF Special Drawing Right (SDR) in 1978. A dual exchange rate system – a market-determined rate and a fixed rate – introduced in 1982, was abandoned for a unified rate pegged to the US dollar in July 1983. In February 1985 the leone was pegged to the SDR once again. A floating exchange rate, introduced in June 1986, was abandoned in October 1987 for a peg to the SDR. Finally, in April 1990, a floating exchange rate was introduced as part of an adjustment program. The frequent policy reversals in the 1980s were in response to balance of payments difficulties and the ensuing problems. These policies created rents, criminalized economic activity, and discouraged socially productive activities: price and exchange controls, and the ensuing black market spread – often exceeding 200 percent in the 1980s and peaking at 280 percent in 1986 (table 19.7) – fueled the smuggling of diamonds, gold, and agricultural produce. The proceeds financed essential imports smuggled into the country, whose sales, in turn, helped finance the smuggling of diamonds, gold, and agricultural produce. As the formal economy shrank, fiscal revenues plummeted: from 15 percent of GDP in the 1970s to 7 percent in 1983–90. The origins of state collapse can be linked to all these circumstances.

4.3   The labor market[5]

Sierra Leone's renowned educational system, inherited from colonialism, offered a missed opportunity for human capital-led growth *à la* India. In 1863, Fourah Bay College became SSA's first university-level educational institution and subsequently educated many of anglophone West Africa's

---

[5] The analysis of rural households also encompasses labor market issues.

first African cadres. Ironically, however, Sierra Leone's human resource base remained under-developed over time. Adult literacy was less than 10 percent in the 1960s and less than 40 percent in 2000, among SSA's lowest. The low literacy rate in the 1960s was partly because access to education was initially largely available only to the minority Creoles in coastal Freetown. Even in the hinterland (Protectorate), access was initially selective. The Bo School, the hinterland's first and (for many years, only) secondary school, was founded explicitly for the sons and nominees of chiefs (Clapham 1976). Post-independence governments did not adequately exploit the education infrastructure to promote widespread literacy.

By the 1980s, a mismatch between educational output and labor market needs became obvious. Tertiary education was skewed towards the liberal arts, with little skills formation. In 1987–97 only 17 percent of students in tertiary institutions pursued science and engineering courses. Although agriculture engages 70–90 percent of the national population, Fourah Bay College never taught or researched agriculture. Over 70 percent of its students pursue liberal arts or social science disciplines. Although reliable statistics are not available, graduate unemployment in these disciplines is known to be widespread. Njala College, set up in 1964 for agricultural studies, also later veered towards the liberal arts. The preference for an academic, liberal arts education is primordial, driven in the colonial and immediate post-colonial period by high returns and prestige when educated African cadres were in demand. The prestige of academic education, and low social esteem of agricultural and vocational studies, endured, despite the growing need for technical and vocational training. In the 1990s a new educational system ostensibly emphasizing technical and vocational training was introduced.

5. Key agents

5.1 Rural households

Rural households, accounting for 70–90 percent of Sierra Leone's population, produce the bulk of agricultural output (which in turn accounted for 37 percent of GDP in 1961–2000). However, rural households faced major constraints: poor soils and infrastructure, disease prevalence, underdeveloped credit and commodity markets, and explicit and implicit agricultural taxation. Unsurprisingly, agricultural productivity has been low. Rice, the staple food, accounts for about 67 percent of the total area cropped (Agricultural Sector Master Plan 1993). In 1970 rice output was estimated at 1,180 lb per acre compared with an average of almost 2,000 lb world-wide and 1,360 lb in Africa (IMF 1970). Although 75 percent of the land area is arable, 84 percent of the arable land is low-fertility uplands (Agricultural

Table 19.8 *SLPMB, prices and purchases, 1961–1989*

		Cocoa		Coffee	
Year	Palm kernels: producer price (% export price)	producer price (% export price)	SLPMB purchases (% total)	Producer price (% export price)	SLPMB purchases (% total)
1961–5	66				
1966–70	56	48		49	
1971–5	62	56		54	
1976–9	50			43	
1980	53	104	87	64	50
1981	62	98	68	90	50
1982	22	17	58	20	52
1983	8	10	74	11	30
1984	21	10	71	14	8
1985	37	19	52	27	44
1986	30	11	38	43	25
1987					22
1988		33	33		
1989		48	21		

Source: World Bank (1993).

Sector Master Plan 1993). The remainder is fertile lowlands. For the uplands, natural fertility is low due to low pH, organic matter content, and cation-exchange capacity. Water-holding capacity is also low due to a coarse topsoil and years of weathering from high rainfall of 130 to 190 in. a year (Levi 1976; Agricultural Sector Master Plan 1993). The rains from April to November cause inundation and flooding while the dry season from December to March causes dessication, constraining irrigated agriculture. Fertilizer use is rare. Malaria and other tropical diseases are endemic, while health facilities are poor and urban-based. Rural life expectancy is much lower than the national average of about thirty-two–thirty-six years in 1960–2000. The country had the world's highest infant mortality rate of 200–220 per 1,000 live births.

Prior to structural adjustment in the early 1990s the government intervened extensively in the markets for agricultural produce. It imposed a 30 percent tax on agricultural exports in the 1980s. Under-pricing by the monopsonistic Sierra Leone Produce Marketing Board (SLPMB) (see table 19.8), and exchange rate over-valuation (as shown in table 19.1) implicitly taxed these exports. The ratio of producer price to export price for palm kernels, the leading agricultural export, declined from 66 percent in 1961–5 to less than 25 percent in 1982–6. The same ratio was below 15 percent for cocoa and less than 25 percent for coffee in 1982–6. Unsurprisingly, the share

Table 19.9 *Liberia and Sierra Leone, producer prices, 1976*

	Price per tonne (US$)	
Commodity	Liberia	Sierra Leone
Palm kernels	156.75	85.80
Cocoa	582.40	430.08
Coffee	560.00	376.32

Source: Clapham (1976).

of total output sold to the SLPMB declined from 87 percent for cocoa in 1980 to 38 percent in 1986, the share for coffee declined from 50 percent in 1980 to 25 percent in 1986. As these crops are grown principally for export, most of the quantity not sold to the SLPMB was presumably smuggled abroad. Indeed, price differentials between Sierra Leone and Liberia on the south-eastern border were large. In 1976 the price per tonne of palm kernels was US$157 in Liberia and only US$86 in Sierra Leone (table 19.9). Moreover, it was cheaper for farmers near the border to cross over to Liberia with their produce than to travel longer distances on bad roads to sell to the SLPMB in Sierra Leone.

Additionally in the 1970s and 1980s, import subsidies and price control turned rice to a source of rents and leverage. The subsidized price of imported rice was one-fortieth its market price in 1986 (Reno 1995). Agricultural export taxes helped finance such subsidies (IMF 1989), with the SLPMB sometimes undertaking rice importing and marketing.

Adaptation to the high-risk, high-cost environment induces a low pro-duction equilibrium trap. Rudimentary markets and low technology induces subsistence small-scale farming. In the 1990s, farm size averaged 1–2 ha of land per family, the size readily manipulable with family labor using hoes, knives, and axes as main farming implements (World Bank 1993). Credit constraints, in a high-risk environment, force consumption-smoothing through accumulation of food grains and livestock, with possible losses due to poor storage facilities and animal disease morbidity. Not surprisingly, rural poverty is widespread and savings low. The 1989 Survey of Household Income and Household Economic Activity estimated that over 80 percent of the population of Sierra Leone lived below the poverty line of US$1 a day and that poverty was more prevalent in rural areas than urban.

Soil infertility has led to shifting cultivation. Rice yields decreased by about 30 percent as population pressure forced a decline in fallow periods from ten to three–four years (Agricultural Sector Master Plan 1993). Moreover, shifting cultivation necessitates clearing of new forest land every one–three years and burning to restore carbonates, phosphates, and silicates of the cation (Nye and Greenland 1960), sometimes leading to deforestation and erosion, and considerable time loss. Little (c. 1951) estimates that the Mende of south-eastern Sierra Leone spent a third of total farm work time on clearing operations.

Crop and activity diversification reduces risks. Thus, some 95 percent of farmers produce rice along with a selection from over seventy other crops while also raising livestock and engaging in non-farm activities such as hunting and fishing. Mixed cropping prevents erosion and leaching of cultivated land by providing a green cover to the land throughout the crop season as the crops mature at different times (Jones 1961). Waldock, Capstick, and Browning (1951) observed more than nineteen subsidiary crops growing in "rice" fields in Sierra Leone. However, diversification precludes economies of scale and specialization, and impedes learning-by-doing, while time is lost moving across activities. Furthermore, multiple cropping as a response to risk is costly, forcing households to engage in low-return activities just because they are safe or have risks uncorrelated with other activities. It also reduces the scope for learning-by-doing (Collier and Gunning 1999). In the 1960s farmers in Sierra Leone planted cassava on previously cropped land for harvesting only if other crops faied (Saylor 1967).

Collective land ownership by families or communities, perceived as an insurance mechanism, prevails in rural Sierra Leone. Outsiders require the consent of the proprietary family or community to obtain land. They may be barred from growing tree crops, a potential basis for claiming access to land. Land titling is gradually emerging in some rural regions. Critics contend that collective land ownership inhibits agriculture by precluding land collateralization while inducing uncertainty, especially for outsiders. A counter-argument is that other constraints, such as the dearth of financial institutions, have been binding, and that if land titling were implemented it would displace and further impoverish rural communities. Given the prevailing conditions of relative land abundance, it is likely that the introduction of marketable individual ownership rights would generate low land prices and land illiquidity. Rural land tenure remains a sensitive political issue, with the tensions between stability and efficiency yet to be satisfactorily resolved.

5.2 Manufacturing firms

The manufacturing sector can serve as a catalyst for economic growth. It is the main vehicle for productivity increase, through economies of scale and scope and through the creation, adoption, and application of new technology. It is also an agent of modernization and a source of dynamic comparative advantage. Lack of industrial transformation is thus a key factor underlying

Sierra Leone's poor growth performance. The manufacturing sector has always been small, accounting for about 5 percent of GDP in 1965–2000 as compared with about 15 percent for SSA. Manufactured exports are virtually nil.

At independence in 1961 the industrial sector was weak. The domestic market was small with a national population of only 2.3 million and low *per capita* income of about US$260 (in 1995 dollars). Rudimentary financial markets constrained capital accumulation and risk insurance. It was generally claimed that the foreign-owned commercial banks favored foreigners and the more profitable and less risky mining and trade in loan allocation. The urban location of commercial banks and the courts aggravated loan default risks for rural-based SMEs, constraining their access to the formal sector credit. The informal sector credit was short term, usually less than three months, reducing its scope for generating investment funds. While deficient everywhere, infrastructure was worse in the rural areas which lacked electricity, telecommunications facilities, a pipe-borne water supply, or good roads. Skilled human resources were also scarce. An elitist educational system provided mostly academic rather than technical training, and only 5–10 percent of the population was literate.

After independence the government embarked on an import-substituting industrialization (ISI) program, the prevailing development paradigm. It offered generous incentives to local and foreign investors – tax holidays, duty free imports of equipment and raw materials, repatriation of capital and dividends in foreign currency, and tariffs on import substitutes; the Wellington Industrial Estate was set up in Freetown. These measures and direct government investment led to the setting up of some large manufacturing enterprises. However, the economic decline of the 1980s buffeted manufacturing firms; large enterprises operated below capacity due to lack of foreign exchange, poor electricity supply, and competition from cheaper smuggled imports. The import-substitution strategy failed in Sierra Leone, as in SSA as a whole, for reasons documented in the literature (see, for instance, Bruton 1998). The adjustment program's liberalization measures since the 1990s removed the macroeconomic distortions (Davies 2002); however, other constraints endure, notably poor infrastructure, rudimentary financial markets, and widespread corruption in government (see sections 6 and 8).

6. Political-economy analysis

Many authors have highlighted the role of political-economy factors in explaining Africa's poor growth performance (see, for instance, Ndulu and O'Connell 1999). The following explanation for the two big stories in

Sierra Leone's growth experience – growth collapse by the end of the 1980s and civil war from 1991–2001 – corroborates this view.

6.1 Growth collapse

Alesina *et al.* (1996) distinguish technocratic dictators, associated with high economic growth in Chile, Indonesia, South Korea, Taiwan, and Turkey; and kleptocratic dictators associated with growth tragedies like Mobutu's Democratic Republic of Congo (DRC). The literature places Sierra Leone's President Siaka Stevens, who ruled from 1968 to 1985, among the kleptocrats (Clapham 2001; Reno 1995; Smillie, Gberie, and Hazleton 2000). Stevens erected a "shadow state" characterized by the informalization and control of markets and their rewards and the "replacement of true political competition with a struggle for his favour" (Reno 1995). The markets for diamonds, rice, petroleum, and foreign exchange were at the epicenter of this parallel government structure (we mentioned on p. 681 the 40:1 ratio of the market price of rice to its subsidized price in the mid-1980s). Although market intervention pre-dates Stevens, its scope was much smaller then and rents did not occupy political center stage. Extensive intervention, starting with the 1970s oil shocks, favoured urban communities enjoying the bulk of subsidized imports and official foreign currency. The taxation of export agriculture, in turn, hurt the productive anti-APC south-eastern regions, producing an ethno-regional bias. Urban groups, particularly university students, posed the main threat to Stevens (Abdullah and Muana 1998).

Stevens undermined or violently repressed institutions that posed a challenge, culminating in one-party rule in 1978 (see Abdullah 1997; Rashid 1997). The shadow state also had no room for agencies of restraint such as an independent central bank: the governor was murdered in 1979, allegedly for objecting to lavish government expenditures on the 1980 OAU summit in Freetown. The hotels, villas, and limousines that were constructed or acquired became mostly redundant or were unaccounted for afterwards (see Reno 1995).

Stevens consolidated power by centralizing it in Freetown, exacerbating rural isolation. He abolished traditional government structures such as chiefdom and district councils, and arbitrarily appointed and dismissed traditional rulers, the opposition SLPP support base. The railway had been dismantled by the mid-1970s, without a rural road network being first or subsequently developed, hurting rural agriculture; in many areas, transporting produce to urban markets became impossible. Some argue that President Stevens' motive was to under-develop the productive south-eastern regions where the pro-opposition SLPP was based and the rail network concentrated. This argument is consistent with Acemoglu and Robinson's (2002) model, in which political elites block institutional and technological developments for

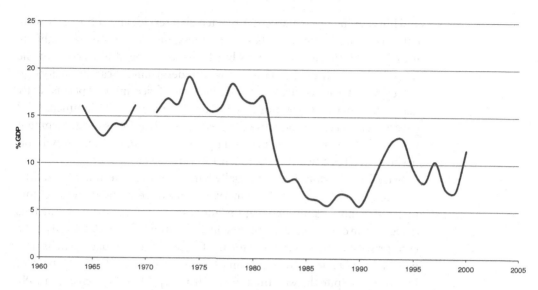

Figure 19.2 Sierra Leone, fiscal revenues, 1964–2000, percent of GDP
Source: IMF (various years).

fear that these may undermine their own political security by strengthening the capabilities of opposition movements. Objective reasons for dismantling the railway also existed, however: a World Bank study, for example, recommended their shut-down because of operating losses.[6]

Stevens precipitated the corporate diamond sector's collapse in order to garner political support and establish personal control of diamond resources. In the 1967 general elections, as opposition leader, Stevens promised greater scope for artisanal diamond mining, claiming it represented "the little man's only hope for wealth" (Smillie, Gberie, and Hazleton 2000: 41). His victorious APC won parliamentary seats mostly from the diamond-rich Kono District, the northern regions, and Freetown. The defeated SLPP won virtually all the seats in the south-eastern regions except Kono District. This voting pattern reflected the political importance of diamonds and ethno-regional rivalries. The new government appeared to be deliberately frustrating efforts to curb illicit mining on SLST concession areas. It deported three successive Chief Security Officers of the Trust within eight months without explanation (Harbottle 1976). As the corporate sector declined, Stevens reinforced control over the diamond trade through a cabal of Lebanese businessmen (Reno 1995).

Government revenues plummeted from 17 percent of GDP in the 1970s to 8 percent in 1985–9 (figure 19.2), driven by collapsing diamond revenues

---

[6] Stevens was selective with regard to the advice of the international financial institutions, once dismissing such advice as political suicide (Reno 1995).

and burgeoning black markets. A bloated civil service and subsidies to state enterprises and basic imports – with smuggling of imports to neighboring countries increasing the fiscal burden – kept expenditures high. By the mid-1980s, much of the economy was underground. Scarcity of foreign currency and price controls left basic imports of rice and fuel permanently scarce. Infrastructure deteriorated. Public sector real wages plummeted and government services gradually collapsed. By the late 1980s the government was hardly functional. Not surprisingly, annual *per capita* GDP growth was negative in all but two years between 1981 and 1990.

Blacklisted by donors and virtually bankrupt, the government had little option but to launch a SAP late in 1989. Subsequently, aid donors became major stakeholders, influencing the adoption of reform measures such as deregulation of foreign exchange, credit and commodity markets, and public enterprise and public sector reforms. Consequently, budget deficits as a percentage of GDP decreased from over 8 percent in 1976–85 to 5 percent in 1991–5, despite the war. Inflation fell from a peak of 180 percent in 1987 to an average of less than 20 percent after 1993. However, the political and economic environment was soon to be buffeted by the onset of civil war in 1991.

6.2 Civil war, 1991–2001

Domestic and external factors combined to induce the 1991–2001 civil war. The economic decline of the 1980s and the use by the government of drugged youths as thugs produced a recruitment base for the rebellion – unemployed, disillusioned youths. The large army of illicit diamond diggers in the eastern regions widened the base. Nepotism and corruption eroded morale and discipline in the military, which prolonged the rebel war by producing a weak government military response. With widespread political repression, culminating in a one-party system of government from 1978 to 1992, university students became the vanguard for political opposition. University authorities, beholden to the government, expelled radical students in the mid-1980s. Some of these students underwent military training in Libya to overthrow the APC, leading to the formation of the rebel movement (Abdullah 1997; Abdullah and Muana 1998). The rebellion actually began as a spillover from neighbouring Liberia.

In terms of its nature and organization, the rebel movement, the Revolutionary United Front (RUF), did not appear to be ethnically based. Nor did ideology play a major role in its operations. The rebel leader, Foday Sankoh, was from the northern regions, while most of the rebels initially came from the marginalized southeastern regions where the war began. The movement's ideological barrenness has been attributed to the low social standing and educational status of its leadership (Abdullah 1997). Most of the former students and other "intellectuals" associated with the antecedents of the rebel movement did not participate in the rebellion.

The rebel movement initially enjoyed some support in the south-eastern regions where the war began. However, its main strategy involved atrocities against civilians and forcible recruitment. Recruits were made to commit atrocities against their own communities in order to bond recruits to the rebel organization by making them no longer welcome at home. Communities were also sometimes terrorized into supporting the rebellion. The rebels were generally not trained fighters; many were children who could hardly carry an AK47 rifle (Davies 2000). New recruits, women, and children were often used as guinea pigs or human shields in battle.

Diamonds, poor government response, ethno-regional grievances, and external support helped prolong the rebellion. The RUF obtained an estimated US\$25–125 million a year from diamonds from 1997 when it controlled some 90 percent of Sierra Leone's resources, compared with government annual defense expenditures of US\$15–30 million in 1995–2000. Diamonds also produced a war-prolonging congruence of interests among the protagonists, whose private control of diamond resources was contingent on an overall security vacuum (Davies 2000). Late in 1993, the military government declared a unilateral cease-fire which enabled the routed rebels to reconsolidate. Abraham (1997) hints that this was deliberate.

Libyan and Liberian support aided the rebellion. Libyan support was apparently part of Colonel Gaddafi's grand plan to spread the Libyan "revolution" to West Africa by financing and training dissidents (Abdallah 1997). Liberian warlord Charles Taylor launched civil war in Liberia and then aided the rebel movement to do likewise in Sierra Leone. Taylor's action may have been due initially to Libyan influence, and to his frustration with Sierra Leone for aiding an Economic Community of West African States (ECOWAS) force which sought to contain him in 1990 by intervening in Liberia. However, Taylor subsequently became involved in an arms-for-diamonds trade with the rebel movement, as documented in a special UN report (United Nations 2000). Foday Sankoh, leader of the RUF, lived in Côte d'Ivoire during much of the rebellion. Mercenaries from Burkina Faso fought for the rebel movement; Burkina Faso also served as a transit point for arms shipments to the rebel movement (United Nations 2000). Côte d'Ivoire and Burkina Faso apparently supported the rebellion for reasons personal to their heads of state (Reno 1998). Nigeria led a pro-government intervention force with troops from Ghana and Guinea under the aegis of ECOWAS.

Special interests, perceived poor leadership, and a weak military stultified the government's response to the rebellion (Musah 2000; Clapham 2001). Although forewarned by military intelligence about the advent from Liberia of the rebellion, the ruling APC failed to deploy substantial defensive troops and materiel in the vulnerable border area (Abdullah and Muana 1998). To some observers the government appeared to be deliberately encouraging the war in the anti-APC south-eastern regions, with a view to disenfranchising them in imminent multi-party elections or/and delaying the elections. That the APC was overthrown in 1992 by soldiers from the war front also raises the possibility that the government deliberately failed to equip the military out of distrust. The military National Provisional Ruling Council (NPRC), which overthrew the APC, also unsuccessfully attempted to delay multi-party elections in 1996 on the grounds of "peace before elections." The military government, headed by a twenty-nine-year-old captain, replaced top military officers appointed by their predecessors with relatively inexperienced ones (Abdullah and Muana 1998); this helped turn the tide in favor of the rebel movement.

Tejan Kabbah and his SLPP, elected in 1996, were overthrown by the military in alliance with the rebel movement in 1997 before being reinstated in 1998 by an ECOWAS intervention force. In January 1999 the rebels occupied much of Freetown before the intervention force repulsed them once again. Musah (2000) aptly captures the view that the Kabbah government's management of the crisis was flawed: "Tejan Kabbah's Sierra Leone People's Party ruling since 1996, complacent in the knowledge that regime security was being provided by foreign forces, all but abandoned any efforts at nation rebuilding. Instead, political infighting for control of resources and power within the SLPP hierarchy had dominated the agenda of leading SLPP figures since the restoration (of the SLPP in 1998)" (2000: 107). Kabbah's leadership skills have often been criticized. According to Clapham (2001) "he had, however, only very limited leadership capacities, and when his regime was challenged both in May 1997 and in January 1999, his immediate response was to take refuge under foreign protection" (Clapham 2001: 15).

Ethno-regional rivalries leading to Kabbah's Presidential candidacy in 1996 partly account for his leadership problems. A minority Madingo, Kabbah was chosen to deflect criticism of historical Mende dominance of the SLPP. Brought in through a marriage of convenience, Kabbah lacked a support base within the party. Finally, although the war never took the form of an "ethnic" war, ethno-regional grievances initially induced voluntary enlistment in the rebel movement in the south-eastern regions where the rebellion began.

Estimates of war deaths range from 25,000 to 75,000. The war also displaced 40 percent of Sierra Leone's population of 4.6 million. The outreach of the government was often largely limited to Freetown. Production activities in all sectors were disrupted or halted, and Sierra Leone came to depend increasingly on foreign aid which averaged 22 percent of GWI in 1992–2000. The war also claimed the ruling APC: disillusioned war front soldiers, storming Freetown ostensibly to protest their neglect, ended up overthrowing the government in April 1992.

The following factors helped to end the war by January 2002. First was the decimation of the rebel movement's military capability in 2000 by Guinean troops (who repulsed an RUF-assisted rebellion in Guinea) and the British military, which intervened to support the government. Second, the government's own military capability increased with the building of a new army with British assistance. Third, the size and mandate of the UN peacekeeping force, UNAMSIL, was expanded, permitting it to respond robustly to rebel attacks. Fourth, UN sanctions forced Liberia to reduce its arms-for-diamonds support for the rebel movement. An existing arms embargo was extended to include diamond exports, and a travel ban was imposed on selected government officials and political leaders. Fifth, and speculatively, was war fatigue. It was widely believed that the rebels were tired of warfare; some rebel leaders were believed to have amassed wealth and were looking forward to returning to civil society to enjoy it. Sixth was the incarceration and replacement of the intransigent rebel leader, Foday Sankoh.

These developments facilitated a peace plan, and the disarmament and demobilization of combatants was completed in January 2002. General and Presidential elections were conducted peacefully in May 2002, producing the re-election of President Kabbah and his SLPP. The RUF and other parties accepted the results.

6.2.1 Perspectives on state failure

Some commentators perceive the seemingly anarchical post-Cold War civil wars in Africa and elsewhere as a clash of civilizations. Kaplan (1994) predicts anarchy for these fault-line regions and attributes his archetypal Sierra Leone civil war to "ancient economic hatreds," age-old African superstitious beliefs, and contemporary problems of population explosion, environmental pollution, drugs, and ethnic rivalry. Abdullah (1997) disagrees, attributing the rebels' anarchic behavior to their social background and war tactics. In Collier and Hoeffler (2004), economic factors, especially natural-resource dependence, are the high-risk factors for civil war. In Sierra Leone, diamonds played a key role in sustaining the rebellion although the rebels did not gain access to the diamond mines at the outset. The destabilizing and corrupting influence of diamonds discussed in section 4 did play an indirect role in the war's onset, inducing state failure. Furthermore, expectations of diamond revenues might have motivated Liberian warlord Charles Taylor's support for the launch of the rebellion in Sierra Leone.

The seemingly self-destructive ethos and survival strategy of the APC poses a conundrum. Bates (1981) famously sought to 'rationalize' poorly chosen economic policies by appealing to the political influence of narrow interest groups. But to paraphrase Bates,[7] why should a government, whether captive to narrow interests or not, do things that ultimately induce its own demise? One explanation for the APC conundrum is the inability to attain the optimal level of corruption (from the government's standpoint). Up to a certain level, corruption might reinforce a government's hold on power by inducing loyalty and weakening opposition. Eventually, however, corruption could deny the government the resources to govern, inducing state collapse as in Mobutu's Zaire. Targeting the optimal level of corruption requires co-ordination; otherwise, in the extreme case of kleptocracy, the optimal level of corruption can easily be exceeded as members of the government adopt self-seeking, rivalrous behavior. Co-ordination would be more difficult with natural resources that could be looted before the state collected the rents, as with Sierra Leone's alluvial diamonds.

Another explanation is that, for a self-seeking government, hysteresis increases the attractiveness of anti-growth measures such as inflation taxation, pricing intervention, and unsustainable foreign borrowing: the government passes on the consequences, at least partly, to future generations. However, the consequences may catch up with the government before it leaves office, as in the case of the APC. This leads to a related explanation, the government's time horizon, which is likely to vary positively with the government's life expectancy and apparently, as in the case of the APC, the head of state's life expectancy. A shorter time horizon induces policies that discount the future and, in the extreme, risk state collapse in the long term for short-term benefits. The APC faced a volatile and uncertain political environment, characterized by ethno-regional divisions, a chaotic diamonds sector, and the prospect of a coup. The military had already staged three successful coup in 1967–8, the first preventing and the third permitting the inauguration of the APC after its electoral victory in 1967. Several coup attempts were alleged in the 1970s and the alleged plotters executed. These factors may have shortened the APC's time horizon. Also, although his true age was a matter of speculation, President Siaka Stevens was believed to be in his sixties and thus already aging when he gained power in 1967. This may explain why Stevens' policies did not reflect any concern for long-term economic growth. He died in 1987 before the onset of war (in 1991).

7. Sierra Leone and Botswana: a comparative analysis

Sierra Leone and Botswana are both diamond-rich. However, Sierra Leone has experienced growth and state collapse while Botswana has been one

---

[7] "Why should reasonable men adopt policies that have harmful consequences for the societies they govern?" (Bates 1981: 3).

of the world's fastest-growing economies and one of Africa's most politically stable countries. Four key factors can explain this contrasting performance. First, Botswana's diamonds occur in Kimberlite deposits, which require sophisticated mining techniques. Furthermore, Kimberlite diamond mining is a "point" activity with the deposits geographically concentrated. These factors tend to induce a natural monopoly in the exploitation of Kimberlite diamonds, unlike Sierra Leone's alluvial diamond resources.[8]

Second, labor movement is not problematic in sparsely populated Botswana with a population density of 2 persons per km^2 in 1990, unlike in Sierra Leone with a population density of 56 per km^2. In fact, labor movement does not matter for Botswana: that the diamonds are a "point resource" and require capital-intensive mining techniques precludes the artisanal mining that is otherwise likely to result, with open access for labor.

Third is a sharp difference in the ethos and political survival strategy of the two countries' governing elites. Botswana's rulers benefit from the stability of an ethnically homogenous and generally deferential society, and their hold on power has not been seriously threatened. The dominant Tswana ethnic group has integrated non-Tswana ethnic groups into the polity (Parsons and Robinson 2006). Sierra Leone's leaders have often to scramble for allies in a fragmented, ethnically polarized, political system in which access to diamond resources is the critical source of leverage (Clapham 2001).

Fourth, Botswana's political elite invested heavily in farming (ranching and beef exporting) and therefore did not adopt anti-agricultural policies such as export taxation, or permit the "Dutch disease" that afflicted other mineral-rich economies. Their agricultural interests gave the elite a strong incentive to promote rational state institutions and private property (Parsons and Robinson 2006). On the other hand, Sierra Leone's rulers had no underlying agricultural interests, private access to diamond deposits was a much quicker source of wealth. Furthermore, the APC which ruled from 1968 to 1992, heavily taxed export agriculture, concentrated in the opposition south-eastern regions.

8. Conclusions

Despite certain seemingly favorable initial conditions, Sierra Leone's post-independence growth performance over 1961–2000 ended in growth collapse and civil war. The preceding analyzes have identified four principal culprits for this tragedy: diamonds, corruption, ethno-regional rivalries, and external actors. First, informalization of access to the diamond resources in

---

[8] Sierra Leone also has Kimberlite deposits, which were unexploited up to 2003.

turn informalized and criminalized overall economic activity. Diamonds also sustained the war by financing it and generating a war-prolonging congruence of interests among the protagonists. Second, kleptocracy in the 1970s and 1980s prompted policies that undermined the state and the economy and ultimately induced growth collapse and civil war. Such policies included distortionary government intervention in key markets and the dismantling or vitiation of key political and economic governance institutions. Third, ethno-regional rivalries had a deleterious effect on governance. Such rivalries were divisive and helped explain the explicit and implicit taxation of agriculture. Ethno-regional rivalries also facilitated the kleptocracy of the 1970s and 1980s. Lastly, external actors – Libya and Liberia – catalyzed the war. Later, other external factors – British military intervention, UN peacekeepers, UN sanctions on Liberia, and intervention by ECOWAS – helped to end the war.

Economic reform measures since the early 1990s improved the macroeconomic environment and reduced market distortions. Peace stimulated large aid inflows of about 40 percent of GDP between 2000 and 2003, democratic reforms since the 1990s saw the return of multi-party politics.

However, the four factors that induced growth collapse and civil war – diamonds, corruption, ethno-regional rivalries, and external threats – endure to varying degrees. Politics is still dominated by the two parties that historically evoked strong ethno-regional rivalries: the SLPP and the APC. Political competition and accountability remain limited, with the APC, now the main opposition, enfeebled by infighting. While peace has returned to Liberia, with the warlord Charles Taylor facing an international criminal court in The Hague, external threats to Sierra Leone's security prevail. In particular, as of this writing, peace talks to end Côte d'Ivoire's civil war appear to have stalled and the prolonged illness of a despotic head of state in Guinea has sparked fears of an imminent power struggle. Domestic threats to Sierra Leone's peace and security also abound: doubts about the reliability and capability of the country's military, widespread unemployment among ex-combatants and youths, and grievances from the war. Diamond mining remains largely informalized and a key source of political leverage; the most promising policy, which would favor large-scale mining given the problems associated with small-scale operations, remains elusive. Widespread corruption appears to have largely survived the war and the various reform measures. An International Crisis Group report (ICG) (International Crisis Group 2003) says: "there are consistent signs that donor dependence and the old political ways (corruption) are returning . . . The government's performance has been disappointing, and complacency appears to have set in. Reform rhetoric abounds but action is yet to follow." The Economist Intelligence Unit Sierra Leone Country Report for March 2006 (Economist

Intelligence Unit 2006) speaks of "chronic maladministration of the country."

After a decade of pernicious civil war, therefore, and at a time when donors are increasing aid to poor countries, Sierra Leone is at a crossroads. The above two reports highlight the possibility that the country has returned to the old status quo and is failing to seize a major opportunity for sustained growth.

References

Abdullah, I. (1997), "Bush Path to Destruction: The Origin and Character of the Revolutionary United Front," *Africa Development* 23(3): 172–93

Abdullah, I. and P. Muana (1998), "The Revolutionary United Front of Sierra Leone: A Revolt of the Lumpen Proletariat," in C. Clapham, ed., *African Guerrillas*. Oxford: James Currey

Abraham, A. (1997), "War and Transition to Peace: A Study of State Conspiracy in Perpetuating Armed Conflict," *Africa Development* 23(3): 101–16

Acemoglu, D. and J. Robinson (2002), "Economic Backwardness in Political Perspective," NBER Working Paper 8831

Agricultural Sector Master Plan (1993), Freetown: Government of Sierra Leone, mimeo

Alesina, A., S. Ozler, N. Roubini, and P. Swagel (1996), "Political Instability and Economic Growth," *Journal of Economic Growth* 1, June: 189–211

Alie, J. A. D. (1990), *A New History of Sierra Leone*. London: Macmillan

Auty, R. M. (1993), *Sustaining Development in Mineral Economies: The Resource Curse Thesis*. London: Routledge

Barro, R. (1991), "Economic Growth in a Cross Section of Countries," *Quarterly Journal of Economics* 106(2): 407–73

Barro, R. and J. W. Lee (1994), "Sources of Economic Growth," Carnegie Rochester Conference Series on Public Policy 40: 1–46

(2000), "International Data on Educational Attainment: Updates and Implications," CID Working Paper 42, Harvard University, Cambridge, MA

Bates, R. H. (1981), *Markets and States in Tropical Africa*. Berkeley, CA: University of California Press

Bruton, H. J. (1998), "A Reconsideration of Import Substitution," *Journal of Economic Literature* 36: 903–36

Cartwright, J. (1970), *Politics in Sierra Leone 1947–67*. Toronto: University of Toronto Press

Clapham, C. (1976), *Liberia and Sierra Leone: An Essay in Comparative Politics*. Cambridge: Cambridge University Press

(2001), "Sierra Leone: The Global–local Politics of State Collapse and Attempted Reconstruction," http://www.ippu.purdue.edu/info/gsp/FSIS_CONF4/papers /clap_Sierrra Leone

Cohen, D. and M. Soto (2001), "Growth and Human Capital: Good Data, Good Results," Technical Paper 179, OECD Development Centre, Paris

Collier, P. and J. W. Gunning (1999), "Explaining African Economic Performance," *Journal of Economic Literature* 37(1): 64–111

Collier, P. and A. Hoeffler (2004), "Greed and Grievance in Civil War," *Oxford Economic Papers* 56: 563–95

Collins, S. M. and B. P. Bosworth (1996), "Economic Growth in East Asia: Accumulation versus Assimilation," *Brookings Papers on Economic Activity* 2: 135–203

Davies, V. A. B. (2000), "Sierra Leone: Ironic Tragedy," *Journal of African Economies* 9(3): 349–69

 (2002), "Liberalization and Implicit Government Finances in Sierra Leone," AERC Research Paper 125, Final Thematic Research Report. Nairobi: African Economic Research Consortium

 (2006), "Alluvial Diamonds: A New Resource Curse Theory," Unpublished PhD dissertation, University of Oxford

Davies, V. A. B. and A. Fofana (2002), "Diamonds, Crime and Civil War in Sierra Leone," Paper prepared for the World Bank and Yale University Case Study Project, The Political Economy of Civil Wars

Economist Intelligence Unit (2006), "Country Report: Sierra Leone." London: Economist Intelligence Unit, March

Gelb, A. H. and associates (1988), *Oil Windfalls: Blessing or Curse?* New York: Oxford University Press

Gylfason, T. (2001), "Natural Resources, Education and Economic Development," *European Economic Review* 45: 847–59

Harbottle, M. (1976), *The Knaves of Diamonds*. London: Seeley Service

Heston, A., R. Summers, and B. Aten (2002), "Penn World Table Version 6.1," Center for International Comparisons at the University of Pennsylvania (CICUP), October

Hoeffler, A. (2000), "The Augmented Solow Model and the African Growth Debate," Framework Paper prepared for the Explaining African Economic Growth Performance Project. Nairobi: African Economic Research Consortium

International Crisis Group (2003), "Sierra Leone: Security and Governance," September, http://www.crisisweb.org

International Monetary Fund (IMF) (1970, 1972, 1989, 1994, 1997, 2001), "Sierra Leone: Recent Economic Developments," Washington, DC: International Monetary Fund

 (various years), *International Financial Statistics Yearbook*. Washington, DC: International Monetary Fund

 (2001), "Senegal: Selected Issues," Country Report 01/188, October 26

Jones, W. O. (1961), "Food and Agricultural Economies of Tropical Africa," *Food Research Institute Studies* 2

Kaplan, R. (1994), "The Coming Anarchy," *Atlantic Monthly* 273(2), February: 48

Levi, J. (1976), "Introduction," in J. Levi, ed., *African Agriculture: Economic Action and Reaction in Sierra Leone*. Oxford: Commonwealth Agricultural Bureau

Lewis, S. R. (1984), "Development Problems of the Mineral-rich Countries," in M. Syrquin, L. Taylor, and L. E. Westphal, eds., *Economic Structure and Performance: Essays in Honor of Hollis B. Chenery*. Orlando, FL: Academic Press: 157–77

(1989), "Primary-exporting Commodities," in H. Chenery and T. N. Srinivasan, eds., *Handbook of Development Economics Vol. II.* Amsterdam: Elsevier Science Publishers: 1541–1600

Little, K. L. (c. 1951), "The Mende Upland Rice Farmer," mimeo

Mankiw, N. G., D. Romer, and D. Weil (1992), "A Contribution to the Empirics of Economic Growth," *Quarterly Journal of Economics* 107: 407–37

Musah, A. F. (2000), "A Country under Siege: State Decay and Corporate Military Intervention in Sierra Leone," in A. F. Musah and J. K. Fayemi, eds., *Mercenaries: An African Security Dilemma.* London and Sterling, VA: Pluto Press

Ndulu, B. J. and S. A. O'Connell (1999), "Governance and Growth in Sub-Saharan Africa," *Journal of Economic Perspectives* 15(5): 41–66

North, D. (1987), "Institutions, Transactions Costs and Economic Growth," *Economic Inquiry* 25(3), July: 419–28

Nye, P. H. and D. J. Greenland (1960), *The Soil under Shifting Cultivation.* Farnham Royal, UK: Commonwealth Agricultural Bureau

O'Connell, S. A. and B. J. Ndulu (2000), "Africa's Growth Experience: A Focus on Sources of Growth," AERC Growth Working Paper No. 10. Nairobi: African Economic Research Consortium, April (downloadable: www.aercafrica.org)

Parsons, Q. N. and J. A. Robinson (2006), "State Formation and Governance in Botswana," *Journal of African Economies* 15(1): 100–40

Rashid, I. (1997), "Subaltern Reactions: Lumpens, Students and the Left," *Africa Development* 23(3/4): 19–44

Reno, W. (1995), *Corruption and State Politics in Sierra Leone.* Cambridge: Cambridge University Press

(1998), *Warlord Politics and African States.* Boulder, CO and London: Lynne Reinner

Richards, P. (1996), *Fighting for the Rain Forest: War, Youth and Resources in Sierra Leone.* Oxford and London: The International African Institute in association with James Currey and Heinemann

Sachs, J. D. and A. M. Warner (2001), "Natural Resources and Economic Development: The Curse of Natural Resources," *European Economic Review* 45: 827–38

Saylor, R. G. (1967), *The Economic System of Sierra Leone.* Durham, NC: Duke University Press

Smillie, I., L. Gberie, and R. Hazleton (2000), "The Heart of the Matter: Sierra Leone Diamonds and Human Security," *Insights Series.* Ottawa: Partnership Africa Canada

Torvik, R. (2002), "Natural Resources, Rent Seeking and Welfare," *Journal of Development Economics,* 67: 455–70

United Nations (2000), "Report of the Panel of Experts Appointed Pursuant to UN Security Council Resolution 1306 (2000)," Paragraph 19 in Relation to Sierra Leone, December

Van der Laan (1965), *The Sierra Leone Diamonds.* Oxford: Oxford University Press

Waldock, E. A., E. S. Capstick, and A. J. Browning (1951), "Soil Conservation and Land Use in Sierra Leone," Freetown: Government of Sierra Leone, mimeo

World Bank (1993), "Sierra Leone: Policies for Sustained Economic Growth and Poverty Alleviation," Report 11371-SL, Washington, DC: The World Bank
(1994), "Sierra Leone: Public Expenditure Policies for Sustained Economic Growth and Poverty Alleviation," Report 12618-SL, Washington, DC: The World Bank
(2002), *Sierra Leone: Tapping the Mineral Wealth for Human Progress – A Break with the Past.* Poverty Reduction and Economic Management Sector Unit, Washington, DC: The World Bank
(2003), *World Development Indicators 2003.* Washington, DC: The World Bank
Zack-Williams, A. (1995), *Tributors, Supporters and Merchant Capital: Mining and Underdevelopment in Sierra Leone.* Brookfield, VT: Avebury

Index

Printed in the United States
By Bookmasters